THE SUNDAY TIMES

Countryside
Companion

A stately, pollarded beech adorned with autumnal russets and golds in the ancient forest of Epping

THE SUNDAY TIMES
Countryside
Companion

Geoffrey Young

Introductions by Brian Jackman

GUILD PUBLISHING
LONDON

In Search of the Greenwood

The Open Patchwork

This edition published 1985 by
Book Club Associates
by arrangement with Country Life Books,
an imprint of Newnes Books,
84–88 The Centre, Feltham, Middlesex, England

Text © The WATCH Trust for Environmental Education
Artwork illustrations © Country Life Books, a Division
of The Hamlyn Publishing Group Limited 1985.

First published 1985

PRINTED BY ROYAL SMEETS OFFSET - THE NETHERLANDS

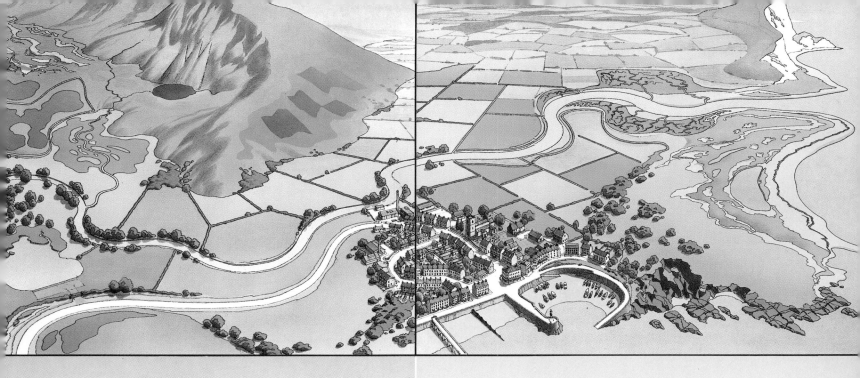

General editor: Andrew Branson
Design editor: Christopher Pow
Associate editor: Trevor Dolby
Designer: Karel Feuerstein

Most of the artwork and schemes were designed and prepared by Ken Oliver.

Many of the photographs were taken by Peter Loughran especially for Country Life Books.

The Artists

Martin Camm – Linden Artists
Peter Crump
John Michael Davis
Brian Delf
Ian Garrard
Roger Gorringe – R. P. Gossop
Pat Harby – Linden Artists
Delyth Jones
Kate Lloyd-Jones – Linden Artists
Josephine Martin – The Garden Studio
Robert Morton – Linden Artists
Kenneth Oliver
Peter Stebbing – Annabel Milne
Charles Stitt

Photographers include:

Heather Angel
Frank Blackburn
Adrian Davies
Geoff Dufeu
Robin Fletcher
Bob Gibbons
Brian Hawkes
Peter Loughran
John Mason
Owen Newman
Judy Todd

Foreword by David Bellamy

"Oh no! At this rate there will be more trees sitting on the nation's bookshelves than there will be adorning its hedgerows. Not another book about the British Countryside."

Well, don't blame me, I didn't write it, but I hasten to add, I wish I had and must settle to do the next best thing, write the foreword.

It is a super book, an ideal colour supplement to add to anyone's library, and an ideal companion to the vibrant living British Countryside.

It really lives up to its name as a companion, for it is like being taken by an old friend who reveals the innermost secrets of their detailed knowledge about something which is very special and almost private to them.

It is like being led along the River Bank by Ratty and Mole, across the Downs and Wildwood with Fiver the prophet, and over the fells and mountainsides by Strider himself. It is a celebration of facts drawn from history both natural and man-made, and rejoices in the knowledge that our landscapes are not natural and must be managed, warning of the perils of mismanagement. All is not well in our small corner of this one Earth, which we must learn to share with all the other products of creative evolution.

Please enjoy this book with the care it deserves, and then go out and join your local branch of the Royal Society for Nature Conservation and, with them, fight the good fight. If you are already a member, then go out and enrol two more.

I write this foreword as a botanist and conservationist and as the President of WATCH, a position I am very proud to hold. The royalties go to them, and so will help put both trees and hope back in our hedgerows.

DAVID BELLAMY
Bedburn, 1984

Photographic Acknowledgements

AEROFILMS, BOREHAM WOOD 212–13; HEATHER ANGEL 10, 11 top, 38, 74–5, 154 bottom, 154–5, 156–7, 159, 174–5, 188–9, 204, 216–17, 242–3; ANGLING PHOTO SERVICE, HOUNSLOW, Bill Howes 189; BARNABY'S PICTURE LIBRARY, LONDON 78, 79; ANDREW BRANSON 18 right; CAMBRIDGE UNIVERSITY COLLECTION 128–129; COMMITTEE FOR AERIAL PHOTOGRAPHY, UNIVERSITY OF CAMBRIDGE 252, PETER CRUMP 32; BOB GIBBONS PHOTOGRAPHY, RINGWOOD: Robin Fletcher 20, 29, 158–9, 180, 232, Bob Gibbons 119, 122, 170–1, 205, 217; BRIAN HAWKES 76–7, 78–9; PETER LOUGHRAN 2, 17 top, 26, 198; JOHN MASON 12, 15, 22, 127, 154 top, 166, 204–5, 216; S. & O. MATHEWS 11 bottom, 74 top, 134; NATURE PHOTOGRAPHERS LTD, ALDERSHOT: T. Andrewartha 144, Leo Batten 90, 90–1, Frank V. Blackburn 18 left, 31, Derick Bonsall 36, Kevin Carlson 16, 54, 210, Hugh Clark 50, Chris and Jo Knights 43, R. Mearns 230, Owen Newman 42, 52, 56 bottom, 147, 238, J. Russell 112, Patrick Sellar 130, Roger Tidman 241; NEWNES BOOKS: Adrian Davies 82, 86, 94, 97, 130–1, 136, Geoff du Feu 92, 115, 167, Peter Loughran 14, 33, 34, 39, 40, 41, 48 top, 48 bottom, 56 top, 59, 67, 68, 69, 80–1, 84, 87, 88, 95, 96, 98 top, 98 bottom, 99, 104, 106 top, 106 bottom, 108, 110, 118, 120 top, 120 bottom, 124 top, 124 bottom, 126, 132–3, 138, 138–9, 140, 142, 146, 150, 151, 158, 160 top left, 160 top right, 168, 172–3, 174, 178, 178–9, 184, 190–1, 191 top, 191 bottom, 193, 194, 196, 200, 202–3, 207, 208, 211, 218, 218–19, 219, 220–1, 221, 222 top, 222 bottom, 224, 226 top, 226 bottom, 227, 233, 240; THE ROYAL SOCIETY FOR THE PROTECTION OF BIRDS, SANDY 17 bottom; R. J. SCHEFFER 80; JUDY TODD 66, 74 bottom, 116–17, 160 bottom, 250; M. W. F. TWEEDIE 46.

Artist Acknowledgements

Martin Camm – 21, 22, 23, 24, 25, 26, 27, 28, 29, 30, 31, 68, 69, 182–3
Peter Crump – 244, 245, 251
John Michael Davis – 58–9, 60, 61, 62, 63, 64, 65, 70, 71, 114–5, 146, 147, 162–3, 164, 165, 168–9, 176, 184–5, 240–1
Brian Delf – 4, 5, 8, 9, 72–3, 152–3, 214–5
Ian Garrard – 176–7, 192–3, 206–7, 208–9
Roger Gorringe – 36, 37, 49, 80, 81, 82, 83, 102–3, 104–5, 108–9, 111, 125, 142–3, 181, 189, 194–5
Pat Harby – 39, 40–1
Delyth Jones – 84–5, 86–7, 88–9, 92–3, 126–7, 131
Kate Lloyd-Jones – 33, 35
Josephine Martin – 234, 235, 236, 237
Robert Morton – 51, 53, 55, 113, 145, 201, 211, 231, 233, 239
Ken Oliver – 17, 19, 44–5, 46–7, 56–7, 100–1, 107, 141, 186, 187, 197, 199, 203, 213, 243
Peter Stebbing – Annabel Milne – 223, 225, 227, 228–9
Charles Stitt – 95, 97, 117, 121, 123, 135, 137, 148, 149, 151, 161, 167
All diagrams Ken Oliver/Peter Crump

Author's Acknowledgements

The author is deeply grateful to the following for discussion, help and advice on various stages of the drafts of this book:

Dr Oliver Gilbert
David Glue
Dr Bryn Green
Dr Nigel Holmes
Nigel Ajax Lewis
Dr Ian Mclean
Dr George Peterken
Dr Ed Rispin
Dr Jeremy Thomas
Dr Nigel Webb
Derek Wells

He would also like to thank all the talented artists and photographers that have contributed to the book

Introduction

THIS BOOK LOOKS AFRESH at the modern countryside. It helps you to identify a thousand different wild plants and animals. It also explains why you see them where you do. This insight is relatively modern.

In past centuries, countryside lore was gained by those who lived and worked all their lives in the fields and woods. Though their observations were acute, their interpretations of what they saw were often misleading. But a few centuries ago, some people of enquiring mind were trying to produce order from the chaotic folklore; some compiled floras, lists of plants they saw, and they delighted in finding new specimens on their journeys through the lanes of Britain. Botany became a popular hobby, and by Victorian times the collecting and naming of birds, butterflies, beetles and other wildlife had also become fashionable.

The Victorians also witnessed the revelation of evolution, deduced by Charles Darwin. Some of its implications (that man was on a par with the rest of nature) took some digestion, but it founded a new inquisitiveness in science and today the natural world is seen as something much more than lists of names and places. It is now realised that it is an intricate system of lives, or even, as is now the fashion, flows of energy passing from one type of organism to another.

Many notions about wildlife, from quaint cobwebby folklore to the modern concept of the ecosystem make their appearance in this book. Also included is the history of the countryside we see today, the modern changes to it, and the effects of such things as pollution. They are all, however, the setting of the heart of this book – the sheer fascination of wild plants and animals. The more we learn about their lives, the more interesting they become. None of them can be properly understood out of the context of the place in which they are seen – their habitat, their living place in the countryside. We are in charge of that countryside. Many of its classic features such as old hay meadows and pastures, even the old oak wood, are by and large our creation – if we let nature take its course they would become something else, often a poorer else. These traditional features of our countryside and the life in them were taken for granted by our grandparents, but in recent years they have been changing, even disappearing, at an accelerating rate. What remains of the old richness is in scattered patches.

Although now ragged, the traditional landscape is, nevertheless, part of our heritage. Some of the fascination of wildlife lies with the way that it reflects our own, human involvement with it. Many of those early floras were beautifully illustrated, they were works of art. So, too, in their way were the meticulous collections of the Victorian enthusiasts. Zoos perennially fascinating places, reflect our own fascination with other creators on this planet. So do the vast audiences for TV wildlife programmes. Today's match for all of these are the fragments of our remaining ancient countryside, with the wildlife they contain. They are far subtler places than a museum or zoo, not only to recognise for what they are (they need not look special) but to protect. They contain long-established communities of plants and animals which cannot be replaced. Extinction for them is for ever. Many of these jewels lie within the boundaries of protected landscapes, many form nature reserves in their own right, but as many do not. These gems, of all kinds, lie close to hand, unknown, unrecognised for what they are. This book hopes to help you recognise them, the real countryside. And it hopes to persuade you that such places are worth fighting for.

How to use this book

1 The book helps you to identify places in the countryside and the wild animals and plants to be found in rural Britain.

2 Decide on your section. Wildlife is not limited to one section but we have chosen typical places for them. Reference to other places where they may be seen can be found in the captions and in the introductions to each page as well as the index.

3 The book is arranged in double page modules, each of which is self-contained although linked to others before and after it. Sometimes the pages show an assemblage of species from a particular kind of habitat (living place); sometimes groupings of species. The introduction to each page often describes interesting aspects of the lives of the animals or plants shown. Other insights appear in the boxed sections.

4 Plants often show a marked preference for certain conditions of light or shade, or soil. This is often not so much a positive preference, however, as they may be seen growing elsewhere, but it does reflect the circumstances in which they have the edge over other competitors for space. Examples in the book illustrate very clearly how changes made by man can have a dramatic result and sometimes wipe out whole communities of plants. Some pages carry soil preference charts. These charts can be matched with each other to explain, for example, why you see certain shrubs and spring flowers growing together in a wood.

5 Some of these 'habitat' links are so marked that plants can be used as indicators of soil or of old established communities. Some plants help us identify old hay meadows, others old woods, for example. Similarly animal life can help us identify such things as clean streams and ancient pasture. That an animal or plant is an indicator of this kind is noted in its caption and in the index entry.

6 Some pages describe 'classic' habitats – old meadowland, lowland heaths, salt marsh, for example. Much of the interest of many of these elements of the countryside results from their use by man in past centuries, as this book explains. Indeed, many have been created by traditional farming. They were once seen in profusion, they *were* the countryside, but many have been lost in recent years. This book, by use of captions, indicator species and other information given in it, helps you to identify these remaining fragments for yourself.

7 All words used are either explained briefly in the index or reference is made to a page carrying an explanation. The index also gives some soil preferences of plants, and tells you when a species is a useful indicator.

8 It is often interesting to compare related species of plants and animals. Certain sequences of pages explain aspects of the lives of, for example:

birds – pages 50–54, 112, 144, 200, 210, 230, 232, 238
butterflies – pages 44, 100, 140.

Similarly the description of such things as habitats and ecosystems can be found on pages: 42, 98, 138, 178, 220.

Groupings of dragonflies and mammals, wild grasses and orchids and other animals and plants can be located from the contents or from the index.

GEOFFREY YOUNG 1984

In Search of the Greenwood

Woods and trees clothe the view, and even hedgerow trees **1** share this important role.

Few if any unaltered relics of the original wildwood remain, but woods which have never been anything but woodland since the Ice Age can still be found. Look for them on parish boundaries: they often have an irregular shape **2,** but a more uniform wood **3** may still be old, its boundaries having been trimmed in recent times.

In the past, nearly all our woodlands played an integral part in the rural economy. Some were used for grazing or as hunting forests or chases **4,** but most were coppiced. Here, you can see newly cut coppice **5** with its accompanying timber, standard trees. Such woods, often old, may have the remnants of rambling boundary banks set with pollards **6.** As they have never been ploughed, ponds may be found in them **7.**

Natural woods can be expected to contain a mixture of tree species, and some of this variety may remain even after centuries of use **7.** Many coppice woods have, however, been planted up in recent·times as single-species hardwood high forest **8** or even with conifers **9.** Vast blocks of conifers are a feature of heaths, and moors. They can, however, be found also in the lowlands, on poorer farming land **10.**

In this section we look at the structure of trees and woods, but also at the life they contain. These woodlands are an important habitat for a host of wildlife

In the past, trees were also planted in shelter belts **11**, and as ornamental landscaping in a park **12** or even in the nearby countryside **13**. Many game coverts have been planted **14**. Alien trees and shrubs are often a clue to these.

Finally, and intriguingly, we can also find woods which have recently regenerated themselves on abandoned land **15**: the plants they contain may mark them out.

W OODLAND IMAGES are with us from childhood. To smell bluebells in a dappled oak wood, or walk in the silence of a Chiltern beech wood when all the autumn leaves are falling is to grow up believing that Britain is a land of woods, as indeed it once was.

It is a dream maintained by the large numbers of hedgerow trees and innumerable small woods, clumps, groves, hangers and spinneys which, unless you happen to live among the Fenland prairies, perpetuate the illusion of a leafy Britain.

Yet ours is a country where less than ten per cent of the land is covered with trees. Of these, the greater part – something like three quarters – are less than 65 years old, having been planted since the creation of the Forestry Commission in 1919.

It was not always like this. After the last Ice Age, Britain was a treeless tundra; but as the climate improved, dwarf birch and Scots pine, willow and juniper rooted and spread. The pines which had followed the ice northwards were themselves replaced in southern Britain by a surge of broadleaved trees. Glades of birch covered the drier soils; crack willows and alder carr filled the boggy bottoms; and oaks took root in the lowland clays. Together with other broadleaved colonists – hazel, ash, elm, lime – they became dominant over much of the landscape. Only in the far north, in the Great Caledonian Forest (of which the Black Wood of Rannoch is a precious relic), did the native pine remain unchallenged.

Meanwhile the sea level was slowly rising with the melting of the ice sheets and in time waves began to wash over what is now the North Sea, and the English Channel was cut. By about 5000 BC Britain had become an island. One of the last trees to arrive before this break with the continent was the beech – the last of our truly native trees and shrubs, which number nearly seventy in all.

This was the heyday of the primeval British wildwood, which could then boast a spectacular variety of animals, including the wolf, brown bear and wild boar. But the climate which had encouraged the growth of trees also lured other colonists in the shape of man; and even in the Stone Age, the early neolithic farmers were clearing the forest from the thin soils of the Wessex chalk and East Anglian Breckland to graze their animals and grow their crops.

From the Stone Age onwards, every fresh invasion by Celt, Roman and Saxon hastened the process of deforestation, beating back the wildwood with axe and plough, laboriously hacking out the hand-made landscape of Medieval Britain. Even though the Norman kings set aside vast tracks of land, much of it wooded, for hunting, of which Hampshire's New Forest survives as a splendid remnant, the destruction continued, though at a slower pace. In parts of Britain, the woods were still large enough to hide wolves and outlaws, but the ancient wildwood was now largely a folk memory. Many of the remaining fragments were now carefully maintained, enclosed with banks and ditches (many of which survive to this day) and managed under a widespread system known as 'coppice-with-standards', to yield a regular supply of poles, brushwood and timber. Other woods were 'wood pasture' and consequently set aside for grazing with the trees frequently pollarded – cut out of the reach of browsing animals. Both methods, coppicing and pollarding, greatly extended the life of a tree. Consequently the gnarled pollards and huge coppice stools to be found in old woods such as Epping Forest and Burnham Beeches are some of the oldest living things in Britain. And sometimes, when you look at such trees, you are seeing the ghosts of a forest which has been used by man for perhaps a thousand or more years.

By the 17th century, good timber was becoming scarce as the native oaks were devoured by ship builders and were cleared by an expanding agriculture. Firewood was gradually replaced by coal, and the hornbeam woods of Essex and Hertfordshire, once London's favourite fuel, no longer rang to the song of the woodman's axe.

In our own century we have witnessed the replacement of the traditional greenwood by faster-growing and more profitable conifer plantations. With the virtual ending of coppicing and other traditional management methods, many woods have simply been grubbed out to make way for yet more fields, continuing the process begun by our Stone Age ancestors. We may yet see the return of a valuable new market for British hardwoods; but meanwhile, our

remaining broadleaved woodlands have acquired other, no less precious values, both as living monuments from our Medieval past, and as literally irreplaceable wildlife habitats for rich communities of native woodland plants and animals.

Climate and the structure of the land itself determine the character of our native woodlands. For the best ash woods you must look to the limestone gorges and river valleys; Dovedale in Derbyshire, Ebbor Gorge in the Mendips. For beech woods, the chalk hills of Surrey and the Chiltern scarps are unsurpassed, rising and falling in fathomless aisles of magical light and distance.

Woods dominated by the durmast or sessile oak are more common in the western half of Britain, with fine examples at Borrowdale in Cumbria, in many parts of Wales and in the hanging woods of the North Devon coast west of Porlock. Britain's other great oak, the pedunculate oak, prefers the heavier lowland clays; but often the two species grow together, for more often than not a wood is a mixture of trees: oak, birch and hornbeam together, with maybe an understorey of old hazel coppice, holly or thorn.

Every wood, whatever its composition, is enriched by the communities of wild plants and animals which thrive within it. The old practice of coppicing was especially beneficial to many species, from the nightingale which skulk in the hazel thickets to the pearl-bordered fritillaries and other butterflies which frequent the clearings in which dog violets and other foodplants grow. Sadly, they have become much less common as the old coppice woodlands have become neglected and overgrown.

Today our biggest forests are the man-made plantations created by the Forestry Commission. (Kielder, in Northumberland, is the largest man-made forest in Europe). Comprised mostly of alien conifers, their dense ranks march across our northern uplands with unrelieved monotony. Yet one cannot deny that there is also a powerful magic in their damp and resinous gloom, and they have provided a new habitat which some species of animals and birds have been quick to exploit.

Many of our most interesting mammals are woodland species. Badger sets – some of them centuries old – and fox earths are commonly excavated in woodland banks, especially where the soil is sandy. At dusk the shy deer emerge from the shelter of the woods to browse in the surrounding fields. Their two-toed 'slots' or prints are easy to spot, particularly along the narrow winding 'racks' worn by the passage of generations.

Much rarer is the dormouse, an inhabitant of southern hazel coppice woodlands, and the predatory polecat, an agile denizen whose main strongholds are the woods and dingles of wild Wales; while the red squirrel and pine marten favour the coniferous woodlands of northern Britain

Birds are legion, from the sparrowhawks which hunt the woodland rides to the goldcrests, warblers and long-tailed tits which flit through the forest canopy in search of insects. Many birds nest in holes in trees: woodpeckers, nuthatches, tawny owls, redstarts. Food is abundant: acorns for the jays, mice for the owls and insects for the treecreeper to winkle from the bark.

The fragmented remains of the Royal Forests and chases of Medieval Britain can still be found today often within old deer parks such as this relic of the once extensive Charnwood Forest at Bradgate Park in Leicestershire. Centuries of grazing by deer and removal of timber has produced an open view with a few gnarled oaks and a bracken or grass covered floor.

An autumn scene in the Black Wood of Rannoch, Perthshire. This is part of the ancient Caledonian pine forest and is one of the most natural woodland scenes left to us – the variety of shapes and frequent branching of the trees contrasts markedly with the serried ranks of plantation conifers. The presence of dead stumps and a dense shrub layer of heather and bilberry are also typical of these magnificent woods.

At no time of the year is a wood entirely silent. In winter the bare oaks echo to the harsh cries of carrion crows, the chinking alarm notes of blackbirds at dusk, and the sweet, sad song of the robin. From March onwards, new voices are heard; chiffchaff and willow warbler, heralding the spring; the green woodpecker's mocking laughter and the drowsy summer sound of woodpigeons.

In spring and summer, too, glades and rides are alive with woodland butterflies. Oak woods in the south and Midlands are the home of the handsome purple emperor. Some of our rarest butterflies are woodland species, as is one of our most numerous – the speckled wood.

But perhaps the true glory of a wood in spring and summer is its wild flowers. First to bloom are the snowdrops, appearing in February in the damp woods of the West Country. Then follows the miraculous pageant of primroses and violets, pale wood anemones and early purple orchids, the white and garlic-smelling ramsons, and most wondrous sight of all, the misty carpets of bluebells which flourish more beautifully and more generously in the woods of Britain than anywhere else on earth.

Bluebells are also among the most ancient of our woodland ground flora. Together with other species such as dog's mercury, and much scarcer flowers such as solomon's seal and the true oxlip, they can be clues which reveal the existence of a truly ancient wood; tenacious survivors which may once have bloomed in the age of the long-vanished wildwood.

A beech wood on the North Downs in Kent. The beech was one of the last of our truly native trees to colonise the British Isles and it is thought that its natural distribution only extends as far north as the Cotswolds.

The way that a wood is used changes its structure. Two main traditions of woodland management are described on pages 14, 15; forestry (another kind of management) on page 66. The bird life is one aspect of woodland which reflects its structure, page 50.

Looking at woods

Many of our woods have been in existence ever since the land was colonised by trees at the end of the Ice Age. Others grow on ground that was once cleared, but even these may now be hundreds of years old. However, old age does not mean that the wood is completely natural.

In a natural wood the vegetation tends to grow beneath the leafy canopy of the trees in rather patchy layers. There is plenty of dead wood lying rotting on the ground. When old trees die and fall, youngsters thrust up to replace them, so that in time the wood contains trees of many different ages and sizes, and often trees of many different kinds, each competing for space.

Through the centuries, our woods have been used in ways which have changed their structure and appearance. One important tradition was 'coppice-with-standards', when a supply of poles, staves and brushwood was extracted by regularly cutting the woody growth back to ground level. This was the coppice, and dotted through it were standard trees, allowed to grow tall for their timber. Other woods were set aside for livestock and this 'wood pasture' developed a more open look, as the animals browsed back the underwood.

Over the last three centuries there has been a gradual change of emphasis away from the woodmanship traditions, which essentially relied on producing a sustainable yield from the existing trees, to silviculture which concentrates on producing new crops from seeds or seedling trees. Oak, beech and other native timber trees were often planted, to form a type of 'high forest' hardwood timber plantation where the trees were grown in close proximity to discourage side branching and provide tall straight trunks. The latest step in this direction is today's alien conifer plantations. So, when looking for indications of the original woodland diversity it is often safer to be guided by the ground plants and non-timber trees.

Natural woods untouched by man no longer exist in Britain, but we do have a variety of woods large and small, which have been in existence for a long time, whatever their origin. Perhaps they contain many different kinds of trees, shrubs or other plants, and are not much disturbed. These 'semi-natural' woods are, from a conservation point of view, the best we have, and sometimes their variety can be safeguarded only by continuing or restoring the former management practices.

Many of our more ancient woodlands have a richness and variety of structure which enables them to support a wide variety of wildlife. This view from a woodland ride clearly shows the multi-layering that can result in a semi-natural wood. The towering oaks provide a backcloth to a shrub layer of hazel and sallow, whilst the open nature of the ride has allowed two oak saplings to establish themselves. The dark green spikes of rush amidst the herb layer in the foreground indicate that the drainage is poor.

Natural, unmanaged woodland will exhibit a wide variety of structures: in parts the canopy will be closed with young trees growing close together pushing up to reach the light; in other areas, perhaps where a large tree has been felled by a storm, the wood will be more open with the decaying timber left to rot on the floor and surrounded by saplings which have sprouted up to take advantage of the light. At the woodland edge and around these glades the tree will branch strongly towards the more open areas. The wood will therefore have trees of many different ages and shapes and, if old, will have many different species as well.

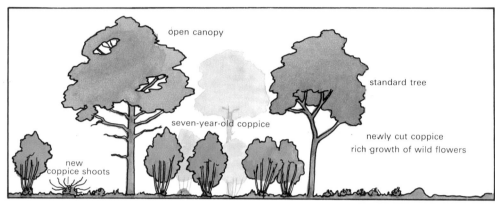

Coppice-with-standards woodland has a lower profile than natural woodland as the smaller trees and shrubs are regularly cut (coppiced) leaving a scattering of single high-crowned standard trees for timber production. The woods are usually divided into small compartments marked by low boundary banks, whilst the whole wood may be enclosed by a large sinuous bank to keep livestock and deer out. Neglected coppice can still be identified by the presence of 'many-trunked' trees.

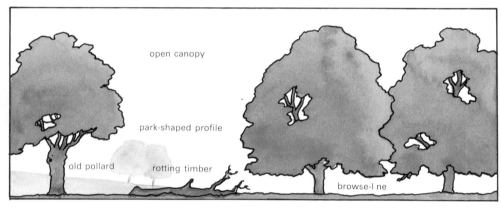

Wood pasture has a more open feel to it, with widely spaced trees exhibiting a broad, 'parkland' profile with, perhaps, a clear browse line at the base if there are deer or cattle still present. Some of the trees will have been pollarded – regularly cut at about head height – to provide a supply of poles for fuelwood or for fodder. This practice, like coppicing, can extend the life of the tree.

In a plantation the trees, whether they are hardwoods or softwoods, are usually planted close to each other in order to promote strong upward growth. There will be obvious blocks of even-aged trees with little underwood and few, if any, saplings. Dead wood will have been removed and the planted trees will be usually all of one species, e.g. beech. If the plantation is neglected it will start to show signs of natural high forest, as woodland glades may form as the result of felling or damage. The wide woodland rides and fire breaks may still contain some of the plants of the original wood.

Primary and secondary woodland

Primary woodland is a direct descendant of the wildwood. It has never been cleared since the site was first colonised after the last Ice Age. These woods are often found in places that are relatively inaccessible, such as steep slopes, or occupy wet ground which was less suitable for farming. An important aspect of the wildwood was its local variety. In one place the low banks along a stream may have slipped and the resultant bare soil may have been colonised with plants which we now find widespread in the open countryside as 'weeds'. A short distance away there could be a permanent patch of marsh indicating a spring line. Further on, an outcrop of soft sandy rock could be marked by very different ground plants and shrubs beneath the trees. These differences are mostly smoothed away when man clears a wood so you are more likely to see them in a primary wood.

You will sometimes come across clear signs of disturbance beneath the trees – diggings of some kind, perhaps, or the unmistakable ridge and furrow pattern of medieval ploughing. In the long history of our countryside, countless patches of open land must have been abandoned to be colonised anew by trees. Such secondary woodland, as it is called, may be hundreds or even thousands of years old by now and would have been subject to the same management practices as primary woodland.

Native trees to be found in woodland are shown on pages 20–26, and pages 28, 82 show the variety of shrubs, many of which were useful as coppice. Coppiced woods are noted for their spring flowers (pages 32, 34), butterflies (44) and birds (52, 54).

Coppice woodlands

If the wood is at all old, then there is a good chance that it was once worked as coppice-with-standards. This is a tradition which has survived well into this century, though only a relatively few woods are still being coppiced today.

Depending on the kinds of shrubs and young trees growing (and maybe the use for the crop of poles), the coppice or underwood is cut back to ground level when it is between 7 and 15 years of age. The timber trees or standards are felled in their prime, at ages between 70 and 150 years, often as a direct multiple of the coppice. The coppice cut encourages growth in the field layer with the spring flowers reaching a peak of profusion two or three years afterwards. Birds are also attracted by the growing coppice, as it gives good, but well lit cover. They often occupy it for a definite span of years, when the height and denseness exactly suits them. Nightingales, for example, use coppice from its third year, but tend to forsake it after the seventh, even though it may remain uncut for a further number of years. A short coppice rotation encourages this fine songster.

A coppice woodland was often divided up into compartments, sometimes marked out with low banks. Each was cut in turn to give a regular, annual crop of poles and brushwood. Therefore the butterflies, birds and other animals did not have far to migrate from one compartment to another, seeking conditions which suited them. Plants, too, could seed themselves successfully into the lighter, recently cut compartments or remain dormant until the next cut brought with it light to stimulate them into new growth. In other words, the reason why many of our woods are so rich in variety with many species of plants and animals, is partly *because* of centuries of coppice management.

Research has shown that some trees and shrubs are to be found only in ancient woods. Some groups of woodland flowers which take time to establish themselves can also indicate ancient woodland.

An old wood is often the result of addition and subtraction of trees; the underwood too, but to a lesser extent. The trees may not be as 'natural' to the site as the shrubs and the spring flowers below them.

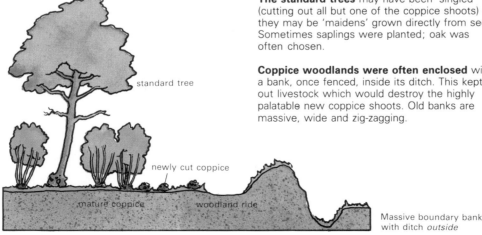

An area of coppice woodland carpeted with dog's mercury. The freshly cut ash stools in the foreground are probably over 350 years old and will soon begin to put up a fresh crop of 'poles'. The standard trees are mostly oaks with some recently singled birches. In the background is another compartment with coppice that has put on seven years' growth.

Though many of our oldest trees are pollards, the oldest living thing in Britain may be an ancient coppice ash stool growing on wet ground in Felsham Hall Wood in Suffolk. It is about 6 metres across, and maybe over a thousand years old.

Coppice stools renew their vitality at each cut – the outer ring of living bark throws up a strong growth of new shoots even though the heartwood at the centre of the stool may decay, and even disappear.

standard tree

newly cut coppice

mature coppice   woodland ride

Massive boundary bank with ditch *outside*

The standard trees may have been 'singled' (cutting out all but one of the coppice shoots) or they may be 'maidens' grown directly from seed. Sometimes saplings were planted; oak was often chosen.

Coppice woodlands were often enclosed with a bank, once fenced, inside its ditch. This kept out livestock which would destroy the highly palatable new coppice shoots. Old banks are massive, wide and zig-zagging.

Pollarded trees are a feature of wood pasture – and they are often our oldest surviving trees, a natural scrapbook of incidents which you can learn to read, page 18. Do not forget that rabbits (page 146) can be as important grazers within woods as elsewhere.

Wood pasture

Although grasses may crowd out the other woodland plants on wet or sandy soils, carpets of grass under the trees or clearings with lawns often mean that animals are grazing the wood. This has an old tradition.

Rough grazing for the villagers' livestock was an important part of the villagers' common land rights. This practice was usually allowed on 'manorial waste' land, and the livestock freely wandered in these woodlands as well as over the waste heath and marshes on which the villagers also had other rights such as to collect firewood or smallwood for fencing. Forests and chases were also partly wooded grazing land, but they were set aside in particular, for deer for the hunt and were subject to specific laws. The king had the right to hunt the forests, whilst other magnates had rights to hunt in the chases. Here, strict 'forest' laws took precedence over the legal commoners' rights.

Sometimes areas were fenced off to allow trees to grow and grazing was resumed once the trees had established themselves. Sometimes, too, the local bye-laws controlling grazing changed, with the result that what was once wood pasture may now contain trees of two or more different but clearly distinct ages. Parts of the New Forest are a good example of this. Many of the trees in these woods were pollarded giving the woodland a distinctive profile.

Wood grazings and forests were not normally fenced – the deer stayed in the forests from force of habit. Deer parks, however, were fenced – they could almost be called deer farms, as they gave a supply of fresh winter meat, as well as providing sport for the landowners. There were once over 2000 deer parks.

As a tradition, wood pasture is all but dead. True, in the hills of the west and north, old parish coppice woods are sometimes used for sheltering and grazing sheep, and with their grassy floors they resemble the wood pastures of centuries gone by. The trees, however, are not quite the same. Only in a few places can you find the last true echo of the ancient tradition – in Borrowdale and Langdale in the Lake District, for example, where the ash trees are still regularly pollarded.

Wood pasture could create an attractive view, with old and widely spreading trees set in grassy open ground. It is an especially English view – there is nothing quite like it elsewhere. This 'park' view was admired and copied by the Georgian landscape designers when they laid out their own new 'parks' for the gentry.

Grazing reduces the variety of plant life in a wood, though some flowers may survive. Cattle and deer also attack trees and shrubs. They strip both bark and leaves from ash, elm and hazel, but the less palatable oak and beech they leave to last, so that really old wood pasture can come to contain these two trees and few, if any, others.

Holly can also suffer – though prickly, it is eaten in winter. In the Scottish Highlands, deer still cause serious problems, reducing the pine forest to heather moor.

A stand of grand old oaks in the ancient forest of Sherwood in Nottinghamshire. The long history of grazing has produced a typically open grassy ground layer, with bracken dominating some areas later in the year. The absence of shrubs and lack of regeneration has meant that the trees have developed broad open profiles with strong branching low down the trunk. These trees are probably not much older than the ash stools shown opposite!

The bank of a deer park, with its fence (the park 'pale') on top of it, was outside the ditch – the idea being to keep the animals in. This is the opposite to the coppice boundary bank.

Pollards were no use for timber, and so they were left to grow. Many of our most ancient trees are pollards. Decayed in parts, they are nature reserves in their own right – beetles and other insects, as well as many lichens, flourish on the rotten timbers, and birds find plenty of nest holes. Pollarding is seldom practised today except by water authorities on riverside willows.

old pollard

Massive boundary bank with ditch *inside*

The spring flowers and other plants you see in a sporting covert will reflect its own particular history – some are rich, others poor. But in such a wood, often gutted of its sound timber and let-go, look for the story markers shown on page 36.

Sporting woods

Pheasants mean more than just an exotic flash of colour; they mark an important use of many small woods today. These woods have frequently been gutted of their sound timber, especially in the early years of this century, and without the sporting interest there would be every pressure to fell them for the plough or for new plantations. As a pointer to identifying a small sporting wood, also known as a 'covert', look for small strips of kale, sunflower or maize planted in open ground near the wood as well as thickets of bushy shrubs such as snowberry, planted as cover for the pheasants. Another clue may be a patch of apparently uncleared scrub, also for cover, in the middle of cultivated farmland.

The management of sporting woods is exclusively tailored to the needs of the pheasant. For cover, the wood needs a dense underwood, which may be provided by a neglected coppice cut from time to time to thicken it. In older, more open woods, rhododendrons were specifically planted for the purpose. Yew trees may also have been grown in small clumps to provide the birds with roosting sites away from predators, such as foxes.

The pheasants themselves are as closely managed as the woods they live in. At the end of the shooting season – which runs from the 1st of October to the 1st of February, but not Sundays or Christmas Day – the gamekeeper traps enough hens to produce the next season's eggs. The hens' wings are 'hobbled' with leather brails to stop them flying, and then they are released into laying pens. The eggs are collected and incubated until the chicks hatch. Before they are released the chicks are acclimatised in heated brooders in the wood. The adult birds are given supplementary feed at regularly placed feeding stations in the woods. Without all these measures the birds would be able to maintain themselves quite successfully, but there would be too few for the sportsmen.

The management of these woodlands for the benefit of the pheasants also creates oases for other wildlife which would otherwise have been unable to survive in the surrounding farmland.

Pheasants are common in open wooded areas and mixed farmland with reasonable cover as well as 'sporting woods'. It is thought that they were originally introduced to Britain during the Roman occupation but there are no firm records of their existence here until the 11th century when they featured on various banquet menus. These early introductions were almost certainly the Southern Caucasus pheasant or Old English black-neck. In the 18th century further birds from China were imported with a distinctive white collar and these together with later introductions freely interbred with the original stock so that today the wild pheasant is a true hybrid. The brightly coloured cocks are at their most noticeable in spring when they can be heard loudly crowing and strutting as they establish their territories. The cock takes no part in the incubating of the eggs or the rearing of the chicks and may well mate with other hens. They are normally shy birds, and although they will fly strongly over the guns when flushed out by beaters, if you disturb them on a walk they will usually run, head down, to hide rather than fly.

A cock pheasant proclaiming his territory. In the spring they are very vocal, crowing loudly, ruffling their feathers and flapping their wings in a similar manner to a domestic cockerel. This bird is surrounded by hens, which frequently follow the cock on his territorial rounds.

The golden pheasant and Lady Amherst's pheasant were introduced into this country in the 19th century, mostly by releasing birds on the large sporting estates. The golden pheasant came from the mountains of central China and first bred in the wild in this country at the end of the last century. The cock is a splendidly gaudy bird – in the worst possible taste many would think. In spite of his colouring, however, he is retiring in habit and something of a prize to see. Feral populations can be found in the Brecklands of East Anglia and Galloway.

Lady Amherst's pheasant also comes originally from China, although it was named after the wife

Pheasant
Phasianus colchicus

male

female

chick

Lady Amherst's pheasant
Chrysolophus amherstiae

'white collared' male

Golden pheasant
Chrysolophus pictus

At night pheasants roost off the ground on the lower branches of the covert trees (*left*). Like many birds, they take dust baths which may help rid them of ticks and other parasites.

of the Governor General of India, who first sent specimens to England. It is found mainly in the Bedfordshire area in a few conifer plantations, and deciduous woodlands where there is dense undergrowth. It is very elusive and if disturbed runs and hides rather than flies.

Vermin such as grey squirrels, stoats, weasels, rats and crows are trapped and poisoned for the threat they pose to the young pheasants. They are hung up on a gamekeeper's gibbet in the hope they will frighten off any other predators which might be around.

A pole trap. These lethal traps, now illegal, were once frequently used by gamekeepers to kill 'vermin' on the large Victorian woodland estates. Often the trapped animal would be left to a slow death with its leg or foot caught in the trap.

The gall-makers are only some of the invertebrate animals that the generous oak provides a home for: others are shown on page 48. Birds are attracted by these insects: see pages 52, 54; hole-nesting birds (page 50) are likely to be seen in woods with old trees.

Reading an oak tree

An old oak, especially one at the edge of a wood or in a hedge, often has the look of a battle-scarred veteran. Its wide expanse of trunk may have been used as a convenient village noticeboard or, indeed, some carving may have been carried out on the bark itself. Frequently fencing wire will have been nailed to it and various inconvenient limbs will have been removed, all leaving their own distinctive scars. A change in the drainage as the result of the piping of an old stream may result in the topmost branches dying back as the tree retrenches its growth. This 'stag-heading' may also be the result of a combination of defoliation by caterpillars and drought. In a warm spring an abundance of caterpillars can strip a tree of its leaves and, although there may be a second flush of growth ('lammas growth') later in the year, the outer branches will be weakened and may die, especially if there is drought later in the year.

Each epidemic has its own particular history. In 1927, many oaks died in the south of England when oak-leaf roller caterpillars defoliated the trees, and a mildew weakened the second flush, followed by attacks of bark fungi. In 1965, in Norfolk, when durmast oaks were the victim, the epidemic was started by drought. Then the moth caterpillars and mildews attacked the already weakened trees. One way or another, drought seems always to play a part. Below the dead limbs the oak may put on vigorous new growth and continue to thrive for many further years. However, a red danger signal for the tree may be the sight of a parasitic fungus such as a bracket fungus high up on the bark, or the lethal honey fungus.

Honey fungus

In woodland, honey fungus can play an important part in the destruction of dead and old trees. However, there are reports of oaks growing healthily on sites that carry the fungus, and it may be that the fungus is the nail in the coffin of a tree that is already dying back. Without the fungus, it could live on. With it, it has no hope.

The fungus spreads in two ways, by means of spores and by long black strands, called 'rhizomorphs', which look like long, black bootlaces. These can spread through the soil for up to ten metres; and on reaching a tree they force their way up between bark and heartwood and permeate it with fine white feeding threads – this pure white 'rot' shines in the dark as a result of enzyme action. Honey fungus is seen as groups of twenty or more caps in autumn on stumps, dead trunks, on the soil under a tree (where it may be attacking the roots), and even on living trees. The cap is 2–10 cm across, honey coloured and covered with brownish hairy-looking scales.

The fungus is poisonous when raw – though it is said to be delicious when thoroughly cooked. It is probably safer not to try!

Recipe for an old tree Look for an oak or similar long-lived species, on poor soil (and therefore growing slowly), out of woodland and pollarded in the past (so that its timber is valueless and not worth the trouble of felling). Burrs on the trunk are a good sign; they can produce new branches should the crown above them die, or branches fall.

How old is the tree? Here is a simple way of estimating the age of a tree.

Measure the girth, the distance around the trunk, at head height (about 1.5 m from the ground).

If the tree is growing in a wood, close set with others, and with a straightish trunk

1.25 cm }
½ inch } girth = 1 year of age

If the tree is standing by itself out in open, with widespread branches

2.5 cm }
1 inch } girth = 1 year of age

Rough and ready? Yes, but better than cutting the tree down to count its rings!

Lichens are often seen on trees – but only if the air is clean. These are classic pollution indicators. Lichens are rootless and rely on rain for nutrients, so are sensitive to any poisons dissolved in it. One such is sulphur dioxide, a gas released when oil, coal and even smokeless fuels are burnt.

Mark the air pollution with lichens

	clean air	some pollution	heavy pollution – are you in a town?
crusty (miniature crazy paving)	●	●	●
leafy (flat rosettes stuck to the bark)	●	●	
shrubby (miniature bunches of ribbons)	●		

It is only in recent centuries with increased pollution that the bark of most trees has been exposed to view. Before then they would have looked like this old poplar, bedecked with the fine ribbons of *Usnea* and *Evernia* lichens and covered with the leafy fronds of *Parmelia* lichens.

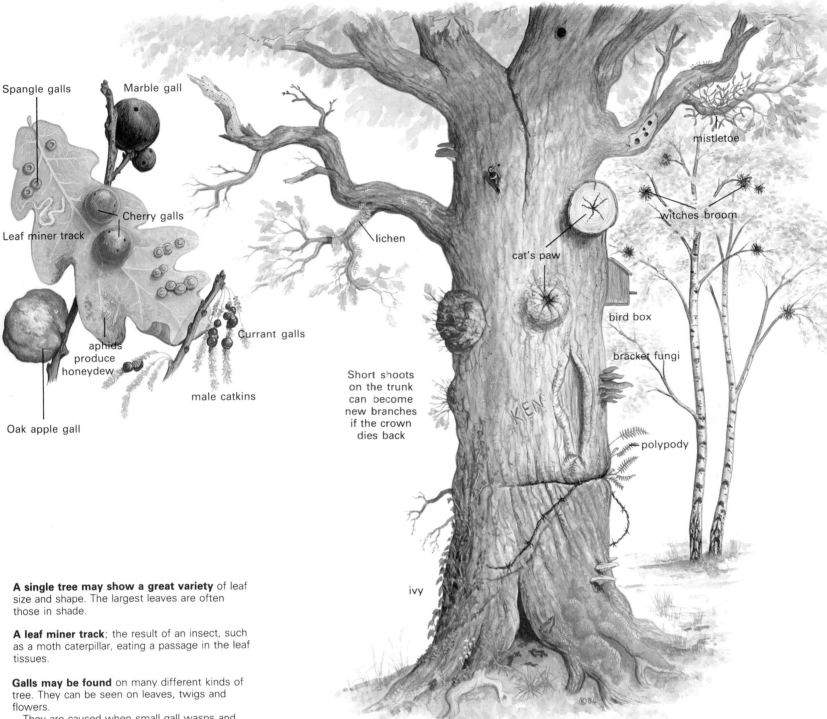

Spangle galls

Marble gall

Leaf miner track

Cherry galls

aphids produce honeydew

Currant galls

male catkins

Oak apple gall

lichen

cat's paw

bird box

bracket fungi

Short shoots on the trunk can become new branches if the crown dies back

polypody

ivy

mistletoe

witches broom

A single tree may show a great variety of leaf size and shape. The largest leaves are often those in shade.

A leaf miner track; the result of an insect, such as a moth caterpillar, eating a passage in the leaf tissues.

Galls may be found on many different kinds of tree. They can be seen on leaves, twigs and flowers.
   They are caused when small gall wasps and other invertebrates lay their eggs in the living tissues, which then swell, to create a home for the grub. They are very noticeable on oaks and willows. Some galls, such as witches broom, may be caused by fungi.

Dark stains may be mildew (a type of fungus), but may be the rotting honeydew released by aphids and, consequently, are harmless.

Ivy uses the tree solely for support; it has its own root system and photosynthesises its own sugars. It is harmless to trees.

Numbers of insect species which trees play host to, for at least part of their lives

NATIVE TREES		INTRODUCED	
oak	284	spruce	37
willow	266	larch	17
birch	229	fir	16
hawthorn	149	sycamore	15
blackthorn	109	sweet chestnut	5
poplars	97	horse chestnut	4
apple	93	plane	0 (!)
Scots pine	91		
alder	90		
elm	82		
hazel	73		
beech	64		
ash	41		
small leaved lime	31		
rowan	28		
hornbeam	28		
field maple	26		
holly	7		
yew	1		

Oak wilt and the wilting treescapes of Britain

Oak trees face a threat rather similar to Dutch elm disease (described on page 80). This is oak wilt, and it is also spread from tree to tree by bark beetles. This disease affects the tree by interfering with the free flow of water and sap within the bark. It has already caused great havoc amongst red oaks in North America and many fear its arrival in Britain.

Oak wilt would create havoc, of course, to a treescape already threadbare in many counties as a result of the death of the elms. But even if it did not reach Britain, will the traditional tree'd countryside view remain? This vista is created largely by the hedgerow trees. However, a scrutiny of these trees shows something very disturbing. You will find that most of them are mature or semi-mature, as there are precious few young saplings growing above the tops of the hedges. Although in some counties there has been a definite policy to encourage

tree planting along hedgerows, much new planting is in pockets, along laybys and similar places, where maintenance is easier. An educated guess is that to maintain existing tree stocks in the landscape, let alone increase numbers, at least six saplings should be growing for every mature tree, which assumes that five will at some time fall victim to disease, accidental hedgerow fires and other hazards. A glance along any hedgerow will speak for itself.

On the other hand, plenty of healthy young saplings are growing within the hedges. They could become trees and, in the past, many of them were encouraged to do just this, for the value of their timber or foliage. Today, they are chopped by the mechanical flail. In a way, it would make more sense to protect those saplings already rooted rather than plant others. But then, the hedge would be more trouble to trim!

As a result of soil, climate and history, the two native oaks each form different kinds of woodland, examples are seen on pages 60 and 61. Match the soil chart shown here with that on page 35 to explain some of the plant communities you find.

The oaks

For most people our classic broad-leaved tree must surely be the majestic oak. It might come as a surprise, then, to find that there are two species of native British Oak: the common or pedunculate oak and the durmast or sessile oak. Both are found throughout Britain, although woodlands on heavy lowland clays usually contain common oaks, whilst the poorer hill soils of the west and north often carry durmast oak. These oaks are now one of our most common native timber trees. However, analysis of pollen preserved in peat bogs shows that historically other species such as lime, elm and ash were as numerous for long periods. The population and distribution of the oaks has been considerably influenced by man. He has not only widely planted them, particularly the common oak in the past, as a timber tree but often selectively thinned out other species in preference for these. This was because for many years their timber was highly valued for ship and house building.

Where the soils were too shallow or poor to encourage a reasonable growth, the oaks were often managed as coppice. In this instance, the oak bark was an important product as tannin could be extracted, providing the raw material for a large leather tanning industry. This reached a peak at the beginning of the 19th century – in the period 1810 to 1815, England alone produced 90,000 tons of oak bark for tanning. The bark was stripped from the coppice poles which were cut on a twenty-year cycle as the tannin content declined with age. Imported bark, particularly from France, eventually led to the decline of this trade.

As a free standing tree, the common oak is broader than the durmast oak, and has clearly 'zig-zag' branching, which provided usefully curved timbers for ship building. Both oaks grow 30 metres tall or more. The tallest oak in Britain is a durmast oak in Hereford – 41 metres high.

The reason for the 'zig-zag' branching is interesting: the shoot from an end bud of the twig is often weak, and fails, and a strong side shoot then continues last year's growth.

The leaf of common oak has deep lobes and two (often curled) ears where it joins the short stalk. The underside of the leaf is hairless. The acorns are carried, maybe two or three together, on a long stalk. The acorn is blunter than that of the durmast oak. The male catkins can be seen in April, the female flowers (bud-shaped catkins) open later with the leaves. The pollen is wind blown.

The durmast oak leaf has shallow lobes, and the leaf runs smoothly into the longish stalk (maybe 2.5 cm long). The ribs under the leaf are usually hairy.

The acorns have a very short stalk or no stalk at all; hence the other name for this tree – sessile oak. The durmast oak is less often found outside woods. The common oak is frequently met in hedgerows.

Intermediate forms between the two species are often found as the trees can hybridise producing offspring which will readily 'back-cross' with the parent trees – a type of hybridization known as 'introgression'.

Hearts of oak

A heart of oak, the dictionary tells us, is a stout, courageous person; a man of strength and endurance; part of the national character, as popular belief would have it.

There is no doubt at all that oak trees were in part responsible for the power and influence of Britain in past centuries. Oak trees were used to build ships – men-o-war and trading vessels; a 74-gun warship needed 4,000 tons of timber. Everything on a ship could be made of oak, except for the masts, which were usually pine. Moreover, the corkscrewing branches of the common oak provided handy 'compass cuts' or 'knees' – curving timbers which needed only surface-finishing to be used. They were extremely durable as there were no cuts across the curving grain. These shaped pieces, as well as lengths of straight timber, could be obtained from the tall trees of the coppice-with-standard plots, but larger timbers – needed for the larger vessels – would have been supplied from free-standing 'park' and wood pasture trees. It is also thought that hedgerow or laneside trees were a valuable source of large timber in those days.

It is not at all certain, indeed, the facts seem to lie the other way, that the demand for ships' timbers finally destroyed the remaining forests of Old England. The navy's needs were often met from managed woodlands and royal forests, and usually only from those areas near the ports (with the addition of field trees, as mentioned above). But there was a degree of scaremongering and journalists, true to their tradition, found it a splendidly splenetic subject. By the late 17th century large areas of the Forest of Dean and the New Forest were being taken over to grow oak timber. They were the first large scale plantations. Many coppice woodlands were planted up with oaks in the early 19th century in response

to high timber prices. In the event, however, only a small proportion of this oak was used. Before a century had passed, supplies of cheap Baltic softwood had become important for many uses and the pressure was taken off the existing groves of oak.

In the first half of the 19th century, more than half the wooden vessels ever built in Britain were constructed, yet there

seems to have been trees enough. If anything, the woodland was being, and had been, destroyed by the relentless push for improved arable and pasture farming. Much the same can be concluded about the destruction of the Wealden forests. Here iron was smelted locally, but the charcoal for the furnaces would have been sensibly supplied from coppicing.

An ancient oak in the New Forest in Hampshire. This is one of the best surviving Royal Forests in England and still contains thousands of hectares of old woods, some of which may well have an ancestry dating back to the original wildwood.

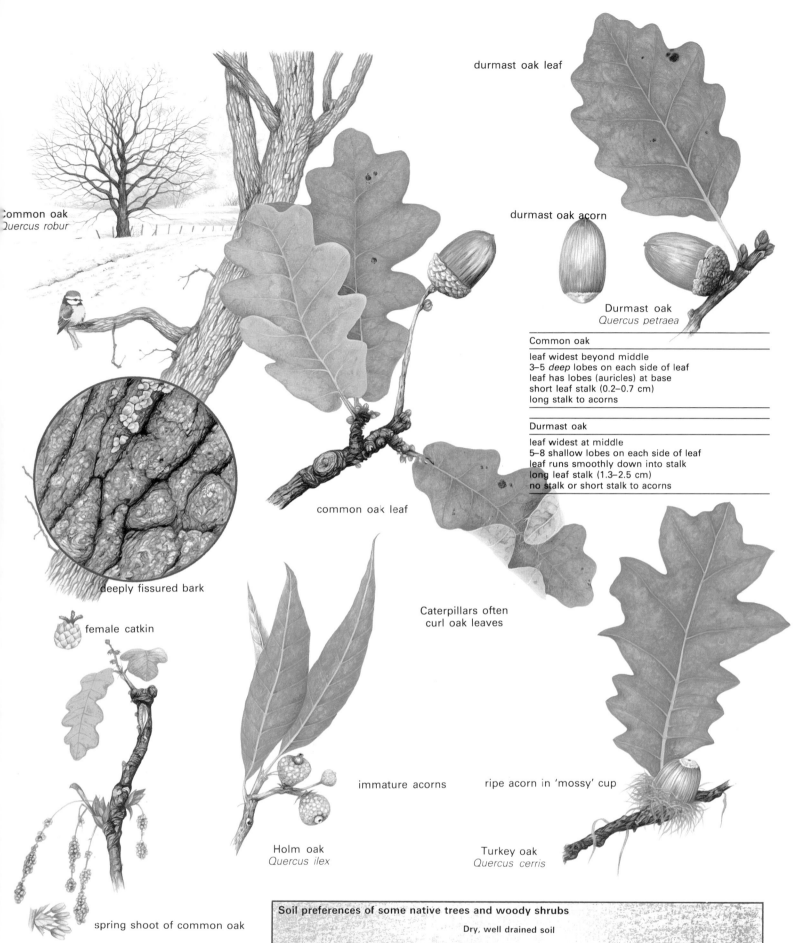

durmast oak leaf

durmast oak acorn

Durmast oak
Quercus petraea

Common oak
Quercus robur

deeply fissured bark

female catkin

common oak leaf

Caterpillars often
curl oak leaves

immature acorns

ripe acorn in 'mossy' cup

spring shoot of common oak

male catkins

Holm oak
Quercus ilex

Turkey oak
Quercus cerris

Common oak
leaf widest beyond middle
3–5 *deep* lobes on each side of leaf
leaf has lobes (auricles) at base
short leaf stalk (0.2–0.7 cm)
long stalk to acorns

Durmast oak
leaf widest at middle
5–8 shallow lobes on each side of leaf
leaf runs smoothly down into stalk
long leaf stalk (1.3–2.5 cm)
no stalk or short stalk to acorns

Holm oak is a Mediterranean tree and can
sometimes be found naturalised, growing in dry
woods in the south. It is evergreen, with glossy
dark green leaves, woolly-white underneath,
which become khaki coloured with age.

The Turkey oak is native to southern Europe
and southwest Asia, but grows well in Britain. It
is now naturalised in many places. Its leaves are
rather variable in shape; hairy-rough above. Note
the 'mossy' cup to the acorn.

Soil preferences of some native trees and woody shrubs

Dry, well drained soil

Alkaline (limy) soil

Acid soil

BEECH   spindle   wayfaring tree   DURMAST OAK   BEECH

BOX   YEW   broom

            SMALL-LEAVED LIME   ROWAN

                        privet

WHITEBEAM   HOLLY

dogwood

    FIELD MAPLE   BIRCH

            ASH   WILD SERVICE TREE

        elder   heather
                                                        bilberry
        ELM   COMMON OAK

            hazel   dog rose

                HORNBEAM   blackthorn

    midland hawthorn   common hawthorn

The TREES
named here are   ASPEN   SALLOWS
shown on pages   buckthorns   The shrubs
20–30, and can be   named here are
located via the index   guelder rose   ALDER   WILLOWS   shown on pages
                                                              28 and 82
Wet, poorly drained soil

21

Woodlands formed by beech and ash trees are described on pages 62, 63, but we see that a good many of those natural-looking woods have been planted or arisen naturally in recent centuries. These two trees are also prominent in hedgerows in some areas, page 80.

Beech and ash

Although the elegant beech is certainly one of our native trees, the British Isles are on the very fringe of its natural range and probably only in the south of England and Wales can it be considered to be truly indigenous. Today, however, beech can be found growing almost throughout Britain as it has been widely planted for its dense, even-grained timber, which makes excellent furniture, and its ability to grow successfully on shallow hill-top soils forming first-rate shelter belts. For example, many of the famous Chiltern beechwoods are growing on what 400 years ago was open sheepwalk. The trees were planted to supply timber for the nearby furniture workshops.

Contrary to popular opinion, beech will grow well on either sandy or chalky soils provided they are well drained. On these soils it forms the natural climax vegetation as its seedlings will grow strongly under the shade of other trees, including oak and may be ready to replace them when they die.

Over the years, the distinctive smooth grey bark of the beech has often fallen victim to the need for people to carve out a record of their presence. Some of the larger park trees are often severely defaced as a result. However, some of the carvings that were carried out in the last century were often stylishly done.

The beech can grow to 30 metres, reaching maturity in 80 years or so. Though large, it is not very long lived – though pollarding will extend its normal span. Usually when it is about 150 years old, it begins to decline, and may begin to drop massive branches. Beech has thin, smooth grey bark.

The unmistakable fresh translucent green of young beech leaves darkens as the summer gets under way. Some young trees keep their dead leaves through the winter.

The flowers are seen with the opening leaves in April and May. The males are somewhat more obvious, hanging tassel-like on a long stalk. The female flowers stand up on the twigs.

The mast or beech nuts are shed in October; they are enclosed in a woody case which splits open. They are poisonous if eaten in large numbers, causing severe stomach cramps. The mast is not produced in quantity every year – good mast years occur every four or five years.

Beech is a shallow rooting tree – part of the reason why it can grow well on the thin soils of steep slopes (page 62). Its fine roots strike up an association (a mycorrhiza) with a soil fungus. The mycorrhiza forms a whitish cloak around the rootlets, and helps the tree take up water and nutrients – a distinct advantage in such soils.

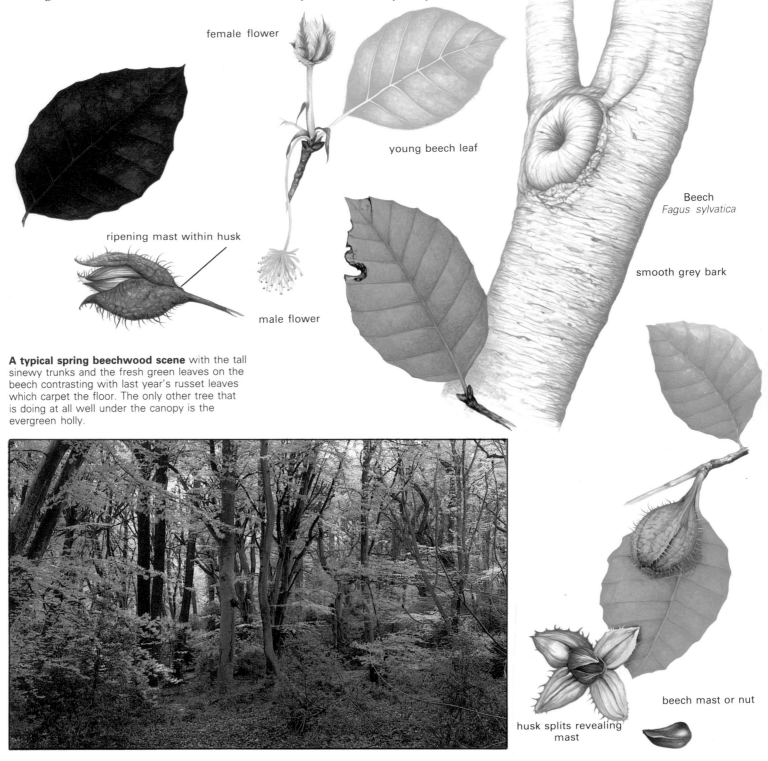

female flower

young beech leaf

ripening mast within husk

male flower

Beech
Fagus sylvatica

smooth grey bark

A typical spring beechwood scene with the tall sinewy trunks and the fresh green leaves on the beech contrasting with last year's russet leaves which carpet the floor. The only other tree that is doing at all well under the canopy is the evergreen holly.

beech mast or nut

husk splits revealing mast

Did beech trees give their name to Buckinghamshire?

. . . for the Old English name of the beech tree is *bece*, which easily becomes buck.

Some place names recall animals of the old wildwood: Beverley in Yorkshire, the beaver; Catford in Kent, the wild cat. Other names are certainly derived from trees: Ashton and Esher from the ash; while alder has named Allerton and Ellerbeck. The Old English name for the oak was 'ac' which has become Acton, but also Cressage, Dart, Eakring, Hodsock, Knockholt, Matlock and Oxted; deciphering names is a complicated business. We are interested in the history of Britain's woodland, however, so were those places named after the oak because there were many

oaks (hardly unusual) or from one giant old oak? We will probably never know. In the case of other trees, however, the modern name does hold an ecological clue. Chestyns in Essex tells us that the sweet chestnut grew there in the Dark Ages, and Hulver Street in Suffolk recalls the holly, which today is rather uncommon in East Anglia, especially towards the fens. That classic wildwood tree, the small-leaved lime, is alluded to in the names Lindfield and Lyndhurst (the old name for the tree was 'lind').

'Spinney' itself means spine-dense or thorny and 'carr' a wood of alders. Wayland Wood in Norfolk comes from a Norse 'lund' meaning 'grove'. 'Hurst', as

part of a village name, seems to have come from the Saxon meaning isolated grove on a hill, while names ending in '-spring' could indicate coppiced woodland.

A village name with 'ley', 'ly' or 'leigh' as part of it could be interesting. It seems to have meant a woodland clearing – a permanent one – maybe a first settlement in unbroken forest. There are plenty of examples in Cambridgeshire, suggesting that the Anglo Saxons cut themselves clearings in wildwood left untouched by the Romans. Furthermore, by marking those 'woodland' names on the map, it is possible to draw the boundary of that now long vanished wilderness. There are usually plenty of place name books in local libraries for you to do your own detective work.

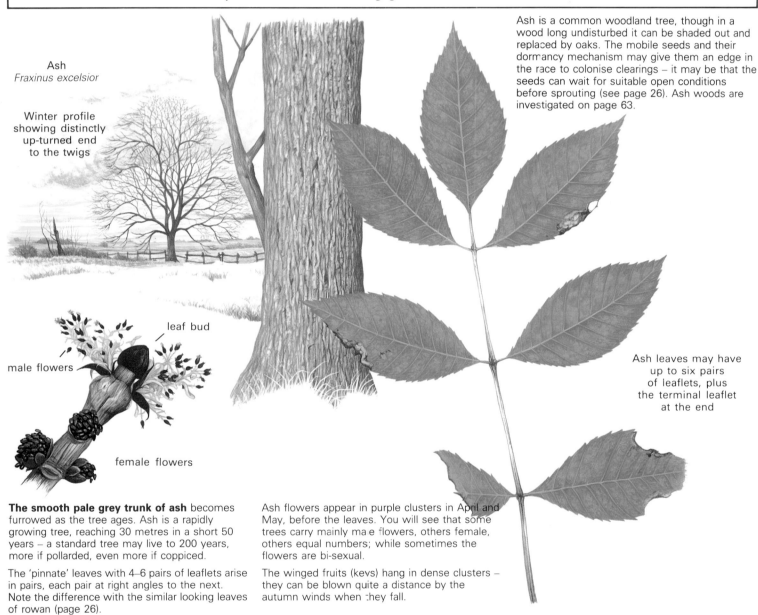

Ash
Fraxinus excelsior

Winter profile showing distinctly up-turned end to the twigs

leaf bud

male flowers

female flowers

Ash is a common woodland tree, though in a wood long undisturbed it can be shaded out and replaced by oaks. The mobile seeds and their dormancy mechanism may give them an edge in the race to colonise clearings – it may be that the seeds can wait for suitable open conditions before sprouting (see page 26). Ash woods are investigated on page 63.

Ash leaves may have up to six pairs of leaflets, plus the terminal leaflet at the end

The smooth pale grey trunk of ash becomes furrowed as the tree ages. Ash is a rapidly growing tree, reaching 30 metres in a short 50 years – a standard tree may live to 200 years, more if pollarded, even more if coppiced.

The 'pinnate' leaves with 4–6 pairs of leaflets arise in pairs, each pair at right angles to the next. Note the difference with the similar looking leaves of rowan (page 26).

The leaves of the ash open late and fall early, whilst still green. The winter twigs with their pairs of black buds are easily recognised.

Ash flowers appear in purple clusters in April and May, before the leaves. You will see that some trees carry mainly male flowers, others female, others equal numbers; while sometimes the flowers are bi-sexual.

The winged fruits (kevs) hang in dense clusters – they can be blown quite a distance by the autumn winds when they fall.

Ash

The ash is one of our commonest trees, growing alongside field maple or oak and hazel in lowland areas, but also sometimes forming impressive woods in its own right in some regions. It is, also, since the disappearance of the elms, one of the commonest trees of the hedgerow, where its sparse winter profile, with up-turned twigs at the end of the branches, is unmistakable. You will often notice that the trees have a ragged crown, dying back at the top. Like beech, they seem to be sensitive to damage and although this 'die-back' is becoming more frequent it is still not certain what is causing it.

Ash was frequently pollarded and giant old pollard trees can still be found, especially in hedges. It was also coppiced as it produced high quality straight poles which were frequently turned into tool handles. Indeed, a small factory in Suffolk still produces rakes from ash coppice. The combination of toughness and elasticity meant that it was also used to construct frames for carts and wagons, and more recently even for aircraft and sports cars.

ash 'keys'

Alders, willows and sallows create woods of the kind shown on page 65. Such woodland was once very extensive in the wetlands. Birch, too, can form a grove within a wood, or sometimes an entire woodland of its own, with a unique character, see page 64.

More native trees

An ancient wood is likely to be an intricate patchwork of different trees, some of it perhaps mixed ash-maple wood, some oakwood and damper areas with stands of alder. Although selective growing of oaks and coppicing may have smoothed out some of this variety it is still often possible to detect it. However, a stand of birch, which is a quick coloniser but does not live much past 70 years of age, may mark a comparatively recent woodland clearing. It will not grow well in shade, but can sometimes be found in small numbers sprinkled through woods with an open canopy.

Sycamore, which was brought here in medieval times, is particularly hardy and was for this reason often planted as a windbreak. Now, however, it is thoroughly established in the wild, and you will often find it invading native woodland. Unfortunately, its large slowly decaying leaves tend to inhibit the ground flora. For this reason it is often disliked by naturalists. However, unlike many alien trees, it does support a small number of insect species, probably those originally associated with field maple, but nowhere near as many as most native trees.

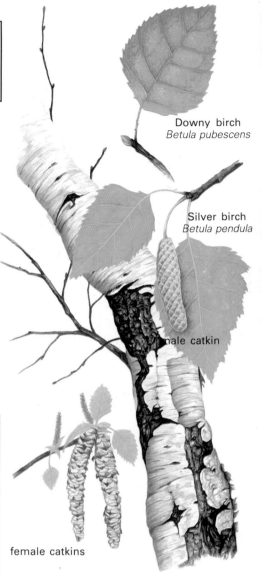

Downy birch
Betula pubescens

Silver birch
Betula pendula

male catkin

female catkins

The black poplar

The black poplar is one of our rarest trees – it is a true native, a tree predominantly of watersides on the flood plains of lowland rivers. Today, as this map shows, its headquarters seem to be in East Anglia.

The map is of a kind used for recording animals and plants in the countryside – a dot represents a positive sighting within a grid of 10 kilometre squares. This map tells you its national distribution at a glance – but, of course, nothing of the local habitats, which are crucial. A large number of sightings within one 10 kilometre square still only warrants a single dot. Therefore, although one dot in Worcestershire represents a common which has no fewer than 80 black poplars, the two dots in Hampshire represent one tree apiece.

Black poplars can grow to become fine trees, with rugged black bark, the trunks often carrying large bosses. The lower branches arch down, giving the tree a distinctive profile. However, it was often pollarded – those 80 trees in the Worcestershire common have been cut in this fashion; and so is the black poplar in the middle of the village of Aston on Clun in Shropshire. This is one of our historic trees – not so much for its age (275 years at least) but for the fact that on Arbor Day, 29th May (which happens to be the date of Oak Apple Day), the villagers usually decorate it with the flags of all nations – as they do for some local

weddings – according to a custom which dates back at least two centuries.

The native wild black poplar is rare, but you may not have to look far to find *a* black poplar. It is resistant to air pollution and was much planted into Manchester and other cities, from cuttings. Those cuttings were taken from the male tree – which has red catkins – as the female makes a nuisance of itself, shedding masses of white fluff from its catkins in June. Many planted black poplars are, in fact, hybrids with American trees. Only in a marlpit in Cheshire and in two other places throughout the country do male and female true native trees grow close enough to each other to set seed.

The research on the distribution of the black poplar was carried out by a retired enthusiast, Edgar Milne-Redhead, with the help of the Botanical Society of the British Isles. This definitive 'map' has had one positive result, for the National Trust and some county conservation Trusts, now they know where the genuine stock can be found, are now planting the authentic breed back into the countryside.

Which birch is it, for there are two closely related species? The **silver birch** is commonest in the south, often marking light dry soil, though it can tolerate wet soils, but not flooded ground – its shallow roots spread near the surface. It is a short-lived tree, reaching 20 metres in 50 years, and rarely surviving 100 years. The outer branchlets hang down and the twigs are smooth with white dots or 'warts'.

The **downy birch** is commoner in the north, often seen on wet moorland. The twigs, which never hang as noticeably as with its cousin, are downy. Its bark is often brownish.

Birches carry male catkins at the ends of the twigs, the female further back. They are seen in April when the leaves are opening.

They produce profuse, light, wind-blown seed, which is easily carried to colonise clearings.

Silver birch
branches hang down
twigs smooth
noticeably triangular leaves with sharp point
double teeth on edges of leaf

Downy birch
branches do not hang down
twigs downy
leaves more rounded
single teeth on edges of leaf

Willows and their kind (and their names) are easily muddled. But they are not too difficult to identify. They are trees of stream sides and other wet places.

The crack willow has fragile twigs which crack when snapped off. Crack willows are still pollarded along river banks, but if allowed to grow, they can reach 20 metres, with a recognisable winter profile given by the side branches running horizontally off the trunk. These branches are weak, however, and often fall (as do the larger branches of old pollards), tearing the bark.

The 'willow-shaped' leaves are green and bare – those of its close relative the white willow are silvery grey with down underneath. (Cricket bat willows are a variety of white willow.)

Willows can easily be grown, quickset, by sticking a green but woody twig into damp soil. Catkins (with male and female flowers on separate trees) are open in April and May.

Willows (and sallows) are extremely important to insects, especially moths – willows can host 266 species, almost matching the generous oak.

The catkins of the willow tribe are pollinated by bees and other insects and are a valuable source of nectar and pollen for them early in the year. Masses of silky-haired wind-blown seeds are produced later in the year.

Sallows are broad-leaved willows, often shrubby. They carry the well-known catkins ('palm' – they are also called 'pussy willow') in

March. Though a quick colonist, a sallow can tolerate some shade and may be found in woodland and often on drier soil. Here we show this **grey sallow** with leaves barely hairy below. The leaves of goat willow (which is a sallow) are densely hairy underneath.

Osiers were once grown extensively in regularly flooded osier beds – they were coppiced for 'rods' for basket making. The common osier (which can grow to a tree of 10 metres) is easily recognised by its long narrow leaves, dark green above, silvery below, with their edges curled over.

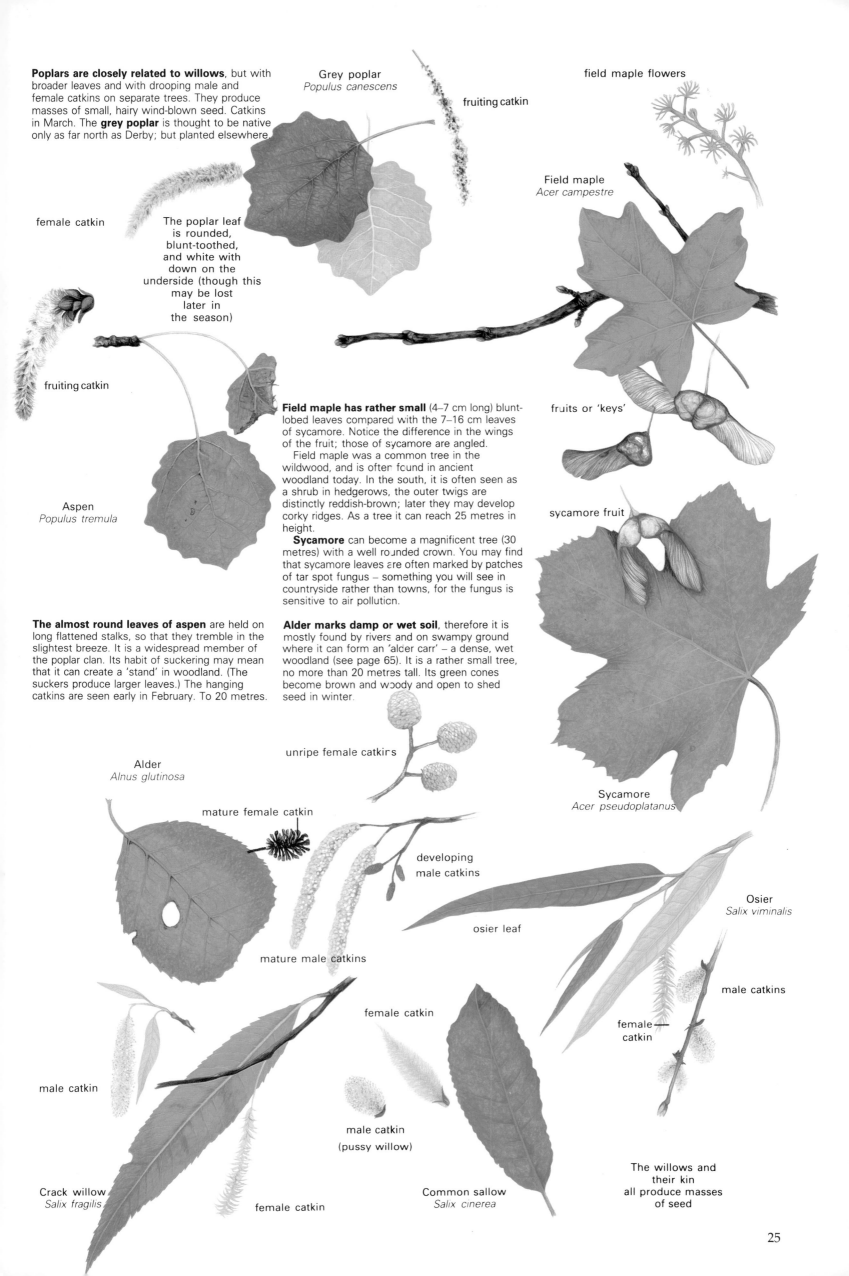

Poplars are closely related to willows, but with broader leaves and with drooping male and female catkins on separate trees. They produce masses of small, hairy wind-blown seed. Catkins in March. The **grey poplar** is thought to be native only as far north as Derby; but planted elsewhere.

Grey poplar
Populus canescens

fruiting catkin

field maple flowers

Field maple
Acer campestre

female catkin

The poplar leaf is rounded, blunt-toothed, and white with down on the underside (though this may be lost later in the season)

fruiting catkin

fruits or 'keys'

Field maple has rather small (4–7 cm long) blunt-lobed leaves compared with the 7–16 cm leaves of sycamore. Notice the difference in the wings of the fruit; those of sycamore are angled.
 Field maple was a common tree in the wildwood, and is often found in ancient woodland today. In the south, it is often seen as a shrub in hedgerows, the outer twigs are distinctly reddish-brown; later they may develop corky ridges. As a tree it can reach 25 metres in height.
 Sycamore can become a magnificent tree (30 metres) with a well rounded crown. You may find that sycamore leaves are often marked by patches of tar spot fungus – something you will see in countryside rather than towns, for the fungus is sensitive to air pollution.

sycamore fruit

Aspen
Populus tremula

The almost round leaves of aspen are held on long flattened stalks, so that they tremble in the slightest breeze. It is a widespread member of the poplar clan. Its habit of suckering may mean that it can create a 'stand' in woodland. (The suckers produce larger leaves.) The hanging catkins are seen early in February. To 20 metres.

Alder marks damp or wet soil, therefore it is mostly found by rivers and on swampy ground where it can form an 'alder carr' – a dense, wet woodland (see page 65). It is a rather small tree, no more than 20 metres tall. Its green cones become brown and woody and open to shed seed in winter.

unripe female catkins

Alder
Alnus glutinosa

mature female catkin

developing male catkins

Sycamore
Acer pseudoplatanus

Osier
Salix viminalis

osier leaf

mature male catkins

male catkins

female catkin

female catkin

male catkin

male catkin
(pussy willow)

Crack willow
Salix fragilis

female catkin

Common sallow
Salix cinerea

The willows and their kin all produce masses of seed

25

Although all these trees are to be found within woods, some are also characteristic of open habitats. Holly and rowan are frequently seen in the uplands, often rooted amongst streamside rocks, out of reach of the grazing sheep: see pages 156, 158.

More native trees

Pollen deposits tell us that many of the trees shown here were common in the original wildwood. The small-leaved lime was one of these. It has been declining due to changes in climate and man's activities for at least 5,000 years. Early farmers probably stripped the lime's succulent leaves for animal fodder and, as it sets very little fertile seed, it was not able to colonise easily suitable new areas and so largely failed to survive the shifting cultivation of those times. It can still be found in old coppice woodland, particularly in East Anglia, where it may mark a long link stretching back to the original wildwood. If small-leaved lime is not cut as coppice, it can grow to become an elegant domed tree.

It is also interesting to look out for wych elm: an important component of the ancient primary woodland. It tends to prefer rich loamy soils and consequently was one of the first trees to disappear when the forests were originally cleared for agriculture. Wych elm can still be found growing in woods in the north, where elm disease has not yet exacted its full toll, unlike the common elm which is essentially a hedgerow tree. In the south it has survived in a few places as ancient coppice stools, which, if cut regularly, may escape the disease.

Standing like some fairy-tale tree in the autumn mist, this old hornbeam clearly displays the marks of many years of pollarding. The wood of the hornbeam is so hard that it was used to make the teeth in the cog wheels of mills.

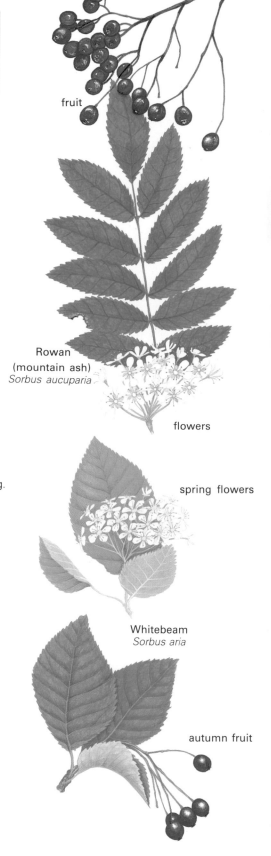

fruit

Rowan
(mountain ash)
Sorbus aucuparia

flowers

spring flowers

Whitebeam
Sorbus aria

autumn fruit

Growing tree seeds

If you have a female holly bush in the garden, then you will certainly know that seedlings are common, especially in rough, undisturbed ground – you may well find them on the rockery if you have one. But there's a bit more to the whole business than a seed falling (or being ejected by a bird which has eaten the berry) and then germinating the next spring. For holly will not germinate until the second or third spring after shedding. Ash is the same, although some say that the keys will germinate at once if they are gathered and planted while they are still green.

These seeds, like those of some other species, undergo a dormant period, during which presumably they ripen and the internal chemistry of the embryo matures (some chilling over a winter or two may be part of the process). But is there an advantage in this? For, on the face of it, the longer the seed remains dormant the greater the chances of being eaten by inquisitive mice, which will nibble out the smallest fragment of nourishment from any seed they find.

There could be one advantage. Ash seedlings, for example, cannot tolerate shade – they need light to thrive, which could be a disadvantage in a forest tree. However, an ash produces many seeds. These are easily scattered and if they have a long dormancy period then the wood around will contain a good many viable seeds, ready (when germination is triggered) to exploit new circumstances, such as a clearing created when an old tree dies and falls.

Rowan or mountain ash can be found growing high on hillsides and it is certainly native in the hills of the west and north, and may have been introduced into the south and east, for it is a popular garden tree and can seed itself easily back into the countryside. Its pinnate leaves, though they rather resemble the ash, arise alternately along the twigs. The insect-pollinated flowers (May-June) develop into the familiar red berries in August. Rowan is a rapid grower – reaching 10 metres or more in 25 years – some trees in the north are long lived.

The leaves of whitebeam open silvery grey; the topside becomes dull green, but the underside retains an attractive woolly greyness. The flowers open in May and June, in heads up to 10 cm across, and the berries ripen red in September and are often eaten by birds.

Stands of whitebeam are a feature of chalk and limestone downs and hills in the south, where it is certainly native. It has, however, been much planted in the north of Britain. It can grow to about 10 metres in 30 years.

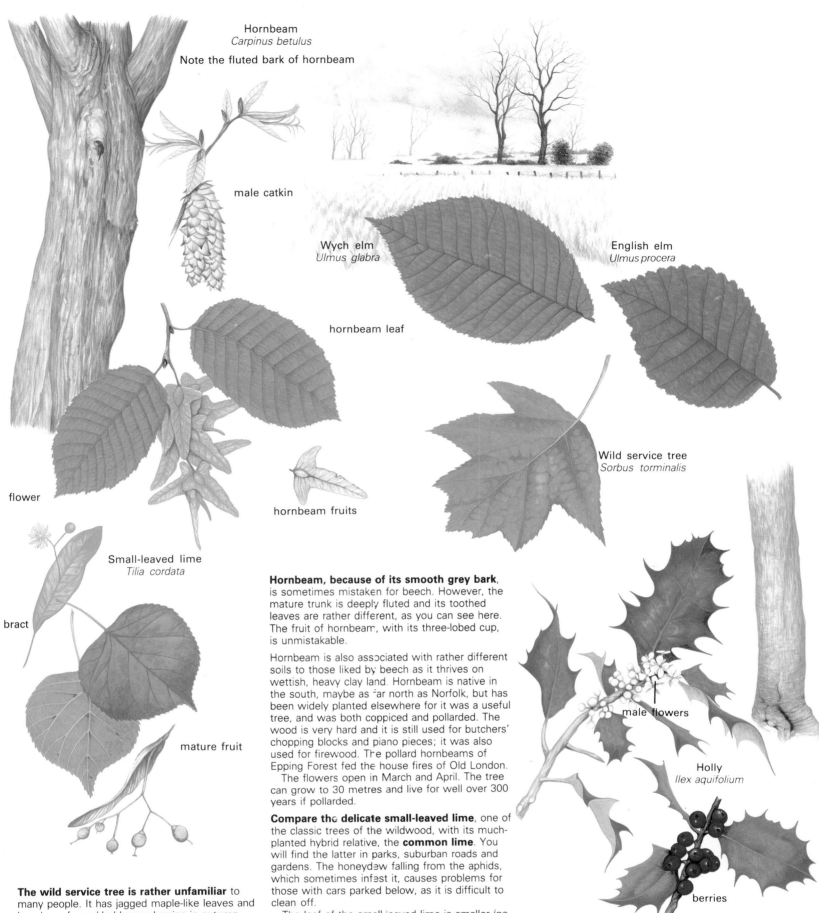

Hornbeam
Carpinus betulus
Note the fluted bark of hornbeam

male catkin

Wych elm
Ulmus glabra

English elm
Ulmus procera

hornbeam leaf

flower

hornbeam fruits

Wild service tree
Sorbus torminalis

Small-leaved lime
Tilia cordata

bract

mature fruit

male flowers

Holly
Ilex aquifolium

berries

Hornbeam, because of its smooth grey bark, is sometimes mistaken for beech. However, the mature trunk is deeply fluted and its toothed leaves are rather different, as you can see here. The fruit of hornbeam, with its three-lobed cup, is unmistakable.

Hornbeam is also associated with rather different soils to those liked by beech as it thrives on wettish, heavy clay land. Hornbeam is native in the south, maybe as far north as Norfolk, but has been widely planted elsewhere for it was a useful tree, and was both coppiced and pollarded. The wood is very hard and it is still used for butchers' chopping blocks and piano pieces; it was also used for firewood. The pollard hornbeams of Epping Forest fed the house fires of Old London.

The flowers open in March and April. The tree can grow to 30 metres and live for well over 300 years if pollarded.

Compare the delicate small-leaved lime, one of the classic trees of the wildwood, with its much-planted hybrid relative, the **common lime**. You will find the latter in parks, suburban roads and gardens. The honeydew falling from the aphids, which sometimes infest it, causes problems for those with cars parked below, as it is difficult to clean off.

The leaf of the small-leaved lime is smaller (no more than 6 cm long) than that of the common lime. Its underside is bluish, and hairless except for small tufts of rust-coloured hairs in the angles between some of the veins. Its flower clusters (pollinated by bees of different kinds) are somewhat erect on the twig.

Common lime, on the other hand, has leaves with tufts of white hairs between the under-veins, and flowers that hang in clusters.

The fruits of small-leaved lime are smooth; those of common lime are faintly ribbed.

Small-leaved lime flowers in early July; it can grow to 25 metres.

Holly leaves high on the tree, out of reach of browsing animals, are said to be without spines. Also the leaves on old and shaded trees are supposed to be less spiny. Have a look and see. Holly is one of our few native evergreens, the leaves lasting up to four years.

Holly was an important iron ration for livestock

The wild service tree is rather unfamiliar to many people. It has jagged maple-like leaves and bunches of speckled brown berries in autumn. The bark has a chequered appearance – hence its other name of chequers tree, which can still be traced today in pub names and other place names, particularly in Kent. It is said that the name 'service' comes from the Latin 'cerevisia' meaning 'beer', in that the Romans used to flavour their beer with the mildly astringent berries of the related, true service tree. The wild service tree is an uncommon, classic tree of ancient woodland but is probably native only in the south of Britain. It is found mostly on clay or hard limestone soils. Note the jagged leaves; the off-white flowers are seen May-June.

Wych elm has larger leaves than other elms, with more main veins on them (15–20 compared with 8–10). Note that the large lobe at the base of the leaf hides the short stalk when seen from above. Wych elms rarely if ever sucker, and so are usually found singly within woodland. More about elms in general on page 80.

in winter and, especially in the north and west, it was sometimes pollarded to give a handy supply of foliage. Apart from this use, its hard wood was often used for engraving blocks, and its twigs were boiled for bird lime – glutinous stuff spread on twigs and branches to catch small birds for the pot. The wood is also excellent for burning.

Found on all but very wet soils, holly grows as a large shrub or small, short-trunked tree, to 15 metres. The male and female flowers are pleasantly scented and pollinated by insects and are usually borne on separate trees; in other words, some holly bushes never bear berries.

Hollies grow slowly (at about 15 cm a year), and can be relatively long lived – some must be well over 100 years old. The holly is found in woodlands (see page 62) but is also a frequent hedgerow tree. It is often the only tree species left in one that has been severely cut.

Other native shrubs are shown on page 82. Shrub species can be found in hedges (page 76) and scrub (page 128) as well as in woodland. Many have strong soil preferences, and make excellent soil indicators (see the chart on page 21).

Shrubs and coppice

A shrub puts up many shoots at ground level and most broad-leaved trees will also grow in this way when cut back, so that many native trees such as oak, ash and birch, as well as shrubs, make good coppice. The underwood and shrubs that grow in a wood usually reflect the soil type. However, like the extensive planting of oak standards, certain species were sometimes encouraged or planted in preference to others. Hazel and sweet chestnut were both extensively planted for coppice in the past. Even as recently as the mid-1950s over 60,000 hectares of woodland were worked as hazel coppice. This has declined dramatically in recent years and in the 1979–82 Forestry Commission survey only 3,000 hectares were recorded as being actively worked. Hazel was used to construct fencing hurdles, and was also cut for thatching spars and wattle and daub plaster. Sweet chestnut, however, now constitutes over 50 per cent of all worked coppice in England, out of a total of almost 37,000 hectares. This is because it still has a reasonable market in fencing poles and pulpwood. A great deal of sweet chestnut coppice was also planted in the mid-19th century for the hop industry which needed long straight poles.

Though the Romans fed their legions on sweet chestnut porridge, this country produces only small nuts. It is thought that the Romans introduced the sweet chestnut tree to Britain. It is a most useful coppice tree; the split poles are still made into roll-up fencing.

If not coppiced, sweet chestnut grows to become a fine tall tree, with the bark fissured spirally around the trunk. It is sometimes seen as an ornamental parkland tree; up to 35 metres.

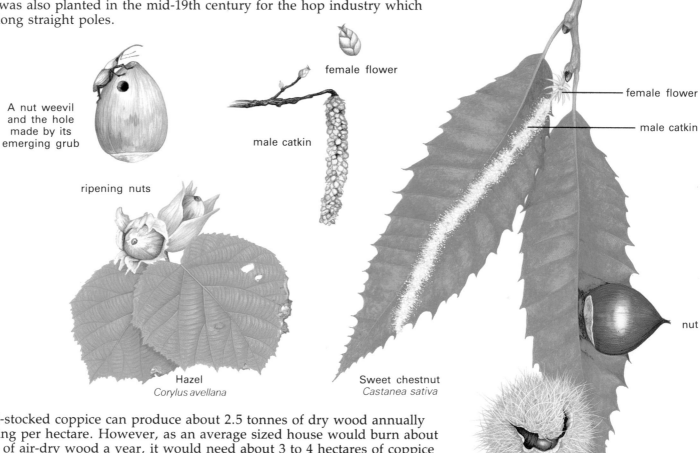

A nut weevil and the hole made by its emerging grub

female flower

male catkin

ripening nuts

Hazel
Corylus avellana

Sweet chestnut
Castanea sativa

female flower

male catkin

nut

Mature nuts in prickly husk

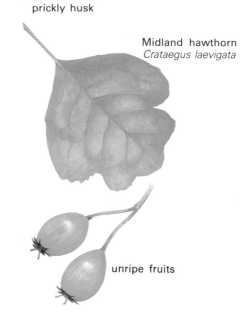

Midland hawthorn
Crataegus laevigata

unripe fruits

A well-stocked coppice can produce about 2.5 tonnes of dry wood annually for burning per hectare. However, as an average sized house would burn about 8 tonnes of air-dry wood a year, it would need about 3 to 4 hectares of coppice to provide it with a sustainable yield of fuel wood!

Judging by recent memories, it took one man about a year to work up 1.5 hectares of hazel coppice – that is, to cut the poles and fashion them into whatever was needed or would sell locally. On a seven-year cutting rotation, about ten hectares of woodland would give a coppice craftsman a full-time job. The coppice obviously was a major labour market in past centuries.

Hazel is one of our commonest shrubs, and can be found in hedges as well as woodland. It is a big bushy shrub – but it may sometimes grow a short stem, barely a 'trunk' in the real sense. The male catkins appear before the leaves, as early as February in some years – they are a familiar sight hanging from the bare twigs. The female flowers are less noticeable as they are bud-like, but look for the red hair-like style at the end. The nuts (the orchard varieties are chosen for their heavy crop) are in clusters of up to four; ripening in September.

The small neat holes that mark many hazel nuts are made by nut weevils. The female bores into the young green nut and lays a single egg. The grub that hatches feeds on the kernel until the nut falls in autumn, then bores its way out to burrow in the soil.

Another interesting weevil can sometimes be found, with rather different habits. The female lays her egg on the main vein of the leaf, biting it through so that half the leaf hangs; this she then wraps around the egg for cover. The grub hatches and makes forays from its hanging lair to eat the rest of the leaf.

The Midland hawthorn has a broad-lobed leaf and haw with two pips. Unlike its relative, the common hawthorn, it is not a pioneer onto open ground – its presence often marks old woodland or an old hedge. In a wood it may be wide spreading, almost creeping, close to the ground. There is more about this shrub on page 82.

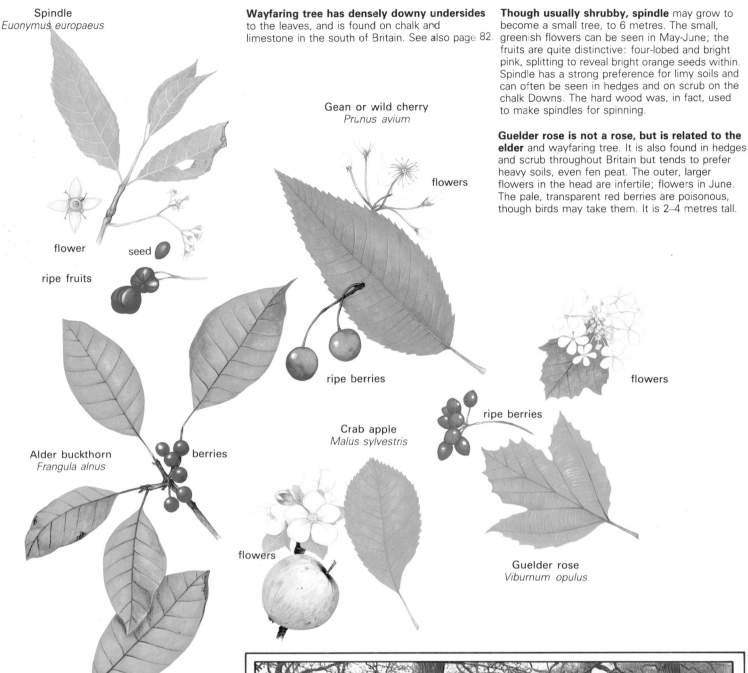

Spindle
Euonymus europaeus

flower

seed

ripe fruits

Alder buckthorn
Frangula alnus

berries

flowers

Wayfaring tree has densely downy undersides to the leaves, and is found on chalk and limestone in the south of Britain. See also page 82.

Gean or wild cherry
Prunus avium

flowers

ripe berries

Crab apple
Malus sylvestris

flowers

ripe berries

flowers

Guelder rose
Viburnum opulus

Though usually shrubby, spindle may grow to become a small tree, to 6 metres. The small, greenish flowers can be seen in May-June; the fruits are quite distinctive: four-lobed and bright pink, splitting to reveal bright orange seeds within. Spindle has a strong preference for limy soils and can often be seen in hedges and on scrub on the chalk Downs. The hard wood was, in fact, used to make spindles for spinning.

Guelder rose is not a rose, but is related to the elder and wayfaring tree. It is also found in hedges and scrub throughout Britain but tends to prefer heavy soils, even fen peat. The outer, larger flowers in the head are infertile; flowers in June. The pale, transparent red berries are poisonous, though birds may take them. It is 2–4 metres tall.

Alder buckthorn is reputed to have provided even better charcoal for gunpowder than alder. It is a small tree or shrub; 4–5 metres. In spite of its name, thorns may be absent. The greenish-white flowers are seen May-June; the berries start green then turn red to black when ripe. The 'buck' comes from the male fallow deer, not the beech tree (see page 22). Rather a specialists' species but we have included it because the brimstone butterfly lays her eggs on it. It is a local species growing on damp peaty soils.

The gean or wild cherry is the ancestor of cultivated cherries and has edible but rather bitter, thin-fleshed fruits. The **bird cherry** has smaller, black, and sour fruits. Its flowers are carried in a raceme – a long head – and the cherries hang in a lengthened bunch as a result. It is the cherry tree of northern Britain.

The wild cherry can grow to become a tall tree (20 metres), and is often seen on the edges of old woods. It produces suckers. Flowers April-May; cherries ripen in July – though you will have a job getting to them before the birds!

Crab apple grows as a shrub or a small tree. Unlike descendants of garden apples growing wild, crab apple is thorny with hairless leaves. The fruit is smaller than cultivated varieties, often streaked with red.

Wattles and heatherings

The prime product of hazel coppices was an interwoven hurdle of split wattles which was made on a wooden frame or 'break' without the aid of nails or wire – the way the rods were bound together made the hurdle rigid and strong. Other uses for the poles were for thatching spars, hoops for wooden barrels, wattle and daub plaster, clothes props, bean rods, rods for fish traps, hedge stakes and the 'heatherings' used in hedge laying (see page 78); the brushwood was used in baking bread. This last was important – in the old days, bread was baked in a closed bread oven, a recess alongside the open fire range, which was heated up by burning brushwood inside until the bricks were piping hot.

Conifers, which are usually evergreen, are shown on page 68. Only three conifers are native to Britain – yew and juniper (below) and Scots pine (68). Holly is another important evergreen, 26. Evergreens often play a role in the formation of woodland (page 128).

The yew and other evergreens

The yew is a slow-growing, long-lived tree. Its rugged appearance of antiquity may be misleading, for many of the larger trees seen in churchyards throughout Britain will be no more than 300 years old. The real age of one of these veterans is impossible to certify as the heartwood of the yew trunk, which would carry the annual rings, tends to rot away when the tree ages. An old tree, however, can still be very vigorous as the life and growth is preserved by the sap ring in the bark.

You will sometimes come across a yew wood on a steep slope or an abandoned sheepwalk, often on chalk or limestone (though yew can be found on other soil types). The story here is perhaps that initially the other native downland conifer, juniper, managed to establish itself and yew, which is shade tolerant, grew in its protection, safe from livestock. (Nearly all parts, including the bark, of the yew tree are very poisonous. It is considered by some authorities to be one of the most toxic wild plants in Britain.) In time, the yew grew to overtop the juniper, which can still be seen as a dead skeleton underwood below the dense yew canopy.

If the yew did not quickly produce a dense cover, then ash and beech, in particular, could in turn overtop the yew which, being itself shade tolerant, would still exist as a green understorey. A superb example of a natural yew wood can be seen at Kingley Vale in Sussex. Isolated yews in mixed woodland were sometimes planted as a boundary tree.

You might see juniper on the chalk Downs of the south growing as an upright shrub, but high up the mountainsides of the north it hugs the ground. The prickly, 2 cm leaves grow in whorls of three, usually more densely than shown here. Juniper has separate female and male bushes; the berries ripen in September. It likes well-drained soil and cannot stand deep shade. It can grow to 6 metres in height.

Juniper was once quite common on British open land. Sometimes you will come across a thicket of junipers all of one age – at some time in the past they will have colonised a new site. And the bottom of the 'mini-wood' may be quite bare, nibbled clean by rabbits.

The smell of crushed box leaves is striking. The small flowers are seen in April and May; the seed case 'explodes' open in September to scatter seeds up to 3 metres away. Sometimes, but not often, it grows to 10 metres tall.

Box is frequently planted for hedging throughout Britain but is found only in a handful of localities as a native tree, Box Hill in Surrey being one. Box has probably been growing there for 5,000 years. It was also sometimes planted into game woods – you may still see it there. It likes chalk and limestone soils.

Yew berries ripen in October, sometimes earlier. The fleshy red cup is not poisonous, the seeds however are very poisonous.

seed

Ripe, berry-like female cone

Although the leaves of the yew arise from around the twig, they tend to be twisted into two rows

Yew
Taxus baccata

Juniper
Juniperus communis

On the left, juniper cones ('flowers'), and below the berries. Juniper berries take two or three years to ripen on the twigs, and are seen ripe in autumn. They are used for flavouring gin.

Ripe, berry-like, female cones

flowers

Box
Buxus sempervirens

Box is a flowering plant and here we see the clusters of minute flowers

ripening fruits

box leaves are leathery

Yew berries are, in fact, cones with fused and very swollen scales. The seeds are poisonous. The male and female cones grow on separate trees. The needles (1–3 cm long) form a pair of flat rows down the shoot. A variety known as the Irish yew is often found in churchyards. It has a more upright habit and the leaves grow around the shoot.

The historic yew tree

Many myths have grown up around the yew tree. There may be some truth in some of them. Tradition has it that the evergreen boughs of yew sheltered the first Christian missionaries to Britain. Thereafter, yews were planted in churchyards as a symbol of the faith, and as a symbol of immortality. They were also a source of 'palm' for Easter, though there was usually a supply of hazel or pussy willow never far away.

However, it may well be that the link with churchyards arose from another direction. It has been proposed that yews marked the sacred sites of the Celtic tribes and these places retained their potency throughout Roman times. Such places would be the prime sites for the new churches. Quite often there are two yews in a churchyard, one close by the lych-gate. Another tradition has it that those churchyard yews were planted to provide bows. The longbows that won Crecy and Agincourt were fashioned from straight boughs cut from selected trees. These, however, are more likely to have been found in woods. There seems also to have been quite an early trade with Spain in yew for longbows.

flower spike

ripe berries

Cherry laurel
Prunus laurocerasus

The fruits of cherry laurel are a great favourite of thrushes and blackbirds

Cherry laurel with its striking flowers and black, cherry-like berries is a garden favourite but can spread past the garden fence. The leaves are 5–15 cm long and emit prussic acid when crushed. They were often used in the 'killing bottles' of Victorian entomologists.

Rhododendron
Rhododendron ponticum

Rhododendron is a relative of the heathers and, like them, indicates acid soil – if growing on chalky soil it cannot gain enough iron and its leaves turn yellow. The evergreen leaves are 6–12 cm long, those of azaleas are smaller.

Purple-flowered rhododendrons are native to Spain and Portugal. They are often planted for game cover and decoration. They have now naturalised themselves and have spread rampantly in many woods, shading out all else below.

The Selborne yew

A grand old yew tree stands in the churchyard at Selborne in Hampshire. It serves as a memorial to one of Britain's best known and loved naturalists. He was Gilbert White, who spent much of his life as vicar of the parish of Selborne. He died aged 73 in 1793. Gilbert White wrote letters to two friends – Thomas Pennant, a Fellow of the Royal Society and the Hon. Daines Barrington, recorder of Bristol. The letters are entrancing, inquisitive and filled with affection for the countryside around him. They were published as 'The Natural History and Antiquities of Selborne in the County of Southampton' in 1789. The book was an immediate success and has since been issued in countless editions worldwide.

When White was alive, there were still plenty of unsolved puzzles. Did swallows fly away in winter or did they hibernate in the muddy bottoms of ponds, where, indeed, some had been found? And if the early swallows find frost and snows, 'as was the case of two dreadful springs of 1770 and 1771, they immediately withdraw for a time. A circumstance this much more in favour of hiding than migration, since it is much more probably that a bird should retire to its hybernaculum just at hand, than return for a week or two only to warmer latitudes.' That was written in 1774.

Another extract written in 1770 shows his meticulous eye for detail: 'Hedgehogs abound in my garden. The manner in which they eat their roots of the plantain in my grass-walks is very curious; with their upper mandible which is much longer than their lower, they bore under the plant and so eat the root off upwards, leaving the tuft of leaves untouched.'

White was interested in newts, and deer; in the warning colours of wasps; in linnets, crocuses and crickets. He found some unusual mice; non-descript, unknown to science. He popped them in a jar of brandy to preserve them; they were in fact harvest mice . . . .

Gilbert White has become the 'patron saint' of natural history. He lies buried in the same graveyard as that old yew; it was 23 feet round in his day. Early in this century another famous Hampshire naturalist, W. H. Hudson, measured many of the churchyard yews around Selborne including the Selborne yew which then, over a century later, had a girth of 27 feet. He also felt that it was 'the best-grown, healthiest and most vigorous-looking yew of its size in Britain'.

A further selection of flowers of the woodland floor is shown on page 34: see also 60–64, 71. Many woodland species will also be found out of woodland, along shaded hedgerows or in scrub. Some of these are shown on page 88.

Flowers of the woodland floor

Some of the most attractive features of our woodlands are the colourful displays of flowers that bloom in succession from the depths of winter through to June. Everyone knows the nodding heads of the snowdrops, which seem to defy the worst that the winter weather can bring down on them, heralding the true spring plants such as the carpets of lesser celandine, the bright yellow primrose and the star-like flowers of the wood anemone. But, perhaps, it is the bluebell which is considered the woodland flower *par excellence*. Its dense blue pools of flowers almost seem to shimmer under the May sunlight, reaching their best just before the leafy canopy closes over. Whereas the leaves of the bluebell soon die back in the shade, others such as dog's mercury remain in leaf throughout the summer. Coppicing, which produces a regular cycle of light and shade through the wood, encourages the growth and spread of these plants. Anyone who has seen the effect on the ground flora of re-coppicing a neglected wood will immediately appreciate this. The seeds and plants of these flowers may have lain dormant or survived at a low ebb for many years and suddenly spring into life with the return of the sun's warming rays.

This will be the case, however, only if the wood has a long history of such management, as many woodland plants are slow to colonise new sites. If you find a woodland spangled with many different wild flowers, therefore the chances are that it has a long history. Planting up a coppice with conifers unfortunately is a complete break with traditional management and eventually the dormant seeds will no longer be viable.

Early purple orchids are one of our indicators of ancient woodland. The blotches run lengthwise along the leaves. It has a 'tom-cat' smell, especially at night. (Details of it are on page 124.)

Enchanter's nightshade is as lovely a plant as its name, flowering in the shade of high summer. The fruiting stalks all tend to point downwards and the fruits have small bristles on them to catch on to the fur (or trouser leg!) of passing animals, thus dispersing the seeds. June-August; 20–70 cm.

The unusual green 'flowers' of wood spurge are, in fact, leaf-like bracts. Have a close look at them. The actual 'flower' is made up of a cluster of tiny male flowers with a single female flower in the centre. There are no petals or sepals. Wood spurge cannot stand much disturbance. It is not found north of Lincolnshire. March-May; 30–80 cm.

Flowers of wood anemone open fully only on sunny days. It cannot stand much disturbance. When it carpets the ground it can indicate old woodland. March-April; 6–30 cm.

Observations on a bluebell wood

Bluebells carpet many woods in England and Wales; and in Scotland, too, where the flower is known as the wild hyacinth (the Scottish 'bluebell' is otherwise known as the harebell, a plant of open grasslands!). It is a typical 'Atlantic' plant: our mild winters allow it to come into leaf early, something which drier, colder 'Continental' winters would not allow. You will not see bluebells far into Germany or even in Scandinavia; in Denmark it is one of their rarest plants. But in the wetter west of Britain, bluebells can be seen flourishing out of woods and along hedgerows, even out in open pastures. Moist, rarely very cold conditions suit them best.

Climate, which includes both daily and annual changes of temperature, humidity, etc., is one of the three main factors which affect the distribution of wild plants. The other two are the type of soil and the effects of animals, including man. As a result of the history of Britain, and man's use of the land, we not only have Atlantic plants, which are confined to the ocean seaboard of western Europe, and Continental plants, which are common in Central and Eastern Europe, but also Arctic and Alpine plants, which are generally found in the high mountainous regions as relics of post-glacial climates. These climatic links run as a flowing counterpoint to other more obvious habitat factors. Of these, man himself is now often the most influential. In the case of the bluebell, the coppice in which it thrives was usually cut in autumn or winter so that during the following spring the woodland floor was fully open to the sun. Consequently, the leaves of the bluebells, and other low plants, could photosynthesise strongly, allowing the bulb below to build up good reserves.

When the next spring arrived, the now potent bulb could put up a strong head of flowers, and maybe another in the spring after that. But by now the heads of shoots from the coppice stools would already be taking some of the light, and the spring flowers would begin to decline until the next cut. So, when people complain that their favourite woodland is not as colourful as it was, this is often the reason. Management has ended within it. Dog's mercury and, maybe, also enchanter's nightshade on calcareous soils, seize dominance.

A southern hazel coppice flanked by tall beeches provides the perfect setting for a bluebell wood.

Does picking the bluebells destroy them? It is damaging if the whole of the flower shoot is pulled out; but equally damaging is trampling of the leaves around – without them the bulb starves. But picking wild flowers today is a contentious topic – see page 246.

You will often see, amongst the blue, a white bluebell. All being well, it will be there again the next year – for this colour change is a genetic factor, unlike some of the other variations met in this book.

These delightful plants are relatives of the onion family and have small underground bulbs.

The common violet has no scent. It is the commonest violet of the woods. It is easily picked out from other violets as its spur is generally lighter in colour than the rest of the flower. March-May, but it may put up late flower buds which do not open – they are self-fertilising; 2–20 cm.

Note that **sweet violet** – the scented violet – has darker blue flowers without the pale spur. You may see that it sometimes sports white flowers. It often puts out runners.

Stitchworts (narrow-leaved relatives of chickweeds) have weak, square stems which can sprawl. This one is the greater stitchwort, the smaller lesser stitchwort is a plant of sandy grassland and heath. Named because the plant was thought to ease a stitch, the white flowers can also be seen amongst the grass of hedgerows, but not as a weed of recently dug ground. April-June; 60 cm.

Wood sage has a strong preference for dry and usually rather acid soil, and may be found on heaths and dunes as well as woods. Sometimes found in grazed woods. July-September; 15–60 cm.

▲ **The wood spurge** is one of our tallest spurges and can form impressive stands, such as this one, in old woodlands usually with rich soils. In the foreground are the blue flowers of bugle, a common plant of woodland clearings and rides (see page 89).

Early purple orchid
Orchis mascula

Pignut
Conopodium majus

Wood spurge
Euphorbia amygdaloides

Wood sage
Teucrium scorodonia

Bluebell
Hyacinthioides non-scriptus

Greater stitchwort
Stellaria holostea

Wood anemone
Anemone nemorosa

Enchanter's nightshade
Circaea lutetiana

Primrose
Primula vulgaris

Lesser celandine
Ranunculus ficaria

Wood avens
Geum urbanum

Common violet
Viola riviniana

As we explain on the next page, specific combinations of certain woodland flowers can sometimes be an indicator of ancient woodland. Hence, if you see the early purple orchid, wood anemone and bluebells together in the wood, there is every likelihood that it is an old wood.

Pignut is an umbellifer. The smooth stem becomes hollow after flowering, May-June; 30–50 cm. It grows well in dry soils, and may survive in grazed woods. It is also sometimes seen out on old grasslands on dry, non-calcareous soils.

The wrinkled leaves of primrose are downy beneath. Essentially a woodland plant, it may be found on damp roadside banks and sea cliffs. March-June; 5–12 cm.

The glossy leaves and flowers of lesser celandine brighten woods and hedgebanks from March to May. It has up to twelve petals; to 20 cm. It prefers damp soils.

Bluebells can spread quickly on light soils and may pick out a patch of gravel in a wood. April-June; 20–50 cm. On heavy soils in the east they may mark old woods.

Wood avens is distinctive but beware, for when growing near its cousin water avens (page 35) the two plants may hybridise producing plants of a mixed character, May-August; to 60 cm.

See also page 32. The woodland rides and established clearings contain a different selection of plants, some typical of open grassland perhaps (see, for example, pages 92 and 122), but flowers of classic ancient grasslands (148, 150) are less likely.

Flowers of the woodland floor

The woodland floor may vary from place to place, being damp or dry, fertile or infertile, and so several plant communities may be present in one wood. The chart on the right shows that some woodland plants do make good soil indicators. There is, however, another factor to be considered. It seems that a fair number of truly woodland plants are poor colonisers of new sites, being mostly slow-growing perennials. Moreover, some are rather sensitive to disturbance. Those plants that are on the fringe of their natural distribution, and therefore only infrequently encounter conditions which enable them to set seed easily, are even more restricted. This inability to spread rapidly by some plants means that it is possible to draw up a list of species which indicate ancient woodland. This list will vary from region to region as, for instance, the bluebell can indicate ancient woodland on some of the heavy boulder clays of East Anglia but is far more adaptable in the west, colonising recent hedges and woodland. There is, however, a core of species which are generally reliable indicators. These include solomon's seal, lily-of-the-valley and herb paris. Perhaps a better indication, however, is the actual assemblages of plants, rather than single species. For example, if you are in southern Britain and you have a woodland with early purple orchid, wood anemone, herb paris and yellow archangel there is a fair chance that it is ancient.

Some plants that often indicate more recent woodland include ivy, cow parsley and also, on occasions, sweet violet and lords-and-ladies. The claim that recent broad-leaved plantations will in time become as rich as ancient woods stands only if there is a reserve of woodland plants either adjoining or in close proximity – even then, the process could take centuries. Unfortunately, in today's fragmented landscape, this is rarely the case, making it doubly important that we sympathetically manage the ancient woodland that we still have.

Indicators of old woodland: species which have been found to be associated with ancient wood in Britain.

Very strongly associated throughout whole range	Strongly	Often some link, especially when seen growing in profusion and/or with others on the list	
lily-of-the valley (if not a garden escape) oxlip wild service tree small-leaved lime	herb-paris midland hawthorn	often seen together in old woods	wood anemone early purple orchid bluebell (heavy soil)
		yellow archangel wood sorrel dog's mercury	

Match this soil preference chart to that on page 21 to see why different combinations of species are seen together in the same place in the wood.

A carpet of wild garlic or ramsons on damp clay soil at the edge of an ancient coppiced wood. This strong smelling plant can form dense stands in woods and wet hedge banks sometimes picking out heavier soils amidst seas of bluebells.

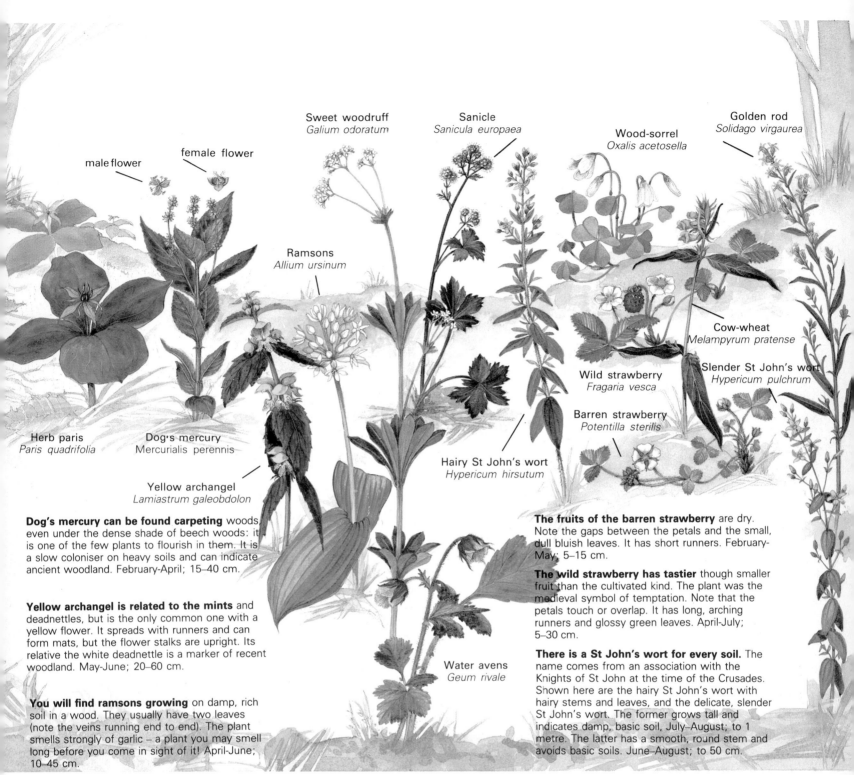

male flower

female flower

Sweet woodruff
Galium odoratum

Sanicle
Sanicula europaea

Wood-sorrel
Oxalis acetosella

Golden rod
Solidago virgaurea

Ramsons
Allium ursinum

Cow-wheat
Melampyrum pratense

Wild strawberry
Fragaria vesca

Slender St John's wort
Hypericum pulchrum

Barren strawberry
Potentilla sterilis

Herb paris
Paris quadrifolia

Dog's mercury
Mercurialis perennis

Hairy St John's wort
Hypericum hirsutum

Yellow archangel
Lamiastrum galeobdolon

Water avens
Geum rivale

Dog's mercury can be found carpeting woods, even under the dense shade of beech woods: it is one of the few plants to flourish in them. It is a slow coloniser on heavy soils and can indicate ancient woodland. February-April; 15–40 cm.

Yellow archangel is related to the mints and deadnettles, but is the only common one with a yellow flower. It spreads with runners and can form mats, but the flower stalks are upright. Its relative the white deadnettle is a marker of recent woodland. May-June; 20–60 cm.

You will find ramsons growing on damp, rich soil in a wood. They usually have two leaves (note the veins running end to end). The plant smells strongly of garlic – a plant you may smell long before you come in sight of it! April-June; 10–45 cm.

The fruits of the barren strawberry are dry. Note the gaps between the petals and the small, dull bluish leaves. It has short runners. February-May; 5–15 cm.

The wild strawberry has tastier though smaller fruit than the cultivated kind. The plant was the medieval symbol of temptation. Note that the petals touch or overlap. It has long, arching runners and glossy green leaves. April-July; 5–30 cm.

There is a St John's wort for every soil. The name comes from an association with the Knights of St John at the time of the Crusades. Shown here are the hairy St John's wort with hairy stems and leaves, and the delicate, slender St John's wort. The former grows tall and indicates damp, basic soil, July–August; to 1 metre. The latter has a smooth, round stem and avoids basic soils. June–August; to 50 cm.

Herb paris is a dramatic looking flower of damp woods on chalk and limestone, although sometimes hard to pick out amongst dog's mercury. It only sometimes sets seed (the fruit being a black berry); and spreads by its roots. A good indicator of ancient woodland. May-August; 15–40 cm.

Compare this damp-loving water avens with the wood avens (page 33). The swarm of hybrid forms is interesting to find. The hybrid can look rather like the flower shown here, but with the yellow colour of wood avens. April-September; 60 cm.

Sweet woodruff lives up to its name and is hay-scented (some say vanilla scented) when dry. It has square stems and is a member of the bedstraw family, often forming patches. May-June; 15–45 cm.

Sanicle is a member of the umbel family found mainly on chalky soils in the south. The long stemmed leaves arising from the rootstock are rather ivy shaped – deep cut, but *toothed* in outline. May-September; 20–60cm.

Cow-wheat is an annual and a semi-parasite attached to the roots of woody plants. So named from its grain-like seed. Usually found in old woods on well-drained acid soil. The flowers all face one way. May-October; 8–60 cm.

The clover-like leaves of wood sorrel close downwards at night, and also droop after being repeatedly touched. April-May; 15 cm.

Goldenrod indicates acid soil. It is smaller than its familiar garden cousin, with a looser flower head. July-September; 5–70 cm.

Soil preferences of some woodland flowers

Alkaline (limy) soil

Acid soil

Dry, well drained soil

woodruff

wood sorrel

cow wheat

wood melick grass

pignut

wood sage

wood spurge

dog's mercury

sanicle

goldenrod

herb paris

greater stitchwort

enchanter's nightshade

wild strawberry

slender St John's wort

early purple orchid

wood anemone

bluebell

hairy St John's wort

primrose

barren strawberry

Other flowers seen in woodland (e.g. on page 88) have their soil preference if it is a marked one, mentioned in their caption

common violet

ramsons

lesser celandine

See also page 32 for illustrations of some of these flowers

rushes

Wet, poorly drained soil

You will see many of these story markers in abandoned quarries, on refuse tips and other scrap sites, often in towns (page 130). Their pioneering strategy means they make an early appearance in such places. Details of bracken, bramble on pages 38, 86.

Story markers in a wood

It is sometimes not too difficult to hazard a guess at the previous history of a patch of woodland. The visual clues to coppice management, previous wood pasture or to more recent plantation forestry can be clear enough. Yet some plants, because of the strategy they adopt, can act as 'story markers', telling of incidents of a lesser kind. Some are favoured by disturbance to the wood floor, for example, or rapidly invade if a part of the wood is burnt.

We show some of those plants here. The interpretation can never be completely certain: the only conclusive proof would be written evidence of a contemporary observer. The experts consult a whole range of documents when deciphering the history of a wood.

The forest and the fireweed

One of the memorable sights of the 1939–45 war – without exaggerating its importance in those unhappy times – was the flourishing of rosebay willowherb on bombsites in London and other cities. This striking plant produces masses of light, fluffy, windblown seed and is a speedy pioneer of suitable ground. It is by origin a woodland plant, and until the mid-19th century was fairly uncommon. It is thought that it underwent some genetic change at this time and by the Second World War was becoming more prominent everywhere in woodlands, and not just in the devastated cities. The standing timber in many woods was being felled for the wartime emergency, and conditions were just right for it. Today, it can be seen on disturbed ground everywhere as well as in many woodlands – a plant that you might encounter casually on a walk through a wood. It is a plant which colonises bare soil. These pioneers have small seeds, produced in prodigious quantities, but with only the reserves within the seed to sustain a small first root which cannot work down through a thick tangle. Pioneering trees and shrubs such as birch and willow are much the same.

So in a clearing created by felling or by fire and without the mass of ground flowers associated with coppice, you might see rosebay willowherb, or fireweed as it is also known, as well as foxglove, ragwort and thistles. They are all biennials so they will be in flower in the second summer after the disturbance. Following them will come bracken, brambles and wild roses and through that may grow birch, willow and hawthorn. Finally the seedlings of the larger trees such as ash and oak may get away and if left, in time, the clearing will heal over. From this it is possible to see why, in theory at least, an accidental fire in the wildwood could result in the appearance of a 'stand' of one species within a mixed woodland in later centuries.

Ivy
Hedera helix

flowers   berries

climbing roots

Ivy does not harm the tree it is on, using it only for support. Although it can tolerate shade, ivy will put out flowering shoots only in good light. These bear oval leaves. The greenish-yellow flowers are held in umbels. Opening in autumn, they are a boon to late appearing bees, hoverflies and some butterflies. The berries of ivy are poisonous. Ivy can be of great age; some plants may be over 400 years old. Ivy grows well on all but very acid, very dry or water-logged soil.

If ivy covers the ground, it could mean a fairly young wood. Plantations and working coppice rarely let in enough light. It quickly invades disturbed ground in a wood, and is often limited to it. When it reaches a vertical surface it climbs with the help of sucker-like rootlets. Flowers September-November. See also page 18.

Foxglove seeds can remain dormant in the soil for 40 years, to be triggered by light reaching the ground when trees are felled or burnt. Often a good indicator of acid soil. June-August; 15–150 cm.

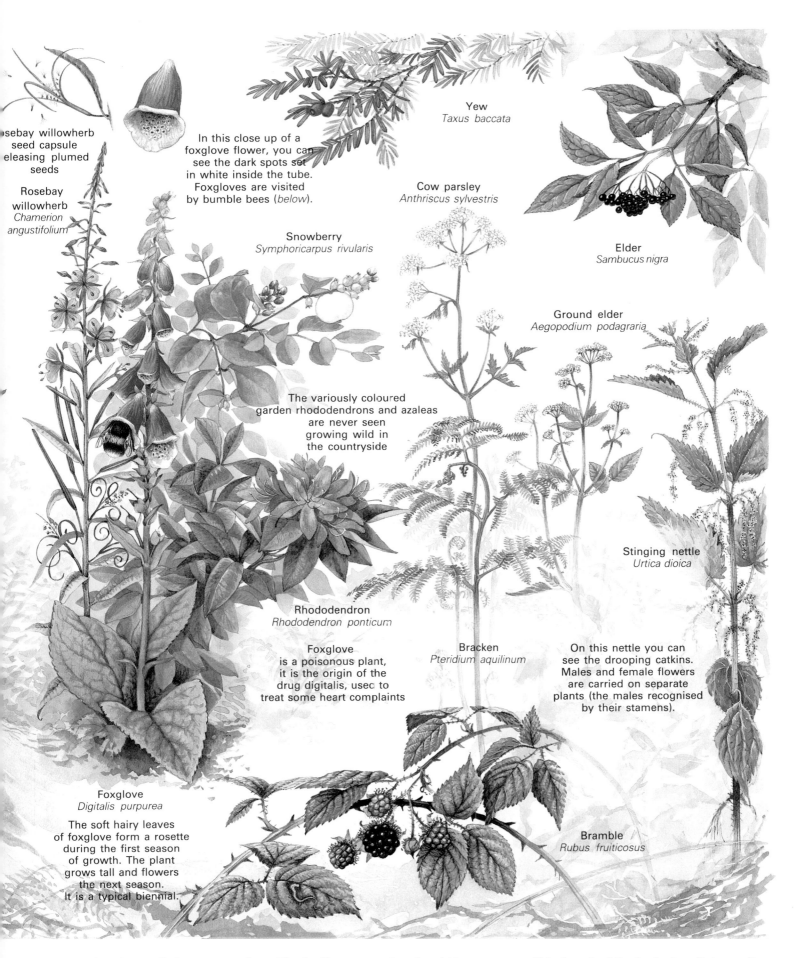

sebay willowherb
seed capsule
eleasing plumed
seeds

Rosebay
willowherb
*Chamerion
angustifolium*

In this close up of a
foxglove flower, you can
see the dark spots set
in white inside the tube.
Foxgloves are visited
by bumble bees (*below*).

Yew
Taxus baccata

Cow parsley
Anthriscus sylvestris

Snowberry
Symphoricarpus rivularis

Elder
Sambucus nigra

Ground elder
Aegopodium podagraria

The variously coloured
garden rhododendrons and azaleas
are never seen
growing wild in
the countryside

Stinging nettle
Urtica dioica

Rhododendron
Rhododendron ponticum

Foxglove
is a poisonous plant,
it is the origin of the
drug digitalis, used to
treat some heart complaints

Bracken
Pteridium aquilinum

On this nettle you can
see the drooping catkins.
Males and female flowers
are carried on separate
plants (the males recognised
by their stamens).

Foxglove
Digitalis purpurea

The soft hairy leaves
of foxglove form a rosette
during the first season
of growth. The plant
grows tall and flowers
the next season.
It is a typical biennial.

Bramble
Rubus fruiticosus

Yew, though found naturally in some woods
on chalky soil, may have been planted in small
clumps into other woodland to provide roosts for
pheasants.

Rhododendron and snowberry also suggest
that the wood is managed for pheasant rearing
as they have both been extensively planted as
cover for game.

Bramble is a vigorous plant, and can flourish,
though not flower, in the half light of a mature
wood. Deep shade, however, does check it. It is
quick to take over disturbed ground, especially
on heavy acid soil. May-September; up to 3
metres.

The familiar cow parsley of roadside verges
(page 92) can be found scattered through many
woods. If it grows strongly, dominating the field
layer, the wood is likely to be a secondary wood
on land that was once a field. April-May;
60–100 cm.

Rosebay willowherb or fireweed may mark past
fires; it can stand some shade. July-September;
50–120 cm.

Bracken vigorously colonises open grassland,
but does less well in shade. It can flourish in
woodland that has become rather open. See
page 38.

Ground elder, as every gardener knows, invades
disturbed ground. It is a member of the umbel
family. May-July; 40–100 cm.

Elder is a short-lived coloniser. Badgers will eat
its tasty fruit, so it may mark the latrine areas
near their sets. Rabbits (sometimes important
woodland grazers) find the bark of the elder
distasteful and it may therefore mark the site of
rabbit warrens, growing where other shrubs
have been nibbled down. June-July, fruits August-
September; up to 10 metres.

A thick patch of stinging nettles in a wood could
indicate the site of an old hut, cattle shed, or
maybe a rubbish dump, because they are
phosphate-greedy plants. June-August; up to
150 cm.

Adder's tongue, an unusual looking fern, is shown on page 149, and moonwort on page 151. The important moss *Sphagnum* (bog moss) is shown on page 160. Ferns and mosses flourish in wet woods (page 65), but are also typical of others (pages 61, 71).

Ferns, mosses and liverworts

Ferns are non-flowering plants; they reproduce with spores which are usually released from small capsules (sori) on the undersides of the leaf fronds. Very often the shape of these cases is important in identifying the fern. Note that many flowering plants have fern-like leaves.

Most ferns are perennial plants; some of them are evergreen. The reproductive cycle of a fern needs moisture as the male sperms have to travel through water in order to reach the female ova. Therefore many ferns are restricted to damp and humid areas, growing particularly well in the wetter woods of western Britain. Some, such as bracken, can spread vegetatively from underground stems, forming dense stands.

Mosses are small primitive plants which, like ferns, need moisture to reproduce and therefore thrive in undisturbed moist woods. They consist essentially of a stem with leaves, producing stalked capsules containing the spores. Some woodland mosses, such as the pin-cushion moss, *Leucobryum*, form attractive cushions on the ground. Others grow as mats or loose fronds sometimes in crevices in bark or rocks.

Liverworts are similar to mosses but have a more simple structure. These plants can be found on the moist banks of shaded woodland streams where the constant humidity prevents the delicate leaves from drying up.

Bracken

Bracken is by origin a plant of rather open woods. It flourishes in clearings, and outside woodland it rapidly spreads by underground stems, especially on deep, well-drained and usually acid soils, of the kind you may find on many heathlands, for example.

Its roots cannot stand waterlogging, and if you see bracken blanketing a hillside look at the foot of the slope. You may see a sharp edge to the invasion, where marshy ground begins. Bracken is also rather sensitive to late frosts.

Bracken is a feature of our upland grazings, although it is in some places being eradicated (sprays do exist which can control it). However, it really marks land let go, not worth the effort of clearing. Cattle will eat the young shoots, but sheep will not. Rabbits also avoid it. It is poisonous, if eaten in quantity, to livestock.

A damp ash-hazel wood in the West Highlands showing a profuse growth of mosses both on the boulder-strewn woodland floor and on the trunks and branches of the trees themselves. These humid conditions also suit ferns such as the bracken shown here.

Both male and lady ferns grow as a clump of fronds from a dense rootstock. The shape of the spore-cases helps to identify them: those of the lady fern are hooked into a narrow open comma shape; the male fern's are closed with a kidney-shaped flap. Both have a feathery appearance. Lady fern prefers acid, very damp soils; male fern is common everywhere. Fronds to 90 cm.

Broad buckler fern is so called because the spore cases look like bucklers (round shields). The spores are ripe in late summer. A common woodland fern. Fronds to 150 cm. A relative, the hay-scented buckler fern, which smells of hay when crushed, can indicate old woodland.

The hard fern is unmistakable: the rosette of sterile fronds lies flat; the fertile stems, looking rather like the bones of a finished kipper, rise up to between 15 and 70 cm tall. A good indicator of acid soils, and often abundant on heaths and moors in the north.

Hart's-tongue fern is easy to recognise with its overwintering strap-shaped leaves; it is very common in the wetter west. Fronds to 60 cm.

Polypody is a fern which requires particularly sharp drainage. It is the only British fern that is regularly found growing on tree trunks. The fronds (10–40cm) grow singly from a creeping rootstock.

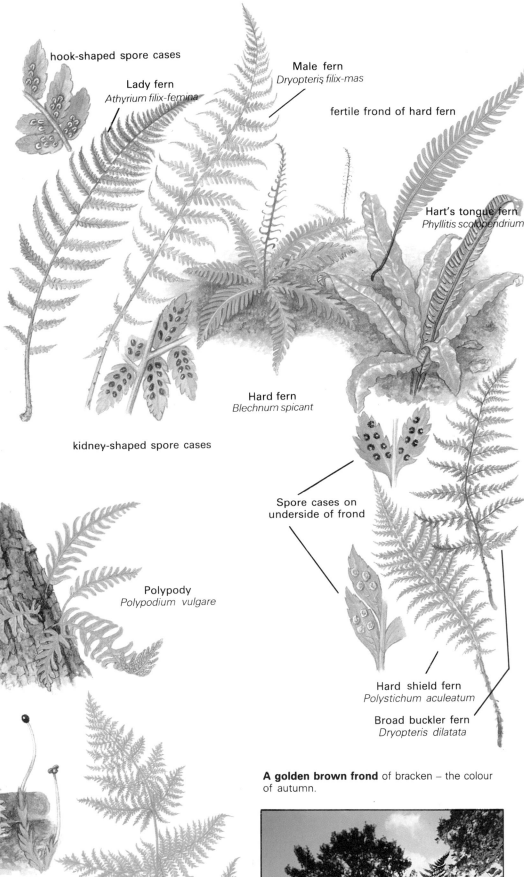

hook-shaped spore cases

Lady fern
Athyrium filix-femina

Male fern
Dryopteris filix-mas

fertile frond of hard fern

Hart's tongue fern
Phyllitis scolopendrium

Hard fern
Blechnum spicant

kidney-shaped spore cases

Spore cases on underside of frond

Hard shield fern
Polystichum aculeatum

Broad buckler fern
Dryopteris dilatata

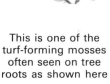
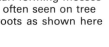

Moss
Mnium hornum

spore capsule

Polypody
Polypodium vulgare

This is one of the turf-forming mosses often seen on tree roots as shown here

Liverwort
Lophocolea bidentata

Liverwort
Pellia epiphylla

Liverworts are primitive plants with either a rather thread-like form with unveined leaves, or simple flat, fleshy lobes. Look for the small cups which hold the bud-like new plants. Found by ditches and on rotting logs.

The moss above is one of the commonest of all woodland mosses: in spring, its spore capsules grow on reddish stalks curved like a swan's neck, 2–10 cm tall.

The fronds of bracken are almost triangular in shape, with a strong stem that may be half the total height which may be up to 200 cm or more. Look for the spore cases under the fronds: they form a thin line around the margin of the leaf segments.

A golden brown frond of bracken – the colour of autumn.

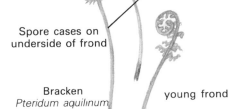

Spore cases on underside of frond

Bracken
Pteridum aquilinum

young frond

Colourful toadstools are associated with birch trees, see page 64. Beech woods often contain a fine array (page 62). Mushrooms and other fungi of grassland are shown on page 122. Fungi may be found on heaths (page 166). See also page 82.

Some common fungi

Toadstools and other fungi are important in the survival of a woodland as they enable nutrients stored in the leaf-litter or decaying wood to be recycled through the soil, thus enabling the trees as well as animals to continue to thrive.

The colourful shapes that you see are the fruiting bodies of the fungus which consists largely of an unseen web of threads known as the mycelium. The fruiting bodies produce the spores by which the fungus is spread. These spores are microscopic and one toadstool can produce many thousands of millions of them. The ways in which these spores are dispersed varies considerably. Most mushrooms and toadstools have a cap with rows of gills hanging below which are, in effect, spore bearing surfaces from which the ripe spores fall. In the stomach fungi, such as the earthstars and puffballs, the spores are produced inside the fruit-body and, when mature, are ejected through a hole in the top. The disc or cup fungi, such as the orange peel fungus and the morel, have the spores on minute club-shaped sacks on their upper surfaces. These sacks burst at the tip shooting the spores out into the air.

Many fungi are edible and in other European countries they are enthusiastically collected for the pot. However, some species are extremely poisonous and as there is no simple guide to identifying them it is best to discover these unusual plants by joining one of the many autumn 'fungus forays' organised by local Naturalists' Trusts and Field Societies, where experts will be able to help you.

Earth stars (their shape is created when the outer skin of the fungus folds back) are seen in summer and autumn, mostly in beech woods, but also under other trees.

Orange peel fungus is found in autumn and winter on open ground, in bare woods, often by paths.

Stinkhorn or wood witch grows in woods and gardens. The stalk lengthens in a few hours, carrying up the cap, which is coated with a dark, sticky spore mass with an offensive stench. This smell attracts flies, which carry off the spores to new grounds.

Morel is a springtime fungus. It is edible, but it must be blanched in boiling water before cooking. Found in woods and hedges.

Candle snuff fungus develops light grey tips to its leathery stems, resembling a snuffed candle wick. It can be found throughout the year on dead wood.

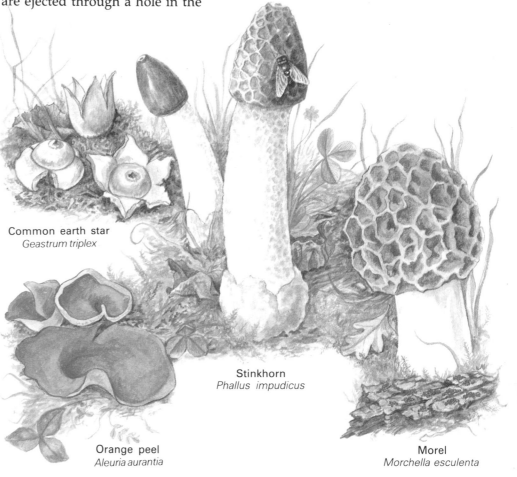

Common earth star
Geastrum triplex

Stinkhorn
Phallus impudicus

Morel
Morchella esculenta

The green-staining fungus, *Chlorosplenium aeruginascens*, tints the wood it infects a blue-green colour. Oak infected in this way was used by cabinet makers, particularly in Tonbridge in Kent, where it was used as an inlay in Tonbridge Ware. The stained wood is found quite commonly, but the fruiting bodies which are similar in shape to 'elf cups' are more infrequent.

Orange peel
Aleuria aurantia

Death cap is found in oak and beech woods in late summer and autumn. Its cap is pale greenish or yellowish and slightly slimy, with white gills and stalk. Note the 'cup' at the base of the stalk. This is the remnant of a membrane which was burst apart as the fruiting body swelled. This fungus is extremely dangerous and can prove fatal if eaten.

Beefsteak fungus, named after its appearance, grows on living oak and sweet chestnut trees. It is seen in late summer and autumn. It is edible but not good to taste.

Mycorrhizas

When walking in woodland, particularly during the autumn, you may notice that some fungi keep cropping up under the same species of tree. For example, orange birch-boletus, *Leccinum versipelle*, is found almost solely under birches, as is the familiar fly agaric. While some species of *Russula* seem to be found most frequently under oak or beech trees. This association between some types of fungi and trees is called mycorrhizal. Each involves a definite relationship between the fungus and the roots, since the fungal mycelium, as it grows, actually infects the smaller tree roots. These soon become distorted, with a characteristic swollen and much branched appearance. Such fungus-root structures are termed mycorrhizas. Each is enclosed in a dense sheath of hyphae, some of which penetrate between the outer cells of the root.

It is assumed by many experts that the association is a symbiotic one, that is, of mutual benefit to both organisms concerned. Maybe the fungus gains some nourishment from the tree, in the way of sugars that flow down to the roots in the sap, and it may give nourishment to the tree, from its processes of decomposition of the decaying matter of the soil. It may, however, be that the relationship was originally a parasitic one, with the fungus the sole benficiary. Over fifty years ago it was shown that seedlings of pine and spruce would grow normally in poor soils only when they had developed mycorrhizas, and that uninfected seedlings in the same soil would die. It has actually proved possible to induce mycorrhizal roots in pine seedlings by adding mycelium from other species of fungi.

The bracket fungus, Dryad's saddle, *Polyporus squamosus*, growing from a living ash stool in an ancient coppiced wood in Suffolk.

Cep is a prized edible fungus, with a nutty flavour which it keeps when dried. Note that, like beefsteak, it has spore tubes, not gills. It is seen in autumn.

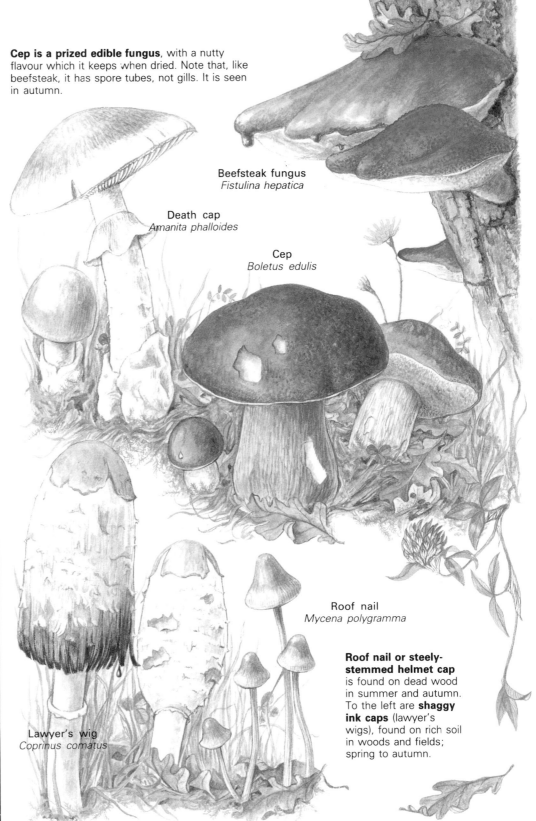

Beefsteak fungus
Fistulina hepatica

Death cap
Amanita phalloides

Cep
Boletus edulis

Roof nail
Mycena polygramma

Roof nail or steely-stemmed helmet cap is found on dead wood in summer and autumn. To the left are **shaggy ink caps** (lawyer's wigs), found on rich soil in woods and fields; spring to autumn.

Lawyer's wig
Coprinus comatus

Candle snuff
Xylaria hypoxylon

Here we explain how a wood works, but the ground rules apply also to grassland, ponds and other kinds of habitat. Pages 98, 138, 178 and 220 continue the description of how living things achieve a working balance – these pages may be read as a sequence.

The woodland ecosystem

When walking through a wood you may hear nothing more than a few snatches of bird song – maybe the echoing *tee-cher* of the great tits. If you inspect the ground closely you may find a network of paths and tunnels in the undergrowth but nothing stirs in them. In fact, you will be lucky to see more than twenty or so different kinds of animals, including flies and other insects, during a half-hour stroll.

Do not be misled. A typical wood is brimful with animal life. If it were not, it could hardly exist. Let us look at the reasons for this.

Plants come first. Only they can capture the energy of the sunlight which makes life possible on this planet. Photosynthesis at the green chlorophyll of the plant's leaves results in the formation of sugars, in which the sun's energy is 'locked up'. From them, and using nutrients obtained from the soil, the living plant builds up starch, cellulose, woody matter and other carbohydrates, the fats and oils found in seeds and (with nitrogen and sulphur) proteins are also formed. Some animals (herbivores) consume this plant matter to gain the energy they need – they often specialise in the leaf, bark, sap, nectar or seeds of particular plants. Other animals (carnivores) gain their energy ration by preying on the plant-eaters, while they themselves may be the prey of other (usually larger) predators.

In woods, a large group of animals including worms, woodlice and many different beetles gain their energy input by taking part in the process of decomposition – they eat dead matter and waste. They are to be found with the leaf mould, the rotting twigs and branches and the animal droppings on the floor of the wood. It is interesting that fungi (which play an important role in the later stages of decomposition) are now considered to be a third living kingdom, neither animal nor plant. Bacteria, too, are important decomposers.

We take it for granted that a wood has a recognisable structure, with spaced

Nutrient cycling in a woodland

Nutrients taken up by trees and other plants

leaf and twig fall

Leaf mould and decomposers release nutrients into the soil

This fox looks harmless enough sunning himself at the woodland edge, but his fierce array of teeth betrays his position as one of the top carnivores in the woodland ecosystem. The fox is also a master opportunist. It will readily take carrion and can even survive for periods on berries and other fruit.

out trees, shrubs and a field layer. Yet, without the important, very small but very numerous decomposers, it could not exist – the space between the trunks would gradually fill up with unrotted leaves, twigs, fallen branches and dead tree trunks! Furthermore, they all contain between them a vast treasure store of nutrients, and unless these are released by decomposition to become available for re-use, the whole growth system would run down.

So, in a wood that is anything like natural, there is a thriving but hidden world of animal life. Much of it is small, much of it is active only after dark. The plant-eaters and the predators and the many scavengers, together with the vegetation, the soil and the local climate, create the wood *ecosystem* – a strongly interlocked system of living things.

An ecosystem is a very complicated network of energy transfers and nutrient recycling in which all the living things play a part. A habitat comprises the plant structure, the soil and the climate to which an animal (or plant) is adapted and in which it plays out its role in life. As animals and plants lead such interlocking lives, it is quite usual to talk of a wood or a hedge or a pond as a 'habitat' – an ecological unit. Every species has a 'niche' (a role) in its ecosystem.

In managed woodlands, the balance may be swayed by removing dead wood – for the 'pests' (beetles, etc.) could spread out and invade healthy timber.

The female sparrowhawk and her hungry brood are an excellent barometer of the health of a woodland. Their place at the head of the foodchain means that they are very sensitive to any fluctuations in the fortunes of woodland wildlife. It was the dramatic decline in birds of prey, such as the sparrowhawk, that provided the first clear indication of the effect of certain toxic pesticides in the countryside in the 1960s.

The difference in the size of the young hawks shown here is deliberate. The eggs are laid at intervals so that in times of hardship the eldest and strongest nestling will be able to dominate and survive his siblings. This brood looks well-fed and they will probably all fledge successfully.

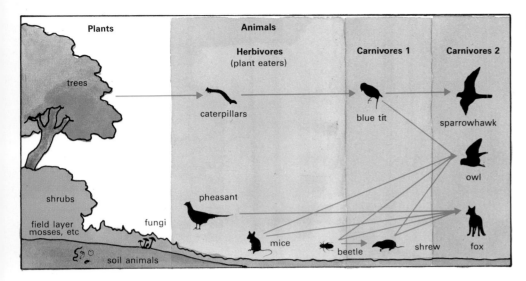

Plants

Animals

Herbivores (plant eaters) **Carnivores 1** **Carnivores 2**

trees

caterpillars

blue tit

sparrowhawk

owl

shrubs

pheasant

field layer
mosses, etc

fungi

soil animals

mice

beetle

shrew

fox

Life plan of an oak wood
The upper diagram shows the interactions of
plants, and animals . The lower
diagram shows the flow of energy through the
system. It is interesting that in a wood,
90 per cent of the energy moves down the
decomposer side of the energy
flow diagram.

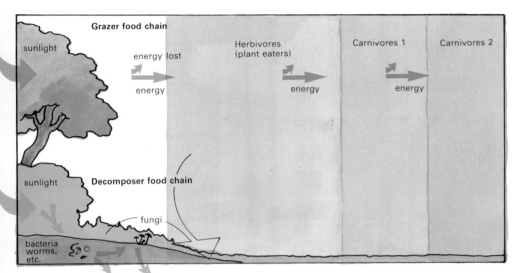

Grazer food chain

sunlight

Herbivores
(plant eaters) Carnivores 1 Carnivores 2

energy lost

energy

energy

energy

sunlight

Decomposer food chain

fungi

bacteria
worms,
etc.

These butterflies are typical of woodland, but others shown on pages 100, 140, 243 may be seen in the open glades. Most species of butterfly are more often seen in the south than the north, but northern woods need not lack the fritillaries and other species shown here.

Woodland butterflies

If you see several species of butterfly in one site it is likely that there will be a good variety of other invertebrates and plants in the same locality. These superbly coloured insects provide an excellent indication of the richness of a habitat, as most of them have very specific requirements when choosing suitable plants on which to lay their eggs. This is certainly true of those that grace our woodland glades and rides – in fact, some of our better woodland areas in southern England can support thirty or more species. Surprisingly, however, few of these rely on the trees as such. They are in the wood because of the profusion of flowers growing in the sunny glades and newly coppiced areas.

Recent research has shown that the butterfly is very fussy about the individual plant on which she is to lay her eggs. Initially the plant is chosen by sight and this is then probably confirmed by scent. Furthermore, the plant has to be at a certain height and stage of growth. For some species, the plants also have to be in exactly the right degree of sun or shade.

In order to avoid heavy predation by birds, the caterpillars are often camouflaged to blend in with the food plant. They will often be most active at night, making it very difficult to find them, unless one knows precisely where to look. Interestingly, some species even change their coloration after each moult to match the changing colour of the maturing foliage.

Purple hairstreak
Quercusia quercus

male

This is the male, the female has a bright purple flash on her forewings

male underw[ings]

male

Purple emperor
Apatura iris

The pearl-bordered fritillary has declined greatly in recent years and is now rare throughout the eastern half of England; it was always rather scattered and scarce in the north. It has a rapid fluttering flight close to the ground, often difficult to follow – though it usually glides in to land on a flower. The violet is the food plant of the caterpillar. This butterfly is early on the wing: May-June; 45 mm ws.

All fritillaries have suffered massive declines in recent years as they prefer their larval food plant, the violets, in freshly-coppiced woods.

You will find silver-washed fritillaries (so called from the streaked or 'washed' underwings) flying with power and grace in open rides in woods in the south, but in the West Country they may also be seen along hedgebanks. Violets are the food plant of the caterpillar but the eggs are laid in the bark of a nearby tree. June-September; 70 mm ws.

The speckled wood, like the ringlet, is a butterfly of the brown family, laying its eggs on shaded grass. You will see them (well camouflaged in the dappled light) in woodland glades, flying with a weak zig-zag flight. The males are fiercely territorial and chase others of their kind from their own patch of sun. A butterfly more of the south and west of Britain. Speckled woods increased in the 1940s – 60s, but have been stable since then. They can be seen in young conifer plantations, but do not expect to see them when

the blocks of trees mature. The speckled wood overwinters as a chrysalis and is seen flying in March-April. These mate and a second generation of adults flies in August, September and into October; 40 mm ws.

In spring, the brimstone newly emerged from hibernation wanders erratically down the hedges in search of energy-priming nectar. Then it mates and lays its eggs on buckthorn bushes, finding them in the hedges but also in woodlands. The females are whitish and rather similar to a 'cabbage white' but they fly more strongly. The next generation, which will hibernate in ivy or evergreen bushes, is seen flying by July. 50 mm ws.

The holly blue is a woodland butterfly – though also seen in gardens, especially old ones; it is more common in the south than north. The pale blue underwings and lavender blue upperwings identify it – the male has a narrower dark border to his wings. You will see these blues flying with hesitant movements around bushes and trees, settling high up. There are two generations a year. The spring butterflies seen in April, lay on holly, dogwood and ivy (the caterpillars feeding on buds, blossom and later on berries). The second generation is on the wing in August when the females lay their eggs on the flower buds of ivy; the hungry caterpillars give the flowers a withered look. They spend the winter as chrysalises; 28 mm ws.

The purple hairstreak is most often seen by birdwatchers using binoculars, for it flies in the crowns of oak trees on which the eggs are laid; the flight is a fluttering dance. It is often at rest however, so is easily overlooked. The female has bright purple patches on her forewings. July-August; 35 mm ws.

Purple emperors are perhaps commoner than is realised where they occur – many woods in the south have colonies – but they are often missed as they fly high in the canopy. The males gather above a 'master tree' in the wood and await the females. From time to time they may descend, maybe to feed on the juices of a rotting carcass. The brown females (they lack the imperial purple sheen of the males) lay their eggs one at a time on low sallow bushes, over a wide area. The communal master tree draws them together to mate. Their flight is a majestic gliding and soaring. Seen in July and August; 60 mm ws.

The female ringlet (with ringed spots on the wings) scatters her eggs at random over grass, very often the lush damp grass of woodland rides (for 90 per cent of our colonies are found in woodland). The ringlets will sometimes be seen flying in light rain – the flight is a slow and rather feeble fluttering, often around a bush. July-August; 40 mm ws.

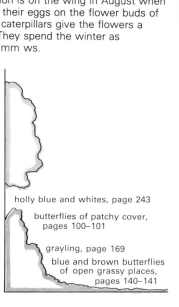

Where to look for woodland butterflies

- purple emperor
- purple hairstreak
- white admiral
- speckled wood
- silver washed fritillary
- brimstone
- pearl bordered fritillary
- ringlet

Dappled glade   Tall trees   Underwood   Open ride   Damp ditch

holly blue and whites, page 243

butterflies of patchy cover, pages 100–101

grayling, page 169

blue and brown butterflies of open grassy places, pages 140–141

female

Holly blue
Celastrina argiolus

male underwing

The brimstone gave us
the name 'butterfly'.
Note the leaf-like
appearance when its
wings are closed.

male

Brimstone
Gonepteryx rhamni

female underwing

Many butterflies
can be seen feeding
on bramble flowers

female

male

Speckled wood
Pararge aegeria

male

Silver-washed fritillary
Argynnis paphia

Pearl-bordered fritillary
Clossiana euphrosyne

Ringlet
Aphantopus hyperantus

White admiral
Limenitis camilla

White admirals lay their eggs on mature honeysuckle, but choose only shaded spindly plants of the kind found in coppice which has been let-go this century. The butterflies spread from the south-east to the Midlands in the 1930s and 1940s as coppicing declined (the warm summers also helped). You would not expect to see them in light, newly cut coppice nor in the deep shade of timber forest. Graceful fliers, gliding effortlessly. Seen in July and August; 60mm ws.

The black hairstreak butterfly is chocolate brown rather than black; both sexes sport short wing-tails. The eggs are laid in July on blackthorn (sloe) bushes and the caterpillars hatch the following March. The black and white chrysalis, which looks exactly like a bird dropping, is bound to a twig with silky threads. The butterfly breaks out from it and is on the wing in June-July; 35 mm ws.

The survival of the black hairstreak

The female black hairstreak butterfly will only lay her eggs singly on the high, end shoots of old blackthorn (sloe) bushes. Blackthorn is common enough, out of woodland as well as in it, being a typical hedgerow shrub, but the butterfly is confined to woods, and it is, in fact, extremely rare, being found only in a few woods in the East Midlands.

In 1969, only a dozen colonies of the butterfly were known, but a search was put in hand, which revealed sixty locations where it had been known to fly – and it still was flying at thirty of them.

Some of these surviving colonies were large, others small.

Those sixty sites were carefully assessed, and it was clear that the large colonies were always located on blackthorn bushes growing thickly in sheltered but sunny woodland sites. It seemed that the colony could survive even when the rest of the wood was felled, provided its crucial blackthorn thickets survived.

In these prime breeding spots, the butterfly bred for many years, but did not easily colonise suitable places which

man or chance created, for it was reluctant to fly far. And it seemed that the habitats of the remaining colonies were being destroyed by modern forestry faster than new ones close by could be found and colonised. In the past, those Midland woods had been coppiced in small compartments with long rotations so that there was usually some dense scrubby blackthorn nearby.

A dozen of the surviving thirty colonies were in woods which were already nature reserves, or in which conservation agreements between owner and local naturalists were in force.

Willows, sallows and poplars are excellent moth trees (page 26). Some splendid moths are shown elsewhere – the emperor on page 130, merveille du jour and green oak moth on 49; see also 82. Gaudy day-flying moths are shown on pages 130, 142.

Moths

What is the difference between a moth and a butterfly? Not at all an easy question to answer, because our division of these supposedly easily recognised insects into two main groups is rather artificial. Butterflies are merely one of the several groupings within the order Lepidoptera. Therefore it is hardly surprising to learn that whilst there are only sixty or so species of butterfly in Britain there are over 2,000 species of moth. Admittedly, a butterfly is very different from a hawk moth, but there is also a good deal of difference between a hawk moth and some of the other moths shown on this page. To confuse matters further, some of the butterflies, such as the skippers, are very moth-like, while some of the moths are brightly coloured and fly by day! However, there is one simple clue to look for in order to distinguish the two groups. Look at the antennae. If they end in a small club, then it is almost certainly a butterfly. Moths have many different types of antennae but they never end with these small clubs. But beware, the day-flying burnet moths (page 142) do have a gradually thickened end to their antennae.

Many of the moths are tiny dull-coloured insects, and the caterpillars of some of these can do enormous damage to stored food and fabrics. Some of the larger moths, however, have wing patterns which are every bit as beautiful as the butterflies' and the Victorian collectors often gave them delightful names – black arches, Hebrew character, true lover's knot, garden tiger, rosy footman, peach blossom, square spot rustic, to name but a few.

The peppered moth

The peppered moth is in its own way a classic animal. It is quite large for a moth (60 mm wingspan), and flies by night from May to July in woodlands, parks and also in suburban and town gardens throughout Britain. The eggs are laid on oak, birch and other trees. The 'normal' form of the moth is white mottled with black. There is, however, another, 'melanic' form – with black wings mottled with white. This kind of colour variation within a species, caused by excess of the dark pigment melanin, can be seen in about twenty other moths.

A century ago, the dark form was just noticed in the smoke-laden city of Manchester. It became the commoner of

the two. Presumably this dark form was at an advantage, for when it rested in the daytime, with its wings spread, it was hard to see against the sooty bark or brick. Birds did not notice it, whereas the pale normal form stood out against the dark background.

However, things may not be as simple as that – for it is now quite common even in the open, 'soot free', countryside. Perhaps its darker pigmentation is linked to an improved hardiness in general. It will be interesting to see if the 'normal' white form again becomes commoner in the cities, for the Clean Air Acts of 1956 and 1968 prohibited 'dark smoke' entirely, and created smokeless zones in towns. The bricks and trees are now often clean again.

A normal and 'melanic' form of the peppered moth on a soot-blackened tree trunk. Notice how the normal form stands out, making it prone to predation by birds.

Puss moth
Cerura vinula

Goat moth
Cossus cossus

eyed hawk caterpillar

The goat moth is so called from the smell of its caterpillar which feeds on the wood of various deciduous trees. The tunnel made by the caterpillar drips sap, which attracts many other insects. A large, scarce moth, it spends its day resting on trunks and fences. 65 mm ws.

The puss moth has a thick 'fluffy-cat' body. The caterpillar is striking – when disturbed it draws back its head and whips its tails of long red threads. Though the outline of the caterpillar is clear enough when pictured, in the field the dramatic markings break up its outline and make it very difficult to see on the sallow or willow leaves on which it feeds. 80 mm ws.

The eyed hawk moth sits with forewings held apart, but if disturbed the wings open further to show the two startling eyespots on the hind wings. The caterpillars of hawk moths are distinctive, with a 'horn' at the rear. The eyed hawk moths seen here are mating. 90 mm ws.

The hairy vapourer moth is common everywhere, even in cities where the unusual caterpillars thrive on ornamental bushes. Their hairs cause a rash on the skin. The female is wingless and usually seen fat, full of eggs. Female 15 mm long; male 25 mm ws.

The oak eggar is one of a family of stout brown moths. The males fly in a fast zig-zag pattern by day over rough ground, seeking the scent of the female. 50 mm ws.

The resting camouflage of the buff tip moth makes it look like a freshly broken, lichen-covered twig on hazel or oak. The caterpillars, which feed together initially, separate when fully grown, leave the tree and can be seen walking on the ground looking for a secluded site when ready to pupate. 55 mm ws.

Both the adult magpie (or currant) moth and its caterpillar flourish warning colours. The latter can be found on many plants; the moth is slow flying; often seen in gardens. 40 mm ws.

The wings of the male ghost moth are pure white. The moths weave backwards and forwards like pendulums over a grassy place at dusk, and so attract the females to them. However, in the extreme north of Scotland in the Shetland Isles, where summer nights are short and light, such

puss caterpillar

Willows, sallows and poplars
are very important food plants
for moth caterpillars. Hawthorn
and oak are also
good moth trees.

Magpie moth
Abraxas grossulariata

magpie caterpillar

Oak eggar moth
Lasiocampa quercus

Buff tip
Phalera bucephala

buff tip caterpillar

Canary-shouldered
thorn moth
Ennomos alniaria

White plume moth
Pterophorus pentadactyla

The unusual looking white plume moth is
common in hedges, flying by night but also in
daylight if disturbed. Its caterpillars feed on
bindweeds. 15 mm ws.

male

Ghost moth
Hepialus humuli

Eyed hawk moth
Smerinthus ocellata

Large yellow underwing moth
Noctua pronuba

Pug moth
Eupithecia sp.

Hart and dart moth
Agrotis exclamationis

The large yellow underwing baffles birds.
Camouflaged at rest with its wings closed, it flies
off erratically if disturbed, flashing its underwings,
to plunge into cover. It then closes its wings and
'disappears'. Often flushed out from long grass.
It is on the wing from June to October.
55 mm ws.

Angle shades moth
Phlogophora meticulosa

Garden tiger moth
Arctia caja

Male vapourer moth
Orgyia antiqua

Female vapourer
moth

The angle shades is a lovely moth, but looks
for all the world like a shrivelled leaf when at
rest. The caterpillar is seen on many wild and
garden plants. 45 mm ws.

The garden tiger, when disturbed or attacked,
exposes its bright red hind-wings to tell the
predator that it is distasteful. It flies largely at
night and will often come to lighted windows.
Its 'woolly bear' caterpillars feed on nettles,
dandelion and other plants. 60 mm ws.

vapourer caterpillar

angle shades caterpillar

a ruse will have little effect – the local race of
ghost moths have dark-coloured males. 55 mm
ws.

Heart and dart (so called from the black marking
on its forewings) flies during June and July at
night. One of a large family of 'noctuid' moths,
often attracted by lighted windows. The
caterpillars are 'cutworms' – they nibble the stalks
of young cabbage plants. 35 mm ws.

Many thorn moths have two broods, spring and
autumn. They are of the geometer family, so
called because of the way their caterpillars move,
'measuring' their paces. They are also called
'loopers'; when rigid they are well disguised.
These geometers rest with wings closed
upwards in butterfly fashion. The canary-
shouldered thorn shown here is seen flying in
August. 40 mm ws.

Pug moths are small and rest with wings spread
flat. The caterpillars feed inside flowers or seed
pods. 25 mm ws.

**Hawk moths are all rather dramatic looking
insects** – as neat and functional as a jet aircraft.
Many of the larger hawk moths are day-flying
migrants, arriving here from the continent in
summer, breeding and then eventually being killed
by the frosts of autumn.

The hummingbird hawk moth is one of these.
It is easily recognised when it comes into a
garden to hover at the flowers, darting from one
to the other with wing beats too quick to see,
just like a miniature hummingbird.

Another is the death's head hawk moth – one
of the prizes of the Victorian collectors. It is the
largest insect seen here (120 mm ws.) with
distinctive markings, which include a 'death's
head' – a skull or mask – on its back. When the
moth is alarmed it will squeak, quite loudly,
which presumably frightens the predator. It is a
night-time flier. Whether you have a chance of
seeing it depends more on conditions overseas,
for like many migrants, it cannot survive the
British winter. It can be counted as British for it
breeds here when it arrives in spring – the eggs
are laid on potato, woody nightshade and other

leaves, and the caterpillars are seen in July.
Often a second generation of adults is on the
wing in October, but are killed by the first frosts.
There is more about the rather puzzling migration
of insects on page 101.

Although butterflies cannot hear sounds in the
way animals equipped with ears can, some of
the moths may be able to do this. The large yellow
underwing, for example, has a pair of sacs closed
with a thin membrane on each side of its body.
The moth reacts to high pitched noises: the
squeak of a stopper turned in a glass jar, for
example, will cause it to run around, vibrating its
wings.

When flying, these 'ears' can act as a bat
'detector' – the moth can pick up the high-
pitched sonar calls of the bat, and take avoiding
action, dashing wildly about and often diving into
cover.

To this selection of easily seen invertebrates add species shown on pages 102–110, for many of them will be found in the shelter of woods. On the wood's grassy rides look for species shown on pages 142.

Woodland invertebrates

Although you may be aware of a background hum of insect life in a wood on a warm summer's day, you may well be hard put to see many of them. What you do see is just a token of the vast community of animals of all kinds which may surround you. Some are hidden by the curtain of leaves whilst others are retiring and active only at night. Indeed, many small animals spend almost their entire lives within the trunk or bark of a tree or in the soil. We may only see the mating dances of the adults from time to time.

So, although woods can contain a vast variety of animal life, you may be disappointed when you walk into one and not see very much at all.

Here we show some interesting animals to search for in a wood. Look for them on the lower branches and at the edges of the glades and rides. The border zone between two habitats, such as the edge of a wood, is usually quite rich in wildlife, and many different species can be seen.

Bush crickets, once known as long-horned grasshoppers because of their long antennae, are akin to crickets and sing by rubbing their forewings together; rather feebly in the case of the oak bush cricket shown here. The female has a curved egg-layer or ovipositor; it is not a sting. Found in tree foliage, hedges; adult in later summer. They can fly weakly. Body 12 mm.

Other bush crickets make a noise by drumming their legs on a leaf. One, the great green bush cricket, sings a penetrating continuous song on warm nights in the south of England.

The caterpillars of the green oak moth can strip the oak twigs of their leaves. They are frequently met in spring, hanging down on a thread after they have been dislodged from the rolled leaf within which they feed; this habit also gives them the name green oak roller moth. The adult moth flies in June; 20 mm ws.

This green spider Micrommata can sometimes be seen silhouetted against a thin leaf. The larger green spider is the longer-lived female. In the summer the female constructs a retreat by binding together several leaves. She then lays many bright green eggs and encloses them in a white silky sac; body 8–15 mm.

Wood ants

The social organisation of ants is astonishing – and well known. Less well known, and equally astonishing, is their part in the ecology of their habitat.

The nests of the wood ant, which may house 100,000 ants, are easy enough to see – large domes of leaf and twig fragments, or pine needles. In beech woods, the ants collect the dry outer scales of the buds for the nest. The overground nest contains a labyrinth of passages, connected to others running underground. There are many exits – gateways guarded by sentinel ants and closed by the worker ants at night (they often drag twigs across them). From these gateways run tracks – some as long as 100 metres – to the colony's foraging grounds.

A colony may build more than one nest in a wood, two or three maybe, within a short distance of each other, but the wood may contain other communities and they all have their own foraging grounds. Indeed, the way that these dovetail into each other in a wood is fascinating – it can be as intricate as a three-dimensional Chinese puzzle. Not even the trackways meet or cross.

In their foraging grounds, the ants have a massive effect. They take large numbers of caterpillars and other insects from all layers of the wood – from the ground to the highest canopy. Studies have shown that in a wood with these ants, the trees can be expected to lose about one per cent of their leaves to caterpillars and other insects, while in a wood with no ants, the trees lose nearer ten per cent. From a forestry point of view this is vital, for good leaf cover equates with good timber production! However, it does not seem to be a British practice to encourage these ants in timber woodland, although in some European countries wood ants are protected, even encouraged in woodlands as a form of pest control.

The ants also farm aphids – they guard the sap-sucking aphid colonies, and gain supplies of the sweet honeydew that the bugs exude.

Wood ant colonies are long-lived – they may be permanent if undisturbed. Within the nest, the cycle of life continues, repeating itself from year to year. The nest may contain several queens, laying the very small eggs from which the grubs hatch. These are attended and fed by the workers (which are sterile females), and when full grown they spin themselves a white cocoon. These cocoons are sold as 'ant eggs' for feeding aquarium fish, but they are much larger than the real eggs.

In June, small numbers of winged male and female ants are produced amongst the numerous sterile workers – they fly out of the nest to mate, and the female then usually returns to her old colony, to become in her turn one of the egg-laying queens on which it depends.

Wood ants are still to be found in woodlands in England and Wales, especially the larger ones, and particularly in woodlands with pine trees. They have been disappearing from smaller woods however, and disturbance may be part of the cause. In Scotland, a related species of ant fills the same 'niche' in the woods.

Wood ants moving a pupa or cocoon to a safer place.

A wood ants nest made of thousands of pieces of heather, twigs and pine needles.

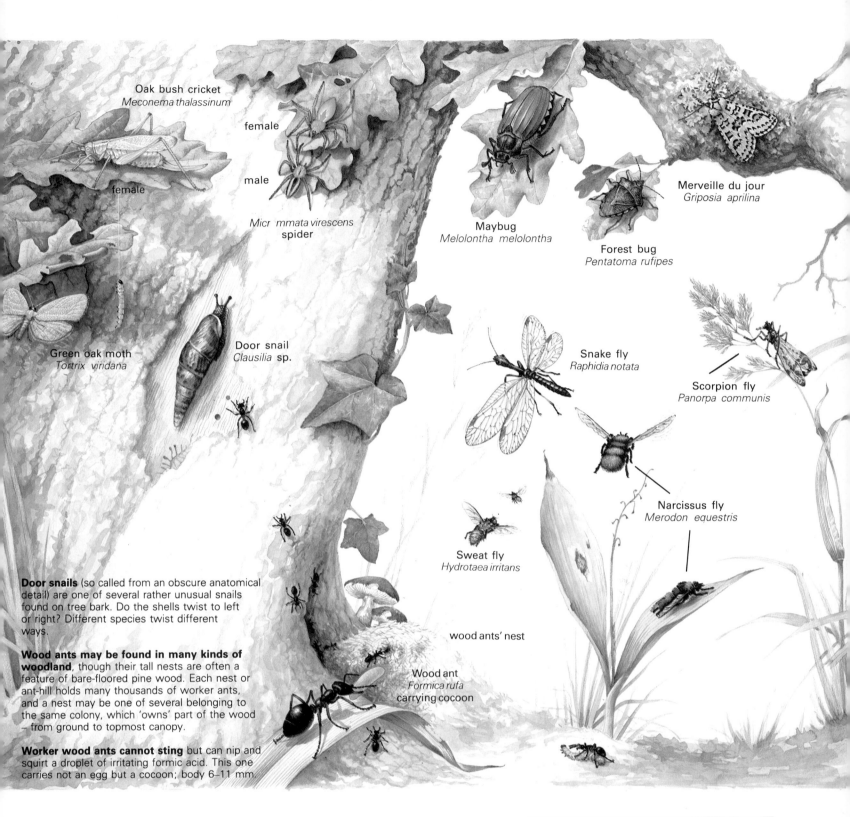

Oak bush cricket
Meconema thalassinum

female

female

male

Micrmmata virescens
spider

Maybug
Melolontha melolontha

Merveille du jour
Griposia aprilina

Forest bug
Pentatoma rufipes

Green oak moth
Tortrix viridana

Door snail
Clausilia sp.

Snake fly
Raphidia notata

Scorpion fly
Panorpa communis

Narcissus fly
Merodon equestris

Sweat fly
Hydrotaea irritans

wood ants' nest

Wood ant
Formica rufa
carrying cocoon

Door snails (so called from an obscure anatomical detail) are one of several rather unusual snails found on tree bark. Do the shells twist to left or right? Different species twist different ways.

Wood ants may be found in many kinds of woodland, though their tall nests are often a feature of bare-floored pine wood. Each nest or ant-hill holds many thousands of worker ants, and a nest may be one of several belonging to the same colony, which 'owns' part of the wood – from ground to topmost canopy.

Worker wood ants cannot sting but can nip and squirt a droplet of irritating formic acid. This one carries not an egg but a cocoon; body 6–11 mm.

Once very common, but not so today, the maybug or cockchafer (actually a beetle) is to be seen in the south, even bumbling into houses with a buzzing, heavy flight, and crashing noisily into lighted windows. The grub nibbles roots in the ground, and is a favourite food of rooks; adults eat oak leaves; body to 30 mm.

The forest bug is one of the shield bugs. The bugs overwinter as larval nymphs hidden in cracks in the bark – they are a food for blue tits. In spring the nymphs become active and feed on caterpillars and leaves. Adults are seen in July; body to 12 mm.

The snakefly is made unmistakable by the snake-like way it moves its 'neck'. This is really an extension of the thorax, the part of the body which carries the wings. It is seen from May-July. It is an uncommon predator but worth looking out for, especially around aphids; body to 15 mm.

The male scorpion fly curls its tail as a threat when disturbed: but this is display only, as it is stingless. You will see it making short, rapid flights seeking dead insects. The scorpion fly belongs to a very ancient family of insects, from which butterflies probably evolved. Note its 'beak'; body to 20 mm.

The forewings of the lovely merveille du jour (day's wonder) **moth** camouflage it against lichen-covered bark. The moth is 25 mm long, seen only on autumn nights. The caterpillars feed on oak leaves.

Female sweat flies follow you in swarms, wanting not to bite but to sip your perspiration. The grubs feed on cow pats and horse droppings. The adults are common, May-October, and will annoy you in many woods; 10 mm.

Narcissus flies are hoverflies and look rather like bumble bees. In spring the males take territorial possession of grass tussocks in glades and rides, hovering over them and flying away if disturbed but returning afterwards. They are waiting for the females. The females lay their eggs near bluebells; the grubs work their way down to the bulbs and eat them out; 20 mm.

Tally of life in a wood. Here is a tally of the life in an oak wood in Oxfordshire, more or less in the centre of England. It is a semi-natural woodland which has been coppiced in the past and is now being managed as a nature reserve. The lists were compiled not only from amongst the trees but also in the glades and along the woodland edge, which is often an important habitat.

	Number of species
Mosses	12
Liverworts	1
Other plants, including trees	206
Fungi of all kinds	36
	Plant total 255
Insects	
crickets and grasshoppers	3
alderflies, lacewing flies and their kin	1
scorpion flies	1
bugs	7
butterflies	29
moths	167
beetles	9
bees, wasps, ants	3
true (2-winged) flies	3
	Insect total 223
Spiders	99
Harvestmen	1
Snails, slugs	8
Frogs, newts	2
Snakes, lizards	2
Birds	44
Mammals	9 + 1 (!)

The birds on this page are rather more tree-linked than those on pages 52, 54, some seeking tree holes for nesting. They are, all of them, typical of broadleaved woodlands, but may be seen with conifers if conditions suit them, see page 67.

Birds and trees

Although there is a close link between the plant life of a wood and its history this is not so for birds. The structure of a wood is important for bird life and, of course, its management history is a critical factor in this. But there are no birds that are limited to ancient woods in the way that some flowers are.

It is often difficult to discover why some birds are seen in one wood and not in another, given that they are within their broad geographical range. There is a difference between the birds you might expect to see in deciduous and coniferous woodlands but that is usually a result of the structural difference rather than the type of tree. For example, you are as likely to see the great spotted woodpecker in an old pine wood as in an ancient broad-leaved wood – provided they both have suitable breeding and feeding places. The crossbill is an exception in that it is a specialist feeder on conifer seeds. In general, however, birds are not restricted to particular kinds of trees in the way that some species of butterflies or other insects are.

Apart from the structure, does the size of the wood matter? You can usually expect to find a greater variety of birds in a large wood, mainly as a reflection of the greater diversity of types of living place that are likely to be present. An isolated small wood also has a greater risk of losing its resident breeding population in a hard winter. It might take several seasons before neighbouring birds have filled these vacant sites. However, a small wood might have a high density of breeding birds as it will have more woodland edge in relation to its overall area.

Climate obviously plays an important part in the lives of birds, as it controls the supply of food and often dictates their movements. The spring arrival of warblers and swallows when the insects are available is well known. Less realised is the dispersal of our 'resident' birds during the winter months. Many species that are tied to woodlands for breeding will forage along hedgerows and fields in winter, while others that are seldom found in large woodlands in summer, such as rooks, may use them for roosting in the winter months. Some woods in the milder south-west may actually have larger numbers of birds in the winter than in the summer. Some woods suit specialist feeders more in winter than in summer—beech woods are one example, where flocks of finches visit in winter for the beech mast.

A sparrowhawk slips fast among the trees or courses down hedgerows to take the finches and other small birds on which it preys by surprise. It does not hover, but may glide high up to prospect. It has a *kek kek* chatter. Both sexes look greyish-brown, but, as you can see, the male (shown here) has an orange-barred breast; the female is brown-barred. Resident. The flattish nest of twigs is built in a tree. The male is the shorter of the two, less than town-pigeon sized, 28 cm; the female is 38 cm.

The spotted flycatcher is misleadingly named, for the adults have streaked breasts. The birds perch alertly, and make sudden short twisting 'flycatching' sorties, often returning to the same perch (unlike their pied cousins, page 61). They prefer rather roomy woods to fly in (where the sunny glades attract flying insects), and they have adopted gardens and town parks where suitable nest sites can be found. A *zee* call. Summer visitor. The nest is a cup of grass built tight up against a tree trunk, in a hollow in the rotting bark, or in ivy, usually 2–4 metres above ground. They will nest behind drainpipes and ivy on buildings. Sparrow sized; 14 cm.

Both male and female tree sparrows resemble male house sparrows, but with a brown crown and cheek spot. They will sometimes flock together at the end of the nesting season, but tree sparrows are not often seen in gardens; they are birds of woods and fields. A sharper *chirrup* than the house sparrow. Tree sparrows breed where they can find nest holes – in trees, but also in quarries. 14 cm.

Woodpigeons nest in woods, but feed out in the surrounding fields and nowadays they will also be seen nesting in copses, hedges, even gardens and far into towns. In the warmth of towns, with plenty of food, they may breed for much of the year. Their song is of five-phrase sequences *co-coo-coo coo-coo*, and often ends with a 'cuk' note, but just as characteristic is a loud wing clap when they take off in alarm. The nest, a thin platform of twigs, is in a tree or shrub, and may be high or low. Somewhat larger than town pigeons; 41 cm.

Stock doves have a gruff, far-reaching double coo-COO. They lack the white rump of the feral rock dove (the classic town pigeon pattern, see page 130) but are otherwise rather similar. They often flock with woodpigeons. They nest in woods, parks and farmlands where there are old trees with holes, but also sometimes nest in suitable holes in buildings, cliffs, and often with others of their kind close by. 33 cm.

You will often see turtle doves perched openly on branches in the open woods or hedges they choose for nesting when they arrive from West Africa in May. A soothing, purring call. The nest is low, and is a thin platform built 3 metres or below in small trees or shrubs. A summer visitor to south and east England. Note the neck markings and fine chequered back. About the same size as town pigeons; 32 cm.

A male great spotted woodpecker (told from the female by his red patch at the back of the head) leaving his nest hole in the bole of a tree. It has a fast bouncing flight.

Sparrowhawk
Accipiter nisus

male

Tawny owl
Strix aluco

Great spotted woodpecker
Dendrocopus major

Spotted flycatcher
Muscicapa striata

Green woodpecker
Picus viridis

Woodpigeon
Columba palumbus

Jay
Garrulus glandarius

Tree sparrow
Passer montanus

owl pellet

Stock dove
Columba oenas

Turtle dove
Streptopelia turtur

Woodcock
Scolopax rusticola

Predatory and insect-eating birds cough up pellets of undigested waste – those of the tawny owl are 3–7 cm long and contain the bones, fur, wing cases of their prey. You find them scattered under favourite roosts.

'Tu-whit tu-whoo' calls the tawny owl? In fact, what you hear is one bird announce *ker-wick*, and its mate reply with a snatch of territorial hoot – *hooo-hoo-oo*. They usually hunt at night, dropping down on their prey of voles and mice (they also take worms and beetles) from a perch, their keen sight aided by acute hearing. They use any suitable hole to nest – in a tree, a rock crevice, sometimes using the nests of other birds such as crows. Larger than a town pigeon; 28 cm.

The woodcock is a wader of woodland. It likes a wood with a dense bottom to it, and nests on the ground in dry areas but likes some wet nearby where it can probe for worms in the damp soil. Secretive, well camouflaged birds, they are usually best looked for on spring evenings, when the males can be seen roding – carrying out a tree top patrol of their territory, calling a loud *tswick* or a soft croak. Resident, but some from northern Europe winter here. Town-pigeon sized; 34 cm.

Great spotted woodpeckers hack away loose bark to reach beetle grubs and other insects, but the loud drumming they make in spring is a territorial signal, made by knocking on a dead branch. A loud *tchick* call. Rarely seen on the ground. They bore a nest hole, 3 metres or higher up a tree. Smaller than a blackbird; 23 cm.

Green woodpeckers rarely drum, but are vocal in spring with a satanic *plew plew* laugh – they are also known as 'yaffles' because of it. They fly bouncily, and, unlike other woodpeckers', you will often see them on the ground, feeding on ants, sometimes far from trees – they are attracted by parkland with old trees to nest in and plenty of open ground. The nest is bored in a trunk of a tree, at least 1 metre from the ground. Town-pigeon sized; 32 cm.

Jays are members of the crow family, but are wary woodland birds though they may venture out of the trees to cache acorns they have collected. A harsh screech, but some of the warning calls they make seem to imitate the threat – the pop of a gun or the snitter of squirrels. They nest in the fork of a tree, from 2 metres upwards. Town pigeon sized; 34 cm.

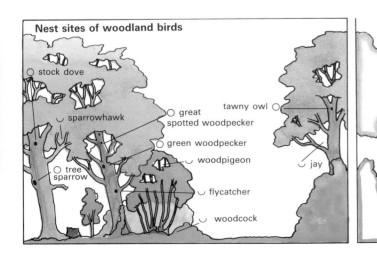

Nest sites of woodland birds

○ stock dove

sparrowhawk

tree sparrow

○ great spotted woodpecker

tawny owl ○

○ green woodpecker

⌣ woodpigeon

⌣ jay

⌣ flycatcher

⌣ woodcock

More birds of deciduous woodland on pages 52–53 and 54–55

kestrel, page 113
buzzard, page 162
rook and crow, pages 144–145
pied flycatcher, page 61
birds of coniferous forest, page 70
redpoll, page 64
birds of the hedgerow, pages 112–113
pheasant, page 17

⌣ nest construction
○ nest hole

The community of birds you find in any one wood depends on its structure, both vertical and horizontal, each species shopping for certain elements they need for nest site and territory/feeding ground. Shown here are the preferred woodland nest sites for the birds illustrated on this page.

Birds usually choose a wood, or patch of scrub or a hedge, not for the kinds of tree or shrub, but because its structure suits them.
Nevertheless, some trees do have an interesting bird-link because of the food they provide or the woodland they create: pages 61–65; 70.

Birds and trees

Blue tits (the word 'tit' is Norse for 'small bird') are so familiar outside the window at the bird table in winter that it is always something of a surprise to see them searching the tops of the trees for caterpillars when they are food gathering for their brood in spring. Their relatives the great tits, search the tree lower down so that the two are not in direct competition for food at this crucial time of year. However, there is nothing very neat and tidy about these zones, and if there is a heavy crop of caterpillars on the highest leaves, the great tits will join the blue tits at the feast.

Competition for food is fierce – and so birds tend to remain in the habitats to which they are best suited by body, diet, way of life, and in which they can

find good nest sites. By and large, competition for food is between members of the same species rather than between members of separate clans. During the breeding season the prime food of the species is sought, and the holding of territory means that birds become spread out and so share out the available food supply.

When breeding, many birds take and defend a 'territory' – a patch of land which includes the nest site itself and often a feeding ground around it. Possession is nine-tenths of the natural laws now operating, and usually the presence of the resident pair of birds is enough to caution away others of their kind. However, song birds also proclaim their holding with their distinctive songs. If they prefer to sing from a tall song post, this too can be an important element of the territory.

The size of the territory can vary enormously. Predators have large ones – a tawny owl may possess a whole 20 hectare wood, that of a redstart may be only 0.5 hectares of the same wood. Birds, like ourselves buying a house, often have to put up with second best, and woodland birds are often found in what seem to us to be very different places. It is interesting that the birds most often encountered in surveys of nests in woods (robin, wren, blackbird, song thrush, willow warbler, blue tit, great tit, chaffinch) are also the birds you are most likely to see in the garden. Indeed, many mature gardens have the structure of a woodland edge with many suitable song posts and 'woodland glades'. All the birds in that list are British residents, except the willow warbler (see page 54) which is a summer visitor, and though not as common as the others in gardens, it certainly can sometimes be seen in them. It is, however, the ground nesting habit, requiring a dense undergrowth, that prevents the willow warbler from more effectively colonising gardens.

Blue tits are acrobatic birds on the thin twigs where they search for caterpillars for their young. They often flock with other tits after breeding, when they regularly visit gardens and will feed from ground scraps. They have large clutches of eggs, but mortality is high. They call a scolding *tsee-tsee-tsee-tsit*; the song includes this with *tsirruptsee* trills. Their nest is a hole or cavity in a tree or wall and they will quickly occupy nest-boxes. Hundreds of individual blue tits may visit one garden in the course of a winter, but they come in small groups at a time. 11.5 cm.

Treecreepers move jerkily, searching for bark insects, spiralling their way to the top of one trunk, then flying down to begin again at the base of another. They have a shrill *tsee* call, and a faint song. The cup-like nest is in a crack or behind loose bark or ivy on the trunk of a tree. They therefore seek out large trees in mature woods, parkland and even farmland. These birds have the unusual habit of occupying holes when they roost in winter. Blue-tit sized; 12.5 cm.

The nuthatch is a bird of mature woods or parkland where large trees are likely to be used for nest holes – sometimes disused woodpecker holes are used. The entrance to the hole is often narrowed by the birds (by plastering mud around it) to keep out intruders. They feed on insects, actively running up and down trunks and branches. They also eat seeds, and in winter jam nuts in the bark and hammer them open. Some of their song sounds like a kestrel's. Resident in England and Wales, but rarely seen in Scotland. Great-tit sized; 14 cm.

The tail of the redstart is an eye-catching chestnut colour ('start' is an Old English word for 'tail'). Redstarts are active birds and will perch, quivering, before making an energetic sally after an insect. The female often feeds also on the ground. They prefer spacious woods (but not beech woods), but are also seen around villages and towns, even on open heathlands. A *hweet* call, and brief warbling song from a high song post. Summer visitor. The nest is high up in a hole in a tree or in a tree stump, wall or sometimes in a hollow in a bank. The number of visiting redstarts has declined in recent years, maybe as a result of drought in their winter grounds south of the Sahara. Sparrow sized; 14 cm.

Great tits have a clearly recognisable, echoing see-sawing *tee-cher* song and many different calls, a *pink pink* being common. They are often seen feeding on the ground. The bold black chest stripe (only glimpsed here) is shown off while protecting the breeding territory. The nest is a hole in a tree – or in a wall or rocks, but normally with trees nearby. 14 cm.

A parent long-tailed tit (*left*) **feeding** its offspring with a succulent green caterpillar. The carefully camouflaged nest may take two weeks to build and hold up to twelve young.

Marsh tit or willow tit? They are closely related, but can be distinguished by their calls – the former a harsh *pit-chew*, the latter an *eez-eez-eez* and *tchay* repeated many times. Their names are misleading. Willow tits excavate nest holes in soft wood, e.g. tree stumps, and so are often seen in wet woods where rotting timber is not uncommon, but they may be found in drier conifer plantations. Marsh tits use holes they have found in trees or stumps, and are to be sought in drier woods, though rarely in conifer plantations. Both are resident. 12 cm.

Chiffchaffs arrive early in spring, often to sing from bare boughs. They occupy mature woods with dense undergrowth, or scrub or old hedges with trees for song posts. They take insects from the leaves, and may hover to do so, or take them in mid air. The chiffchaff is a restless bird. Its *tsip-tsap-tsap-tsip* ('chiff-chaff') song identifies it from the willow warbler (next page). One of the first summer visitors from Africa, often arriving in March. The nest is low in cover, sometimes in creepers on a wall. About blue-tit sized; 11 cm.

Blue tit
Parus caeruleus

In springtime, the male wood warbler is often seen displaying to the female, spiralling down to perch beside her, singing while he does so

Wood warbler
Phylloscopus sibilatrix

Chiffchaffs, like other warblers, may sometimes be seen 'fly-catching' on the wing.

Chiffchaff
Phylloscopus collybita

male

Redstart
Phoenicurus phoenicurus

Treecreeper
Certhia familiaris

Blackcap
Sylvia atricapilla

This is the male blackcap, the female has a brown crown

Long-tailed tit
Aegithalos caudatus

Great tit
Parus major

Nuthatch
Sitta europaea

The nuthatch can be seen running head first down tree trunks

Marsh tit
Parus palustris

male

Bullfinch
Pyrrhula pyrrhula

Robin
Erithacus rubecula

Wood warblers arrive in late April from central Africa. They choose woods of all sizes, but with little undergrowth. They like exposed song posts and often feed high in the tree canopy, but nest on the ground amongst scant cover. They are seen in beech woods and open-floored hillside oak woods. They are quicksilver movers, and shake while singing. The song is either a repeating *duu* or a single note repeated, ending in a shimmering trill. Somewhat larger than blue tit; 13 cm.

Long-tailed tits gather food at the top of the underwood. The domed nest is amongst the outer twigs of brambles, shrubs, up to 6 metres; higher in a tree, when it is in a fork or near the trunk. A thin piping *tsi tsi* call when they flock in winter. Small groups huddle to keep warm on cold nights, but mortality is high. Sparrow and great tit length; 14 cm, but note the tiny body.

Wren
Troglodytes troglodytes

Both sexes of robin sing a liquid song from a small tree or other lowish song post, even in winter, for they each hold a 'territory' throughout the year, flaunting the red breast in aggressive displays. Common garden birds in Britain (you can watch them feeding, darting to the ground from a perch), they are shy deep forest birds in Europe, where only their *tic tic* alarm note gives them away. 14 cm.

The melodious song of the blackcap can be said to match that of the nightingale – it is certainly richer than the similar song of the garden warbler (page 54). As well as a rich, varied warbling, it has a *tack* call. Though a summer visitor, some birds overwinter in the milder west and south west of Britain, where they can often be seen in gardens at this time. The nest is in thick undergrowth, brambles or rhododendrons up to 2 metres from the ground. Great-tit sized; 14 cm.

Dumpy wrens have a shrew-like run and a low whirring flight. They have a *tic tic* alarm, but their song, which is heard all year, is very loud and marks their extensive territory. Maybe our commonest bird with possibly 10 million birds in Britain and Ireland; numbers can fall dramatically in hard winters. With no need of trees, they are seen in many different habitats, even open moorland if nest crevices can be found. Tiny; 9.5 cm.

Bullfinches mate for life – you may see the pairs feeding on apple buds in spring, when other food is scarce; ash seeds are an important food in winter. They seek dense, lowish cover for the nest and are birds of wood edges, though they will occupy hedges and any tangled, scrubby areas. They have a piping call. Slightly larger than a sparrow; 15 cm.

Nest sites of woodland birds

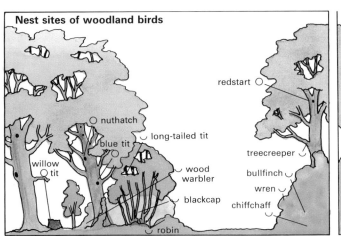

redstart

nuthatch

long-tailed tit

blue tit

willow tit

wood warbler

treecreeper

blackcap

bullfinch

wren

chiffchaff

robin

More birds of deciduous woodland on pages 50–51 and 54–55

buzzard, page 162
rook and crow, pages 144–145
pied flycatcher, page 61
birds of the coniferous forest, page 70
redpoll, page 64
birds of the hedgerow, pages 112–113
pheasant, page 17

⌣ nest construction
○ nest hole

Following on from the previous page here we show preferred woodland nest sites of the birds illustrated on this page. The birds shown here, although woodland species in the broad sense, by and large nest amongst the underwood and low cover.

Blackbirds and thrushes are among our most familiar birds, partly because they are such fine songsters. They will often be seen alongside birds shown on page 112 – song birds occupy a great variety of bushy places.

Birds and song

The birds on this page are prime songsters. It is interesting to note how many require a tall song perch within the territory. Some, however, are more often heard than seen.

It would be pleasant to think that songs which pleased our ears also gave pleasure to the birds. Perhaps the furthest one can go in this noble sentiment is by assuming that when birds are singing, they feel some kind of security – as they are holding territory with a nest nearby.

Bird song is complicated but a good example is always close to hand in the lovely song of the blackbird. Although we notice the blackbird's song in early spring (often in February) the story begins the year before. By late summer the nestlings have flown and the family ties have been loosened, though the hen birds seem to remain and roost in the vicinity of the old nest site. At this time of year and through the winter one of the typical sounds of the dusk is the lengthy, irritating 'chinking' of the blackbird males . . . *mik-mik-mik* . . . often ending in a noisy rattle. The males are, in fact, pulling rank on each other – and through this process attract the females. The birds are often paired up by the New Year.

The pair then occupy a suitable territory, near the centre of which they nest

in the fork of a tree or shrub. The male drives away others of his kind with that aggressive chinking, though rivals rarely intrude close to the nest. He is now singing from a tallish song post near the nest. The song is therefore loudest at the centre of the territory, weakening to the edges (there is no hard and fast line) where the territories of neighbouring birds may adjoin it.

During winter, the birds use a soft song as part of their courtship ritual – it is rather harsh, and can only be heard for a metre or two. This soft song, however, seems to become the raw material for the splendid territorial song. In early spring, the latter consists of a set of phrases (some people have counted twenty or more different ones) which are repeated one after the other, time and time again. Each phrase is short, sometimes ending with a rather unmusical *cluck*.

By the end of a few weeks, however, that early repertoire has changed. The old phrases are mixed, some seem joined together, new ones are heard. The birds may mimic other birds – sometimes they pick up phrases from other species. One researcher found his garden blackbird copying the dog whistle he used to call his pet, but raised by a fifth. Soon the reworked notes of that dog whistle were appearing in the songs of all the neighbouring blackbirds!

The song of the blackbird appeals to our ears, accustomed as they are to trills and rhythms. The song is functional, however, so what is the reason for its continual change throughout the season? Is the bird bored by singing the same notes? The blackbird's memory can hardly be faulty if sequences of twenty or more phrases can be followed for days at a time. Perhaps the variation is to prevent neighbouring birds getting used to the song so that it always remains a fresh territorial flag.

Sound pictures

It is easy enough to record bird song with a small cassette recorder. The quality will not be professional but you can play it and replay it until you can recognise some of the phrases and see if they have changed a week or two later. A useful professional tool is a sound spectrograph, which produces a *sonagram*, a 'picture' of the sound. Here is one blackbird phrase in March:

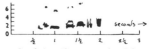

By the end of April, notes had been added on at the end, as the sonagram clearly shows:

By the end of the season, the blackbird was linking the first phrase with another and then adding extra notes. But the two extra notes added earlier are not now being used:

The song of the grasshopper warbler (*left*) is usually delivered unseen amongst low scrub. It is sometimes very difficult to locate the singing bird as, apart from remaining hidden, the warbler often changes the pitch and volume of its 'reel' producing a ventriloquial effect.

The willow warbler seems to be less tree-linked than its twin the chiffchaff (page 54). It breeds in open woodland, or on the edges of woods, scrub, high hedges – places where it can nest on or near the ground with the bushes around sheltering it. It is our most numerous summer visitor, with maybe three million pairs nesting in Britain and Ireland. The yellow in the plumage can vary, some birds appearing brown and white. Its song is a fine waterfall of notes quite unlike that of the similar-looking chiffchaff. Blue-tit sized; 11 cm.

Garden warblers are secretive birds; best located by their song. This is, however, very similar to that of the blackcap (page 52). If you cannot see the bird, the habitat may offer the clue as to which is singing, for garden warblers (they are rarely heard in gardens) do not need the tall song post of the blackcap, and may often be heard from scrub or young plantations. Summer visitors from Africa. The nest is a cup in a low shrub or young tree, usually with 0.5 metres of the ground. Somewhat larger than a sparrow; 15 cm.

The blackbird often begins the dawn chorus, starting to sing 40 minutes before sunrise, joined at intervals by the song thrush, wood pigeon, robin, mistlethrush, turtle dove, pheasant, willow warbler and wren (usually in that order). The male blackbird is a deep black with a yellow-bill; the female is brown with a somewhat spotted breast (the juvenile is also speckled). The blackbird can be recognised even from a distance by the way it moves – the way it raises its tail on landing is distinctive. The bird searches the ground for worms, insects, fruit and berries, cocking its head to eye the ground and turning over dead leaves. Resident, with some from Europe wintering here. Blackbirds breed in many different habitats – woods and wood edges are their origin, but they will nest anywhere there is low tree or shrub cover. The nest is a cup in the fork of a tree or shrub, 1–10 metres up. They will also nest on or in buildings, but trees or bushes are usually close by. 25 cm.

Note the willow warbler's pale legs compared with those of the chiffchaff.

Willow warbler
Phylloscopus trochilus

female

young blackbird

Song thrush
Turdus philomelos

Garden warbler
Sylvia borin

Blackbird
Turdus merula

male

Nightingale
Luscinia megarhynchos

Mistle thrush
Turdus viscivorus

Nightingales benefit from coppicing, which produces the low song posts and cover they need for their nest, built on or very close to the ground. They are most numerous in coppice between three and six years after the cut – and their decline in numbers in recent decades may be due to the abandonment of coppicing, though they will also occupy suitable scrub. They are summer visitors, usually arriving here in mid-April from central Africa, the male birds arriving first. Nightingales are restricted to the south-east of Britain – roughly east of a line from Exeter to Humberside. They have a loud, rich repetitive song, building to crescendoes that other birds cannot match. They sing in daytime, but are better heard at night, when most other birds are quiet (though not all song heard at night is a nightingale's!). Song apart, they are highly secretive; if you do manage to glimpse one, you will notice its cocked tail; it looks rather like a large uniformly brown robin; 16.5 cm.

Grasshopper warbler
Locustella naevia

Grasshopper warblers reel an insect-like high-pitched whirring song which elderly people with failing hearing may not be able to catch. These are birds of open, scrubby places, fens and marshes, even heathland and moorland as long as it has some dense tangled cover. If you hear it in woodland, it will be in the open scrubby areas; it may have benefited from coppicing – today it is one of the birds occupying young plantations. Summer visitor. Sparrow-sized; 14 cm.

Poets have tried to put bird song into words. Tennyson wrote:

Summer is coming
Summer is coming
I know it I know it I know it

– yes, the rhythm of the song of the song thrush, made up phrases, each repeated and then discarded. The nest is low, in a bush or hedge, or in thick ivy against a tree. The diet consists mainly of small animals; song thrushes smash the shells of snails on a stone 'anvil', wiping the snails on the ground before eating them. In autumn, however, thrushes take berries, including many yew berries (which blackbirds ignore).

Some of our blackbirds and thrushes move southwards or even cross the Channel in winter; some birds from more northerly Europe come here.

The mistlethrush requires high song posts and few garden trees are high enough to provide it with a nest site. It will sing from a lofty perch even in windy weather, one of the few birds to do so – hence its name 'storm cock'. The song is rather shriller than a blackbird's. It has a recognisable rasping flight call; 27 cm.

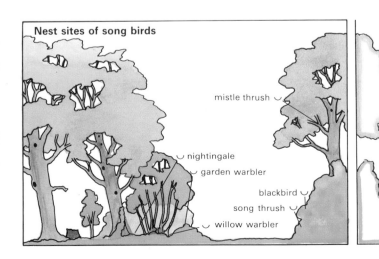

Nest sites of song birds

mistle thrush

nightingale

garden warbler

blackbird

song thrush

willow warbler

More birds of deciduous woodland on pages 50–51 and 52–53

buzzard, page 162
rook and crow, pages 144–145
pied flycatcher, page 61
birds of the coniferous forest, page 70
redpoll, page 64
birds of the hedgerow, pages 112–113
pheasant, page 17

⌣ nest construction
○ nest hole

Badgers and especially foxes are mobile animals, often seen far out from the cover of trees and scrub. Woods also carry a large number of smaller mammals, see page 114. Rabbits and moles (page 146) may also be present in the wood.

Woodland mammals

Grey squirrels are probably the simplest British mammal to observe – their bold, almost cheeky behaviour in town parks and gardens has won them many admirers. They are unfortunately looked upon very differently by foresters as they can cause considerable damage to trees, feeding on leading shoots and leaf buds in late winter and spring as well as stripping bark.

Watching badgers and foxes is a very different matter. There is always the possibility of a chance sighting, particularly of a fox which may suddenly bound across a road or perhaps be seen patrolling a hedgebank across a field. Foxes are often active by day and in undisturbed areas can be quite bold. Badgers, on the other hand, are more creatures of the night and close to human settlements will seldom venture out until after dark. The best places to watch both these mammals is at their set or earth.

If you suspect there to be badgers in an area, the first thing that you should do is to have a good search round for typical signs of activity – look for well-worn paths which pass under low vegetation and branches (thus eliminating deer), perhaps you might find a few distinctive hairs on a low fence (look for the black tips at each end). If the ground is soft enough, you should find tracks – look for a broad central pad with a parallel row of four or five toe pads. The

The track of a badger (*below*) showing five toe pads and a broad interdigital pad.

Badger sets, which may be centuries old, are often at the edge of a woodland as the badgers will frequently feed on earthworms in nearby fields. Watch for their stern-high ambling waddle as they make their way along their well-worn paths. Some say that badger paths were the original country paths through the wildwood.

Elderberry bushes may grow at the latrine site having germinated from swallowed pips.

The badger is still quite common throughout Britain, being most plentiful in the south and west. Although it is a protected animal it is gassed under licence in some areas as there is evidence that it can carry bovine tuberculosis. There has also been a disturbing increase in the incidence of badger baiting and digging in recent years. The badgers are usually located using terriers and then dug out to be savaged by the dogs.

Magpie beside its domed nest

Badger
Meles meles

mound of bedding outside set

latrine

Badgers (*bottom*) do not usually run down their prey and are therefore rather ambling creatures; even at full speed a human would usually be able to outrun one.

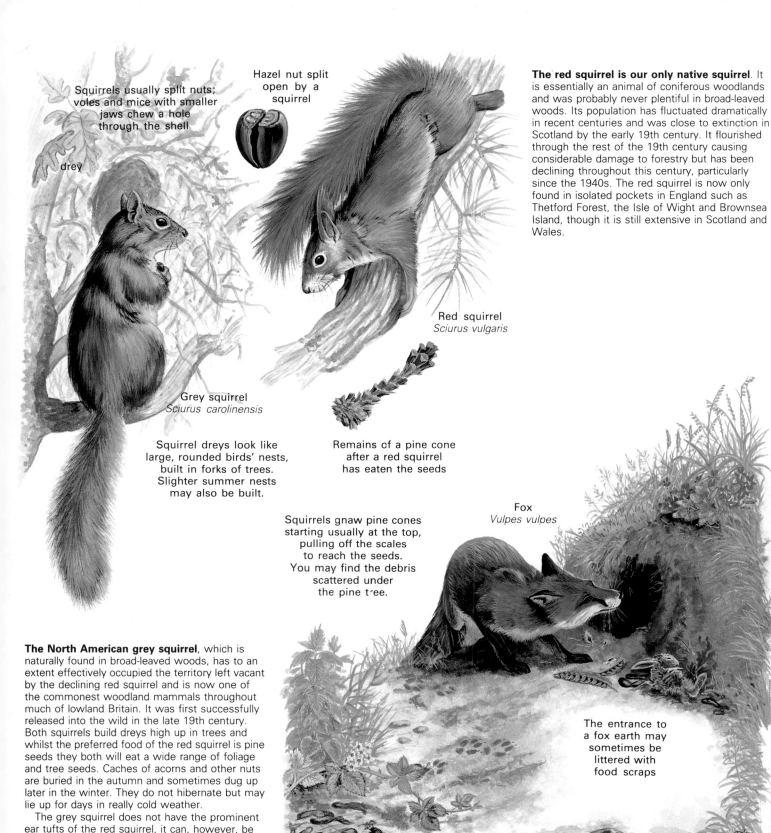

Squirrels usually split nuts; voles and mice with smaller jaws chew a hole through the shell

Hazel nut split open by a squirrel

drey

The red squirrel is our only native squirrel. It is essentially an animal of coniferous woodlands and was probably never plentiful in broad-leaved woods. Its population has fluctuated dramatically in recent centuries and was close to extinction in Scotland by the early 19th century. It flourished through the rest of the 19th century causing considerable damage to forestry but has been declining throughout this century, particularly since the 1940s. The red squirrel is now only found in isolated pockets in England such as Thetford Forest, the Isle of Wight and Brownsea Island, though it is still extensive in Scotland and Wales.

Red squirrel
Sciurus vulgaris

Grey squirrel
Sciurus carolinensis

Squirrel dreys look like large, rounded birds' nests, built in forks of trees. Slighter summer nests may also be built.

Remains of a pine cone after a red squirrel has eaten the seeds

Fox
Vulpes vulpes

Squirrels gnaw pine cones starting usually at the top, pulling off the scales to reach the seeds. You may find the debris scattered under the pine tree.

The North American grey squirrel, which is naturally found in broad-leaved woods, has to an extent effectively occupied the territory left vacant by the declining red squirrel and is now one of the commonest woodland mammals throughout much of lowland Britain. It was first successfully released into the wild in the late 19th century. Both squirrels build dreys high up in trees and whilst the preferred food of the red squirrel is pine seeds they both will eat a wide range of foliage and tree seeds. Caches of acorns and other nuts are buried in the autumn and sometimes dug up later in the winter. They do not hibernate but may lie up for days in really cold weather.

The grey squirrel does not have the prominent ear tufts of the red squirrel, it can, however, be quite reddish brown in colour. Alternatively, the red squirrel can look quite grey in winter

The entrance to a fox earth may sometimes be littered with food scraps

set itself is unmistakable. This is usually sited on a well-drained slope with more than one entrance, the large hole (approximately 30 cm) being partly hidden by the large mound of excavated earth, perhaps with bundles of discarded bedding (dry bracken or grass) nearby. Look also for latrine pits in the vicinity as, unlike foxes, badgers are relatively clean animals and will use these in preference to soiling the underground chambers. The latrines are also used to mark out the badger's territory. Once you have located your set, make sure it is in use – fresh signs of digging or freshly moved bedding are good points.

Then return at least half an hour before dusk, making sure you are down wind from the set, as badgers have an acute sense of smell. Remain perfectly still, preferably with a tree or large object behind you, masking your silhouette. Raisins, peanuts and even peanut butter sandwiches have been suggested as suitable food items to encourage them to forage around the set entrance. Remember, if you have had a good view of these delightful creatures, to leave the set as carefully and quietly as you arrived, preferably after they have left the area. The best months to watch are from April to August.

Foxes often use unoccupied badger sets, or enlarged rabbit burrows. They usually venture out earlier in the evening than badgers and if disturbed will move the cubs to an alternative earth. Dawn is also a rewarding time to watch and regularly baiting the entrance can be successful. The fox is more opportunistic than the badger and outside the breeding season (March-July) will use whatever cover is available – so watching a feeding area, such as a rabbit warren, will probably be more useful than returning to one of the earths.

Foxes are common everywhere, even in towns where they have exploited the rich pickings of suburban life. Usually the first indication that they are in the neighbourhood is the barking of the dog fox and the strangled, screaming call of the vixen during the mating season (December to February). The scent of foxes is very noticeable particularly in damp weather. The cubs are born in early spring and are fully weaned at six weeks, often surviving on beetles when they first start hunting. At least 50,000 foxes are killed annually in Britain, their ability to exploit available food sources, whether they be earthworms, free range ducks or still-born lambs, has given them a perennially bad reputation. Research has shown that in lowland areas the main food items are small rodents, insects, berries and carrion. Fox hunting has had a curiously ambiguous effect on the fox population as overhunting in the 19th century meant that many thousands of foxes were introduced from the continent; furthermore coverts and small copses are deliberately left to encourage the fox in the area of the hunt, even though the huntsmen say they are providing a service to the farmer by keeping numbers under control. The foxhunting season runs from the first Saturday in November to early spring.

Red deer are also seen on page 164, in an upland setting, what now seems to us to be their 'natural' habitat. They are, however, by origin woodland animals. More woodland mammals are shown on pages 56 and 114.

Deer

Culling towers and high wire fencing around new conifer plantations remind us that deer are not uncommon in today's countryside. Indeed, there may well be over half a million of them in Britain. Most large woodland areas, especially in the south, contain clues to their presence. They are not easy to see, however, as they are usually very secretive animals, feeding at dawn and dusk and hiding up during the day in dense cover. The best way of establishing their presence is to look for their tracks or 'slots', particularly near water or where a suspected deer path crosses a ride. The male deer will often clean off the velvet from their antlers by rubbing them against young saplings. They may also scent mark trees in this way, so, if you find a series of frayed trees, this might well indicate the edge of a deer's territory. Bark gnawing is often blamed on deer as well and, although they will do this if there is a shortage of their preferred food, hares and rabbits are often the real culprits.

In the absence of any natural predators culls are frequently organised to check deer populations, particularly in densely wooded areas. In the open hills of the Highlands the shooting of red deer by stalking on foot is still widely practised. These activities are controlled under The Deer Act of 1963, which applies to England and Wales, and The Deer (Scotland) Act 1959, both of which

Fallow deer have been hunted in English woods probably since Roman times when they were introduced from the Mediterranean, and although it is said that there may once have been a closely related native species in Britain, those that roam the chases and deer parks today are certainly the result of these early introductions. They show a greater range of colour variation than any of the other British deer, and 'white' and 'black' herds can be found, as well as a 'menil' variety which has larger spots than the normal form. In winter the normal tawny, spotted coat turns grey-brown and the spots all but disappear. One distinguishing mark, however, is constant: the rump is white with a black border and black tail making an unmistakable pattern. This marking is very noticeable when you chance upon a small group which, if alarmed, will 'pronk' (bound with all four legs held stiffly) away before running into cover. Smaller than red deer; 90 cm at the shoulders.

The red deer is our largest native land mammal, measuring 120 cm to the shoulder. The truly wild herds are to be found in Scotland, and north-west England. However, long-established feral populations occur in Exmoor and Devon and in the Breckland and New Forest. Though by origin the red deer is an animal of dense woodland, in Scotland it will spend the day resting in quiet corries in the hills, coming back down into the valleys to feed in the evening. In wooded lowland areas such as the New Forest it will lay-up during the day in dense undergrowth moving out to more open areas to feed as evening approaches. During the summer the Highland deer will graze on grasses, sedges and heather, browsing conifers and holly in the winter months when the snow has covered the ground plants. This habit has caused considerable problems in some areas of Scotland and northern England as an adult red deer will bark-strip conifers if no other food is available. During the rutting season the bellowing of the stags is a clear indication of their presence. Their value as a source of venison and as a game animal has ensured their position in the Highlands, and in some regions they are farmed commercially.

Roe deer are small (65 cm to the shoulder) with relatively simple antlers, a white rump and a scarcely visible tail. They have a dog-like bark when alarmed. They are woodland deer, but small family groups and individuals will feed in glades and adjoining fields at dawn and dusk. One of their favourite foods is bramble and they can develop a taste for garden roses. In Scotland heather, particularly in winter, is an important food. They probably became extinct in most of England in the 18th century but survived in the Border counties and Scotland. Following introductions in Dorset in 1800 and Brecklands in the late 19th century, the roe is now widespread in England, as well as Scotland; it is not found in Wales. The increase in conifer plantations has benefited this deer, which uses them for cover

Red deer
Cervus elaphus

Frayed tree
damaged by scent marking

Roe deer
Capreolus capreolus

fallow deer droppings

slots

and shelter during the day. The habit of browsing young coppice shoots particularly in early spring, has caused problems in some areas. However, more worrying for commercial forestry is their scent-marking and fraying of young trees in plantations in early spring and summer.

establish closed seasons for the different species. Essentially the closed season in England and Wales for stags and bucks runs from 1st May to 31st July and for does and hinds from 1st March to 31st October. In Scotland the closed seasons are usually longer. The Act also makes it illegal to shoot a deer at night or from a vehicle, and outlaws the use of traps, arrows, snares and poisoned baits. It also carefully stipulates which type of firearm and ammunition should not be used.

Unfortunately there has been a steady increase in the amount of indiscriminate poaching in recent years, as there are dealers who are willing to buy venison from any source. Interestingly, something like eighty per cent of British venison is exported to the continent, principally to France.

	Red deer	Fallow deer
male	stag	buck
female	hind	doe
young	calf	fawn
rut	Sept-Oct	Oct
antlers shed	March	Apr-May
calves born	May-Jun	May-Jun

	Muntjac	Chinese water deer
male	buck	buck
female	doe	doe
young	fawn	fawn
rut		Nov-Dec
antlers shed	any time	
calves born	any time	May-Jun

	Roe deer	Sika
male	buck	stag
female	doe	hind
young	fawn	calf
rut	July-Aug	Sep-Nov
antlers shed	Nov-Dec	March
calves born	May-Jun	May-Jun

A red deer wallow. The function of these wallows remains uncertain but it may be to rid the animals of parasites and loosen dead hair.

The sika deer was first introduced into this country in the 17th century and is now well established in Dorset and Hampshire, West Yorkshire and scattered localities throughout Scotland. It is a relative of the red deer with which it can interbreed and has the same shaped antlers although it is a smaller animal; 70–80 cm at the shoulder. It prefers mixed woodland with a dense groundcover in which it can rest during the day.

culling tower

Sika deer
Cervus nippon

Fallow deer
Dama dama

Muntjac deer
Muntiacus reevesi

Chinese water deer
Hydropotes inermis

The muntjac is a small (45 cm at the shoulders) pig-like deer with simple antlers which has escaped into the wild from the Woburn Abbey estate where it was introduced at the turn of the century. Its native home is the mountains of southern China. In recent years the muntjac seems to have been spreading gradually from its base in Bedfordshire, frequenting woods with a dense groundcover. Another name for this curious, hunched deer is the 'barking' deer, for it can bark at short intervals for up to an hour. Nobody is sure why it does this but it probably has some link with the breeding ritual.

The Chinese water deer, as its name suggests, originates from river valleys of eastern China. It has escaped since the Second World War from Woburn Abbey and Whipsnade Zoo establishing itself in and around Bedfordshire. It has no antlers but the large rounded ears and small size are noticeable (up to 60 cm at the shoulders). The buck has distinctive long upper canines which can sometimes be seen. It prefers open countryside with reedbeds and long grass.

The red deer rut

Like most herding animals the red deer has a complex social life with the stags and hinds forming separate herds for most of the year. The young calves and stags up to two years old will remain with the hinds. During the 'rut', however, (usually from the beginning of September to the end of October) the adult stags take harems of hinds and defend them against rivals. The master stags proclaim their dominant position by bellowing, which is often enough to keep other stags at bay. If this does not work the rivals will 'eye-up' each other. Here, the size and development of each other's antlers are probably crucial and only if they are fairly evenly matched will conflict actually take place. The two animals will then push against each other with their antlers, twisting and grunting, each trying to gain ground or twist his opponent off his footing. The action is often over quickly but occasionally it can last for more than twenty minutes. The victor will often give chase to the fleeing stag. The master stags have to keep on constant alert. They will also frequently wallow in muddy pools during this period. By the end of the rut they are often exhausted and return to their winter feeding grounds to make up lost weight.

Within an old oak wood the soil may vary from place to place and the vegetation may change (see the charts on pages 21, 35). The management may also vary. A great variety of bird and other wildlife is to be expected: see pages 44–58.

Lowland oak woods

The natural cover of much of our lowlands is a rich mixed woodland containing many oaks and a variety of other trees and shrubs. Much of it has been cleared for fields, but numerous fragments remain as small woods scattered amongst farmland, where perhaps the soils are heavy and more difficult to plough. Such relics may have been managed as coppices.

What they contain can reflect the natural distribution of the trees and shrubs. Only about half our natives are able to grow throughout the whole of Britain; the rest seem to reach the end of their range in the English countryside. Field maple, spindle, dogwood and buckthorn are commoner in the south (they are rarely seen in Scotland), while the Midland hawthorn and wayfaring tree are only found south of a line from Bristol to Hull. On the other hand, the bird cherry, which is a smaller tree than the wild cherry, with bitter black fruit, is locally quite common in the north, but only found as far south as Wales and East Anglia. The small-leaved lime, a very common tree in the prehistoric wildwood, is now found most frequently in a broad belt stretching between the cathedral cities of Lincoln and Gloucester, where it indicates ancient woodland. For much of lowland Britain, ash is probably the most likely companion to the oak on the richer soils. The most typical understorey shrub is hazel.

It may well be, however, that man has changed the make up of the wood during the long centuries of coppicing. Some of the oaks may have been planted while other native trees such as ash and field maple could have been removed or cut as coppice. What is more certain is that if the wood is old then the floor will carry an interesting assemblage of flowers. More than any other woodland type, these oak woods are marked by their rich array of spring flowers – the sheets of bluebells are one of the most spectacular botanical sights of the whole of Europe.

common oak

bluebells

Mistletoe
Viscum album

Winter aconite
Eranthis hyemalis

Nettle-leaved bellflower
Campanula trachelium

Oxlip
Primula elatior

Moschatel
Adoxa moschatellina

Snowdrop
Galanthus nivalis

The Druids looked upon oak trees with mistletoe as sacred, for it is rarely seen on them. It is far more common on apple, poplar and lime trees. Mistletoe is a semi-parasite, taking sap from the tree. The sticky berries are out in November and December.

Winter aconite is one of the earliest spring flowers to bloom (January-March). It is, surprisingly, a native of southern Europe but is well established in some woods in the south of Britain. The green ruffs of leaves beneath the flowers are actually bracts; the true leaves do not come out until later. It is poisonous; 15–25 cm.

Snowdrops can be found in old damp woodlands, where they may be native; in other places the swarm originates from bulbs thrown away in garden rubbish. January-March; 15–25 cm.

Moschatel, is easily overlooked amongst the bluebells, but is well worth looking for. It is also called town-hall clock, as its head of five green flowers are arranged like four clocks around a tower with the fifth one pointing upwards. It is quite unlike any other plant. April-May; 5–12 cm.

Nettle-leaved bellflower is a tall plant with coarsely toothed leaves. It is found in woods and hedgebanks on chalk or limestone soils, but not in Scotland. July-September; 50–100 cm.

The oxlip is an interesting flower as it is found in some ancient woods where Suffolk meets Cambridgeshire and Essex but nowhere else in Britain; the soil here is a rather limy clay. Its leaves narrow abruptly into the long stalk, continuing as wings and are a rather paler green than the leaves of primrose, as well as being less wrinkled. The flowers, which are similar in cowslip, are clear yellow. March-May; 10–30 cm.

Oxlips replace primroses in the woods that they occupy; but at the zone where the two meet, there is a flourish of hybrids of mixed character. There is another flower which is quite common in many parts of Britain, called the false oxlip, which is a primrose – cowslip hybrid. You will know it is the false oxlip because you are not standing in a wood a few miles from Cambridge.

Oak woods of the hills

You find woods of durmast oak on the acid soils of the Welsh hills and in the uplands of the west and north of Britain, but they can also be found in the lowlands. There are patches of such woodland on the greensand soils of the Weald in Sussex, for example. These durmast woods were often coppiced; the poles were turned into charcoal (you can sometimes find flat charcoal burners' platforms cut into the hillsides), and the bark was stripped for its tannin content.

That was some time ago and often when the charcoal burning ceased, the coppice stools were singled – one shoot was chosen to grow to mature height – and a rather top heavy 'high forest' was allowed to develop. The trees were, however, likely to fall on their weak bases. Rowan and birch are associated with this type of wood. In the west and north today, most of these woods are used for sheltering livestock and, as a result, contain very few interesting flowering plants. But they have a thick carpet of grasses and mosses. Where the grazing is not too intense, such as in deep gullies and steep hillsides, there will be a rich growth of ferns. Look out for polypody, a fern which is often seen growing from boughs and forks of trees or from cracks in rock faces. Hard fern and the almost ubiquitous bracken are also common. On the trees and boulders there may be a dense covering of lichens of many kinds, marking the fact that the air is not only damp but clean as well. These luxuriant western woods are unfortunately threatened by clearing for coniferous plantations and lack of regeneration due to the browsing of sheep.

A feature of the drier woods, may be carpets of honeysuckle. This plant will flower only when it can climb high up a tree or shrub.

Pied flycatchers can be found in loose colonies in upland woods, nesting in holes in trunks or main branches. They use the branches as song posts and hunting perches, leaving one perch to swerve after a fly, then returning to another (unlike the spotted flycatcher); there they wait, tail bobbing and wings flicking. Listen for the *whit* call and simple song of repeated *zee-it* notes followed by a trill. Smaller than the sparrow; 13 cm.

Pied flycatchers are summer visitors and are often found with two other typical summer migrants to these western woods – the redstart and the wood warbler. Both the redstart and pied flycatcher have been encouraged to increase their range by placing nest-boxes in suitable woods.

Great woodrush is most common in the oak woods of north and west Britain. Its broad leaves have a sparse covering of silky white hairs. The flowers are seen in May-July; 30–80 cm.

The moss, *Leucobryum*, forms dense cushions on the raw leaf mould of the wood floor, soaking up water like a sponge. Also found in beech woods.

Other typical plants of these woods include bilberry, wood sage, tormentil, wood sorrel and wavy hair-grass.

Pied flycatcher
Ficedula hypoleuca

male

Female

durmast oak

Wood sage
Teucrium scorodonia

Golden rod
Solidago virgaurea

Great woodrush
Luzula sylvatica

Bilberry
Vaccinium myrtillus

Pin-cushion moss
Leucobryum glaucum

Birch woods

If botanists were ever in danger of taking the birch tree for granted, then surely the rest of us would set them to rights. 'The Lady of the Woods', as it is sometimes known, is certainly a most elegant tree. Birch is often planted in towns, parks and gardens for its quick growing habit and silvery-grey bark but in woods foresters often count it as a weed and cut it out. In the Scottish Highlands you often meet birch in relic patches of Scots pine forest alongside Lake Rannoch, for example. Further north it can form its own woods, sometimes with an understorey of hazel and rowan. It is an extremely hardy tree and birch woods are sometimes the first type to be found below the tree line in mountain districts. Sometimes, in these upland areas, the birch is mixed with durmast oak and some pure 'birch woods' may have resulted from the felling of oaks in previous centuries. Often the 'woodland' birch of the north and west is the downy birch, although, as with the native oaks, it is not uncommon to find both silver and downy birches growing together.

The birch, like the Scots pine, is seen in a different light south of the border. Here it is very much a quick seeding, fast growing colonist of abandoned land, fated in the course of time to form a 'nurse-crop' for other more dominant and longer-lived trees, such as oak. A pure stand of birch in a wood could therefore mark an abandoned clearing. Though birch is often found in old woods, it is on commons and heaths, where grazing has ceased or fire has burnt off the heather, that it is at its most prolific, often causing a management problem if the open heath is to be retained.

Redpoll
Carduelis flammea

witches broom

Common bent grass
Agrostis tenuis

silver birch

Razor strop fungus
Piptoporus betulinus

Fly agaric
Amanita muscaria

Tinder fungus
Fomes fomentarius

Earth ball fungus
Scleroderma aurantium

Witches broom is a cluster gall – a mass of deformed, distorted tissues, triggered by a fungus. Other tree galls are more usually caused by insects.

The beautiful but poisonous fly agaric is, like many fungi, a saprophyte, gaining nourishment from decaying matter. This attractive fungi often forms a mycorrhizal association with the roots of birch trees. The fruiting bodies can be seen in late summer and autumn.

The tinder fungus grows on birch trees in the Scottish Highlands and, surprisingly, on beech trees in Knole Park, Kent. Tinder was essential for fire lighting in the days before matches: the spark from the flint caught on the tinder. This fungus, soaked in saltpetre was often used for this.

The fine, corky, dry flesh of the razor strop fungus was used for sharpening razors. Though widespread on birch trees, it only arrived in Britain about 100 years ago.

The earth ball is a fungus most often, though not always, seen under birch trees. It has a rather sour inky smell.

Common bent grass indicates acid soil. It is fine leaved, with a delicate flower head. June-August; 70 cm.

The redpoll is at the south of its breeding range in Britain; it is a circumpolar bird. They often nest in loose colonies often high in trees. Redpolls are attracted to the seeds of birch and alder and are active, acrobatic birds feeding at the ends of the branches. They are also seen in conifer plantations. They have a bouncing flight, and a buzzing, nasal flight call. The song consists of trills and buzzing sounds. Blue-tit sized; 13 cm.

See also page 26 for details of willows, sallows and osiers as well as alder. Ferns are shown on page 38. As well as yellow flag, shown here, look for other wetland flowers (page 208). Kingcup should be prominent, although it is not as common as it was.

Wet woodlands

Wet woodlands can be jungles. Between the alder and willow trees there can be a knee-deep tangle of rotting branches and thin trunks. Everywhere mosses and ferns flourish, some growing unexpectedly tall in the rich peaty soils and dappled shade. Lichens add muted colour to the decaying bark of the trunks, but also grow profusely on the branches overhead.

Straggling hop, bindweed and bittersweet hang in festoons. The waterlogged soils, unexpected streams and tussock sedges make walking rather hazardous, as well as very slow going. In more open areas a splash of bright colour may be provided by a clump of marsh marigolds or yellow flags. In winter flocks of tits and finches, including siskins, cavort

through the tree tops, their jangling calls filling the woods.

These woodlands have a distinctive character all of their own, one which was probably all too familiar to the first settlers. There can be little doubt that such woods were once common, edging rivers in the flood plains and fringing extensive wetlands. Centuries of drainage and clearance have turned these dense woodlands into important farmland, but relic patches can still be found alongside many rivers and larger areas still exist, for example, in the Norfolk Broads. Look out for them also on valley sides where they mark moving water near the surface resulting from spring line or seep.

Some of our native trees cannot stand even short periods of waterlogging (beech and sycamore are sensitive) but most of them grow well on slightly damp soil.

Neglected alder coppice is probably the most typical type of wet wood today. The water-resistant straight-grained wood was frequently used for clogs and its charcoal was used in the manufacture of gun-powder.

The yellow flag iris, with its tall sword-shaped leaves, is found in many other wet places as well as damp woodland. In October its seed capsules split to reveal an array of flat brown seeds. May-July, to 1.5 metres.

The royal fern has an attractive stately appearance so is often planted in gardens. It is a true native of boggy land, and wet acid woodlands, mostly in the south and west. The fronds of the royal fern can be as much as 1.5 metres tall, and grow in a dense clump, with the brown spore fronds arising from the centre in June, July and August.

The pendulous sedge is also an attractive plant, and can be quite tall (up to 1.8 metres). It is commonest in the south.

The massive fibrous base of the great tussock sedge can grow to a metre high and broad. It is one of the most distinctive plants of wet alder woods, forming almost impenetrable stands in the more peaty areas.

Apart from marsh marigold and other waterside and marsh plants (shown on page 207) look also for the golden saxifrages. They often carpet wet woodlands, and flower from March to July; commonest in the north and west.

alder

redpoll

siskin

goldfinch

Great tussock sedge
Carex paniculata

Yellow flag iris
Iris pseudacorus

Pendulous sedge
Carex pendula

Royal fern
Osmunda regalis

Where to find trees of wet woodlands

Alder can survive some waterlogging, but roots need aeration in growing period

alder

willow

sallow

waterline   great tussock sedge

Marsh marigolds may mark rich soil or that washed by fertile river water

Sallows need drier ground but can tolerate some shade

We describe here a type of woodland management which is, in many ways, quite different from the much older traditions of coppice-with-standards (page 14) and wood pasture (page 15). Forestry often entails a break with past regimes, which is damaging to wildlife.

Forestry

The practice of modern forestry started as far back as the 16th century. It was not a natural development from the traditional coppice-with-standards management, but a completely new kind of land use, in which woods were managed for their timber alone. The first of these timber plantations were on open ground – the very first being an oak plantation in Windsor Great Park (1580) – but by Victorian times much old wood pasture and many coppiced woods had been converted to the forestry regimes.

The timber trees can be encouraged by simply fencing off land and allowing it to scrub up, eventually forming a wood, or selected coppice shoots can be 'singled', but the most prevalent method in recent years has been to plant seeds or seedlings. The trees are grown close together to promote a tall, straight trunk and, as a result, the underwood is often sparse. When mature, this type of woodland is aptly called 'high forest'. The trees will probably be of one age and one kind, with fashion often dictating the choice of species. Many of the oak groves in the New Forest and the Chiltern beech woods were established in this way. The uniformity of these woods has been weakened with the passing of time as some trees have been removed and other trees have filled the gaps. As the majority of the trees may well have originated from one batch of seed from a single tree, the variety of shape and size that you would expect in a natural woodland is likely to be missing.

When a timber compartment is felled, it is often clear felled – all the trees are removed – and the ground may be treated before new saplings are planted. The link with the past, which makes coppice woodlands so rich in plant and animal life, is broken. An ancient wood felled and replanted for timber can be counted as an ancient wood lost. Things are rarely that clear cut, however, and even plantations of foreign conifers may offer something to wildlife.

A familiar sight in upland Britain today is the regimented stands of conifers broken by wide fire-breaks. The foreign spruces and pines grow well on the poor upland soils providing a new source of income to the landowners. Unfortunately, these vast plantations frequently upset the tenuous balance of the hilltop ecosystem and bird species as the golden plover and dotterel, which need the open scene, disappear.

Some of the conifer species likely to be met in a plantation are shown overleaf, page 68. Although generally poor in insect life (there will be few butterflies past the 'heath' stage) a plantation can attract birds for periods of its growth, as shown below.

Conifer plantations

Though conifers have been planted for centuries, most of our large conifer plantations date from the present century and, in particular, since the creation of the Forestry Commission in 1919. This government agency has established many plantations in its own right and offered advice and finance to private landowners. Its main effect has been to promote the planting of conifers, which are faster growing and thrive on the poorer soils of the west and uplands.

At first, Scots pine and European larch were chosen, as they grow well on many different types of soil. In recent times, however, other trees, such as the Japanese larch and its hybrid, the lodgepole pine and sitka spruce, have been planted, the latter of which grows well even on poor high moorland soils.

The effect of these vast new forests on the view is obvious enough and in the uplands they have replaced the delicately balanced communities of animals and plants. Young plantations can have considerable wildlife interest, however, as they are fenced to keep the sheep out, enabling the ground plants to grow profusely and attracting large numbers of animals, including birds. That specialist feeder on pine seeds, the crossbill, seems to have spread as a result of the older plantations. The plantation regime is a harsh one and the benefits of enclosure in the early stages are lost as the trees grow and shade out the ground flora, leaving a relatively lifeless, rather gloomy interior carpeted with a thick mat of acidic pine needles.

Look along the plantation rides and you might see some interesting communities surviving from earlier years.

The erection of a fence around newly planted conifers does not mean the instant disappearance of the birds that occupied the open heath or moorland. The changes are more gradual, and for a time, the plantation may attract a rather interesting bird community as shown here.

Plantations receive regular management. 'Beating up' means replacing saplings which have died. When 'wolf trees' outstrip their neighbours, they are often removed. 'Brashing' means clearing the trunk of side branches to promote knot-free timber; the cut branches are left on the ground to discourage the growth of brambles and other plants, which are considered weeds. From time to time the ground may be sprayed to kill such growth. By the time the trees are six metres tall, thinning may have started to yield an intermediate cash crop and to enable those trees left to grow more strongly.

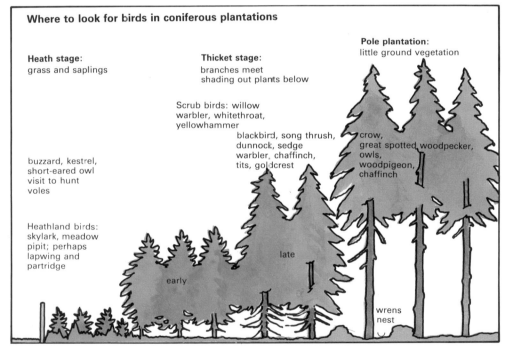

Where to look for birds in coniferous plantations

Heath stage:
grass and saplings

Thicket stage:
branches meet
shading out plants below

Pole plantation:
little ground vegetation

Scrub birds: willow warbler, whitethroat, yellowhammer

blackbird, song thrush, dunnock, sedge warbler, chaffinch, tits, goldcrest

crow, great spotted woodpecker, owls, woodpigeon, chaffinch

buzzard, kestrel, short-eared owl visit to hunt voles

Heathland birds: skylark, meadow pipit; perhaps lapwing and partridge

early

late

wrens nest

A mature plantation of Scots pines showing the uniformly straight trunks. Any side shoots low down on the tree would have been brashed at an earlier stage. The plantation is now more open as many of the trees have been thinned out at intervals during the life of the wood.

Scots pine is one of our three native conifers – the other two (yew and juniper) are shown on page 30. Note the difference between it and the commonly planted Corsican pine, shown opposite.

Scots pine and other conifers

Scots pine is one of our most handsome native trees and formed extensive woodlands throughout Britain until it was replaced by oak, ash and the other deciduous trees which invaded Britain as the climate improved at the end of the Ice Age. Scots pine, being resinous, is quickly burnt by fire and, as it does not coppice, cutting or grazing it down can kill it. Therefore any stands of pine that did remain in the wildwood of the south of Britain were very vulnerable to the slash-burn-and-graze management of the Stone and Bronze Age farmers. Patches of native Scots pine do remain, however, in some of the Scottish glens.

You will often see Scots pine growing in the south, where it has been extensively planted for ornament and in plantations on sandy barrens. It has sometimes seeded itself from these out onto surrounding open land where, with birch, it can quickly create woodland. These pines are often of a European strain which develops a flat-topped crown, while the native Scots pine keeps a pyramid-shaped crown that can become rounded with age, although individuals can show considerable variation. Scots pines are sensitive to sulphur dioxide pollution and so are rarely found downwind of our industrial cities, unless recently planted. Though Scots pines are associated with sandy soils, you can find them growing well on dry chalk soils, lining farm tracks in downland counties in the south.

Scots pine grows quickly when young but more slowly later. It may top 30 metres and reach 200 years of age. The bark on the lower part of the tree is red-brown and rather split. Higher up it is an attractive reddish-orange. The needles are 3–7 cm long, blue-green in colour, and twisted.

The male cones are in clusters set back from the end of the shoot. They shed their pollen in May and June. The female cones are at the ends of shoots; they grow to about 1 cm by the end of the first season; next spring growth is resumed. They become woody and by autumn have turned brown. The seed ripens within and is shed when the cones gape open (often with a pop) on dry days in the following spring. The seeds have a wing and spin down to the ground. The seedling is rather unusual, having twelve or more seed leaves.

Scots pine
Pinus sylvestris

one-year-old

young cone

old female cone

two-year-old

female flowers

three-year-old branch

male flowers

crested tit

Larches have clusters of needles which turn yellow and die in autumn; it is therefore a deciduous conifer.

Larch is a tall, symmetrical tree growing to 40 metres in height. Its young spring needles are a vivid pale green and very noticeable. Older plantations of larch are usually seen on valley sides and other land which was difficult to farm but near to hand. It is only recently that plantations have spread to the really bleak conditions of moors and hills, where foreign conifers can hold their own. Larch was once very popular as a plantation tree.

Larch is native in Europe, and (doubtfully) may have been so in Britain. This species, the European larch, has young shoots bearing pale yellow bark. Japanese larch has recently become popular – its shoots have dark orange bark. The vigorous hybrid of the two is, also, often planted.

The male cones are at the tops of the twigs and the red female cones below; they are known as 'larch roses'.

Larch does not thrive in shade, but it does let some light down through its canopy, so larch plantations are often much richer in ground flowers than other conifers.

A sprig of larch in spring showing the red larch 'roses' which are in fact, the female flowers; the male flowers are yellow.

Larch
Larix decidua

mature female cone

whorled leaves on old gro

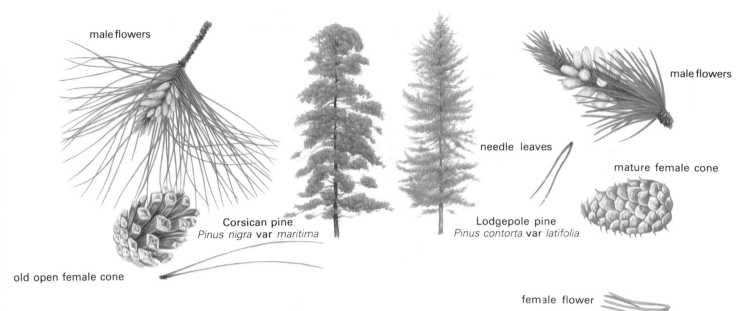

male flowers

Corsican pine
Pinus nigra **var** *maritima*

old open female cone

needle leaves

Lodgepole pine
Pinus contorta **var** *latifolia*

male flowers

mature female cone

The Corsican pine is a plantation tree of southern Britain and has long (10–15 cm) needles, close set on younger shoots. It has been planted on sandy soils on Thetford Chase, and other places.

Spruce trees have stiff sharp needles which leave pegs on the twigs when they fall. Their cones hang. The familiar Christmas tree is, in fact, the Norway spruce. The custom was introduced into this country in 1844, by Prince Albert, Queen Victoria's Consort.

In the west of Britain, the most frequently planted spruce today is the sitka spruce, introduced from the west coast of North America. It is faster growing and thrives on poorer soils.

Lodgepole pines were brought to Britain from British Columbia. They are now widely planted by the Forestry Commission in Scotland and Ireland where rapid timber production is required. The record height for a lodgepole pine is 28 metres.

Norway spruce
Picea abies

female flower

male flowers

Douglas fir
Pseudotsuga menziesii

female cone

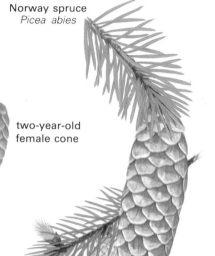

Sitka spruce
Picea sitchensis

mature female cone

two-year-old female cone

male flower

young female cone

mature female cone

Fir trees have needles which fall (or can be pulled) off the twig to leave a scar. Note the unusual cone of this Victorian favourite, the Douglas fir, which was introduced from Canada in 1827. It was initially planted as an ornamental tree.

new shoot

The true Scots pine *Pinus sylvestris* var *Scotica* in a glen in the Cairngorns. Winter browsing by red deer has meant that this Caledonian wood is suffering from lack of regeneration and may have to be fenced if it is to survive.

An old plantation (perhaps thinned at some time in the past and then let go, so that it contains large old trees) may attract hole-nesting birds shown on page 50. The scheme on page 67 explains the sequence of bird life in a plantation.

The birdwatcher's plantation

Upland conifer plantations are often fenced against sheep, and the grass, heather and bilberry are then able to grow tall around the young saplings. The grass gives cover and food for short-tailed voles (field voles) – they nibble it and make runways, perhaps helping to create grassy tussocks. Sometimes the voles reach plague numbers, to the advantage of the short-eared owl which can be seen hunting the moors.

Skylarks and meadow pipits may also be attracted by the tussocks and come to nest, and then begins an interesting sequence of bird life. It can also be seen in lowland conifer plantations. Though it must be stressed that when an old oak wood is felled and replanted with conifers, a priceless habitat has been lost. The new birds never match the variety of the old – nuthatches, tree creepers, nightingales and even tree sparrows will no longer be seen or heard.

The birds to expect at the different stages of the conifer plantation's existence are shown on page 67. Skylarks will be gone long before the branches of the low trees begin to meet, but the cover provided by the luxuriant heather or bilberry can attract merlins. All in all, there is quite a bit of bird interest.

Within a few years, the trees are 3–4 metres tall. It is rather dark below them and plants are finding it hard to survive in the shade, though the sunny rides may be lit with flowers.

By the time the trees are six metres tall, brashing of their lower branches will have taken place, and some will have been removed to give the rest more room. Crows may nest in the canopy. Then, when the trees are mature, some interesting and typical pine wood birds may move in. There has been, for instance, a big increase in the range of the siskin as a result of the Forestry Commission's work.

Siskin
Carduelis spinus

male

Coal tit
Parus ater

Long-eared owl
Asio otus

male

male

Goldcrest
Regulus regulus

Crossbill
Loxia curvirostra

female

The coal tit has benefited from plantations. It feeds on insects in summer and seeds in winter. Its song is a quick ringing *teachoo*, rather like the great tit's. Commonest in the north; 11 cm.

Siskins are sometimes hard to see like the others here, as they feed in the canopy. They often visit gardens in winter to feed on nuts from peanut bags; some say these might look like enormous pendulous cones to them. 12 cm.

Goldcrests are our smallest birds (9 cm). They are canopy feeders but can sometimes be located by their loud *zi zi zi* call. The song has the pattern: *cedar-cedar-cedar-sissu-pee*.

Long-eared owls, unlike short-eared owls, are strictly nocturnal, showing a marked preference for breeding high up in pine trees. They prefer isolated plantations with surrounding open hunting grounds rather than large uniform areas of forest, which the tawny owl seems to exploit more successfully. Their territorial call is a low, mournful triple hoot. 36 cm.

Crossbills are unmistakable with their uniquely crossed bill with which they prize open conifer cones which are still on the branch. 17 cm.

Crossbills shed a fascinating light on some of the checks and balances operating in the natural world.

While in the nest, the crossbill brood may consume near to 100,000 conifer seeds, which their parents have painstakingly extracted from the cones. Most trees, conifers included, do not produce a large crop of seeds every year; in this they differ from herbaceous plants, which have a more regular seed production.

In good seed years, large numbers of crossbills may survive; but the following year (when seed is in short supply) they may have to roam far to look for food. This wandering movement of birds is not quite the same as migration, and their arrival is called an *irruption*. Siskins, redpolls, redwings and bramblings, as well as crossbills show irruptive behaviour in some years.

Conifers ripen in very early spring: so crossbills nest from February onwards.

Heather, bilberry and the other acid-soil plants mentioned here are pictured on pages 160 and 166. (These relics of the ancient pine forest are, of course, set in moorland.) Ferns and mosses are common beneath the trees, see page 38.

Pine woods

The Black Wood of Rannoch alongside Lake Rannoch in Perthshire is one of few fragments of ancient pine forest that you can visit in Scotland. These areas of woodland are almost living museums, for, as far as we can tell, they are much the same as the forest which covered much of the land long ago, until it was invaded and shaded out by the broad-leaved trees of the wildwood. The Black Wood and other relics have had their timber trees removed from time to time, but those trees you see today have sprung up naturally; they have not been planted. So the Scots pines in the wood are not only of many different ages, but also exhibit a wide variety of shapes: some have broad profiles with many horizontal branches, some are almost pyramidal, others lean at awkward angles. Look for this kind of variety in most pine woods and you will seldom find it, as the seedlings will have been selected for their long straight trunks which provide the best timber cuts. Furthermore, they will have been planted too close together for much side development.

Parts of these ancient Scots pine woods have an unexpected feel to them: there is plenty of open sky overhead. With the pines themselves may be a scatter of birch, holly and rowan. The ground may have a dense cover of heather, bilberry and cowberry, growing tightly together with shrubby junipers. On the ground beneath these there may be plenty of mosses as well as some unusual flowering plants.

You can also find pine woods in the south. Scots pine was a fashionable plantation tree, and a rather open wood may once have been a plantation in which some of the trees have been felled. A younger pine wood may be the result of trees invading heathland, in which case the plants below the trees will be those of heathland which can survive shade. Scots pines are amongst the commonest conifers in Europe, and so you can compare our forests with those you see abroad on holiday.

Cowberry grows as a low shrub, 30 cm tall, with evergreen leaves rather like those of box. The red berries ripen August to September and make a fine sweet relish. It is found on acid soils on hills in the west and north and is absent from low ground.

Though many birds are typical of pine woods crested tits are the flag-birds of the Scots pine forests of the Scottish Highlands. They are our rarest resident tit. They are unmistakable if seen. You may only hear their high pitched, purring trill, however, as they search for insects in the tree canopy. They need old decaying stumps in which to excavate their nest holes, which limits their choice of woodland. 11 cm.

The coal tit is also often seen: details of it are given opposite, but here you can clearly see its distinctive black cap, white nape, and white cheeks.

Members of the wintergreen family are typical of these ancient woodlands. As their name implies, the light green leaves remain throughout the winter. The small white flowers can be seen from June to August; to 25 cm.

Chickweed wintergreen, despite its name, is not related to the wintergreens or the chickweeds, but is a member of the primrose family, and looks like a wood anemone. It is rare outside Scotland's pine woods, but is quite common in oak and beech woods elsewhere in northern Europe. It flowers in June; 10–20 cm tall.

Creeping lady's tresses is a member of the orchid-family. Its oval basal leaves are evergreen. This local plant of Scottish pine woods can also be found in the pine plantations of East Anglia. July-August; 10–25 cm tall.

coal tit

Crested tit
Parus cristatus

Chickweed wintergreen
Trientalis europaea

Wintergreen
Pyrola minor

Cowberry
Vaccinium vitis-idaea

Creeping lady's tresses
Goodyera repens

The Open Patchwork

With this bird's eye view of the open countryside we can detect the subtle fingerprint of history. Near the village (itself an ancient settlement site) are the irregular small fields and winding lanes **1** of the 'ancient and ornamental' countryside. There is a small village green **2**, a relic of the extensive 'commons' of years gone by. It is, typically, lined with pollarded trees **3**, a clue to a grazing ground in the past.

Alongside the river lie the tawny hay meadows **4**, which can be as old as the village church itself. Equally ancient open grazing land can still be seen on the higher ground but only patches of it remain, maybe on the steep slopes and perhaps scrubbed up from disuse **5**. Surrounding these old fields and ancient grazings are the more recent 'enclosure' fields, marked by regular hedges or stone walls **6**.

The hedges of the enclosure landscape are ruled straight **7**, as are the ditched roads **8**. This is hard-worked countryside as the seasonal colours of the fields tell you. Grass itself is a crop, and often old grass fields have been 'improved' and resown. They are a vivid green, but if the soil has not been ploughed, ancient features such as the ridge and furrow of medieval arable may be seen **9**.

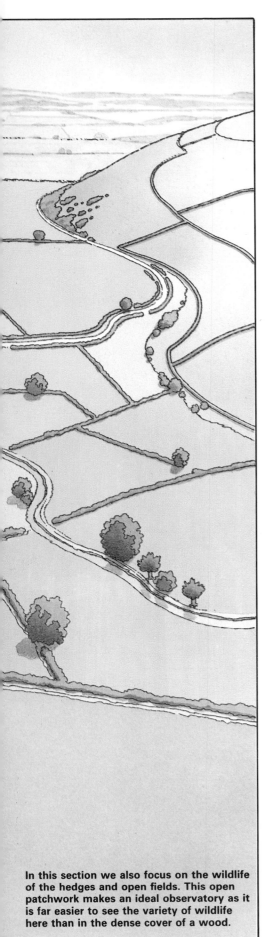

WHEN we look at the British countryside we are gazing at the living pages of our own history; for ours is a land deep-etched by centuries of unbroken habitation. There is nothing special about that. Many countries have civilisations at least as old as ours. But few have produced a farming landscape to compare with our gentle vistas of fields and hedgerows. Dotted with villages, plumed with trees, cobwebbed with trackways and crooked lanes, stitched together with thousands of miles of walls and hedgerows. It is this pleasing patchwork that makes our counterpane countryside admired the world over.

From the 12th century onwards, the monasteries were a driving force in the opening of the landscape, draining the fens around Glastonbury, pushing deeper into the Yorkshire Dales, bringing prosperity wherever the great stone abbeys took root. Then in the mid-14th century came the Black Death, which cut down close on half the population, ended the medieval era and left England alone with a legacy of at least 1300 deserted villages.

In the aftermath, so great was the shortage of labour that arable farming was largely abandoned by many landowners, who set about transforming the ancient pattern of open fields into cattle enclosures and sheep walks. By 1500 England's population was creeping towards three million, but the numbers of sheep had soared to nearly eight million. Theirs was the golden fleece which spread the prosperity of a booming wool trade through Tudor England.

With the coming of the Georgians, Britain saw several major innovations in the rural scene. One was the fashion for landscape gardens which reached a golden age with the parkland vistas of Capability Brown. Another was the virtual completion – hastened by innumerable private Acts of Parliament – of the enclosures which has given the British landscape its most characteristic texture: the orderly patchwork of pasture and ploughland, cross-hatched by hawthorn hedges or, in the uplands, drystone walls.

In the Midland shires where the new Georgian fieldscape was most firmly established, hunting squires made their own quirky contribution to the local scene in the form of coverts and spinneys where foxes could thrive.

In time the rawness of the new enclosures wore away. Great blowsy hedgerow trees arose; sycamore, field oaks and lofty elms; and every May the hawthorns burst in breakers of white blossom, filling the air with their sultry sweetness.

Alas, it was not to last. Intensive modern farming has ripped out thousands of miles of hedgerows to make bigger and more efficient fields. Chemical sprays and fertilisers have banished the once familiar scarlet poppies from our cornfields; while Dutch elm disease has added its own devastating hammer blow, removing many millions of trees from the landscape. Yet still the pattern remains, too deeply entrenched to obliterate; and with it, the wildlife it has harboured for so many years.

In the traditional countryside, hay was a vital resource, keeping cattle and horses alive through the winter until the first bite of fresh spring grass. Land which grew good grass was greatly prized and seldom ploughed. The fields were 'shut up' and the cattle moved off in spring to allow the grass to grow tall. Here grew the flowers of the fields: hawkbit and meadowsweet, buttercups and ox-eye daisies, nodding among the ripening panicles of fescue, foxtails and sweet vernal grass. Here partridges ran among the toppling stems, disturbing clouds of meadow brown butterflies; and in the long June evenings, when ghost moths whirred over the fields, barn owls would emerge to hunt for voles in the gathering dusk.

Often the richest grass grew beside rivers in water meadows which were flooded in winter – often deliberately by means of an intricate system of hatches and ditches – to provide a greater flush of growth. Where such areas survive they are greatly favoured by certain species of wading birds. In winter, snipe probe for worms in the soft mud; and in spring the sharp piping cries of breeding redshanks fill the air.

Nowadays, old, undisturbed hay meadows are hard to find. When they do occur, as in the localities in the Thames Valley where the lovely snakeshead fritillary still grows, they have acquired the status of nature reserves, so rare has that ancient mingling of wild flowers and tawny grasses become.

Scarce, too, is the thin green skin of downland turf which once covered the chalk hills of England from Dorset to Flamborough Head. Close-bitten, springy underfoot, smelling of thyme, here was a different grassland habitat, able to

In this section we also focus on the wildlife of the hedges and open fields. This open patchwork makes an ideal observatory as it is far easier to see the variety of wildlife here than in the dense cover of a wood.

In this intensively farmed countryside, wildlife maintains its variety in those long-established habitats which have escaped modern improvement. But the opportunities offered by abandoned quarries **10** and scrub **11** are seized. Old hedges are interesting **12**; the wildlife they contain can be affected by their management **13**. Verges too can be rich in variety **14**, carrying species lost from the improved fields alongside.

thrive on the porous chalk and withstand the constant nibbling of sheep and rabbits. Today most of these ancient sheep walks have gone under the plough, and barley blows where harebells once shook in the wind. But in places, on slopes and scarps too steep for ploughing, and among the ramparts of the prehistoric downland hillforts, magical tracts of old sward remain, loud with skylarks, pocked with anthills, alive in summer with marbled white butterflies and chalkhill blues.

Below the downs, in the shelter of the sprawling hedgerows and on the grass verges, birds and flowers find food and shelter. Every hedge is a linear jungle, a narrow strip of rampant wilderness, stuffed with goosegrass, bright with dog roses, smelling of elder and rank nettle beds. Hidden amongst its thorns and brambles are hedge sparrows' nests with sky blue eggs. (Some 10 million birds are said to breed in our remaining 600,000 miles of hedgerow.) Its margins are a haunt of butterflies: brimstone and orange tip, ringlet and gatekeeper; and in winter the blood red haws attract hungry flocks of fieldfares and redwings.

In areas like the Cotswolds, the Pennines and the Lake District, where stone is abundant, the hedgerows give way to drystone walls, which in turn provide an ideal habitat for mosses and lichens, stoats and weasels, lizards, slow-worms and plants such as toadflax and red valerian.

Other plants are more commonly associated with footpaths, roadside banks

A field in the Derbyshire Dales bright with buttercups and red clover. Despite this lush summer scene the stonewalling indicates that the growing season is probably fairly short compared with lower areas. This coupled with the colder upland winters would mean that a healthy stockproof hedge would be difficult to maintain.

A typical Shropshire country lane in May with well-kept hedgerows and the roadside verge white with cow parsley. Lush roadside scenes such as this can harbour a wealth of small insects and birds.

A view across the Weald from the South Downs Way showing both a declining agricultural landscape and a prosperous new one. In the foreground is an area of chalk grassland which once would have been grazed by large flocks of downland sheep. The economics of modern farming are such that it is more profitable to plough any suitable level ground for arable crops and to leave the steep grassy slopes to be gradually colonised by scrub and trees. Until the arrival of myxomatosis in the 1950's rabbits helped keep the encroachment of the scrub in check but since then many rich open grassland areas have disappeared.

Beyond this the modern field patchwork of yellow-flowered oil-seed rape and the bright green of wheat and new ley pasture can be seen. Only the winding route of the old roads breaks the geometric precision of the large fields.

and verges. In springtime many lanes and minor roads in southern Britain are banked high with cow parsley, red campion and other wayside flowers. According to the AA, Britain now has more than 210,000 miles of public highway, of which some 1,600 miles are motorway, all with banks or central reservations where wildlife often thrives between the hurtling streams of traffic.

And finally, at the heart of the open patchwork, is the village or country market town. At first glance, such centres of concentrated human habitation may not appear to be likely wildlife habitats. But many wild plants and animals are remarkably adaptable, and a country village offers all kinds of refuges: barns for swallows, eaves for house martins, ponds for moorhens, newts and dragonflies. Here, too, a host of garden birds find food: blackbirds, song thrushes, tits and robins. Lilac and privet are the favourite foodplants of the large and handsome privet hawk moth caterpillars; and in summer the fragrant mauve flowering spikes of buddleia attract red admiral and peacock butterflies by the score. Village churches are traditionally the haunts of bats and owls, and in many parishes the churchyard is an oasis of wildlife in an increasingly hostile environment. Outside the graveyard walls, old grassland is disappearing so fast that in some areas these relic graveyard patches are doubly sacred, representing virtually the last surviving remnants of the ancient communities of wild flowers, which were once the glory of our open countryside.

During World War Two, the Germans prepared hedge maps to aid their bomber crews flying over Britain, as not only do hedges and field patterns vary within a single parish, they also change from one part of Britain to another. Stone walls are described on page 156.

Old hedges

The history of hedges is as old as our need for protection or boundaries. Dead hedges were probably the first to be used. These were stockades of cut thorn bush like African 'bomas'. Anglo-Saxon documents mention 'thorn rows'. Earth banks were constructed in earlier times – the Giant's Hedge is an earthwork which stretches from Lerryn to Looe in Cornwall and is a splendid example of a defensive structure. In Cornwall, too, can be seen very ancient field boundaries, made of small boulders topped with turf, perhaps with bushes growing on them. They are known to this day as hedges.

The earliest written reference to a hedge of the kind very common today is in Caesar's *Gallic War*, which describes a type of defensive hedge used in France and Belgium and which is very much like the laid hedge found today all over Britain. The word 'hedge' is of much later origin than the Roman description. It comes from the Anglo-Saxon word *gehaeg*, a word which also gave rise to hay and haw (thorn). Saxon settlers brought with them the concept of the village as we know it and some of our oldest existing hedges may well follow the parish boundaries they originally marked out. It is also possible that in Saxon times hedges were planted to make cattle paddocks using shrubs collected from woodlands. The rectangular plantings of hawthorn, blackthorn and elm, that we generally think of when confronted with the term 'hedge', date, in the main, from the 18th and 19th centuries when the 'enclosure' laws were passed allowing farmers to take over large open fields and common land and divide them into smaller enclosed fields in the cause of more efficient farming. The new fields needed to be marked quickly and hawthorn quicksets were used – living twigs thrust into the ground to root. Contrary to the popular belief that most of our existing hedges originated at that time, it may be that perhaps half were established by the 17th century before enclosure.

The older a hedge the more likely it is to contain an interesting variety of plant and animal life. One fact to remember is that hedges growing alongside ploughed fields are usually on excellent soil.

Not only does the make-up of hedges differ from county to county, their location dictates their chances of survival. Hedges are sometimes hard to find in the barley prairies of eastern Britain as many have been grubbed up to create larger fields.

A hillside view across the tiny Devon village of Widecombe on the western edge of Dartmoor. The apparently jumbled pattern of small fields marked out by ancient turf hedges and stonewalls contrasts vividly with the uniform rectangles of later 'enclosure' fields of the Midlands and elsewhere.

Today's hedges originated in three ways. Some grew up naturally along parish boundaries, waysides and other strips of unused or abandoned land. Some are the remains of woodland left when fields were cleared on each side. These 'wood relics' need not look like a strip of woodland, for they may have been trimmed and managed for centuries. They may contain woodland plants which are slow colonisers of other habitats.

Many of our hedges have been planted, either with quicksets, or with saplings collected in nearby woods. These planted hedges can also be old.

Clues to the origin of hedges

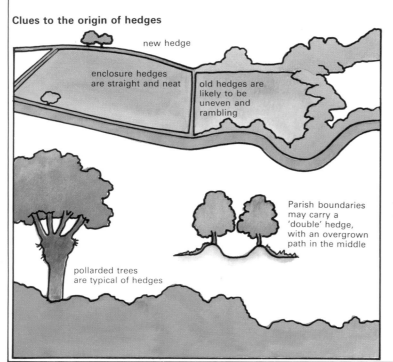

new hedge

enclosure hedges are straight and neat

old hedges are likely to be uneven and rambling

A row of trees striding across a field may mark the line of a hedge which has been grubbed up

Parish boundaries may carry a 'double' hedge, with an overgrown path in the middle

If a hedge is let go, the shrubs grow tall, and may become gappy at the bottom

pollarded trees are typical of hedges

Very rarely does a hedge have in it a tree older than itself. This fact can be a way of estimating a hedge's minimum age. If you can date the tree (page 18) you can therefore date the hedge. A row of trees across a field may mark the line of a hedge now grubbed up.

Oaks and elms were often planted for their timber, along the enclosure hedges of the 18th and 19th centuries.

A hedge may be a woodland relic if it contains shrubs and other plants usually found in ancient woodlands. Midland

hawthorn may mark a wood relic, as could wych elm and even the sun-loving blackthorn (sloe).

Hazel can quickly colonise light soil but if found in a 'hedge' on heavy clay soil it may signify a woodland relic. Remember that a planted hedge running up to an old wood can in time be colonised by woodland species, such as bluebells.

Enclosure hedges were planted with hawthorn; but look for other single-species hedges, planted by smallholders. There are holly hedges in Staffordshire, (the leaves were fed to livestock in winter), and even laburnum hedges in Pembrokeshire, planted for decoration.

Dating hedges

Whatever its origin, you can expect to find a greater variety of woody shrubs in an old hedge, because they seed themselves along it in the course of time. This gives us a way of dating hedges. The method works well in much of the Midlands and south, and is safe for telling a Saxon hedge from a Tudor hedge, or a Tudor one from a Victorian hedge.

Pace out 30 strides along one side of the hedge, and count how many different woody species (trees and shrubs) you see.

Disregard ivy, brambles and climbers. Count all roses as one.

Find the average number per length, and multiply it by one hundred to give you the approximate age of the hedge in years. A thousand years old Saxon boundary hedge may have nine or ten species of woody shrub in each 30 stride length.

Note that this simple method may *not* hold good on calcareous (lime-rich) soils, on which a large number of native shrubs can usually be found growing.

Compare coppicing (page 14) with the craft of hedge laying. Though coppicing is definitely an ancient tradition (Stone Age causeways were made of coppiced poles), there is no evidence that hedge laying pre-dates the enclosure movement of two-three centuries ago.

Laying hedges

Apart from acting as a boundary marker to a field, a hedge is usually there to keep farm animals in (or out), and the thicker it is, the better it is for this purpose. The shrubs and young trees of the hedge strive to grow tall, and unless the hedge is managed, it will quite quickly become gappy, and useless for confining animals.

Regular trimming will keep the hedge thick, but it can need other management if it is to perform its job effectively. Left to their own devices the branches of hedgerow shrubs interlace to form a dense network – something you do not see among the branches of a woodland tree canopy. If this interwoven woody mass is simply cut back, there is a danger that the lower branches will, in time, weaken and die (as they are in almost permanent shade), resulting in gaps. The craft of 'laying' or 'layering' a hedge (see below) overcomes this problem by creating a dense barrier right from the base.

Any management of the hedge has an effect on the variety of plants. Many typical hedgerow climbers have long-lived rootstocks, but regular clearance can prevent seeding and may in time eliminate them. Animal life may also be affected by hedge management. Birds will nest if the hedge is dense enough and provides good shelter, but the presence of a bird's nest does not by itself mean that the hedge is particularly rich in plants and animals. The insect life is a much better clue to general wildlife diversity. If the hedge is old established and with a good mix of plants, vast populations of different insects will be seen along it.

Today many hedges are trimmed with a flail: the tractor moves down the hedge leaving a wall of twisted and torn branches in its wake. This is not as damaging as it seems as the branches heal and grow back into a thick tangle. From a wildlife point of view, the best way of trimming is one which leaves the sides of the hedge sloping out with a triangular cross section, so that the lower branches are not shaded.

Hedgerow trees were a valuable source of timber and in the south of England they were frequently pollarded to gain 'smallwood'. Villagers sometimes had commoners rights to such pollarded trees.

If hedges are let go, the shrubs and trees will, in time, grow tall and lose their bushiness – a line of small hawthorn trees across a field is a fairly common sight, and may be a result of this.

A well finished cut and laid hedge in Wales. These hedges have to contain sheep and are therefore more densely packed and lower than the typical Midlands hedge. This one has its top reinforced with a strong plait of woven branches.

'Laying' a hedge

During the last two centuries, hedges have been regularly laid or layered. This is done in the following way. The hedge is cleared of climbers and soft plants, and the ditches cleaned out. A row of strong upright stems is chosen to be 'pleachers'. The rest are lopped off, perhaps to be used later for stakes. The crucial skill of the hedge layer is making the angled cut down into the base of the pleacher, with a billhook, almost severing it but leaving a strip of living bark untouched. The pleacher is then bent over and the bark 'hinge' becomes the lifeline of the now inclined branch. Its undamaged sap tubes allow the pleacher to sprout new shoots which will tangle to create a thick barrier. Stakes are banged in to hold the pleachers firm until these new shoots do interlock. Sometimes the stakes are joined together at the top with a plait of supple hazel or climber stems.

There are many local laying styles. The 'bullock hedges' of the Midlands have their pleachers turned to one side: the wood faces the road, while the twigs face into the field to deter the cattle. The 'sheep hedges' of the Welsh borders have the prickly twigs of the pleachers facing both ways.

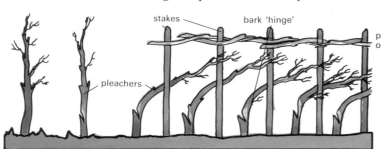

A Midland hedge being cut and laid. The photograph on the right shows the upright stakes being positioned between the cut pleachers, before they are firmly knocked into the ground. The photograph on the left shows the 'wattle' or 'heathering' of woven sticks (usually hazel) in position, binding the upright stakes together. The workman is trimming the tops of the stakes using a billhook and bracing them against a piece of stout wood known as a 'billet'. These hedges have to be able to withstand buffeting by cattle and a firm framework is essential.

Many native tree species can be seen growing in hedges (pages 22 to 26). Some counties have typical hedgerow trees – holly in Staffordshire, ash in Northumberland, as well as the Norfolk oaks mentioned here. Sometimes you will see Scots pine (page 68).

Hedgerow trees

You will often see old hedgerow trees which have been pollarded, for they were once an important source of branches as well as timber. Today, however, the importance of hedgerow trees is rather for their aesthetic value, giving the English lowlands their delightfully 'bosky' appearance.

Trees of many different kinds grow in hedgerows although some counties have their own specialities. For example, most of the hedge trees in Norfolk are oaks. Hedges are also the place to look for trees of foreign origin such as horse chestnut, which is rarely planted in woodland, and Lombardy poplar. Above all, the typical hedgerow tree was the English elm. Before the ravages of Dutch elm disease it was this tree which gave the English lowlands their character.

The English elm is a distinctive, lofty tree. It is probably a hybrid between the wych elm and other elm species; it rarely set good seed. It does, however, produce vigorous suckers growing up from the roots, and these suckers can grow to become trees themselves forming a line along the hedge – a habit that was encouraged in the past, because elm timber was very useful (for everything from water pipes to coffin planks) and its leaves could be fed to livestock. It was rarely found in woods, but because of its suckering habit it could sometimes invade recent woodland from a neighbouring hedge, producing a pure stand of elm trees within it. The elms died of Dutch elm disease, a fungal disease which blocks the sap tubes of the tree and which is carried from one tree to another by the elm bark beetle or through the roots. Today you will often see a dead elm surrounded by healthy young suckers, which have arisen from the rootstock of the stricken giant. Sadly, they usually grow only a few metres tall before dying, infected either by beetles or from the contaminated roots.

Wych elm is rather different from the English elm in that it can set good seed, does not sucker and is often found in woodland. It is widespread throughout Britain, but is commoner in the north and west, where perhaps two-thirds of the elms are wych elm. It is sometimes called the 'Scottish elm'.

You may still see it alive in the north, for the disease seems to spread more slowly there; maybe the northerly bark beetles are lazier travellers in the cooler climate and the relative separateness of the trees protects them (unlike the English elm, you will rarely see wych elms standing shoulder to shoulder).

The elm's last stand

A few decades ago, there were no less than 23 million elm trees alive south of a line from Birmingham to the Wash. Dutch elm disease has raged unchecked through these southern counties, and now most of these trees are dead, all that remains is perhaps a line of dead stumps along the hedgerow, a visual reminder of just how important an asset elms were to the delightful lowland scenery. Today, in many places it is threadbare, reduced in scale to the size of the tallest hedge shrubs. There are a few pockets where the English elms survive in the south, usually the result of a concerted effort by local authorities to combat the disease. There is (or was) one such pocket around Brighton. Here a 'sanitation' approach was taken, which included amputating dead branches and felling contaminated trees and digging trenches between neighbouring elms to sever the links between the roots. This did save many trees. Elms could perhaps have been protected in this way in other areas, but it is a costly business, and few councils were willing to commit money to it.

Interesting experiments are being conducted in Merseyside and a few other places in the north where the disease seems to spread more slowly than in the south. At the start a tree is found which is beginning to die. The elm bark beetles are attracted by the rotting wood, and this attraction is heightened by purposefully killing the tree outright and then baiting it with chemical 'smell' which attracts the beetles. They lay their eggs under the bark of the tree then die naturally – their job being done. Their grubs hatch, but it

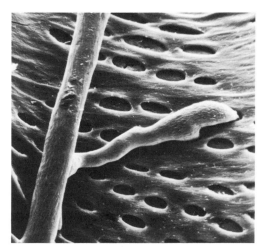

This photograph was taken with a powerful electron microscope and shows the pipe-like hyphae of the Dutch elm disease fungus within the tree. The hyphae are growing into, and blocking, the tubes which convey nutrients to and from the roots and leaves so that the elm almost literally starves to death.

The elm bark beetle is specific to the elm and will not attack any other tree. The female elm bark beetle flies in April or May, feeding on the thin bark around the twig crotches of healthy elm trees. As it feeds any fungus spores it may be carrying can contaminate the tree. The female is attracted to dead or dying elm timber to breed. She tunnels a main gallery under the bark of a dead or weakened tree, laying eggs along the tunnel. The grubs hatch and then chew out the side galleries, producing the distinctive pattern you see etched into the underside of the bark and slightly scored into the hard timber below. Another generation of adult beetles is often flying in July and August.

English elms struck down in their prime by Dutch elm disease.

fruit cluster

English elm
Ulmus procera

flowers

english elm fruit

fruit

flower

Wych elm
Ulmus glabra

flower

flower panicle

Horse chestnut
Aesculus hippocastanum

catkin

flower

Lombardy poplar
Populus nigra var *italica*

Fruit splitting to show ripe conker

conker

seems that the timber is now, for some reason, unpalatable. The grubs do not feed, and they die, so that these vectors (carriers) of the Dutch elm disease may be wiped out from quite a sizeable area. This is a long term approach to combating Dutch elm disease and there is no way of knowing whether it will succeed, but a similar strategy employed in North America has saved many trees.

It is interesting to note that there have been other outbreaks of elm disease in this country; one in 1927 was not devastating and pollen deposits have thrown light on another, much earlier, elm catastrophe. It occurred around 3000 BC, when the wildwood more of less completely covered Britain and when man was first beginning to cut it down. There was a sudden, massive elm decline. The reasons are not certain, although it may have been disease. On the other hand, it was the time when the first 'farmers' were stripping the elm foliage for their livestock, and, perhaps, added to this, a possible change of climate meant that no viable seed was being set. We have no real way of telling.

Obviously many elms did survive, to become the great feature of our open countryside. There is a chance they may again but not for some generations to come.

Wych elm is widespread but commoner in northern England and Scotland. It has longer leaves than the English elm, 8–15 cm, and 15+ pairs of veins. The shape of the leaves is also rather different being rather more pointed and, when viewed from above, the bottom bulge hides the short leaf stalk. The trunk may also be divided. Look also for **smooth-leaved elms** especially in the east Midlands and Cornwall. The leaves are often shiny and smooth on top.

As with all trees, there is much variation in leaf pattern: so when identifying elm trees, choose leaves growing in short shoots on one of the main branches.

English elms are found predominantly in the Midlands, southern England and the Welsh borders. They have leaves 5–8 cm long, with 8–14 pairs of veins and a longish leaf stalk. The leaves of branches infected with Dutch elm disease die and turn a rust-brown colour in July or August.

Lombardy poplar is one of many foreign trees which grace our hedgerows. It was brought here from Turin, Italy in 1758. This tree is a variety of the black poplar.

Horse chestnut is a tree which is native to a few mountains in Albania but it grows and sets seed well in Britain. It is rarely found in woods.

Conkers

Conkers used to be played with snail shells (the word comes from a dialect word for snail, akin to the word 'conch'). Recommended strategies for winning at conkers are to soak the nut in vinegar beforehand or (truly dastardly this) spray it with wood seal and claim that it is highly polished.

The conker – lovely, shiny but highly inedible – is a nut, the seed of the tree. It is carried in the spiky fruit – usually singly, but 2-3 flattened nuts are sometimes found. It is interesting to see how few conkers the tall spikes of flowers produce.

Those flowers, too, are well worth a second look; they are as intricate as orchids.

Mature conker trees of some age can now be found – the oldest still alive grows in Surrey, it was planted in 1664.

81

Apart from the age of the hedge, the soil can be a factor in determining the number of shrub species. You may expect to find more species in districts with limy or chalky soil. See page 28 for more of the shrubs to be seen growing in hedges.

Profiles of hedgerow shrubs

In the 18th century, our calendar was adjusted, so that May Day (1st of May) fell on what had been the 13th day of May. There were riots, for those who were not very good at maths thought they had been robbed of 11 days of life! The hawthorn (the may tree) ignored the fuss, and now usually begins to flower in the middle of May, rather than the beginning. This is the common hawthorn. Its relative, the Midland hawthorn, flowers earlier by a week or so, and it may well bring in the month of May. The Midland hawthorn is easy to distinguish from the common hawthorn not only by its blunter leaves but by the fact that its flowers and young haws have two styles, and the haws have two pips. Their lifestyle is also different. Common hawthorn is found in woods of many different kinds and ages. It also forms scrub and, of course, is a common element of hedges. The Midland hawthorn, which is not restricted to the Midlands, is more likely to be seen in old woodland, and it may also indicate old hedges. However, these two hawthorns can hybridise when they grow near each other.

The Midland hawthorn leaf has lobes which are more broad than long; the common hawthorn leaf has them longer than broad.

Hawthorns may grow to be a shrub or small tree, up to 10 metres tall. The pink to red garden hawthorns are a cultivated variety of the Midland. The early leaf and heavily scented flowers attract a host of insects, some of which are shown below.

An overgrown blackthorn hedge in full blossom in April. The later flowering hawthorn blooms after it has come into leaf. It is dense thickets like the one shown here that provide ideal nesting sites for retiring birds such as the nightingale and garden warbler.

Blackthorn (sloe) **creates 'blackthorn winter'**, with pure white flowers between March and May before the leaves open. It grows to about 4 metres and its suckers spread to create thickets on cleared ground, and occasionally in woodland clearings. It does need good light, however; the spines are weak in shade. The fruits (sloes) are bitter, but edible. They can be added to gin to make 'sloe gin'. The Shillelagh, a stout club or cudgel, which was exported to the whole of the British Isles from its eponymous town in Ireland, is made from blackthorn or sometimes oak.

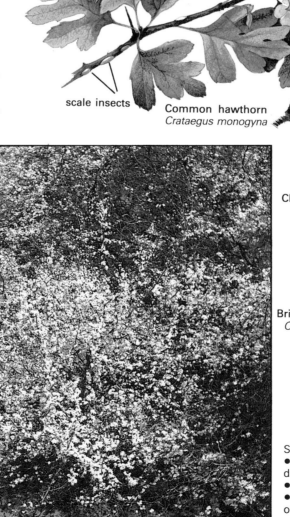

Midland hawthorn
Crataegus laevigata

flowers

fruit showing seeds

ripe fruit or 'haws'

unripe haw

scale insects

Common hawthorn
Crataegus monogyna

ripe haw

Chinese character moth
Cilix glaucata

fruit showing seed

Webs of small ermine moth caterpillar

Brimstone moth caterpillar
Opisthographis luteolata

Small ermine moth
Yponomeuta padella

Some insects to look for on hawthorn:
● Chinese character moth disguised as a bird dropping.
● Brimstone moth caterpillar disguised as a twig.
● Small ermine moth – its caterpillars spin webs or silky tents down the hedge and may be there in such numbers that the shrubs are stripped of their leaves.

Elder is a quick coloniser with a shortish life and it can be abundant in hedges. Though birds rarely nest in it, its flowers and fruit are highly attractive to insects. It may mark manured soil and rubbish tips. It often carries ear fungus on dead branches. June-July; to 10 metres.

Wild privet is a relative of the garden privet and can sometimes be found, especially in chalk or limestone country. The flowers are heavily scented and the black berries are very poisonous. June-July; to 5 metres.

Dogwood sports red twigs in winter. Its wood is useless, hence the name 'dog'. This shrub can be found growing up to 4 metres tall, in woods, scrub and open chalky grassland in the south. June-July.

Wayfaring tree was named by an early botanist who found it all along the lanes he rode. It is a shrub that is common only south of the Wash-Bristol line on limy soils. It has sickly smelling flowers and poisonous berries. May-June; to 6 metres.

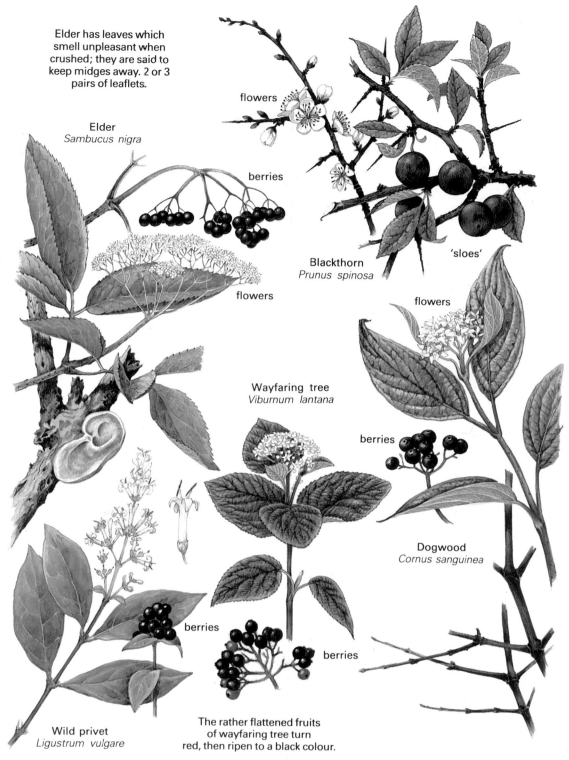

Elder has leaves which smell unpleasant when crushed; they are said to keep midges away. 2 or 3 pairs of leaflets.

Elder
Sambucus nigra

berries

flowers

flowers

berries

'sloes'

Blackthorn
Prunus spinosa

flowers

Wayfaring tree
Viburnum lantana

berries

Jew's ear
Hirneola auricula-judae

Ear fungus has a membranous texture, and may have an ear-like appearance.

Dogwood
Cornus sanguinea

The wild privet has narrower leaves than its garden relative, which is a Japanese species.
Wild privet is not truly evergreen, though many of its leaves do remain throughout the winter.

berries

berries

Wild privet
Ligustrum vulgare

The rather flattened fruits of wayfaring tree turn red, then ripen to a black colour.

Hawthorn trees of Old England

In 944 AD, King Edmund granted to a local bishop some lands on the downs above Blewbury in south Oxfordshire. In the days before maps, the boundaries had to be described in words. Here is part of the charter describing the estate:

'. . . then up to the great tumulus beneath wild garlic wood, then from the tumulus up along stone way to the tall crucifix at hawk thorn, then from hawk thorn to the tall thorn tree at Icknield Way, then to the third thorn tree at bog myrtle hanger . . . then to the olive tree, [which may have been a wild privet] then west along the little way up to the hill of trouble, then to the rough lynchet . . . .'

It is interesting to see how often thorns appear in these old documents. They were perhaps quoted because they were considered in those days to be potent, mystical trees.

Hawthorn trees may live to be extremely old. There is one such ancient specimen at the hamlet of Hethel a few miles south of Norwich. A century ago, when it was in its prime, its girth measured 14 feet 1 inch (nearly 4.5 m)

and it was then estimated to be around 500 years old. It may be far older, for an already old thorn was mentioned as a boundary marker thereabouts in a document of the 13th century. The thorn is still alive today, though its trunk is now shattered into separate strands, and many old boughs lie rotting on the ground.

Whether they were old or not, hawthorns were important trees in myth. They featured in pagan spring rites and this tradition continued until quite recently. Chaucer described how 'forth go all to Court, both most and least, to fetch the [hawthorn's] flowers fresh.' And there may be a very ancient folk memory in the name 'bread and cheese', given to its fresh green spring leaves. True, they can be nibbled and they give a fine nutty taste to a salad, but they are not like a cheese sandwich! However, part of the ancient spring ritual was the 'green man' who dressed in foliage and demanded food (a token sacrifice) from the people. This pagan figure was possibly dressed in hawthorn foliage.

It was once thought that hawthorn leaves deterred witches, and they often form part of the design carved into the roof bosses of churches. There is still a superstition that to bring 'may' flowers indoors invites death into the house. The origin of the belief could be historical, for hawthorn (being a rapid coloniser) was soon seen growing out onto farmlands abandoned after the terrible plagues.

The Glastonbury Thorn was a famous hawthorn that grew at Glastonbury. It was a variety of the common hawthorn but came into leaf and flowered in winter. It was often in flower on Christmas Day and again in May. The legend that the tree grew from the staff that Joseph of Arimathea stuck into the ground on his arrival in England was first published in 1722, making the claim rather more than dubious. It seems that the original tree was felled by soldiers in the Civil War, however, cuttings from it can still be seen flowering twice a year nearby.

Compare woody nightshade with deadly nightshade, described on page 62. Black nightshade is an arable weed, page 96. Ivy, page 36, is frequently seen in hedges. Vetches (92) often sprawl over hedgerow shrubs. Climbers are also to be expected in wet woodland, page 65.

Hedgerow climbers

Climbers, as their name implies, use other plants as supports to raise themselve from the ground. They are not parasites; they need no nourishment from their support and you may often see them climbing up fencing.

The types of climber present in a hedge may indicate the way the hedge is managed. Bryonies and bittersweet are more often found in undisturbed hedges, but the vigorous annual cleavers can survive even when the hedge is 'cleaned-up' before laying. Honeysuckle will survive in hedges which are regularly trimmed.

All these plants have devised special ways of assisting their climbing; some twine their stem or leaf stalk around their support, others have specialised tendrils which do the same job. Often they have poisonous stems, leaves or berries, such as those of the nightshades and bindweeds.

White bryony is one of the gourd family and has bristly stems with tendrils which grow straight until they contact a support. They then attach themselves by a sucker and coil, pulling the plant up. It is found predominately on calcareous (chalky or limy) soils except in Scotland and south-west England. May-September; climbs to 4 metres.

Black bryony is the only British member of the yam family and has stems without tendrils which twine to the left. It likes rich or chalky soils. The berries are ignored by birds. May-July; climbs to 4 metres.

White bryony
Bryonia cretica

berries

berries

Black bryony
Tamus communis

— tendril

Whilst most climbing plants are relatively harmless to the shrubs and trees that support them, the binding stem of honeysuckle can severely deform a sapling such as this ash.

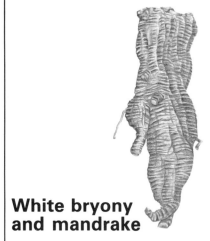

White bryony and mandrake

White bryony is associated with mandrake, one of the most important plants of the ancient herbalists. There is an echo of its potency in these lines by poet John Donne:

'Go and catch a falling star,
 Get with child a mandrake root,
 Tell me where all past years are,
 Or who cleft the devil's foot?'

The true mandrake grows around the Mediterranean, from Spain to Israel and in North Africa. It was the 'male plague god plant' of the ancient Assyrians; the Greeks called it mandragonas. Mandrake was important in antiquity because it was believed to help women conceive and is even quoted in Genesis XXX, 14–17 as being used for this purpose. Mandrake has a split root, which looks rather like a body with legs, and is said to give an unearthly shriek when pulled out of the ground. It does not grow wild in Britain, but it was such a valuable plant that a substitute was found – white bryony, whose roots can (or can be trimmed to) look like a child!

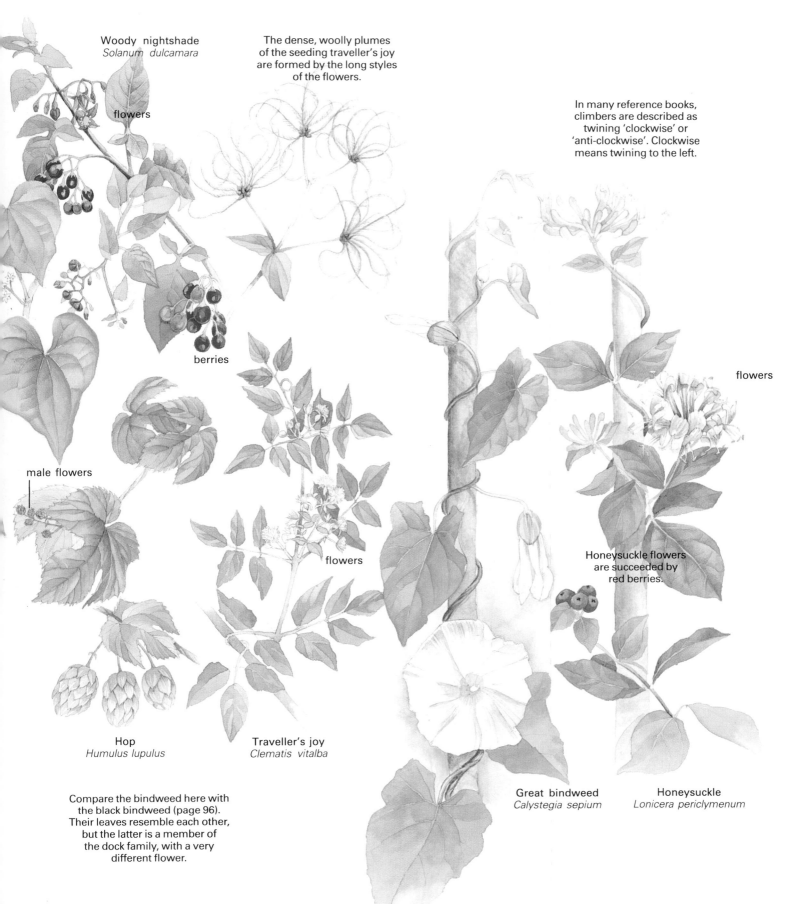

Woody nightshade
Solanum dulcamara

flowers

berries

The dense, woolly plumes
of the seeding traveller's joy
are formed by the long styles
of the flowers.

In many reference books,
climbers are described as
twining 'clockwise' or
'anti-clockwise'. Clockwise
means twining to the left.

flowers

male flowers

flowers

Honeysuckle flowers
are succeeded by
red berries.

Hop
Humulus lupulus

Traveller's joy
Clematis vitalba

Compare the bindweed here with
the black bindweed (page 96).
Their leaves resemble each other,
but the latter is a member of
the dock family, with a very
different flower.

Great bindweed
Calystegia sepium

Honeysuckle
Lonicera periclymenum

Woody nightshade (bittersweet) **belongs to the potato family**. The oval red berries are poisonous. Note the small lobes at the bottom of each leaf. June-September; clambers to 2 metres high, threading its stems through others.

Cleavers (not illustrated) **has stems which are more or less square** in section and together with the leaves and fruit have backward-pointing bristles or prickles. Like bramble, cleavers is commonest in disturbed or managed hedgerows. It is an annual related to the coffee plant. June-August; to 1 metre or more.

Hop is a fast growing square-stemmed plant, which twines to the left. As with many other climbers, the male and female flowers are seen on separate plants – the male flowers in clusters, the females are cone-like catkins, which become the 'hops'. It is a native plant, though those usually seen may be an escape from cultivation: it is grown for brewing. June-August; to 5 metres.

Great bindweed (bellbine) **twists to the right**, and grows so quickly that its tip may complete a full circle within an hour or two. The stem is so pliable you can tie a knot in it. See if the scentless flowers (white trumpets up to 4 cm across) stay open at night; some say they remain open in moonlight. Another even larger 'bindweed' can sometimes be seen with white flowers, 7–8 cm across. This exotic – a garden escape – is a native of south-east Europe. July-September; to 3 metres.

Traveller's joy (old man's beard, clematis) **is an indicator of chalk** and limestone soils. Its woolly fruits create the impression of wreaths of smoke along the hedge. It has rope-like, but woody, peeling stems, which climb by twisting the leaf stalks around a support. It will grow along the ground, if it can find no support. Native south of the Humber-Mersey line, July-August; to 20 metres.

Honeysuckle (woodbine) **is often seen growing low and trailing**, but can reach 6 metres high, climbing, by twisting its stem to the left, and so tightly that it may deform the young tree or branch supporting it. This produces weird 'barley sugar' walking sticks, once very popular with countrymen. Thomas Hardy wrote in 1887: '. . . [they were] mostly woodland men who on that account could afford to be curious in their walking sticks, which exhibited various monstrosities of vegetation, the chief being corkscrew shapes in black and white thorn, brought to that pattern by the slow torture of the encircling woodbine, as the Chinese are said to mould human beings into grotesque toys by compression in infancy.' Honeysuckle plants may carpet the ground in woods but they flower only when they reach good light. The flowers are white, becoming yellow when pollinated. Pollination is by moths attracted by the heady scent, which is strongest at dusk. Honeysuckle is a plant of dry, acid soils – it is typical of some sessile oak woods. June-September; to 6 metres.

Brambles and roses are often seen in hedgerows, though bramble is common enough in some kinds of woodland (see page 36) and sometimes plays a part in scrub development (page 128). Stone bramble is shown on page 63.

peacock butterfly

wasp

leaf miner tracks

Brambles and wild roses

For many people their first contact with nature is when they are taken blackberry picking as very small children. There are several hundred closely similar 'microspecies' of brambles or blackberries. They can be distinguished from one another by the way their stems arch or lie along the ground, by the size, shape and direction of their prickles, by the shape of the leaflets on the leaf, and by other fine characteristics. Generally only the experts are interested in these microspecies; for most of us 'bramble' is good enough.

Brambles are widespread plants with easily spread seed. These seeds can remain dormant in the soil for long periods, and therefore they are favoured by any disturbance likely to bring the seeds to a suitable germination ground. Their arching stems can root at the tip, even in soils inhospitable to the seeds. Brambles are also interesting for the large variety of animals that can be seen visiting them to feed or making a home among them.

Capturing the scent of a rose

Two centuries ago, scents became fashionable and with them the new fashion of cleanliness also brought soap into vogue.

At first, wild flowers were the only source of sweet scents, and the rose was prized for, 'It has a fragrant and odoriferous smell,' as Gerard, the well-known herbalist, wrote in 1597. He was describing garden roses, which were popular by his time. It was Gerard who first called our commonest wild rose, the 'dog rose' to distinguish it from the headier scented cultivated varieties.

The dog rose does have a scent of its own, which you can capture by an ages old, and simple method. Pick the flowers at the peak of opening, in the morning but when dry of dew. Take the petals off and lay them on white paper (not newspaper – the smell of modern inks is likely to deaden the wild scents) in a coolish, dry place. Spread the petals thinly, never more than one layer deep otherwise they will begin to brown and rot. Turn them every day for a week or two, until they are quite dry.

They can be kept in a jar or bowl – a pot pourri – to sweeten the smell of a room. Old English and Damask garden roses have the strongest rose scent and pot pourri can be made from them.

The same technique can be used to preserve the smell of hay. Indeed, most leaves and flowers can be dried in this way. Choose what you fancy as a reminder of summer for winter evenings.

Brambles are often scrambling shrubs, with many stems arching up from the rootstock, rising to 3 metres high. Each leaf has three to five leaflets. The fruit (the blackberries) of the various microspecies differ in shape, colour and flavour, some more succulent than others. Flowers May-September. Bramble watching can be interesting: large numbers of insects visit the flowers and fruit. Wasps have jaws strong enough to tear the skin of the berries: flies and butterflies then come to sip the oozing juice. In autumn, the green chlorophyll of the leaves breaks down and yellow and red pigments are revealed. You can sometimes see leaves coloured and dying from rust fungus. Look also for the tracks of leaf miners, made by small moth caterpillars, beetle and fly grubs, chewing in the body of the leaf. Some of these miners create sinuous tunnels, others create clear blotches in the leaves. Most brambles are self-fertile, though some may be pollinated by bees and butterflies.

Dewberry (*Rubus caesius*) **is the only bramble microspecies** which is easily identified from its cousins. Its leaves have three distinct leaflets and the stems have weak spines. The fruit has a noticeably waxy bloom. It is found on heaths and dune scrub. (Photograph on opposite page.)

Dog rose has sharp, hooked, shark-fin prickles on strong arching stems. It is the common pink rose found in hedges and scrub where the soil is neither too dry nor too wet. The fruits are the familiar rose hips. There are few prickles on the flower sprigs. The flowers are pink, or sometimes white and sweet-smelling. June-July; to 3 metres.

Sweet briar (eglantine) **has apple-scented leaves** (with smaller and more rounded leaflets than the dog rose), hooked prickles similar to dog rose but unequal in size up the weaker stems. Found on limy soil especially in the south; June-July; to 3 metres.

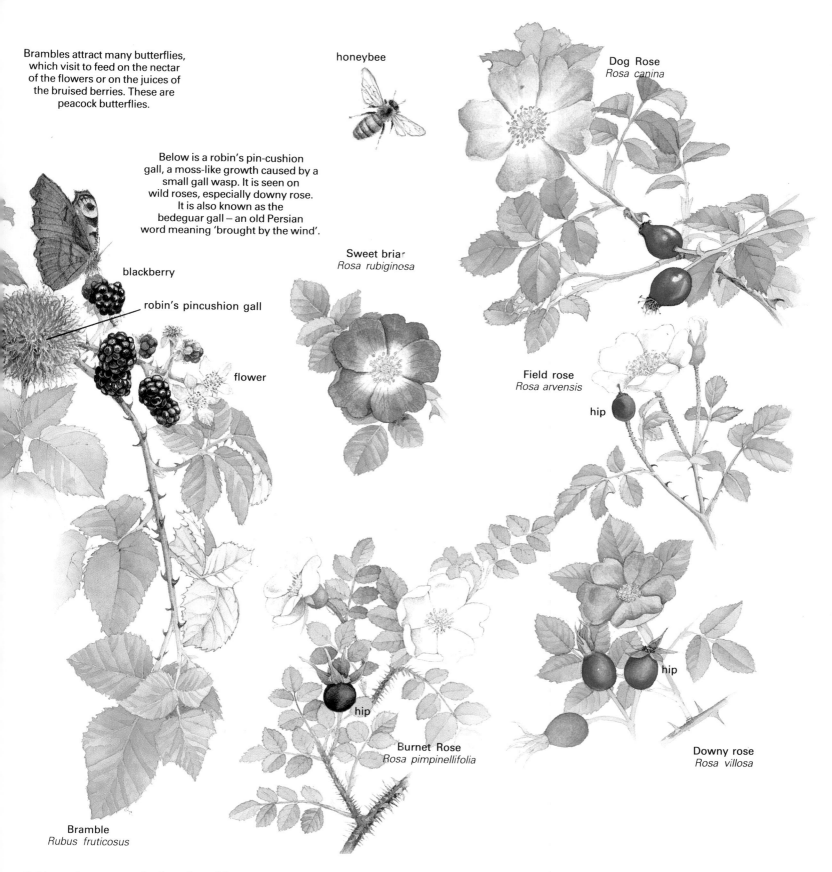

Brambles attract many butterflies, which visit to feed on the nectar of the flowers or on the juices of the bruised berries. These are peacock butterflies.

honeybee

Dog Rose
Rosa canina

Below is a robin's pin-cushion gall, a moss-like growth caused by a small gall wasp. It is seen on wild roses, especially downy rose. It is also known as the bedeguar gall – an old Persian word meaning 'brought by the wind'.

blackberry

robin's pincushion gall

flower

Sweet briar
Rosa rubiginosa

Field rose
Rosa arvensis

hip

hip

Burnet Rose
Rosa pimpinellifolia

hip

Downy rose
Rosa villosa

Bramble
Rubus fruticosus

Field rose forms mounds of weak, arching or trailing green stems with arching prickles. Despite its name, it is usually seen in shade, mostly in the south, being rare in the north. The 'styles' at the centre of the flower are fused into a single beak sticking up above the stamens. The flowers are white, unscented. June-July; 1 metre tall.

Downy rose is commonest in Scotland, rare in the south. It has down on both sides of the leaf and has straight spines on 2 metre tall stems, and deep pink flowers. June-July.

Burnet rose is found on limestone or shelly dunes in the north and west where it can create wide areas of scrub. Its prickles are straight and thin. The name comes from the French *brun* – 'brown': the leaves are often flushed purple-brown, its hips being purple-black. It forms suckers to make patches. White flowers. May-July; 1 metre tall.

Hedges combine light with a fair degree of shelter and provide a home to many flowers of woods and wood margins, including some of the flowers shown on pages 32 and 34. The flowers in the hedge often reflect its age and history – see page 76.

The foot of the hedge

None of the plants you see at the foot of the hedge is restricted to this habitat. After all, hedges are rather unnatural creations in many ways. Nevertheless, they do combine well-lit surroundings with shelter, and many of the characteristic plants are those of wood margins or open woodlands. Bugle and ground ivy are good examples of such plants as, although they are common in hedgerows, they also carpet the wood floor after the trees or underwood have been cut. One of our most fascinating plants, the wild arum, is found predominately in hedges, especially on richer soils.

Stinging nettles have hairs on their leaves which break on contact to release irritating acid. This acid, which causes the sting, is destroyed by cooking and young leaves can be boiled and eaten. The flowers of the nettle are held in small catkins. The roots of the perennial nettle form a dense mesh under the surface of the soil: each spring these throw up a dense stand of fresh stems. This growth strategy is quite different from that of the other British nettle, the annual nettle. Possibly introduced here by the Romans it has a milder sting than the stinging nettle, and has smaller, more deeply toothed leaves. Stinging nettle, May-September; to 1 metre.

A carpet of bugle flowering in May with their distinctive 'pagodas' of blue flowers.

Stinging nettle
Urtica dioica

White deadnettle
Lamium album

Red deadnettle
Lamium pupureun

Wild arum – Britain's most exotic wild plant?

Wild arum is also commonly called cuckoo pint or lords and ladies. Indeed, it is so noticeable and unusual a plant that it has nearly 100 dialect names, compared with the bluebell's 40. Most of them have sexual connotations due to the unusual shape of the flower. The word 'arum' may be derived from a Greek term referring to the fiery taste of the tubers.

Wild arum was once an important plant. In the reign of Elizabeth I collar ruffs became popular and a starch was needed to stiffen them. It was the tubers of wild arum that provided it. The extracted starch was very hard on the hands, making them itch, and eventually it was replaced by starch from the potato, which had been recently introduced from the Americas.

Even more interesting is the botany of the plant. Sometimes the leaves are spatted with red or bluish-black spots, which are either small or quite large blotches. They were once thought to be drops of blood from Christ on the Cross. The spots seem to have a fading distribution across Britain – blotched leaves are commoner in the south where

up to a quarter of the plants may have them, but rare in the north where the plants are also smaller. This kind of gradual change in character as you travel across a plant's range is a common feature.

Another difference you may notice is in the way the sheath or 'spathe' is folded – left over right, or right over left. You may see equal numbers of both. It may be that the overlap is simply a result of the way the young leaves are packed in the bud.

Most fascinating of all is the way that the plant ensures cross-pollination. Small midges are attracted by the colour of the flower and by the scent of rotting meat which is emitted when the spathe opens fully, usually in the afternoon. The spadix also heats up and can be warm to the touch. As many as 30 midges can be attracted to the spadix and follow the scent down into the closed cup at the base of the spathe, crawling past a fringe of hairs around its entrance. Once there, these hairs make escape difficult. At this stage of the flower's existence the ovaries, which are at the bottom of the

rod-like spadix, are receptive and can be fertilised by any arum pollen that the midges may be carrying. After pollination the stamens, which are in a ring above the ovaries, open and shower pollen onto the insects. The spathe hairs begin to wither, and the midges can escape to visit another plant nearby, carrying the pollen with them. The process may take days to complete, and is speedier in dry, fine weather.

Arums are quite sensitive to climate and shelter. You will see the plants on hedgebanks and in woodland but never in dark gloom. They grow better at the edge where there is more light. They need some shelter and they are rarely seen right out in the open. The leaves appear early in the year, sometimes in February; the flowers in April and May. The leaves remain into the summer but they are hard to notice, for the grasses and other plants will by then have grown up around them. In autumn the bright red berries become obvious. They are poisonous (as are all parts of the plant) even though birds eat them.

Red and white deadnettles do not sting; moreover they have interesting flowers, pollinated by bees and other insects. The white deadnettle is a perennial with green, nettle-like leaves. May-December; 20–60 cm. The red deadnettle is annual with purplish leaves and flowers earlier, often beginning in March. It may flower all year if the winter is mild; to 50 cm.

Butterbur is a strange plant, that may be seen by the roadside when it dips to damp ground at a valley bottom. The flowers open before the leaves which may grow very large (60 cm across). This is the female flower found in the north; the male is tighter bunched, and more widespread. March-May; flower spike is 10–40 cm tall.

Ground ivy can remain green all year, surviving all but the hardest frosts. The softly hairy leaves have a harsh, very distinctive, minty smell. It is found on all types of soil, in woods, open ground of all kinds. March-May; to 20 cm.

Bugle creeps and roots to form mats. Its blue turrets of flowers can be seen growing in drifts in woods and along hedges. The frosts kill off the stems but new plants grow from the rooting points. The hairless leaves are sometimes a striking bronze. Found mainly in damp places. April-June; to 30 cm.

Rushes at the hedge bottom indicate damp conditions. A great variety of conditions may be met along one stretch of hedge.

Red campion is an elegant woodland plant. Its flowers are scentless and presumably they are pollinated during the day by flies and butterflies. May-November; to 80 cm.

White campion is an annual (sometimes perennial) 'weed' of more open places, and only opens fully at evening, emitting a trace of scent, to be pollinated by moths.

It s said that red and white campions cross pollinate to give (unusually) fertile pink-flowered campions. It is not known whether these hybrids are pollinated by day or night. May-October; to 80 cm.

Bladder campion is often found growing with the rather similar white campion. It has a bag-like swelling just below the petals. This is a plant found more often out on open ground. May-September; to 80 cm.

Wild arum (cuckoo pint; lords and ladies) **is also common in woods**, especially on richer or calcareous soils. April-May; to 50 cm.

The leafy *spathe* encloses the upright *spadix* of wild arum. Lords and ladies and many of the "his-and-her" dialect names may have originated from the fact that the spadix is sometimes purple (Lord) rather than yellow (Lady). There are many more Ladies!

White campion
Silene alba

berries

Red campion
Silene dioica

Rush
Juncus sp.

Wild arum
Arum maculatum

Ground ivy
Glechoma hederacea

Butterbur
Petasites hybridus
Compare the butterbur with
its close relative, the
yellow coltsfoot, page 96.

Bugle
Ajuga reptans

A grass verge can resemble a meadow, and, indeed, may carry wild grasses (page 120) and flowers (pages 122, 148) which have disappeared from the 'improved' fields alongside. Skipper butterflies can form colonies along these scraps of land. Other hedgerow wildlife 100–114.

Roadside verges

Roadside verges are immensely variable habitats, found running from dry hills to damp valleys, over changes in the bedrock and other hidden features. Some may be open to full sunshine, others permanently in the shade where the road passes by a wood. Unlike hedges, verges are not limited to the lowlands – they can accompany roads across mountain fells, and being ungrazed they may carry an unexpected range of plants for such wild areas.

As a reservoir of plants and wildlife, verges are in some ways more important than hedges. Because of centuries of traditional management, they often carry relic communities lost from the intensively farmed fields alongside. For hundreds of years, up to the beginning of this century, each parish had a 'lengthman', whose job it was to maintain the roads. He worked along them through the seasons, cutting back invading shrubs and mowing the grassy verge with his scythe. Often a hay crop was taken from the wider verges, and many were used for grazing cattle and sheep as they were herded to market.

Today motor-mowers have replaced the lengthman but some flowers can survive if the blades are not set to cut too short. Sometimes verges are mown in strips: the strip next to the road is kept short to protect the drivers' sight lines (and for appearance); while a middle swathe is left to grow taller; and at the back of the verge cow parsley and its relatives grow tall, with only one cut per year.

The cost of maintaining verges is a crucial factor in their management. Present day economies mean less frequent cutting, and the denser mowings are left on the ground to rot. This mulch increases soil fertility encouraging cow parsley and other tough plants to take over the verge, thereby reducing the variety of plant life.

▲ **A Cornish hedgebank in spring**. The milder more humid western climate means that sheets of bluebells are often found in the open. Here they are seen with a mix of red campion, greater stitchwort, buttercups and sorrel. Fronds of bracken are just beginning to show through and will probably dominate the bank later in the year.

◀ **Looking rather like a floral display** in a cottage garden, this West Country hedge is a riot of colour and form. The hedge itself is covered in goosegrass, while the foreground is dominated by the tall spikes of foxglove and lower down, red valerian and cow parsley.

Old drove roads, which were once used to move flocks of sheep and herds of cattle across country to market, may be very wide from hedge to hedge, with only a narrow tarmac strip in the middle.

Verges may be teeming with animal life. Throughout the country twenty of our fifty native mammals; all six reptiles and forty of our two

hundred nesting birds all frequent verges, and twenty-five of our sixty or so native butterflies breed there.

Motorway verges sown with clover attract bees. The tussocky grass encourages voles which are hunted by kestrels. Some motorway verges are now decades old, and are being rapidly colonised by many grassland and scrub plants.

Large amounts of salt for spreading on icy roads in winter may quickly kill trees nearby, even those on the other side of walls and hedges.

Look for plants which grow on one side of the verge but not the other. The balance of sun and shade is the most obvious factor in this but the difference may reflect management.

All plants except dandelion, plantains and other low or rosette plants are eliminated by regularly close cutting of the strip next to the road. If a short turf is left, bird's-foot trefoil and other pasture plants may be found.

Meadow crane's-bill, melancholy thistle and other meadow and grassland plants can be found on the centre strip.

Cow parsley dominates ground on the back strip which is cut only once a year.

The ditch may contain small aquatic communities, including amphibians.

Some of these plants are soil type indicators. Heather or broom will indicate acid soil, while meadow crane's-bill will indicate a limy one.

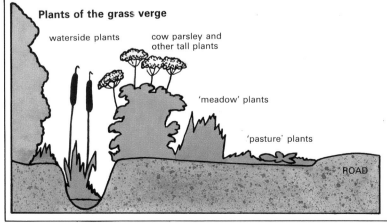

Plants of the grass verge

waterside plants

cow parsley and other tall plants

'meadow' plants

'pasture' plants

ROAD

As this scheme shows, the cutting regime of a grass verge can create a series of different plant communities running from the 'scorched' low plants at the edge of the tarmac to the dense vegetation close to a hedge or wall

The family of the umbelliferous plants is a good one on which to sharpen botanical teeth. Other umbellifers are to be seen on pages 32, 34, 36, 149, 187, 192, 236, 237. Pea-family plants, relatives of the vetches, are also shown on pages 122, 134, 148, 166.

Cow parsley
Anthriscus sylvestr

Plants of the tall verge

Many of the tall plants seen along roadside verges are members of the cow parsley or carrot family – the umbellifers. Their name comes from a Latin word which also gave us 'umbrella', and if you look at the flowering heads of cow parsley, hogweed, wild carrot and others you can see why. There are more than 70 'umbellifers' growing wild in Britain and at first glance they all seem very similar. However, a close inspection of their leaf-shapes, stems and especially their fruits will usually enable them to be easily identified. Furthermore, the different species flower in a predictable progression through the spring and summer making an interesting botanical calendar. May is the month when cow parsley can be seen flowering in glorious profusion along southern roadsides. The similar-looking rough chervil comes out in June and July, followed by the upright hedge parsley in July and August. In the north sweet cicely replaces cow parsley as the commonest early roadside 'umbel'.

Most of the umbellifers cannot survive frequent cutting but late-flowering species, which can set seed after the cutting season, can be found. It is well worth getting to know these apparently confusing plants as some of them, such as hemlock, are very poisonous.

A road in May fringed with cow parsley. The other name for this abundant plant is Queen Anne's Lace which probably refers to the delicate fern-like leaves. In the north of Britain this plant is replaced by sweet cicely.

Cow parsley has downy, furrowed, unspotted, hollow stems and fresh-green fern-like leaves which are 2–3 pinnate. The flowers are white, the outermost flowers having unequal petals. The fruits are rather cone-shaped and smooth. 'Cow' means false; the plant has another name, 'keck' meaning retch, so do not chew it! Found more in the south, April-June; 60–100 cm.

Hogweed (cow parsnip) **has rough-haired, furrowed, hollow 'pea-shooter' stems,** and broad-cut, once-pinnate leaves. As with cow parsley, the outermost petals are larger; its fruits are flattened. June-September; up to 2 metres.

Giant hogweed is Europe's tallest herbaceous plant. It looks rather like a hogweed but has a red-spotted stem and it can grow 5 metres tall! It is poisonous, and merely to touch it produces such a violent rash of blisters hospital treatment is usually required. June-July.

Wild carrot has rough-haired, furrowed, solid stems which smell of carrot. There is a red flower at the centre of the flowerhead. Notice the leafy green 'ruff' under the flowerhead, and the long flower stalk. The fruit is bristly. Found especially on chalky soil. June-August; to 1 metre.

Sweet cicely is rather like cow parsley (with downy, hollow stems) but smells unmistakably of aniseed. It is a plant of northern hillsides often found in pockets of rich soil near settlements. It may be native but is more likely to be introduced from Europe. It has long, stout, sharply ridged fruits. April-June; to 1 metre.

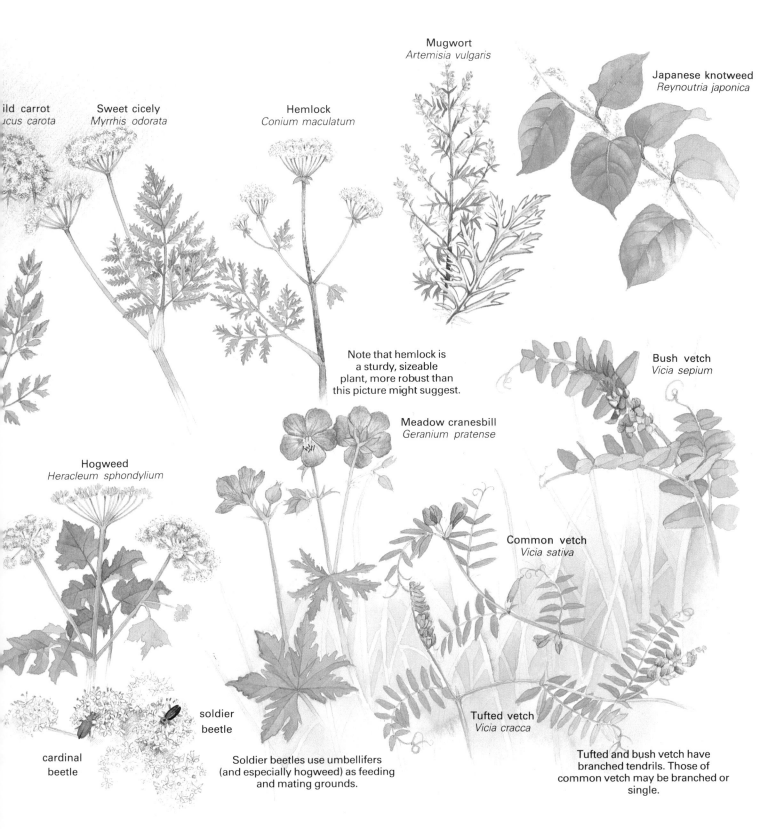

Mugwort
Artemisia vulgaris

Japanese knotweed
Reynoutria japonica

Wild carrot
Daucus carota

Sweet cicely
Myrrhis odorata

Hemlock
Conium maculatum

Note that hemlock is a sturdy, sizeable plant, more robust than this picture might suggest.

Bush vetch
Vicia sepium

Hogweed
Heracleum sphondylium

Meadow cranesbill
Geranium pratense

Common vetch
Vicia sativa

cardinal beetle

soldier beetle

Tufted vetch
Vicia cracca

Soldier beetles use umbellifers (and especially hogweed) as feeding and mating grounds.

Tufted and bush vetch have branched tendrils. Those of common vetch may be branched or single.

Hemlock can be identified by its purple-blotched, hairless stems which have a waxy bloom, and also by its fine cut leaves. Its fruits are rounded and ridged. It smells unpleasantly of mice and is very poisonous; its juice can blister the skin. It likes a soil with a good deal of nitrogen, so thrives on damp rubbish dumps. June-July; to 2 metres.

Mugwort is a relative of wormwood. 'Mug' means 'midge'; the plant was once used as a fumigant, being burnt to keep away flies, and clear houses of fleas. Like wormwood, it is strongly smelling with white down under the leaves. Found on verges recently dug or disturbed. July-September; 50–100 cm.

Meadow crane's-bill should remind you that verge cutting may create something like a meadow. This fine plant is found especially on limy soil. The flower stalks droop after flowering and straighten again when the seed pods ripen. June-September; 30–80 cm.

Vetches are climbers of the pea-family, and are easily recognised by their flowers.

Tufted vetch climbs up into the hedge, with stems up to 2 metres long. Note the flowers are carried down one side of the stalk only, in heads of 10–40 flowers. The pods are brown when ripe. June-August.

The geranium family

The geranium family gives us some very attractive wild flowers such as the meadow crane's-bill shown here. The word 'geranium' comes from a Greek word for the crane and the plants are so named from the long seed pods, which look like cranes' (or storks') bills. These wild geraniums are distinct from the scarlet and other highly coloured garden 'geraniums', which are more correctly called pelargoniums and originate from Southern Africa.

Common vetch can trail or climb, with slightly zig-zag stems, single or branched tendrils and single or paired flowers. The small leaf-like stipule at the base of the flower stalk has a dark spot. It is not the most common vetch. May-September.

Bush vetch has zig-zag stems, branched tendrils, and a 'spike' of 2–6 flowers producing pods which ripen black. June-August.

Japanese knotweed can be a scourge, swamping all other plants on the verge with its ranks of 2 metre tall canes. The broken stems exude an irritating juice. It only inhabits disturbed ground and is a garden escape. August-October.

The pinnate leaf is a common pattern of compound or divided leaves. The separate leaflets are ranged on each side of the leaf stalk, often in opposite pairs. The leaflets themselves may be divided up – the leaves are then known as 2-pinnate. Those 'leaflets' may themselves be divided, to form leaves of 3-pinnate pattern.

In theory, this is a good recognition aid. In real life, however, individual plants may show some variety as we note with the cow parsley here and may be 2- or 3-pinnate.

93

Dandelions may sometimes be seen growing in established grasslands, alongside some of the plants shown on page 122. They provide a tasty bite for cattle. More examples of the great daisy family are seen on pages 88, 96, 122, 126, 130, 148.

Weeds of roadsides

A large number of apparently similar plants or 'look-alikes' colonise roadsides and waste ground. The key to their identification is not only in the way they look, but also in their 'life-style'. Some have a surprising character: the dainty nipplewort and goat's-beard, or Jack-go-to-bed-at-noon, hum with insects on a sunny morning but any insects visiting in the afternoon will be unlucky, for they close their flowers soon after midday. They will also close in the morning if it becomes cloudy.

These are both typical plants of the great daisy family, the Compositae, the world's largest family of flowering plants, with more than 14,000 different species worldwide. Each 'flower' is, in fact, made up of many small petal-like flowers called florets, tightly held together to form a dense flowering head. The florets are either tubular or strap-like. With some of the family you will find tubular florets in the centre surrounded by strap florets. These are yellow in the coltsfoot, ragwort and groundsel, or white, as in the common daisy. The introduced pineapple weed is an example of a plant which has no surrounding florets.

Thistles are also members of the daisy family but their florets project like a shaving brush from a green mug. Coltsfoot (next page) and butterbur (page 88) are also members of the daisy family, as is yarrow (page 122). If you look at the flowers of this last plant, you will see five outer florets broadened to appear like 'petals'. By looking closely for these subtle structural differences one is able to spot the underlying character of the family in what, at first sight, appear to be very different kinds of flowers.

Dandelion flowers are typical of the daisy family. The flower is held on a longish flower stalk and is made up of 200 separate florets. Each floret produces a parachute seed which when combined with others forms the familiar 'clock'. March-October; to 35 cm.

Nipplewort is unlike many of the daisy family in that the branching stems do not exude juice when broken. The name comes from the shape of the bud. The many small flowers form a loose head. The seeds have no parachute. July-September; to 90 cm.

Hawkweed seeds have a stalkless parachute of brittle brown hairs which do not form a clock. There are around 400 closely similar 'microspecies' of hawkweed, making it one of the most difficult groups of plants for the botanist to identify. June-August and beyond; to 35 cm.

Smooth hawk's-beard has smooth, narrow dandelion-like leaves, and a many-flowered, pale yellow head. Seeds have white parachutes. June-September; to 75 cm.

◄ **The tall spikes of great mullein clustered with yellow flowers** tower over the other roadside plants in mid-summer. The large leaves are arranged around the stem so that they funnel any rain water towards the roots.

Goat's-beard or Jack-go-to-bed-at-noon closes its flowers at midday but will keep them closed in cloudy weather. It has greyish grass-like leaves and a large, dirty-white 'clock'. Note the starfish look of the spreading sepals under the flower. May-July; to 60 cm.

Chicory has blue flowers and no parachute on the seeds and is most often seen on chalky soils. It may not be native. The roots were once collected, dried and roasted to make either 'coffee' in their own right or to add to coffee to improve the flavour. A close relative yields, after very complicated cultivation, the tight, green-salad chicory heads. July-October; to 1 metre.

Great mullein is a typical biennial. It grows a rosette of woolly leaves in its first year and a tall flower stem the next. In the days before cotton was imported into Britain, mullein 'wool' was collected from the leaves to be made into candle wicks. Another name for the plant is 'Aaron's rod'. An Old Testament story tells how the rod of Levi (with the name of Aaron inscribed upon it) produced buds and flowers when planted in the tabernacle. June-August; to 2 metres.

Common mallow is found on roadside and waste places, possessing dark-veined, mauve, spreading flowers. Marsh mallow is similar, but with broader pale pink petals and is found in ditches and brackish wetlands. A flour made from the roots of the marsh mallow was once used to flavour the sweet of that name. June-September; to 50 cm.

Horse-radish can be identified by the smell of its crushed stalk; the sauce is made by mashing the root with vinegar; the root is boiled first and mixed with cream if a milder taste is required. Note the shiny leaves. May-June; to 1 metre.

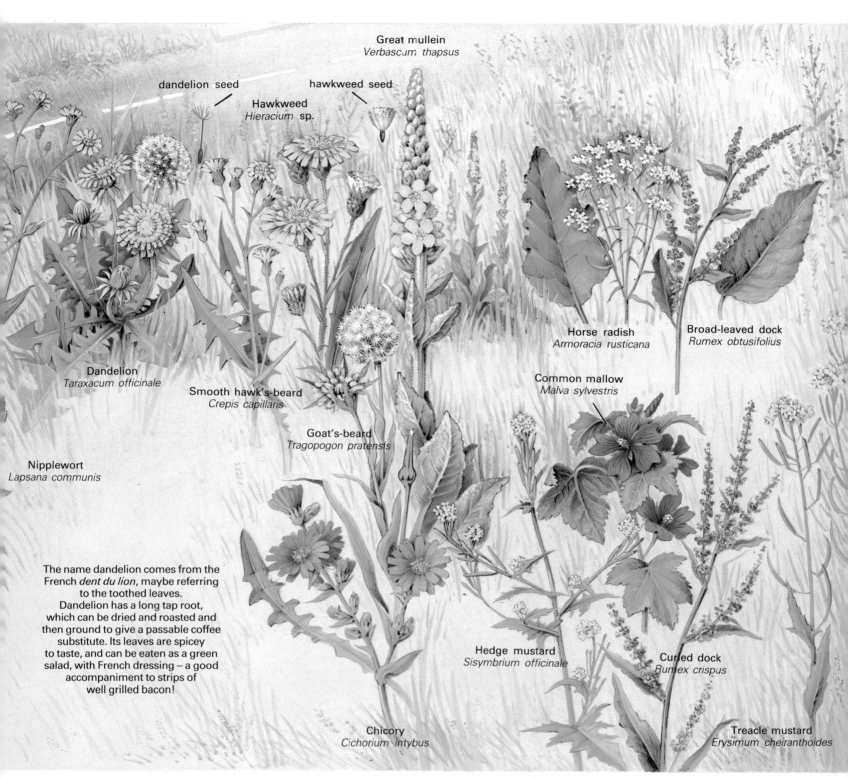

Great mullein
Verbascum thapsus

dandelion seed

Hawkweed
Hieracium sp.

hawkweed seed

Horse radish
Armoracia rusticana

Broad-leaved dock
Rumex obtusifolius

Common mallow
Malva sylvestris

Dandelion
Taraxacum officinale

Smooth hawk's-beard
Crepis capillaris

Goat's-beard
Tragopogon pratensis

Nipplewort
Lapsana communis

The name dandelion comes from the French *dent du lion*, maybe referring to the toothed leaves.
Dandelion has a long tap root, which can be dried and roasted and then ground to give a passable coffee substitute. Its leaves are spicey to taste, and can be eaten as a green salad, with French dressing – a good accompaniment to strips of well grilled bacon!

Hedge mustard
Sisymbrium officinale

Curled dock
Rumex crispus

Chicory
Cichorium intybus

Treacle mustard
Erysimum cheiranthoides

Treacle mustard is rather similar to hedge mustard but has a square stem. Mustards belong to the crucifer or cabbage family of plants, along with the cuckoo flower – which explains why you see the caterpillars of some butterflies on both. June-August; to 60 cm.

Hedge mustard keeps its seed pods close to its stiff stems. A member of the cabbage family, it is rarely seen in hedges, more often on open ground. June-July; to 80 cm.

Broad-leaved dock possesses small green flowers and leaves which are twice as long as broad. June-October; to 1 metre.

Curled dock has narrow leaves, five times as long as broad, with wavy edges. Found on waste ground like its relative the broad-leaved dock, but also on shingle beaches by the sea. June-October; to 1 metre.

The mouse-eared hawkweed (*Hieracium pilosella*) **is one of the more easily recognisable roadside** members of the hawkweed clan with its single lemon-yellow flowers and rosettes of hairy leaves.

Compare these commonplace weeds with close relatives linked with particular habitats. The hoary plantain is a flower of chalk grassland, see page 148; the wood spurge is seen on page 32. See page 84 for more bindweeds and nightshades.

More weeds

The most quoted definition of a weed is 'a plant out of place', and as every gardener will tell you the success of weeds in colonising disturbed ground is undeniable. Many of the plants shown here are successful because they produce vast amounts of seed which quickly germinate and grow. Shepherd's purse and chickweed may even have several generations of plants growing and seeding in one year. Other weeds are successful because they spread rapidly by their roots. These types of plants are ideally suited to life on recently disturbed ground. They are so common today that we take them for granted. But how did they evolve and where was their place in the wildwood before man started to clear open ground for the plough? Were occasional landslips enough to ensure their survival in early times? Most weeds need a bare soil surface upon which to grow – they are not fussy about what kind of soil it is – but cannot stand much competition from other plants. Some of these plants are often seen on roadside verges especially where cars have parked and churned up the soil.

Redshank. Note the leaf blotches. June-October; to 70 cm.

Field bindweed has a rootstock which grows new plants if broken up. It is a serious garden weed, difficult to eradicate from borders. June-September; climbing to 3 metres.

Black bindweed resembles other bindweeds only in its leaves; it is a relative of redshank. July–September; climbing to 3 metres.

Fat hen seeds and leaves were eaten in the past and used to make an orange dye. June-September; to 1 metre.

Great plaintain (rat's tail) **is a broad-leaved, hairless plantain**; often seen on well trodden places. May-September; to 15 cm.

◄ **Seen in close up, the tiny flowers of the speedwells** have a symmetry and beauty all of their own. This is one of the most common speedwells, germander speedwell (*Veronica chamaedrys*). It is easily told from others of the family by its deep blue flowers and the two rows of dense hairs on opposite sides of the stem.

Chickweed is one of our commonest weeds. Compare it with its close relative, greater stitchwort (page 33). March-December; to 30 cm.

Shepherd's purse is named after its purse-shaped pods. Flowers all year; to 35 cm.

Knotgrass is not a grass but a member of the dock family. It grows on bare soil. June-September; forms dense patches to 1.5 metres across.

Tansy is a stiff, upright plant of the daisy family with an aromatic smell. July-October; to 1 metre.

Sun spurge flowers all winter if it is mild. It has a single upright stem with five flowering stems branching off this in an umbel. To 45 cm.

Common orache is one of the highly confusing orache family which are also successful colonists of shingle beaches. The leaves of the common orache taper into the stalk more gradually than in the similar halberd-leaved orache. July-September; to 1 metre.

Coltsfoot is one of the earliest spring flowers. The large rounded leaves appear after the flower has died down. A rapid colonist of disturbed ground. March to April; to 25 cm.

Pineapple weed smells of pineapple when crushed. It was accidentally introduced to this country in the late 19th century and is now very common along field edges and roadsides. June-October; to 20 cm.

Field and ivy-leaved speedwells are both common garden and arable weeds. The first flowers all year; the second, April-July.

The common fumitory is one of the favourite foods of the turtle dove. Some think that the sites visited by the dove, and chosen for the nest, reflect the distribution of fumitory. This delicate weed with its feathery leaves and pink flowers is a very common arable weed throughout Britain (except in the west). May-September; to 50 cm.

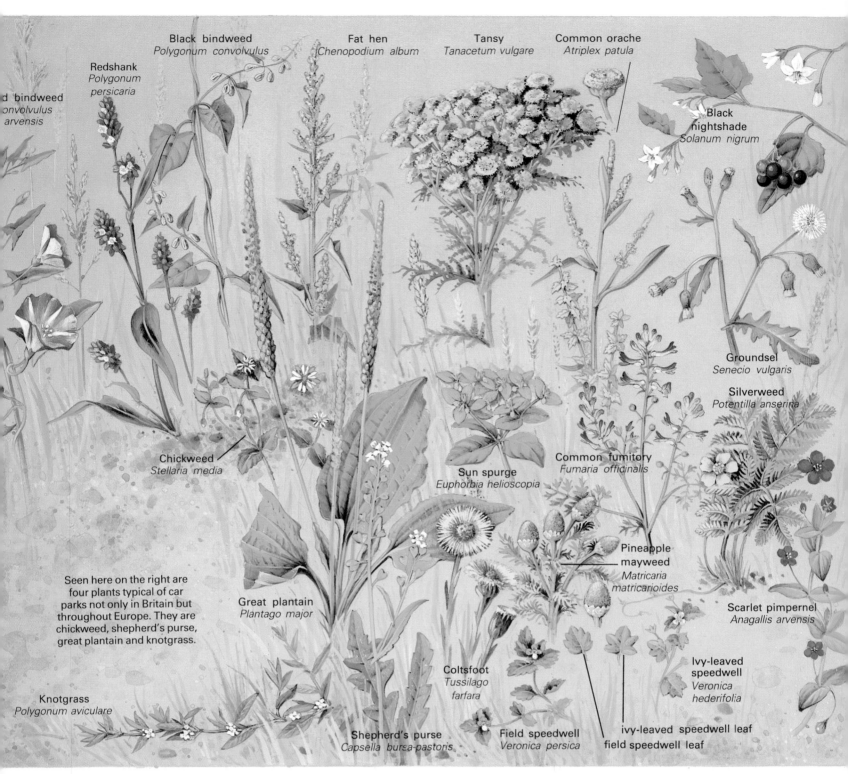

Black bindweed
Polygonum convolvulus

Redshank
Polygonum persicaria

d bindweed
onvolvulus arvensis

Fat hen
Chenopodium album

Tansy
Tanacetum vulgare

Common orache
Atriplex patula

Black nightshade
Solanum nigrum

Groundsel
Senecio vulgaris

Silverweed
Potentilla anserina

Chickweed
Stellaria media

Sun spurge
Euphorbia helioscopia

Common fumitory
Fumaria officinalis

Seen here on the right are four plants typical of car parks not only in Britain but throughout Europe. They are chickweed, shepherd's purse, great plantain and knotgrass.

Great plantain
Plantago major

Pineapple mayweed
Matricaria matricarioides

Scarlet pimpernel
Anagallis arvensis

Ivy-leaved speedwell
Veronica hederifolia

Coltsfoot
Tussilago farfara

Knotgrass
Polygonum aviculare

Shepherd's purse
Capsella bursa-pastoris

Field speedwell
Veronica persica

ivy-leaved speedwell leaf
field speedwell leaf

Groundsel flowers all year. It is a widespread weed of wasteland and gardens; to 40 cm.

Black nightshade berries are poisonous. Flowers July-September; to 50 cm.

Silverweed resembles the yellow buttercup flower but has silvery, feathery leaves. It is closely related to tormentil. Tea can be made from the leaves and flowers, to help ease diarrhoea or piles. June-August; to 15 cm.

Scarlet pimpernel flowers can sometimes be blue. It is common in the south, but rare in the north, a distribution which reflects the general change of climate in Britain. Its flowers open around 8 am and close again at 3 pm, but it is also sensitive to the dampness of the air, and may close when the sun clouds over and rain is imminent. This plant is therefore not only a clock but also a barometer. June-October; to 25 cm.

▶ **If you see a bright patch of yellow flowers** along the roadside in March it will probably be coltsfoot. Once established this plant spreads by an extensive system of underground stems or rhizomes from which new shoots can arise.

Here we continue to investigate the ways in which nature keeps in balance. See also page 42, and pages 138, 178 (for aquatic ecosystems) and 220 (seashore). Ladybirds and aphids are shown on page 110; and one of the important parasitic flies on page 242.

Numbers down the hedgerow

Little of today's countryside is completely natural. Even tangled woods are likely to have been managed at some time in the past. Hedges are an extreme case of man's control but this does not limit their wildlife interest. A hedge is rather like a woodland edge in some ways, and 'edge' habitats, where two different sets of conditions overlap, are often particularly rich. You can therefore expect to find a great variety of life where wood merges into scrub, scrub meets grassland, and at the water's edge.

Though many birds nest in hedges, that in itself need not indicate that the hedge contains a great variety of other animal life. Birds may use the hedge simply for its cover, and feed elsewhere. The insect life is a more convenient yardstick.

Some insects are typical of hedges, being found in them more often than in any other habitat. The gatekeeper butterfly – also known as the hedge brown – is a good example. When you see the insects along the hedge, remember that the journeys they are making are purposeful ones – food gathering, searching for a mate, or perhaps seeking suitable sites to lay their eggs.

A hedge can be a very complex place – with a multitude of 'micro-habitats' meshing into a network. As with any habitat, however, the plants are the base – they are the primary producers, capable of creating and producing their own food. Animals of many different kinds feed on the plants – eating leaves, fruit, bark, or sucking the sap. Carnivores and omnivores consume the plant-eating animals, and may themselves fall prey to other animals. There cannot be more animals than there is food to feed them and so a delicate balance is achieved.

Pyramid of numbers in the hedgerow

The network which links predators to their various prey is complex and is continually changing as different food sources are exploited and as populations fluctuate. By and large, plants, which are the primary producers, are fed upon by hordes of invertebrate animals – aphids and caterpillars, for example. Ladybirds, lacewings and hoverflies consume aphids at various times in their lives. Blue tits also take aphids, as well as caterpillars.

There are fewer blue tits than caterpillars and aphids – it takes a good many of the latter to keep one bird alive. Sparrowhawks take blue tits and other small birds.

It is convenient to imagine this ladder of food and feeder as a pyramid of numbers, with many smaller organisms feeding fewer, larger organisms above them. This is a simplification, however, and parasites are often influential in controlling numbers.

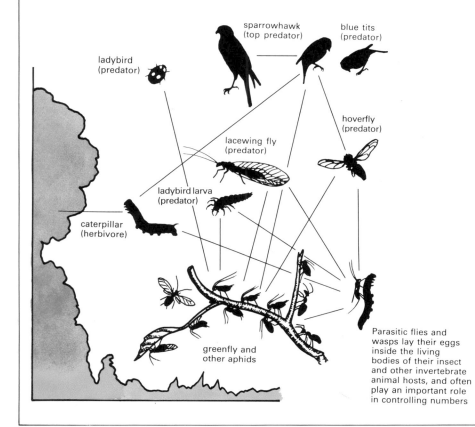

sparrowhawk
(top predator)

blue tits
(predator)

ladybird
(predator)

hoverfly
(predator)

lacewing fly
(predator)

ladybird larva
(predator)

caterpillar
(herbivore)

greenfly and
other aphids

Parasitic flies and wasps lay their eggs inside the living bodies of their insect and other invertebrate animal hosts, and often play an important role in controlling numbers

▲▲ **This young bush cricket**, climbing amongst the flowerhead of a bird's-foot trefoil, looks like a minute version of the adult. Crickets feed mostly on animal matter while their cousins, the grasshoppers, are essentially herbivores.

▲ **A very common insect of hedgerows is the hawthorn shieldbug** (*Acanthosoma haemorrhoidale*) which feeds primarily on haws, when they are available. It will also feed on the leaves.

▶ **Spiders are important hedgerow predators**. This is an orb-web spider in its daytime retreat, concealed in the flowerhead of a knapweed.

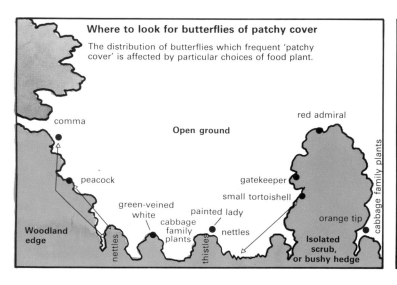

Where to look for butterflies of patchy cover

The distribution of butterflies which frequent 'patchy cover' is affected by particular choices of food plant.

Open ground

comma
red admiral
peacock
gatekeeper
small tortoishell
green-veined white
painted lady
cabbage family plants
orange tip
Woodland edge
nettles
thistles
nettles
Isolated scrub, or bushy hedge
cabbage family plants

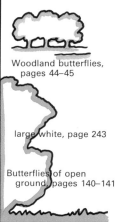

Woodland butterflies, pages 44–45

large white, page 243

Butterflies of open ground, pages 140–141

Orange tips lay their eggs on lady's smock, charlock and other cabbage-family plants. The caterpillar feeds on the flowers and pods. Their underwing markings provide excellent camouflage when they rest on cow parsley and other hedgerow plants – the males hide their orange markings. They can be seen flying in May and June, with a weak fluttering flight. They spend the winter as chrysalises. 30 mm ws.

Commas take their name from the white, comma-shaped mark on the underside of their wings. The tattered-looking wings disguise the butterflies at rest and when they are hibernating (often on the sheltered side of tree

Red admirals seen in Britain are often migrants from the Continent; the numbers arriving vary from year to year. Unlike the peacock and small tortoiseshell, these butterflies lay their eggs singly on nettles. The new brood, which flies in early autumn, either hibernates or begins a return migration. They are strong, purposeful fliers. 70 mm ws.

Red admiral
Vanessa atalanta

Painted lady
Cynthia cardui

peacock caterpillars

small tortoiseshell caterpillars

Small tortoiseshell
Aglais urticae

Peacock
Inachis io

hedge brown caterpillar

Small tortoiseshells hibernate in garden sheds and other sheltered places, and fly in spring. The next generation emerges in June-August. Some also migrate here from Europe. The eggs are laid in batches on nettles, and the young caterpillars spin a communal silken web over the head of the plant, below which they feed. When the leaves are stripped, they move to another nettle plant nearby. There is little difference between the male and female butterflies, although the female is the one usually seen hovering around nettles. They have a fast, rather wild flight, often following one another. 50 mm ws.

Peacocks hibernate in sheds and among ivy. They rely on excellent underwing camouflage to hide themselves. The large 'eyes' on top of the wings are thought to be a shock defence mechanism. If the resting butterfly is disturbed by a bird it suddenly opens its wings, hopefully startling the bird. Peacocks may be seen first in spring as overwinter survivors from the previous year. The main flight is from June onwards. The smaller males often chase the females in a figure-of-eight courtship dance. The black, spiny caterpillars spin a silk web on their food plant between a leaf and stem, within which they pupate. 60 mm ws.

Large white
Pieris brassicae

Hedge brown
Pyronia tithonus

Painted ladies migrate here from the Mediterranean. The first arrivals are seen in April when they are at risk from late frosts. They are powerful fliers. Their eggs are laid singly on thistles; the new generation flying between July and October. 65 mm ws.

trunks). They have a rapid jerky flight and may perch or rest on the ground with wings held open. The eggs are laid singly on nettles, elm suckers and hops, the next generation flying between July and October. A century ago comma numbers were declining and they became virtually unknown outside the Wye Valley. Now they are seen widely in southern England and Wales. Comma caterpillars disguise themselves as bird droppings.

Hedge browns or gatekeepers are found more in the south and are common where they occur. They are a butterfly of high summer, on the wing in July and August, hibernating as caterpillars. The flight is weak and fluttering; the butterflies rarely move more than a hundred metres from where they emerge from the chrysalises. The eggs are laid on grasses in lightly shaded places, and you can often see adults feeding on the nectar of brambles. 40 mm ws.

Many of these butterflies are mobile – they may be seen in other habitats: woods (page 44), scrap sites (130) and gardens (242). You often seen large or small white butterflies at a hedge (242); sometimes green hairstreaks (page 140) are also present.

Hedgerow butterflies

These are butterflies of the tangled corners of fields, hedgerows, clearings in woods where nettles and thistles may flourish, and where plants grow lush in the damp soil. The peacock, small tortoiseshell and red admiral lay their eggs on nettles, as will frequently the comma butterfly. They are all mobile insects, and so are often seen in gardens, sipping nectar from the flowers and basking in the sun in secluded corners. They can be encouraged to breed in the garden by leaving a patch of nettles behind the greenhouse. They are very selective, like all butterflies. The small tortoiseshell chooses young nettles on which to lay its eggs, and will sometimes lay on a plant right out in the open. The peacock and comma, on the other hand, choose older, taller, sheltered plants at a woodland edge or hedge, perhaps (peacocks are typical woodland butterflies). The garden would have to match up to these requirements for them to breed.

Like the small tortoiseshell, the painted lady often lays (in its case on thistle) out on open ground. Nettles and thistles are often the only two 'weeds' seen in improved grass fields and so these two butterflies may be the only ones to expect on 'modern' farms.

Orange tip
Anthocharis cardamines

male

female

comma caterpillar

Comma
Polygonia c-album

green-veined white caterpillar

Green-veined white
Pieris napi

Green-veined whites have two generations which fly, in April and August, the winter being spent in the chrysalis stage. The eggs are laid on much the same plants as the orange tips – sometimes on the very same one – but the caterpillars feed on the leaves not the flowers. The adults have a fluttering flight and on the wing they are difficult to tell from the small white. They do, however, have a less erratic flight. When perched, the green veins can be clearly seen on the undersides of the wings. You can often see them sunning themselves, angling their wings to control the heat gain from the sunshine. 45 mm ws.

Butterfly migration

One of the folk tales of this century is that one day early in the Second World War, a cricket match in Kent had to be abandoned. It was not the bombers that stopped play, nor the weather, but butterflies. Cabbage whites had crossed the Channel in such numbers that they put the batsmen off their strokes!

Large swarms of butterflies crossing the Channel were not uncommon in the past and today we still have a regular tide of arrivals reaching us each spring and summer. Some are rarely seen and have never been known to breed here. One such example is the legendary Camberwell beauty, a large butterfly with purply-brown wings edged in white which occasionally crosses the North Sea (it has been reported passing lighthouses) from northern Europe.

Some migrant butterflies are regularly seen here and do breed, but they cannot survive our winter. The clouded yellow is just such a migrant – 1983 was an excellent year for it, as was 1947. The 'good years' do not seem to follow any obvious rule, but a dry spring with southerly winds seems to help these butterflies move north from their home base in southern Europe. Clouded yellows mate when they arrive and if they arrive early enough there is time for the first British-bred generation of the year to produce a second, and for these offspring to fly before autumn. Numbers, although scattered, can become large enough to give everybody in the south the possibility of seeing one before they are killed by frosts.

The painted lady is another well known migrant. It is, in fact, one of the world's most widely ranging butterflies, seen in every continent except South America. Those that arrive here seem originally to come from North Africa. They fly across the Mediterranean and up through Europe; some even fly on to Iceland, a total journey of some 2,000 miles (3,200 km). The early summer arrivals mate and lay their eggs on thistles and the new

brood is on the wing by August when still more migrants are crossing from Europe, though too late to breed. By recording the flight directions of these migrant butterflies in late summer, evidence has been collected which seems to suggest that they attempt a home run southwards in autumn. Though they do not usually get far before the frost kills them.

The picture is rather different for another common migrant, the red admiral. It arrives in spring and breeds here. Some of this British generation usually manage to hibernate in Britain and survive the winter. Again, there is evidence that red admirals tend to fly in a southernly direction in autumn. successful residents, but whose numbers are swelled each year by the arrival of migrants from Europe – the peacock, and the cabbage white butterflies are two examples. It is not only butterflies that migrate here in this way – many moths, such as the death's head hawk moth and the silver Y moth, make the trip.

The migration of these insects is rather different from the well catalogued migrations of birds. Butterflies are fragile animals and mortality on the journey must be immense, not only from sudden changes in the weather but also from birds and other predators. When swarms of cabbage whites do reach our shores, sparrows and flycatchers have a field day, and observers have seen the ground littered with butterfly wings. The rarer migrants, reaching us in smaller numbers, are even more at risk from predators.

The reasons for butterfly migration are not clear and we can only speculate that it is triggered by overcrowding or by a substantial increase in the number of predators. If the instinct to migrate was present in all the painted lady butterflies, for example, the result would be that, given time, their homeland in North Africa would be emptied with fewer and fewer returning.

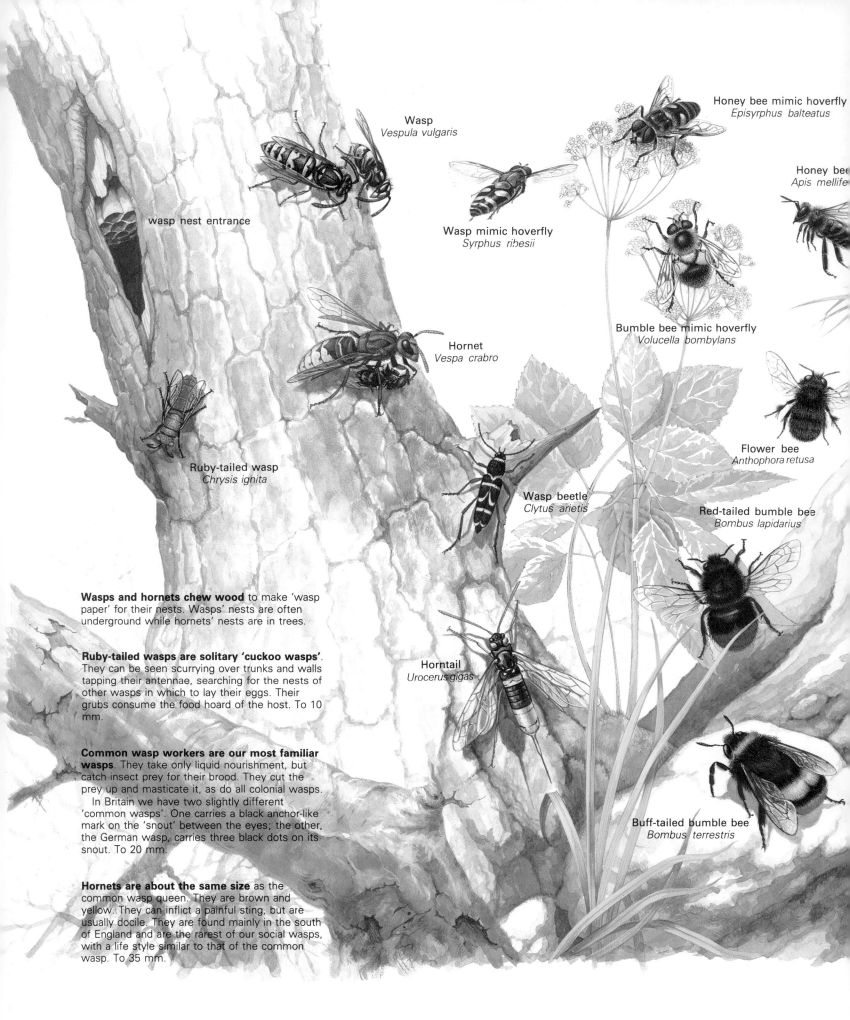

Wasp
Vespula vulgaris

Honey bee mimic hoverfly
Episyrphus balteatus

Honey bee
Apis mellife

wasp nest entrance

Wasp mimic hoverfly
Syrphus ribesii

Hornet
Vespa crabro

Bumble bee mimic hoverfly
Volucella bombylans

Ruby-tailed wasp
Chrysis ignita

Flower bee
Anthophora retusa

Wasp beetle
Clytus arietis

Red-tailed bumble bee
Bombus lapidarius

Horntail
Urocerus gigas

Buff-tailed bumble bee
Bombus terrestris

Wasps and hornets chew wood to make 'wasp paper' for their nests. Wasps' nests are often underground while hornets' nests are in trees.

Ruby-tailed wasps are solitary 'cuckoo wasps'. They can be seen scurrying over trunks and walls tapping their antennae, searching for the nests of other wasps in which to lay their eggs. Their grubs consume the food hoard of the host. To 10 mm.

Common wasp workers are our most familiar wasps. They take only liquid nourishment, but catch insect prey for their brood. They cut the prey up and masticate it, as do all colonial wasps.
In Britain we have two slightly different 'common wasps'. One carries a black anchor-like mark on the 'snout' between the eyes; the other, the German wasp, carries three black dots on its snout. To 20 mm.

Hornets are about the same size as the common wasp queen. They are brown and yellow. They can inflict a painful sting, but are usually docile. They are found mainly in the south of England and are the rarest of our social wasps, with a life style similar to that of the common wasp. To 35 mm.

Wasp beetles are harmless common wasp mimics which, when crawling, also copy the jerky movements of a wasp. They have a narrower waist than is usual in beetles and are often seen on wooden posts and gates, places wasps visit to collect wood for the construction of their nests. To 12 mm.

Horntails or wood wasps are not true wasps, and do not have a sting – their tail is an egg layer. Note that they have no true 'wasp waist'. They are seen most often on pine trees in Scotland, laying their eggs beneath the bark. To 40 mm.

Hoverflies can hover for minutes at a time and then dart off much more quickly than a wasp or bee. Being flies, they have only one pair of wings. The three different hoverflies shown are harmless, and imitate particular wasps or bees. Note that they all have a flat abdomen.

Worker honey (hive) bees are sterile females; they collect nectar and pollen, held in sacs on the hind legs. The food is for the brood, but enough is stored to keep the colony alive through the winter. To 12 mm.

Flower bees are stout and look much like bumble bees but have a quicker flight. They also have a long tongue. They are usually seen in early spring. To 15 mm.

Queen bumble bees can sting and are similar to the workers, though slightly larger. To 30 mm.

Red-tailed bumble bees nest in mouse holes and other underground sites. To 20 mm.

102

Leaf-cutter bee
Megachile centuncularis

Carder bee
Bombus agrorum

Digger wasp
Mimesa equestris

Mining bee
Andrena sp.

Field digger wasp
Mellinus arvensis

Remember that a small fly is not a young fly, but one of another species! Further species are seen on page 110. Some of the insects of page 48 will be found on hedge shrubs. Further examples of warning colours can be seen on pages 110, 130.

Bees, wasps and their mimics

Bees and wasps can be broadly divided into colonial (hive) and solitary species. Both honey and bumble bees are colonial, but the whole honey bee colony survives the winter whereas only the egg-laying, queen bumble bee hibernates to found a new colony the next spring. Common wasps are also colonial and again the queens alone survive the winter. They found new colonies in spring, and later in the year the workers can be seen searching for food for the brood.

The solitary bees and wasps do not fend for their offspring. They leave food by the egg, for example, nectar and pollen in the case of the lawn bee, stunned flies, greenflies or caterpillars in the case of wasps. They then seal up the egg chamber and go on to the next one.

Look closely when you spot what you think is a bee or wasp. You may be watching a fly. They often mimic the bees and wasps to delude their enemies. You can tell fly mimics because they have a single pair of wings which do not fold back across their body when at rest. Flies have mouth parts which are modified for sucking or piercing, they cannot chew food with them. Flies are never armed with stings.

Mimicry is a fascinating strategy adopted by many animals to increase their chances of survival. The three hoverfly mimics on this page closely resemble their 'models'. One hoverfly resembles a wasp, another a bumble bee, while the third resembles a honey bee. This last, a drone fly, is often seen feeding at flowers alongside its model.

These hoverflies mimic insects which can sting a predator and which may also be foul tasting. For this kind of survival mechanism to work, some ground rules must hold true. The predator must be fooled by the disguise and the mimic must obviously live in much the same habitat as the model. The (presumably tasty) mimic must also be less common than the model, if we assume, for example, that a bird learns by experience that bees sting, it is not going to help hoverflies if they are eaten before the birds learn this.

There is another, rather different kind of mimicry, where two animals which are protected, say, by a sting, use the same colour or pattern which tells predators they are dangerous. In this case, a young bird tasting them is as likely to try one as the other and so there is no disadvantage in either being numerous, in fact rather the reverse, for the sooner birds learn that they sting the safer the rest of their collective species will be. The yellow and black markings of wasps and their kin are an example of this. Red seems to be a signal meaning distasteful, as shown by ladybirds and burnet moths.

Lawn bees are short-tongued mining bees which dig holes in dry grassy places (and lawns), leaving a small mound. They are similar in appearance to a hive bee, but the sting is too weak to pierce human skin. The bee is solitary. It is seen flying in early summer. To 12 mm.

You will find solitary wasps of many different hues and kinds crawling over flowers, looking not for nectar or pollen but for insect prey for their brood. Here, a typically large-headed field digger wasp is stocking its brood cells with flies. To 10 mm.

Buff-tailed bumble bees are our bulkiest bees and nest below ground. Queens have a buff tail; workers a white one. Queens to 20 mm; workers to 16 mm.

Leaf-cutter bees are rather like a broad honey bee in appearance. They often nest in a hole in rotting wood. They build their brood cells from pieces cut from leaves, especially from roses and lilac. To 12 mm.

Hairy carder bees are a type of bumble bee, but their nest (often looking like a small bird's nest) is often above ground, among grass stalks.

Bee colonies

At the heart of a colony of honey bees is a single queen, the mother of the whole hive. At 16 mm long she is slightly larger than the other bees and moves around the hive, laying eggs one at a time into the wax cells created by the worker bees. These are sterile females whose egg-laying mechanism has been transformed into a sting. The queen may lay up to 1500 eggs a day, and at the height of the summer the hive may hold 60,000 worker bees.

From time to time the queen lays an egg in a slightly larger cell; from this a drone (a male) develops. At very rare intervals she lays an egg destined to become a queen. The workers in the hive attend and feed the grubs that hatch from all these eggs, but for those destined to become workers themselves, attention slackens after a few days. Not so for the future queen. Food is brought to her up to the time she is to pupate.

The worker bees start with household tasks within the hive, but as they age, they begin to forage outside. A new source of nectar is communicated to the other bees in the hive by means of a 'figure-of-eight dance', performed by the bee on her return. The long axis of the 'eight' shows the direction, the speed of the dance the distance, or at least, an idea of the time spent flying there.

At some time in the summer, bees swarm. When a hive becomes crowded, the old queen leaves taking with her some of her workers. The swarm leaves and clusters on a low bush or other support often not far from the old hive. Scouts leave and return and at some stage the swarm moves off – nobody has much idea how the mass makes up its communal mind to do so – for a new site found by one of the scouts. These swarms are regretted by beekeepers; they do not like to see half their stock fly off and attempts are made to prevent them leaving. But many do escape, and there are a good many 'wild bee' colonies in Britain which are little noticed. The only clue to the whereabouts of a 'wild' colony may be a line of bees flying to a hole high on the side of a building or tree.

For the bees, swarming is a vital part of their species survival. Swarming is a way of creating new colonies. There is, for social animals, no species advantage in simply larger colonies – what is needed is a greater number of colonies.

These invertebrates may be found in many different situations – snails of various species can be found in woodland, on grassland and even out on sand dunes (235). Their aquatic relatives are shown on pages 180, 194. Seashore snails are shown on page 224.

Glass snail
Oxychilus cellarius

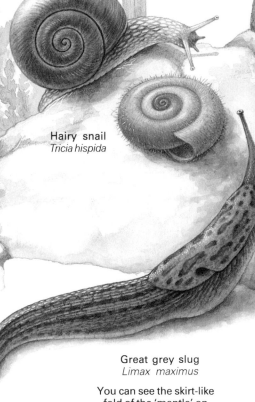

Hairy snail
Tricia hispida

Life on the ground

The soil, far from being of benefit only to plants, is a bustling powerhouse of animal life. The cool, humid conditions close to the ground provide an ideal home for an immense number of slugs, snails, woodlice and hundreds of other creatures which are sensitive to water loss. Many of them are most active at night, so escaping the drying sunshine, particularly garden snails and slugs which can forage for tens of metres before returning to their home base by morning.

Many of these soil surface dwellers feed on plant and animal remains, playing a vital role as decomposers in the re-cycling of material for later generations of animals and plants.

Slugs and snails are closely related molluscs and, although slugs have no obvious shell, some do have the remnants of one. To build their shell and maintain their body, snails need calcium and so are more numerous in chalky areas than in acid ones.

There are three main kinds of slugs: those with a small relic shell at their tail; those with a 'keel'; and the 'roundback' slugs which lack a keel and any sign of a shell. Keeled slugs are often found under rubbish heaps. Their skin is dry, with deep furrows along their flanks. The keel can be clearly seen on their sides.

Great grey slugs have a very unusual mating habit. Pairs climb tree trunks or walls then drop on a thread of slime and mate in mid-air. They are keel slugs and feed on fungi and decaying matter. They are aggressive and will outlaw other slugs from their home patch. Common in gardens. To 20 cm long.

Great black slugs may also be grey-brown or orange. They are roundback slugs which feed on rotting vegetation. They may sway from side to side if disturbed. To 15 cm long.

Great grey slug
Limax maximus

You can see the skirt-like fold of the 'mantle' on the back of this great grey slug. Below it is the lung: you can see its opening.

A great black slug feeding on broom in the early morning. As slugs quickly lose moisture from their bodies they usually feed in the cool of the night and during wet days.

Netted slugs secrete a milky slime when handled. They are keel slugs, which feed on vegetable crops. To 5 cm long.

Garden slugs are common in all situations. They are a serious crop and garden pest. To 5 cm.

Garden snails are commonly found in woods. They hibernate in winter, often in clusters with others of the same species, under bricks or in cracks in rocks. To 3.5 cm tall.

Glass snails are not common. They have a translucent shell and are found in damp places. To 4 mm tall.

Hairy snails have fine hairs on their shell which wear off in patches. Found in damp places, for example under mossy stones. To 5 mm tall.

Grove or banded snails have a variable shell pattern which camouflages them against their surroundings. For all their camouflage, they seem to be easy prey for thrushes. Their broken, empty shells can be seen littering thrush's anvils. To 2 cm tall.

Common woodlice are found under stones, in rotting wood and behind dead bark. They feed on decaying vegetable matter. To 1.8 cm long.

Pill woodlice have a characteristic habit of curling into a ball to prevent water loss. To 1.8 cm long.

Earthworms

Earthworms play an important role in churning up the soil and recycling vegetable matter by pulling leaves down into their holes. They 'eat' soil which they pass through their bodies, removing the organic content. Some excrete the remains as worm casts on the surface. Their importance in soil ecology was described by Gilbert White, the eminent 18th century naturalist, who wrote, 'They are though in appearance a small and despicable link in the chain of Nature, yet if lost would make a lamentable chasm. For, to say nothing of half the birds, and some quadrupeds which are almost entirely supported by them, worms seem to be the great promoters of vegetation which would proceed but lamely without them, by boring, perforating, and loosening the soil, and rendering it pervious to rains and the roots of plants, by drawing straws and stalks of leaves and twigs into it, and most of all by throwing up such infinite numbers of lumps of earth called wormcasts, which, being their excrement, is a fine manure for grain and grass. Worms probably provide new soil for hills and slopes where the rain washed the earth away . . . .

Gilbert White's interest in worms was shared by Charles Darwin who a century ago re-interpreted the whole of nature in a framework of evolution. Darwin noticed that worms kept on his piano popped back into their holes when he played, but took no notice when they were not in direct contact with the piano. He concluded that they are sensitive to vibration, a sense which enables them to dart back into their holes if a predator approaches. Earthworms are extremely abundant and Darwin estimated that they recycle ten tons of new soil per acre per year. If this is so, they may be partly responsible for much of the smooth rolling character of our downs and hillsides.

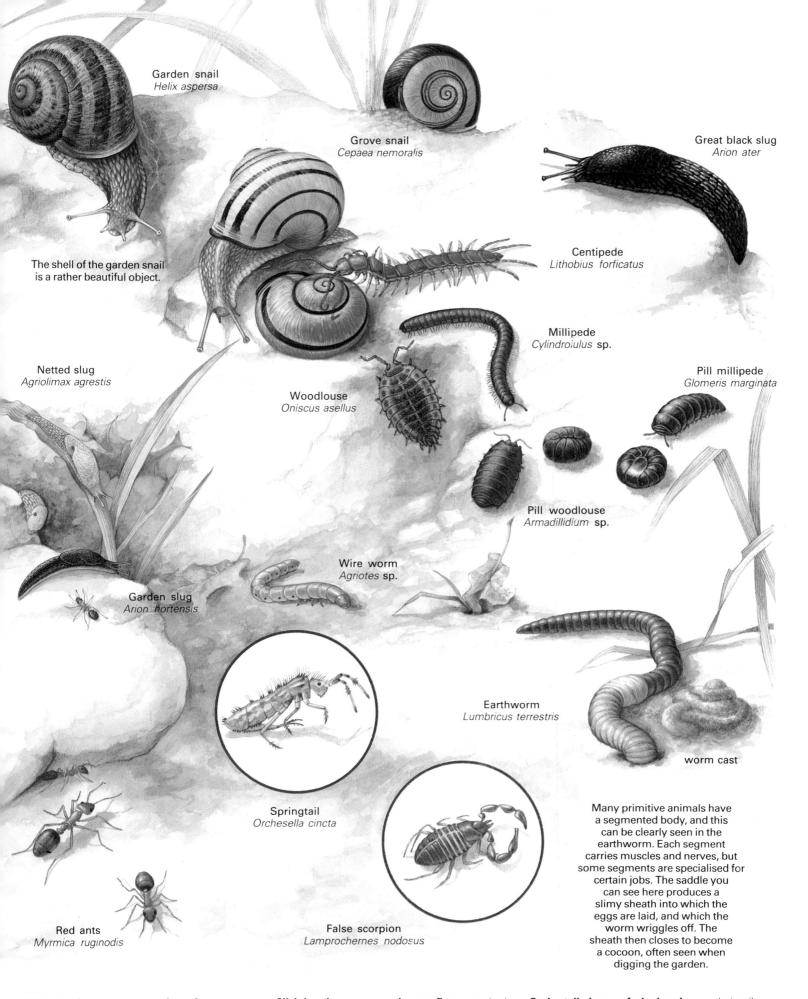

Garden snail
Helix aspersa

Grove snail
Cepaea nemoralis

Great black slug
Arion ater

The shell of the garden snail
is a rather beautiful object.

Centipede
Lithobius forficatus

Millipede
Cylindroiulus sp.

Netted slug
Agriolimax agrestis

Pill millipede
Glomeris marginata

Woodlouse
Oniscus asellus

Pill woodlouse
Armadillidium sp.

Wire worm
Agriotes sp.

Garden slug
Arion hortensis

Earthworm
Lumbricus terrestris

worm cast

Springtail
Orchesella cincta

Many primitive animals have
a segmented body, and this
can be clearly seen in the
earthworm. Each segment
carries muscles and nerves, but
some segments are specialised for
certain jobs. The saddle you
can see here produces a
slimy sheath into which the
eggs are laid, and which the
worm wriggles off. The
sheath then closes to become
a cocoon, often seen when
digging the garden.

Red ants
Myrmica ruginodis

False scorpion
Lamprochernes nodosus

Millipedes have many more legs than centipedes and curl up in a spiral when disturbed. To 5 cm long.

Pill millipedes are often confused with pill woodlice. The pill millipede has fewer tail segments, more legs and is much shinier than the pill woodlouse. It is said that both these creatures gained their names from their use as a stomach medicine to cure the gripes. Their struggles inside the stomach would have had a remarkable effect on anybody whether ill or not. More likely, the names come from their habit of rolling up into a tight ball, like a small pill, when attacked. To 2 cm long.

Click beetles may spend up to five years in the grub stage. The grubs, called wireworms, feed on plant roots and can be a serious crop pest. Adult to 1.6 cm long.

Centipedes are active predators which catch slugs, worms, etc. They live in soil, under stones and in leaf litter. They often curl up if disturbed. Over 5 cm long.

False scorpions are very small and therefore difficult to recognise. They may be seen on the backs of harvestmen in autumn, hitching a lift to new feeding grounds. Look out for them in leaf litter taken from under a hedge. To 3 mm long.

Springtails have a forked spring on their tail which propels them away when disturbed. They are often present in vast numbers in leaf litter. To 5 mm long.

Common earthworms are just one of many types of worm. All earthworms are hermaphrodite, each individual possessing both male and female reproductive organs. 10–30 cm long.

Red ants are common throughout the British countryside. They nest under stones or in tree stumps, and will sometimes share an earth mound with meadow ants. They have a sting. To 10 mm long.

The process of evolution is described on page 229. More beetles can be seen on pages 48, 80, 142 and some handsome species are shown on pages 110 and 170. Page 194 shows aquatic beetles and a fascinating array of bugs. Aphids – also a type of bug – are on page 110.

Beetles and a bug

At the turn of this century, some clerics were cross-examining an eminent biologist on his view of God, 'He has an inordinate fondness for beetles' was his studied reply.

There are more than 3,700 different species of beetles found in Britain and over a quarter of a million in the world. These insects are one of the most successful types of animal life on earth. They come in all shapes, sizes and colours, and live in almost every habitat in the world.

Unlike many other insects, beetles have only one pair of functional wings – the other forms a horny wing case which sometimes hides the body and which meets along the centre of the back. You can see it clearly on the stag beetle. Beetles usually have biting mouthparts, an exception are weevils which are plant-feeding beetles with a head drawn out into a snout for piercing and sucking.

Names and classification

Specialists today use a logical system of naming animals and plants which avoids confusion. Every species has an official name which is recognised by scientists in countries throughout the world.

The system was devised about 200 years ago by a Swede, Carl Linnaeus. The unit of animal and plant life is the species – a species is different from and does not normally breed with, other species, not even with those closely related to it. The species usually carries an everyday English name – blue tit, stag beetle, meadow buttercup, for example.

In the Linnaean system, the species receives two names which are latin-like, if not true Latin. The stag beetle shown on this page is *Lucanus cervus*, where *Lucanus* is a group, a genus, of beetles sharing common features such as, in this case, elbowed antennae. The name *cervus* pinpoints the species, stag beetle. Similarly, the blue tit is *Parus caeruleus*, and the great tit, *Parus major*. The meadow buttercup is *Ranunculus acris*, while its close relatives (page 126) have different specific names.

Classification is the science of arranging living things into a ladder of life, or into groups which have features in common. This ladder also sheds light on the way they may have evolved from each other. Similar species are grouped into a genus, similar genera into a family, similar families into an order, orders into classes.

Beetles make up one of the orders of the insect class, and they, in turn, belong to a division (a sub-class) of insects which show *complete* metamorphosis, passing through a pupa stage. Bugs belong to a separate order of insects, and together with dragonflies and some others belong to a division which has *incomplete* metamorphosis – the young resemble adults.

Click beetle
Agriotes obscurus

Clover weavil
Apion pisi

Longhorn beetle
Stenocorus meridianus

male

Rose chafer
Cetonia aurat

Stag beetle
Lucanus cervus

Violet ground beetle
Carabus violaceus

female

Though at first sight this bug may resemble a beetle, note that its front wings overlap, and are not hardened right to their ends.

Bombardier beetle
Brachinus crepitans

Devil's coach-horse beetle
Ocypus olens

Sailor (soldier) beetle   Capsid bug
Cantharis rustica   *Lygus pratensis*

male

Burying beetle
Necrophorus vespillo

Glow worm
Lampyris noctiluca

female

A bug has a precise meaning in classification, for an order of insects with mouthparts modified into a sucking beak. Unlike beetles, bugs have incomplete metamorphosis (see index). Though some bugs are beetle-like (above), others are not – aphids, for example are bugs.

Clover weevils are beetles, though their head and mouth parts are drawn forward into a long snout. Weevils are plant feeders. To 3 mm.

Rove beetles (sometimes known as cock-tail beetles) are a family of more than a thousand species. The one shown here is called the devil's coach horse. Both it and its grub are nocturnal predators and can give a sharp bite. To 25 mm.

▲**The bloody-nosed beetle** *(Timarcha tenebricosa)* **has an intriguing defense mechanism:** if it is agitated it will exude a red, blood-like liquid from its mouth parts; hence its name. It is a beetle of grasslands and heaths where it feeds on bedstraws.

◄ **Black-tipped soldier beetle** *(Rhagnycha fulva)* **are commonly seen in late summer** on the spreading umbels of members of the parsley family. Their fierce looking mouth parts, however, betray their carnivorous diet. They use the flowers to search out other nectar-feeding insects.

Click beetles drop to the ground if disturbed. If they fall on their backs they can right themselves with a flick somersault. The grub of one species of click beetle is known as the wireworm which is a serious crop pest. This beetle may be seen in bracken in early summer. To 10 mm.

Violet ground beetles have a violet sheen. They are very common and can be seen scurrying over the ground especially at night as they hunt for worms. They cannot fly. To 25 mm.

Bombardier beetles eject a puff of caustic liquid from their back-end if attacked. Found under stones in August, especially in chalk country. To 7 mm.

Burying beetles are attracted by rotting carcasses. They dig away the soil under the dead animal and sink the corpse into the hole. They then cover it and feed on the remains, laying their eggs alongside. 20–25 mm.

Longhorn beetles are very elegant and have long antennae. This one is seen on flowers, feeding on nectar, its grubs feed in timber; to 20 mm. The wasp beetle on page 102 is also a longhorn.

Rose chafers are, as their name implies, often seen on rose bushes, especially in the south. Larvae are found in rotting tree stumps. To 20 mm. (Compare with the cockchafer, page 48).

Soldier beetles are usually found, sometimes in large numbers, on nettles and hogweed, during the summer. They are predators, and will even attack each other. They visit flowers to mate and look for insect prey. To 20 mm.

Glow worms are now rather rare. They are beetles, although the female, which glows at the tip of the tail, looks rather like a woodlouse. They feed on snails and are most likely to be seen in chalk and limestone areas. 10–15 mm.

Stag beetles are our largest and most easily identified beetles. They are seen in the south in May-June. The beetles fly at dusk. Their horns cannot pinch, and, if threatened, the male beetles will rise up on their forelegs presenting the horns. (Compare its antennae with those of chafers and dung beetles page 142). Their grubs burrow into dead wood. Male to 60 mm. Female to 35 mm.

Spiders can be surprisingly numerous in a habitat. They are seen in woods, hedges, on grassland and on walls (page 116). Page 194 shows a water spider and see page 48 for a green one. The purseweb spider is shown on page 170; it can be plentiful where it occurs.

Spiders

Spiders are possibly the most feared and misunderstood group of creatures in the whole animal kingdom. They are often regarded as dangerous, even malevolent. Despite this most of us would prefer not to have to squash a spider. The fact is that almost all spiders are harmless to man, certainly those found in Britain, and they have fascinating life stories. Furthermore, many are beautifully coloured and patterned.

Spiders are not insects: they have four pairs of legs and a body in two parts. They do not have insect-like antennae, nor do they have wings. There are many different kinds of spider and in some places they occur in vast numbers – an acre of old grassland, for example, may carry more than two million, some building their webs between the grass stalks.

Web-spinning spiders do not all spin the same kind of web; a selection is shown here. The differences between webs are not only in size and pattern, but also in subtler ways such as the angle at which they are spun and whether they are sticky or not. Many spiders do not spin webs at all.

All spiders are predators. Some catch their prey by waiting in ambush, others stalk small insects and jump on them from a distance. They have varied diets, but seem rather fussy about what they will eat.

At mating time the ferocity of spiders puts the (usually smaller) males at risk. Male jumping spiders sooth the female with tic-tac leg dances. Some male web-spinners pluck a strand of the female's web until she rushes up to him. In some species, the male spider presents the female with a present of a parcelled fly, to distract her while he mates with her.

A female nursery-web spider (*Pisaura mirabilis*). She holds her egg sac under her body unlike the wolf spiders.

Meta segmentata spider

The web shown here is quite sophisticated, with a touch-telephone wire which alerts the spider, lurking in cover, as soon as an insect is snared. The spider then moves to the central 'platform' that you can see in the web, discovers where its victim is caught, and then rushes across to poison it with a bite and wrap it up – it is then carried back to the silky retreat to be sucked dry at leisure.

Money spiders are tiny and build their familiar hummock webs in grass, or low in hedges. They can be seen picked out by dew on autumn mornings. The webs are not sticky, the prey is taken from below while trying to walk along the filaments. To 5 mm.

The cross, diadem or garden spider, spins a vertical 'orb' web. **Cross spiders** may sit at the centre of the web at night (use a red torch to see) but usually spend the day in cover, ready to rush out and grab trapped prey. They have no 'telegraph wire' to tell them that the web is vibrating. Much of their diet consists of small midges; every few days the entire web is eaten by the spider together with its catch of stricken midges and a new web is then spun. The spiders are perhaps too well-programmed because they are unable to repair a broken web. Young spiderlings can be seen in early summer just out from the cocoon, congregating in a golden mass, ready to disperse. To 15 mm.

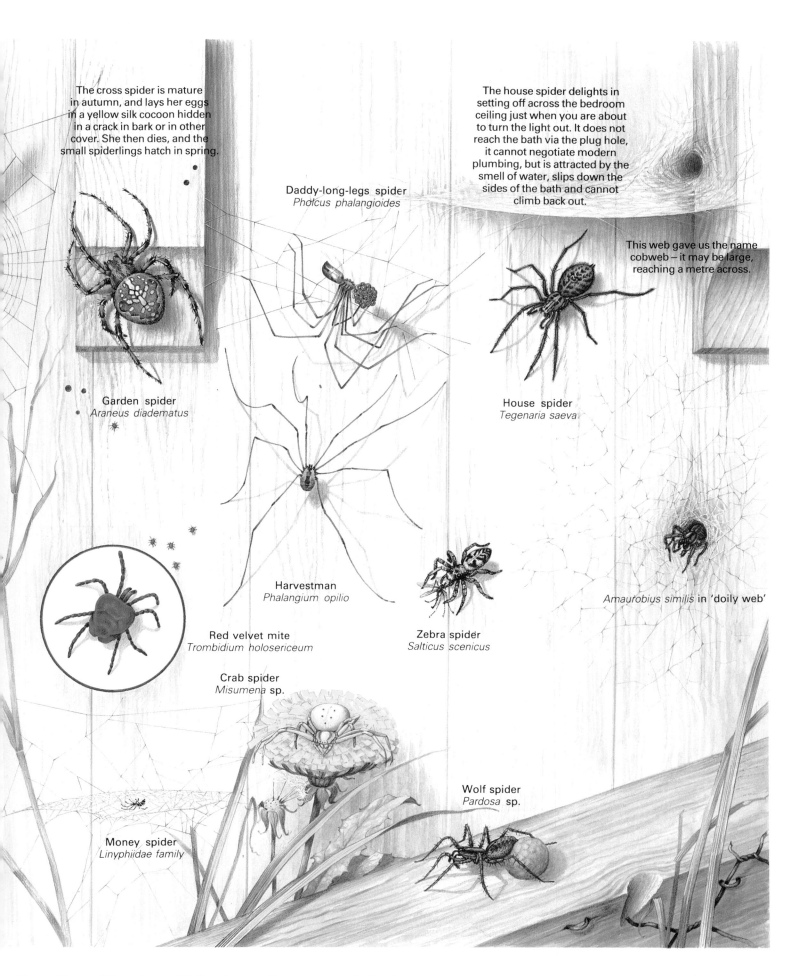

The cross spider is mature in autumn, and lays her eggs in a yellow silk cocoon hidden in a crack in bark or in other cover. She then dies, and the small spiderlings hatch in spring.

The house spider delights in setting off across the bedroom ceiling just when you are about to turn the light out. It does not reach the bath via the plug hole, it cannot negotiate modern plumbing, but is attracted by the smell of water, slips down the sides of the bath and cannot climb back out.

This web gave us the name cobweb – it may be large, reaching a metre across.

Daddy-long-legs spider
Pholcus phalangioides

Garden spider
Araneus diadematus

House spider
Tegenaria saeva

Harvestman
Phalangium opilio

Red velvet mite
Trombidium holosericeum

Zebra spider
Salticus scenicus

Amaurobius similis in 'doily web'

Crab spider
Misumena sp.

Wolf spider
Pardosa sp.

Money spider
Linyphiidae family

Crab spiders wait in ambush with their legs splayed ready to seize their prey with a jump. They can be white, yellowish or another colour to match the flower on which they live. To 12 mm.

Wolf spiders live on the ground, where they chase and pounce on their prey. Look for the females carrying their egg cocoons. To 10 mm.

Zebra spiders are likely to be seen on walls. They stalk and jump on their prey, leaping many times their own length. To 7 mm.

Mites are small relatives of spiders. The small red mites you see scuttling over paths in summer are pollen eaters but the one shown here is a parasite or predator. To 1 mm.

Harvestmen, with their long legs, can reach 7 cm across. They are not closely related to spiders: their body has no true waist and they do not spin webs. They are active predators. They need to drink and can often be seen sipping from drops of dew. Occasionally they can be found with legs missing. If they are trapped they will deliberately sever the limb.

Daddy-long-legs spiders (named after their resemblance to the daddy-long-legs or crane fly) make a three dimensional web, like a mini-scaffolding attached to a wall. If they are disturbed they will rock; it is presumed this is a kind of threat display. To 8–10 mm.

House spiders have very long legs and can reach 5 cm across. They have an organ on their legs which detects water. The large triangular web (to 20 cm across) is a mesh of threads. They catch prey which cannot walk across it – the web is not sticky. To 18 mm.

Some spiders have specific locations for their webs and tailor their construction accordingly. Walls have their own web spinning spiders. The web shown here looks like a small doily with a tunnel into a knot in the fence at the end of which the spider waits.

Hedgerow hawthorn is an ideal shrub for insects – it leafs early and its flowers provide plenty of pollen and nectar. Hedges are visited by many butterflies (100). The snake fly (48), an insect predator, could indicate insect diversity in a hedge.

Greenfly are aphids and are also called plant lice. They are, in fact, bugs with piercing and sucking mouth parts.

Ladybirds are beetles which lay their eggs near aphid colonies, as both adults and larvae feed on them. Two weeks after hatching a ladybird larva becomes inactive and its skin splits to reveal the pupa which looks like a small bird dropping. After a further ten days the pupal skin splits, and the adult emerges. You will often find ladybirds hibernating indoors in winter. To 5–8 mm.

Two-spot ladybirds can vary in pattern, some have red spots on a black background, others black spots on a red background. Sometimes they carry four spots or up to a total of six. All these different forms interbreed. You may come across a seven-spot ladybird or a small, neat 22-spot ladybird with black spots on a yellow background. These are both more constant about their pattern.

Hedgerow insects

A wood keeps its vast community of animals hidden while a hedge is not shy of revealing them. From spring until high summer, the hedgerow sees a succession of insects following the leafing, flowering and fruiting of the plants. The herbivorous insects form the basis of the insect population which is highly complex with many complex interrelationships developing between predator and prey. The brightly coloured ladybirds, despite their story-book image, are voracious carnivores and feed on large numbers of aphids (green- and blackfly) which means that most gardeners should welcome the hibernating groups in his shed. Flies also play an important role in hedgerows. Many of those seen early in the year are nectar feeders, such as the bee-fly, with its long tube-like mouthparts, and the St Marks fly. As the summer progresses and the numbers

Greenfly and blackfly

Greenfly (aphids) can be closely observed even without the aid of a magnifying glass. They wriggle as they pierce with their mouthparts the soft green stem below them. They seem to feed for much of the time, sucking up large amounts of sap to obtain nourishment. They take in more liquid and sugar than they can deal with, and the excess is excreted as honeydew, a sweetish, sticky substance. This is sometimes discharged in large amounts, coating leaves, the ground and any cars parked below the trees they live in. They are sedentary animals, and channel the energy gained from their large food intake into achieving an incredible breeding rate. The greenflies normally seen are females and, in warm weather with plenty of food available, each female may produce two or three live young females each day – with patience, you may watch a 'birth' for yourself. They do not need to mate, neither do their offspring, and so the latter, after a few day's hearty nourishment, are ready to start producing in their turn. Numbers would soon become astronomical, were it not for the large numbers of predators of all kinds, from birds (blue tits and others) to many of the insects shown on this page. Parasites, too, are important in keeping down greenfly colonies, though these parasites are very small and difficult to observe.

From time to time in the summer, when the colony is tightly packed on the stems, winged females are produced. These fly off to colonise new plants and can carry plant virus diseases with them. This dispersal is usually aided by the rising streams of warm air and breezes. On a warm day, the air over Britain up to 1500 metres overhead can contain a thin 'soup' of greenfly, small flies and other insects all being dispersed by the wind.

In the autumn, some male greenfly are produced. Mating can take place and eggs are laid which survive the winter to hatch new females the next spring.

Normally greenfly are one element of a balanced community of animals kept in check by their predators, and numbers do not become formidable. This can even be noticed in a garden in which sprays are not used. Gardens, however, are by definition somewhat unnatural creations, and an imbalance can set in. In theory,

it is perfectly possible to leave nature to control the greenfly on the roses. Remember that sprays can kill the predators as well as their prey.

'Biological' control is a viable alternative to costly chemicals in many cases, and often it is a parasite rather than a predator which can be introduced to control a

pest. In commercial operations, forestry for example, parasites may be introduced to attack moths which have arrived in this country with their host tree, but which have left their natural controls behind in their home country.

Early this century, the greenhouse whitefly was a pest which attacked cucumbers and tomatoes, making them lose colour and hence rendering them unmarketable. Sprays helped, but were expensive for commercial growers. The problem was solved with the introduction of a minute wasp. It was not a native, but it was noticed in a greenhouse in 1926 where its grubs were seen eating the young whitefly. Stocks were bred and by 1930 it was being sent to nurseries all over Britain. This wasp is still used today as a control for greenhouse whitefly and, is likely to be present in many established glasshouses.

The kind of control is really a job for the experts. If you are inclined to bring ladybirds into the garden to deal with the greenfly on the roses, half a dozen will not be effective. You need to know when the ladybirds breed and how to time things so that large numbers of ladybirds are present when the aphids are likely to increase their numbers.

Ants have a remarkable relationship with aphids. Some ants take them down to the nest, where the aphids suck the sap from roots and the ants harvest the honeydew they exude. Usually, however, the ants adopt colonies of aphids. They keep parasites and predators at bay, and in return they milk the honeydew from the aphids – persuading them to yield it by stroking them with their antennae. This link is an old one, for ants and aphids are found together in amber – fossilized tree resin many millions of years old. Moths and hoverflies are also often seen feeding on honeydew.

Blackfly have much the same life story as greenfly, but in late summer winged females leave the beans, roses and other plants, on which they have been feeding, and fly to spindle or guelder rose bushes where they give birth to wingless but egg-laying females. Males join them to mate. The eggs survive the winter on the bushes, and in spring wingless females hatch from them – these produce living young, and a colony grows, in which winged females are produced, which fly to that year's crops of beans.

of active insects increase, the true predators, such as the robber flies, become more evident.

Parasites also play an important role. They are usually small and inconspicuous insects but they lay their eggs in the living bodies of other insects, and exert a considerable influence on their numbers. The rotting fruit of the autumn provides a final orgy of food for the plant eaters and many species can be seen clustered around damaged berries. Often the different sexes and stages of these insects will have remarkably different feeding requirements. For example, some hoverfly larvae are carnivorous while the adults are nectar feeders.

The open nature of a hedge means that, without hardly moving, it is possible to watch many different types of insect with highly different life-styles. Watch for the lacewings and their carnivorous larvae. These delicate insects are also attracted to lighted windows. Bush crickets can be heard and occasionally glimpsed in the ranker vegetation. Butterflies will be patrolling the hedge continually seeking out brambles and other flowers on which to feed. A closer look at some of the lower branches may reveal froghoppers – jumping bugs – whose nymphs protect themselves in a mass of foam known as 'cuckoo-spit'. The adults and young pierce the plants and feed on the sap and are, in turn, preyed on by many larger insects.

Green lacewings are often seen indoors in late summer when they can turn a dirty pink colour. These beautiful insects feed on nectar and pollen. The larvae feed hungrily on greenfly. To 1.2 cm. To 3 cm wingspan.

Froghoppers lay eggs in autumn. The nymphs hatch in spring on plant stems and produce a mass of froth – cuckoo spit – to protect themselves against desiccation and predators. To 3 mm.

Brimstone butterflies are just one of the many butterfly species which can be seen along hedges. They may be looking for buckthorn bushes on which to lay their eggs. To 6 cm wingspan.

Swarming hoverfly larvae prey on greenfly and can consume large numbers. To 2 cm.

The male bush cricket shown here is worth comparing with the female on page 48. This dark bush cricket is found in rank vegetation and can be detected by its long chorus of fruity, metallic chirrups. To 1.5 cm when adult.

Earwigs are adept flyers, although you will only see them fly at night. Note the difference between the male with its curved 'pincers' and the female. Neither can nip. Earwigs seek out dark places in daytime and can even be found curled up in flowerheads. To 1.5 cm when adult.

Cardinal beetles are a handsome, though scarce, insect of woodland edges and hedges in the south. The larvae are found under the bark of fallen trees or branches. The adults are flower feeders. To 1.5 cm long.

Flesh flies are relatively common. Their grubs feed on carrion. Unlike similar flies, flesh flies are rarely seen indoors. To 1.5 cm long.

Cluster flies justify their name in autumn when they swarm on warm walls or trees, before hibernating. You can also see them clustering in summer. You will sometimes see one or two fly off and return, flying in a figure of eight. This may be a ritual courtship flight. The grubs are parasites of worms.

Bluebottles (blow flies) **come indoors to lay eggs** on exposed meat. Smaller greenbottles lay in carrion along hedges and scrub. To 2.5 m.

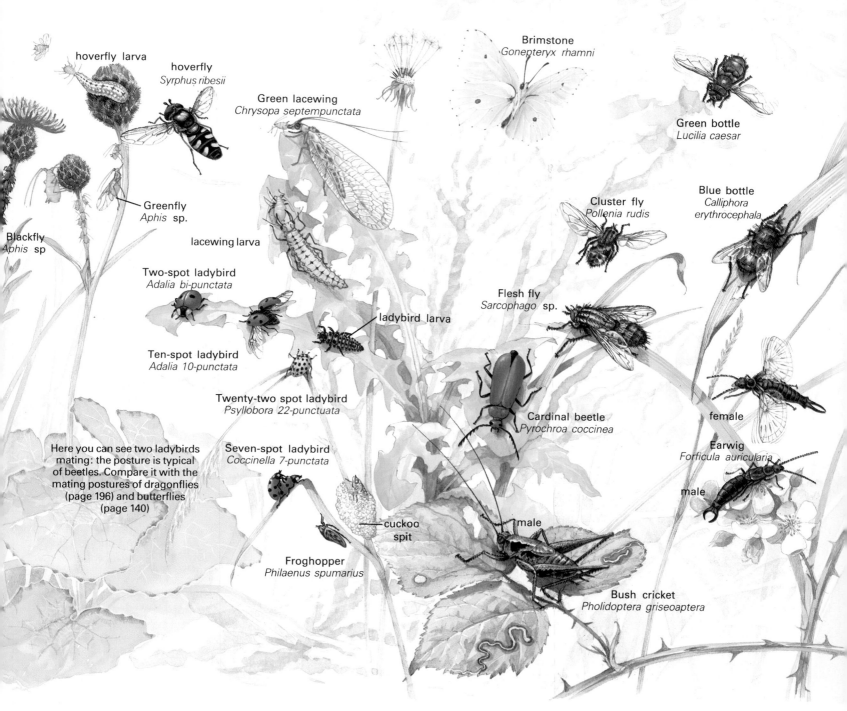

hoverfly larva

hoverfly
Syrphus ribesii

Green lacewing
Chrysopa septempunctata

Brimstone
Gonepteryx rhamni

Green bottle
Lucilia caesar

Greenfly
Aphis sp.

lacewing larva

Blackfly
Aphis sp

Two-spot ladybird
Adalia bi-punctata

Cluster fly
Pollenia rudis

Blue bottle
Calliphora erythrocephala

ladybird larva

Flesh fly
Sarcophago sp.

Ten-spot ladybird
Adalia 10-punctata

Twenty-two spot ladybird
Psyllobora 22-punctuata

Cardinal beetle
Pyrochroa coccinea

female

Here you can see two ladybirds mating: the posture is typical of beetles. Compare it with the mating postures of dragonflies (page 196) and butterflies (page 140)

Seven-spot ladybird
Coccinella 7-punctata

Earwig
Forficula auricularia

male

cuckoo spit

male

Froghopper
Philaenus spumarius

Bush cricket
Pholidoptera griseoaptera

111

Many of the birds of pages 52 and 54 will also be seen in hedges. Hawthorn itself forms part of the attraction for birds, as it provides good nest cover, while it also attracts hosts of insects for the insect-eating birds; plants growing in its shelter provide winter seeds.

Hedgerow birds

Many of the birds that nest in hedges are woodland species, although you can expect to see less variety than in any good area of woodland. Out of 27 different species regularly seen on one Dorset farm, 21 were found to be nesting and only 14 nesting in the hedges nearby.

Although there may be fewer birds nesting in hedges, they are much easier to see than those confined to woodland. Hedges make excellent observatories, especially to watch out-of-breeding-season activities such as flocking and roosting. Many birds which are fiercely territorial while nesting will fly and

A fieldfare feeding on rotten apples. Mixed flocks of this winter visitor can often be seen feeding on orchard windfalls with blackbirds and redwings.

feed together in flocks at other times of year, often outside their strict breeding habitat. Also, birds of different kinds may flock and roost together.

The advantages of flocking are, perhaps, obvious. There are more eyes to spot new sources of food. There are also more eyes to see predators. Flocking is an important part of the survival strategy of many birds.

At a certain point in a hedge or patch of scrub, you may regularly see a noisy throng of birds at dusk in the winter. The birds roost together at these places, and by ringing them scientists have discovered that these favoured spots often house different individuals each night.

Magpies are easily recognised (note their large tail) They are birds of woodland edge or scrub, and do not feed far from cover. They take food of all kinds, including pheasants' eggs, a habit they have been persecuted for in the past. They are now recovering and can even be found breeding in towns. Their bulky nests, loose domed, are built in deep cover in trees and bushes.

There is a saying that one magpie means bad luck but, fortunately, they are usually seen in pairs. Their call is a raucous *chak chak*; they sometimes chatter. 46 cm.

Cuckoos can be seen as well as heard, flying strongly with hawk-like, rapid downbeats of their wings. The males call *cuc-coo*, the females have a bubbling note. Cuckoos specialise in eating the woolly caterpillars of moths, found along hedges,

but earlier in the year they possibly survive on leatherjackets. Their eggs are laid in the nests of small insect-eating birds, such as dunnocks, meadow pipits and reed warblers. They winter in southern or central Africa. 33 cm.

Whitethroats, unlike other, more retiring, warblers, perch in full view on bushes to sing. They also have a very noticeable song-and-dance act of a display: they fly up a few metres singing a wheezing warble, then tumble back down to the perch. The nest is usually within 0.5 metres of the ground amongst tall plants or in low shrubby growth in rather open habitats – scrub or heathland, for example. A few years ago numbers of these summer visitors declined dramatically, as a result of drought in the Sahel region of Africa where they winter. 14 cm.

Linnets are birds of hedges, scrub and bushy waste ground. They have a bouncing, erratic flight. The males sing twittering songs from a low perch. Note their bills, which are adapted for seed eating. They flock and feed with chaffinches and greenfinches when breeding is over. They nest in bushes, in groups with, perhaps, half a dozen other pairs. 13 cm.

Greenfinches like to perch in fairly tall trees where they perform a twittering territorial song – a nasal *dzwee* (not very pleasant on the ear) – which can be heard in spring. The birds often launch off into a wavering display flight, with tail spread and colours showing. Note the heavy bill. The nest is in a bush or tree, in a fork or against the trunk; often in loose colonies. 14.5 cm.

Dunnocks are often called hedge sparrows, though they are not related to sparrows. Dunnocks have the thin bill of an insect-eating bird. They are often overlooked because they are secretive, though are not uncommon in farmland, woodland and gardens. They are often mistaken for sparrows when they come to the bird-table for scraps. But are always below, never on the table itself, moving with a mouse-like shuffle over the ground. Dunnocks have a loud *tseep* call and a wren-like *sweedle-deedle-deedle* song. The nest is usually between 1 and 3 metres above ground, well hidden in a bush or sometimes a bank. 14.5 cm.

Whitethroat
Sylvia communis

Cuckoo
Cuculus canorus

Magpie
Pica pica

Barn owl
Tyto alba

Kestrel
Falco tinnunculus

female

Chaffinch
Fringilla coelebs

male

male

female

Yellowhammer
Emberiza citrinella

Redwing
Turdus iliacus

male

Linnet
Carduelis cannabina

Fieldfare
Turdus pilaris

male

female

Dunnock
Prunella modularis

Greenfinch
Carduelis chloris

Yellowhammers sing a persistent, hammering song, really hitting home its message – a *chitti-chitti* song with the rhythm *a-little-bit-of-bread-and . . . noooo . . . cheese*. The song is delivered from the top of a bush. Yellowhammers are buntings, with a heavy beak adapted for seed eating. They form flocks in winter, often with other birds. The nest is usually on the ground hidden in grass against a bush or hedge. They are birds of open farmland. 16.5 cm.

Kestrels are our commonest bird of prey – they can be seen hovering with fast beating wings, tail dropped. They are a common sight along motorways, for the long grass often carries a fair number of the voles they hunt. They fall in stages until within striking distance of their prey and then finally drop. They also sometimes attempt to take small birds. They possess a high *kee* or *kek* call. The nest is on a ledge on a rock outcrop, tree, or sometimes on a building far into town. 38 cm.

Barn or 'screech' owls have a long, blood curdling eerie shriek. They hunt at dusk, flying slowly about a metre or two from the ground with a wavering flight, swooping down to take rats, mice and shrews, located by hearing as much as by sight. They have a monkey-like look to their face.

We now have maybe fewer than 5,000 pairs of these owls left in Britain. They were once much more numerous and were, in fact, encouraged – many old barns have an 'owl hole' high on a side

wall to allow the owls to enter to hunt for rats and mice amongst the stored crops. Their decline may be due to disturbance while nesting; poisoning from pesticides, or any number of other reasons. The nest is in a cavity in tree or building. 34 cm.

Chaffinches are among our most numerous breeding birds. They are strongly territorial. Their song has an emphatic flourish at the end of

each rattling phrase – *tissi-cheweeoo*. The song has distinct 'dialects', differing from one part of the country to another. They also have an easily recognised *pink pink* alarm call. They flock in winter and range widely for food, when resident birds are joined by continental birds.

The chaffinch is primarily a bird of woodland and woodland edges, but it also breeds in scrub, thickets, parkland, hedges and gardens. The nest is usualiy in the fork of a tree or taller shrub. 15 cm.

Redwings and fieldfares migrate here from Scandinavia in autumn and during the winter feed in small flocks, often with our resident thrushes and blackbirds. The orange underwing of the redwing shows as it flies, the fieldfare shows a white underwing.

On clear autumn nights you might hear the hissing *seep* flight call of redwings as they fly over head. Ground calls include chuckles. Redwing 23 cm. Fieldfare 26 cm.

Nest sites of hedgerow birds

Wood edge, scrub or thicket

greenfinch

barn owl

kestrel

magpie

linnet

whitethroat

yellowhammer

dunnock

birds which may nest in hedgerow trees, pages 50–53

birds and buildings, page 131

more birds of thick low cover, pages 53–54

birds of open ground, pages 144–145

In many ways a hedge resembles the edge of a wood; however nesting birds are likely to choose a hedge for the cover it provides, rather than the species of the woody plants or its aspect. The kestrel is a good example of the adaptability of birds: it nests in holes in trees, but also in buildings and cliff ledges.

Rabbits, moles and hedgehogs are associated also with hedgerows and are shown on page 146 – both these mammals and the ones on this page are to be expected in woodland, scrub and on waste land. Mammals associated with water are shown on page 184. Deer are on page 58.

Roadside mammals

At first sight the roadside seems a most hostile environment for a mammal. The thundering noise of the traffic, fumes from exhausts and the continual stream of litter that cascades from cars all appear to deter wildlife. In fact, a few mammals have been quick to exploit the environment. Mice and voles can be seen scurrying along amongst the grass and thistles. In some counties stoats and weasels have taken up residence in roadside rock crevices and tree hollows. Bats can also be seen flying around hedgerow trees at night.

The domed nests of the harvest mouse (left) **and dormouse** (right). Dormouse nests are usually made from the stripped papery bark of honeysuckle and can be found above the ground amongst hazel coppice stools. Harvest mouse nursery nests are usually built amongst the stems of tall grasses, including at one time, growing grain crops. Initially built within a few centimetres of the ground they are slowly raised as the grass grows.

Hibernation

Many animals become lethargic when the weather is cold. Warm-blooded animals counteract this by maintaining a high body temperature whatever the weather. This uses up a great deal of food, however, and some animals hibernate during winter, when food is scarce.

Insects become dormant during the winter – their inert body (whether as larva or adult) appears to freeze without damage. Vertebrate animals suffer from frostbite if ice forms inside their body cells, so that hibernating mammals need the insulation of fat and fur to prevent this disaster. During hibernation, their breathing slows and body temperature drops – hibernation is something more than simply a deep sleep. Although many mammals spend some time dormant, only the dormouse truly hibernates. Also known as the sleep mouse, this attractive animal is totally inactive over winter. Bats and hedgehogs, however, are usually active for short periods in the course of the cold season.

Winter activity especially puts bats at risk. They rely on the fat reserves built during the summer – if they do wake and fly in winter, they have no hope of catching flying insects to replace the wasted energy.

Weasel
Mustela nivalis

Weasels prey on mice, voles and young rabbits which are much larger than themselves. They will also attack rats. They are active at night and also during the day, when they can be seen coursing a hedgerow with a sinuous, gliding run and also swim for fish and climb for birds' eggs. They nest in holes or hollows in trees. To 25 cm.

Stoat
Mustela erminea

stoat in winter ermine coat

Common shrew
Sorex araneus

The stoat is larger than the weasel and more clearly white under the belly. In winter, the northern stoat becomes white – but the tail always keeps its noticeable black tip (the winter fur is ermine). It moves by a series of low bounds, hunting animals and fish. To 40 cm.

The pygmy shrew is our smallest mammal, distinguished from the common shrew by its proportionally longer tail. To 6 cm; tail is two thirds as long as the head and body.

The common shrew has a fine, toothed snout which shows that it is an insect eater. It is rarely seen, but sometimes heard screaming loudly when it meets another. To 7 cm long; tail half as long as the head and body.

Bank voles are reddish-brown and make shallow runs in the cover of hedgebanks where they may sometimes be seen foraging. They have a catholic diet, even climbing bushes for leaves and fruit.

The long-tailed field mouse or wood mouse has an underground burrow, though it may use empty birds' nests as a food cache. It is active in winter and will bound away when disturbed, zigzagging in a bouncy fashion. To 19 cm.

Bank voles eat seeds. They are larger than field voles and seen in many different places, usually in more open ground. They nest in a small tunnel system. To 15 cm.

Field or short-tailed voles eat grass and do not compete with bank voles. They have rather shaggy coats, snub faces and short, pink tails. To 15 cm.

Dormice live in some old coppiced woods in the south of England where they collect hazel nuts and strip honeysuckle bark for their nests. They hibernate in a ground nest. They have bushy tails, orange-brown backs and large eyes. To 15 cm.

Feeding remains

Hazelnuts are a favourite food for several hedgerow mammals including mice, voles and squirrels. A close look at the discarded nut can sometimes reveal which mammal (or bird) has eaten the nut. Squirrels tend to split the nuts in two with their powerful incisors. Voles hold the nuts away from them and leave a neatly gnawed rim showing no incisor marks on the outer surface. Nuts eaten by mice show faint lower incisor marks on the surface. Birds tend to leave jagged broken holes.

A store of hazelnuts left by a woodmouse underneath a tree.

Pipistrelles are our smallest and commonest bats, roosting in trees and buildings. They have a high jerky flight and can be seen soon after sunset. They need to catch about 3,000 insects a night. 21 cm ws.

Noctule bats fly before sunset. They have golden-brown fur which gleams in the evening light. They roost in trees and have a quick, dashing, swift-like flight. They have short rounded ears. 40 cm ws.

Long-eared bats often pick insects from leaves on the wing. They have very large upright ears and are sometimes found hibernating in clusters in attics. 25 cm ws.

Pipistrelle bat
Pipistrellus pipistrellus

Long-eared bat
Plecotus auritus

Field vole
Microtus agrestis

Noctule bat
Nyctalus noctula

Dormouse
Muscardinus avellanarius

Field mouse
Apodemus sylvaticus

Pygmy shrew
Sorex minutus

Bank vole
Clethrionomys glareolus

Bats

Bats have had a very mixed history of popularity. Through the ages they have been regarded as demons and portents of evil. With their nocturnal lifestyle and unearthly looks, perhaps this is hardly surprising. In more recent times they have been looked upon with more benevolence as we have begun to understand their astonishing sense of direction finding, and to forgive them for their ugliness and crepuscular habits.

Bats navigate and find food by way of their sophisticated echo-locating system. They emit a series of high pitched shrieks usually above the human range of hearing (children and those with more sensitive ears can sometimes hear them). These sounds echo off anything they hit and the bats' ears detect these echoes, enabling them to build up a 'sound picture' of all that is around them. This natural radar system can detect flying insects only one centimetre across. Some moths seem to have an anti-echo device – see page 47.

In recent years, there has been a sharp decline in the number of bats in Britain and they are now protected animals. This decline is the result of many factors – one is that there are far fewer insects for them to catch as a result of the disappearance and 'improvement' of old meadows and other rough grassland.

Different kinds of bat prefer different roosts: some choose trees, while others select buildings, where they seek out draught and dust-free attics and cavities. Colonies of bats are more likely in modern houses, not derelict barns. Half of the bats found in buildings roost in houses less than 25 years old. All bats hibernate, but in mild winters when few insects are about they may wake and waste their precious food reserves.

Lichens are excellent air pollution indicators, as is explained on page 18. Walls make good habitats for spiders (page 108) as well as bees and wasps. They are often covered with ivy and other climbers (36, 84). Page 156 shows how stone walls are made.

Wildlife on walls

Some stone and brick walls are centuries old and present a curious habitat for colonisation by all kinds of plants and animals. A wall with crumbling mortar or tumble down stones is ecologically almost a miniature cliff and its vegetation may reflect this. Dry stone walls tend to be the oldest walls and many are rather delapidated now. Sometimes, in the Lake District, for example, they may still mark out steep hillsides, almost in the same condition as when they were built.

From an ecological point of view walls are a harsh habitat for animals and plants. The drainage is very fast and they are usually exposed. If the air is moist, as it is in the west of Britain, then you can at least expect to see plenty of lichens. If the wall is built of limestone, or the mortar between the rocks is limy, there will be a different selection of lichens compared to a wall composed of acid stone, such as granite.

Some kinds of plants are more often seen on walls than anywhere else, for example, ivy-leafed toadflax and red valerian. Pellitory-of-the-wall is, as its name implies, also found typically on walls. The first word in its name is a corruption of the Latin adjective for wall, so its name literally means 'wall of the wall'. Many mosses are also found on walls.

Look for plants that have seeded themselves from nearby gardens. You may see them flowering, but somewhat dwarfed as a result of the dry, minimal amount of soil. Wallflowers are frequently seen living up to their name; most are garden escapes. The wild wallflower, brought here from cliffs in southern Europe many centuries ago, has bright yellow flowers.

Pellitory-of-the-wall is a true native, also found on sea cliffs, which is its original home. The leaves have soft hairs. Note their alternate arrangement up the stem. May-September; to 70 cm.

Ivy-leaved toadflax is as common as pellitory but is not a native, although it has grown wild for 300 years. After flowering the seed stalks curl to escape the sunshine and so 'plant' the seeds in cracks. May-September; stems to 70 cm long.

Red valerian is a thriving foreigner, often seen growing wild in the south. May-July; to 70 cm.

An old stone wall in the Peak District with a fine covering of lichens and mosses. The moist upland climate is ideal for the growth of these sensitive plants but even up in these hills their growth may be affected by the aerial pollution carried from the surrounding industrial areas.

Tortula forms small cushions and is one of our most familiar mosses. It is commoner on walls than anywhere else. The hairs at the end of the leaves are straight when moist, curled when dry. Here we show just a few shoots; in time they will grow thickly together to create a low cushion on the surface. The wall feather moss is shown far right.

Lichens are complex plants – a delicate partnership between an algal plant and a fungus. They have no roots and rely on rain to wash down a mineral supply which makes them sensitive to any poisons the rain may be carrying.

Red osmia bees are rather like honey bees but they collect pollen on their bellies (honey bees have their pollen baskets on their hind legs). They nest in cracks in stone walls or buildings. To 15 mm.

Red osmia bee
Osmia rufa

Pellitory-of-the-wall
Parietaria judaica

Red valerian
Centranthus ruber

Ivy-leaved toad flax
Cymbalaria muralis

Web of
Amaurobius
spider

Wall feather moss
Camptothecium lutescens

wolf spider

Lichen
Caloplaca heppiana

Wall moss
Tortula muralis

Lichen
Physica caesia

Lichen
Parmelia saxatilis

LIMESTONE

ACID

Lichens

Although fragile looking plants, lichens are extremely slow growing and long-lived – they can often be proved to be 100 years old or more. The Victorians were dedicated lichenologists and we have inherited their careful records.
Sometimes the age of the rock face can be 'dated' by the size and character of the lichens growing on it.

Some lichens have a strong link with the past history of Britain. A maritime lichen *Ramalina* (related to the sea ivory) is common at certain places around our coasts. It is, however, also found on the ancient sarsens of Stonehenge and on the stones of the ancient circles of Avebury. Stonehenge is almost 100 kilometres from the nearest coast. Furthermore the hard rock the lichen needs is not found before the West Country several hundreds of kilometres to the south-west.

Churchyards are good places to study lichens. Often the older gravestones are beautifully patterned with many different species. Furthermore, it is probable that several different types of stone will be found in a churchyard with some being made from acidic granite or volcanic rock and others from limestone, each with their own array of lichens. These also benefit from the often plentiful bird droppings, as graveyards are frequently favourite bird roosts.

Plants of old grassland can be seen on pages 122, 124, 148 and 150. As many as thirty different species are sometimes found growing in each square metre – they flower in succession as the summer advances. There may also be ten or more wild grasses (page 120).

Old grass fields

Until recent centuries the only way of keeping farm animals alive during the winter was by feeding them hay cut from meadows during the summer. The importance of these grass fields to the farmer was therefore immense; they were never ploughed and had their own management regime. Animals were grazed on them after the cut, but other fields were used solely for grazing. They too, were rarely ploughed and over the centuries wild flowers colonised the undisturbed soil of these grasslands.

Over the past 50 years these ancient grasslands, more than any other part of our countryside, have faced a quiet but lethal revolution; almost all have already changed beyond recall. Herbicides (weedkillers) are routinely used to kill the wild flowers for the benefit of grasses and improved drainage may parch out a host of damp-loving plants. It often makes good economic sense to plough up an old grass field and resow it with modern hybrid high-yield grasses which, if sown as a 'ley' is ploughed up again after two to five years. This is much too short a time for the wild flowers to re-establish themselves.

Animals are often grazed on these ley fields, but hay is rarely cut. Instead the grass is mown short when young and green, and cut more than once a year to be stored as slightly fermented green silage for winter cattle fodder. Some farms have silo towers for this, but often the silage is piled under black polythene sheeting weighted down with old car tyres – a familiar sight in the countryside today.

All these changes in management have led to changes in the character of grass fields and, surprising as it may seem, wild flowers will also suffer if nothing is done to the field except treating it with fertiliser. The fodder grasses flourish and smother their wild flower neighbours. Some of the delightful wild grasses also disappear from this fertilised grassland; sweet vernal grass with its strong hay smell is one of the first to go.

The way that the field is grazed can also have an effect: sheep (and rabbits) produce a fine springy sward, cattle and horses tear the grass. Horses are somewhat choosy about taste, and may leave patches of grass. Cattle will not graze around cow pats, leaving tall dark green tufts of grass. Here there may also be nettles or thistles which seed into the rich soil. If overgrazing of any type occurs large bare areas appear and tough plants, such as nettles, docks and thistles, invade. One way or another almost any change to the traditional management of these old grass fields adds up to a catastrophe for the wild flowers.

The abandoned workings of these ancient chalk pits in Hampshire have been colonised over the centuries by many grassland plants including these cowslips which not only provide a glorious display in spring but are also the food plant of the local Duke of Burgundy fritillary butterfly. Old abandoned workings such as this often provide important reservoirs of old grassland plants, as they would have been re-colonised at a time when the surrounding fields would have been far richer in plant species. The uneven terrain means that they cannot easily be ploughed or sprayed.

Ant hills, like this one covered in thyme, are usually a reliable indicator of old unploughed pasture as the mounds may take many centuries to reach this size.

Finding an old grass field

Permanent grassland, in origin cleared woodland, and maintained by centuries of grazing, is a balanced community of plants and animals.

The colour is an important clue to identifying old grass fields. The modern ley field is a vivid green whereas an old grass field is tawny in colour, the exact shade varying from month to month as some plants flourish then die down.

The colour also varies from place to place, as slight differences in soil favour some plants over others.

Old grassland carries bumps and hollows, features which would be smoothed down by ploughing. The pattern of medieval ridge and furrow is quite often seen under grass, showing the land has not been ploughed for centuries.

The slight changes created by these ridges are frequently marked by a change in the mix of plants. Rushes, for example, may be scattered along the valleys of the damper furrows.

The variety of plant life can be astonishing, with up to thirty different flowers and ten wild grasses growing in each square metre. This is exceptional, but as a rule of thumb suspect that the field is old if more than five species of wild grass are growing abundantly in it.

Ant hills are a good clue to an old pasture field as they make mowing difficult and are cleared from hay meadows as well as improved pastures.

Some flowers such as the yellow rattle are good indicators of old grassland, because they cannot survive disturbance or only establish themselves slowly. Examples of these are shown on pages 122, 148 and 149.

A scatter of bushes is often a feature of unimproved grassland

Long hauls with the plough in medieval times created a pattern of 'ridge and furrow', still to be seen under many ancient grasslands today. Very often the ridge and furrow crosses below the more recent enclosure hedges.

drier ridges   damper hollows

Three important fodder grasses are shown on page 134; they will also be found growing wild. See page 62 for wood melick, and page 64 for common bent, an acid-soil indicator. Moorland grasses are shown on page 160, aquatic and other grasses on pages 176, 206, 240.

Grasses

1 Tor grass (*Brachypodium pinnatum*) **is commonly found on abandoned chalk** or limestone grazing and it can spread rapidly with its underground rhizomes to form dense yellow patches. It does well on burnt ground, and only ploughing will remove it. July; 30–90 cm.

2 Sheep's fescue (*Festuca ovina*) **is classically found on grazed land**. It has fine leaves, which are curled round to keep down water loss. It can form tufts, and covers the ground, but it does not possess runners. It is a favourite of sheep. One variety is found on chalk, another on acid soils. May-July; 5–60 cm.

3 Creeping bent (*Agrostis stolonifera*) **can be found in many different open habitats**. It is a tufted perennial with yellowish, sometimes purplish, flowerheads. It spreads via creeping runners. July-August, 10–40 cm.

4 Quaking grass (*Briza media*) **is arguably our loveliest grass** with its hanging purplish spikelets which dance in the breeze. It produces few leaves. It is found in many different open habitats, particularly on calcareous soils. June-July; 20–50 cm.

5 Crested dog's-tail (*Cynosurus cristatus*) **grows in tight clumps** with an abundance of flat smooth leaves – it creates the tall spikes seen on ill-kept lawns. The spikelets are all turned one way, forming a one-sided head. It is a rather tough grass, avoided by cattle when found in pasture. June-August; to 75 cm.

6 Yorkshire fog (*Holcus lanatus*) **is a gorgeous grass** which holds the morning mist creating, it seems, a mist of its own along the ground. It is covered with soft hairs which give it a downy feel. The flowerhead is pinkish or rather purple. It is often seen as a 'weed' in older grass leys. June-September; 20–60 cm.

7 Red fescue (*Festuca rubra*) **is a darker green than sheep's fescue**, with stouter flowerheads, forming dense clumps of fine leaves. A rather pretty pink or purple flowerhead. It has runners which easily root to produce new plants. May-July; to 70 cm.

◀ **An area of limestone grassland**, fenced off from sheep, allowing the grass to flourish uncropped. The distinctive flower heads of crested dog's-tail and cocksfoot can be seen against the sky line.

▼ **The evening light** catching the flower head of one of our most common grasses – cocksfoot.

Grasses are, in fact, flowering plants, even though their flowers are hard to see. Instead of petals, they have reduced leaves which enclose the male and female parts of the flower. These small florets are grouped, two or more, in spikelets, and these in turn are grouped together to form the head or panicle of the grass. This head may have a distinctive and easily recognised shape, which makes the wild grasses not as difficult to identify as may seem at first sight. Other identification clues are the way that the thin green leaves join the stem, as well as the general appearance of the plant.

Grasses are outstandingly successful plants. Some of them can quickly create carpets, spreading by overground runners, or underground stems called rhizomes. Many grow in a tufted fashion, often quite tall. But when grazed they may form a compact sward. They are able to survive grazing, cutting and trampling because the growing areas of the shoots are not at the tip as in most plants, but well down close to the ground. Some grasses are annuals, dying down in winter to grow again from seed the next spring. The perennial grasses are sometimes evergreen, but most die down to the rootstock in the autumn, to grow again in the new year.

Different grasses grow best under different conditions and (as with other plants) the mixture of grasses you see growing in any place reflects the soil and management history of the site.

Grasses are wind pollinated and produce large amounts of pollen which, along with the pollen of nettles and plantains, constitutes one of the prime causes of hay fever. It is estimated that upright brome produces the most pollen. It has also been discovered that different grasses release pollen at different times of day. Timothy releases pollen very early, at break of dawn, but to do so it needs sunshine the previous evening. Cocksfoot and many fescues release pollen at about 6 am, rye grass at noon, while Yorkshire fog releases its pollen twice a day, at 8 am and again in the afternoon.

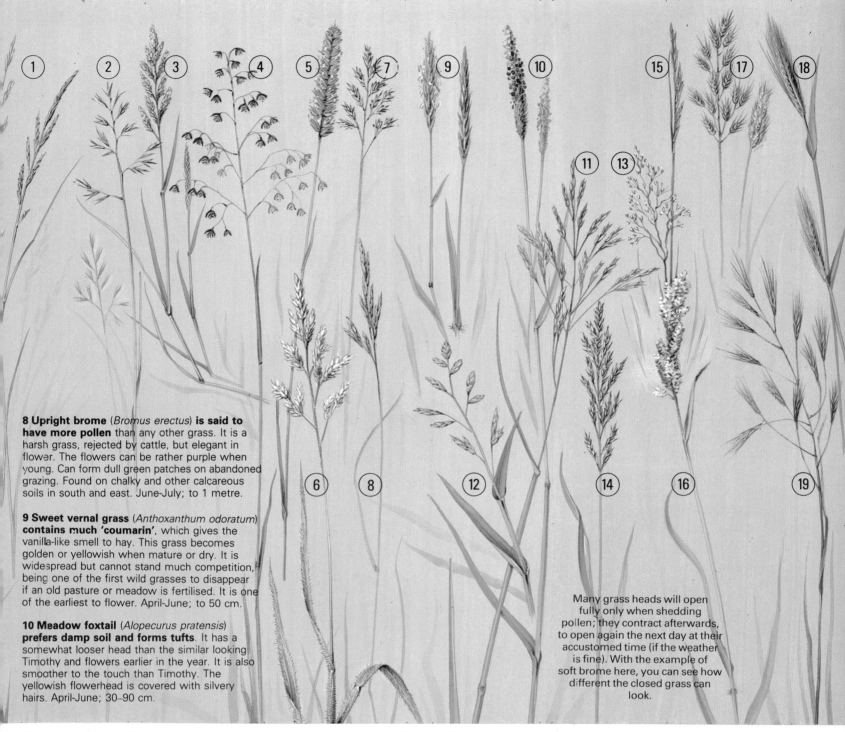

8 Upright brome (*Bromus erectus*) **is said to have more pollen** than any other grass. It is a harsh grass, rejected by cattle, but elegant in flower. The flowers can be rather purple when young. Can form dull green patches on abandoned grazing. Found on chalky and other calcareous soils in south and east. June-July; to 1 metre.

9 Sweet vernal grass (*Anthoxanthum odoratum*) **contains much 'coumarin'**, which gives the vanilla-like smell to hay. This grass becomes golden or yellowish when mature or dry. It is widespread but cannot stand much competition, being one of the first wild grasses to disappear if an old pasture or meadow is fertilised. It is one of the earliest to flower. April-June; to 50 cm.

10 Meadow foxtail (*Alopecurus pratensis*) **prefers damp soil and forms tufts**. It has a somewhat looser head than the similar looking Timothy and flowers earlier in the year. It is also smoother to the touch than Timothy. The yellowish flowerhead is covered with silvery hairs. April-June; 30-90 cm.

Many grass heads will open fully only when shedding pollen; they contract afterwards, to open again the next day at their accustomed time (if the weather is fine). With the example of soft brome here, you can see how different the closed grass can look.

11 Tufted hair-grass (*Deschampsia cespitosa*) **is found on heavy wet soil**, the sides of ditches, old damp grazings, where it forms dense tussocks. The tough, rough leaves can cut your fingers if you pull them. June-August; may be more than a metre tall.

12 Annual meadow-grass (*Poa annua*) **is a classic grass of paths**, tufted but sometimes creeping. It is self-fertilising. It is found in many different places. Note that the leaves are often wrinkled at their base. Flowers all year; 5-30 cm.

13 Wavy hair-grass (*Deschampsia flexuosa*) **is found on moorland** and heaths on acid soils. It grows in tufts, and is rather slender, with narrow bristle-like leaves. It possesses delicate flowers, which create a pink mist across the ground. The flowerhead is spread when open, but contracts tight before and after flowering. June-July; 25-40 cm.

14 False oat-grass (*Arrhenatherum elatius*) **can hold its shiny stems very tall**. It is a classic roadside grass. Its flowerhead is covered in long bristles (awns) which are green at first then become brown or purplish. June-July; to 1.5 metres.

15 Mat-grass (*Nardus stricta*) **is very tough and wiry** and occurs in dense tufts in upland areas. Except when young in spring, the shoots are not eaten by sheep or cattle making this grass stand out as dense patches in grazed meadows. June-August; 10-40 cm.

16 Creeping soft-grass (*Holcus mollis*) **usually grows in woodlands**. It is rather like Yorkshire fog in appearance but less common. Note that it has a ring of hairs around each 'node' on the stem. It has extensive creeping shoots which have made it a troublesome weed. June-August; to 1 metre.

17 Soft brome (*Bromus mollis*) **has large wheat-like heads** which are upright at first then droop. The whole plant is covered in soft hairs. It is widespread, but most common in the lowlands of Britain. May-July; to 1 metre.

18 Wall barley (*Hordeum murinum*) **is an annual grass of roadsides** and waste places. Meadow barley is similar but less 'barley-like', with shorter bristles. June-July; 30-70 cm.

19 Barren brome (*Bromus sterilis*) **is an untidy looking grass**, sprouting from a slightly creeping root with soft, flat, downy leaves. It is common on waste or cultivated land, particularly in hedgerows and field margins. May-July; to 1 metre.

Where to look for grasses

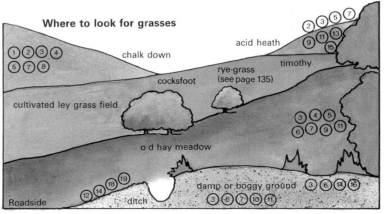

acid heath
chalk down
rye-grass (see page 135)
timothy
cocksfoot
cultivated ley grass field
o d hay meadow
damp or boggy ground
Roadside
ditch

The grass species on open ground may change as the conditions change, for example, traditional grazing of calcareous rocks produced sheep's fescue and bent grass swards. When grazing stops, upright brome grass can invade; or (in the Cotswolds and South Downs) tor grass can form large yellowish patches the first clue of imminent scrub invasion.

The plants shown here tolerate a range of soils, so add them to those on pages 148 and 150. Meadow vetchling, daisy, yarrow and self-heal do not like the soil too acid; yellow rattle does not like it too limy. Ox-eye daisy, knapweed and hawkbit mark neutral soil.

Grassland flowers and fungi

An incredible variety of flowers can be found on old established meadows or pasture, provided it has not been improved by modern agricultural methods. Most of these flowers can only be found where there has been a continuity of sympathetic management for many hundreds of years and so will not be found on recently ploughed land or temporary leys. Some flowers characterise certain types of grassland. Others, such as the daisy, will be found almost anywhere and will even thrive when the soil is improved. In upland regions, however, the presence of the daisy can be used to pick out lime-rich soils. The difference in the diversity of wild flowers found in old and disturbed grassland is very marked. Certain types of fungi are also common in grasslands, not least the edible mushroom.

Bird's-foot trefoil trails long stems from a woody rootstock on all except very acid soils. The pea-like pods carried in a bunch resemble a bird's foot. Though the flowers are yellow, the buds may often be deep red, hence another name for it is 'bacon and eggs'. May-September; stems 10–40 cm.

Kidney vetch is a good indicator of dry, limy soils. A downy perennial, its yellow flowers can be tinted orange or even fiery red. June-September; to 30 cm.

Meadow vetchling has weak scrambling stems. It is a plant of long grass, damp meadows and grass verges. Note the unusual, arrow-shaped 'stipules' at the bottoms of the stalks. May-August; to 1 metre.

Ox-eye daisy is a widespread and smaller relative of the garden 'Shasta daisy'. It has small, dark green, toothed leaves. June-August; to 70 cm.

Daisies may indicate infertile soil, or heavy grazing or trampling. They are sensitive to light and close in dull weather. April-October, may flower all year; to 10 cm.

This ancient hay meadow in the New Forest provides a glorious display of flowers in May and June before the cut. The tall ox-eye daisies and yellow composites colour the top layer of the meadow, while below red clover, plaintains and yellow rattle form an intricate counterpoint.

Parrot toadstools are multi-coloured and grow in small clusters on old grassland. May-October; to 3 cm across.

Ribwort plantain is a familiar lawn weed but is also common in grasslands. The leaves are arranged in a rosette around the flower stalk (note that this is deeply furrowed). April-May; to 40 cm.

The fairy ring fungus produces nitrates which stimulate a ring of lush grass visible before the 'toadstools' appear. The ring is formed as the fungus grows away from soil from which it has taken the nutrients. The 'toadstools' are up to 3 cm in diameter and the ring is up to 3 metres across.

Common mouse-ear is common in grass on a wide range of soils. The name 'mouse ear' refers to its hairy basal leaves. April-October; to 20 cm.

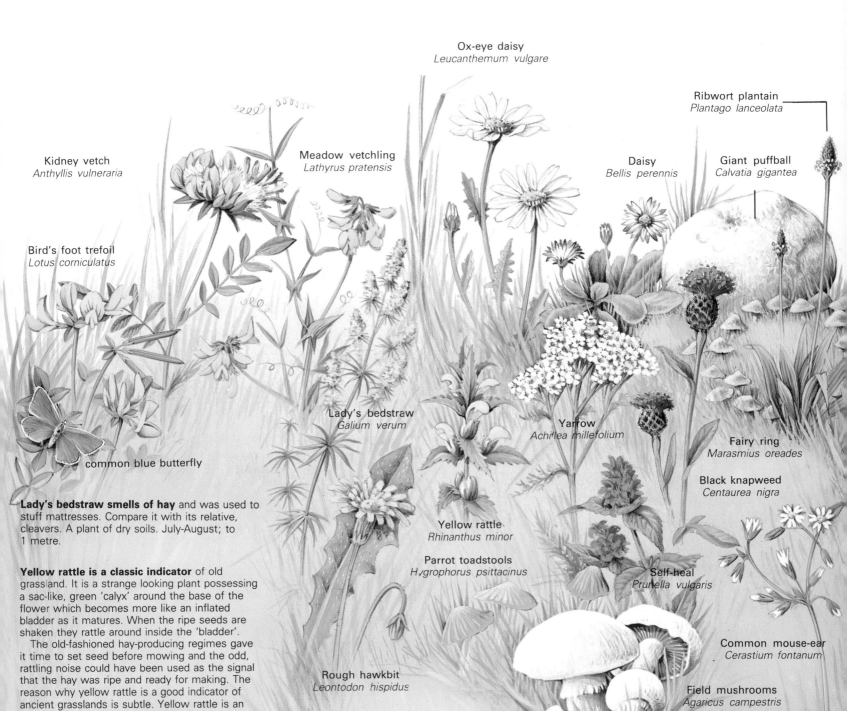

Ox-eye daisy
Leucanthemum vulgare

Ribwort plantain
Plantago lanceolata

Kidney vetch
Anthyllis vulneraria

Meadow vetchling
Lathyrus pratensis

Daisy
Bellis perennis

Giant puffball
Calvatia gigantea

Bird's foot trefoil
Lotus corniculatus

Lady's bedstraw
Galium verum

Yarrow
Achillea millefolium

Fairy ring
Marasmius oreades

common blue butterfly

Black knapweed
Centaurea nigra

Yellow rattle
Rhinanthus minor

Parrot toadstools
Hygrophorus psittacinus

Self-heal
Prunella vulgaris

Common mouse-ear
Cerastium fontanum

Rough hawkbit
Leontodon hispidus

Field mushrooms
Agaricus campestris

Lady's bedstraw smells of hay and was used to stuff mattresses. Compare it with its relative, cleavers. A plant of dry soils. July-August; to 1 metre.

Yellow rattle is a classic indicator of old grassland. It is a strange looking plant possessing a sac-like, green 'calyx' around the base of the flower which becomes more like an inflated bladder as it matures. When the ripe seeds are shaken they rattle around inside the 'bladder'.

The old-fashioned hay-producing regimes gave it time to set seed before mowing and the odd, rattling noise could have been used as the signal that the hay was ripe and ready for making. The reason why yellow rattle is a good indicator of ancient grasslands is subtle. Yellow rattle is an annual flower, sprouting from seed each year. It is, however, semi-parasite and though green and able to photosynthesise, it feeds on, and requires the presence of, the roots of established grasses to supplement its food intake. May-September; 10–30 cm.

Field mushrooms were once very common but are now hard to find. These are an edible mushroom. July onwards; to 8 cm across.

Yarrow (milfoil) **is strongly scented**. It is a plant of the daisy family, though the flowerheads resemble umbellifers. It is a common flower of all grasslands possessing long, narrow, feathery leaves. June-October; to 50 cm.

Black knapweed (hardhead) **is a relative of the cornflower**, with broader leaves. It has a hard, compact, purple flowerhead. Visited by many insects. June-September; to 90 cm.

Rough hawkbit is a dandelion-like flower found on old established, dry grasslands. The fruits make a dirty, white 'clock'. It is a rather hairy plant and the leaves tend to lie on the ground in a rosette around the flower stalk. June-September; 10–40 cm.

Puffballs are round and when ripe have a small opening at the top to release the spores. The giant puffball, shown here, is white at first, turning brown with age and can grow to the size of a football. Late summer.

Self-heal is a member of the labiate family, together with the woodland bugle, which it resembles. It is very common in most types of grassland and flowers later than the bugle: June-October; to 20 cm.

Mushrooms in the grass

The proverbial rapid 'mushrooming growth of the field mushroom takes place after heavy rain in warm weather. They sprout up in large numbers from the parent fungal threads in the soil below, taking no more than a few hours to grow from a small white 'button' to the open mushroom. Nevertheless, they are easy to miss, for they are generally hidden by long grass.

The word mushroom is often used to describe any edible fungus or their look-alikes, the poisonous ones being known as toadstools. These names are not used very exactly.

The field mushroom is a much prized countryside delicacy and was once very common. It seems to have a distinct liking for horse manure, for it flourished in pastures where horses were grazed. It can still be found, but rarely whitens the fields as it once did.

Make sure you pick the edible field mushroom as other poisonous grassland fungi can easily be mistaken for it. The white cap of the field mushroom is from 3 to 8 cm across, and the gills are pink when fresh and young but darken with age to purple-brown. It has a short stem and a ring where the cap was joined to the 'stem' during the young 'button' stage. There is no sheath wrapped around the bottom of the stem. Cut it in half: if the flesh is pure white and/or quickly stains pink or yellow where it has been bruised, it is probably not an edible mushroom. If you are not sure DO NOT TAKE ANY RISKS!

The field mushroom has a larger relation, the horse mushroom, which is also edible. Its cap may be 20 cm across, and it also grows in pastureland.

The shop mushroom is akin to the field mushroom, but another species, with nothing of that sinful taste of its wild cousin!

123

Orchids may be seen in many habitats – not only in woods and grass-lands but also on shelly dunes and spoil tips! Some further species are shown on pages 62 and 71. The scheme below right shows the soil and habitat preferences of some of these intriguing flowers.

Orchids

There are approaching 30,000 species of orchid worldwide, of which only 54 grow in Britain. Our native orchids are not the large tropical species, those ultimate symbols of exotic beauty, grown with such religious enthusiasm by gardeners. British orchids are much more unassuming. One thing that they do have in common with the large tropical species is their fragile and complicated lifestyle. Orchids have minute, dust-like seeds which are spread by the wind, and they must encounter exactly the right conditions if they are to germinate. The seeds carry little or no food reserves, and growth is slow – two or three years may elapse before the first green leaves appear. The twayblade variety takes 12 or more years to flower.

The orchid seedling gains the energy-giving food it needs from mycorrhiza – a helpful soil fungus. The latter invades the roots of the young orchid, but continues in its fungus-like way to obtain food by breaking down decaying matter in the soil. Some of this food is taken by the orchid.

Certain orchids have evolved fascinating methods to lure insects to pollinate them. The bee-orchid flower resembles a female bumble-bee and so attracts the male. Some such as the fragrant orchid have a vivid smell that attracts moths; others such as the twayblade actually glue the pollen to the backs of visiting insects. The complicated lifestyle of orchids possibly makes them ultra-sensitive to local conditions, especially as many of them are at the edge of their geographical range in Britain. Many of our rare orchids are common in France or (in the case of the northerly species) Scandinavia.

▲ **A close-up of the flowers** of the man orchid, (*Aceras anthropomorphum*), showing the 'helmeted' lip, shaped like a human figure. The fantastic shapes and patterns of the orchid flowers are reflected in their unusual names – frog, lizard, lady, butterfly and spider orchid, for example. Some flowers do resemble particular insects in order to attract potential pollinators but many names are purely fanciful.

Bee orchids are found in calcareous grasslands in the south of Britain and in sand dunes in the west. The velvet-like lip resembles the back of a bumble-bee. The grey-green leaves form a basal rosette. It is said that in Europe these orchids are pollinated by bees but in Britain are self-fertilised. June-July; 15 – 40 cm.

The common spotted orchid can be seen in woods, scrub and grassland. The dark blotches are elongated across the leaves. Note that the rosette leaves at the base of the stem are broad. This orchid can be seen throughout Britain. June-July; 15 – 40 cm.

◀ **Three flowering spikes** of the dense-flowered variety of the fragrant orchid growing in damp meadowland amongst sedges and rushes. This variety has a more deeply coloured flower than its more common cousin and a rich carnation scent.

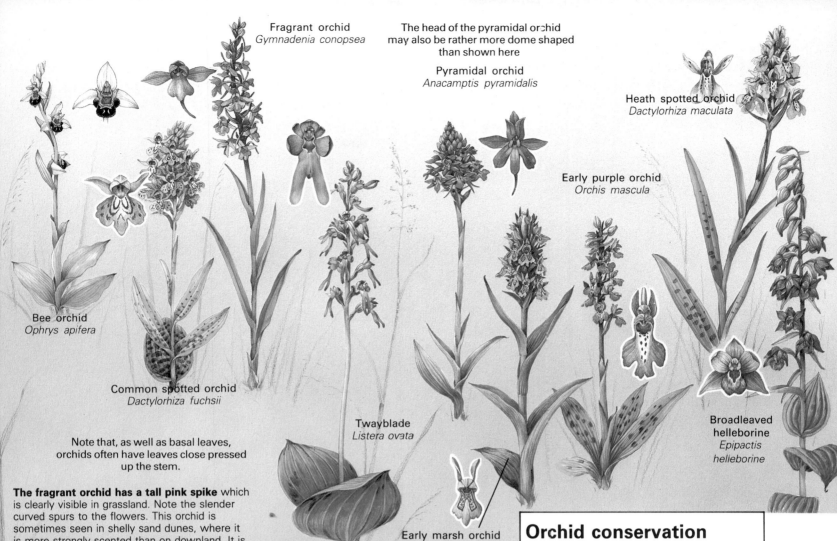

Fragrant orchid
Gymnadenia conopsea

The head of the pyramidal orchid may also be rather more dome shaped than shown here

Pyramidal orchid
Anacamptis pyramidalis

Heath spotted orchid
Dactylorhiza maculata

Early purple orchid
Orchis mascula

Bee orchid
Ophrys apifera

Common spotted orchid
Dactylorhiza fuchsii

Twayblade
Listera ovata

Early marsh orchid
Dactylorhiza incarnata

Broadleaved helleborine
Epipactis helleborine

Note that, as well as basal leaves, orchids often have leaves close pressed up the stem.

The fragrant orchid has a tall pink spike which is clearly visible in grassland. Note the slender curved spurs to the flowers. This orchid is sometimes seen in shelly sand dunes, where it is more strongly scented than on downland. It is the only British orchid to possess a scent which is sweet and musky, but with a rather rancid overtone. Its glossy green leaves are keeled, and ranked up the stem in two rows. June-August; to 40 cm.

Twayblade has a pair of strongly ribbed leaves arising from the stalk a few centimetres above ground. Seen flowering in woods, scrub and open ground. June-July; to 60 cm.

The early purple orchid has a loose flowerhead that smells of cats! The leaf blotches run lengthwise up the shiny leaves. It is found in woods, grasslands and, as it likes some chalkiness, often at the foot of chalk downland slopes. April-June; 15 – 60 cm.

The pyramidal orchid has foxy-smelling flowers. It can often be seen on dryish, chalky rather than chalk, grassland with the fragrant orchid; and sometimes on verges, in easterly counties. June-August; 20 – 30 cm.

The early marsh orchid (meadow orchid) can be common in fens and wet meadows. It has yellow-green, keeled, spotted leaves. Flower colour may vary from yellow to purple. May-July; to 40 cm.

The heath spotted orchid is a flower of wet, acid soils, mainly in the north and west. Unlike the common spotted orchid, all its leaves are narrow, with more or less round dark spots. June-August; 15 – 40 cm.

Broad-leaved helleborine is found in woods and at woodland edges. It has dull green leaves spiralling around its tall stem. Rarely found north of Edinburgh. July-September; to 80 cm.

Orchid conservation and sheep

The frail, weird flowers of orchids, found almost accidentally on walks in the countryside, have always intrigued people. It is, perhaps, rather puzzling that they should be found in some places but not in similar locations nearby, and why in some years the flowers are hard to find and in others they are plentiful.

One of the County Conservation Trusts looks after a scattered handful of chalk grassland nature reserves. They are all small, but full of flowers, including many orchids, although these occur as unpredictably here as anywhere else. The growth of scrub in these pastures chokes the orchids and the Trust has invested in sheep to keep the scrub down. These sheep are not the common meat-producing whites you see crammed into fields today, which close-crop the turf, but more ancient breeds such as the St Kilda. These are scrawny animals, sometimes sporting four horns, and they nibble the young scrub and coarse grasses quite effectively. Another breed used is the Beulah from Wales which does not eat the scrub but lightly crops the grass.

Modern stockmen try to keep sheep on one patch of grass for as long as possible before moving them on, but by moving these unusual sheep in a most unfarmer-like way from one nature reserve to the other, the conservation managers hope to create a diversity in the plant community which will echo the diversity of the ancient chalk downs. On these downs, the sheep used to roam in large flocks following their appetites under the eye of their shepherd (and now there are housewife shepherdesses from the Trust). The hope is that the plant diversity will encourage orchids to flourish, perhaps by stimulating the soil fungi on which they rely. But it may be years before the results are visible.

Soil preferences of some common orchids and helleborines

Dry well drained soil

Like its cousin, the white helleborine, the broadleaved helleborine is a woodland orchid. Twayblade and early purple orchid may be found in woodland as well as in more open habitats.

pyramidal orchid

bee orchid

Bird's-nest orchid

white helleborine
(Beech hangers, page 62)

broadleaved helleborine

early purple orchid

common spotted orchid

fragrant orchid

← twayblade →

Alkaline (limy) soil

Acid soil

creeping lady's tresses
(page 71)

heath spotted orchid

early marsh orchid

Marsh and common spotted orchids can, on occasion, be found on slag heaps, in old quarries and on soil enriched with industrial waste

Damp, poorly drained soil

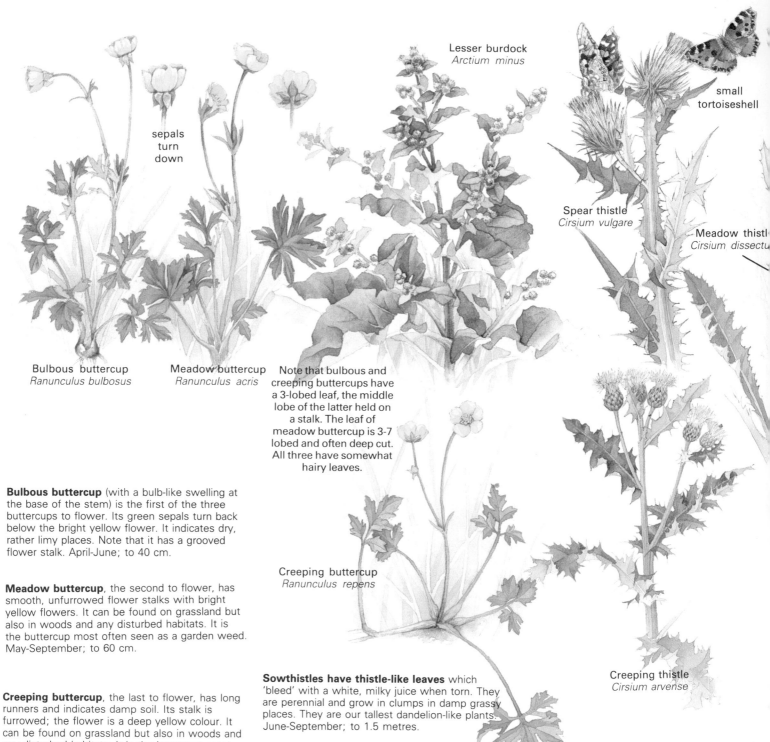

sepals
turn
down

Lesser burdock
Arctium minus

small
tortoiseshell

Spear thistle
Cirsium vulgare

Meadow thistl
Cirsium dissectu

Bulbous buttercup
Ranunculus bulbosus

Meadow buttercup
Ranunculus acris

Note that bulbous and creeping buttercups have a 3-lobed leaf, the middle lobe of the latter held on a stalk. The leaf of meadow buttercup is 3-7 lobed and often deep cut. All three have somewhat hairy leaves.

Creeping buttercup
Ranunculus repens

Creeping thistle
Cirsium arvense

Bulbous buttercup (with a bulb-like swelling at the base of the stem) is the first of the three buttercups to flower. Its green sepals turn back below the bright yellow flower. It indicates dry, rather limy places. Note that it has a grooved flower stalk. April-June; to 40 cm.

Meadow buttercup, the second to flower, has smooth, unfurrowed flower stalks with bright yellow flowers. It can be found on grassland but also in woods and any disturbed habitats. It is the buttercup most often seen as a garden weed. May-September; to 60 cm.

Creeping buttercup, the last to flower, has long runners and indicates damp soil. Its stalk is furrowed; the flower is a deep yellow colour. It can be found on grassland but also in woods and any disturbed habitats. It is the buttercup most often seen as a weed in damp gardens. May-September; to 50 cm.

Lesser burdock grows tall, woolly, branched stems on disturbed ground. It is not a thistle but has prickly heads. The huge leaves are oval in outline. July-September; to 1 metre.

Spear thistle has spiny wings down its tall, cottony stem and spines on the leaves. It generally grows singly. This thistle is the one chosen for the Scottish emblem. It is a 'plume thistle'. The flower is shown here blowsy and about to seed. July-October; to 1.5 metres.

Creeping thistle grows from fragments of underground stems, and so is a tiresome garden weed. The plant produces dense stands of stems. This is perhaps our commonest thistle and the only one with pale lilac flowers (the others have reddish-purple flowers). Note that the flower shoots do not carry spines or 'wings'. It is a 'plume thistle'. June-September; to 90 cm.

Melancholy thistle is often seen with a nodding flowerhead, hence the name. It has soft, toothed (not prickly) leaves. It can be found on wet hillsides in the north, while the somewhat similar meadow thistle is found only in the south. The two do not overlap their range. It is a 'plume thistle'. June-August; to 1.5 metres.

Sowthistles have thistle-like leaves which 'bleed' with a white, milky juice when torn. They are perennial and grow in clumps in damp grassy places. They are our tallest dandelion-like plants. June-September; to 1.5 metres.

Musk thistle has single, drooping flowerheads. It is an indicator of dry, limy soils. May-August; to 1 metre.

Meadow thistle is a slender version of the melancholy thistle – both have leaves that are white below. This, our least spiny thistle, is often seen in wet meadows. It is a 'plume thistle'. June-August; to 50 cm.

A meadow brown butterfly feeding at a creeping thistle flower-head.

Musk thistle
Carduus nutans

Perennial
sow thistle
*Sonchus
arvensis*

Teasel
Dipsacus fullonum

Melancholy
thistle
*Cirsium
heterophyllum*

Teasels are often mistaken for thistles, but note the flower is surrounded by long spiny 'bracts', unlike the thistles. They are most often seen on damp clayey ground. June-September; to 2 metres.

The photograph below shows how plants can precisely reveal slight differences in the soil. Thistles are often busy with bees and other insects. The painted lady butterfly (page 100) lays her eggs on thistles. Goldfinches (page 144) eat the thistle seeds.

Buttercups and thistles

Buttercup is a fairly recent name, only about two hundred years old. Before that the plant was usually (apart from hundreds of local dialect names) called crowsfoot – its waterdwelling relatives still bear that name.

If you can find two, or even all three, of the buttercups shown on this page growing near to each other in a grassy field, it is possible that they may mark out with fine exactness slight differences in the soil. If they are growing on ancient ridge-and-furrow land, for example, you will find the creeping buttercup in the wetter hollows while the meadow buttercup has the competitive edge on the drier ridges. Another interesting fact is that these buttercups have different, but overlapping, flowering periods; the bulbous buttercup is the first to flower, the creeping buttercup the last.

If the grazing on a field is badly managed from a farming point of view, the result may be a field of buttercups. Cattle find them unpalatable. Nowadays, however, buttercups can sometimes 'signpost' a rare unimproved field. There are two main types of purple-coloured thistles. The 'plume thistles' have a very feathery head of 'thistledown' to each seed and their stems may sometimes have a winged profile. The other group of thistles, of which musk thistle is a good example, have seeds which, though haired, lack a real plume and their stems are edged with very spiny wings.

There are also the yellow thistles. These are relatives of the hawkweed tribe and have softish hollow stems which exude white 'milk' when they are snapped.

Thistles can be found most frequently growing out on grassland as they are easily spread by their underground stems or their seeds to colonise bare patches of ground. Spear and creeping thistle can be found on grass leys.

The teasel is thistle-like but does not belong to the daisy family to which all true thistles belong. Teasels are in a family of their own, and are related to the attractive scabious flowers.

The tops of the contours cf ancient ridge-and-furrow patterns have been neatly picked out by meadow buttercups in this area of hawthorn scrub and open pasture.

The shrubs that play a role in succession are shown on pages 82 and 28. Heathers are shown on page 160, gorse on 166, and the tree species on pages 20–26. The original scrub may persist as one of the noticeable 'layers' of the wood – see page 13.

Commons and scrub

England and Wales still have about one and a half million acres (600,000 hectares) of common land ranging from small village greens to vast tracts of fell grazing in the Lake District and other wilderness areas. (Scotland does not have common land as such.) This land is not 'common' in the sense that it automatically belongs to the public. Each parcel of common ground has an owner, originally the lord of the manor, but nowadays it is more likely to be the local council, or a commercial company of some kind. Historically, commons were unused or waste lands belonging to the lord of the manor but to which the cottagers (commoners) of the manor had certain rights. They could pasture their animals on rough grazings or feed their pigs on the acorns of the wood pasture and could dig for peat and collect branches for fuel. In some parishes they had rights to any coal and other minerals they could collect. Today the public has right of access to all commons owned by the local authorities, and those in the wider countryside are usually freely open, though the right to graze animals may be vested with only a handful of local people.

Commons include many different kinds of habitat – woods, open grassland, heaths and moors. Much of the land has always been considered marginal, and grazing may well have ceased. If so, scrub will have invaded. Commons are ideal places to observe the succession from grass to scrub through to woodland.

Two aerial photographs of the ancient quarries of Barnack, near Stamford, showing the effect that removal of grazing pressure has on the vegetation. The left photograph was taken in July 1948 and it can be seen that, apart from a few areas of scrub in the far left of the picture, the site was largely open grassland. Up until that time a combination of sheep and more recently rabbit grazing had helped to keep the scrub out. In the photograph right, taken in late June 1976, the encroachment of scrub, mostly Turkey oak, from the wood was quite extensive. The more open area in the top left of the picture had been kept clear by the local Trust. Today, with fencing and the reintroduction of sheep grazing, as well as physical clearance of the scrub, the ancient grasslands of the quarry have become more open again.

Hawthorn and blackthorn (sloe) **are often found in scrub**. Their prickles help to protect oak and other saplings which would otherwise be destroyed by grazing. Blackthorn is a prime thicket shrub. It is light-demanding and sends up shoots some way from the main stem, creating a dense tangle.

The first woody colonisers are usually spiny. In their shelter, safe from grazing animals, the tree seedlings can grow.

On chalky soils in the south, these pioneering shrubs may include dogwood and wayfaring tree. Juniper, too, may appear early on, and be a 'nurse' to yew (page 30).

Plant succession in scrubland

As soon as managed land is left to its own devices, a succession of plants invades. First, if the soil is bare, come annual weeds. Then long-lived grasses and other perennials invade, perhaps creating dense stands. In time the seeds of woody shrubs and trees reach the site and if there is no grazing or cutting they grow to form scrub and eventually a tangled thicket. The young trees in time grow tall, and in about 60 years from bare ground, a wood is formed. Woodland is the natural 'climax' cover of much of Britain.

The bushes and young trees invading abandoned grazings will usually include hawthorn and elder. Those invading heathland will include birch and gorse. Obviously, what does invade depends on local seed sources. If there is a plantation nearby, pine may be an early arrival.

On exposed hills and near the coast, you may find scrub 'held' and not developing further. The wind and cold are the reasons for this.

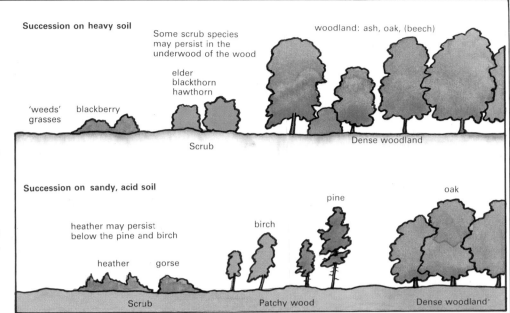

Succession on heavy soil

'weeds' grasses — blackberry — Scrub — elder blackthorn hawthorn — Some scrub species may persist in the underwood of the wood — woodland: ash, oak, (beech) — Dense woodland

Succession on sandy, acid soil

heather — gorse — Scrub — heather may persist below the pine and birch — birch — pine — Patchy wood — oak — Dense woodland

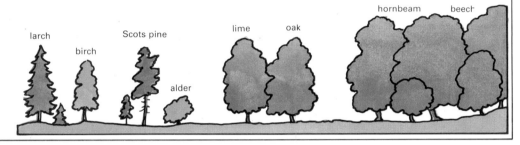

Light demands of growing trees

Least tolerant of shade: light demanding   Most tolerant of shade when growing

larch — birch — Scots pine — alder — lime — oak — hornbeam — beech

Some of the first colonists of bare soil are to be found on pages 94 and 96. Even on urban wasteland you may see some of the plants shown on page 36. Climbers are also common – see page 84. See page 100 for likely butterflies, besides the white butterflies of page 242.

Waste ground: a tomato's tale

Imagine, if you will, a pub in any town. Most, today, provide lunches of all sorts to accompany the beer. Often there is a yard at the back, with tables to sit by in summer, and a patch of waste ground alongside where cans and other litter collect. Look closely and you may find healthy tomato plants growing from the sandwich ends thrown out of the pub garden.

Waste ground is a haven for plants of unexpectedly bizarre origin. Almost everyone has dumped garden rubbish on waste ground, so you can expect plenty of garden plants, but look also for more exotic plants.

If you plant some bird seed you may be surprised to see what comes up apart from the expected sunflowers. This is just one of the sources of exotic plants that appear on refuse sites. Not many decades ago waste tips in the north sprouted plants grown from seeds brought from all over the world in the wool used to make cloth.

Waste ground is not hard to find in today's built-up areas – but also in the

mechanised and developed countryside.

If the ground is being colonised from scratch, then you will see much the same kind of succession as appears on an abandoned field – with the quick-seeding opportunist plants growing first, followed by taller scrub and then trees. What is interesting about waste land is the cosmopolitan origin of its colonisers. For example, Japanese knotweed from Japan, buddleia from China and sycamore, which was introduced into Britain from central and southern Europe.

Waste land often attracts a distinctive animal life. You cannot draw hard and fast boundaries for mobile animals such as birds, which are quick to exploit new sources of food. The town pigeon, for example, will make a home almost anywhere, as will kestrels, which have nested right in the heart of London. Gulls regularly feed on city waste-tips.

It is only in this century that we have looked on this wildlife on our doorstep with anything like a benevolent eye. In Victorian times, birds were to be eaten – Mrs Beeton gives recipes for blackbird pie – and tens of thousands of skylarks each year were sold in London's markets.

One serious threat to the bird (and animal) life of waste lands in towns does remain today: the cat. Not the family moggy, but the large, feral populations of cats. Hundreds have been removed from old hospitals, warehouses and similar structures in Birmingham and elsewhere. They find security in the labyrinth of ducts and low tunnels below such buildings – and their effect on the local population of birds, mice, rats and other mammals must be immense.

The town pigeon

Town pigeons are descended from rock doves – which can still be found breeding wild on the coasts of western Scotland. Domesticated rock doves may have been brought to Britain by the Romans. They have a long breeding season, almost all year if they have plenty of food. They provided fresh winter meat, the young 'squabs' being regarded as a delicacy. Dovecots owned by the lord of the manor were common in the countryside, and were much hated by the medieval peasants for the birds took much of the grain they laboriously sowed on the fields.

Pigeons eventually escaped and took to living in towns, which provided ledges similar to those of their ancestral cliffs. They were also bred for show purposes and some of these escaped. Homing pigeons that did not make it home, joined the feral town flocks. All in all a bewildering variety of plumage, both in pattern and colour, resulted, but it is possible to pick out three main kinds today. Bars are nearest to the wild rock dove pattern. They are greyish blue with white rump and a sheen to their neck and two dark wing bars. Checkers (which can be various colours) have speckled plumage. Velvets (again, various colours can be seen) are plain. They all have marginally different breeding habits or other preferences. For example, bars are rather more frequent in the flocks of town pigeons in the north of Britain than in the south, and there are more of them to be seen out of the big cities—more in Cheshire than in Manchester.

Oxford ragwort, photographed appropriately in front of a passing train. These alien plants produce masses of wind-blown seed and it has been suggested that the seeds are sucked along the track by the draught created by the trains.

The silver Y moths, so named from their wing marks, often fly in daylight and are seen on waste ground. Each year migrants cross from Europe and breed. They occur in large numbers in autumn in some years, but do not survive the winter. Note the unusual 'hump' of the wings behind the head. To 39 mm long.

Buddleia is very attractive to butterflies (and other insects) – hence its name 'butterfly bush'. It is familiar on many waste sites, having seeded from gardens during the last two or three decades. The purple flower spikes are seen July-September; to 5 metres.

Common ragwort can be seen growing stiffly upright. It is found on poor grasslands, and is usually a sign of overgrazing. It is also common on waste ground. June to October; to 1 metre.

Cinnabar moth and its caterpillar possess classic examples of warning coloration. Both are extremely unpleasant-tasting. The colonies of caterpillars feed quite openly on ragwort, sometimes on groundsel. 20 mm or more long.

Wall barley has long bristly seed heads which make those familiar darts thrown by children. Wall barley is an annual grass, though it often overwinters. It is one of the world's most widespread plants, though it is not found in either Iceland or Albania! See other grasses typical of waste places on page 120.

Orpine is a succulent plant, with rather waxy leaves. It is more likely to be seen on sand or gravel but always in dry places. Orpine can often be seen in old-fashioned cottage gardens, where it may have been grown for centuries. It can therefore mark the site of a derelict cottage. July-September; to 60 cm.

Monk's-hood is mainly a garden plant. It can be found 'wild' in shady places by streams in South Wales and south-west England, but the plant most likely to be found is an escape from garden stock. This garden variety has less narrowly-cut leaves than the wild one. It is very poisonous and was, perhaps, first grown because of this. It is an attractive flower and, like orpine, may mark the site of an old cottage garden. May-September; to 1 metre.

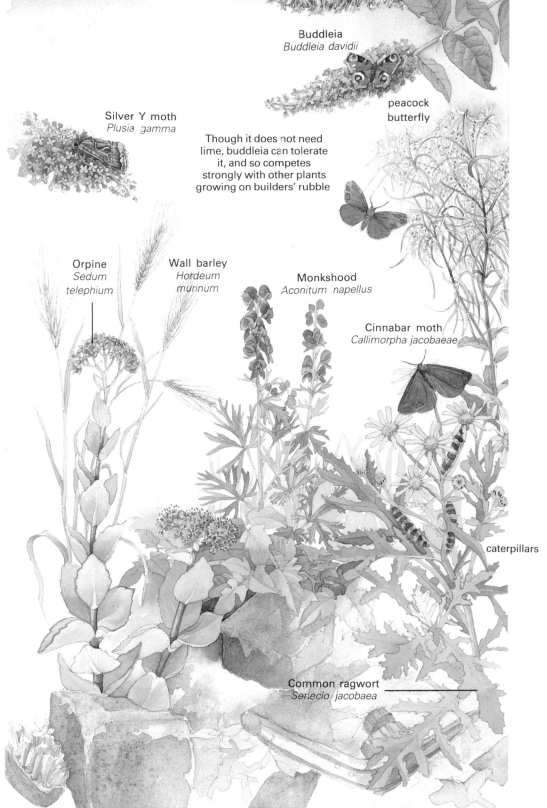

Buddleia
Buddleia davidii

peacock butterfly

Silver Y moth
Plusia gamma

Though it does not need lime, buddleia can tolerate it, and so competes strongly with other plants growing on builders' rubble

Orpine
Sedum telephium

Wall barley
Hordeum murinum

Monkshood
Aconitum napellus

Cinnabar moth
Callimorpha jacobaeae

caterpillars

Common ragwort
Senecio jacobaea

Oxford ragwort is a relative of the common ragwort and possesses an interesting history. It was first brought here in the 17th century as a botanist's specimen for the Oxford Botanic Garden. Its native home is lava soils on the slopes of Mount Etna and other volcanoes. By 1800 it had escaped from the botanic garden and was growing on old walls in the town. In 1879 it was seen growing on cindery railway lines, which were very like its original habitat. Passing trains spread seeds across England, to Cornwall, London and the Midlands. During the blitz of the last World War, it gained a hold on the bombed sites of London, together with rosebay willowherb. Today it seems to be extinct in London, but can be found elsewhere in England, on dry soil, but especially along railway tracks. Note the brilliant yellow of its flowers, which are 16–20 mm across. April-December; to 30 cm.

Nesting places of birds found on waste ground

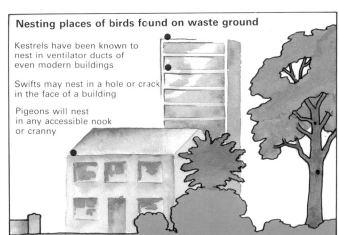

Kestrels have been known to nest in ventilator ducts of even modern buildings

Swifts may nest in a hole or crack in the face of a building

Pigeons will nest in any accessible nook or cranny

Hole-nesting birds are not attracted by the young, healthy trees of built-up areas (if the trees are not healthy they are felled!). Neither are the shyer birds of deep woodland

The most typical birds of towns are starlings and sparrows, which nest almost anywhere

Open grass spaces, may seem like wildlife deserts, but they may be feeding grounds for gulls, thrushes and starlings

Wasteland of all kinds can attract a good many birds. Most visit to feed: we must remember that for nesting their needs may be rather more precise, and that wasteland may not offer the structural diversity which makes a wood such a good bird habitat.

Of all our birds and mammals, only the skylark and lapwing (pages 144, 210), long-tailed fieldmouse (114) and brown hare (146) are truly adapted for life in today's gigantic open arable fields. And even they are disadvantaged by the sheer busy-ness: page 134.

Farming and wildlife

Today, farming is an industry with innumerable techniques to maximise production. Pesticides, herbicides and fungicides used in bulk have the effect that crop fields are now a uniform green, containing not much more than the crop itself. This blanket approach to crop production does have grave dangers, for although sprays may eliminate a pest for a while, if, or when, the pest does return it may multiply rapidly in this monotonous expanse as its natural enemies will also have been wiped out. Farming produces a new kind of ecological instability, and it has been said that today's pests are the creation of farming itself.

Along with the change in arable farming the farm animals themselves have changed. The sheep and cattle we take for granted certainly do not look much like their ancestors of Georgian times when stock breeding began. One sheep breed, the Dorset, can even be pushed to produce three crops of lambs in two years – you may see them gambolling unseasonably in autumn. Cattle have their diet supplemented with food concentrates and they are given hormones to boost productivity. Indeed, they have to be treated in this way to be productive, as grazing alone may no longer be enough to achieve the quick results on which profits are dependent.

It is easy to condemn modern farming as the destroyer of a patchwork countryside that was so pleasant to visit and picnic in. It is also easy to argue that the farmer is actually being paid to wreck, receiving subsidies from the government for his activities. That is rather unjust – today's farming continues a system that originated in wartime necessity. In theory at any rate, with modern methods it would be possible to grow sufficient temperate foods for our needs in a reduced acreage, leaving wildlife as a worthwhile 'harvest' in the rest.

There are signs that the expansionist approach to farming may be coming to an end. Chronic surpluses – who has not heard of butter and grain mountains and milk lakes? – make a mockery of ever-increasing production.

Pesticides and foodchains

A voluntary ban has stemmed the use of persistent pesticides such as DDT, which do not quickly break down in the body of an animal which has eaten treated crops. Their danger was highlighted twenty years or so ago, when falcons and other predators at the top of food chains suffered serious declines. Mice and other animals ate seed corn dressed with these pesticides and every time the predators made a kill they took in the pesticide, until enough was built up in their tissues to kill them or prevent them breeding successfully.

Straw (stubble) **burning** is subject to a voluntary code of practice aimed at reducing damage to trees and hedges. Burning the waste straw reduces smuts (fungal diseases), which persist in the stubble, and may also kill off weed seeds. The main argument, however, is that it is a speedy method of destroying the straw at a time when every day counts if the ground is to be made ready for the winter wheat. There is little to be gained by ploughing the stalks in, as they only rot slowly.

Barley straw, which is quite nutritious, is sometimes baled for stock food.

An early 19th century painting of a Lincolnshire, prize short-horn cow. These grossly proportioned animals were the toast of the Georgian and early Victorian agricultural changes. They resulted from controlled breeding which would have been impossible in the days of open field systems and common grazing.

A classic view of lowland agriculture with a rich mixture of arable and grazing land. Notice the tall hedgerows and stands of trees, all of which indicate the richness of the soil.

Hedges are removed to create larger fields to allow today's massive farm machines to operate. Grubbing up a hedge removes a whole habitat. Cutting it to the ground (coppicing) may seem less destructive and means that the shrubs may grow again, but many of the shade-loving plants are lost. This loss of hedges is already causing problems of soil erosion in some parts of the country.

The invertebrates of ploughed land attract crows and gulls; but you rarely see signs of mole activity in arable fields.

Some crops can give short-term food or cover to wildlife. Pheasants may use the cover of potatoes, which are planted into bare soil (kale is also sometimes planted alongside shooting coverts to give the birds winter cover). Winter wheat (sown in autumn) may be grazed by rabbits, deer and, in some places, flocks of brent or greylag geese.

The clovers sown in ley grass mixtures can attract hive bees. Oil-seed rape is often busy with bees, but the honey from it is somewhat bland, and tends to crystallise in the comb.

Grain crops do not root well in damp soil, and so improved field drainage can often increase the yield by boosting growth in the vital weeks in spring. This improved drainage often follows river engineering which may also sacrifice another habitat.

In spite of the efficiency of modern farming, nature is not 'defeated'. Even some of the wild grasses shown on page 120 may appear as 'weeds' on recently seeded grass leys. More about leys, silage and modern grassmanship on page 118. Arable weeds are on 136.

An arable farmer's year

Some of our hedged and walled fields are very old and have names which recall long-forgotten village matters or sometimes even battles. They may still bear these names but the style of farming which is practised within them has little to do with the apparently leisurely pace of yesteryear. Today, arable farms are usually busy efficient places, with the whole year packed with activity.

The farming year finishes in autumn when the combine harvester has greedily sucked up all but a few cereal grains, leaving scant pickings for any woodpigeons. The straw has been baled and the surplus burned. Now starts a race against the weather as the soil has to be prepared for the next year's crops before the frost and snows set in. The tractor is out early dragging a cultivator – a large rake-like instrument – across the fields, disturbing the soil and encouraging any weed seeds to 'chit' or germinate. A few days later the ground is again cultivated to uproot the seedlings so that they die in the sun. If the weather holds dry this may be repeated in an attempt to kill as many weeds as possible including, with luck, the hardy couch grass.

The soil is then ploughed ready for sowing, or in some places seed is drilled directly into the unploughed soil. Ploughing has the advantage of 'pan busting'

or breaking up the crusty layer that forms below the surface of unploughed soil. The disc harrow then breaks down the deep plough furrows and makes the ground smoother, creating a fine 'tilth' in readiness for sowing.

If the weather holds, all this will have been done on the arable fields within six weeks of harvest. The weather is the crucial factor, for a day's rain can make the soil too wet to work. If the winter wheat or barley is not sown before the weather closes in, the chance to sow is lost until February. But assuming the weather holds, the seed is sown and fertilizer applied, the seed soon sprouts, producing a green sward which looks like young grass. Winter barley is susceptible to mildew fungus and if the seed is not already dressed – treated with fungicide before sowing – the crop must be sprayed with fungicide.

As winter sets in, the fields are left to their own devices and the farmer turns to maintenance work: hedge-cutting, cleaning out ditches and repairing fences.

Come January supplies of seed corn and fertilizer are ordered and by February farmers in the south of Britain are sowing potatoes, oats and spring barley. In the north, the weather usually delays this activity until early April. At the time of spring sowing, the 'winter' crops are treated with nitrogenous fertilizer, a process repeated in April and May.

Through spring and summer, pests and weeds are treated with pesticides. Twenty years ago a farm would have used only five or so chemical sprays; today the number is nearer thirty – each herbicide, fungicide and insecticide now more specific than it was. Even though the crops themselves are bred for disease resistance they are still susceptible to numerous pests. As one set of problems is eradicated so another steps in. Twenty years ago, poppy and

Fodder grasses planted in 'leys' are cultivated varieties (cultivars) of wild grasses. The mixture of grasses planted on a ley is chosen with care. Rye-grass and cocksfoot are rarely planted together: the latter can resist drought and flourish on light well-drained soils where rye-grass falters. Timothy with rye-grass and some clover is a good mix to fatten sheep. Fields which are cut for silage are repeatedly scattered with nitrogenous fertiliser in early summer and usually irrigated in dry weather. If the grass has too high a nitrogen content, it gives sheep diarrhoea, therefore their grazing areas are not usually intensively fertilised. Dairy cattle, however, can use the nitrogen to produce milk; they can be grazed on intensively managed grass leys and fed on silage cut from them.

Perennial rye-grass can be found in grasslands of many kinds and in waste places. It is a valuable grass for grazing and hay, and is prominent in new pastures. Its round shoots are purple at the base. May-August; to 50 cm.

Timothy (cat's-tail) **has close-packed flowerheads.** The bases of the round shoots are clothed in dark brown sheaths. It is now a widespread ley grass but was native only to water-meadows and other low-lying grasslands. Its name comes from a Mr Timothy Hanson who introduced it into America in 1720. June-September; to 1 metre.

Cocksfoot is a large, coarse-looking grass found in many places. It grows quickly after cutting, to give a good 'aftermath' for grazing. The basal sheaths on the stems are pale green, and its shoots are noticeably flattened. June-September; to 1.5 metres.

Couch grass or squitch (twitch) forms large tufts. It is a persistent weed in arable land and is almost impossible to get rid of since a small fragment of the underground rhizome will produce a new plant. June – August; to 1.2 metres.

Wild oats can be recognised by their spreading clusters of spikelets, which have dark awns. June to September; to 1.5 metres.

A lone tractor spraying a wheat field in Dorset. Thomas Hardy would barely recognise some of the new agricultural landscapes in his beloved county. The new strains of wheat are bred to be resistant to disease but are still susceptible to numerous pests and are subject to carefully timed applications of insecticides and fungicides.

Field names in a farm near Bury St Edmunds, Suffolk

The fields in this farm still retain their ancient names. Malcolm Reid, who compiled the map for WATCH, reports local folklore as maintaining that a Saxon battle was fought on Blood Hill and that people were hanged afterwards in the field below. Although modern farming methods tend to destroy the boundaries of these types of old field it is interesting to note that most farmers and farm labourers still refer to the areas of their farm by the old names even though the fields themselves may no longer exist.

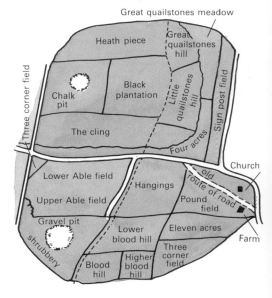

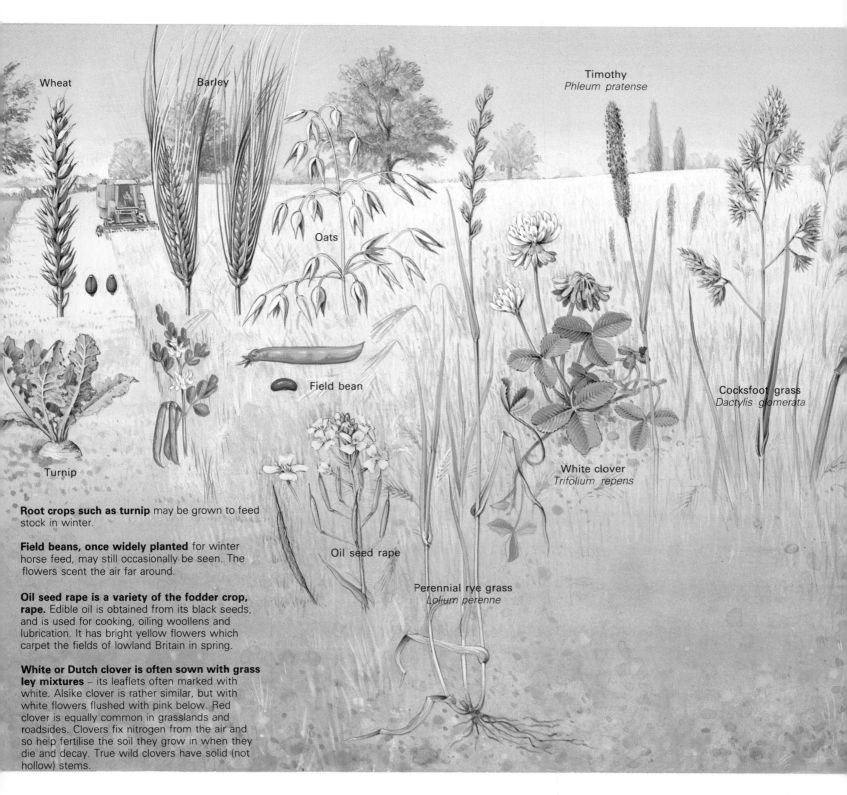

Wheat

Barley

Oats

Timothy
Phleum pratense

Field bean

Turnip

Oil seed rape

White clover
Trifolium repens

Cocksfoot grass
Dactylis glomerata

Perennial rye grass
Lolium perenne

Root crops such as turnip may be grown to feed stock in winter.

Field beans, once widely planted for winter horse feed, may still occasionally be seen. The flowers scent the air far around.

Oil seed rape is a variety of the fodder crop, rape. Edible oil is obtained from its black seeds, and is used for cooking, oiling woollens and lubrication. It has bright yellow flowers which carpet the fields of lowland Britain in spring.

White or Dutch clover is often sown with grass ley mixtures – its leaflets often marked with white. Alsike clover is rather similar, but with white flowers flushed with pink below. Red clover is equally common in grasslands and roadsides. Clovers fix nitrogen from the air and so help fertilise the soil they grow in when they die and decay. True wild clovers have solid (not hollow) stems.

Its long bristles (awns) make barley easily recognisable. The most widely grown variety is 'two-rowed barley'. Barley is our most abundant cereal, mainly used for livestock feed, but much is used to produce malt for brewing. Its straw is sometimes baled for fodder.

Wheat is second only to barley in the amount grown. Most is used for making bread when mixed with the 'harder' wheats of Canada and America. The seed-heads are carried upright until just before harvest when they bend over.

Oats are probably native to Britain. The grain hangs in open pyramidal seed-heads. It is grown less now than in the past when it was fed to horses. Scotland produces more oats than anywhere else in Britain, not just because they are used to make porridge but because oats grow well on areas with poor soil.

charlock were important weeds; today it is cleavers and chickweed. Other problems still persist even with this battery of chemicals. Wild oats still grow in profusion, as does the ubiquitous couch grass, and aphids are a major pest one year in four.

As summer approaches harvest again becomes imminent. The combine is taken out of mothballs, or hired, and the farm's electronic moisture meter is checked every day to see if the grain is ready for harvesting. In years gone by the farmer would bite the grain to see if it was ready.

The grain can be cut when it contains no more than 18 per cent moisture; this must be reduced to 16 per cent before storing. In a good summer it may dry naturally down to 12 per cent moisture but a wet summer may increase the moisture to 25 per cent. If the harvest is delayed too long and the air is damp, the grain may germinate in the ears, making the field look as if it has had a touch of frost. Overnight rain can dramatically increase the moisture content of the grain, but 20 minutes of sunshine can do the same as a day in a grain dryer. The situation may change from hour to hour and the combine driver may have to drive miles at short notice to cut grain that is just right.

The grain in, the year starts all over again.

Larkspur, familiar from gardens, was with corncockle a 'weed' brought here by farmers. Many plants with an opportunist strategy (pages 94, 96) may be seen around the edges of the arable fields.

Cornfield weeds

Any plant that contaminates the monoculture of an arable farm-crop is regarded as a weed. The farmer tries to get the best yield he can from his crops and any plants that compete for soil nutrients must be removed.

Many of the traditional weeds of cornfields are Mediterranean plants which probably arrived in Britain with the first neolithic farmers thousands of years ago. They are essentially open-ground annual colonisers, adapted to life in regularly disturbed ground – a good strategy for survival in ploughed land. Even if their seeds are buried deep by ploughing, many will lie dormant until they are brought to the surface again.

The farmer has a varied armoury with which to fight cornfield weeds. Traditionally they were pulled out by hand, but in recent decades herbicides have been used to poison the weeds and leave the crop unharmed. The grain is also cleaned after harvesting so that any weed seeds are not passed on from one year to the next in the seed corn.

The field, or common, poppy may sometimes be seen in scarlet lines when trench digging has brought dormant seeds to the surface. Sometimes you can see a cereal field dotted with them. Field poppy is a rather bristly, erect plant, the red petals often carrying a dark blotch at their base. The flowers are popular with insects for the large amounts of pollen they produce. June-October; to 60 cm.

The rough poppy is rather similar to the field poppy but with hairy pods. June-July; to 50 cm.

The long-headed poppy has flowers very similar to those of the field poppy. June-July; to 40 cm.

The opium poppy is different. It is taller than the other poppies and the flowers have white or lilac petals. It was once frequently grown in Britain – fields of it were a common sight in Victorian times. The drug opium is obtained from the 'milk' that exudes from the unripe pod. In Victorian times the opium was extracted with alcohol to make laudanum, which was drunk as a painkiller. The opium poppy also yields a rather fine poppy oil used for oil painting, and sometimes for cooking. June-August; to 80 cm.

A patch of common poppies showing their distinctive smooth pods and drooping buds.

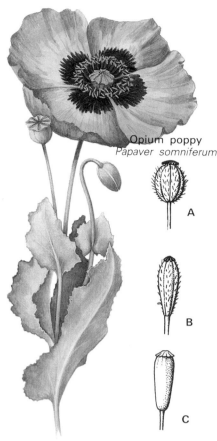

Opium poppy
Papaver somniferum

A

B

C

Corncockle is a tall, hairy plant with long green sepals that show above the reddish-purple flower petals. It is now a rare and decreasing plant. June-August; to 1 metre.

Before the introduction of more efficient seed cleaning methods, corncockle was the bane of farmers' lives at harvest-time. If it got into the corn the flour could be unpalatable and even mildly poisonous.

In many hamlets around Britain it became traditional for villagers to 'walk the wheat', pulling up the corncockle in April. In Gwent it was customary for the children to do this on Easter day. Cider and cakes were handed out at the end of the day, with double rations for those who found any corncockle. The plants were then ceremoniously buried.

For all its faults in the farmers' eyes, corncockle is a handsome plant and one farmer at least, who farms in East Anglia, sows a stand of corncockle each year in a corner of his land for old time's sake.

Charlock is often seen flowering with poppies. Its seeds will remain dormant in the soil until brought to the surface by deep ploughing or trenching. It is a hairy annual. May-July; to 80 cm.

Opium poppy can frequently be found naturalised in wasteland. Beside it are the seed capsules of three less common 'red' poppies: (A) rough poppy; (B) prickly poppy; (C) long-headed poppy.

Hairy tares are pea-family plants; only their pods are hairy. May-August; to 15 cm.

Common hemp-nettle is a weed found especially in potato fields but is no stranger to cornfields. Its hairs are coarser than those of the dead nettles. July-September; to 50 cm.

Corn marigold, unlike the cornflower, can still be seen dotting cornfields. It is an annual, with grey-green leaves. The flowers are a clear beautiful yellow. June-August; to 50 cm.

Field pansy is usually creamy yellow (it can be variable); note the green sepals reaching out past the petals. It is a relative of the violets. April-October; to 28 cm.

Scentless mayweed, unlike many of its kin, is, as its name implies, scentless. It has thread-like leaf divisions inland in Britain, but a coastal race has blunter and fleshier lobes. July-September; to 50 cm.

Scented mayweed looks similar to the scentless species but has a rather pleasant smell. Stinking chamomile looks much the same but has a foul smell. Note that its flowers are rather smaller than those of scentless mayweed, often with turned-down rays. June-September; 10–30 cm.

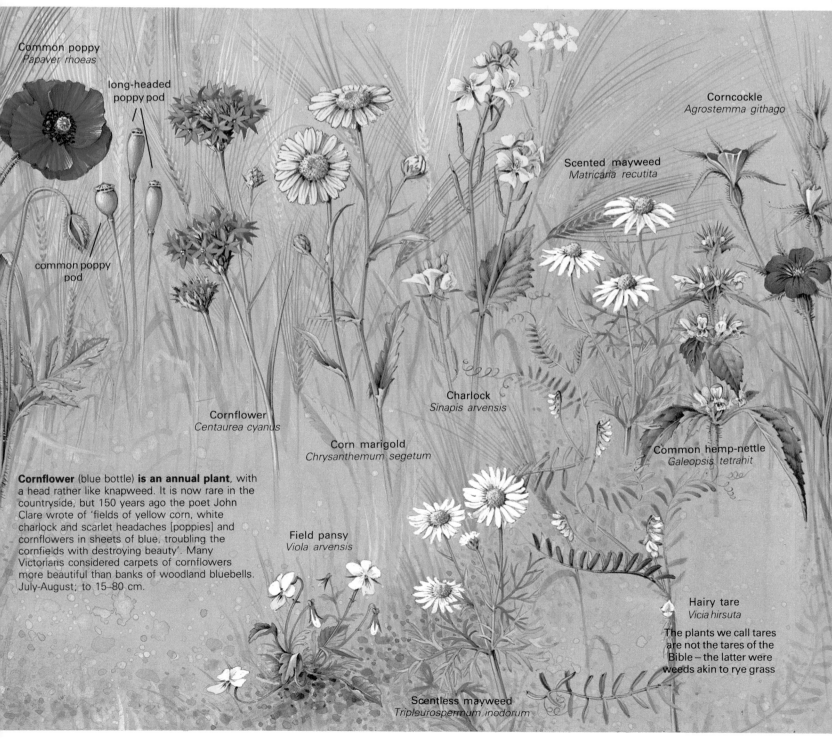

Common poppy
Papaver rhoeas

long-headed poppy pod

common poppy pod

Corncockle
Agrostemma githago

Scented mayweed
Matricaria recutita

Charlock
Sinapis arvensis

Cornflower
Centaurea cyanus

Corn marigold
Chrysanthemum segetum

Common hemp-nettle
Galeopsis tetrahit

Cornflower (blue bottle) **is an annual plant**, with a head rather like knapweed. It is now rare in the countryside, but 150 years ago the poet John Clare wrote of 'fields of yellow corn, white charlock and scarlet headaches [poppies] and cornflowers in sheets of blue, troubling the cornfields with destroying beauty'. Many Victorians considered carpets of cornflowers more beautiful than banks of woodland bluebells. July-August; to 15–80 cm.

Field pansy
Viola arvensis

Hairy tare
Vicia hirsuta

The plants we call tares are not the tares of the Bible – the latter were weeds akin to rye grass

Scentless mayweed
Tripleurospermum inodorum

See also pages 42, 98, 178 and 220 for insights into nature at work. Grass fields are usually intensively managed though not for the benefit of foxes! More about 'improvements' and grazing regimes on page 118. Wildlife as a whole suffers from this disturbance.

Pyramids in a grass field

The seemingly thin layer of grass on a well maintained field can provide enough fodder each year to support four sheep or maybe one cow per acre, but it is not only sheep or cows that crop the grass. With them may be any number of rabbits, and grasshoppers and other grass-eating insects that rely on the energy stored in the grass leaves, stems or seeds. And the grass is just part of the picture, for in established grasslands such as old meadowland, the weight of earthworms below the soil may equal the weight of the sheep or cows on top. The earthworms and other decomposers play an important role in redistributing the energy in a field.

The rich plant communities of the downland slopes have developed in conjunction with hundreds of years of sheep grazing. The constant nibbling of the sheep has kept the plants low prevented coarser grasses and scrub from encroaching. Grazing sheep cause a net loss to the overall biomass as the energy that they consume is lost when they are removed. Sadly, this type of scene is now on the decline and vast areas have been turned over to cereal production, as can be seen on the hill top opposite.

Ants

Red ants may sometimes build their nests in rotting tree stumps but both they and the black ants generally build their nests below flattish stones. The reason for this is not simply protection: ants are very sensitive to warmth, needing some but not too much. (The species that are active above ground are usually dark with protective pigment.) A flat stone acts as a storage heater, absorbing the heat of the sun during the day.

Black ants are often found in gardens, and sometimes nest below well-trodden paths – the trodden soil can also store heat. Black ants are often seen tending colonies of greenfly and other aphids which they milk of their honeydew. Red ants can 'sting', but black ants have lost that capacity.

Yellow ants are responsible for the ant-hills, often mistaken for mole-hills, which can cover old grazing grassland. You may see that these hills are rather elongated in an east-west direction. Research in Switzerland has shown that the ants tend to add to their nests on the east side, so that there is more area to catch the warmth of the morning sun. Guides claim to be able to find their way by these 'ant-hill compasses' when mists suddenly fall on the high Alps. The same may be true of British yellow ants. Yellow ants keep aphids in their nests and milk them for their honeydew, and even store aphid eggs in the nest during the winter to start a new 'herd' the next year.

A biomass pyramid

Like any food, grass is a kind of stored energy and grazing animals such as rabbits tap this energy. Foxes and other predators gain their energy in turn by feeding upon rabbits and other small mammals such as voles. There are, of course, fewer foxes than there are rabbits and voles because it takes many rabbits and voles to keep one fox alive. This pyramid of numbers is quite usual in nature, there always being fewer carnivores than herbivores.

A better way of gaining a picture of the energy movement between each consumer level is to show the total weight (or mass) of the animals and plants. The rather imprecise pyramid of numbers then becomes a more regular pyramid of 'biomass'. A small amount of energy is locked up in body matter; it is only this energy which is available to the next consumer level.

Part of the energy is used up driving the life processes; maintaining body heat, for example. Part of the energy is passed on in droppings, urine and dead matter – this is available to the decomposers for recycling.

Each level of the pyramid of biomass provides enough energy to support the smaller level above it. A pyramid results because of the energy loss, at each consumer level. The shape (slope) of the pyramid depends on how efficient the feeders at the different levels are at converting the energy. Efficient energy users produce a steep-sided pyramid of biomass, because less energy is wasted.

Together with the sheep, rabbits have traditionally been responsible for keeping the grassy swards of the Downs closely cropped. Too many rabbits competing with the sheep and other herbivores can cause overgrazing effectively breaking down the food pyramid.

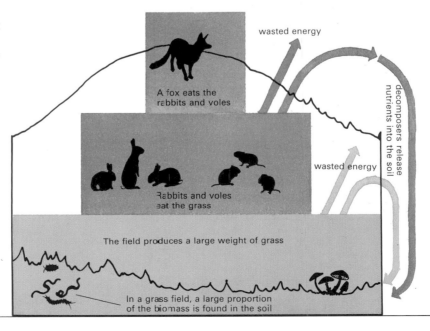

wasted energy

A fox eats the rabbits and voles

decomposers release nutrients into the soil

wasted energy

Rabbits and voles eat the grass

The field produces a large weight of grass

In a grass field, a large proportion of the biomass is found in the soil

These butterflies are mainly of the south, but green hairstreak, small copper and small and common blue are not so limited. Pea-family plants mentioned can be seen on pages 122, 148. Rock-rose on page 150. Pages 44, 100, 168 show other brown butterflies.

Butterflies of open ground

Butterflies are more likely to be seen flying on still, warm days. As well as searching for food, they fly to find a mate, which they recognise by colour and pattern, and also perhaps scent. You may see courtship dances with the males fluttering around the females. This is very often seen with the 'blues', as well as many other butterflies.

When mating is over, the female butterfly seeks a special food plant for her eggs. This is usually a very subtle choice, often explaining why you sometimes find butterflies confined to very local areas. Most 'blues' are rather weak fliers, which restricts them to sometimes dense colonies at a suitable site.

The reasons behind the siting of a 'blue' colony are complex. Most 'blue' butterflies have a curious relationship with ants. Some types of ant milk the 'blue' caterpillars of honeydew while protecting these caterpillar 'cows' against predators. The ants associated with the rare adonis blues are commonest in short turf, on hot, sunny, south-facing hillsides.

Common blues show how striking the difference can be between male and female colouring. The male is a clear, violet blue, while the female is brown, with maybe just a dusting of blue. These butterflies are never seen in large numbers in any one place. The female lays her eggs on bird's-foot trefoil, which is widespread. A quick fluttering flight over short distances: they often perch, wings half open. Two generations fly between May-September. 30 mm ws.

Small blue males have only a dusting of blue. The female is sooty brown. She lays her eggs on kidney vetch, choosing secluded corners. Small blues have a quick fluttering flight for short distances, low over the ground. They fly May-June, and occasionally August, not often in large numbers. 30 mm ws.

Adonis blues lay their eggs on horseshoe vetch like the chalkhill blues. The male is a more silvery, iridescent blue than that of the common blue; the adonis female is dark brown. A lively flight up and down the hillsides where they breed. They fly in colonies, in May-June, with another generation on the wing in August-September; 30 mm ws.

The adonis blue

A few years ago enthusiasts were hoping to protect a colony of blue butterflies on a nature reserve. They put a fence up around the site to prevent the butterflies being disturbed. The fence also prevented sheep from grazing the site. The grass inside grew tall, and it smothered the wild flowers growing there, including the plants the blue butterflies laid their eggs upon. Without those plants, no eggs were laid; so the colony of blue butterflies was inadvertently wiped out.

Hampshire, where a few years ago they had disappeared. This is an example of positive conservation.

The eggs of the adonis blue are laid on horseshoe vetch which grows on short, old turf. The butterfly is obviously limited by this, but that is not the only restricting factor, for the chalkhill blue butterfly also chooses horseshoe vetch, yet it is nothing like as rare as the adonis blue.

By the late 1970s, the adonis blue could be found at fewer than 80 places in Britain. It had gone from Old Winchester Hill and it was even disappearing from some (professionally run) nature reserves. Its complete ecology was studied. It was realised that it flies only on really hot, south-facing hillsides, the real sunspots of the south of Britain. Moreover the females lay their eggs only on very sheltered short plants (less than 3 cm high) in pockets in the turf. The caterpillars of blue butterflies are often attended by ants. Some are never without four or five ants in attendance. The ants guard the caterpillar when it is moulting its skin, and they even cover it up at night. More crucially, they keep at bay the parasite flies and wasps which lay their eggs inside the bodies of living caterpillars and which normally inflict high mortality on caterpillar populations.

In return, the caterpillar of the adonis blue exudes a sweet juice from a gland in its skin, which is milked by the ants. Ants are also generally choosy about where they themselves set up colonies, and so the combination of sunshine, hillside, short turf 'plants' and ants needs to be finely tuned to ensure the butterfly's survival.

Old Winchester Hill has been short-grazed for centuries, but during and after the last war, grazing was being run down. Rabbits continued to keep the turf short, but then in the 1950s they were stricken by the disease myxomatosis. Large areas of the hill became tangled scrub – and the adonis blue disappeared. For the sake of the flowers, however, grazing regimes were restored, and it was realised that conditions again suited the butterfly. However, there were no colonies near enough to reach it (all blues are weak fliers). In 1981, 65 adonis blue butterflies were introduced to the site, and now more than 5,000 can be seen on the wing there.

Small heaths are among th   commonest browns; flitting lazily with a slow flight above and among the grass blades. Their caterpillars are found on fine-leaved grasses. When their wings are closed at rest, the two eye spots on the underwing are obvious. These may be to distract any birds so that they peck at the 'eye' instead of the body, allowing the butterfly to escape with merely a torn wing. Two generations in summer; 25 mm ws.

Marbled whites are one of the few butterflies to scatter their eggs, apparently at random, while flying over the grass. This butterfly is, in fact, one of the 'browns'. Its caterpillar eats sheep's fescue and other grasses, but is localised to tall grasses. A rather slow flapping flight. July-August; to 50 mm ws.

Meadow browns were once one of our commonest butterflies. They are now harder to find in many places because of the widespread elimination of hayfields and tall grass. Their caterpillars feed on many different kinds of grass, and numbers may revive when grazing is restricted for a year or two. They remain in the same area (even the same field) for generations. A rather lazy flier, resting often with wings closed. June-September; to 50 mm ws.

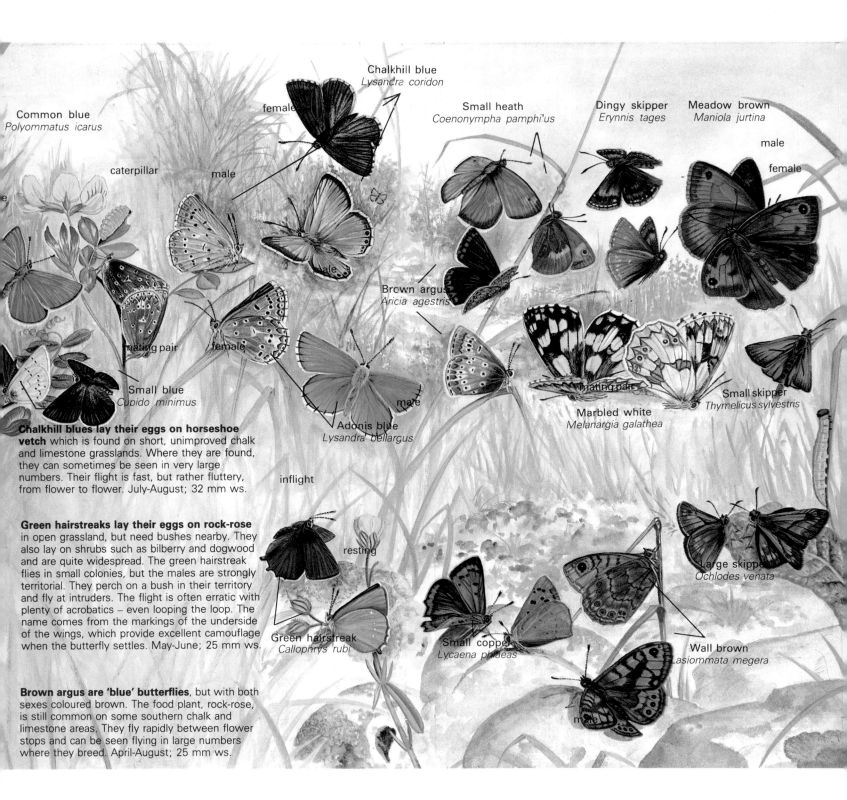

Common blue
Polyommatus icarus

caterpillar

male

mating pair

female

Small blue
Cupido minimus

Chalkhill blue
Lysandra coridon

female

male

male

in flight

Adonis blue
Lysandra bellargus

Brown argus
Aricia agestris

Small heath
Coenonympha pamphilus

Dingy skipper
Erynnis tages

Meadow brown
Maniola jurtina

male

female

mating pair

Marbled white
Melanargia galathea

Small skipper
Thymelicus sylvestris

resting

Green hairstreak
Callophrys rubi

Small copper
Lycaena phlaeas

male

Large skipper
Ochlodes venata

Wall brown
Lasiommata megera

Chalkhill blues lay their eggs on horseshoe vetch which is found on short, unimproved chalk and limestone grasslands. Where they are found, they can sometimes be seen in very large numbers. Their flight is fast, but rather fluttery, from flower to flower. July-August; 32 mm ws.

Green hairstreaks lay their eggs on rock-rose in open grassland, but need bushes nearby. They also lay on shrubs such as bilberry and dogwood and are quite widespread. The green hairstreak flies in small colonies, but the males are strongly territorial. They perch on a bush in their territory and fly at intruders. The flight is often erratic with plenty of acrobatics – even looping the loop. The name comes from the markings of the underside of the wings, which provide excellent camouflage when the butterfly settles. May-June; 25 mm ws.

Brown argus are 'blue' butterflies, but with both sexes coloured brown. The food plant, rock-rose, is still common on some southern chalk and limestone areas. They fly rapidly between flower stops and can be seen flying in large numbers where they breed. April-August; 25 mm ws.

Small coppers have as many as three generations in a season. They feed on sheep's sorrel and common sorrel. They are rather restless butterflies and strongly territorial – you may see them hassling other small coppers when they intrude into their area. Two broods, in April and September/October; To 25 mm ws.

Wall butterflies are easy to recognise from their habit of settling for a moment or two, wings outspread, before moving on. They bask even more than is usual among butterflies, often on warm walls. They have a quick zig-zag flight if disturbed. As with all 'browns', the caterpillars feed on grasses. The first generation is seen in May, then another in August; to 45 mm ws.

Skippers are moth-like butterflies, with a quick, darting, buzzing flight; note the way the wings are held at rest, with hind wings flat and forewings raised at an angle. The dingy skipper lays eggs on bird's-foot trefoil; flies May-June; 25 mm ws. Small skippers lay on creeping soft grass. June-September; 25 mm ws. Large skippers choose mainly cocksfoot grass for their eggs. May-August; 30 mm ws.

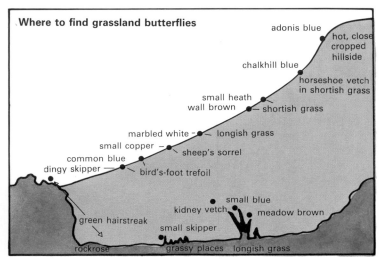

Where to find grassland butterflies

adonis blue — hot, close cropped hillside

chalkhill blue

horseshoe vetch in shortish grass

small heath
wall brown — shortish grass

marbled white — longish grass
small copper —
sheep's sorrel
common blue
dingy skipper —
bird's-foot trefoil

small blue
kidney vetch
meadow brown

green hairstreak
small skipper
rockrose
grassy places
longish grass

grayling, page 169

visiting white butterflies, page 243

more butterflies associated with patchy cover, pages 100–101

Out in the field you may find patches of sheep's sorrel growing higher up the hillside than the close cropped sward which attracts the adonis blue. In other words the scheme shows you the plant links of the butterflies, not where to expect them on a hillside.

See page 110 for further possible species. Beetles are shown on pages 106, and the important place of ants is discussed on page 138. Some grassland moths can be seen amongst those on page 46 (on page 140 are shown butterflies). Mosquitoes and other biters on page 194.

Hoverfly
Syrphus sp.

Meadow grasshopper
Chorthippus parallelus

Insects of the grassy field

There is always a frenzy of purposeful activity in a grassy field in summer. Above the ground flying insects can be seen gathering food, mating or looking for places to lay their eggs. Many moths make an appearance. Look for the six-spot burnet whose caterpillar weaves itself a pale yellow cocoon which can often be seen attached to the tops of grass stems.

In amongst the grass, grasshoppers may be heard but seldom seen. Camouflaged by their green and brown colours, the males chirrup by rubbing their hind legs against their forewings. The females hear the call with 'ears' on each side of their abdomen. Each grasshopper species has its own characteristic sound which experts find as recognisable as individual bird songs.

Look out for the numerous beetles, such as the soldier beetle. Spiders, such as the money spider and the wolf spider, are also common in grasslands, as are ants scurrying from their nest to scavenge for food or defend their territory. The insects you see will depend very much upon where you are in Britain and the time of year. Many have but a brief flying-mating adult stage and most of the lifespan is spent as a food-gathering grub.

Grasshoppers are more likely to be heard on sunny days, the hotter the better. The insects shown here are all active in summer, but their season may extend well into autumn if the weather is favourable. You will sometimes hear the chirrup of field grasshoppers until mid-November. Young grasshoppers hatch as 'mini-adults'; they grow and moult many times before becoming mature, so beware of trying to identify them by size. The mature adults can be seen from June to November. Their colour varies from brown through to green.

Meadow grasshoppers prefer damp grass. The males have a very short chattering song to lure the females to them. The wings of this grasshopper are almost lost – a good way of telling them from other grasshoppers. To 20 mm.

Common field grasshoppers sing a series of short chirrups, often in chorus, as this is a gregarious species. They are found most on dry grass or waste land. They have long wings and fly most often in hot sunshine. The colour is variable. To 20 mm.

Ground hoppers are well camouflaged in black and grey and can leap well to escape predators. They are also excellent swimmers. They are active on warm days, feeding on green algae found on the ground surface. They do not chirrup. To 10 mm.

Robber flies are morbidly fascinating to watch. They dart from their perch almost faster than the eye can follow, to return with an insect caught on the wing. They then set about sucking their prey dry. To 10 mm.

Craneflies ('daddy-long-legs') can, with legs dangling, rise vertically in flight. Notice the pair of balancing mini-clubs or halteres, set just behind the wings. These are modified hind wings and all true flies have them. Craneflies have fragile legs and while they can grasp with them, they cannot usually walk well. Pairs may often be seen mating. The grubs (leather jackets) eat grass roots and are an important food for rooks and also cuckoos when these birds first arrive in spring. There are many kinds of cranefly, some with dramatically coloured yellow and black bodies. To 20 mm.

Thunderfly thrips have a little-known life story. They are so called because they are blown or fly into houses in large numbers in sultry weather. To 2 mm.

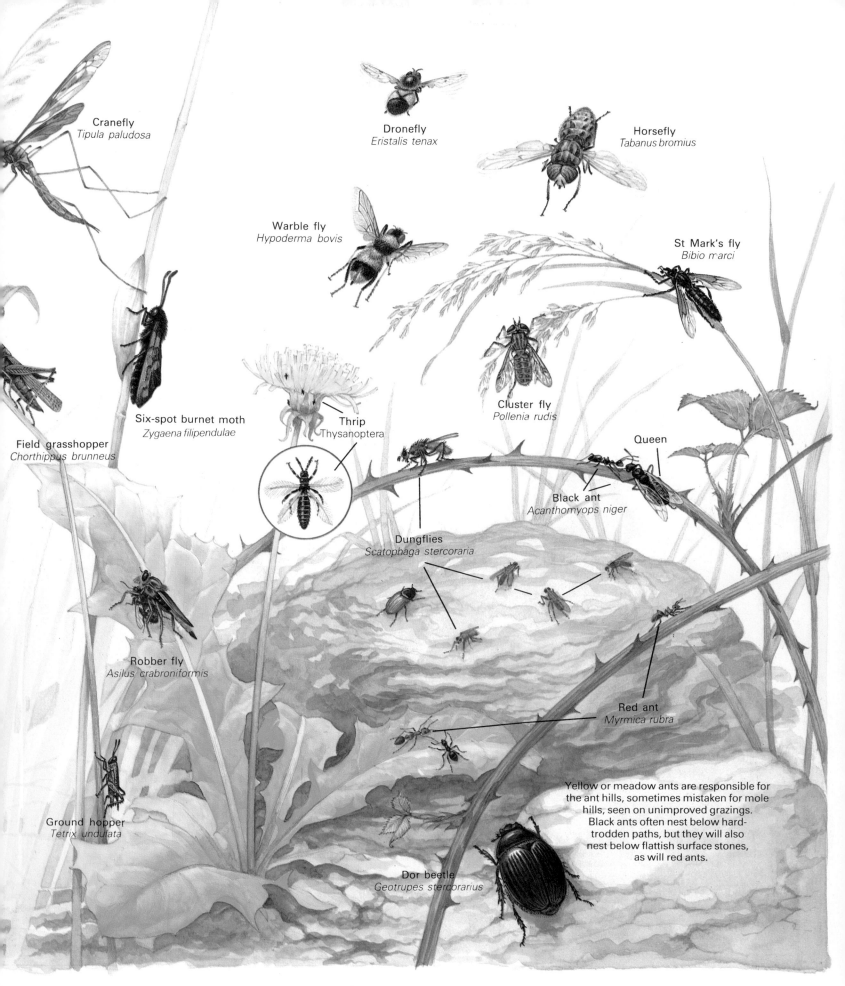

Cranefly
Tipula paludosa

Dronefly
Eristalis tenax

Horsefly
Tabanus bromius

Warble fly
Hypoderma bovis

St Mark's fly
Bibio marci

Cluster fly
Pollenia rudis

Six-spot burnet moth
Zygaena filipendulae

Thrip
Thysanoptera

Queen

Field grasshopper
Chorthippus brunneus

Black ant
Acanthomyops niger

Dungflies
Scatophaga stercoraria

Robber fly
Asilus crabroniformis

Red ant
Myrmica rubra

Ground hopper
Tetrix undulata

Yellow or meadow ants are responsible for the ant hills, sometimes mistaken for mole hills, seen on unimproved grazings. Black ants often nest below hard-trodden paths, but they will also nest below flattish surface stones, as will red ants.

Dor beetle
Geotrupes stercorarius

Six-spot burnets are day-flying moths, seen in colonies, in grassy places in the south. The eggs are laid on bird's-foot trefoil and the caterpillar cocoons are found at the top of swaying grass stems, where they are difficult for birds to get at. The adults are nauseous to predators. The five-spot burnet is a closely similar species, with five red spots on each wing. It can be seen rather further north than the six-spot species. June-August; to 20 mm.

Dung flies flock to cow pats, obviously attracted by smell, as they approach from downwind. You can see the rather greenish females struggling with maybe two or three of the yellowish, hairy males. They often prey on other kinds of flies. They lay their eggs in the dung. 12 mm.

Warble flies (gadflies) **lay their eggs** on the legs of cattle and horses. The grubs burrow into the skin, migrate to the back of the animal, and create swellings (warbles). Now rare because of a programme of eradication. June-July; 15 mm.

Horseflies are the bulkiest of all our flies; most common in damp, grassy places near woods. The females attack persistently with a loud hum, biting cattle and also humans. They can fly quite fast – 30 mph has been recorded. They are rather fine-looking flies, with glistening iridescent eyes and a golden sheen to the body. June-August 20 mm.

St Mark's flies are seen on the wing from April onwards. The males fly in sluggish swarms, waiting to mate with females when they fly up from the grass. 12 mm.

The female cleg attacks humans and cattle quite silently, often not noticed at all until after the bite. It has mottled wings. May-September; 10 mm.

Dor beetles can be seen on the wing on warm summer nights. They are slow, clumsy fliers, and often blunder into things and fall upside-down to the ground, where you may see that they are infested with small red mites; hence another name for them is 'lousy watchman'. The eggs are laid in holes dug under cow pats and horse droppings. 25 mm.

Ants. At certain times during the summer, winged male and female ants leave the nest in spectacular mating swarms. Once mated, the female loses her wings and settles down to establish a new nest.

143

Woodpigeons and sometimes green woodpeckers (page 50) will be seen feeding out on open ground. Blackbirds and thrushes (page 54) tend to keep to the shelter of the hedge. More waders can be seen on pages 210, 230, 232; the meadow pipit again on page 165.

Birds of the open fields

Some of the birds seen making regular use of the open fields are of woodland origin. Blackbirds are one example; notice that they keep close to the shelter of the hedge. Field birds such as rooks are more generally regarded as 'park' birds, needing tall trees for roosting and nesting but always feeding out on open ground. It is sometimes possible to see the rooks feeding in a definite order – called a peck order – with the top birds taking food first. There is an advantage in this hierarchy for the species as a whole: when food is short, some of the stronger birds at least will survive.

Some of the community of birds are true 'steppe' birds, birds of open and treeless plains to be found in eastern Europe. The skylark is one. It sings fiercely, declaring its territory high above the nest, which is a slight hollow in the ground, often sheltered by a tuft of grass.

If the field is low-lying and the soil damp, then you may regularly see waders probing the soft earth with their delicate bills. The chicks especially need soft soil for they feed themselves after hatching.

As feeding grounds, these wet grasslands are generally more important to birds in winter. Not only waders, but wildfowl, gulls and sometimes geese will visit them, and some of this country's washes are vital habitats for our resident British birds and many migrants.

Rooks feed out on open ground, probing into the soft soil for worms and insects, though they will also take grain. They have 'baggy pants' of loose feather and (when mature) a greyish-white face which makes the bill seem longer – very different from the face of a crow. Rooks fly with faster wingbeats than crows, and are slightly smaller. Calls include *caw, kah* and other harsh notes. They are seen in flocks, often with jackdaws. The nests are bulky cups of twigs on branches high in the treetops, often in colonial rookeries which were traditionally found in groups of elms near houses, but are more often seen now in ash and other tall trees, sometimes in broken woodland. Rooks are strongly territorial, even though they nest in colonies. The nests are defended vigorously and there are numerous twig-stealing disputes, but the birds mingle happily when feeding. This territorial nest behaviour may be the origin of the term 'rook parliaments', when the birds seem to be in noisy debate, clustered around one of their number at the treetop – perhaps a rook attempting to take another's nest site. To 46 cm.

Jackdaws both walk and fly more jauntily than crows and rooks. They can often be seen flying acrobatics high above farmland and woods. Close up, their grey nape and shortish bill identify them. They nest in holes in trees or buildings but show no preference for town or country – they are less tied to farmland than crows. *Jak* and *kyow* calls. They are inquisitive birds and will take (and hide) bright trinkets and pluck wool from sheep's backs. 34 cm.

The boldly patterned red-legged partridge now outnumbers our grey partridge in parts of east England, where it thrives amidst the dry arable farmlands.

Lapwings can be seen in swerving flight above the fields in spring. See page 210.

Skylarks sing a long unbroken song (other birds may sing for only seconds at a time). They may spend up to 20 minutes of an hour singing high in the air, rising, circling, hovering, sometimes drifting down. The open country they choose offers no song post – though they will sing from a perch if one is close to the nest. The song itself is a clear bubbling warble. They nest in a grassy cup on the ground. They feed on seeds, crop leaves, insects. To 18 cm.

Black-headed gulls can often be seen inland following a tractor, and may be found nesting, in colonies, on tussocks of grass by lakes and reservoirs, and on the moors and salt marshes. The dark cap is lost in winter, but a dark ear spot remains. Note the red legs and bill. A *kwaar* call.

A hundred years ago, these gulls were seen only on the Thames estuary. They now breed in towns throughout Britain – a classic example of exploitation of a 'new' habitat by a bird species.

Meadow pipits have a song flight, in which they climb 30 m above the ground and then 'parachute' down singing all the time. Sparrow-sized, to 15 cm. Tree pipits are very similar looking birds. These too sing a flight song, also parachuting down singing as they go. However, they prefer to perch above ground, and so a glance at the habitat should tell you which of these twins you have spotted. Both nest on the ground, in the shelter of bracken, grass tussocks or heather.

Starlings have an all year charm. They are flashy but attractively plumaged birds, and opportunists, always taking any advantage offered. They nest in holes – anywhere – and can be very common indeed in woodland, although better known from town and village sites, even behind shop signs! Their voice includes an extraordinary series of wheezes and chuckles, but they mimic other birds, and even telephones, remarkably well! They probe the soil for food with an open bill, but also take scraps, etc.

Their winter roosts are well known, where they congregate each evening in noisy multitudes on city buildings. At dawn they leave, a kind of reverse rush hour, back to suburb and countryside feeding grounds where they feed in small groups, perhaps as many as fourteen miles from the night roost. In the evening again, you can see the feeding groups join others nearby to form bigger flocks and move back to the city. To 21.5 cm.

Grey partridge coveys (flocks) **run or whirr up**, and skim away with quick wingbeats and glides, making them fine sporting birds (the shooting season is 1st September to 1st February). But there are far fewer birds than at the turn of the century, as pesticide sprays have killed the insects on which the chicks feed and depend. (Like chickens, they fend for themselves from hatching.) When older, partridge take seeds, leaves, shoots of cereal crops and weeds. They feed out in the open, but the nest is in the cover of a hedge or scrub. They call a loud *kerric kerrick*, at dusk or well after dark. 30 cm.

Corn buntings sing from bushes and other perches, but leave them for a short flight, legs dangling, singing a song sounding like a rattle of keys. The nest is often on the ground, and some consider that the bird has not been deterred by the grubbing up of hedges in recent times – it uses gateposts and power lines for song posts! Larger than the sparrow, to 18 cm.

Little owls, when curious or suspicious, bob and duck. They have markings which make them look cross all the time. These owls are often seen perched during daylight hours. Most of the hunting is done at dawn or dusk, when they fly in bouncy waves close to the ground, taking insects, small mammals and birds. Their cry is a far-carrying, kitten-like *kiew*. Following their introduction about 100 years ago as a means of controlling mice and voles, they are now widespread, with 14,000 pairs in England, Scotland and Wales. They nest in a hole in a tree, building, quarry, etc, or even a deserted burrow in the ground in open country. Starling-sized to 22 cm.

Goldfinches are attracted to areas with scattered trees, park-like countryside or fieldscapes, for they nest in trees and bushes, usually towards the end of a branch. They sing a twittering, tinkling song from a branch (often crooping their wings in display at the same time) but feed on the seeds of thistles and other daisy-family plants found growing on open ground. Goldfinches were once trapped in large numbers for cage birds, their song having made them popular. To 12 cm.

lapwings

Meadow pipit
Anthus pratensis

Skylark
Alauda arvensis

Black-headed gulls
Larus ridibundus

Red-legged partridge
Alectoris rufa

Corn Bunting
Miliaria calandra

Rook
Corvus frugilegus

Crow
Corvus corone

Partridge
Perdix perdix

Starlings
Sturnus vulgaris

Jackdaw
Corvus monedula

Goldfinch
Carduelis carduelis

Little owl
Athene noctua

Crows have for hundreds of years been regarded as vermin. They have been poisoned, trapped and shot to the extent that their natural habitat is not clear and now they survive where they can. They usually nest high in the fork of a tree, taking a variety of food, including birds, eggs and carrion; but, contrary to folklore, rarely (if ever) attacking living young lambs. They have a rather laboured flight and the call is a hoarse *kraah* repeated three or four times. The all-black crow is resident in western Europe, and is the one most often seen in England, Wales and southern Scotland. However, the hooded crow, with the bulk of its body greyish and with black head, neck and wing feathers, can also be seen in Iceland; in Scotland north-west of the Caledonian Canal; and on the Continent. Where the range of these two races (subspecies) meets, they interbreed. In winter, hooded crows sometimes fly some distance south. To 47 cm.

Red-legged partridges were introduced (from France) a couple of centuries ago and have colonised in places, especially in the drier south and east. The call is a *chuka chuka*. The bird is slightly larger than the grey partridge. To 33 cm.

Although we link most of these mammals with the open fields, they can also be active within woodland and scrub. Compare the brown hare with the blue or mountain hare, page 162. More mammals are shown on page 114.

More mammals

In Plantagenet times, rabbits were brought from France to be bred in 'warrens' for meat and fur for the lord of the manor. They escaped and three centuries ago they had become widespread in the wild and constituted the staple meat of the peasants. They also had a great effect on the scenery, being responsible in part for the creation of smooth downland turf.

A principal reason for the success of the rabbit is its phenomenal breeding rate. The bucks are promiscuous; the does (which care for the litters) can begin to mate when three months old, produce a litter of half a dozen in a month or so, and mate again within a few days of giving birth. Litters are less frequent in autumn and winter, however.

The disease myxomatosis almost wiped out our rabbit population in the early 1950s, but numbers are now building up again. Rabbits eat a wide range of plants but will reject ragwort and elder amongst others, which may mark the site of their burrows.

Moles are solitary except for a brief time while mating, though some tunnels seem to have common use by many individuals. Runs are on two levels: one nudging the surface, and many others deeper down. The earth from the runs is pushed up to form mole-hills.

The mole runs along its network of tunnels, collecting worms and other soil animals that have fallen into them. It has a four-hour cycle of activity: four on, four off. To 16 cm.

Brown rats are found wherever there is human habitation both in towns and country. They form large groups and are mainly nocturnal, feeding on almost anything but preferring grain when they can get it, causing vast amounts of damage in the process. To 55 cm.

The numerous mole-hills in this field suggests a great deal of activity. Shallow runs and furrows almost at the surface are created at certain times of the year. These are thought to be used for either breeding or feeding purpose.

House mouse
Mus musculus

Black rat
Rattus rattus

Black rats and house mice

The house mouse is probably as common in the hedgerows and farms of the open countryside as in today's houses. It is not a native mammal, but was introduced very early, perhaps in Iron Age times. It is somewhat greyer than the wood mouse. It can have 10 litters a year if food is available. To 18 cm.

Tradition has it that the black rat was brought to Britain by the returning Crusaders. It flourished in medieval times, but around three centuries ago the brown rat was introduced, larger and tougher than the black. It usurped the place of the black rat, which today is usually seen only near seaports (where its population may be topped up by escapes from shipping) and on a few islands. The black rat has a sharper muzzle and is more slender than the brown rat. To 55 cm.

Rabbits have shorter ears than hares, without black tips to the ends.

hares 'boxing'

Brown hare
Lepus capensis

mole-hills

Rabbit
Oryctolagus cuniculus

Mole
Talpa europaea

Hedgehog
Erinaceus europaeus

rabbit droppings

Brown rat
Rattus norvegicus

Rabbits can be seen in groups, within dashing distance of their burrows, never far out on to the field. They feed at dawn and dusk, but also during the day in quiet places. They digest their food twice: by night they excrete soft pellets which are then reswallowed. The hard, familiar final stools are left out in the open, on raised ground such as ant-hills.

Rabbits have rather short ears and hind legs compared with the hare, and a short scut (tail). Their colour is brownish, though whitish and black rabbits are often seen. Up to 40 cm.

Hares are usually seen singly and far out in the open. They make no burrow, but rest in thick grass. Their normal lope can become a very fast run – so they are considered good sport for shooting, or for hunting on foot with beagles. Up to 70 cm; tail 10 cm long.

Mad March hares are so called from their behaviour in spring, when the males gambol, and are said to box each other to prove their dominance. Breeding occurs also at other times of year, however.

Hedgehogs

The enigmatic, determined hedgehog has become a familiar sight in gardens over the last few years and with a little encouragement in the form of bread and milk, it will readily become a regular visitor. Hedgehogs are essentially nocturnal mammals and are best seen in the late evening – unless you are prepared to stay up all night – making much noise as they forage for beetles, worms and slugs. They are robust little creatures and with their 5,000 or so needle-sharp spines are able to fend off the most tenacious predators and even a playful dog. Their greatest mortality period is during their winter hibernation between October and April. Before settling down for the long sleep in amongst brambles or below garden rubbish, they have to have enough fat stored in their bodies to last until spring. Any young born late in the year will have less time to acquire this fat reserve and will die before winter is through. If they do survive the first winter their chances of reaching a ripe old age of four or five are quite good.

If you take on a hedgehog as a pet it will need more than just bread and milk. The best diet is dog or cat food.

See page 120 for grasses; 122, 150 for other flowers to look for; orchids are on page 124. Many chalkland plants have a liking for the lime-bedded soil, others are there because they tolerate the dry conditions – harebell (page 166) can be found. Butterflies, page 140.

Chalk downland

A wide variety of wild flowers and many wild grasses can grow on the old short turf on chalk downland that has been grazed for centuries but is otherwise undisturbed.

At first sight we might try to attribute this richness of plant life to the soil's fertility, but the thin soil is rather low in phosphates and nitrates and is therefore rather infertile. One possible reason, or part reason, for this diversity of plant life on such poor soil is that the dominant plants, which normally take over a site with good soil, cannot grow vigorously enough to do so. One reason why the soil remains so infertile is the rigour of the grazing, which keeps down the growth and restricts the recycling of nutrients back into the soil. When grazing ceases the turf is soon invaded by tor and upright brome grasses and it is then only a short time before scrub grows up and the downland flowers are shaded out.

Sadly, in recent years many of the flat tops and valley bottoms of our downland have been ploughed and planted with arable crops. The steep slopes between are now yellow with tough grass and dotted with scrub, for today it is not economic to keep a few sheep to graze such a narrow strip of sloping land.

Yellow-wort has an unusual pairing of the leaves, forming a 'ring' around the stem. Its flowers close in the afternoon. Often grows with squinancywort. June-October; to 45 cm.

Hoary plantain has a rosette of greyish downy leaves which lie flat on the ground. The flower is scented and insect-pollinated, unlike that of the other plantains. May-August; to 30 cm.

Restharrow is one of the common downland flowers which is not only confined to chalk: some are found on dunes which may contain a great deal of broken shell, providing an alternative calcium source. It has a creeping, often woody stem and the hairy leaves have a harsh smell. June-September; 30–60 cm.

Squinancywort has thin stems, with leaves in whorls of four. Its name has a strangely convoluted origin. 'Squinancy' is a muddled form of quinsy – the old name for tonsillitis. The plant was thought to cure sore throats if an infusion made from it was gargled. It has vanilla-scented flowers. June-July; 8–40 cm.

Hairy violet leaves grow larger after flowering. It has no scent. The seeds are spread by ants, which throng the chalk pastures. Note that its leaves and flowers rise directly from the roots – there are no stems or runners. The spreading hairs on the leaf stalks and the fruits are a sure way of telling it from other violets. April-May; to 10 cm.

Horseshoe vetch may have got its name from the arrangement of the clear yellow flowers in the flowerhead, or perhaps from the fact that the ripe pod crinkles into horseshoe-shaped sections. The plant has a woody root. The leaves have four to five pairs of side leaflets and one at the end. Horseshoe vetch is a plant with a very limited distribution in modern Britain – hence the fact that butterflies, such as some 'blues', which rely on it for their caterpillar food are also limited. It is found only on old grassland and has not reappeared in suitable grass fields which are known to have been last ploughed 50 years ago. Found mainly in the south. April-June; 10–40 cm.

Carline thistle has an 'everlasting' flower which closes up at night and in bad weather. July-October; 10–60 cm.

Stemless thistle flowers lie in the middle of their rosette of prickly leaves. (This is the thistle you usually find yourself sitting on!) Its flat shape and prickly leaves are a strategy to combat dry situations; it sometimes does have a short stalk. It is really a plant of the south-east, but can be found as far north as Yorkshire and in south Wales.

Carline thistle
Carlina vulgaris

Yellow-wort
Blackstonia perfoliata

Hoary plantain
Plantago media

adonis blue

Horseshoe vetch
Hippocrepis comosa

chalkhill blue

horseshoe vetch seed pods

Restharrow
Ononis repens

Stemless thistle
Cirsium acaulon

Squinacywort
Asperula cynanchica

Hairy violet
Viola hirta

Grassland flowers frequently have rosettes of leaves, or grow in mats close to the soil. Many are waxy to reduce water loss in the dry surroundings.

Wild grasses to look for in the springy turf are sheep's fescue, red fescue, and quaking grass (see page 121).

The soil of a riverside meadow may be neutral, but it may be rather limy if the water comes from limestone or chalk. Many flowers can be expected, including orchids (pages 120–124). See page 208 for water-side flowers. Birds and butterflies are on pages 140, 144.

Hay meadows

Old-established hay meadows contain a long list of plants whose life cycles suit them to traditional hay-making regimes. In the north, the animals are allowed on to meadowland for an early bite in spring, then the field is shut up until mowing in July or August. In the south, the hay is cut in late June or July. The livestock are then allowed back in to graze the aftermath.

Many meadow plants flower and set seed early in the year when the field is shut up. They flourish undisturbed. They suffer, however, if silage is cut from the field.

Many of our remaining hay meadows are as old as the village church nearby. It is a fascinating insight into history to discover that the Domesday Book counted them more valuable than arable land.

Some of our old meadows survive because of an anachronism in their ownership – they may be part common land or worked in joint ownership, or perhaps conservation arguments have been well received, ways maintained.

Typically, however, these priceless relics are found in distant corners of farms where grandpa still does things in the way they were done when he was a boy.

The snake's-head fritillary was once widespread in lowland water meadows but, as these sites have been progressively drained and reseeded, it has become restricted to a few sites in the Thames valley and elsewhere. It has many strange local names: 'dead men's bells' in Shropshire, 'leper's lilies' in the West Country and 'toads' heads' in Wiltshire. To 50 cm.

Great burnet is found mainly in central and northern England. Its unusual deep crimson, plantain-like flowers have no petals. It is closely related to the salad burnet of the chalk grasslands. June-September; to 1 metre.

Pepper saxifrage is a member of the umbellifer family and some say it takes its name from the peppery smell of its fruits. It has yellow flowering umbels and finely-divided leaves. June-August; to 1 metre.

Adder's-tongue fern is found throughout Britain in old grasslands but gets rarer further north. Its spore cases are held at the top of the central stem. To 20 cm.

Cowslips are classic plants of old grass fields. The yellow flowerheads have an apricot scent. The sweet seed stalks, with their seeds, are sometimes taken by ants back to their nest, and this helps to distribute the species. April-May; to 30 cm.

Devil's-bit scabious has short roots which led to the legend that the Devil bit off the root in anger against the Virgin Mary. It is found in damp water meadows and woodland rides. Its mauve-purple flowers are a favourite of bees and butterflies. June-October; to 1 metre.

Cuckoo flower (Lady's smock) **is found mainly near streams** but also in meadows alongside. Its base leaves are watercress-like and can be eaten in salads. Its pinky-white flowers appear in April-July; to 60 cm.

Yellow rattle is a classic indicator of old unimproved grassland (see page 123).

Great burnet
Sanguisorba officinalis

Cuckoo flower
Cardamine pratensis

Pepper saxifrage
Silaum silaus

Snake's head fritillary
Fritillaria meleagris

Devil's bit scabious
Succisa pratensis

green-veined white caterpillar

Cowslip
Primula veris

Yellow rattle
Rhinanthus minor

Adder's tongue fern
Ophioglossum vulgatum

Cowslips can be seen on many different soils, but prefer rather dryish conditions, so you may see them in chalk grassland, opposite.

Look for lime-loving plants noted on page 148, and look also for mountain avens (page 164) and melancholy thistle (page 126). The sheltered grikes may, however, give a home to woodland plants of a limy tendency – see pages 32, 34, 63. Ferns are on page 38.

Grassland of the limestone hills

It might be expected that limestone grasslands would carry many of the plants typical of chalk, because chalk is, after all, just a very pure form of limestone. However, limestone is harder and more widespread than chalk, and it is interesting to find that the more northerly limestone pastures and meadows carry plants that are not found on limestones of the south. What you will find is that many plants are not found in both localities; for example, that exceptionally beautiful flower, the bird's-eye primrose, is found in the Yorkshire Dales but not on the Sussex Downs. Globe flowers too have this rather northerly distribution. The fact that the soil is limy is obviously not the only criterion to be taken into account when predicting what plants can be found where. Limestone and chalk soils are often rather dry, because of their porous bedrock, but the limestone soil can be kept moist by the high rainfall of the north, producing in places a rather unexpected flora which is at home in damp conditions.

A view out across the limestone pavement at Malham Cove in the Yorkshire Dales. This remarkable landscape is produced by a combination of glacial erosion of the original weathered top soil and the effect of rain over many thousands of years.

Limestone pavement

Among the strangest sights of the British countryside are limestone pavements. Originally there were about 2,000 hectares (5,000 acres) of pavement chiefly in parts of the Pennines, but also at a few scattered sites in north Wales and northwest Scotland. Where the limestone rock has been laid bare by glacial action, great 'paving stones', called 'clints', separated by fissures called 'grikes', can be seen. The fissures have been eaten away by rain, which dissolves the lines of weakness in the rock. The exposed surface of the clints is smooth. The grikes can be quite wide and deep, and down within them plants can be found. Little vegetation sticks up out of these grikes, as sheep graze over the pavement, snatching at any mouthfuls they can reach. Sometimes you may find that stretches of pavement disappear beneath soil with trees growing, indicating that once the pavement may have been covered by trees or was exposed only in woodland clearings. It is interesting that many of the plants you see in the gloomy but damp grikes are woodland plants – and in the humid conditions there are always plenty of ferns.

You may catch sight of wrens nesting but few if any other birds can be seen in them.

As a national asset of our countryside, limestone pavement is beyond price. There is plenty to be found in Europe and elsewhere, but here in Britain it is a valuable element of the tight-packed diversity of our countryside. However, it does have a price as stone for rockeries. In 1951, no less than a thousand tons of it were sent to London, to feature in the Festival of Britain as part of an exhibit about the history of the land. Of the original 5,000 acres, only half now remains undamaged.

On this exposed limestone rock, lichens form a patchwork of whites and greys, whilst in the cracks and depressions mosses have managed to establish a foothold. A rich mixture of grasses, bird's-foot trefoil, clover and wild thyme has developed on the thicker soils overlying these limestone rocks.

Globe flower is a typical plant of northern limestone grasslands. The outer 'petals' are in fact yellow sepals – the true petals being hidden inside the flower; to 60 cm.

Rock-rose is a rather shrubby plant with many branches coming from a thick woody stem. It is abundant sometimes where the thin soil is trampled or disturbed, perhaps because its tall grass competitors cannot get hold in these places. It is not one of the roses, but forms its own family with one or two similar plants. June-September and only opens fully in sun; to 5–30 cm.

Wild thyme is often found with the rock-rose. Thyme has a pretty trailing habit with an attractive flower and scent. There are in fact three rather similar wild thymes to be found in Britain. The larger is strongly scented and the common wild thyme is less scented. June-September; to 60 cm.

Both wild thyme and rock-rose exude juices which are washed off by the rain and inhibit the germination of seeds in the soil below.

Lady's mantle has evolved a most unusual system for eliminating excess water if the air is damp with rain. Plants have to lose water through their leaves to be able to suck up soil nutrients through the roots. In damp conditions, lady's mantle forces water out through pores around the edge of its leaves. The leaves often carry pearls of this 'dew' when other plants are dry. June-August; 10–20 cm.

Bloody cranesbill is so spectacular it looks like a garden hybrid. 'Bloody' refers not to its colour; but to its old medicinal use to staunch wounds. July-August; 10–40 cm.

Bird's-eye primrose is especially fond of damp grasslands in the 'intakes' (the enclosed high grazings) of the northern Pennines. May-June; to 15 cm.

Common flax has blue flowers, as does the cultivated species. The tiny **fairy flax** shown here has white flowers. June-September; 5–25 cm.

Moonwort is a small fern. The golden brown 'flowers' on its branched spike are spore fronds. Rabbits seem to like the taste of it. June-August; to 20 cm.

Globe flower
Trollius europaeus

Bloody cranesbill
Geranium sanguineum

Moonwort
Botrychium lunaria

small heath butterfly

Bird's eye primrose
Primula farinosa

large skipper butterfly

Fairy flax
Linum catharticum

Wild thyme
Thymus drucei

Lady's mantle
Alchemilla vulgaris

Rock rose
Helianthemum chamaecistus

You can see here a drop or two of the 'magic dew' on the leaf of lady's mantle. In some weather conditions, the whole of the surface is covered with these brightly shining drops of water.

Wilderness and Freshwater

On the mountain tops **1** can be found plants remaining from the end of the Ice Age. But beware of taking our wilderness lands at face value, for pollen found in ancient pockets of soil tells us that even the high moors **2** were once tree-covered. They were cleared and kept open by grazing, which still takes place within and without the 'intake' walls **3** of the hills.

Many of today's moors are managed for shooting, and the patterning of the burnt heather **4** is easy to see. Heather also forms part of the communities of lowland heaths **5** – heaths are in many ways very similar to high moorland, but even more at risk in today's countryside. Bogs **6** can be an important feature of both moors and wet heaths.

Water is everywhere, shaping the land. It has been called the eye of the landscape, and provides many varied habitats for wildlife. The rushing troutbecks of the hills **7** provide a very different habitat from the slower lowland reaches, where coarse fishing rather than trout can be found **8**. Trout however are often found also in fast, clean lowland streams and rivers.

> 'What would the world be, once bereft
> Of wet and wildness? Let them be left'
>
> *Gerard Manley Hopkins ('Inversnaid')*

Our wilderness lands give refuge to the golden eagle, red deer and other animals. The wildlife of water habitats can be outstanding – the birdlife of rivers and lakes is sometimes exceptional.

WILDEST BRITAIN is the lonely world of the uplands, where the climate is too hostile for man to settle. It is a world of high rolling moors where there are more sheep than people, of rock and scree, sphagnum bog, cotton grass and sullen summits that sulk in the clouds. It is an unforgiving landscape, windswept, rain-lashed and covered with snow for much of the winter. To survive here, wildlife must be tough and adaptable.

In the Highlands, summers are brief, and butterflies such as the mountain ringlet must make the most of the sunny days in late June and July. Now is the time when the bracken grows tall. Higher up it is replaced by heather, that most characteristic moorland plant, blooming in immense sweeps of hazy purple. On many such moors, grouse and heather go together, and the guttural chuckle of these fast-flying game birds is one of the most evocative of all upland sounds.

Sometimes, as you trudge towards the clouds, you may come across an ancient tree stump, preserved like a fossil in the peat: a relic from times when forest clothed much of upland Britain. But above 1,000 metres the land was always bare. At first glance these high tops seem utterly devoid of life and movement. Left behind are the mauve spikes of the heath spotted orchid, the yellow flowers of bog asphodel, the slopes of bent grass and sheep's fescue. Here a new regime takes root, with lichens, crowberry and three-leaved rush. In the silence, there is only the sad cries of pipits, seeping like drizzle from the sky, and the plaintive fluting of golden plovers. But look around you. The feeling of emptiness is an illusion. There are ptarmigan in the rocks and mountain hares. Hidden in the high corries are red deer; and that black speck slowly sailing over the distant mountains could well be a golden eagle. Some 270 pairs of these, our biggest birds of prey, now breed every year in the Scottish Highlands.

Farther south, in the uplands of Wales, it is the red kite which holds pride of place, sharing the wide moors with merlins, buzzards and peregrine falcons. They are joined by carrion crows and ravens, ring ouzels and sweet-throated curlew, whose mournful bubbling cries haunt all our moors, from Scotland to Cornwall.

The heather which feeds the upland grouse also flourishes on the acid lowland sands and gravels of southern England, forming wild heathlands which echo the high moors in almost every respect except altitude. Heaths can be found in many southern counties, from the dry Breckland of East Anglia to the Lizard peninsula in Cornwall. Thursley Common in Surrey is renowned for its wet heathland, rich in dragonflies and orchids; but the greatest remaining concentration of heath lies around the Hampshire basin, in parts of the New Forest and south-east Dorset. Yet even here it is one of our most threatened habitats. Dorset has lost more than four-fifths of its heaths, and those that remain are vulnerable to fire. But where they still exist, as at Arne, the RSPB reserve on the edge of Poole Harbour, they provide a home not only for distinctive heathland species such as adders, stonechats and silver-studded blue butterflies; but also for some of our less common migrants – the nightjar and hobby – and even rarer creatures such as the sand lizard, smooth snake and Dartford warbler.

It is a far cry from the crackling dry summer heaths of Dorset to the remote Highlands and islands of Scotland, where red-throated divers breed on lochans thick with bogbean and water lilies. In the hills of northern Britain, even in summer, the ground squelches underfoot, so great is the rainfall. The bogs and mosses soak up the rain and melting snows like a giant sponge. When the hills can hold no more, the water runs off, feeding the cold lochs and upland tarns of Cumbria and Snowdonia, in whose depths live the char and vendace, Ice Age relatives of the salmon.

Some Scottish lochs are graced by the presence of the osprey. These elegant cream and chocolate fish-hawks were so heavily persecuted by egg collectors that they were not seen in Britain for 50 years. But today, with more enlightened attitudes towards wildlife and round-the-clock surveillance at their nest sites, the osprey has made a dramatic and welcome return to Loch Garten and other Scottish waters.

Rain falling on the uplands returns to the seas as rivers. Even a mighty river like the Severn begins as a trickle in the bogs of Plynlimon. In their infancy, the

Conditions in a river can change by the yard, **9**, **10**, and not only naturally. Pollution can be an important factor **11**. Equally interesting are the swamps, fens and other wetland communities **12**. They were once a major feature of the lowlands, but are now drained for fields **13**. Flooded gravel pits and other new pools can (even if small) have great wildlife interest **14**.

brawling becks come frothing and tumbling out of the hills, splashing boulders where dippers bob, to form clear cidery pools, rich in oxygen, where small brook trout and stone loach swim.

Lower down, as the river grows in size, gathering tributaries, it flows more quietly as the gradient eases, forming deeper pools where trout and salmon might lie. Some of the loveliest rivers in Britain are the classic trout streams of the southern chalklands, such as the Test and Itchen. Here in midsummer the clear waters fill with the floating tresses and white starry flowers of water crowfoot. Demoiselles skitter on dusky iridescent wings above the lush bankside vegetation. By steeper banked rivers, kingfishers perch on overhanging branches, waiting for sticklebacks.

Otters are everywhere becoming rarer, except in the Highlands and islands of Scotland. In the south their old haunts have been usurped by the feral mink, though the spraints (droppings) and seals (prints) of otters still reveal the tenuous presence of these shyest of British mammals along the banks of a few lowland rivers where disturbance is minimal.

More common are the bank-dwelling water-voles, excellent underwater swimmers, which are preyed upon by herons, barn owls and pike. The predatory pike with its dappled flanks and cruel jaws is just one of a host of coarse fish which favour our sluggish lowland rivers. Here, too, can be found quick shoals of silvery dace, the diminutive gudgeon and thick-set chub. Sometimes a sudden gleam of bronze among the lily-pads may reveal the

A rugged upland scene near Glen Coe in the Scottish Highlands. This dramatic scenery has been shaped by thousands of years of action by rain and ice. The steeply plunging valley in the foreground has been cut by the tumbling waters of the stream but the wide, flat bottomed valley behind is the result of action by glaciers which gouged out great U-shaped valleys during the last Ice Age.

Spring in a North Yorkshire river valley with bright stands of yellow marsh marigolds. The banks are covered with the tall spikes of butterbur and their enormous rhubarb-like leaves.

A traditional view of the Norfolk Broads – reed-fringed and covered with water-lilies and marestails. Sadly scenes like this are now rare even in the heart of the Broads, as the combined effects of water pollution and increased disturbance by boating have cleared most of the waters of their larger plants.

presence of a cruising tench. Elsewhere, perch with spiny dorsal fins and tigerish stripes conceal themselves among the submerged reed stems, and heavyweight carp root like pigs along the muddy river bottoms.

These lower reaches burgeon with water plants wherever banks are left unshorn. Between the willows and water-loving alders, flowering rush, purple loosestrife, water mint, willowherb and dense stands of bur-reed build a waterside jungle whose rampant stems are the refuge of dab-chicks, moorhens, reed buntings and sedge warblers.

Many of these water-loving plants and birds will also be found in the wetlands of Britain, in the marshes and reed-beds of low-lying valleys, at the edges of lakes and meres, in the drowned medieval peat-workings of the Norfolk Broads and in the flat fenlands of East Anglia and the Somerset Levels. With the draining of the Fens, wetland species such as bitterns and raft spiders, and plants like the fen violet and fen orchid, have become increasingly rare. Most of our true remaining fens are small and scattered, and can support no more than a few individuals of each species. Therefore if these should meet with any kind of mishap – an exceptionally severe spell of winter weather or a pollution accident – the chance of a recolonisation from other sites is slim. Yet the magnificent swallowtail butterfly still flies in the Norfolk Broad, and the Dutch race of our own extinct large copper has been successfully reintroduced at Woodwalton Fen, to remind us that where now grows nothing but corn and sugar beet, there was once only the wind in the reeds and the boom of the bittern.

Bogs are neither muddy nor smelly, and far from being featureless they are detailed and interesting. This page shows how they form. Some of the plants that grow in bogs are shown on page 160. Stone walls are often part of the scene; see also page 116.

Peat bogs

Peat bogs, more than any other plant community, testify to our wet Atlantic climate. They hold an important place in the story of our countryside, having formerly covered large areas of Britain, particularly in the north and west. Even the lowlands had large areas of peat bog.

Peat bogs can form anywhere conditions are suitably wet. When plant material collects in waterlogged airless situations there are few organisms to break down the dead matter so it gradually accumulates over the years to form layers of peat. The peat tends to keep its nutrients locked up and therefore many plants find it difficult to grow in such a setting. Bog mosses, or *Sphagnum*, are the exception as they can exploit the wet, acid, mineral-poor conditions to the full, taking most of their nutrients directly from the rainfall.

There are many types of *Sphagnum* moss in Britain, but with a few exceptions they are difficult to tell apart. Some, however, are brightly coloured ranging from almost crimson to bright green. They have a porous structure which holds the rainwater like a sponge. Even in the driest of summers a surprising amount of water can be squeezed from them. Gradually, fed by the rain, the mosses flourish, the bog peat accumulates and the surface layer of living mosses becomes higher than its surroundings. You would then expect the top layers of the bog to begin to dry out. However, in our damp climate the spongy bog mosses remain sodden and continue to grow, laying more peat beneath them. Over thousands of years, broad low domes of peat, sometimes ten metres high and up to a kilometre across, rose above the surrounding level of the land. These 'raised bogs' have left us the thick beds of peat in East Anglia, Lincolnshire, Lancashire, Somerset and many other places. If they had not been cut and drained in recent centuries they would still be there. They are still actively growing in a few places: some of the best ones are found along the Scottish border.

Even in mineral-rich areas, once the fen peat, which is made up of dead sedges, rushes, etc., has built up above the general water level, the *Sphagnum* bog mosses can move in to dominate the leached surface leaving only a thin band of the rich fen plants at the edge, where the fresh inflows of water still replenish the mineral content of the community.

Bogs are still an important feature of our upland scenery. Under the British climate, trees once grew to about 600 metres or more up the mountainsides, but it seems that this high-level tree cover disappeared quite early, partly due to clearance by man and partly due to changes in climate. The open ground has provided rough grazing ever since. The story has a twist, however, for once these upland areas became treeless they, too, could develop peat bogs. On the poor and often acid soils of the rainy uplands, bogs flourished and in the flatter areas spread like a blanket over the ground, lapping around boulders and even moving up gentle slopes. These 'blanket bogs' created the thick beds of peat which often cap the slopes of the Welsh hills, the Pennines and the high ground in the west of Scotland.

A blanket bog in Snowdonia showing the areas of open water surrounded by a quaking crust of green *Sphagnum* mosses and cotton-grass. On the drier hummocks rushes and dark green heather have established themselves.

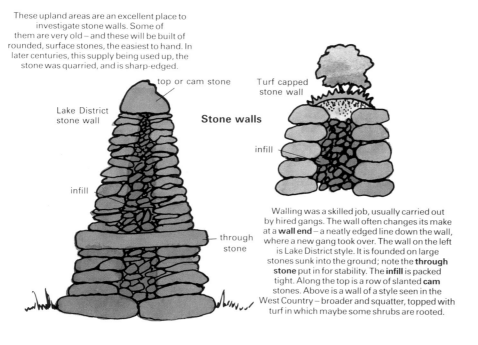

These upland areas are an excellent place to investigate stone walls. Some of them are very old – and these will be built of rounded, surface stones, the easiest to hand. In later centuries, this supply being used up, the stone was quarried, and is sharp-edged.

top or cam stone

Turf capped stone wall

Lake District stone wall

Stone walls

infill

infill

through stone

Walling was a skilled job, usually carried out by hired gangs. The wall often changes its make at a **wall end** – a neatly edged line down the wall, where a new gang took over. The wall on the left is Lake District style. It is founded on large stones sunk into the ground; note the **through stone** put in for stability. The **infill** is packed tight. Along the top is a row of slanted **cam** stones. Above is a wall of a style seen in the West Country – broader and squatter, topped with turf in which maybe some shrubs are rooted.

From a distance, peat wilderness seems monotonous, but close inspection often shows a miniature geography of hummocks and pools, which create different conditions for many kinds of animals, as well as plants. This mosaic is very noticeable on undrained raised bogs.

Some of the plants grow up through the moss from roots in the peat beneath. Some are rooted in the living moss. Others colonise the drier hummocks. This is where heather, bilberry and lichens are found.

Look for flushes along drainage lines, bringing a supply of nutrients to a bog, and allowing rather different plants, such as bog bean, to flourish.

Pollution can affect even these remote areas. A century and a half ago, the Pennine hills between Manchester and Sheffield were a botanist's delight, with many different bog plants growing on the peat. Today, only cotton grass flourishes in their place. It is thought that this is most probably a result of air pollution from the two cities.

Once dry, peat burns well and has always been dug for home fires. Nowadays, peat is extracted on a large scale for gardening and horticulture. In Ireland some power stations burn it. The greatest threats our bogs face are drainage to improve grazing and the spread of commercial conifer plantations.

Bog mosses are surprisingly sensitive to disturbance. A temporary path across a bog may last for well over a year. Sheep trods are often permanent features of bogs.

Look for deep gullies eroded in the peat. Here you may find something interesting. Peat is, in a way, like a history book. Anything buried in it remains well preserved. So, on the sides of the gully look for layers of charcoal from burnings long ago. You may even find pieces of wood or hazel nuts dating from the time when the hills were covered with trees. You may often be able to tell from the bark that the fragment is silver birch, rowan or pine.

157

The rule of thumb is that moors are upland, have heather and grass but few trees and no scrub; there is much boggy ground. Heaths are lowland, marked by heather but often with scrub and trees invading: there may be bog in very wet areas.

Moors and heaths

Both moors and heaths can carry heather and grass as well as share many other plants in common, so there is frequently some confusion between them, and it must be admitted that there is no clear dividing line. Moors are typically wide tracts of untilled ground in the uplands, often covered with heather and with a poor peaty soil. Heaths tend to be found on poor sandy or gravel soils in lowland areas. Bog peat and sand are both acid, so you would expect heather, that classic indicator of acid soils, to grow in both.

Grazing has always been important in these wilderness areas and may affect what you find. Sheep will graze most plants. They quickly nibble down luxuriant bilberry bushes and almost eliminate them. Heather can be killed if the grazing is very heavy and grasses then grow in its place, but if the grazing slackens heather returns and gorse may invade the margins.

It is strange to think of birds as important grazing animals but grouse certainly are; they feed on the young green shoots of heather, but they also need the older woody bushes for cover. To provide both, the grouse moors are regularly burnt, usually in small patches of about an acre (0.4 hectares) every eight to twelve years. Young heather grows vigorously from the rootstocks left undamaged by the fire, or from seed. The mosaic of this 'swaling' (in Scotland it is called 'muirburn') patterns the shooting moors of the north.

In much the same way that many small woods in the lowlands are retained for pheasant shooting, grouse shooting plays a vital role in the uplands. Without the sport, there would be greater economic pressures to cover private grouse moors with conifer plantations.

The burning of heather

The grouse-shooting season begins on 12th August (the 'glorious twelfth') and ends on December 10th; 'swaling' takes place after that – it is an activity lasting through winter to late spring.

The firing has another benefit; it lessens the chances of accidental summer fires.

These could cause great damage, killing the plants, destroying nests and young birds, and scorching the peat, thus starting erosion.

Lowland heaths are sometimes fired, also in winter, to keep them open by destroying gorse, pine and birch seedlings which rapidly invade heathland once grazing stops.

▲ **Burning patterns on grouse moors** in the north-east Grampians.

◀ **Sheep are one of the most important grazing** animals in the Highlands and have had a dramatic effect on the scenery.

▶ **Lowland heath near Hindhead** in Surrey, showing the encroachment of birch and pine on the open landscape.

The unnatural status of our British wilderness can be highlighted by the verges of a road crossing the upland moors. The verge may carry 'lowland' plants while only a metre or two away over the wall the moorland starts.

On the drier slopes, you may see swards of those old familiars, the bent and fescue grasses, perhaps accompanied by harebells. But where it is wetter, two very distinctive grasses replace them. They are mat grass and purple moor grass. These vigorous invaders are only soft and palatable in early spring and under grazing pressure they may take over from other plants, their coarse leaves growing to form dense tussocks. Mat grass does well where drainage is impeded, while purple moor grass flourishes where there is some slight movement of the water through the soil, as there is in the valley bottoms.

If the ground is well drained, bracken may sometimes invade. Cattle help control it by eating the young shoots and trampling the rest underfoot, but sheep do not damage it. Because it is sensitive to frost, bracken fades out above 500 metres.

Some of the heathland plants shown on page 166 may also be met on moorland. Look out for wavy hair grass and sheep's fescue, page 120. Identify the rushes, see page 206. Typical animal life can be seen on the pages following this.

Plants of moors and bogs

Not many plants are capable of growing on the infertile peat of moors or boggy land, but those you do find are usually impressive in their own way. The sundew, for example, traps and digests insects to gain the vital nutrient supply that the peat cannot give.

Heather should not be taken for granted: it does after all produce a rather impressive woody growth in such surroundings. Botanists class it as a dwarf shrub. It can flourish because its roots house fungal threads which help it obtain nutrients. The fungus breaks down dead matter, a job done by the bacteria of other soils.

Heather has four splendid ages: the young carpet-forming pioneer; the vigorous tussock-former; the mature bush; and finally it becomes tall and leggy and the centre stems begin to die – the start of old age. But even the oldest heather bushes are rarely more than 25 years old.

Heather and its close relatives are mostly evergreen and almost all of them are indicators of acid soil. They can also mark other soil differences; bell heather grows on drier ground, while cross-leaved heath favours wetter places, often growing with purple moor grass.

◄◄ **The fluffy white fruiting-heads of cotton-grasses** are a common sight in mid-summer in the boggy uplands of north and west Britain.

▼ **The lovely bell-shaped flowers of cowberry** (*Vaccinium vitis-idaea*). It is a close relative of bilberry but with glossy evergreen leaves. This low-growing shrub is only found in upland moors and woods and produces a red edible fruit in late summer.

▼ **The open fells of the Lake District** in late summer are a blaze of purple when the heather blossoms.

buzzard in flight

Merlin
Falco columbarius

male
Ptarmigan
Lagopus mutus
female

Feral goat
Capra hircus

curlew

dunlin

golden plover

Antler moth
Ceraptefyx graminis

Grouse fly with bursts
of rapid wing beats
followed by long glides,
often closely following
the contours of the ground,
sometimes rolling from
side to side.

male

Red grouse
Lagopus lagopus

female

Short-tailed vole
Microtus agrestis

chick

Red grouse usually occupy lower ground than ptarmigan, being found at 300–600 metres, where the main heather moors occur. The British red grouse is native to only Britain, though it has been introduced to Belgium; it does not become white in winter, unlike the Continental race, known as the willow grouse, which has white wings in summer and is all-white in winter.
Grouse are stay-at-home birds and territorial, though family groups may flock together in winter. As well as the chuckle, they have a *kowk* alarm call.
The nest of grouse is a shallow hollow made by the hen bird, in the shelter of taller heather. 40 cm.

Ptarmigans spend summers at the mountain tops of the Scottish Highlands, but may come down to the lower moors in winter. They are the only British birds to become white in winter. The cocks, in fact, have three moults a year: brown to grey; then to white; then in spring to brown. They are grouse-like in feeding and breeding behaviour. The nest is in a bare scrape out in the open, though it may be sheltered by low cover. A grating alarm call, and croaking, a harsh sounding *uk-uk*; 35 cm.

range) changes in its environment, in today's countryside.

Grouse, too, reflect man's hand. They are native birds, but the large numbers needed to make shooting rents a profitable business are obtained by burning the heather and creating ideal, tight-packed territories. They are strongly territorial birds and some think that the annual shoots take the 'loose' birds making do with second-best territories. Grouse have now become well established where they have been reintroduced on to moorlands in the Pennines. Man's hand, again, has fashioned the distribution of a wild species.

The mountain or blue hare, too, is now seen in what were very probably its old haunts, though not in recent centuries.

An animal of the Scottish Highlands, it has been reintroduced into the hills of southern Scotland, the Lakes and the Peak District, with varying degrees of success. It is interesting that in Ireland where there are no brown hares, the blue hare also occupies lowland fields.

So there are on this page many examples of how wild populations reflect man's design. So far, there has been only one successful reintroduction of a vertebrate animal back into Britain (that is the reintroduction of a native species which had become 'extinct'). The species is the capercaillie, a large (80 cm) turkey-like, woodland grouse which likes older pine forests. Our native stock became extinct in 1785, but some were brought from Europe in 1837, and they now live wild in many places in Scotland. Attempts

are being made at present to re-establish breeding pairs of white-tailed eagles in the Hebrides. These eagles became extinct in Britain in the last century, though in recent history they had been as plentiful as the golden eagle.

This purposeful introduction of species lost to us, or spreading the present range of native animals or birds, or restocking areas in which a few of them already live is not at all the same thing as the spread of animals which were never native. In Britain, we have forty species of mammals; nineteen of them are 'exotics', and these include wallabies (in the Peak District), Himalayan porcupines (in Devon), South American coypus (in the Broads), as well as the thriving populations of house mice, grey squirrels, minks and rabbits!

163

The high mountains

Mountains are essentially harsh places but they do have sheltered gullies and the different rock layers each add their own chemical flavour to the thin soil. So there is scope for diversity and consequently many different plant communities can be found on a single mountain. Our mountains are not very high compared with those of some other countries and sheep can be found grazing right to the summit in many places. Therefore the more interesting plants may be found only on cliff ledges, in gullies and other inaccessible spots.

On the exposed tops, the combined stress of wind and low temperatures may mean that only lichens and mosses are at all common. Look for grey carpets of 'woolly-hair' moss in the lee of boulders. If there is, by chance, a scrap of woody scrub, it is most likely to be low and wind-pruned. This stress coupled with the short, unpredictable summers forces some plants to adopt new reproduction strategies. Sheep's fescue, which is a common upland grass, is replaced by a close relation, viviparous fescue, which produces

young plants or bulbils in the flower cluster. This strategy is stimulated by damp air, for the same plant can be found near the sea in western Britain.

The ground-hugging clumps of arctic-alpine plants that can be found on the ledges and gullies were the first colonists of the environment when the last Ice Age drew to a close, and they are still surviving in isolated patches where the conditions are similar to those of 12,000 years ago. These hardy plants would have then been found over much of Britain but have since retreated to the high mountain climes. Surprisingly you might find thrift and sea campion in these mountain 'alpine gardens', far from the sea shores where you would expect them. On the other hand, in north-west Scotland, mountain avens and purple saxifrage grow down from the mountains to sea level. The cold short summers may encourage these plants both directly and by restricting natural rivals.

In courtship, a pair of eagles will soar in spirals, then plunge to earth. Their eyries are usually seen between 450 and 600 metres (1500 and 2000 ft).

Golden eagle
Aquila chrysaetos

Raven
Corvus corax

Moss campion
Silene acaulis

Red deer
Cervus elaphus

stag

Purple saxifrage
Saxifraga oppositifolia

hind

Mountain avens
Dryas octopetala

Alpine lady's mantle
Alchemilla alpina

Lady's mantle is a member of the rose family, as is mountain avens. Compare the latter with wood and water avens, on pages 32, 34. The meaning of the word 'avens' is not certain – it is French in origin.

Starry saxifrage
Saxifraga stellaris

Golden eagles can survive and breed at higher altitudes than buzzards and ravens. When outspread the wings are 'fingered'. The golden eagle is our largest bird of prey, with a territory of thousands of hectares. On that territory, several different nest sites in trees or on cliffs are used in rotation. For food, these eagles take hares and carrion and grouse, a habit for which they are still persecuted. They are usually silent, but can utter a thin yelp. There are perhaps as many as 300 breeding pairs in Britain. 80 cm (1.8 metre wingspan).

The raven is a bulky bird, larger than a crow. It has a wedge-shaped tail, a heavy bill, and a bearded look to its neck. It is an acrobatic flier. Like the buzzard it once bred in all counties, but persecution has restricted it to the hills and remote parts of the north and west. It is often seen at sea cliffs, for example. Ravens take a wide range of food, including carrion. They have a *pruk pruk* call with other harsh croaks. Ravens nest under an overhang on cliffs or other inaccessible spots, sometimes in trees. 64 cm.

The red deer is our largest game mammal, and 'deer forest' is a traditional land use in the Highlands, with a regular annual 'cull' of animals. This tradition really goes back to the mid-19th century, when much of the Highlands were turned over to game – the red grouse on the heather moor and the red deer on higher ground.

Moss campion grows in dense green cushions dotted with single pink flowers. A plant of cliff ledges, rocks and scree. Flowers July-August.

Purple saxifrage indicates basic (non-acid) **rocks.** It is a mat-forming plant, with tiny thyme-like oval leaves densely covering its stems; the flowers barely have a stalk. It flowers March-May, sometimes later.

Starry saxifrage grows over acid rock, especially on wet ground alongside streams. It can be found quite high up in upland areas of the north of England and Scotland, rare elsewhere. June-August.

Mountain avens has leaves shaped like miniature oak leaves, glossy green above, silvery below. It is a low creeping woody shrub. Mountain avens is found on limestone and other basic rocks. 8 cm high.

Alpine lady's mantle grows well on acid rock if wet, but prefers slightly limy soil if dry. Compare this alpine lady's mantle with the lady's mantle of the lower grasslands shown on page 150.

The acid soil of moors contains few worms. Compare the meadow pipit with the skylark, page 144. Compare the ringlet with other brown butterflies, page 140. Plants seen growing on moorland are shown on pages 160, 166.

The moors

You may be rather surprised to hear cuckoos on the high moors. However, in upland areas the cuckoo will frequently choose to lay its eggs in the nest of meadow pipits. Any rough ground from sea level to 1,000 metres will probably be occupied by meadow pipits – they are our commonest moorland birds. The cuckoos seem not too unsuccessful either: one survey showed one in five of the pipit nests sporting a cuckoo egg.

Another surprising animal often seen on heather moors is the large, day-flying emperor moth, a relative of the silk moths. The large eye-spots on its wings may have the effect of frightening off bird predators. A cuckoo seen hunting over a moor is more likely to be searching for the emperor moth's caterpillars. However, their bright green and black coloration camouflages them beautifully amongst the young heather and bilberry shoots on which they feed.

A noise like a distant free-wheeling bike is made by the common green grasshopper. It is common in the lowlands but is also found further north and higher than the other grasshoppers. Many insects such as members of the grasshopper family reach the northernmost limits of their range in Britain, which sometimes explains the rather surprising fluctuations in their numbers year by year. They are rather like pioneers, laying claim to potentially hostile ground and at risk if circumstances change slightly.

Some insects which are more common in higher and colder regions also have a foothold in Britain's uplands. Consider the mountain ringlet, which is found only above 550 metres in the Lake District but above 450 metres in the Grampians. Its nearest neighbouring colonies are in the Alps. The Scotch argus, shown here, is confined to Scotland (although there are two recent reports of it from the southern Lake District) where it is found on lower ground than the mountain ringlet.

The female emperor moth is larger than the male, and rather lighter and more greyish in colour. You may often see her perched: she emits a scent which attracts the males to her from surprising distances (there is some evidence that moths can 'smell' up to three kilometres away). Scent is picked up by the feathery antennae.

The meadow pipit is seen on any rough ground from sea level to 1,000 metres high. It is the most numerous small breeding bird above 500 metres, and is a major item of prey for merlins as well as playing host to young cuckoos. It is resident, but many birds from northern Europe winter in Britain; these usually remain in lowland areas. You may find the meadow pipit easy to overlook, but listen for its faint *tseep tseep* call carried by the wind. The meadow pipit has an interesting song flight: up to 30 metres, then a slanting glide down, the song becoming faster all the time, ending with a trill. The nest is on the ground, like the skylark's, but is likely to be nearer the cover of a wall, bank or bush.

Dunlin are, perhaps, the least often seen of the waders breeding on moorlands. If you do see one, notice its black belly patch, which is usually lost in winter. For every pair there are ten pairs of curlews and 35 pairs of lapwings.

The mournful call of the curlew can often be heard echoing across the moors and uplands of northern Britain in spring. They probe for insects and other creatures in the soft ground with their long, curved bill. Call a drawn-out *curlee*; 56 cm.

The golden plover has a black chin and underparts in the summer. It is typically found nesting on gently sloping moorland in north and west Britain. Call a single-note whistle *whoo-ee*; 28 cm.

Male emperor moths fly fast by day in search of the females. The cocoon has a ring of fibres around the exit hole to deter invaders. They are large; 65 mm ws (female); 55 mm ws (male).

Dragonflies, such as this brown hawker, often breed in the peaty pools of moorland bogs.

The mountain ringlet is our only true 'alpine' butterfly. Seen on sunny days in June and July, often over boggy ground. It flies with a weak fluttering flight, only in sunshine: the moment the sun clouds over it disappears into the grass. The eggs are laid singly on mat grass. It is one of the browns; 30 mm ws.

The Scotch argus flies with a slow, fluttering flight July-August, lower down the hillsides than the mountain ringlet but like the latter, only when the sun is out. Its name is misleading, for it is not related to the brown argus, and is not a 'blue butterfly' but one of a small family restricted to alpine and sub-arctic habitats. Caterpillars feed on purple moor-grass. 45 mm ws.

The common green grasshopper (often emerald green but it can vary to olive) jumps and flies actively in sunshine. The only grasshopper to be expected on high moors, for it is found higher and further north than other grasshoppers. June-October; body 20 mm.

Heathers and other plants of acid soils are shown on page 160. Look also for wood sage, page 32. Bogs may develop in the wetter parts of heathland, page 156. Look for mosses as well as ferns, page 38. Look for the heath spotted orchid, page 124.

Plants of the lowland barrens

The plants shown here are often to be found on dry lowland heaths, but some of them also occur in 'moorland' communities, if grazing is not too heavy. Gorse is a typical plant of these areas. It is one of our best known flowers, recognised not only by its spines and flowers but by its glorious scent. You will find it on most heathlands, where it can be something of a nuisance because it shades out smaller plants. Nowadays, it is also often seen on the slopes of motorway cuttings as it can easily invade disturbed ground.

Gorse is interesting because it usually grows the typical trefoil leaves of the pea-family only when it is a young plant. In later life it only has spines on the stems. In this mature gorse, most photosynthesis takes place in the green stems. There is an echo here of the strategy adopted by cactus plants, which also have leaves reduced to spines to cut down water loss.

Lousewort is found on damp heaths and moors, on acid soil (it is a good soil indicator). Compare it with its relative, the yellow rattle (page 122) – they are both partial parasites on established grass plants. It is a rather neglected flower, but with some attraction; 'What temperature or vertue this herbe is of,' wrote one old-time herbalist, 'men have not as yet been carefull to knowe, seeing it is accounted unprofitable.'

Needle whin or petty whin is a straggling shrub with sparse spines and waxy green leaves. It flowers May-June; note the swollen pods. It is usually under 50 cm tall.

Many different lichens occur on heathlands, growing either on the soil beneath the heather or on bare peat. These members of the *Cladonia* family have brilliant red fruits which remain throughout the year; 3 cm tall.

Gorse, sometimes called furze, is a spiny evergreen. The heavily scented flowers are out from March-June, though a few may be seen at other times of year. The ripe pods explode, scattering the seeds. The furrowed spines discourage grazing animals. To 2 metres tall.

It was once a useful plant, used to fuel bread ovens and, it is said, was fed to stock after the spines had been crushed by passing the gorse through the cider mill!

This 'common' gorse has two close relatives. Dwarf gorse is smaller, but may grow to 1 metre tall. It is found mainly in the south-east of Britain, never in the south-west and Scotland. The other gorse is western gorse, which is shown here. It is a very prickly, low-growing plant and is found west of a line from Dorchester to Nottingham to Edinburgh, though it may also be seen in coastal sites in East Anglia. It often grows in cushions on the ground, and may be the gorse growing *on* the Dorset heath beloved by novelist Thomas Hardy. The common gorse is found growing around the edge of it. Western and dwarf gorse flower from July-September.

▶ **A rich assemblage of heathland plants** – dwarf gorse, with its late summer flowers, flanked by the purple blooms of heather and spent flowers of cross-leaved heath.

Some of the richest areas of lowland heath can be found in south Hampshire and Dorset. The photograph below shows the heather- and gorse-covered slopes of Studland Heath sweeping down to the sand dunes of Poole Harbour.

Tormentil is abundant in dry acid grassland. It is one of the rose family; compare it with silverweed and other relatives (page 96) and you will note it has four petals to their five. June-September; tufted stems to 10 cm and stalkless leaves; flowers often taller.

Sheep's sorrel is a good indicator of dry acid grassland. You will also find it in bare areas on heaths. Note the halberd-shaped leaves which are rather acid to the taste. May-June; 10–30 cm.

Heath bedstraw is a relative of cleavers (page 84). Both have slender square stems and leaves in whorls. June-August; it forms mats 10–20 cm deep, with taller flowering shoots.

Harebell (the Scottish 'bluebell') is one of the bellflower family. Have a look at its leaves: those from the creeping stems are rounded with long stalks, those from the upright stem are long and thin, the lower ones with a stalk and the top ones without. The flowers droop on their long stalks. Found in many different dry grassy and heathy places throughout Britain, but it is rather less common in south-west England. July-September; 15–40 cm.

The earth fan fungus is a member of the bracket fungus group but grows in sandy ground on heaths and in pine woods.

Unlike the high moors, lowland heaths are frequently surrounded by trees and shrubs and so can quickly turn into scrub and then to woodland. They are sometimes burnt to prevent this. Below, three seedlings to look for: birch, pine and oak.

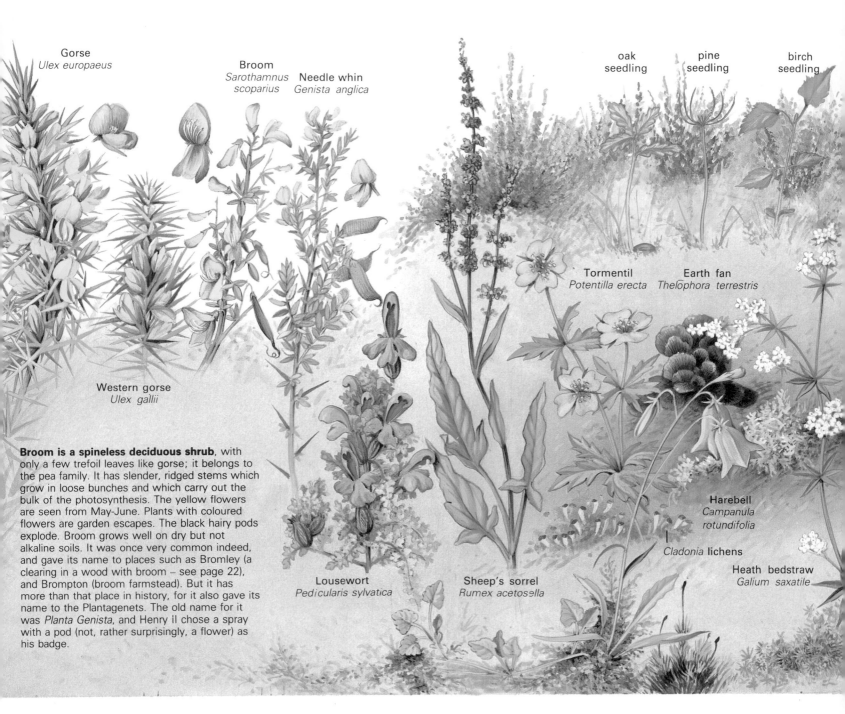

Gorse
Ulex europaeus

Broom
Sarothamnus scoparius

Needle whin
Genista anglica

oak seedling

pine seedling

birch seedling

Western gorse
Ulex gallii

Tormentil
Potentilla erecta

Earth fan
Thelophora terrestris

Harebell
Campanula rotundifolia

Cladonia lichens

Heath bedstraw
Galium saxatile

Lousewort
Pedicularis sylvatica

Sheep's sorrel
Rumex acetosella

Broom is a spineless deciduous shrub, with only a few trefoil leaves like gorse; it belongs to the pea family. It has slender, ridged stems which grow in loose bunches and which carry out the bulk of the photosynthesis. The yellow flowers are seen from May-June. Plants with coloured flowers are garden escapes. The black hairy pods explode. Broom grows well on dry but not alkaline soils. It was once very common indeed, and gave its name to places such as Bromley (a clearing in a wood with broom – see page 22), and Brompton (broom farmstead). But it has more than that place in history, for it also gave its name to the Plantagenets. The old name for it was *Planta Genista*, and Henry II chose a spray with a pod (not, rather surprisingly, a flower) as his badge.

Wildlife of lowland heaths

There are relatively few species of bird on the open heaths, but the insect life can be full of surprises. The surface of the ground is usually an exciting patchwork of bare sunny areas broken by boggy hollows and dry banks, with patches of dense shade under the heather. Here, at the height of summer, you will find grasshoppers and crickets, unusual wasps and bees, many kinds of spiders and, in the wetter areas, dragonflies. Half our native species of dragonflies can be seen on lowland heather barrens, where there are still, perhaps, unpolluted pools in which they can breed.

Sadly, in recent years, much of this heathland has been lost to the plough, built over or planted with conifers. In Dorset, only one-fifth of the heathland of Victorian times remains. This is often in scattered isolated patches, at risk from invasion by scrub and prone to fires and other disasters. The plants may recover from the occasional heath fire but the main danger is that the animal life will not be able to recolonise as the nearest intact heathland community may be too far away.

▼ **A solitary mining bee next to her burrow** in a sandy bank. These burrows can be up to 60 centimetres deep. She constructs a cell at the end of each one which she provides with a ball of honey. She then lays a single egg in the cell and closes it up. She will construct up to six cells in her burrow.

Wheatear
Oenanthe oenanthe

Wheatears are often seen perched upright on the ground. They catch butterflies and moths and flies, often taking them on the grass stalks.

Wheatears are among our earliest summer visitors, arriving in March. Whereas they used to breed on the lowland heaths in large numbers, the destruction of these places means that, today, you are more likely to see the wheatear on the wide, open moors of the north and west. They often nest in a crevice between stones in open ground. They move restlessly, white rump always visible, perching upright on the ground, as shown here. Alarm call, *whit chuck chuck*; song a squeaky warble; 15 cm.

Stonechats seek rough, unfarmed land, and are often seen on heaths and commons, especially near the coast. They are small but easy to see, perching very upright on top of posts or bushes, spreading and flicking their tail and wings restlessly. A clear *tsak tsak* call sounding rather like two stones being knocked together. The song is a jingle of double notes. Stonechats were once seen in every county, but are now more likely to be encountered in the south and west, near the coast. Large numbers die in cold winters, but the population can quickly recover since within a good summer the birds may rear three broods, of which five or six youngsters may survive. Resident. 12.5 cm.

The slow-worm is not a snake, but a legless lizard. You may be able to make out a slight narrowing at its neck and at its tail. The slow-worm may shed its tail if it is grasped, something a snake cannot do. Also, unlike true snakes, it has eyelids.

The slow-worm is an extremely deliberate predator – it will contemplate a slug and slowly move to take it; some observers have seen the slug escape by moving away! To 50 cm.

The common lizard is found in a great variety of dry sunny places with sparse cover. The eggs are kept inside the female until they hatch; the young are born alive. The lizards are often seen stunted, with a tail lost and only partly regrown. The male has an orange belly, the female a yellow one, but the colour of the back can vary. This is a lively, darting animal. 10–16 cm long.

Adders can be recognised by the strongly marked zig-zag pattern down the back and dark dots along the sides against a yellow to red-brown background. They are rather stocky snakes.

Adders mate in late spring, when the males can sometimes be observed fighting – swaying up against each other, but not biting. The female retains her eggs inside her body, and the young adders are 'born live' when they hatch in August. She is, in fact, a living incubator.

Adders prey on mice, shrews and other small animals, sometimes taking young birds. They will climb up to 2 metres in trees and shrubs. They are somewhat retiring animals, though if you disturb a pregnant female she is quite likely to hold her ground. A grass snake will always wriggle away. The bite of the adder is poisonous, and could kill if medical attention is not quickly gained, but only young children (and dogs) are really at risk. Healthy adults may suffer, but they should survive. Adders grow to 60 cm long.

The grayling is one of the brown family of butterflies and the caterpillar is found on fine, dry grasses. The butterfly can be seen in many different dry grassy and heathy places, as well as coastal sand dunes. It often settles on bare ground, where it slides its wings together to hide the wing spots, and then angles them toward the sun to reduce its shadow and make itself nearly invisible and maybe to regulate its temperature.

The grayling is one of the most difficult of all butterflies to approach. At the first sign of your presence, it will fly up and plane away, to land some metres away. The grayling has one generation a year, seen in July; 55 mm ws.

Southern hawker
Aeshna cyanea

male

Stonechat
Saxicola torquata

female

Sandwasps
Ammophila sp.

Grayling
Hipparchia semele

Stonechats feed on the ground more frequently than wheatears. They take insects and other invertebrates.

The holes of digger wasps may often be seen in the sandy banks. They are not colonies in the true sense – each wasp lives its own life, and pays scant attention to the others.

Adders can be surprisingly agile, so beware. If teased with a stick, they can strike it before your own reactions can move it away.

Lizards feed on spiders and insects.

Adder
Vipera berus

Slow worm
Anguis fragilis

Common lizard
Lacerta vivipara

Some of the blue butterflies shown on page 140 are occasionally seen on heathland. Locate beetles, spiders and other animals with the Index. 'Microclimates' are strongly marked on heathlands, and invertebrate life may change by the metre.

Heathland communities

Heathland, like nearly every feature in the British landscape, is inextricably bound up with man's use of the land through the ages. Underlying most heaths are dry, sandy soils which were probably only lightly covered with trees in the days of the primeval wildwood. These areas, being easy to clear, were often an early choice for settlement in Stone and Bronze Age times and may have lost their original tree cover 5,000 years ago. When the trees had been replaced by shallow rooted plants the rain soaked down through the acid sands carrying with it, in solution, most of the minerals from the soil. Reactions took place on the way down, and iron minerals were deposited to form a brown hard 'pan', 50–70 cm below the surface. This can often be seen as a more resistant layer jutting out below the white, bleached soils on the face of a trackside cutting. Apart from giving 'umbrella' protection the trees had, through their deep roots, brought mineral nutrients back up to the surface. It is interesting that birch trees can go some way to reversing this 'podsolisation' process on heathland soils.

Once formed, these leached soils were not much use for crops and so were often grazed. From time to time, patches around the settlements may have been deliberately burnt to keep them clear of invading scrub. Sometimes fires were undoubtedly started by lightning strikes as the summer heaths are often tinder-dry. The heather would have recovered, as it does on grouse moors today, and if the wildlife was destroyed it could soon recolonise from untouched areas of nearby heathland. In time a specialised community of animals exploited these lowland heaths. One such is the attractive silver-studded blue butterfly, so named because of the metallic silver-blue 'studs' on the black spots which edge the underside of its hind wings. Today's distribution map of this butterfly is very largely the map of our surviving southern heathlands.

The Breckland

In the Breckland, a yellow flower glimpsed amongst the grass may turn out to be tormentil, while a few paces away the yellow flowers of horse-shoe vetch may be found. This would normally be unexpected as the former marks acid soils, while the latter cannot tolerate them – it is a calcicole, a plant of chalk and limestone grassland. The Breckland is a mainly sandy region of about 900 square kilometres extent where south-west Norfolk and north-west Suffolk meet. The sand and stony material was thinly spread over beds of chalk at the end of the Ice Age and, in some areas, the chalk gives an alkaline flavour to the soil, with the result mentioned above.

The climate of the Breckland is also rather unusual. It has a wide range in the day and night temperatures with predominantly hot summers and very cold winters coupled with a low annual rainfall. In other words, it has a typical 'continental' climate of the kind found on the steppes of eastern Europe. As a result, it has its own distinct communities of plants. Some of the small annual plants found growing in Breckland are 'winter annuals' – the seeds germinate in autumn and then rest for the winter to flower in spring and early summer before the withering heat makes life intolerable for them.

The Breckland was a country of heaths, sheepwalks and sandy fields. Some areas were managed as large rabbit warrens

which kept the landscape open; place names such as Wangford Warren and Beechamwell Warren are common in the area. Much of it has been planted with conifers in recent times. In the distant past, the region was covered with oak forests, but as early as the New Stone Age the first farmers and cattle grazers were clearing the light soils (Breckland has a fascinating array of prehistoric remains, including Stone Age flint mines).

If the Breckland was once covered with forest, how did the open-ground plant communities establish themselves? They would not have been able to survive beneath the wildwood trees, so where did they come from? This is also a puzzle of the chalk plants of the southern downs. In their case, it may be that originally there were plenty of chalk cliffs alongside the rivers which have now been smoothed away. The plants grew on these, waiting to colonise the open chalky soils once the forest was cleared.

One theory about the chalk plants of the Breckland is that originally, in the days of dense forest cover, they had their headquarters on the hard limestone slopes of the north-west of Britain. Then, as Neolithic man cleared the forests he initially concentrated on the lighter soils of the chalk and limestone uplands. Eventually there would have been a corridor of open land along the uplands of Yorkshire, Derbyshire and the Wolds along which the plants could 'migrate southwards' to the Breckland.

Silver-studded blue butterfly
Plebejus argus

caterpillar

males

These two male silver studded blues have dark edges to their wings: the female is brownish in colour.

Nightjar
Caprimulgus europaeus

When flying, the nightjar shows its hawk-like wings and tail. The flight is silent.

Potter wasp
Eumenes coarctata

Orb web spider
Araneus quadratus

Dodder
Cuscuta epithymum

Dark bush cricket
Pholidoptera griseoaptera

top of web

Purse web spider
Atypus affinis

Green tiger beetle
Cicindela campestris

The purple-blue male of the silver-studded blue butterfly has black borders along the topsides of its wings. The female (as with other blues) is brown. The caterpillar of the silver-studded blue feeds on heather or plants of the pea-flower family such as gorse and broom. They are gregarious butterflies, and large numbers fly together; one generation flies July-August. 25 mm wingspan.

Nightjars are now declining, but the full reasons are not clear. They are now more likely to be heard in south and south-east England. They favour heaths, but will also nest in open woodland, the nest being a slight hollow in the ground. They hunt for moths at night, catching them with their large open mouth, but their days are spent motionless and well camouflaged on the ground.

Nightjars can be heard calling, a strange, rather mechanical rapid 'churr' for minutes at a time at dusk and through the night. The sound changes pitch as the bird moves its head. The first birds arrive here from Africa in mid-May; 27 cm.

An intricate web left by an orb-web spider is picked out by early morning dew. Heathlands are excellent places to see spiders of many kinds.

The heath potter wasps construct flask-shaped cells, attached to heather stems, which they stock with grubs paralysed with their sting, to provide a food store for their brood; 10 mm body.

Dodder is a parasitic plant, festooning heather and gorse. It has no chlorophyll of its own. Its thread-like red stems carry clusters of flowers; August-September.

The purseweb spider builds an unusual tube web at ground level, with itself sealed inside. The tube is camouflaged with leaves. Any insect touching the tube is impaled by the fangs of the waiting spider, and then sucked dry. This is a spider of dry grassy places, on chalk downs or heaths; 7–15 mm body.

Look out for orb-web spiders in late summer amongst the tall gorse and heather bushes.

Compare this bog bush cricket with the oak bush cricket on page 48. This one is found on low vegetation often in boggy places. The song is a series of short chirps; 15 mm body

Tiger beetles have relatively huge jaws, which overlap when not in use. The beetles are seen running actively in spring and summer; 15 mm body.

171

Classic river types are shown on pages 186, 188. Lowland rivers may have fast turbulent stretches which trout like, but the water quality is usually the deciding factor. Canals have a life more typical of still water, see pages 190 and following.

Rivers

Many of our rivers flow through two different landscapes. They start in the uplands as a fast troutbeck, often running over a bed of solid rock, boulders and stones. At this stage the river can be a powerful force, gouging out a steep valley in the hilly landscape. Only in the deeper eddies and where an obstruction changes the flow will any river gravel or silt be deposited, allowing plants to root. Darting in these gentler reaches may be minnows.

Then, often when the first few cornfields are in sight, the river begins to change. It is slowing, and starting on what may be a long journey through many different lowland scenes to end by winding across a wide flood plain to the sea. In the hilly west of Britain, some rivers rush direct from mountainside to sea; they have no lowland stretch. In the south and east of the country, upland sections of rivers are largely absent.

The quality of water the river is carrying can be as important to wildlife as the size or location of the river. The upland troutbeck is fast and cold, well aerated with plenty of oxygen dissolved in it but the mineral content will probably be low, and the water rather acid if the young river is running across moorland and peaty slopes. There will be few plants present as the sudden and dramatic spates mean that it is almost impossible to establish a foothold. There will be mosses encrusting the larger boulders, however. There will also be many insects, mainly the young aquatic stages of mayflies, stoneflies and caddisflies. These are the main food of the trout, which need plenty of oxygen in the water and which feed by sight in the clear bubbly water.

The water of the lowland river is warmer, with less oxygen, and may well contain a good supply of minerals and salts (and traces of chemical fertilisers) washed from the fields alongside or carried in by its tributaries. So the water will be fertile, usually alkaline and with beds of rich silt at the bottom in which a fine array of water plants may root. The insect life is rather different from that of the troutbeck. Coarse fish, which often feed by smell rather than sight, are abundant, replacing the trout in the murky water.

The life of a river

In the hills troutbecks are fast running

The water running from hard hill rocks contains little in the way of dissolved salts. It is *soft* water and probably rather acid.

The water running from chalk or limestone contains limy salts, which make it *hard*. Soap does not easily lather in it.

Where the current slows, minnow reaches can be seen

Tributaries can bring water of different quality to a river. They can enrich a poor-water river. They can also bring polluted water to a clean river.

Waterfalls and pools create different habitats

The erosive power of a stream is not lost in the lowlands: look for the cliff scoured on the outside of a bend

Feeder streams bring in nutrients

On the inside of a bend the water flows more gently and silt may be deposited

Note that lowland rivers may have stretches similar to troutbecks and minnow reaches

Coarse fish are found in weedy, slow running water

An unspoilt lowland clay river in the Midlands fringed with bur-reeds and overhung with alders. In the slower-flowing sections carpets of water lilies cover the surface.

Part of the delight of a lowland clay river or stream is that it offers many different kinds of habitat.

Most clay rivers also cut into deposits left by previous rivers and the retreating glaciers long ago. The greater the variety, the better the chances of finding different habitats.

Look for a patchwork of fast and slow flow, the fast riffles and gravel runs may be picked out by water crowfoots.

Most of our lowland rivers and streams run across heavy, valley clay deposits. These have characteristic high banks cut by rising water after heavy rain. Because of the frequent flash floods, high bridges were built across them. These rivers contrast with the lowland chalk streams which have low bridges, indicating their more constant regime (see page 187).

Water and waterside habitats occupy only about a hundredth of the area of Britain and whether they are still or flowing they are always sensitive to interference and easily destroyed. It is nowadays difficult to find clay rivers offering the variety and vitality shown above. Many are nothing more than polluted drainage channels, dredged deep to reduce the risk of flood.

Cliffs and tall sandy banks are suitable for the nests of kingfishers and sand martins and other animal life.

In spate, a river may carry a thousand times its dry-weather flow, so it may scour the bottom and cut steep banks; but the silt it carries is deposited when the current lessens.

Look for a patchwork of sand, shingle and mud shores or islands appearing perhaps for the summer only, but quickly colonised by certain plants and animals (even birds will nest on them).

Lowland rivers may have fish zones broadly corresponding to the trout stream, minnow reach and weedy coarse fish waters.

Look for patches of swamp or marshy ground, maybe lying alongside a meander.

Look for waterside trees and a lush growth of waterside plants.

Such features disappear when the river is 'improved' as many have been. To prevent flooding, which may occur at any time of year, Water Authorities and other public bodies engineer the river. 'Engineer' is as good a word as any: the river is dredged and deepened, the banks smoothed and graded to a constant slope and the bankside trees grubbed up. Meanders are by-passed and often filled in.

The river can now carry more water, but that is not all. As the river level is lower, the fields alongside can be better drained. Their grass can be improved or they can be ploughed for arable. In this way, river engineering turns the key for the destruction of neighbouring wet meadowland.

The invertebrates that help you evaluate water quality are shown on page 180. Water plants also suffer if the water becomes heavily polluted, page 176. The plants of the water's edge (pages 206, 208) may also be affected: pollution always lessens variety.

Mucking about with water

Quite apart from fish, the water of our lowland rivers should teem with all kinds of animal life. If it does not, the reason is often that we have been using that water insensitively.

We use our rivers in many different ways, all of which create disturbances. Some of the uses are obvious enough: fishing, boating, or for cooling at power stations. You could say that carrying flood water is one important use. However, since most of our cities, towns and villages are sited on rivers, their main function for man has been to provide water for drinking, power for his industries and means of ridding him of waste products.

Treatment of the waste at sewage works imitates a natural process but considerably speeds it up. Sewage is liquid organic waste from our homes together with the muck from slaughterhouses, paper and food factories and the like. It is tumbled and mixed with plenty of air allowing bacteria to work on it, breaking it down into phosphates and nitrates and other matter which is relatively harmless in small amounts. The treated sewage is discharged into the river, where little or no harm is done provided there is enough water to dissipate it. But if the river is low, the arrival of this bonus load of nutrients will stimulate thick growths of green algal slime – blanket weed. This can block out the light and smother most of the existing animal and plant life.

If the sewage treatment is not complete, the bacteria continue to be active in the river taking the oxygen they need from the supply dissolved in the water. Without that oxygen, many animals die quickly: sudden fish kills are caused in this way. The only survivors will be those animals which can store scarce oxygen in their blood, or gain it from the surface. Although only a few pollution-resistant species survive, they may be present in very large numbers, because they no longer have any competitors for food. It is not only near the city that pollution can be a problem as the combined effect of increased abstraction of water from the river systems for domestic and industrial uses, and nitrate fertiliser and slurry-manure run-off from farms, means that the upper reaches of lowland rivers are liable to great enrichment, resulting in dense algal 'blooms' and their consequent effect on the animal and plant life.

All may not be lost, however, as a river can purify itself. The effects of pollution are watered down as it flows along and eventually some distance downstream normal life may be resumed below the surface. The real point, however, is that a clean-looking river may be suffering from a source of pollution far upstream. Only an examination of the life in it will tell you if it is unpolluted.

Sewage treatment and control have been much improved in recent years, and today salmon, which are migratory fish and return up certain British rivers to spawn, are now able to use even the Thames for the first time for a century. Unfortunately some rivers in the Midlands and north are still in a terrible state and have a long way to go before they can be truly called clean.

The edge of this lake in the Lake District is fed by a small river carrying nutrients from the surrounding fields and consequently the richness of the lake has been increased to the benefit of this stand of bulrush and the floating water lilies.

A river downstream of a sewage outflow. The scum on the surface and lack of water plants indicate that it is heavily polluted.

Sewage pollution can be as lethal to the life in a river as poison from a factory, or pesticides washed in from the fields.

Not only rivers but small streams as well can be seriously polluted: not by human sewage, but by the run-off from animal sheds, manure pits and silage clamps.

A 'natural' kind of pollution can be caused by cow pats or even by a colony of ducks on a small stream. A heavy leaf fall can produce the same effects: the bacterial decay of the foliage removes oxygen from the water.

The animal life, especially the small animals living in the muddy edges and bed of the river, will reflect the pollution level, and tell you if the water is clean. Some are shown on page 180. Although small, they can easily be found (if they are there).

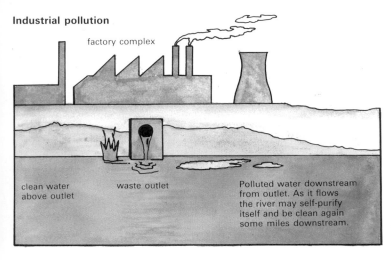

Industrial pollution

factory complex

clean water
above outlet

waste outlet

Polluted water downstream
from outlet. As it flows
the river may self-purify
itself and be clean again
some miles downstream.

A river may be polluted
not only by industrial
effluent but by washings
from quarries. Even
warm water from power
station cooling
towers can affect the
animal life of a river.

Look for sewage fungus; not strictly a fungus
but a spongy growth formed by colonies of
bacteria, microscopic animals, fungi and algae.

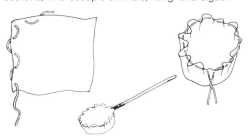

Make a small hand net of wire and curtain
material of 1 mm mesh, then sweep it through
the mud and plants under the bank. Tip its
contents into a white dish full of clear water.
After a short while the indicator animals will begin
to move.

175

The common water crowfoot keeps its thin underwater leaves even when it grows in ponds; it also has floaters. The floaters are usually only produced with the flowers; they are therefore not seen in winter and act as props for the flower stalk, to hold it out of the water. These floating leaves may also be absent from plants growing in deep water. Flowers April-September.

The arrowhead is an exotic-looking plant but grows those arrow-shaped leaves only above the surface. It has oval floaters and thin translucent submerged leaves; in deep or fast water only these are seen. Arrowhead is a perennial plant; it overwinters as submerged buds. The flowers have three petals, the other parts of the flower are also in threes; July-August; 30–80 cm.

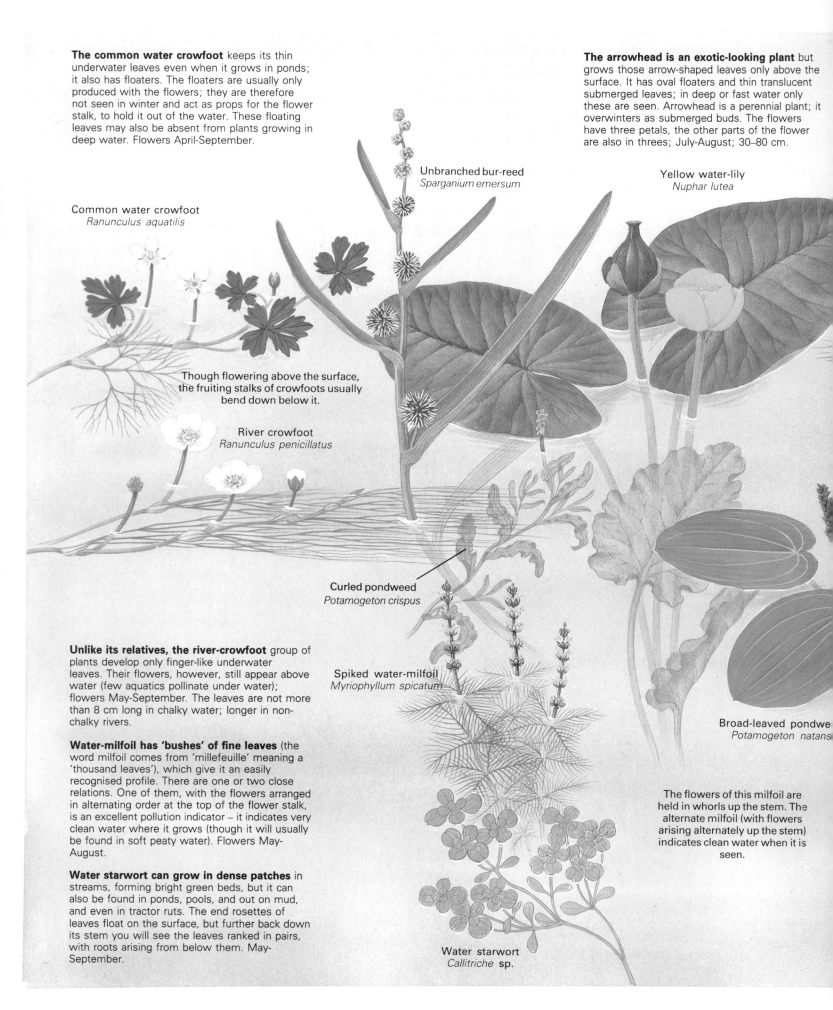

Common water crowfoot
Ranunculus aquatilis

Unbranched bur-reed
Sparganium emersum

Yellow water-lily
Nuphar lutea

Though flowering above the surface, the fruiting stalks of crowfoots usually bend down below it.

River crowfoot
Ranunculus penicillatus

Curled pondweed
Potamogeton crispus

Spiked water-milfoil
Myriophyllum spicatum

Broad-leaved pondwe
Potamogeton natans

Unlike its relatives, the river-crowfoot group of plants develop only finger-like underwater leaves. Their flowers, however, still appear above water (few aquatics pollinate under water); flowers May-September. The leaves are not more than 8 cm long in chalky water; longer in non-chalky rivers.

Water-milfoil has 'bushes' of fine leaves (the word milfoil comes from 'millefeuille' meaning a 'thousand leaves'), which give it an easily recognised profile. There are one or two close relations. One of them, with the flowers arranged in alternating order at the top of the flower stalk, is an excellent pollution indicator – it indicates very clean water where it grows (though it will usually be found in soft peaty water). Flowers May-August.

Water starwort can grow in dense patches in streams, forming bright green beds, but it can also be found in ponds, pools, and out on mud, and even in tractor ruts. The end rosettes of leaves float on the surface, but further back down its stem you will see the leaves ranked in pairs, with roots arising from below them. May-September.

The flowers of this milfoil are held in whorls up the stem. The alternate milfoil (with flowers arising alternately up the stem) indicates clean water when it is seen.

Water starwort
Callitriche sp.

The small bur-reed produces floating ribbon leaves, but also erect, keeled leaves held above the water, if there is little or no current. It can stand some pollution. It is *unbranched* – see page 206 for a *branched* relation. Small bur-reed flowers in June-July; grows 20–60 cm tall.

A water lily in slow-moving water will be the yellow water lily. It needs a hardish bottom with not too much silt, otherwise it is smothered when it dies down in winter. Its cabbage-like, underwater leaves often remain over winter. The leaves arise from a massive rootstock in the bottom of the river or pond. The yellow water lily is also called 'brandy bottle' from the shape of its fruit and their smell, which is somewhat like stale, white wine. They release 'jelly bags' of seeds.

Yellow water lilies appear carved into the roof bosses of many churches (Westminster Abbey,

Bristol Cathedral, for example) but they are also interesting in a botanical way, for the water lily family of plants have no true land relations. The reason may be that though the family is by origin from the land (the fact that the flowers pollinate in air indicates this), the move to water may have taken place a very long time ago, and their land-based kin have become extinct. Flowers June-September.

Still-water plants which may be seen in the quieter reaches of a river are shown on pages 192, 206; more bankside plants on page 208. Watercress and some others are seen on page 187. All except water lilies have close relatives which grow on land.

Arrowhead
Sagittaria sagittifolia

Fennel
ndweed
amogeton
ectinatus

e leaf of broadleaved pondweed hinged to the stalk as you can see here.

Flote-grass
Glyceria fluitans

Fennel pondweed often replaces the crowfoots when the water is cloudy or polluted and is common in nutrient-rich water. Its slender leaves are 5–20 cm long. If you split a leaf you will find it consists of two slender tubes – a good design feature for moving water. Flowers are seen May-September.

The curled pondweed, a submerged plant with dark green, crisped leaves; May-September.

The floating leaves of the broad-leaved pondweed are flexibly jointed at the stalk, so that they float flat. Like other aquatic leaves they quickly become limp if taken out of water. Flowers May-September. Note the stout stalk to the flower.

Flote grass or sweet grass is one of the few truly aquatic grasses. Its leaves do float, but its flowerhead is unmistakably grass like.

Plants in running water

Plants that cannot keep their feet will be swept away in a river or stream, therefore those that have successfully colonised rivers have vigorous root systems to anchor them. These roots can quickly shoot off new stems to replace any that have been torn away by flash floods and under some conditions will form a dense weft which can adapt to the changing contours of the river bottom as silt is moved around.

The underwater leaves of river plants are usually ribbon- or strap-shaped, swaying with the current and therefore offering least resistance. There is another benefit to this shape, as it offers a large surface area to aid exchange of gases with the scarce supply in the water and aids photosynthesis in dim light. This is why pond plants also have ribbon-shaped leaves underwater. Surface-floating leaves also have a smooth, simple working shape. Only those held above the water surface have some of the exotic diversity of land plants.

Most aquatic plants flower out of the water, which indicates that they have colonised the water from the land, but adaptation to the flow of the river has meant that plants from widely different families have developed similar-shaped leaves. Some plants will look markedly different depending on the precise conditions in which they are growing. For instance, the arrowhead, in a strong flow, will produce only strap-shaped leaves but in still or sluggish water it might produce oval floating leaves as well as the extraordinary arrow-shaped aerial leaves. Sometimes all three kinds can be seen on one plant.

Water plants and a pollution check list

The plants growing in a stream or river can be harmed if the water becomes polluted. If the water is enriched when sewage, or the run-off from a factory farm, or even the rain from a heavily fertilised field reaches it, then a new balance is struck between the plants. Some flourish, their competitive edge sharpened at the expense of others. If there is a heavy dose of sewage or other 'organic' pollution, then algal *scums* and *blanket weed* thrive and block off the light reaching the other water plants, and these then die. If the amount of salts of various kinds dissolved in the water rises (a common result of organic pollution) then the water may still be relatively clear of scum but maybe only *fennel pondweed* can cope with the contaminated water. So much so that it can be an *indicator* of water pollution, being the only plant seen growing in a river in a town. It is a rather different matter if the water receives a dose of straight poison – if a weedkiller is washed from the fields, if spray cans are washed out in the water, or if a noxious substance escapes from a factory (many metals are lethal in very small doses). Then all the plant life (and animal life, too) is likely to be killed. Normally, however, pollution changes the variety of life in the river: fewer species are seen.

TOLERANT OF SOME ORGANIC POLLUTION	INTOLERANT
Fennel pondweed*	Quillwort (in peaty water)
Reedmace	Alternate water-milfoil
Water starwort	White water lily
True bulrush	River crowfoot
Duckweeds	
Yellow water lily	
Curled pondweed	
Arrowhead	
Blanket weed*	
*maybe only plants seen in heavily polluted water	

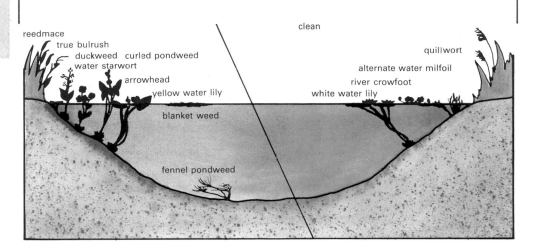

reedmace
true bulrush
duckweed   curled pondweed
water starwort
arrowhead
yellow water lily
blanket weed
fennel pondweed

clean
quillwort
alternate water milfoil
river crowfoot
white water lily

A large family of swans feeding amongst the lush vegetation on the River Itchen in Hampshire. Swans are largely herbivorous and the success of this family is almost certainly related to the healthy state of the river. The main predator of the young cygnets will be pike and the adults keep a watchful eye out for any approaching danger.

This beautifully marked male great diving beetle is an aggressive carnivore and will even try to attack small fish. The larva of this beetle is equally voracious and will soon 'clear' a small aquarium.

See pages 42, 98, 138 and 220 – they also describe nature at work. A river or pool, with clear boundaries, is a good example of a self-balancing ecosystem. The river is not only the habitat for plants and animals; they themselves create its character.

Streamlining is only part of it!

It is all too easy to portray a river in broad terms as having a series of set regimes – a fast-flowing upland section and a more placid lowland stretch as it runs to the sea. However, a walk along most rivers will reveal that the flow and, indeed, the whole nature of a river can change dramatically as it twists and turns across the landscape. At one stage it might be cutting a deep gorge through soft rocks, whilst further downstream apparently imitating a troutbeck as it flows over more resistant ground. On a more intimate scale, the inside of a meander may be shallow and still, almost pond-like, with emergent plants colonising the edges, but at the outside of the same bend the current may run fast and deep, scouring a cliff. Only a few metres away the river may be a few centimetres deep as it bubbles over a gravelly riffle, and carpets of water crowfoot may be present.

Most anglers think they know the best places in a river for fish, as each species is more likely to be found at one particular kind of place, which its body and lifestyle best equip it. So, in the teeth of the current, shoals of dace are likely to be found, while in amongst the pondweeds in the slower reaches, tench and roach may be lurking.

In those muddy parts (muddy because the fine silt that running water can carry is dropped when the current slows) you will find small animals which are typical of ponds. Indeed, some animals, such as freshwater shrimps and other scavengers, will be found almost anywhere there is fresh water, provided the current is not too fierce.

Rivers always flow in one direction, except near the tidal estuary. This constant flow of water is largely advantageous to aquatic animals, which can gain oxygen from the continuously passing water with less difficulty than if they lived in a pond. The water also carries food and certain animals need do no more than lie in wait for it. In fast upland streams there are several species of caddis larvae which spin silken nets among the stones of the river bed and feed on the smaller animals and detritus that float into them. On the other hand, an easy dependence on oxygen can put the animals at risk if the oxygen supply falters, as it may do as a result of pollution. Because the different groups of animals have varying tolerances to low supplies of oxygen, they can be used to 'mark' pollution. See page 180 for further information on this.

Other influences on the freshwater life may be more difficult to discern. The flow of the river will always tend to move the animals downstream. Does this mean that the animals are always on the move upstream? Many insects spend their young immature stages in rivers, therefore do the mayfly nymphs and caddisfly larvae plod up against the current after dark, or do the mature flying adults make this essential correction to the geography of their species?

A freshwater food web

otter
swan
heron
kingfisher
water vole
coot
flowering plants
mosses
fish
water beetle
water weed
water snail
eel
pike
tadpoles
decaying detritus
green slimes
mayfly nymph
dragonfly nymph

A measure of the complexities of ecosystems is that it is extremely difficult to make the patterns neat and tidy. But already in this scheme you can gain an idea of how complex the food chains can be: they are better named food webs.

The predators in the scheme have an importance in addition to their role in the control of numbers. They keep the population of their prey 'healthy' by culling the old, the diseased and the less well adapted. Rarely do they eliminate their prey, unless they are exploiting a 'new' habitat. This can happen in more than one way.

One example is that of a heron setting up shop at a trout farm. Another example is that of a foreign predator escaping to live wild. Mink have escaped from fur farms to establish themselves at many watersides. They are a threat to our native wildfowl, and maybe also to our fish stocks. Some otter hunts (now illegal) have switched their aim to mink.

In other words, native predators have achieved a balance with the rest of their habitat. In a reasonably well stocked, healthy river, they do not harm the fishing. And that includes pike!

In the placid bays of a river or stream you may also see some of the animals shown on page 194. Many insects have an aquatic young phase in their lives, see pages 188, 196. Freshwater fish are shown on pages 182, 186 and 187.

Animal life of running water

You will not see many, if any, of the animals pictured here if you glance casually down into a river or stream. They are mostly small and, like much invertebrate life, they are active only at night. However, they should be present in running water if it is not polluted and if it carries a reasonable amount of dissolved oxygen. With a little effort you can find them, and they can tell you if the water is clean or polluted (see opposite).

Some animals take oxygen from the air and these are often better able to survive in polluted water. But they may be at risk if an oil film covers the surface, while such a film may not affect the animals which have gills and can obtain oxygen direct from the water. It is interesting that while the river snail has a gill, the great pond snail (page 194) goes to the surface for air; it has a simple 'lung'.

Snails were originally aquatic; some colonised the land, developing a simple 'lung' to gain oxygen from the air. So is the great pond snail an animal that has returned to aquatic life? We have already seen (page 176) that some plants have recolonised water; it seems that the same thing has happened with some animal species.

Mayflies, usually 3-tailed but sometimes 2-tailed, are the classic angler's insect. More about that aspect on page 188. This is the large dark olive, which is 2-tailed.

The yellow sally is another fisherman's fly. It is a stonefly – one of the larger kinds which retain the two tails of the nymph. Other stoneflies lose the tails. Stoneflies often fold their wings over the top of their body at rest.

In streams, you will find damselfly nymphs clinging to roots and stems, but rarely to the leaves; the nymphs become motionless if the flow should happen to speed up.

Mayfly nymphs are bottom dwellers: some burrow into the mud, others are seen on gravel and between stones. Some are active swimmers, and can be distinguished from damselfly nymphs which look rather similar by the way their three 'tails' beat up and down, not sideways (like a fish). The 'tails' of the mayfly nymph are sensory; those of the damselfly are gills. Mayfly nymphs have their gills in rows down the side of the body as you can see here.

A nymph is the young stage of a member of the dragonfly, mayfly and stonefly orders, as well as other 'primitive' insects. It resembles the adult in many ways, but has no wings; the adult emerges from this stage by splitting its skin and crawling out.

True flies, butterflies, bees and other 'higher' insects have a young larva or grub stage; this grub must undergo a complete change to become an adult.

Stonefly nymphs are also known as creepers as they are slow and deliberate crawling animals. They are found on gravel or stony beds in clean water. Most of them are plant eaters or scavengers. Body up to 2 cm.

The great red sedge is an angling fly – a caddis-fly, often seen on the wing away from water. The larvae are easy to find as they are the largest we have in Britain.

Caddisflies are known to anglers as 'sedges'. Although they resemble moths in the drabness of their wings and the way they flit at the water's edge, they are not true moths as their wings are coated with fine hairs (the wings of moths are covered with scales). There are nearly 200 species found in this country ranging from 10–50 mm wingspan.

Freshwater shrimps are not insects, but crustaceans. They are not true relatives of seashore shrimps but are akin to the sandhoppers of the seashore (see page 240). They swim actively on their sides. Note the two pairs of antennae on the head. The juveniles are similar to the adults. To 3 cm.

The water louse is a scavenger with a flattened body, rather like a woodlouse. It crawls rather than swims. Juveniles resemble adults; up to 2 cm.

The bright red bloodworm, which loops through the water, has haemoglobin to store oxygen and so can survive in stagnant places. It is the larva of a chironomid midge; up to 12 mm.

A tumbling mountain stream in the Isle of Rhum. Fast-flowing rivers such as these, despite the sudden spates, contain a surprising variety of invertebrate life.

Organic pollution changes the oxygen content of river water, and the sensitivity of different animals to this change gives us a means of visually estimating the amount of the pollution.

A
stonefly nymph
mayfly nymph

B
caddis fly larva
freshwater shrimp
sludge worm
rat-tailed maggot
water louse
bloodworm

C
sludge worm
rat-tailed maggot

D
no life

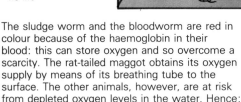

* If you find A, you will probably find many of the others too, and many of the other animals shown here and on page 194.

The sludge worm and the bloodworm are red in colour because of the haemoglobin in their blood: this can store oxygen and so overcome a scarcity. The rat-tailed maggot obtains its oxygen supply by means of its breathing tube to the surface. The other animals, however, are at risk from depleted oxygen levels in the water. Hence:

* Finds of B, but not A, will indicate some pollution (the animals in group B can withstand more pollution than A).

* If you find only C, that will indicate fairly serious pollution. If you find no life at all, D, then the water is indeed very heavily polluted.

The rat-tailed maggot is the larva of the drone fly (see also page 102) and can survive (sometimes in large numbers) in polluted or stagnant water as it has a breathing tube through which it can gain oxygen from the air. The rat-tailed maggot, however, cannot cope with water which has been polluted with oil. The oil forms a skin on the surface of the water and will kill those animals which go to the surface to obtain air, if they cannot break through it. One of the ways of combating mosquitoes whose larvae breathe with a tube (see page 194) is to spread thin oil on their breeding pools. To 2.5 cm; the breathing tube can be 12 cm long.

The banded damselfly chooses slow-flowing streams, and still water. The male sports a distinct band across his wings; those of the female are plain, rather greenish; 6 cm wingspan. These damselflies have a rather flopping flight, somewhat like that of the meadow brown butterfly.

The river limpet has a hooked shell to resist fast-flowing water. It is small, only 0.5 cm tall, and found on rocks and stones. The **pea shell** is also very small. Right, **Jenkins' spire shell**, a recent colonist of fresh water from brackish estuaries.

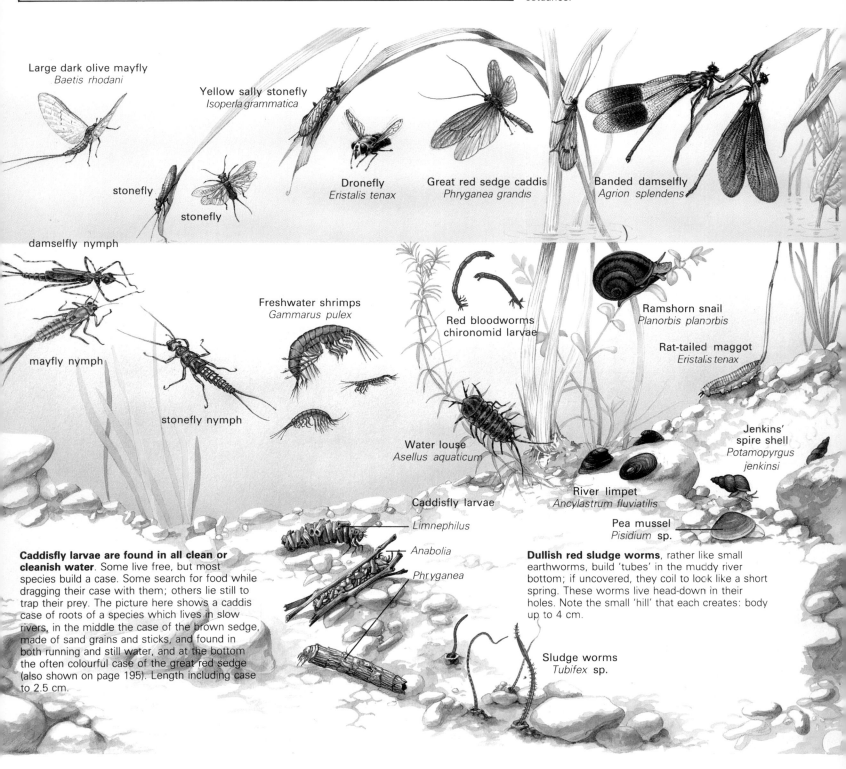

Large dark olive mayfly
Baetis rhodani

stonefly

stonefly

Yellow sally stonefly
Isoperla grammatica

Dronefly
Eristalis tenax

Great red sedge caddis
Phryganea grandis

Banded damselfly
Agrion splendens

damselfly nymph

mayfly nymph

stonefly nymph

Freshwater shrimps
Gammarus pulex

Red bloodworms
chironomid larvae

Ramshorn snail
Planorbis planorbis

Rat-tailed maggot
Eristalis tenax

Water louse
Asellus aquaticum

Jenkins' spire shell
Potamopyrgus jenkinsi

River limpet
Ancylastrum fluviatilis

Pea mussel
Pisidium sp.

Caddisfly larvae

— Limnephilus

— Anabolia

— Phryganea

Caddisfly larvae are found in all clean or cleanish water. Some live free, but most species build a case. Some search for food while dragging their case with them; others lie still to trap their prey. The picture here shows a caddis case of roots of a species which lives in slow rivers, in the middle the case of the brown sedge, made of sand grains and sticks, and found in both running and still water, and at the bottom the often colourful case of the great red sedge (also shown on page 195). Length including case to 2.5 cm.

Dullish red sludge worms, rather like small earthworms, build 'tubes' in the muddy river bottom; if uncovered, they coil to look like a short spring. These worms live head-down in their holes. Note the small 'hill' that each creates: body up to 4 cm.

Sludge worms
Tubifex sp.

181

Trout are described on page 186. Today the natural geography of the fish shown here is blurred as a result of stocking the waters for anglers. On the other hand, spine-chilling pike seem always to be able to get into reservoirs and other fishing preserves!

Freshwater fish

Fishing is our most popular participation sport, with nearly 3 million anglers applying for club licences each year. As would be expected with this level of interest, many waters are specially stocked with fish, although some of these are of foreign origin. The home of our native brown trout includes fast rivers and, if they are cold and hold enough oxygen, slow rivers as well as deep, cold, upland lakes, and the tumbling becks, in which it spawns. An American relative, the rainbow trout, is stocked in slow rivers and also reservoirs and gravel pits. However, it breeds successfully in only a few rivers (the river Loddon is one of them).

Some fish, such as pike and perch, are major predators in rivers. But in natural waters, with a balanced mix of plant and animal life, the predators do not reduce the total fish population. In fact, they keep it stable by culling disabled and less active fish, and thereby generally enhance the vitality of the prey species.

The angler places freshwater fish into two major groups. Salmon, trout and their kin are classed as game fish. They require cool, well-oxygenated water which need not be rich in nutrients. They move to special areas to breed, often the place where they themselves were born, and the eggs are laid in clean gravel. Sight plays an important part in feeding. The rest are classed as coarse fish. These have a variety of lifestyles and habits, as this page shows. In general, they feed by smell. These lifestyles and habits are as important as the size and shape of the body in fitting the animal to its 'niche' in the river ecosystem. The niche is a role, more like the part in a play, than an address. Feeding is only one aspect of the niche, but the requirements of breeding are as important. The behaviour of the fish is also an aspect of their niche. For example, fish that feed on small creatures picked up from the bottom of the river also tend to be found swimming in shoals, because there are more eyes to spot the places where such food is abundant, and more eyes to watch out for predators while they are busy head down on the mud.

There is yet another way of looking at fish. They are an obvious expression of the sheer productivity of what may seem at first glance to be empty-looking water!

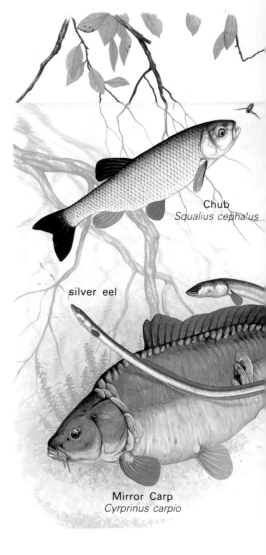

Chub
Squalius cephalus

silver eel

Mirror Carp
Cyprinus carpio

Classic courtship

The courtship of the stickleback is extraordinary. The colour red is the emotive tint – and one researcher found that the sticklebacks in his desk-side aquarium were set off whenever the day's post arrived: they could glimpse the flash of the red mail van through the window!

The male develops a brilliant red belly and throat – a warning signal to other males – and he pugnaciously defends his own home territory against them. He makes a shallow pit by removing the sand with his mouth, and then builds a nest of plant stems and pieces over it. A tunnel is constructed inside the nest. This is the marriage den. A female stickleback is enticed by the male's colours and by the zig-zag dance that he executes for her. Once she is in the den, he butts her flank and this stimulates her to release eggs. She then leaves and he fertilises the eggs. The male may then look out for yet another mate.

The male cares for den and precious eggs, fanning water over them, which ensures that they receive a good supply of vital oxygen. When the young fish hatch he guards them for up to a fortnight – even to the extent of chasing after adventurous small fry and bringing them back to the nest in his mouth.

Chub eating anything that moves, with their large leathery mouths. They prefer deep, shaded places, often below overhanging trees, for they like the shelter. Solitary when older. Note the brassy scales. Up to 60 cm.

The story of the eel is awesome. Eels are born in the Sargasso Sea and swim (aided by the current of the Gulf Stream) to Britain and Europe. They run up the rivers to fresh water, where they remain for up to ten years, feeding and growing. They may even clamber out of water and cross dry land to reach new feeding grounds. These are the yellow eels and if kept in these waters (by accident or design) they can remain yellow and live for up to 50 years.

However, for most a change occurs: after some years they become silver eels ready to swim back down to the sea, and eventually back to the Sargasso, 5600 kilometres away, where they spawn. Up to 100 cm.

Hump-backed perch move to shallow water to spawn in March-May. They are active predators of smaller fish and are solitary when old, ambushing their prey in the manner of pike. Found in ponds, fast rivers; to 45 cm.

When threatened, the strong-bodied tench becomes a living torpedo. It is a shy but powerful fish. If the water dries up, tench can survive in the damp mud for short periods. They are very tolerant of low levels of oxygen in the water and so can survive in some polluted rivers; 40 cm.

The bleak is a fast-moving fish, catching insect prey at the surface. Often seen in large surface-feeding shoals, disturbing the serious angler. It is a rather slim silvery fish found usually in slow rivers, but sometimes in still water. 12–20 cm.

Carp are Asiatic, brought here in medieval times, now established over a wide area up to southern Scotland. They stir the mud with the barbels alongside the mouth and suck out the food. 'Leather' carp are dull skinned; 'mirror' carp have rows or blotches of large shiny scales down their flanks. They are quite tolerant fish: trout die when the water is 25°C, carp can tolerate 38°C – like a warm bath. May live to 40 years; 25–100 cm.

Pike are the most important predators of British freshwater habitats. In April the females swim at traditional breeding sites, in sheltered shallow water, accompanied by the males. The eggs are shed and stick to the water plants. The feeding pattern of the young pikes (called 'jacks') is established early. For the first year they remain in the shallows, catching freshwater shrimps and water insects, but when they reach 3.5 cm in length, they are already taking other small fish fry. Even now they seize their prey with the lightning strike which is so characteristic of the adult. If taken sideways on, the prey is mouthed until head on, then gulped down.

By late summer, the 5 cm pike is taking 1 cm minnows and as it grows it takes larger prey, including young water birds, with the 5:1 ratio operating. Pike are reasonably long-lived; and they can be 'dated' by the annual growth rings on their body scales. Their growth depends on water temperature but also on the amount of energy they have to expend catching food.

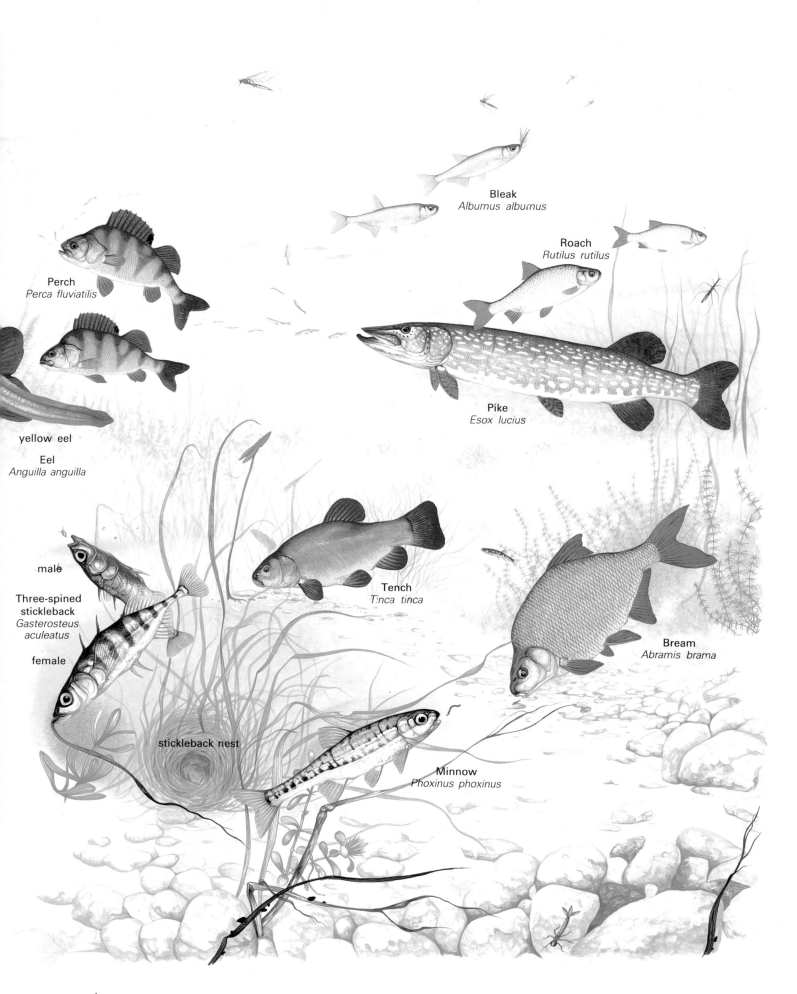

Bleak
Alburnus alburnus

Roach
Rutilus rutilus

Perch
Perca fluviatilis

Pike
Esox lucius

yellow eel

Eel
Anguilla anguilla

male

Three-spined
stickleback
*Gasterosteus
aculeatus*

female

Tench
Tinca tinca

Bream
Abramis brama

stickleback nest

Minnow
Phoxinus phoxinus

The stickleback shown here is the three-spined species. It is found in most types of fresh water and can even survive in brackish pools. Up to 8 cm. The three-spined may have its hind spine incorporated with the rest of the back fin.

How many anglers first got 'hooked' by catching minnows with a bread-baited bottle? Seen in breeding shoals, May-July, in shallow water with a gravel bottom. The largest recorded is 8 cm.

Our picture shows the course of the lateral line down the flank of the minnow. Below the skin is a long thin sac, which is extremely sensitive to changes in pressure in the water. It can act as a kind of 'ear' (fish have sometimes been seen leaping around when heavy lorries pass by quiet pools), but it is also important in warning one member of a shoal when the others flash away in alarm, and in telling the fish which way is upstream – a fact of which it needs to be continually aware. If it were not, the fish would in time be swept out to sea.

Roach wander in shoals, and are easy to fish with maggots and casters (these are the chrysalids of the maggots), but left to themselves they eat more plant food than animal. Note the reddish eyes and fins. Roach are found in more or less any kind of water; 10–25 cm.

Bream have long anal fins and forked tails. Often seen 'standing' on their heads, sucking food particles from the mud. These fish are usually seen in vast shoals. Up to 60cm.

Compare the water vole and shrew with their relatives on page 114. Look also at the coypu, page 212. The mute swan is not the only swan seen in Britain, page 232. More birds of water and water's edge are to be seen on pages 186, 188, 200, 210, 212.

More animal life at the riverside

A sudden 'plop' as you walk along the bank of a slow lowland river often means that you have disturbed a water vole (often mistakenly called a water rat). Another clue to its presence is a roughly cropped lawn on the bank, or even a pile of grass stems and shoots ready for eating, as grasses are its main food. The water vole makes a burrow in the bank, and some of the many entrances will be under water. It has a small territory, rarely feeding far from its burrow, and has regular swims as well as runs. It is active day and night. Despite the report in 'The Wind in the Willows', it cannot row boats.

The water vole is a very successful animal; even rivers where drastic bankside clearances have been carried out are recolonised as soon as the plants grow again. Such clearances, however, have had a much more serious effect on otters and kingfishers – and on swans too, to some extent, helping to bring about their decline.

Water shrew
Neomys fodiens

Diving for a

Water vole
Arvicola terrestris

Compare the water vole and shrew above with their close relations shown on page 114.

The decline of the swan

Although disturbance caused by vastly increased use of rivers by pleasure boats and by major river engineering schemes is a contributory factor to the decline of the swan population in Britain, the fact is that prime breeding territories remain unfilled. The birds themselves have gone. This decline is fearsome on some rivers. A regular annual count has been kept for centuries on the swans of the Thames below Reading. These birds belong to the monarch and at a regular annual 'swan-upping' – a ceremony which dates back 400 years – they are counted and their bills notched for identification. In 1956, when swans on the river were thought to be a nuisance, 1000 swans were counted, of which 200 were cygnets, the future breeding stock. In 1984, the census found around 200 adults and only 32 cygnets, not enough even to maintain the already much lower total.

Swans are bottom feeders and take up gravel to help them grind the fronds of the water plants on which they feed. This puts them at risk from lead angling weights and shotgun pellets which lie among the gravel. The lead is worn down in the gizzard and poisons the bird. There is no doubt that swans have died, and are dying, from poisoning due to discarded fishing weights. Symptoms of this poisoning are listlessness and the neck drooping back with a recognisable kink (see illustration). Lead weights have been found in the gizzards of swans at post-mortems, and blood tests show high lead levels. The habits of the birds put them more at risk, for in winter they (and especially the flocks of young immature birds) often seek food scraps in and near towns, where angling is a common pastime and lead weights are more likely to be taken up from the bottom.

Heavy putty-like substances to replace the lead weights have been developed, but these alternatives are not generally available, at least at the date of writing. There will always be some swans in Britain but unless the use of lead fishing weights is curtailed, flocks of swans on rivers in towns (where most people can see them) will become a thing of the past. The domestic flocks at such places as Abbotsbury in Dorset will be safe enough: their waters are kept free of lead weights.

The water vole is an excellent swimmer and is common wherever there is good bankside vegetation to provide cover and food. On the continent it is less aquatic and can become a serious pest of root crops, burrowing like a mole. In Britain this behaviour is rare. To 30 cm (including tail).

Water shrews are not as common as water voles. Part of the reason may be that they need to find their body weight in food each day and so require a home territory of up to 150 metres extent. They are sensitive to water pollution; 10 cm.

Mink are American by origin. They escaped from fur farms in Britain in the 1930s and now breed wild. They are usually seen at rivers – they mainly hunt fish and water birds, causing great loss – and are treated as a pest on nature reserves. To 60 cm long.

The kingfisher is one of our handsomest birds. Unfortunately it is much affected by river engineering, as it needs a steep rat-proof bank in which to dig its metre-long nest tunnel. It also needs bankside trees and shrubs to provide suitable perches. As many as 9,000 pairs nest in Britain. Kingfishers suffer in cold winters when their prey may become locked under the ice. They may also suffer poisoning from pesticides washed into the rivers and streams from the fields and then taken up by the fish on which they prey. They perch on a branch or stone above water, then dive vertically down after fish and water beetles. Sometimes they will dive from a hover. They have rapid flight, and a shrill '*cheee*' call. Larger than a house sparrow; 16.5 cm.

A pair of breeding mute swans will aggressively defend their nest and young. The swan is one of the world's largest flying birds, an adult weighing in at 18 kilos. They are 'mute' only in comparison with other swans, for they can issue a hissing or snorting noise. In flight, a swan holds its neck out and the beat of its wings is unmistakable; it needs a long take-off. There may be 5,000 breeding pairs remaining in England, Wales and Scotland. To 150 cm.

Kingfisher
Alcedo atthis

swan at nest

Mute swan
Cygnus olor

Swan with a
'kink' in its neck –
a symptom of
lead poisoning

cygnets

otters at play

American mink
Mustela vison

Otter
Lutra lutra

otter spraints

Otters are fish-eaters, with a particular taste for eels. They seem to hunt one stretch of water for a night or two before moving on, but their entire territory may encompass many rivers, and extend many kilometres; they may use the main river as a main road, and feed and lie up in the tributaries. The dog otter moves vast distances even in one night; but the female is much more 'house bound'. 'Boss' dog otters defend larger territories, two or three times larger than those of the other males. The bitch and the young cubs have smaller areas for feeding. Otters tend to feed more in slower water, where the fish are often larger than in fast flows.

Otters grow to 1 metre. They mark their territory with spraints – tarry-looking droppings, 5 cm long, full of fish bones and rather pleasant smelling. Spraints are usually left on rocks, bridge foundations and other hard places on the water's edge.

Otters

Otters are shy of man, and so rather difficult to survey. Sightings of wild otters are rare. However, an idea of their numbers can be gained from a census of their tracks and holts and the spraints (dung) they leave as territory markers.

To try to clear up once and for all the arguments about the numbers of British otters, an Otter Survey was conducted during 1977–79. Volunteers took part, organised by different conservation groups and also employees of the Nature Conservancy Council and other bodies. All major rivers in England, Wales and Scotland were checked.

The otter's distribution was found to be more restricted than had been feared: it was absent from much of England and Wales, as this map shows.

Only in the north of Scotland could sightings be termed at all 'frequent'. From many places in England where

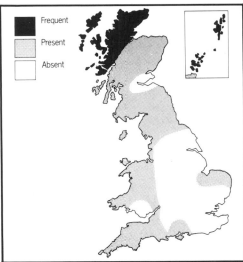

Frequent
Present
Absent

sightings had been known to be frequent in past decades (in southern Sussex and Kent, for example) came nil reports.

We can make an informed guess at the causes of the decline of the otter. Other species, which were afflicted by the widespread use of persistent pesticides in the past, are recovering now that those chemicals have been renounced. Unfortunately, it is likely that a 'limiting factor' in the case of the otter is the need for long lengths of undisturbed banks. River engineering, which has been more widescale than a casual glance at the countryside would suggest, has created sterile corridors along what were once otter highways. It may well be that pockets of otters exist today, out of reach of others of their kind as a result of these unnatural barriers. Without fresh blood, these isolated families of otters are at risk.

Enthusiasts have built otter holts and set up otter havens – lengths of suitable, quiet riverbank. Unfortunately, these may be out of reach of remaining stocks (for there is no way of telling the otters that such goodwill exists). It is now illegal to hunt otters and the packs of otter hounds chase the feral mink instead.

Adult flying black flies are small, little over 4 mm long. See page 194 for other biters linked with water, and page 142 for others. See page 180 for other invertebrates of running water. Compare the grey wagtail with its kin, page 210.

Profile of an upland stream

The fast-flowing mountain stream sings an unmistakable song as it tumbles along its rocky bed. In some places you will see rowan and other trees and shrubs firmly rooted on the banks, but there is not much to be seen growing under water. But look for swards of mosses and liverworts especially on the larger, firmly-bedded rocks. Perhaps they are only partly covered by that day's flow as the water level can change rapidly in these streams. Along some lengths, the river may flow more slowly across boggy ground. Here is the place to look for surprises, for you might find fragile white water lilies growing in the peaty pools.

Most of the animal life is small. Some of it will be the aquatic young stages of mayflies and stoneflies as well as those of the midges and their kin, including the black flies, the adults of which plague us on still summer evenings. Many of these small aquatic animals spend the daylight hours under stones or in their shelters, and only become lively at night. The trout, therefore, takes much of its food at dawn and dusk, when they are active. Lying on your stomach by the water's edge, look for caddis larvae. You might also see the nymph of the golden-ringed dragonfly half buried in the clean gravel. And birds? Well, you cannot mistake the dipper and the grey wagtail, both typical of upland streams.

The golden-ringed dragonfly can be seen in the lowlands but is typical of peaty, acid-water pools in the mountain streams. 10 cm ws.

Golden-ringed dragonfly
Cordulegaster boltonii

dipper in flight

Dipper
Cinclus cinclus

male

Grey wagtail
Motacilla cinerea

Black fly attach themselves head and tail, to hang on where the current is fiercest. Black fly plague Highland areas – they are small, stout biting flies, usually swarming.

Black fly larvae
Simulium sp.

Salmon fry
Salar salar

Brown trout
Salar trutta

Potamophylax sp.

Sericostoma sp.

Three caddis larvae and their cases found in upland streams

Agapetus sp.

Net-spinning caddis larvae
Hydropsyche sp.

The bobbing, tubby dipper perches on boulders in mid-stream. When feeding it will walk into and under the water in search of insect larvae. The pressure of the river flow against its back holds its body under. The dipper has a fast, direct flight, with whirring wings. A breeding pair may claim a 3 kilometre stretch of stream. The nest is on a ledge or in a hole near the water. The birds remain in their territories throughout the year. Call is a *zit-zit-zit* and wren-like song; 18 cm.

The grey wagtail, tail twitching, keeps watch for flying insects, and will dance into the air after them. It is a colourful bird, despite its name: note the very long tail, longer than that of the yellow wagtail. It may sometimes perch on a branch. Often difficult to spot, but it flies up with loud *chee-ip* note when disturbed; song a high-pitched *tse-tse-tsee-ree-ree-ree*. Seldom far from rushing water, it is mostly seen in the uplands in spring and summer, though it may come down to the lowland areas after breeding. This bird nests in a cavity close to the water; 18 cm.

The story of the salmon starts in November and December when the eggs are laid in depressions in the gravel of the headwaters of rivers. The salmon chooses places with a fast flow and with about 0.6 metres of water. The young fish that hatch are called **fry** until they are finger-length then they are called **parr** and finally when they become silvery in colour and are ready to move down to the sea they are called **smolts**. They move down river, reach the sea and then swim to feeding grounds off Greenland. After one or more years, they are ready to return to their river. They move up it in summer and autumn. This is when the spectacular leaps of the fish up weirs and other obstacles are seen. They return to the headwater where they were born, mate and the cycle starts again. The exhausted fish drift downstream after breeding: some may die, others reach the sea and recover to breed again.

Brown trout do not migrate to sea, though they may leave the headwaters of a river for a lake or pool further down. They are strongly territorial fish, and from an early age the least aggressive are squeezed out downstream. This pressure is relieved by normal mortality – from amongst hundreds of small fry only one pair may mature and breed.

Though trout like cold water and can live in water from 0 to 25°C, they grow fastest between 7 and 19°C. Spawning is triggered by a drop in temperature to 6°C – it is an autumn and winter activity. Their spawning ground, on clean gravel, needs to be washed by running water – they are unlikely to spawn in a pool, unless a stream is connected. Spawning will not take place in water above 13°C. Therefore these fish are closely linked with an aspect of their habitat that we on the bank may not be aware of – the exact temperature of the water. Brown trout are mature when about four years old; and may grow 30 cm or more in lakes, smaller in streams.

You'll sometimes see that the dense beds of water plants of the chalk stream have been cut for the sake of the fishing. There should, however, be a good array of waterside flowers, page 208. You don't expect kingfishers or otters – they need tall banks.

The chalk stream

Chalk streams and rivers have a character of their own, one quite unlike that of clay rivers. Chalk is a porous rock, and the rain soaks down into it, but at a line where the wet chalk presses down on more water-tight rock a spring may gush out, and a chalk stream may begin. The water runs clear and hard as it contains a large amount of calcium carbonate dissolved from the chalk itself. Running from a spring as it does, its flow can be remarkably even – and

there may be a permanently wet marshy strip lining each side. That is where the flowers can be seen – the edges of a chalk stream are often bright with colour. Its temperature, too, can be even, making it relatively warm in winter, which may result in an early blooming of the waterside flowers.

On the other hand, if those chalk layers do become depleted, the spring may cease to flow. Winterbournes (winter brooks) flow only when the chalk has soaked up enough of the

rainful during the autumn.

In the water itself, a profusion of truly aquatic plants often lie in long clumps along the stream bed. Sometimes the spring and summer growth of these is so great that it raises the water level to above its winter mark. The main plants that make up this mosaic of green are the water crowfoots, starworts and lesser water parsnip.

The calcium carbonate in the water also benefits snails: they extract it to build their shells. Crayfish, too, can be found. They used to be very common, but are rather retiring animals (they can best be seen at night with a torch).

Geology and geography, the animals and plants thus combine to create something very distinct and individual: the chalk stream.

Watercress is a common wild plant, but is also grown in streams widened for commercial 'beds'. The older leaves of watercress are the tastier: they contain much vitamin C, and in past centuries were known to be able to prevent scurvy. Watercress sellers roamed the London streets with the other costers. The leaves were often eaten boiled as watercress makes an extremely tasty soup. The lower leaves persist in winter; the flowers are small and white. A cabbage-family plant. May-October; to 50 cm.

Early botanists thought that marestail was the female plant of the water horsetail – hence its name. However, unlike the primitive horsetails it is a flowering plant – look for the tiny petal-less flowers at the junction of the leaf and stem. The stems that emerge from the water are held erect, but others remain submerged and trailing.

Look for the blue water speedwell on muddy stream margins; June-August; stems to 30 cm.

The lesser water-parsnip is another of the umbellifers to compare with those on page 92. This plant has hollow, ridged and hairless stems, often growing up from rooted runners. Note the small flowerhead, only 3–6 cm wide, July-September to 1 metre tall in fast-flowing water it will form large submerged banks. A poisonous plant.

Great willowherb has densely downy stems and leaves; long seed pods. The large cross-shaped stigma and purply flowers are distinctive. July–August; 80–150 cm.

Bullhead or miller's thumb is a fish which you will find in streams with a fine, clean bed. It is common in many kinds of stream, but interestingly it seems to grow larger in chalk ones. It spends the day inactive, under its 'home' stone. It is a solitary predator, catching prey by darting out from this retreat. It resembles the stickleback in the way the male fish guards the eggs. Note the long back fin. The fish is 6 cm long but up to 11 cm in a chalk stream.

Crayfish are not unlike a miniature lobster (they are related) but only reach 10 cm. Once very common, but now hard to find in many waters. Typical of chalk streams with plenty of oxygen.

If disturbed the crayfish will jerk itself back with a quick flick of its tail but during daylight it usually remains inactive in cover.

Great willowherb
Epilobium hirsutum

Blue water-speedwell
Veronica anagallis – aquatica

Watercress
Rorippa nasturtium – aquaticum

Lesser water-parsnip
Berula erecta

Marestail
Hippuris vulgaris

Bullhead
Cottus gobio

Crayfish
Astacus pallipes

Mayfly are shown also on page 180. Swifts, swallows and martins are today as typical of villages and towns (and even cities) as of open countryside. The trout itself is shown and its life described on page 186.

The mayfly hatch

The river seems empty of life, nothing spoils its placid glide. But then a fish breaks the surface with a splash to snatch at something. Some duns float past carried by the current, others attempt flight on weak fluttering wings, while others lie still, posturing with their long tails arched over the water. The hatch has begun and already the swallows are busily feeding, taking the insects from the very surface of the water. The trout are now steadily rising to feed. The angler casts his 'fly' across the water.

The hatch occurs in May, June or July, depending on the species of mayfly, and it is (with bluebell woods and heather moors) a true spectacular of the British countryside – and all the more impressive for being a mass show of animal life rather than plants.

The hatch is the time when mayfly nymphs rise from the bed of the slow river. When they reach the surface, the adults shrug their way out of their nymph skins and fly. But there is something more unusual in this quite common event in the insect world: for the dullish coloured mayflies that first emerge are not quite mature. They are called duns and after a short time (usually only hours) their skin is again shed, and the elegant, mature mayflies emerge. They will never feed, and on still warm days will spend their energy weaving an endless massed mating dance. When exhausted they fall, spinning to the water – hence the anglers' name for them: 'spinners'.

The nymphs need clean water, but being weak fliers, the duns also need bankside vegetation to shelter them from the sun until their final moult before the nuptial dance. If those banks have been cleared, the duns must resort to any grass they can find. This does not offer much protection: so it is not unexpected that many types of mayfly are not as numerous as they once were. On some rivers, the spectacular hatch is no longer seen.

Swifts can be recognised on the wing by their scimitar-shaped wings and short, forked tails; they fly fast with quick wing beats and glides, screaming shrilly. They are not related to swallows and martins but belong to a different order of birds.

Swifts are gregarious birds, though you will never see them perched in lines on a wire. They cannot perch – indeed, except when nesting they do not touch ground. Out of the breeding season they remain airborne for months at a time, flying very high up at night. The nest is a simple cup in a hole in a cliff or building, made of any feathers and grass that they can manage to snatch from the air. They arrive here from Africa south of the Sahara in May and begin to return as early as July. They are larger than martins; 16.5 cm.

House martins flash a white rump as they fly – the tail lacks a distinct fork. The birds arrive at the end of March, and leave by September/October for Africa south of the Sahara. The nest is the familiar upside-down 'mud hut', under overhanging eaves or some similar projection: the entrance hole is at the top. It is made of mud reinforced with grass (so a nearby river or pool is needed). The nests are often in small colonies in suitable places. They are common in suburbs and small towns. A *chirrup* cry and twittering song; 12–13 cm.

Rivers like this one are prized trout-fishing waters. The gravelly bottom and dense, green beds of river crowfoot tell us that this Hampshire chalk stream is in good health. Unlike the upland stream shown on page 186 the constant flow of water means that plants are able to establish a firm foothold in the riverbed creating a brilliant patchwork of gently waving foliage.

One swallow does not make a summer, so the saying goes. And it is true for they arrive in ones and twos in March from southern Africa but most arrive here in late April. Note the long forked tail and red face. This bird is often seen flying low over water in the company of house martins, constantly twittering. Swallows nest in solitary pairs but meet to feed and afterwards to migrate. The nest is a shallow cup of mud reinforced with grass, usually on a rafter inside a building or on a ledge in other cover. Their long, forked tail takes their length to 19 cm.

Thinking fish

At first sight, an angling fly has little similarity with the dainty mayfly it represents. The hook is obvious, certainly not hidden by the twist of thread and feather tied to it. We are not seeing it with a trout's eye; for, looking up at the surface from below, the fly is a blur behind the mirror-like reflection. However, something must be similar, for the trout relies on keen eyesight to catch its underwater food. The secret lies with the feathers, which dimple the water, as they brush it, in exactly the same way as the mayfly's legs. The trout fisherman must maintain this deception, for if his dry fly breaks the surface, the delusion is lost. Other 'wet' flies are tied to dupe the fish into taking them underwater.

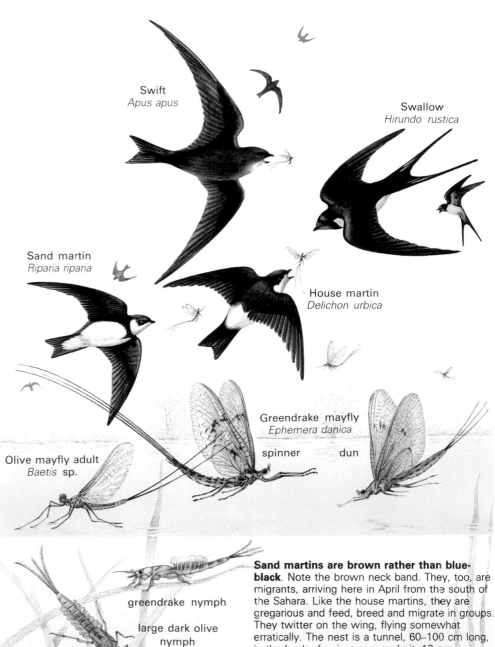

Swift
Apus apus

Swallow
Hirundo rustica

Sand martin
Riparia riparia

House martin
Delichon urbica

Greendrake mayfly
Ephemera danica

spinner   dun

Olive mayfly adult
Baetis sp.

greendrake nymph

large dark olive nymph

These 'dry flies', despite their gaudy appearance, seem to dupe the trout into believing they are a tasty insect. Half the skill, however, is in imitating the distressed movements of the creature as it drifts downstream.

Sand martins are brown rather than blue-black. Note the brown neck band. They, too, are migrants, arriving here in April from the south of the Sahara. Like the house martins, they are gregarious and feed, breed and migrate in groups. They twitter on the wing, flying somewhat erratically. The nest is a tunnel, 60–100 cm long, in the bank of a river or gravel pit. 12 cm.

The dun and spinner of the mayfly shown here is called the *green drake* by anglers. Its nymph lives buried in the mud of slow rivers in the Midlands and south. Other mayfly nymphs are more active, living in the shelter of waterweeds. Swarms of male spinners collect, and fly rising and falling, sometimes over water, sometimes some distance away. When a female spinner approaches, one of the males leaves the swarm to mate with her. Then, exhausted, he dies.

Plankton 'blooms' are a feature of still water – the fragile organisms would be destroyed by the abrasion, if not simply washed away, in a river. Plankton's enrichment of the water in rivers often has a distinctive result, see page 174.

Still waters

In the uplands it is relatively easy to find poor-water lakes and tarns which are not much used or changed by man, and we investigate one on page 202. It is rather different in the lowlands, however, for not only are the lakes and ponds disturbed, but some have unexpectedly unnatural origins. The classic example is that of the Broads, see page 212.

Many of the smaller ponds which remain in the countryside had, until quite recently, a job to do. Village ponds were not only ornamental, they were important for livestock. Many ponds were created for more special jobs: mill ponds to power the water mills that ground the nation's wheat, and hammer ponds, whose water drove iron-smelting machinery. There was also, until quite recent years, a large number of small ponds out in the fields themselves. They were for watering cattle. Most of them were dug out at the time of the enclosures two or more centuries ago. The 1939–45 war also contributed many bomb craters which

The colour code to water

clear	Clear water which remains clear all year is typical of poor, deep upland lakes.	**blue green**	Sometimes blue-green members of the plankton bloom to create a smelly scum in June or July; it is sometimes blown ashore.
brown peat	Sometimes the water of upland tarns and rivers is stained brownish by peat.	**clear blue**	Clear water which is deep has an attractive blue colour, seen in nutrient-poor chalk pools, for example.
clear greenish	This is the colour of a healthy lowland lake (or river) in winter. In summer, these rich lake waters 'bloom' to some extent; the colour deepens but the plankton growths may look like a green underwater snowstorm.	**dark grey**	When bacteria break down decaying matter in airless surroundings, they produce marsh gas (methane), hydrogen sulphide and other substances – the smell and colour of the mud at the bottom of a pond.
snowstorm effect	Green blooms occur in spring or early summer; other members of the plankton bloom brownish in August.	**rust red**	This colour indicates iron salts, released by the action of bacteria.

Here we see some of the water colours interpreted above

The blue of deep, clear water can be seen in the hills but also in nutrient-poor chalk pools. You will often see rust red, where a spring seeps from the ground.

A springhead marked by a bright red deposit associated with the oxidisation of iron compounds brought to the surface in the spring water. A very ancient form of bacteria is involved in this process and derives its energy from the conversion.

Still water contains microscopic plant and animal plankton, and if the water is suddenly enriched, they may undergo a population explosion and 'bloom', creating a thick 'soup' in which larger plants and animal life cannot survive. The plankton when they bloom reduce the light and also the oxygen dissolved in the water. Healthy lakes often carry short-term blooms in spring when the bottom waters mix up with the surface waters containing algae.

▲▲ **This tranquil pond resulted from a Second World War bomb crater.** Today, it is the home to a wide variety of freshwater life including both frog and toad tadpoles.

▶ **This 'dipping pond' at a Sussex nature reserve** has been created out of a neglected ornamental garden pool. It now holds a wealth of plant and animal life.

A pond or lake is more sensitive to pollution than a river. A river can purify itself as it flows downstream: a pond, being still, cannot, though ponds with a stream flowing in and out fare better. When rain washes fertilisers in from nearby fields, or a stream brings in a heavy load of nutrients, the results may be disastrous.

filled with water. Most of these field ponds have now gone: they have been filled in or been left to dry up. Any body of standing water, if it is shallow, will in time become dry land – a natural process described on page 204. That being so, it is probable that ponds which do remain are being maintained from time to time. Many villages keep their duck ponds open – though ducks will pollute a small pond with their droppings and reduce the wildlife potential.

Our wildlife as a whole has suffered from the disappearance of the once common, taken-for-granted pond. Even frogs are now hard to find out in the patchwork countryside. Ironically in many lowland areas they have their last stronghold in ornamental garden pools. But we have also created many new kinds of 'lakes' in recent years: reservoirs are colonised by vast numbers of winter waterfowl, and flooded gravel diggings make excellent haunts for dragonflies and birds. Canals, if they are not too turbid with mud churned up by boats, can also be very interesting habitats.

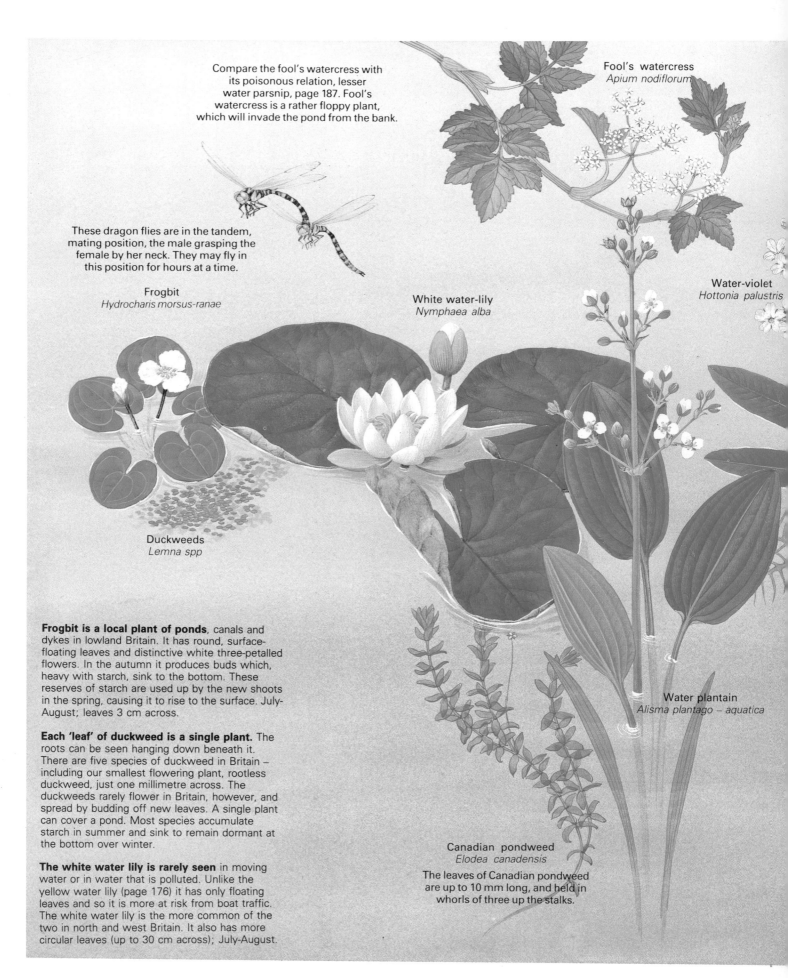

Compare the fool's watercress with its poisonous relation, lesser water parsnip, page 187. Fool's watercress is a rather floppy plant, which will invade the pond from the bank.

Fool's watercress
Apium nodiflorum

These dragon flies are in the tandem, mating position, the male grasping the female by her neck. They may fly in this position for hours at a time.

Frogbit
Hydrocharis morsus-ranae

White water-lily
Nymphaea alba

Water-violet
Hottonia palustris

Duckweeds
Lemna spp

Water plantain
Alisma plantago – aquatica

Canadian pondweed
Elodea canadensis

The leaves of Canadian pondweed are up to 10 mm long, and held in whorls of three up the stalks.

Frogbit is a local plant of ponds, canals and dykes in lowland Britain. It has round, surface-floating leaves and distinctive white three-petalled flowers. In the autumn it produces buds which, heavy with starch, sink to the bottom. These reserves of starch are used up by the new shoots in the spring, causing it to rise to the surface. July-August; leaves 3 cm across.

Each 'leaf' of duckweed is a single plant. The roots can be seen hanging down beneath it. There are five species of duckweed in Britain – including our smallest flowering plant, rootless duckweed, just one millimetre across. The duckweeds rarely flower in Britain, however, and spread by budding off new leaves. A single plant can cover a pond. Most species accumulate starch in summer and sink to remain dormant at the bottom over winter.

The white water lily is rarely seen in moving water or in water that is polluted. Unlike the yellow water lily (page 176) it has only floating leaves and so it is more at risk from boat traffic. The white water lily is the more common of the two in north and west Britain. It also has more circular leaves (up to 30 cm across); July-August.

Canadian pondweed is a completely submerged plant. It has separate male and female plants and it is the female only that is found in Britain, putting out purplish flowers, which reach the surface on long, thin, stalks. This plant was introduced into this country in the 1840s and by 1860 had spread so rapidly that it was blocking up drainage ditches and canals in many parts of Britain. It has now lost some of its original vigour and has been decreasing or just maintaining stable populations in many places. It can continue to photosynthesise under the ice. June to October; up to 1 m long.

Fool's watercress is, in fact, a member of the umbellifer family. It can be mistaken for true watercress as it grows in similar situations in rivers, streams and ponds, but has toothed leaflets and distinct, but small, umbels of flowers. Fool's watercress is not poisonous. However, the similar lesser water-parsnip is (see page 187). July-August; to 80 cm.

Bogbean is one of the most striking of all our wild flowers. Its creamy-pink flowers are fringed with delicate white hairs. The large 'trefoil' leaves can be seen throughout the summer carpeting edges of lakes and in bogs and fens, mostly in northern and western Britain. The delightful flowers are out in May and June before the other vegetation becomes too tall. 10–30 cm tall.

On land, the amphibious bistort grows strong upright stems, with hairy leaves on short stalks, but in water it has hairless floating leaves on long stalks. Both types may be seen on the same waterside plant. July–September; 70 cm.

The water plantain has leaves rather similar in shape to its namesake (page 96), but is not related. As is the case with many aquatics, the leaves have lost the ability to retain water, so they quickly droop if taken from the pond. One water plantain opens its flowers at 9 o'clock, a close cousin soon after noon. The three-petalled flowers are held up to 50 cm high; June–August.

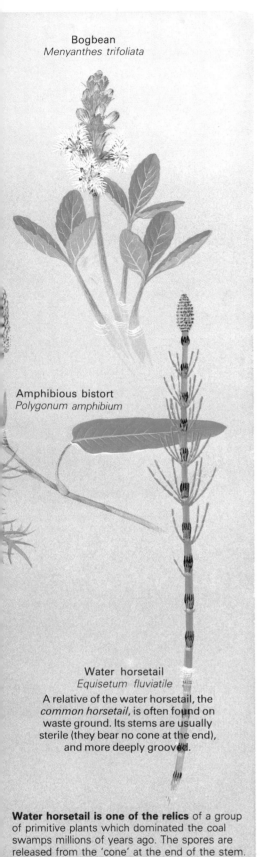

Bogbean
Menyanthes trifoliata

Amphibious bistort
Polygonum amphibium

Water horsetail
Equisetum fluviatile
A relative of the water horsetail, the
common horsetail, is often found on
waste ground. Its stems are usually
sterile (they bear no cone at the end),
and more deeply grooved.

Water horsetail is one of the relics of a group
of primitive plants which dominated the coal
swamps millions of years ago. The spores are
released from the 'cone' at the end of the stem.
Common horsetail is seen on waste ground.

Water violet is rare outside the eastern counties
of England. It is a member of the primrose family.
The flower stem may be 20 cm tall. May-June.

A coot chick swimming amongst a raft of
amphibious bistort.

Aquatic plants can be placed in three main groups:
free floating; submerged, but often loosely rooted; and
rooted with mainly floating or aerial leaves but with some
submerged.

Some of these plants may also be found in the still reaches of rivers;
river plants are shown on page 176. Plants of the water's edge are
shown on pages 206, 208. We see here a pair of mating dragonflies:
more about these fascinating insects on page 196.

Plants growing in still waters

Many of the plants that grow in a slow-flowing river or stream will also flourish
in a pond. The main difference is that free-floating plants, such as duckweeds,
will be expected in the still-water community – in a fast-flowing river they will
obviously be washed away by the current. These floating plants have an
obvious advantage over those with submerged leaves in that they can
photosynthesise directly in the sunlight and will not be hampered by algal
blooms. However, in small ponds, in ditches and dykes they can become so
dense on the surface that they exclude light from all other submerged plants,
eventually leading to their decline.

These plants must, however, have some means of retreating in the winter
months when their delicate tissues are in danger of being frostbitten and
destroyed by ice. A plant that is rooted in the bottom can simply die back to its
rootstock in the mud, as do white water lilies. This is not possible for free-floaters,
and interesting strategies have been evolved to solve this important problem.

Duckweeds build up reserves of starch throughout the summer months, and
the 'leaves' – they are in fact each a complete plant – become so heavy that
they sink to the bottom. The starch is slowly used up in the gloom of winter,
and quickly finished off when the plant becomes active again in spring. The now
much lighter plants rise again to the surface.

Frogbit, however, puts out what are called 'turions', winter buds. They fall
off the plant and lie dormant in the mud over winter, to leaf and float up again
in spring.

Types of aquatic plants

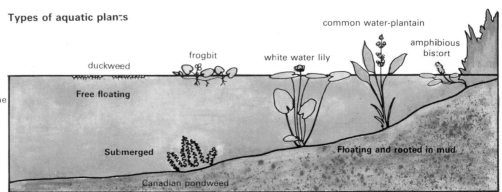

duckweed · frogbit · white water lily · common water-plantain · amphibious bistort

Free floating

Submerged

Floating and rooted in mud

Canadian pondweed

193

In water habitats, just as on land, more snails are to be expected in chalky or limestone areas. Compare these beetles and water bugs with those on page 106. Other biting flies are described on pages 186 and 142. Invertebrate life of running water is shown on page 180.

Animal life of still water

Any established pond, even a small garden pond, is likely to be colonised by many of the animals shown here. It is interesting to discover how these essentially aquatic animals reach isolated patches of new water. Many of the water insects such as the diving beetle and water boatman are strong fliers. They fly mainly at night and might well detect new ponds by reflected moonlight. Snails can colonise ponds through the agency of a passing bird – the slime-covered eggs stick to the feet of waterfowl and can be carried in this way for long distances.

The pond is not the closed world that it might well seem at first, as many of the small animals may be larval stages of flying insects which will move to different habitats once they have emerged and will not necessarily return to the same pond to lay their eggs. Even smaller animals, such as mites, when young may attach themselves to water insects and can therefore 'hitch-hike' to nearby ponds.

▼ **An underwater photograph of a backswimmer** just underneath the surface, replenishing its oxygen supply before diving again in search of prey, including tadpoles.

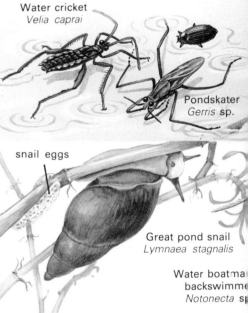

Pondskaters are probably our best-known bug. They can be found almost everywhere in Britain. Their front legs are used to grasp their prey (which they catch by sight aided by 'feeling' vibrations on the water surface). They row themselves with the middle legs, the hind legs being used for steering.

Water cricket
Velia caprai

Pondskater
Gerris sp.

snail eggs

Great pond snail
Lymnaea stagnalis

Water boatman
backswimmer
Notonecta sp

The great pond snail eats carrion. It is one of our commonest water snails, maybe because it comes to the surface to breathe and can therefore tolerate some pollution. Up to 5 cm.

The pond skater preys on insects on the surface. It can dive if escape requires it, and also fly. It is a bug; 8 mm.

Look also for the smaller water cricket which is silent, despite its name; 5 mm.

Whirligig beetles gyrate in small groups on the surface, catching smaller insects. They will dive if danger threatens. They have rather interesting eyes, which are bifocal, the top part giving good vision above the surface, the lower excellent vision below it; 5 mm.

Water boatman or backswimmer is an active and aggressive bug preying even on fish fry – it can be a pest in commercial trout fisheries. It lives, in effect, upside down but rights itself, however, when it flies. 1 cm.

The water spider lives underwater in a silk 'bell' which it fills with air bubbles. The spider secures its bell with threads to the plants but these do not catch its prey, which is hunted down usually underwater. The water louse is a usual victim. The eggs are laid in the bell and when the small spiderlings disperse, they take a small bubble of air with them. They occupy empty snail shells, which they can fill with air brought from the surface. Seen more in the south in ditches and other places with plenty of vegetation. 1 cm.

Mosquitoes and gnats

These names are often used for the same family within the order of true flies. The common gnat is one of the *Culex* mosquitoes. The adult holds its body horizontally and its larva hangs head down from the surface of the water in which it lives until mature. The eggs are laid in a 'raft' on the surface and the larva wriggles down from the surface if disturbed but must return to it to gain air. These mosquitoes breed in many different kinds of place – in ditches, puddles, rainwater butts as well as ponds. They bite birds, however, not humans.

One that does bite humans is the ringed mosquito – with spotted wings and ringed legs. The female, for only she bites (the males prefer nectar), approaches her victim and settles lightly; she feels your skin and then pierces. Her saliva flows, which may be the agent causing the irritation. Most female mosquitoes need

to take blood in order to lay fertile eggs.

The *Anopheles* mosquitoes hold their bodies at an angle and have larvae which lie parallel to the water surface. Brackish-water *Anopheles* mosquitoes once carried malaria which they picked up from one victim and carried to the next when they took a blood meal. These mosquitoes breed more in slow-flowing weedy water.

Malaria was once quite common in Britain – it was called ague – and as recently as Victorian times, people used to talk of it as lightly as we nowadays refer to 'flu. The fact that the larvae rely on their surface air supply held the key to their control, for it was found that spraying the water with thin oil could block their breathing tubes. The drainage of the fenlands for farmland also helped considerably and malaria had been effectively eradicated from Britain by the turn of the century. It was brought back for a short time when soldiers returned from the First World War.

Alder flies fly weakly on warm sunny days, and can be found in large numbers resting on waterside plants; 15 mm.

You will disturb china mark moths from waterside plants – they are common everywhere. Their caterpillars live underwater, in floating shelters made of leaf pieces. Both adult and larvae 12 mm long.

Ramshorn snails are familiar from aquariums, where they are stocked to clear the glass of green slimes, but are common in many still-water habitats. They contain some haemoglobin (some aquarium species are tinged pink by it), which means that they can store scarce oxygen and may not be so at risk from organic pollution. This haemoglobin also allows them to colonise deep water, in large lakes, for example. The coiled, flat shell is often 2 cm across.

Water scorpions are so-called because their long breathing tube looks like a sting. They are bugs and are fairly common predators; 2 cm.

Though the saucer bug, which you will see actively searching the bottom of the pond for prey, has wings it cannot fly, but is said to walk to new ponds; found south of the Midlands. 12 mm.

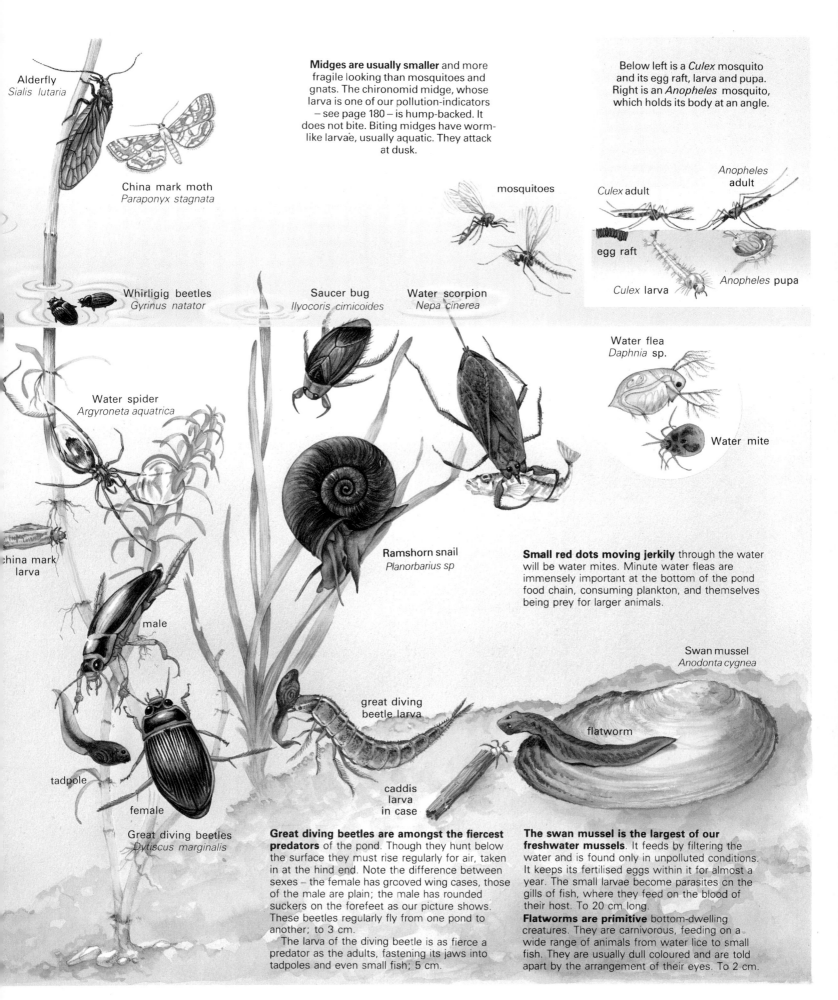

Alderfly
Sialis lutaria

Midges are usually smaller and more fragile looking than mosquitoes and gnats. The chironomid midge, whose larva is one of our pollution-indicators – see page 180 – is hump-backed. It does not bite. Biting midges have worm-like larvae, usually aquatic. They attack at dusk.

Below left is a *Culex* mosquito and its egg raft, larva and pupa. Right is an *Anopheles* mosquito, which holds its body at an angle.

China mark moth
Paraponyx stagnata

mosquitoes

Culex adult

Anopheles adult

egg raft

Culex larva

Anopheles pupa

Whirligig beetles
Gyrinus natator

Saucer bug
Ilyocoris cimicoides

Water scorpion
Nepa cinerea

Water flea
Daphnia sp.

Water spider
Argyroneta aquatica

Water mite

china mark larva

Ramshorn snail
Planorbarius sp

Small red dots moving jerkily through the water will be water mites. Minute water fleas are immensely important at the bottom of the pond food chain, consuming plankton, and themselves being prey for larger animals.

Swan mussel
Anodonta cygnea

male

great diving beetle larva

flatworm

tadpole

caddis larva in case

female

Great diving beetles
Dytiscus marginalis

Great diving beetles are amongst the fiercest predators of the pond. Though they hunt below the surface they must rise regularly for air, taken in at the hind end. Note the difference between sexes – the female has grooved wing cases, those of the male are plain; the male has rounded suckers on the forefeet as our picture shows. These beetles regularly fly from one pond to another; to 3 cm.

The larva of the diving beetle is as fierce a predator as the adults, fastening its jaws into tadpoles and even small fish; 5 cm.

The swan mussel is the largest of our freshwater mussels. It feeds by filtering the water and is found only in unpolluted conditions. It keeps its fertilised eggs within it for almost a year. The small larvae become parasites on the gills of fish, where they feed on the blood of their host. To 20 cm long.

Flatworms are primitive bottom-dwelling creatures. They are carnivorous, feeding on a wide range of animals from water lice to small fish. They are usually dull coloured and are told apart by the arrangement of their eyes. To 2 cm.

Dragonflies can be found alongside many different kinds of lowland water, but they are to be seen also in the uplands: the golden-ringed dragonfly quite often, page 186. Dragonflies may be seen at the bog pools of heaths. The banded damselfly is on page 180.

A bird watcher's insect

With their large size, gaudy colouring and complex behaviour, dragonflies are very much a birdwatcher's insect. If you are interested in watching birds, then the sight of a hawker perched and cleaning its eyes, then flying off to investigate a movement within its range, perhaps catching a smaller insect and eating it in flight, can be just as dramatic as watching a falcon. A further bonus is that dragonflies are very sensitive to pollution and often have strict habitat requirements which means that they are, like butterflies, a good indicator of undisturbed surroundings and that therefore there will probably be plenty of other animals to see. Unfortunately, the unpolluted streams and pools with lush bankside vegetation which dragonflies need have become much harder to find in recent years and many species are far less common than they used to be.

Dragonflies are strongly territorial and this gives rise to chases between males of the same kind, sometimes resulting in aerial battles and torn wings. However, more than any other aspect of their lives, it is their mating ritual which is most astonishing. When ready to mate, the male removes his sperm from its sac at the end of his abdomen, and stores it in another sac under his body. He then prospects for a mate, and when found, seizes her, grasping her head with his legs. Dragonflies, by the way, can use their legs only for grasping and perching: they can't walk with them. Still flying, the male then curls his tail under to grasp the female just behind her head, by the 'scruff of her neck'. He then releases his legs, and the pair is then in a 'tandem' position (it is shown on page 192). They may fly in tandem for some hours – and during this time the female pulls her tail round to take the male's sperm from his body sac under the front of his abdomen. This moment is shown with the mating pair on this page. The eggs are thus fertilised, and sometimes the pair stays in tandem while they are laid. Some of the dragonflies scatter their eggs over the water surface, maybe touching it lightly as they do so. Others perch on plants and lay the eggs

Hawkers are strong fliers and may sometimes be seen flying far from their home patch. Many hawkers roost away from water, in trees and shrubs. Come daytime, they may hunt the canopies of the trees for insects. They are often seen at pine trees, for these grow on the heaths where peaty pools can be found. They return to the pools during the hot, noonday hours.

Darter or 'chaser' dragonflies are rather smaller than hawkers, and spend much time perched, with wings open. They fly off to take prey or to investigate intruders, but return, often to the same perch.

The broad-bodied chaser is a southerly species and is often found in newly cleared water. Old males often have a bluish 'bloom'. 7 cm ws.

The large emperor dragonfly will be seen flying only on sunny days. Dragonflies fly only during the day and the large ones never when it is cold. They are heavy and need to be warm to function fully. The emperor is more likely to be seen over still water in the south; to 10 cm ws.

The common hawker or common aeshna prefers peaty, acid water. The females are greenish. Found throughout Britain; 10 cm ws.

You will often see the brown hawker or brown aeshna take up territory over pools, canals or lake edges, and patrol by ceaselessly flying up and down. Found in England and north Wales, 10 cm ws.

The common darter haunts still water in England and Wales. 5 cm ws.

The four-spotted chaser is named after the black spots on its wings. It is found by ponds and canals particularly in lowland heathy areas. It is a migrant dragonfly in Europe: some may cross the Channel to reach us and add to our resident stock. 7.5 cm ws.

Dragonflies and damselflies, though dramatic looking, are insects of the *primitive* kind. Their young are 'nymphs' – rather similar to the adults, but lacking wings.

The hawker and darter nymphs are equipped with a 'face mask' – a kind of arm which they can flick out to catch prey. By and large they ambush their prey rather than moving in active pursuit. The mask helps them secure their victim.

A head-on view of a common darter showing the enormous compound eyes. Dragonflies, which hunt almost entirely by sight, have excellent vision. Some species have up to 30,000 separate eye facets, each of which produces its own image. The small antennae seen in front of the eyes appear almost redundant.

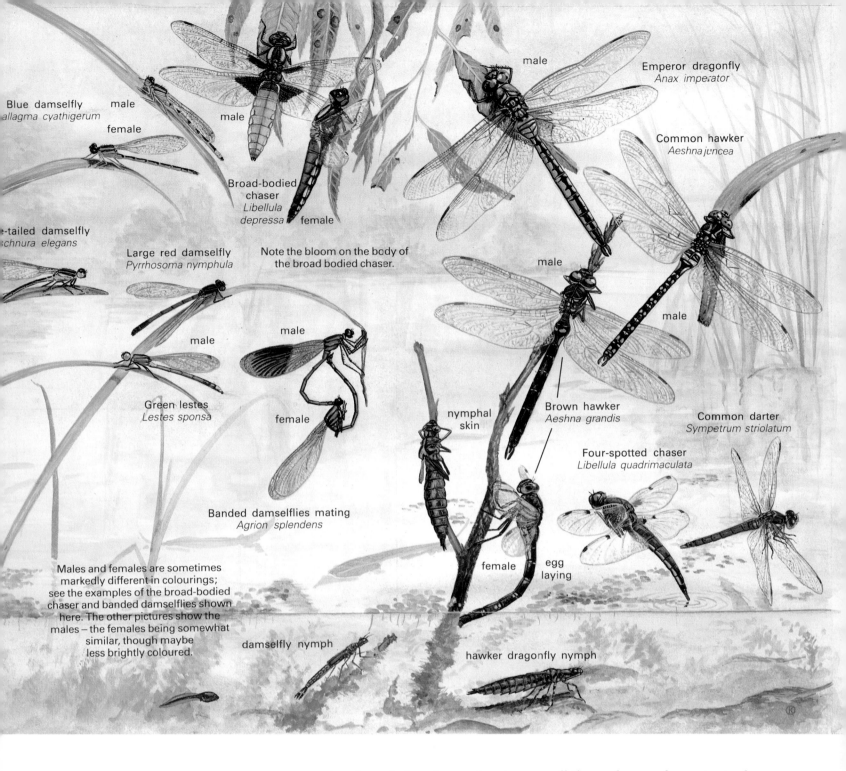

Damselflies are closely related to hawkers and darters, but are smaller, more slender insects which fly weakly and spend much time perched. When at rest they fold their wings back down their body. Their eyes (unlike those of hawkers and darters) do not touch each other on the head.

The blue-tailed damselfly is one of our commonest damselflies. Its nymph can put up with a degree of pollution. 3.5 cm ws.

The blue damselfly is common over still water, throughout Britain. 3.5 cm ws.

The emerald damselfly or green lestes is perhaps more common in acid-water areas, but found throughout Britain. 3.5 cm ws.

The large red damselfly was once common throughout Britain: like others it is now hard to find in the polluted waters of the Midland counties. 4.5 cm ws.

The banded damselflies shown here are mating. The banded damselfly is to be seen at moving but sluggish water, as is the demoiselle. They are both floppy fliers. The banded damselflies are reasonably common and it is relatively easy to observe their territorial behaviour. They usually stake claim to around 2.5 square metres, much of which will be over water, with usually some vantage point on which to perch.

The more agile nymphs of the damselflies have no mask.

on or in the plants below the surface (some pull themselves under water to do so).

The nymphs of dragonflies are important predators in the pond or stream ecosystem, taking many small insects and other animal life. Some nymphs of the larger hawkers will even take small fish and tadpoles. After months for some species but maybe three to five years for the larger dragonflies (the colder the water the longer the time) they are ready for the next stage in their lives.

The nymph will have moulted many times during its underwater life and it will now be full sized (the nymphs of the hawkers can be 5 cm long). It crawls up out of the water, usually pulling itself up the stalk of reeds or other waterside plants. It pauses when it has reached the height its instincts choose, wriggles (maybe to test its grip) and then there is a pause. It is a vital pause, for during this time its breathing pattern is changing under the skin. The skin then splits and the head, thorax and legs emerge and then it rests again, usually hanging head down – a stage which may last for an hour, but nobody knows the reason for it. Maybe it is something to do with the balance of oxygen supply. The abdomen is then finally pulled out. The cast skin remains, the emerging adult clinging to it. Last of all, the wings begin to show, and grow at an astonishing rate – they are full sized after half an hour. The wings are 'pushed' out of the body by pumped blood. They dry and the insect is ready to test them and fly.

This is the sequence of events for a hawker dragonfly; it is much the same for darters and damselflies. The emergence usually takes place at night or just before dawn, though it may take place during the day if the night turns cold. What is interesting is that when the adult dragonfly emerges in this way, it is not quite mature. Its sex organs are not fully developed, nor are its colours fully fashioned, often appearing a dull grey. The first colours to appear are the basic dark brown, black, red and yellow. They will be followed and tinged by green and blue, to create the iridescent sheen of the mating adult. In a long summer season some females gradually attain the males' coloration. These colours, by the way, quickly fade when the insect dies.

197

Frogs, toads and newts

Most of us can put a name to a frog, toad or newt. They are familiar enough. But surprisingly they are not too easy to find nowadays in the countryside. They need a scatter of ponds and pools for breeding, and many rural ponds have disappeared in the last couple of decades. Indeed, there is evidence that frogs are holding their own only in the ponds in suburban gardens and have largely gone from the patchwork open countryside.

Our British amphibians need water for breeding but leave it to spend most of the year on land, feeding on flies, worms and other invertebrates in the shelter and shade of nettle beds and similar places. Only the great crested newt remains in water for much of the year. Frogs and newts hibernate, sometimes in the mud at the bottom of a pool, sometimes in shelter away from water.

Although frogs are not very choosy where they breed, toads will often retrace their hops to an ancestral breeding pool (even if it is no longer there!). They may follow a route which involves crossing busy roads and clambering over recently built obstacles.

If both frogs and toads breed together in the same pool, you will notice that toads choose deeper, more permanent water. Frogs will even lay spawn in day-old puddles, failing all else.

Frogs may have an instinct to move up along rivers, for they can be found higher up the hillsides than toads. If in a high pool, the tadpoles may take two or more years to mature in the water before becoming adult.

Grass snakes have no poison bite; they hunt frogs and are frequently seen near or at water (they swim well). Note the yellow 'band' just behind the head: hence their other name, ringed snake'. They hibernate away from water; and their eggs are laid often in compost heaps – they are not uncommonly seen in gardens on the edge of the countryside. Unlike adders which will sometimes sit you out (page 168), grass snakes will slither away when disturbed.

Grass snakes do not bite, but they have equally dramatic ways of protecting themselves. If picked up, the snake may hiss loudly, dart its head and then void a foul smelling liquid, which is difficult to wash from clothing. If this fails, it may then 'play dead' – become limp and hang from your hand with its mouth open. When placed on the ground, it then turns on to its back as if dead (predators of active prey may sometimes not touch dead animals). 70–150 cm.

Two frogs in a mating embrace in a pond in early spring. The females develop a series of 'warts' along their backs at this time of year, to enable the males to achieve a better hold. A single female may lay up to 3,000 eggs.

Toads often make their summer home in sheds or greenhouses, where they also hibernate. The male toads are first at the breeding pools; they croak to attract the females. The females are grasped, their eggs laid and they then leave the water. The males remain, waiting for further females to join them. 8–12 cm.

The natterjack toad is very rare. A few small colonies exist in sand dunes and heathy places around the country – it s now one of our specially protected animals (see page 247). It is a rather appealing animal. Though largely active by night, it can sometimes be seen in daylight; instead of hopping it *runs* in a mouse-like way, catching

beetles and woodlice. It tolerates brackish water and the spawn may be laid in the dune slacks, but many tadpoles are lost as the pools of these sandy places tend to dry out before development is finished. When mating, the males sing a rather pleasing trill. Rabbit burrows are often used for h bernation. 6 cm.

Common toad
Bufo bufo

Grass snake
Natrix natrix
eating frog

Common frog
Rana temporaria

female   male

frogspawn

Natterjack toad
Bufo calamita
catching a stonefly

Tadpoles are the aquatic young of frogs, toads and newts. They provide a fascinating glimpse of past evolution.

The first amphibians evolved from fish ancestors 300 million years ago. From these early amphibians evolved the frogs, toads and newts we see today. They still show signs of their early origin in their total dependence on water during their young stages. The tadpole cannot survive out of water: it has gills and a tail like a fish, but then changes to become a land-dweller with lungs and legs. Only newts retain the ancestral tail.

Reptiles also evolved early on; however, by coating their eggs with a waterproof skin or shell, they broke the primitive reliance on water.

toad spawn

developing frog tadpole

male
Smooth newt
Triturus vulgaris
female

Palmate newt
Triturus helveticus
male
female

male

Great crested newt
Triturus cristatus

female

newt tadpole

There is a great variation in colour in common frogs; these shown here are fairly common variants. In the breeding pools, the male frogs (7 cm) attract the larger females (9 cm) with croaks, and grasp them, but seize anything in their frenzy, even each other. Often they hibernate at pond bottom.

The eggs of the frog are laid in clusters, a thousand or more at a time. Those of the toad are in strings. Newts lay fewer eggs, planting them singly on water weeds. In the old days when frogspawn was so common as to be not worthy of notice, a sticky 'star slime' was often found out in the fields, far from water. It puzzled people, but it was very likely fresh spawn from a frog eaten by a hungry bird and voided when it began to swell.

All male newts sport a crest when breeding: that of the male smooth newt, though jagged, is unbroken. Like the crested newt, it prefers harder, lowland water.

The first frogspawn

Sometimes the first frogspawn makes as much news as the first cuckoo of the year. But though the cuckoo does herald the summer, the breeding frog cannot be said to do the same for spring. It reacts to some biological trigger in which the temperature and length of daylight presumably play some part. The spawn is usually seen first in the south west of England, and sightings spread north and east as the days pass by. The first Cornish frogspawn is sometimes seen as early as Christmas Day. Hardly spring as we know it.

The great crested newt is our rarest newt, preferring rather deeper ponds than the other newts: the ponds which are most at risk in today's open countryside. Note the dark skin, two-part crest, and the dramatic colouring. 12 cm.

Palmate newts seek soft rather acid water, so they are at home in the northern hills, though they are also found in lowland ponds, sometimes in brackish water. Note the webbed back feet and rather low crest, broken at the end of the body, and the short 'rod' at the end of the tail. 8–9 cm.

Surveys have shown that a good newt pool has half its surface covered with duckweed or pondweed; is more than 200 square metres in area and between 0.5 and 1 m deep; has a low salt content (is not very rich water); is surrounded by scrub or dense waterside cover.

More duck can be identified on pages 210, 230, 232 and 238. More about the hazards facing our swans on page 212. The great crested grebe is shown also on page 212. Compare the heron with its close relative the bittern, page 212.

Birds of open water

Open water is an excellent place to watch birds. Large reservoirs, lakes and gravel pits are often worth visiting in winter as not only will they hold some of our resident waterfowl but larger numbers of Continental birds spend the winter here as well. Our waters do not usually ice over unlike the shallow lakes of northern and central Europe where they breed.

The security provided by the expanse of water means that it is possible to watch the routine behaviour of ducks and other waterbirds without fear of disturbing them. A good pair of binoculars is essential, though, if you want to be able to see the birds clearly. If possible, when approaching a suitable vantage point, try to keep your outline below the horizon and if you then keep still you may be rewarded with some close-up views. Many nature reserves with open water will have a viewing hide alongside – these can be superb places to observe birds and during the winter are also welcome havens out of the cold winds!

The courtship display of the great crested grebe is one of the most exotic sights that a birdwatcher in Britain is likely to see, page 213. These exciting birds were almost lost as a breeding species in the nineteenth century when their breast feathers were extensively used for making muffs and feather hats. The creation of new gravel pits and reservoirs together with the banning of the trade has helped to re-establish this grebe. It prefers larger areas of water and builds a floating nest of weeds and rushes. The young may be seen riding on the back of the adults where they are safe from their main predator – the pike. The adults are expert divers. In winter they lose the colourful neck 'ruff' and crest; 48 cm.

This parent dabchick has just caught a small fish to feed its chick. Like most members of the grebe family, if there is any sign of danger the chick will ride on the parent's back.

Ducks are grouped into two broad categories: dabblers and divers. The dabblers are surface-feeding ducks such as the mallard and shoveler. They usually feed in shallow water, sifting plant and animal material with their broad bills and reaching down below the surface by up-ending. The divers, as their name implies, will frequently dive for food and can swim well underwater. Their feet are usually set well back which makes them ungainly walkers on land; typical species include the pochard and tufted duck.

Courtship rituals begin as early as February when the brightly coloured males or drakes can be seen shaking and bobbing their heads as well as chasing potential mates. By the time the birds depart for the breeding grounds the pair bond is usually well established and the work of nest-building and egg-laying can begin quickly. The gaudy drakes often take little part in the incubation and rearing of the young, leaving the work to the ducks, with their brownish protective colouring. Ducks tend to moult all their flight feathers together in mid-summer and at this time the drakes become more skulking and take on a sombre 'eclipse' plumage which makes them less conspicuous.

Many of our ducks have undergone dramatic changes in their populations in recent history. The drainage of fens and wetlands during the early 19th century robbed many of them of suitable breeding grounds and numbers reached a low about a century ago. Since then the creation of 'new' water in the form of reservoirs and flooded gravel pits has assisted their recovery. Also, from about 1870 to the 1930s long-term climatic changes meant that some of the marshlands in south-east Europe dried up and a milder climate in north-west Europe meant that some of the dispossessed birds moved west to breed for the first time. The pintail and tufted ducks are examples of this.

The heron is unmistakable whether it is seen patiently stalking its prey at the water's edge or slowly flying between feeding sites with its long neck tucked back. It will feed on a wide range of food from frogs and voles to sizeable fish, including those reared in fish farms and garden ponds! Herons nest colonially in treetops, constructing large platform-like nests of twigs and branches. The eggs, which are laid as early as February, hatch at intervals so that, if food is scarce, only the eldest will survive. Their overall population may drop considerably after a harsh winter but soon recovers if this is followed by a series of milder ones. A harsh *frank* call. Up to 100 cm.

Little ringed plovers were a rare sight fifty years ago but in recent decades have been quick to exploit the new gravel pit workings which parallel their more natural habitat – river and lake shingle banks. They are a summer visitor, arriving in early spring when their zig-zagging display flight can be seen. The nest is a simple scrape on the ground. The call is a clear *pee-oo*; 15 cm.

Heron
Ardea cinerea

Little ringed plover
Charadrius dubius

Mute Swan
Cygnus olor

Canada goose
Branta canadensis

Coot
Fulica atra

Tufted duck
Aythya fuligula

Mallard
Anas platyrhynchos

female

female

female

male

Teal
Anas crecca

male

male

male

Pochard
Aythya ferina

female

male

Great crested grebe
Podiceps cristatus

Dabchick
Tachybaptus ruficollis

Moorhen
Gallinula chloropus

The Canada goose is a noisy gregarious bird which was first introduced into Britain in the seventeenth century. It has established feral populations in many parts of England and Wales and in inland areas is the goose that you are most likely to see. Outside the breeding season Canada geese form large flocks which can be a nuisance to farmers as they will graze pasture and winter cereals. In their North American homeland they are migratory and in Britain some migrate to Scotland to moult. Call is a trumpet-like honk; 95 cm.

Teal are dabbling ducks. They are small waterfowl which feed at night and roost during the day. Large numbers arrive in Britain during the autumn from northern Europe and the Soviet Union and are mostly found on coastal marshes and flooded fields. The British breeding teals nest by upland pools and marshes in northern Britain. They are considered good quarry as they rocket into the air when disturbed, testing the skill of the wildfowler. Call consists of high whistles; 35 cm.

Coots are more gregarious than the similar-looking moorhen and can be seen in large flocks on open water in winter. They are, however, very aggressive and can frequently be seen chasing each other. Like the moorhen they require dense waterside vegetation to construct their nests. But unlike the moorhen they often dive for their food, which consists mostly of water plants and insects. The call is supposed to resemble their name; 36 cm.

Dabchicks or little grebes feed singly or in pairs, diving under the water for around 15 seconds to emerge with a distinctive 'plop' some distance away. Their nest is a mound of waterweeds. They can be found on smaller areas of water such as rivers, canals and ponds. They lose their rich chestnut 'bib' and dark underparts in winter, when they have a creamy-white neck and belly; 27 cm.

The mute swan is a familiar freshwater bird. Further described on page 185.

Tufted ducks are gregarious and can be seen diving for underwater plants, insects and molluscs in loose flocks, often with other species. These small, compact birds, with the males' striking black-and-white plumage, are one of our commonest diving ducks They were first recorded as breeding here in the 1830s but have now colonised many lowland lakes and rivers where they can sometimes be found nesting in colonies. Continental birds add to the resident population in winter. 43 cm.

The moorhen can be found almost throughout Britain busily feeding amongst bankside vegetation, in shallow waters of nearly every type of fresh water from small village ponds to edges of large lakes and rivers. The distinctive jerking head movements when it is swimming and flashing white undertail of the alarmed bird instantly identify it. It is strongly territorial for most of the year but can be seen in flocks feeding on waterside meadows in winter. The moorhen builds a platform nest of reeds and other vegetation; the young leave the nest soon after being born and can be seen feeding with the parents in the spring and summer. The alarm call is a loud 'currock'. 33 cm

The mallard or 'wild duck' must be one of the most familiar of our wild birds. It is common everywhere from busy city parks to isolated coastal marshes. It is a dabbling duck and will feed on a wide variety of animal and plant matter. The young leave the nest within hours of being hatched and begin to feed themselves almost immediately but stay with the duck for some time. The brightly coloured drake takes no part in the incubation of the eggs, or the rearing of the young. The populations are kept artificially high in some areas to improve the numbers for wildfowl shoots during the autumn and winter. Many mallards from eastern Europe and Scandinavia come here in winter. The female has the familiar loud *quack*, the male a quieter *aark* call. 57 cm.

Pochards are shy diving ducks. They prefer larger areas of water than the tufted duck and tend to feed more on plant matter. They are scarce as a breeding bird but numbers are substantially increased in winter when large flocks come in from central Europe. Many thousands can be seen on large reservoirs between October and April. Their males have a nasal call or whistle; the female has a 'crouk' call. 46 cm.

See also page 186 for more details of the life of an upland stream. The plant and animal life of moorland is described on pages 160 to 164. Lichens are sensitive to acid rain, and make good air pollution indicators, see pages 18 and 116.

The upland lake

At first glance, an upland lake seems an empty place – far less interesting than a lowland pond or even a gravel-pit pool. However, part of the fascination of ecology is to discover not only the reasons why animals and plants are found in a particular habitat, but also those things which prevent them establishing themselves. An upland lake has many features which are not immediately obvious to the observer.

For a start, lengths of the shoreline exposed to the mountain winds may be as empty of life as a mountain stream – the continual breaking of waves along the edge creating the same harsh conditions as the tumbling waters of the troutbeck. You will find a bare stony beach, or even simply bare rock, which is quite unlike the edge of a lowland pool. The seasonal highs and lows in water level may be marked by zones of green slime or moss. These zones continue out of sight underwater. They may be hard to see but are marked near the shore by the plants growing in them: water lobelia, shoreweed and quillwort shown opposite.

The lake water is poor, low in nutrient supply, with few plankton, hence its clarity. Silt, where it is found, is not very rich; in the shelter of a headland it may support a scanty bed of reeds, but they are rarely as strongly advancing as they would be in lowland, richer water. There will be few snails, but perhaps quite a few freshwater shrimps under the pebbles of the wave-washed shores.

Those remote upland lakes provide relatively undisturbed breeding sites for water birds and consequently they have their own specialities, such as the primeval divers which can still be found nesting in northern Scotland, almost as a relic from the last Ice Age. These places also provide sites for small breeding colonies of common gulls, perhaps our least marine gull. This prim little gull can often be seen feeding on rubbish tips and roosting on large playing-fields in winter but returns to remote areas to breed.

Acid rain

Sweden is a land of countless lakes, but in a good many of them, the fish have either disappeared or are dying out. Large tracts of conifer forest in Germany are also dying back. These two ecological disasters both apparently have their source in what has traditionally been considered the sustainer of life – the rain.

Oxides of sulphur and nitrogen emitted from coal and oil burnt at power stations become dissolved in the water held in the atmosphere, turning it mildly acid, so that it eventually falls as acid rain. It has long been recognised that areas downwind of power stations are likely to be devoid of lichens as these plant are very sensitive to long-term air pollution. Now it seems that lakes and forests are also affected. Moreover, Sweden blames Britain and other countries for the disaster, claiming that the poison rain is blown to these lakes from sources many hundreds of miles away.

More than 5,000 Scandinavian lakes have lost their fish in the last few decades and the natural acidity has been increased, sometimes by as much as ten times. Until recently, however, there was no clear evidence that our waters were suffering a similar effect, but now the

same trend has been found in at least 100 Scottish lakes. It is not the acid water itself which is the direct danger, though salmon are sensitive to it, but the aluminium and other metals which can be released from the soil by the acid conditions. Aluminium attacks the gills of fish and consequently these die of oxygen hunger. Aluminium can be as lethal to plants: one of the reasons for the variety of plant life on chalky soils is that the lime neutralises acids and the poisons are kept locked up.

Scandinavia may be more at risk from acid rain than some other countries because its hard rocks are rather acid to start with; but so are the rocks in many of the mountainous areas of Scotland. In Scandinavia, the quick-melting snow in spring may wash the soil clean of poisons created by the rain, to the benefit of the plant life, but to the tragedy of the fish in the lakes that receive the rushing streams. Much the same could be true of Scotland.

Whatever the precise causes and effects, the only sure way of playing safe and controlling the problem is to reduce the amount of sulphur and nitrogen oxides released from power stations. Unfortunately, this would cost a great deal of money and inevitably progress is slow. Let us hope clear action is taken before more damage is done.

Goosander
Mergus merganser

female

male

Red-throated diver
Gavia stellata

Quillwort
Isoetes sp.

Divers are adapted to swim underwater to catch fish, which is the bulk of their diet, and are ungainly on land.

About 200 pairs of black-throated divers breed in north-west Scotland. They build their nests on the ground, usually on an island near the water. It is thought that numbers of this bird were able to remain in southern Britain during the final part of the Ice Age. In winter, they leave their breeding grounds for the coast where they are joined by others from Scandinavia – and may be seen far south, even off Kent and Sussex. The birds have deep *kwow* and wailing calls; 65 cm.

Black-throated diver
Gavia arctica

Shoreweed
Littorella uniflora

Water lobelia
Lobelia dortmanna

There are about 1000 breeding pairs of goosander in Scotland, with some in the Lakes and Northumbria. Resident, though migrants from Scandinavia come here in winter and can be seen in the south. These birds have a 'sawbill', ideal for grasping the slippery fish on which they feed. They are usually silent, but can cackle or croak. They nest in tree holes or in rock cracks. 66 cm.

In the breeding season, red throated divers emit an extraordinary *kwuk-kwuk-kwuk* call and a long-drawn-out moan. About 1000 pairs nest in north west Scotland. They leave the breeding grounds in winter and, with others from Scandinavia, can be seen on coastal waters throughout Britain. These birds nest on the shores of small lakes, sometimes on an island. The nest is a mound of plants, stems and leaves. About mallard sized; 60 cm.

A bleak upland lake. The rocky shoreline and absence of any shrubs or trees give a clear indication of the harshness of the surrounding land.

Quillwort grows submerged (often deep) in poor-water lakes and tarns. The leaves (to 40 cm) are quill-like. A primitive plant that is allied to club-mosses. Its leaves have four tubes which can be seen when they are split open.

Shoreweed is a common, hardy plant of upland lakes; its leaves contrast with water lobelia because they are sharply pointed and tough but spongy inside. It is equally happy under water or on the damp shore.

Shoreweed and quillwort can sometimes be seen forming dense carpets under water, in the shallows near the shore where there is plenty of light.

Water lobelia brightens the hills in July and August, growing from rooting runners on the stony bottom of shallow lakes; the leaves form soft rosettes. There are two tubes inside the leaf. 20–60 cm.

Compare bogs (page 156) with swamps and marshes. Many of the wintering birds of wetlands are to be seen on pages 200, 210 and others are on pages 230, 232. Wetland flowers are shown on page 208, but see also page 149.

The wetlands

Many of the plants we take for granted at the edge of a river or pond are survivors from very different times.

Swamps and marshlands once fringed our rivers and covered much of the lowlands. Most of this wilderness has long since been drained for farmland, though scattered fragments do remain in East Anglia and in the Spey valley in Scotland; other fragments can be found on the Scottish borders, Anglesey and along the Welsh borders in places where drainage is difficult. Otherwise, all we have left as a memory is a narrow bed of reeds along the shore of a lake, perhaps, spreading to fill the basin of a shallow mere.

Swamp and Fen

The reed marks swamps. It is a quick coloniser, and grows vigorously to create dense beds in shallow water. However, it cannot put up with much of a flow. Its canes trap silt and rot down to create a submerged mushy peat which builds up towards the surface until the fall of the water level in summer begins to lay it bare. When this happens, sedges and other plants can oust the reeds – and these new colonisers also rot down, and in time a firmish peaty 'soil' is created, which is waterlogged for much of the year. This is a fen. In time woody shrubs and trees can root, on what is now becoming dry land. A lake may fill in from its margins in this way. Small ponds dry up in much the same fashion, though different plants may be involved. Bogs could also form (see page 156).

The swamp (fen) peat is, however, not at all like the acid peat produced by a bog. Lowland water is usually fertile – and the swamp peat is rich and somewhat alkaline and many flowering plants will grow on it.

Marsh

A patch of marsh is often found where the water from a spring oozes across pasture or even moorland (its flow prevents a bog forming), or alongside a stream which has not been dredged and deepened, and whose flow nudges up to the top of its bank. Marshy land often spreads away from the standing water of a swamp or fen; and damp meadowland sometimes becomes marshy alongside a river. Marshy land is waterlogged for much of the year, but the soil is never peaty but more like normal garden soil. Marshes are often found on heavy, poorly drained clay sites.

Rushes are found on marshland as well as a whole host of flowering plants. They are also found at the late stages of a swamp and in damp meadows. There are no hard-and-fast dividing lines between swamp, marsh and damp meadowland. They are all now hard to find because of the drastic improvements in drainage in recent years.

If you see marsh marigolds growing with other plants shown on page 208 it could indicate some ancient wetland. Do not jump to conclusions, however, as marsh marigolds are attractive flowers, and are often planted out to brighten the view from a nearby house.

▲ **A traditional view of the Somerset Levels** with sedge-filled dykes and marshy grazing levels. This area is in a National Nature Reserve but elsewhere in the Levels large areas of unprotected land in recent years have been drained and altered out of all recognition.

◄ **A narrow channel winding through vast beds of common reed** at Hicking Broad in Norfolk.

Grazing levels are wet grasslands created by draining peaty fens and marshes; they are found in Somerset and Norfolk and some other places, and their main interest lies in the network of drainage dykes. Where they remain, these dykes contain established water communities of plants and animals. However, they too are threatened by improved drainage and the plough.

Flood meadows lay alongside the Thames and other large rivers; they did flood in winter, and so held some water back, thus protecting the riverside towns downstream. The fritillary and other now rare plants once flourished amidst their damp grass.

Some of the long established damp grasslands alongside rivers, and those created by draining fens and marshes, have acquired a character of

their own. Their names are familiar: flood meadow, water meadow, washes, levels – so what do those names mean?

The washes are artificial flood meadows – grasslands set aside to take some of the water from the winter rivers to prevent it flooding ploughed land. This water brings the invertebrate life of the soil to the surface so that washes attract large numbers of birds, especially winter migrants. The Ouse washes today are a linked series of bird reserves of international importance.

A winter flood keeps frost from the soil and brings the grass on early. The water meadow (traditionally found in the chalk counties of Dorset, Hampshire and Wiltshire) had a network of sluices and channels which flushed the river water across the grass; two or three days of this were all that were needed to bring on that early bite for the sheep or cattle. The meadows were then shut up for hay production and were (and sometimes still are) rich with flowers.

▶ **A series of meadows alongside the Itchen in Hampshire.** These areas are now classed as low-grade agricultural land but at one time were highly prized as they provided the best and earliest spring grazing land.

There is often no clear dividing line between water's edge and an old meadow running alongside it – see the meadow plants shown on page 149. Some of these flowers you will also find in wet woods, page 65. The seasonal change of blooms can be dramatic.

Flowers of the watersides

Many of the plants shown on this page were once very common indeed: you could find them growing in every parish. Alas, this is no longer so as they like some damp around their roots and river engineering and field drainage mean that damp and marshy ground is now hard to find. Look for them also in wet grassland edging streams.

The Himalayan balsam is a fairly recent newcomer, but it has spread fast and far along the river banks of the north – the rivers which are exceedingly polluted. Surprisingly it is an annual, so its seedlings can somehow survive and take advantage of damp ground where the dirty water has killed off other growth. You will sometimes find butterbur doing well in such places, too.

Meadowsweet presents two odours, of fragrant flowers and acrid leaves smelling like a combination of hay and soap! It was a popular plant for strewing on castle floors to keep the muddy medieval smells at bay. Found on damp, less acid soils. June-September; to 120 cm.

Himalayan balsam or policeman's helmet has purple-pink or white flowers and forms dense stands along many rivers. July-October; 1–2 metres.

The yellow iris is one of our loveliest wild flowers. It will sometimes be seen growing in, as well as by, fresh water. Another name for this plant is yellow flag. The word 'flag' is probably by origin a Norse name. Note the large seed pod. May-July; 40–150 cm.

◀ **A magnificent display of purple-loosestrife** amidst a bank of common reeds.

Meadowsweet
Filipendula ulmaria

Himalayan balsam
Impatiens glandulifera

Kingcup or marsh marigold is a flower of spring, its sun-like flowers opening when the air is still cold. Its large leaves are dense green. Not as common as it was – we can no longer take its sighting for granted. A plant of damp shade, it grew in Britain (or where Britain is now) before the last Ice Age. March-May; 30 cm.

Purple-loosestrife has tall handsome spikes of flowers. It is sometimes confused with rosebay willowherb, but the flowering spike of the loosestrife is much more compact.

Purple-loosestrife has one of the most elaborate strategies to guarantee cross-pollination in the whole of the plant kingdom. It has three different versions of its flower, each with a different length of 'style'. (The style is the female stalk to which the pollen from stamens sticks.) There are also stamens of three different lengths; two lengths always being found in each flower.

Flowers with short styles have stamens of middling and long length, but none of short length. Flowers with middling styles have stamens of short and long length. Flowers with long styles have short and middling stamens only. Full pollination takes place only when a style receives pollen from a stamen of its own length. In other words, a flower cannot fully pollinate itself, but can fully pollinate with the other two kinds. June-July; 60–120 cm.

Look for the unusual winged stem of comfrey. This is an erect, rather bristly plant, with broad lower leaves and lance-like upper leaves. It flowers May-June; to 1 metre.

'Organic farming' enthusiasts regard comfreys as companion plants – plants to be grown alongside a crop. The suggestion is that these companions benefit the crop in some way. Some may produce substances which deter insects – many insects home in to their breeding plant by smell – so this could well be true. Comfrey is a plant which concentrates minerals from the soil and accumulates protein much more quickly than the majority of plants. Grown as a companion plant it could, so the enthusiasts contend, be mulched in and save the cost of expensive artificial fertilisers.

What is interesting is that the name comfrey comes from Latin words meaning to be (or to grow) together. Did they grow this plant in the ancient world as a companion? Or did its name arise from its common use as a mixer for potions in medieval times?

Two plants with rather different links with bare mud are shown here. **Bur marigold** is typical of ponds which dry out in summer or places where water stands only in winter. July-October; 60 cm. **Brooklime** flowers May-September; 30 cm tall. 'Lime' here means mud and the plant does root in it. It is usually found near to the coast.

Common valerian can be found by watersides. But you may also find it in wet woods and in a smaller form on dry chalky grassland. June-August; 30–120 cm.

Hemp agrimony is a tall member of the daisy family which can frequently be seen along the edge of streams and rivers in mid-summer when its pink flowers are in bloom. July-September; to 120 cm.

Water mint is our commonest wild mint and is found in many different damp habitats. The cultivated mint is spearmint; peppermint is a hybrid of spearmint and wild water mint. July-October; 15–60 cm.

Ragged robin resembles rather frayed specimens of red campion as it has deep-cut petals. Robin in a flower name usually has evil connotations and it is said to bring bad luck if picked. The Latin name, *Lychnis flos-cuculi*, refers to the cuckoo which should be calling when this plant is in flower. April-June; to 100 cm.

Lady's smock or cuckoo flower can often be found growing in damp meadows and along riversides in spring. The tiny orange eggs of the orange tip butterfly can sometimes be seen on the flower stalks and buds. To 50 cm tall.

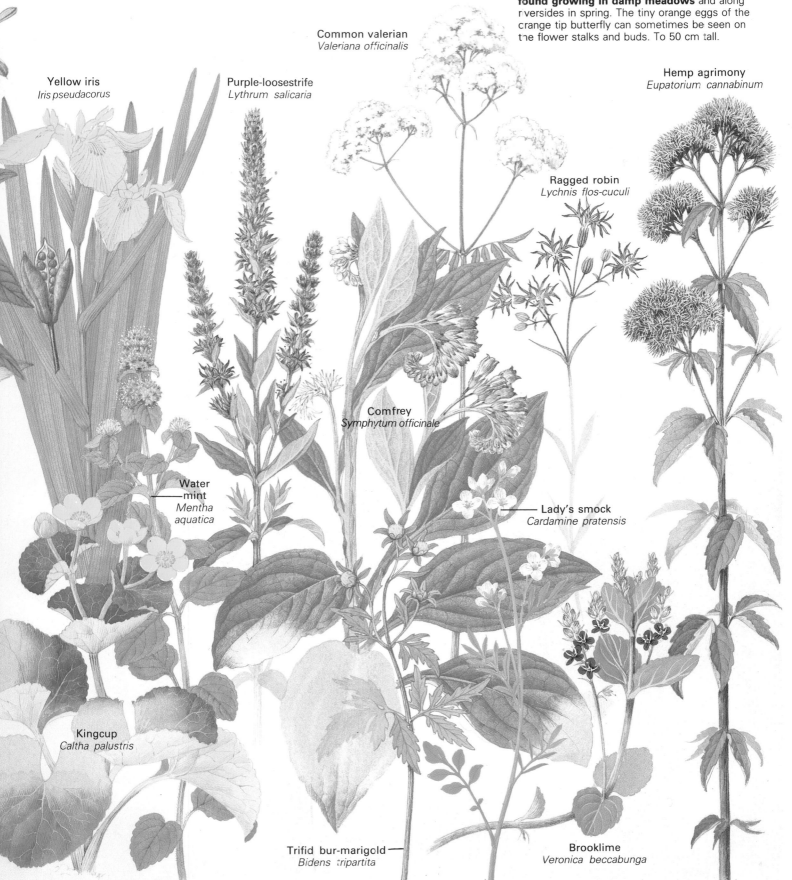

Yellow iris
Iris pseudacorus

Purple-loosestrife
Lythrum salicaria

Common valerian
Valeriana officinalis

Hemp agrimony
Eupatorium cannabinum

Ragged robin
Lychnis flos-cuculi

Comfrey
Symphytum officinale

Water mint
Mentha aquatica

Lady's smock
Cardamine pratensis

Kingcup
Caltha palustris

Trifid bur-marigold
Bidens tripartita

Brooklime
Veronica beccabunga

Here we introduce waders; more of these fascinating birds are shown on pages 230, 232. They often add interest to a summer walk on moorland, pages 162, 165. Reed buntings and sedge warblers may today be seen in young plantations, page 67. See also page 144.

The edge of the swamp

The kind of habitat shown on this page is counted as one of the most at risk in Britain. It is the swampy land which often runs on to large areas of wet, 'unimproved' grassland and, for the birdwatcher, it can be one of the most exciting areas, with waders and wintering wildfowl in the more open areas and small warblers skulking in the dense reedbeds and marshes.

Reed and sedge warblers are closely related birds, and they nest in the same kind of place – the edge of a swamp, where the ranks of tall reeds edge on to dryish land. How they dovetail their habits within this habitat is fascinating.

Reed warblers choose to sling their deep, mug-shaped nest around the stems of the reeds growing in the water. The sides of the nest are woven around several of the close upright stems.

The sedge warblers, on the other hand, choose the 'high marsh' – the dryish land beyond the reeds which (in anything like natural conditions) would be perhaps rather scrubby, with willows and other plants taking root. The sedge warbler's nest (again a deepish cup) is low down amongst this vegetation. Those are typical nest sites but you may also see reed warblers nesting in bushes.

The two birds also feed somewhat differently. They both forage for aphids and other insects and their grubs, and for spiders too, but they tend to look for them in different places within the habitat they share. The reed warbler hunts in both the reeds and bushes encroaching on to the site while the sedge warbler feeds nearer its nest site, on the flote grass and rushes, perhaps – lower down than the reed warbler.

So, in a typical situation the reed and the sedge warbler are able to share the edge of the swamp. From the point of view of these attractive birds, the single habitat is, in fact, divided into two quite separate niches.

The redshank is the 'watchdog' of the marshes, being the first to fly off, giving an early warning to other birds with its insistent piping. Redshanks winter on coastal mudflats and saltmarsh and often breed inland by rivers and in rough grazed marshes. They require damp ground in order to probe for invertebrates in the soil. Redshanks are a good example of the sensitivity of some birds to change. They will quickly desert a field they have previously used for breeding if it is drained or if trees are planted within about 200 metres. They have a low darting flight but also have an aerial display in which they rise steeply and then glide down with wings held stiffly, calling. 28 cm.

Lapwings are probably our best-known wader, with their swerving acrobatic display flights and noisy 'peewit' calls. The destruction of so much rough grazing means that they now rely more on marginal land than in the past. They are, nevertheless, very adaptable and can still be found, though in decreased numbers, nesting in arable and mixed farmland. Large flocks of lapwings arrive in late summer to winter here. Unlike many other waders they fly with slow wingbeats and their rounded wings are not suited to very long journeys. 30 cm.

This reed warbler has been forced to foster this young cuckoo. Both reed and sedge warbler nests are frequently parasitised by cuckoos.

Shoveler
Anas clypeata

female

male

female

Reed bunting
Emberiza schoeniclus

Lapwing
Vanellus vanellus

Sedge warbler
Acrocephalus schoenobaenus

Snipe
Gallinago gallinago

Redshank
Tringa totanus

Reed warbler
Acrocephalus scirpaceus

Yellow wagtail
Motacilla flava

Like other waders, redshank will often be seen swimming when feeding. The pied wagtail below can be recognised from afar by its bouncing flight.

Pied wagtail
Motacilla alba

Snipe probe for worms and other invertebrates in soft ground in marshes, with their long sensitive bills. They are most active at dusk in summer and usually are first noticed when they perform their territorial display flight in which they fan their tail feathers out and plunge at a steep angle with a distinctive 'bleating' or drumming sound. Normally when flushed they have an evasive zig-zag flight and make a *skaap* call. 27 cm.

The shoveler strains watery mud through its large spoon-shaped bill, sifting out small seeds and invertebrates. It breeds in the shallows of scattered lowland lakes, sometimes in small colonies. Our breeders migrate in autumn to be replaced by others from further north. 48 cm.

The sedge warbler is found throughout Britain in 'high marsh' where you might see its brief, fluttering song flights, rising steeply then dropping with wings outstretched. The song is more varied than the reed warbler's, often mimicking other birds. Note the distinct eye-stripe and streaked back. Summer visitor. Numbers have dropped noticeably in recent years following droughts in its wintering grounds south of the Sahara. 13 cm.

The reed warbler is one of a few species largely confined to reedbeds. It has a uniform brown back and indistinct eye-stripe. The song is a repetitive *chirr . . . chirruck . . . chirr* from cover. It is found mainly in central and southern England. Summer visitor. 12.5 cm.

Reed buntings can share dominance of the reeds with reed warblers but are resident seed-eaters, often visiting gardens to feed at bird tables in winter. They can also breed in drier habitats. They have a squeaky repetitive song. 15 cm.

Pied wagtails move restlessly, chasing insects on or near the ground and constantly dipping their tails. They are often seen near water and are territorial when breeding but large numbers may roost together at other times of the year. They will, however, defend a winter feeding territory along a riverbank, patrolling it for washed-up invertebrates. A *chisik* call; 18 cm.

Yellow wagtails arrive from Africa each summer and can be found in lowland marshes and water meadows, where they can be seen feeding around the feet of cattle, catching flies disturbed by the trampling. Nests in drier parts of meadows. Flight call is a *tsweep*, unlike other wagtails. 16.5 cm.

Two snipe probing for food with their long bills in the mud.

Many of the previous pages show plants and animals to be seen in the wildlife tapestry of the unpolluted, classic Broad. See pages 196 for dragonflies, 182 for freshwater fish; see also pages 184, 200 and 210 for some of the rich bird life of this habitat.

The Norfolk Broads

Voyaging through the Norfolk Broads today, you can still recapture the feel of the fenny fastnesses of the past. The Broads occupy the middle courses of three Norfolk rivers and have an unexpected origin; they are the flooded sites of medieval peat diggings of many centuries ago.

Despite their man-made beginnings, they are a magnificent example of wilderness. Reeds soon invaded the flooded pits and in some places they rotted to form a peat; when this reached the surface, sedges took over and, in time, wet alder woodland formed. Parts of the Broads are classic examples of the sequence of events described on page 204 and pictured on page 207.

The Broads are still open water partly because the golden winter reeds have for centuries been harvested for thatching (even some of the local churches are thatched). The saw sedge, which lies behind the reedbeds, is also cut every four years to be used for ridging the thatched roofs. If it was not cut, the tough

You can hear the extraordinary booming call of the bittern night and day, in the early part of the year in the Broads. It is a large heron-like bird, which can be virtually invisible when alarmed. It remains quite still with its neck stretched up, bill pointing skywards, and swaying gently with the reeds around it.

Bitterns were probably extinct in Britain a century ago. They were becoming rare in early Victorian days, and the rarer they became, the more of a prize they were for the taxidermists. However, some birds cross to winter here, and by 1900 bitterns were breeding again in Norfolk. Their stronghold is still in East Anglia, though some are seen elsewhere.

In recent years there has been a decline, perhaps because of the continued disturbance to their Broadland habitat. 75 cm.

An aerial view of Hickling Broad, one of the largest and best known of the Broads. Despite the large area of water it is rarely more than two metres deep except in those channels dredged for sailing. The Broad is mostly owned by the Nature Conservancy Council and is managed as a reserve. All around it the modern arable agricultural landscape dominates the view.

The glamorous swallowtail is one of our largest butterflies, with 7.5 cm wingspan, and it has a strong rapid flight. It is also one of our rarest butterflies. It lays its eggs on the milk parsley, a fen plant of the Broads and some other places. A century ago, the swallowtail was being caught on several southern marshlands by the collectors of that time. Then it became restricted to the fens of East Anglia including the Norfolk Broads. By 1952, only a few flew in the Broads. It is sometimes seen elsewhere, but these sightings are of migrants from Europe which are of a slightly different race.

You will find great crested grebes elsewhere, but they are often seen on the open Broads. A silent bird for much of the time, though it has a variety of calls. These grebes have a remarkable courtship display: the pair, shaking their head plumes, bow to each other and present water weeds, whilst treading water. The fashion for feather hats and muffs in Victorian days spelt the near extinction of these birds. They were down to 32 pairs in 1860, but there are now around 5,000 in the British Isles; 48 cm.

The marsh harrier is one of our rarest birds (20+ breeding pairs) and is associated with the reedbeds. Harriers fly very low and slowly, dropping on to their prey of birds and mammals. The voice is slight – a thin *kwee-oo* or whistle – and the bird is usually silent outside the breeding season. The nest is a mass of reeds. The marsh harrier is found across Mediterranean Europe and North Africa; it is at the end of its range in Britain. To 50 cm.

The coypu is as big as a dog and was bred in Britain for fur but escaped to maintain itself in large numbers in the wild, damaging crops, especially sugar beet, on which it feeds. It also damages the banks of rivers and drainage dykes. Coypu are treated as a pest and control measures cost hundreds of thousands of pounds a year in total: it could cost up to £5 million to eradicate them from East Anglia. Originally from South America. 100 cm long (with tail 140 cm).

saw edge would grow two metres tall or more. However, it is sometimes mown to open up the land for grazing. There are often plenty of flowers amongst the sedges, as well as in the grazed meadows which lie alongside the reedbeds.

The classic open Broad is covered with water lilies and alive with dragonflies and birds, as well as with fish teeming in the water. Giant pike, too, are not uncommon. But the vast increase in boat traffic has polluted the water. Sewage discharge is now more strictly controlled, but the damage has already been done in many Broads. Furthermore, the effect of the turbidity and wash from the motor boats can be very damaging as the reeds cannot survive much water movement.

The Broads that do remain in their original state are either privately owned or are managed as nature reserves.

Marsh harrier
Circus aeruginosus
male

female feeding young at the nest

Coypu
Myocastor coypus

Bittern
Botaurus stellaris

Swallow-tail butterfly
Papilio machaon

Great crested grebe
Podiceps cristatus

213

In Reach of the Sea

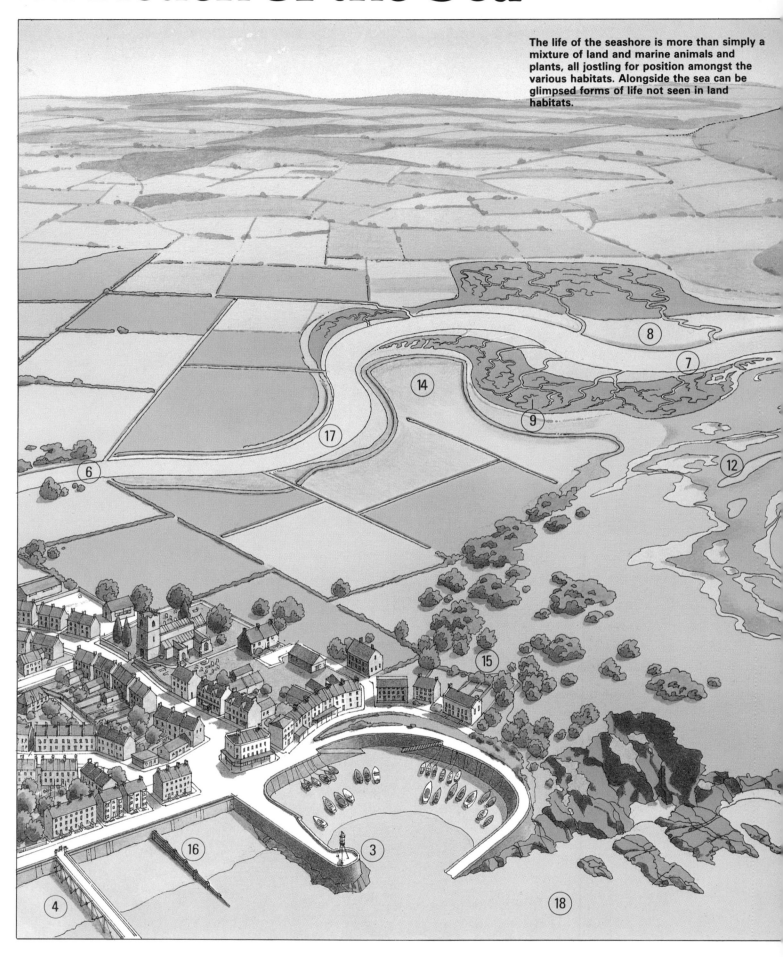

The life of the seashore is more than simply a mixture of land and marine animals and plants, all jostling for position amongst the various habitats. Alongside the sea can be glimpsed forms of life not seen in land habitats.

Where the sea meets the land, an exciting variety of habitats is created. On the shore, the effects of the twice-daily tides is clear, marked by seaweed zones on the rocks **1**. The effect is less marked on the sandy beach **2**, but have a look for the zones on harbour walls **3**, and even pier legs **4**. Rock pools **5**, have a life of their own.

Tidal changes can be seen far up river, although the effects of salt water become diluted **6**. In spite of their dreary appearance, estuaries **7** are one of the most productive of all habitats, as demonstrated by the vast flocks of birds that feed on the mudflats exposed by the ebb tides **8**, and on the salt marshes **9** that are found in many estuaries.

Salt marshes are unique – created by the tides to a great extent, yet colonised by land plants. Other interesting seashore habitats can be found: cliffs **10** and sand dunes **11**. Even the dunes in time become stabilised, to the extent of having permanent ponds or 'slacks' in their hollows **12**. Shingle can support its own range of wildlife if undisturbed **13**.

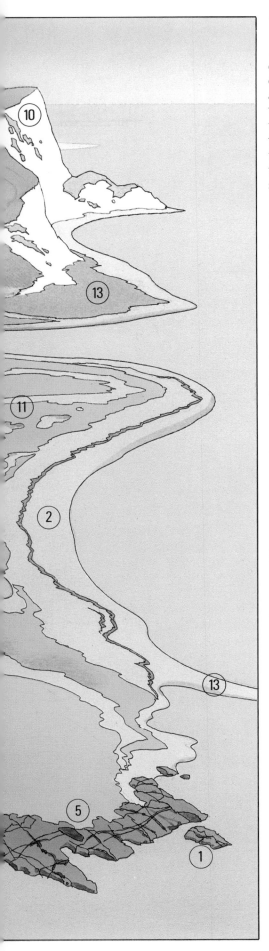

EVERY SUMMER, millions of holidaymakers go in search of the sea. The British seaside with its sandy beaches, cliff walks, rock pools and sheltered estuaries has long been our favourite open-air playground. But the shores of Britain are also home to a host of wild plants and creatures whose lives depend on the presence of the sea. The coast is not always a kind habitat of gentle sands and blue skies. Often stormbound, battered by huge waves, it is truly nature's wildest frontier, an elemental battle-zone where wind and water together batter the land's rocky edge . Sometimes submerged, sometimes exposed to gasping heat or bitter cold, living things at the tide's edge lead a tightrope existence of frequent extremes. Yet such are the miracles of evolution that plants and animals of the shores are able to thrive in the most inhospitable surroundings of sand dunes, shingle spits and wave-washed rocks.

Dunes are hills and hummocks of windblown sand. Some dune systems are very old. Their foundations were begun some 6,000 years ago when our present sea level was established after the last Ice Age. Dunes are found in many parts of Britain, from Braunton Burrows in north Devon to Holkham Meals on the north Norfolk coast; and from Anglesey to the Hebrides. Some dune systems, such as those of the Culbin Sands overlooking the Moray Firth in Scotland, may be 30 metres high. But all are unstable and vulnerable to erosion. If the thin skin of surface vegetation is worn through by tramping feet, the result may be a 'blow-out' in which strong winds punch a gaping hole through the dunes' outer defences.

When this happens, the long, slow process of recolonisation and stabilisation by plant life must begin all over again. Down on the driftline, the first colonisers are tough, salt-resistant plants such as sea rocket and prickly saltwort. Above and behind them, safe from all but the highest tides, other pioneers such as sand couch and lyme grass spring up, followed by the wiry marram grass, the greatest of stabilisers, whose long underground stems bind fast the shifting sand.

At this stage the hillocks are known as 'yellow' dunes. Flowers are few, although the pretty sea bindweed and frosty blue sea holly can be found. As the sandhills grow older, mosses and lichens creep between the marram, creating 'grey' dunes. Sometimes, when the sand is made up of lime-rich seashells, a springy carpet of turf appears. In the Western Isles of Scotland, this is known as the *machair*, beautiful to behold at primrose time, and a favourite breeding ground for wading birds such as redshank and dunlin. Other dunescapes form 'slacks' – hollows that flood with fresh water in winter – where marsh helleborines bloom and the rare natterjack toad croaks in the dusk during its breeding season, which peaks in May.

Shingle beaches are common in Britain, but shingle habitats beyond the reach of the highest tides are few. The best-known are at Dungeness in Kent, Orfordness in Suffolk, and Dorset's famous Chesil Bank. At first glance these massive drifts of sea-heaped pebbles appear even more hostile to wildlife than the shifting dunes. Yet once vegetation takes hold in the shape of orache and sea beet, sea kale and yellow horned-poppy, humus and moisture fill the gaps between the stones, encouraging further flowers such as sea campion and biting stonecrop. Several species of birds also breed on the shingle. They include common, Arctic and little terns, and the ringed plover, whose eggs and chicks are almost impossible to detect even at close range, so perfect is their camouflage.

There could be no greater contrast to the stony inhospitability of a shingle bank than that provided by the rich and teeming expanse of the estuary. Fed by an endless supply of nutrients from both the river and the tide, estuaries are among the most productive natural habitats on earth. In Britain there are at least 300 estuaries, from the Exe and Tamar in the south-west to the gleaming tidal flats of the Moray Firth in the far north. Wherever they are found, their sheltered accumulations of mud and sand contain enormous numbers of aquatic animals: cockles, shrimps, ragworms, green shore crabs and tiny *Hydrobia* snails; and these, together with eel grass and algae, attract great gatherings of waders and wildfowl. Dunlin and oystercatcher, curlew, redshank, shelduck and barnacle goose are among the many typical species to be found feeding or roosting among the breezy salt marshes and exposed tidal flats. Unlike most other plant communities in Britain, our wide salt marshes with their glasswort and sea lavender have evolved naturally, and in winter especially these ancient pastures become a seasonal refuge for huge flocks of ducks and wild geese, many

Parts of this natural canvas have been 'reclaimed' for farming and other purposes since early times. Salt marshes make excellent grazing **14**, houses are built out on to dunes **15**, groynes and other storm defences **16** change what is essentially a mobile series of habitats. Pollution can arrive down river **17** or from a town's hidden sea sewers **18** and disrupt wildlife.

of which drive south from where they breed in the arctic tundra, Greenland, Iceland and northernmost Europe. Many of our major estuaries are therefore internationally important for the survival of Europe's wildfowl and wading birds.

Other seabirds find refuge on rockier shores, where cliffs, stacks and islands echo through the breeding season to the clamour of gulls, auks and other birds of the dizzy ledges. Here, safe and inaccessible, seabirds such as gannets and guillemots congregate in enormous numbers. There are 13 gannetries around the coasts of the British Isles, including the Bass Rock in the Firth of Forth, and remote St Kilda, the largest in Europe, with some 52,000 breeding pairs. Other important seabird islands include Lundy in the Bristol Channel, the Farne Islands off the Northumbrian coast, and the Pembrokeshire islands of Skomer and Skokholm, which between them provide a home for 50,000 pairs of Manx shearwaters and 6,000 pairs of storm petrels. Shearwaters and puffins nest in burrows, but guillemots and razorbills lay their eggs on bare rock ledges. Kittiwakes also nest on ledges, but build true nests of seaweed stuck to the rock with droppings. Keeping them company are fulmars and herring gulls, the former soaring and gliding on the updraughts with narrow, stiff-held wings. But not all the birds that nest on the cliffs are true seabirds. On some of our wilder western coasts you may hear the guttural croak of the raven, and

◄ **The towering chalk cliffs of Bempton,** near Flamborough Head, in Yorkshire provide a spectacular breeding site for thousands of seabirds including guillemots, kittiwakes and fulmars. These 140-metre cliffs also house the only mainland colony of gannets in Britain.

▲ **This flock of farmyard ducks, watched by a lone redshank** are feeding in a salt marsh creek at low tide. Most of this scene will be covered at high tide. The constant replenishing of the marsh with fine salts brought in by the rivers and tides means that these estuarine muds are rich feeding grounds.

►► **A cliff ledge on the Isle of Wight, covered with a mass of plants.** The deeper soils in the crevices are supporting chalkland flowers such as wild thyme and wild carrot. The rocks themselves are mottled with orange and grey lichens.

sometimes, rarer still, the harsh, heckling cry of the peregrine falcon, which also breeds on inland crags.

Of all the habitats within reach of the sea, perhaps none is so fascinating as the colourful and mysterious world of the rock pool. Who has not experienced the pleasure of scrambling over rocks still wet from the tide's last covering, amongst slippery thongs of bladderwrack and blue-black encrustations of mussels, to peer into the crystal waters in search of crabs and prawns and tompot blennies? Here live all kinds of extraordinary animals, each one adapted to the rigours of survival at the sea's edge, where they must withstand not only the crash of mighty waves, but also the twice-daily changes created by the ebb and flow of the tide. Here live starfish, sea slugs, hermit crabs, exquisite sea anemones and thick tangles of seaweed. Here, too, just as on dry land, there are peaceful browsers and remorseless hunters. The limpet, whose familiar pyramidal shell is designed to withstand the battering waves, is a harmless animal that grazes on algae as it crawls across the rocks. But the predatory dog whelk is a carnivore that bores through the shells of mussels and barnacles to reach the soft flesh within. At low tide, other hunters join in, as turnstones and oystercatchers fly in, seeking food among the rocks and pools until all is covered by the return of the replenishing tide.

217

Life in the tide zones

The constant movement of the tides up and down the seashore creates ceaseless change of a kind not seen in other habitats. Periods when the shore is under water are followed by periods of exposure to the hot sun and drying breeze, but the plants and animals have adapted to these extremes. Moreover, they arrange themselves in clear 'zones' down the shore, reflecting the time spent in and out of the water and the amount of pounding they receive from the waves. Parts of the shore may be sheltered from the full force of the waves while others are battered twice a day.

The tides do not end their influence at the seashore – their effect extends far up estuaries and rivers. An estuary has brackish water: salt water and fresh water meet and mix, the 'cocktail' changing with the state of the tide. Not many shore dwellers can tolerate this kind of change nor the rather turbid water of estuaries where the mud is churned by currents. Sometimes the shifting mixture of the waters can create banks of mud and here one of our most fascinating plant communities, the salt marsh, develops.

The tides are the result of the pulls of the gravity of sun and moon on the fluid masses of the world's oceans. There are two high and two low tides each day, but their height varies. The spring tides (nothing to do with the spring season of the year) rise higher and fall lower than others. They occur near the times of new and full moon. In Britain we have some of the most powerful spring tides in the world. In the Severn estuary, there is a rise of 12 metres from the lowest spring water mark to highest tide level.

In between the springs are the neap tides, which have the smallest range, and they occur at the first and third quarters of the moon.

This variation of the tides day by day means, of course, that some parts of the shore are rarely uncovered, others are uncovered regularly twice a day, while others are covered only when the springs build up. The scheme below explains this.

This change in the tides affects the plants and animals of the shore. Some can stand some time out of water; others are very sensitive to drying out. The various kinds of brown seaweeds arrange themselves in noticeable zones down the shore according to the amount of exposure they can tolerate. There is nothing very exact about these zones, for each merges into the next, and rock pools and other features can distort them.

The seaweeds tend to grow lower down on exposed shores, while the rocks are colonised by barnacles. On a rocky headland the splash zone may reach far above the topmost tide mark.

When the tide is rising from low to high water it is called a flood tide; when it is falling it is an ebb tide. The rates at which the tide floods and ebbs usually change as the month progresses.

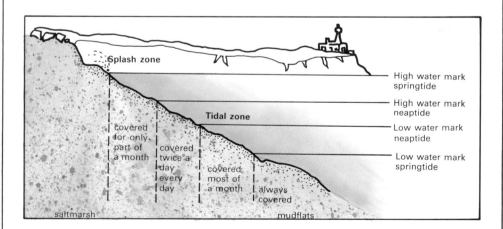

Splash zone

Tidal zone

High water mark springtide

High water mark neaptide

Low water mark neaptide

Low water mark springtide

covered for only part of a month

covered twice a day every day

covered most of a month

always covered

saltmarsh

mudflats

▲**The magnificent, sweeping Dorset coastline at Durdle Dor**. The heights of the recent tides are clearly marked by the strand-lines. The nearest one clearly shows the maximum height of the last spring tide. In the distance the eroded rolling chalk slopes testify to the cutting power of the waves.

◄**The dramatic limestone cliffs of South Wales**. The tides along this part of the coast have a rise and fall of over 12 metres during spring tides. These horizontally bedded rocks are almost sheer as the waves tend to erode the base of the cliff, causing the whole face eventually to collapse along a vertical joint.

▶ **The surface of the cliffs will often be covered by a patchwork of different lichens.** Here great fronds of sea ivory are growing amidst orange, black and grey crust-forming lichens.

This page continues the sequence of 42, 98, 138 and 178. Here we see how the view of nature that emerges when we consider energy flows within an ecosystem can be very different from the conventional picture of speedy hunters pursuing prey.

Seashore life

Forget for the moment that the fox and the seagull are clearly very different-looking animals. If you could spend a day or two following their lives you might find some similarities. They both spend much time restlessly moving great distances to find food. Both have a varied diet of all kinds of small animals, but they will also take plant food and you may even see them both scavenging at the same rubbish dump.

Similarities can be seen, too, in the life-styles of sea anemones (they are animals of course) and spiders – they both sit and wait for their prey. Some sea snails are like caterpillars: both actually live on their food supply – the snails on algae, caterpillars on leaves.

Whether on land or in the sea, all creatures are part of a delicate web of relationships within which each species has a niche or a role to play. In the sea, just as on land, there are herbivores (plant eaters), carnivores preying on other animals, and scavengers. In the sea, as on land, the plants are the primary producers of energy – without them animals could not exist. In the sea, the plants are found as small plankton that float in the sea water, and as the familiar seaweeds and other algae that cover the rocks. Very few higher plants grow in the sea: eel grass is one, it is described on page 234, 240.

Although seaweeds are rubbery, they lack the bulky woody stiffening that many land plants must have. This woody fibre is pretty inedible, and in a woodland ecosystem it passes down the decomposer food chain (page 42). By and large, the seashore plant-eaters, including the shellfish and other animals that strain the plankton from the sea water, are rather more efficient feeders than their counterparts on land, simply because this large element of waste is absent. They therefore have proportionately more energy for body-building and reproduction. This increased efficiency means that the animals that graze on the algae have the potential for a population explosion which is prevented only by a similar increased efficiency in the predators. This unexpected aspect of seashore life often shows itself in food chains with more links than is usual on land, and also, from an efficiency point of view, puts the lowly starfish on a level with those sleek hunters, the fox and the gull!

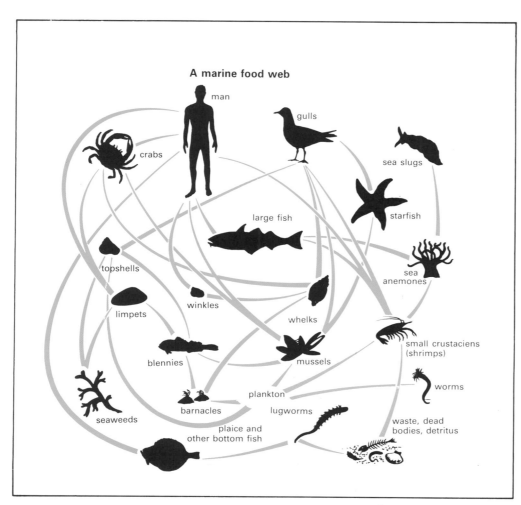

A marine food web

man

gulls

crabs

sea slugs

large fish

starfish

topshells

sea anemones

winkles

limpets

whelks

blennies

small crustaciens (shrimps)

mussels

plankton

worms

seaweeds

barnacles

lugworms

plaice and other bottom fish

waste, dead bodies, detritus

▲ **The dog-whelk is an efficient predator of rocky coasts**, where it feeds voraciously on barnacles. The whelk has a 'tube-tongue' with a rim of hard points at the end, which it forces against the thin internal plates of the barnacle and 'drills' out a hole. It then sucks out the barnacle meat.

The scheme on the left shows just a few of the possible food links on the shore. The balance can be a fine one, and any disturbance easy to spot. The Torrey Canyon oil spill is one example. Quite apart from its effect on the lichen zones on the rocks along the neighbouring coast (see page 237), the oil and the detergents used to clean up the holiday beaches smothered and drugged the limpets. They were then easily picked off the rocks by feeding gulls – or simply fell off. Without them, the lushest growths of seaweed ever seen in Cornwall grew, and lasted for some years, until the populations of the limpets and other grazing snails recovered.

▶ **Barnacles are filter-feeders, collecting drifting plankton** with their feeler-like 'legs'. They are related to the crustaceans and are attached to the rocks at their 'head' ends.

Exposure and pollution can both distort the zonation of the shore. Some pollution effects are short-lived (see page 220); on the other hand the green slimes and weeds of the harbour mud may result from a continuous flow from drains and other pollution sources.

Colours down the seashore

Seaweeds are marine algae that can be found growing on the seashore and in the brackish water of estuaries. They have no roots, although many have distinctive holdfasts that clamp them to rock or other hard surfaces. Only in very sheltered places will seaweeds be seen growing from soft sand or mud, although you will often find storm-torn seaweeds lying along the strand-line of a sandy beach.

Like all plants, seaweeds contain green chlorophyll for photosynthesis, which is most efficient in bright light. Many of our seaweeds contain other pigments that mask the green but allow them to continue food production in what is often quite gloomy, clouded water. In our temperate waters, brown seaweeds are the most common, and red seaweeds can often be seen low down the shore and in rock pools.

The fact that the tides create zones of different conditions down the shore is marked by different species of brown seaweeds. At the top of the shore are those that can withstand extreme desiccation for much of the month, while those at the foot of the shore spend more time immersed. These seaweed zones can often be clearly seen on harbour walls and pier legs.

Green seaweeds are bright green when wet and are found most often on the upper shore where they can photosynthesise most efficiently. Many can tolerate brackish water and even the fresh water of a beach stream.

Enteromorpha coats rocks, floats in pools, and sometimes forms dense sheets where it covers mud washed by sewage-rich sea. The fronds are tubular (enteromorpha means intestine-like). Most abundant in spring. 40 cm.

Sea lettuce is left sprawling when the tide goes out; it can tolerate pollution to some extent and is found in estuaries. Most abundant during the summer. July–August, 15 cm.

Cladophora is found as delicate tufts under other (usually brown) weeds or in rock pools. 15 cm.

Bryopsis is a warm-water weed, found along the edge of deep rock pools and on the lower shore. It does not often survive the winter in Britain, for although the sea water is usually warm enough then, these shore weeds are exposed to cold air when the tide is out. To 10 cm.

Brown seaweeds may appear slightly greenish. They are very slippery when wet and this protects them from bruising and abrasion when pounded by the sea on the shore. They have a holdfast and branching fronds. Some have float sacs that pop when squeezed (poppers).

Some red seaweeds have wide, soft fronds, others are richly branched. Some are hard and brittle. They are most efficient at photosynthesis in dim light and are seen in gullies and heavily shaded pools on the shore. Look for them also growing on the fronds of the kelps washed up from the lower shore.

Coral-weed, seen in rock pools, is often bleached white by sunlight. To 15 cm.

Purple laver is found plastering the rock rather like sea lettuce, but is coloured purple-brown. Also in rock pools. To 25 cm.

Dulse can be very pretty with its iridescent fronds. You may find it on the stalks of kelps. It is one of the commonest red seaweeds of our shores.

Carragheen sometimes replaces the brown seaweeds on exposed shores. It is found on all kinds of shore, occasionally growing so well it makes a thick felt over the rocks. It can be prettily iridescent underwater. 15 cm.

▲ A kelp with a mass of epiphytic red seaweeds, including dulse, growing attached to its stalk.

◄ In the more sheltered bays the knotted or egg wrack can form large clumps amidst the boulders and rocks. On more exposed sections of coast it will be largely replaced by bladder-wrack, which can withstand greater wave action.

Note the unusual 'button' holdfast of thong weed on exposed shores. These buttons may grow to form a dense mat on rocks. From the centre of each grows a long fertile 'thong', a branched strap that is a thin and elongated version of the reproductive sac at the ends of the fronds of spiral wrack. Over 150 cm.

Tangle weeds (kelp) can sometimes be glimpsed below the lowest tide level, swaying back and forth rhythmically with the waves.

The oarweed holdfast adds on a layer of 'branches' each year and can be dated; sometimes it may be more than ten years old. Often found washed ashore. 150 cm.

Sugar weed (sea belt) is sometimes found washed up, attached to pebbles. This shore plant is most often used as a weather forecast. It dries out when hung up but if the air is humid (before rain) it may become soft and limp. To over 200 cm.

Channelled wrack
Pelvetia
canaliculata

Enteromorpha sp.

Sea lettuce
Ulva lactuca

Purple laver
Porphyra umbilicalis

Dulse
Palmaria palmata

Cladophora sp.

Bryopsis

Coral weed
Corallina officinalis

Carragheen
Chondrus crispus

Spiral wrack
Fucus spiralis

Bladder
wrack
Fucus
vesiculosus

Knotted wrack
Ascophyllum
nodosum

Oarweed
Laminaria digitata

Serrated wrack
Fucus serratus

Channelled wrack has fronds (leaf-like parts) that are curled length-wise and have clusters at their tips but no poppers. The tips are often forked. Found at the top of the shore. To 15 cm.

Spiral (flat) wrack has plain-edged fronds, often twisted. It has no poppers. The small sacs at the end of the fronds produce reproductive cells that are released into the sea. It grows slightly higher up the shore than the bladder wrack. To 30 cm.

Bladder-wrack has sturdy fronds with a tough midrib and paired oval poppers each side that buoy up the plants as the tide rises. To 80 cm.

Knotted wrack has large single poppers as wide as its leathery fronds. Its flattened stem has no midrib. 150 cm.

Serrated wrack makes the rocks at the bottom of the tidal zone slippery. It is exposed for only a few hours each day. It has no poppers, and the edges of the fronds are toothed. The midrib is marked by a faint line. 150 cm.

Sugar weed
Laminaria saccharina

The brown seaweeds zone themselves down the shore reflecting the time spent out of water and their tolerance of drying sunshine and wind – as well as the icy cold of winter. In general, the green seaweeds will be found higher up the shore; the red seaweeds around low water mark. Although they live in what appears to be harsh surroundings, seaweeds are as sensitive as other plants to slight differences in temperature (they grow best in cool water) and to pollution.

Thong weed
Himanthalia elongata

Naming brown seaweeds by their shape and position down the seashore

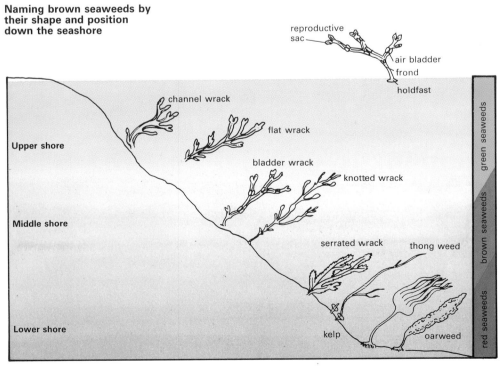

reproductive
sac

air bladder

frond

holdfast

channel wrack

flat wrack

Upper shore

bladder wrack

knotted wrack

green seaweeds

Middle shore

serrated wrack

thong weed

brown seaweeds

Lower shore

kelp

oarweed

red seaweeds

The brown seaweeds are found throughout, from the upper to the lower shore. The green seaweeds are primarily seen on the upper shore and the reds down towards the lower shore

223

It is interesting that we see an echo of the ancestral mollusc in chiton. As a phylum, the molluscs are very varied: for example, they include squids and octopus in which the muscular foot of chiton and limpet has become the tentacles. See also pages 226, 228.

Life on the rocks

Even though they may be quite mobile in their younger stages, many of the animals found on rocky shores are fixed to one spot, either straining the seawater for food or catching passing prey by one means or another. Although the suspension feeders will take floating plant plankton, plant-eaters are not usually immobile. Even limpets, which look as if they are stationary, move around a great deal. Limpets are usually surrounded by a patch of bare rock, and if there are any green weeds growing, they are likely to be on the limpet shells themselves where the limpets cannot get at them. They are mobile grazers, leaving their home spot at night, or when the tide is in, and returning to it after feeding. They return to exactly the same spot – on hard rock the edge of the shell exactly matches the rock's contour, and on soft rock the limpet makes a groove for itself. Many other animals have their own 'geography' within, and under, the broad zones of the seaweeds which range down the shore.

A purple-top shell grazing the algal covered rocks on the middle shore.

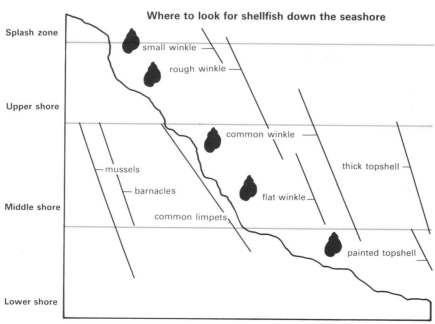

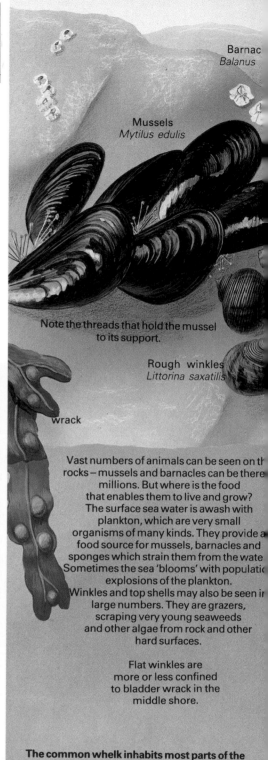

Barnac
Balanus

Mussels
Mytilus edulis

Note the threads that hold the mussel to its support.

Rough winkles
Littorina saxatilis

wrack

Vast numbers of animals can be seen on th rocks – mussels and barnacles can be there millions. But where is the food that enables them to live and grow? The surface sea water is awash with plankton, which are very small organisms of many kinds. They provide a food source for mussels, barnacles and sponges which strain them from the wate Sometimes the sea 'blooms' with populatic explosions of the plankton. Winkles and top shells may also be seen ir large numbers. They are grazers, scraping very young seaweeds and other algae from rock and other hard surfaces.

Flat winkles are more or less confined to bladder wrack in the middle shore.

The common whelk inhabits most parts of the shore. It is edible. You can see the operculum, a plate closing the shell when the animal withdraws.

Where to look for shellfish down the seashore

Splash zone

small winkle

rough winkle

Upper shore

common winkle

mussels

thick topshell

barnacles

Middle shore

flat winkle

common limpets

painted topshell

Lower shore

Mussels can sometimes be found in vast beds, from near high water to below the low water mark. They are particularly common in estuaries. They are suspension feeders. Up to 23 cm (in the shops only) to 10 cm.

Winkles (sometimes known as periwinkles) have a horny plug, an operculum, which closes their shells. There are four common types on the shore.

Small winkles occur in crevices high on the shore, even in the splash zone. They release their eggs to be washed out to sea, where they become part of the plankton. The young winkles later settle on the shore, then move up to their living zone. To 0.5 cm tall.

You also find rough winkles high on the shore. They give 'birth' to fully developed young. The gills of the adults can 'breathe' very damp air, hence they can colonise the high shore. To 1 cm.

Common (edible) **winkles inhabit most parts** of the shore. Up to 2.5 cm tall.

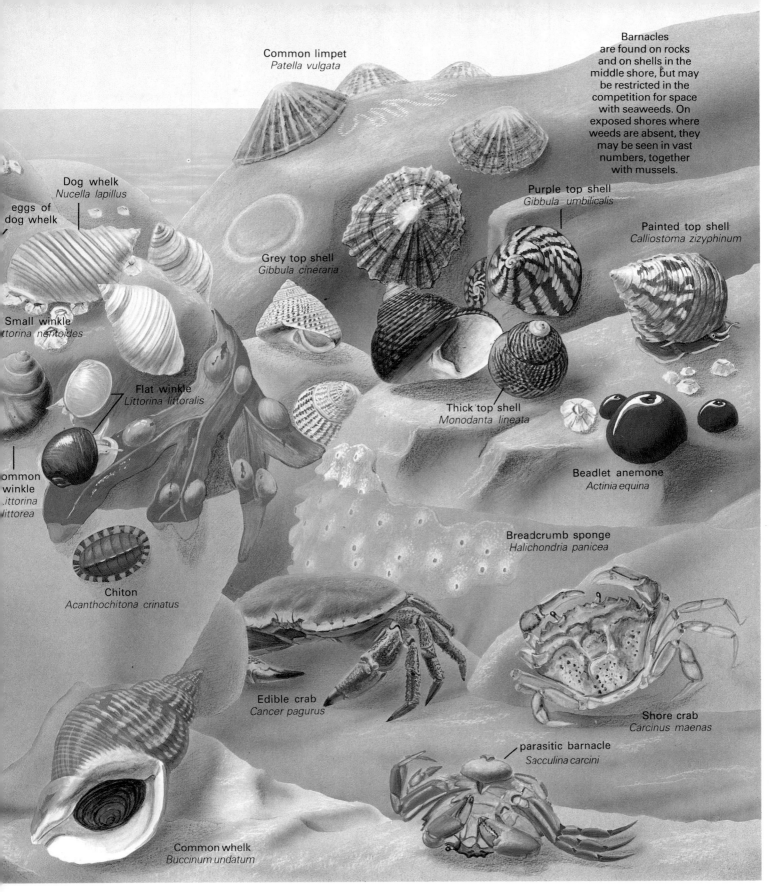

Common limpet
Patella vulgata

Barnacles are found on rocks and on shells in the middle shore, but may be restricted in the competition for space with seaweeds. On exposed shores where weeds are absent, they may be seen in vast numbers, together with mussels.

Dog whelk
Nucella lapillus

eggs of dog whelk

Purple top shell
Gibbula umbilicalis

Painted top shell
Calliostoma zizyphinum

Grey top shell
Gibbula cineraria

Small winkle
Littorina neritoides

Flat winkle
Littorina littoralis

Thick top shell
Monodanta lineata

Common winkle
Littorina littorea

Beadlet anemone
Actinia equina

Breadcrumb sponge
Halichondria panicea

Chiton
Acanthochitona crinatus

Edible crab
Cancer pagurus

Shore crab
Carcinus maenas

parasitic barnacle
Sacculina carcini

Common whelk
Buccinum undatum

Flat winkles live on the bladder and knotted wracks. The reason for their different colours is not known. To 1 cm.

The chiton's coat-of-mail shell resembles that of the mollusc ancestor. It has eight shell plates on its back and clings to the rocks whilst feeding on seaweed. To 1 cm.

Barnacles are related to shrimps, not molluscs. They can cover the rocks in vast numbers; maybe as many as 50,000 to the square metre. Those shown here are all closed, as they would be at low tide; when covered by water, they open, and their food-straining legs are pushed out. Look for empty barnacles, cleared out by dog-whelks. To over 0.5 cm.

Dog-whelks that feed on mussels are dark coloured and those that feed on barnacles are pale. Since barnacles are their preferred food, most are white. Their shells may be thicker, blunter and smoother in more exposed places as an adaptation to harsh conditions. They copulate and lay their eggs hidden in cracks in the rock; dog-whelks will eat the eggs of their own kind. To 3 cm.

Limpets are related to snails and have a head and muscular foot: their cone shell is the end portion of a coiled shell that does not develop. 5 cm.

Top shells – unlike winkles, which copulate – simply spend eggs and sperm into the open sea for fertilisation. 'Flat tops' are found high on the shore, 'thick tops' on the middle shore, and 'painted and grey tops' mark the lower shore. Various sizes over 1 cm.

Breadcrumb sponges obtain food by filtering plankton from the sea water. They are found on rocks and their colourful patches can vary in size and hue, through yellow and green to brown.

Small edible crabs found in shelter near low tide mark are often mistaken for shore crabs: but note the edible crab shell is twice as wide as long.

Female crabs 'in berry' carry a mass of small eggs protected by the rounded apron tail. There may be 150,000 eggs in all. Sometimes instead of the eggs you may see a parasitic barnacle.

The tails of the males are rather pointed. Crabs moult their hard shell and swell and then a new case hardens. The shells seem to increase in size by about a third at each moult: beginning at 3 mm across, the largest shore crabs can be 150 mm across after about a dozen moults. You can often find the discarded skins.

Shore crabs are our commonest crabs. They are aggressive and tough, can resist exposure and changes in water saltiness and are seen everywhere on the shore. Their shell is as wide as it is long. Note the three blunt 'teeth' between the eyes, and the five sharp notches on either side. Note also that the end of each hind leg of the shore crab is flattened to form a paddle for swimming. It appears that shore crabs move in seasonal migration up and down the shore, commonly in deep water in winter but all over the beach in summer. This may reflect the overall shift of the seashore population. Although, individuals may never wander far. To 10 cm across.

Species shown on the previous and following pages may also be seen in rock pools if conditions are suitable. Remember that sudden movements will make them hide. Much can be seen after dark, using a red torch – many animal eyes are blind to red light.

Rock pools

Rock pools are *not* just places where the inhabitants of the ocean gain refuge while the tide is out. The conditions of life in rock pools are quite special. The problems met by rock-pool plants and animals are not the same as those of the open shore, as they do not face the weight of crashing waves or the grinding sand. Their problems are much more subtle.

First, although the rock pool may not totally dry out, the quality of the water in it may change by the hour. When the sun beats down it becomes warm, even hot, and the evaporation can make it highly salty. On the other hand, a heavy rainstorm running off the rocks into a small pool may be lethal since most sea life cannot live in fresh water. Then, in winter, a small pool can become extremely cold, and even freeze over.

Plants and animals respire, taking in oxygen to 'burn up' food and giving out carbon dioxide. In daytime, plants, as a result of photosynthesis, take in carbon dioxide and give out oxygen. In a small pool, the two can balance, but only in daylight. At night, without the incoming sea to dilute the effect, not only does the vital oxygen in the water become scarce, but carbon dioxide may accumulate, bringing a rise in acidity that can be lethal. The plants and animals you see in permanent pools on the rock shore can, by and large, cope with such effects, but the size of the pool is the major factor. The conditions are more extreme in a small pool.

So the rock pool is a unique habitat of the seashore. Moreover, one pool is never quite like another. They are, however, living natural aquariums where you can observe with ease many sea-living creatures.

Breadcrumb sponges are often seen in rock pools or crevices at the bottom of the shore, usually sheltered beneath an overhang of some kind as patches of yellow or green on the rock. Sponges are very primitive animals – the various cells of their body are not coordinated in any way (the movements of the sea anemone are a classic example of how the cells of quite simple bodies can be coordinated to the benefit of the animal as a whole).

Not many sponge fossils are found because of their soft bodies, but it does seem that they have been an evolutionary dead end – no other groups of animals have evolved from them.

▲ **The green breadcrumb sponge** with smaller areas of the orange sponge, *Hymeniacidon*. The sponges are simple animals that feed by drawing the seawater in through tiny pores in their surface and then expelling the waste water through tiny communal 'volcanoes'.

Sea anemones are soft-bodied animals with a mass of stinging tentacles that surround a mouth into which they channel any small animals that stay near them. They attach themselves to rocks or piers where they themselves may be eaten by sea slugs. There are about 40 British species of sea anemone.

The snakelocks anemone cannot contract its tentacles, so prefers quiet pools that do not dry out. To 10 cm across.

The beadlet is our commonest sea anemone. It retracts to a blob of jelly when uncovered by the tide but when the tentacles are half open you may catch a glimpse of a ring of 24 bright blue spots around the top of the stalk. Relatives of the common beadlet may be strawberry-spotted—the body-stalk is red with green dots; about 2 cm across.

Dahlia anemones are the largest shore anemones, generally found in the shelter of seaweeds. Their warty appearance comes from grains of sand and shell stuck to the body-stalk. They may have banded tentacles. To 10 cm across.

The gem anemone is often strikingly coloured, hence its name. It is commonest in the south west. To 3 cm across.

Common (edible) prawns are most often seen walking the sand in rock pools. They have a 'beak' between the two pairs of feelers (antennae). To 10 cm.

Shrimps will suddenly vanish when disturbed by burrowing into the sand. Their body is rather flatter than that of the prawn, and they have no beak and one pair of feelers. They can tolerate a wide range of water conditions and are found in rock pools – even those that have been concentrated by evaporation and have become very salty – and up estuaries where fresh water mixes with the salt water. Shrimps are scavengers, but may take young fish and other crustaceans. They are best observed in rock pools, but shrimp fishing takes place on the open beach; the shrimp net has a cross strut which disturbs them from the sand, and they are caught by the net. To 8 cm.

Hermit crabs have to squat in empty shells to protect their soft bodies. They are very common; sometimes they can be seen with a sea anemone on top. As they grow they move to bigger shells. To 10 cm.

Sea hares and sea slugs are found in deeper pools at the foot of the shore. They are brightly iridescent. Some sea slugs feed on sea anemones anemones, whose strings they can transfer to their own tentacles. To 15 cm and 7 cm respectively.

The common goby is camouflaged to match sand. Often found in estuaries as well as shore pools. To 7 cm.

The blenny is a true shore-dwelling fish. Such fish all have a rather similar character. They are, as a start, usually of the 'goldfish' type – flat fish are ocean fish, visiting the shore for food. Shore fish lay few eggs and they usually guard them: this means that a formal relationship between the pairs is likely. This can explain the rather dramatic markings of shore fish – they are important for recognition during courtship. To 12 cm. Tompot blennies are larger, to 20 cm.

◄ **The range of creatures to be found in a large rock pool is quite staggering.** Here, amidst the seaweeds is a colony of orange sea-squirts or turnicates. Although the adults are fixed to one place, the larvae are tadpole-like and have bodies that are stiffened by cartilaginous thread. This is lost when they change into adults. The presence of this spinal stiffening shows that sea-squirts are akin to vertebrates. A tube worm can also be seen.

► **The writhing medusa-like tentacles** of a snakelocks anemone.

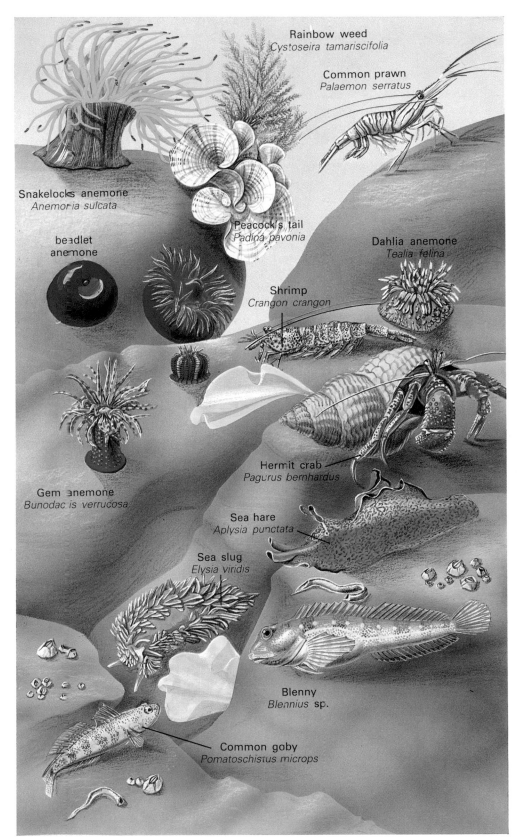

Rainbow weed
Cystoseira tamariscifolia

Common prawn
Palaemon serratus

Snakelocks anemone
Anemoria sulcata

Peacock's tail
Padina pavonia

Dahlia anemone
Tealia felina

beadlet anemone

Shrimp
Crangon crangon

Gem anemone
Bunodactis verrucosa

Hermit crab
Pagurus bernhardus

Sea hare
Aplysia punctata

Sea slug
Elysia viridis

Blenny
Blennius sp.

Common goby
Pomatoschistus microps

Winkles and mussels (224) may also be found on muddy shores – the shrimp is shown on page 226. Fishmonger's dabs and plaice follow the tide in, biting the heads off worms as they come, but the fish shown here are true shore fish, not reliant on deeper water.

Sandy and muddy shores

Grains of sand are usually of quartz stained yellow by iron, but other minerals and sometimes large amounts of ground-down shell can be seen. Sand is finer than gravel, but not as fine as silt – the latter when mixed with quantities of decaying matter makes mud.

Although it might seem rather monotonous the sand on the beach holds some

The sand gaper or soft clam is the 'American clam' mentioned in countless novels and thrillers – the clam of the beach party 'clambake'. It can be fried, steamed, made into stew as clam chowder. It can be found around British shores, but is not a popular food in this country.

It has an enormously long siphon, which can be five or more times as long as the shell, and the full-sized clam makes its home at a depth of 40 cm below the muddy sand. The different species of the bivalve shellfish that burrow all have a level at which they are to be found when adult: the sand is thus 'zoned' down from the surface, though their food is obtained, via their siphon, from above the surface of the sand itself. To 40 cm.

Venus shells, including the striped and warty venus, are one of the commonest shells found on our shores. Growth rings, one a year, can be seen running across the shell. To 12 cm.

The common sunstar is found mainly below low tide mark, but is occasionally washed up. It may have eight to thirteen arms and is a predator of the common starfish. To 25 cm.

The pod razor is our largest razor shell and like all razor shells it is an adept digger and can sink itself faster than you can dig. To 20 cm.

Peacock worm tubes litter the low shore when the tide moves out. They stand up to form miniature forests when the tide is in, their tentacles filtering food particles from the sea water. To 12 cm.

Scallops swim to escape predators by jetting water or flapping their shells. The one shown here is the variegated scallop, with unequal ear-like projections at the end of the shell. To 3 cm.

The shiny beautiful shells of thin tellins sometimes litter the clean sand; the ligaments that hold them together decay after death, so the shells open like a butterfly. To 2 cm.

The necklace shell takes its name from the circle of eggs which it lays. It is carnivorous, boring holes in tellin and other shells to eat the flesh. To 2 cm.

Although dab, sole and other deep-water fish visit the beach to prey on worms and other creatures, the **weever fish** is a true shore fish, feeding on shrimps. The spines of its back fins have a poisonous sting, even when the fish is dead. If you are stung, let the wound bleed profusely before cleaning it up. It is painful but not fatal. To 15 cm.

The sand eel (not a true eel) often swims in shoals and is a favourite food of terns. To 20 cm.

Slipper limpets were introduced to Britain last century from America. They have spread from their original site at Southampton Water to become a pest of oyster farms, where they compete for food. Slipper limpets are often seen in stacks: the young settle on the backs of others. They change sex as they age, with the young males at the top and older females below. They rejoice in the damning scientific name of *Crepidula fornicata*! To 5 cm.

The common starfish is one of seven species commonly found on Britain's coasts. It is carnivorous, attacking shellfish, and can be a pest of oysterbeds. This starfish carries tube feet, small suckers that project in rows along the arms and help it both to move and to feed. The tube feet are used to get a good grip on the shell of its prey. When the shell is partly open, the starfish can extrude its own stomach into the prey and begin digestion. Four to six arms. To 20 cm.

The cockle can move through sand – it extends and swells the end of its muscular foot, then pulls itself up to this anchor. Permanent burrows are not possible in wet sand (they are in wet mud), so the sand dwellers must have an efficient way of boring through hard-packed sand. The evolution of the bivalve body made this possible. When the tide is in, cockles spend most of their time quietly buried with 'siphon' tubes sticking above the sand or mud, feeding themselves by

filtering the water. They may be present in enormous numbers, up to 10,000 per square metre in beds in such places as the Wash and Morecambe Bay. To 2.5 cm.

Edible cockle
Cerastoderma edule

Prickly cockle
Acanthocardia echinata

Pod razor
Ensis siliqua

Peacock worm
Sabella pavonina

Razor
Ensis ensis

Varigated scallops
Chlamys varia

Warty venus
Venus verrucosa

Striped venus
Venus striatula

Thin tellin
Tellina tenuis

Banded wedge shell
Donax vittatus
with hole bored
by necklace shell

eggs of
necklace shell

Necklace shell
Natica alderi

The small hydrobia snails can be found in vast numbers on muddy shores and in estuaries. During the last 100 years one of the hydrobia family has even invaded rivers. To 6 mm.

Lugworms produce a string-like coil of wet sand which marks the back end of their U-shaped burrow. They obtain food like earthworms, by eating the muddy sand. A small pit can be seen at the mouth end of the burrow. To 15 cm.

Ragworms (their floppy appendages make them look like limp cloth) are important burrowing carnivores. They can also bite! They are dug up as angling bait. Over 6 cm.

Sea urchins and starfish are both echinoderms – a large group of marine creatures with 'radial symmetry'. The **sand urchin** or **sea potato** shown here is commonly found burrowing on sandy shores. The sea urchin shells or 'tests' seen for sale in souvenir shops, are usually deep-water species.

surprises. Coarse sand drains and dries quickly under pressure: it hardens and whitens under your foot. A few steps away, however, where the grains are smaller, the reverse can happen – it becomes more liquid when you stand on it, a property shared with non-drip paint, which runs under pressure from the brush! Such factors will obviously influence the sand-dwelling animals.

You would expect more animal life in wet sand than in the mud further down the shore, suspecting perhaps that finer particles of mud would choke the gills and other delicate structures. However, permanent burrows for worms and other creatures seem much commoner in mud.

Many of the animals living in sand and mud are filter feeders, straining plankton from the sea when the tide is in. Their often bizarre shapes are no more than the result of ingenious filtering systems. Others are deposit feeders, 'eating' the rich mud. With plenty of food, these seashore animals may be present in vast numbers.

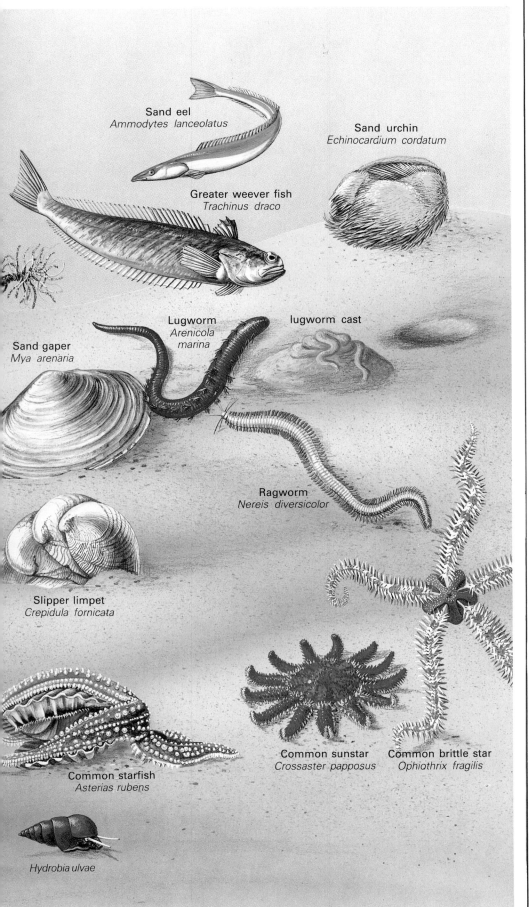

Sand eel
Ammodytes lanceolatus

Sand urchin
Echinocardium cordatum

Greater weever fish
Trachinus draco

Lugworm
Arenicola marina

lugworm cast

Sand gaper
Mya arenaria

Ragworm
Nereis diversicolor

Slipper limpet
Crepidula fornicata

Common sunstar
Crossaster papposus

Common brittle star
Ophiothrix fragilis

Common starfish
Asterias rubens

Hydrobia ulvae

Evolution

The differences between the many types of shells on the seashore are a good example of the results of evolution. Why is life so diverse? Why is there not one 'perfect' shell?

The key to the answer was provided by Charles Darwin in his book *The Origin of Species by Means of Natural Selection* published in 1859. The book was conceived after a voyage around South America during which Darwin meticulously noted a vast variety of plant and animal life. Earlier in the century, fossils found in rocks dug out for the canal and railway systems had shown an increase in the diversity of life from one rock layer to the next. Darwin took these observations and tried to explain why this progression of life occurred.

Essentially Darwin knew that many more individuals are born than survive to breed, and those that do survive are usually the ones better equipped to deal with life and pass their winning characteristics on to their progeny. He also noticed that members of the same species are not identical and some of these individual characteristics better fit one animal for survival at a particular time. Since the organism that is better matched with or 'fitted' to its own niche survives, we see the 'survival of the fittest'.

He explained how separate species might arise by imagining that a population of plants or animals might be split into two parts – for example, by the flooding of a land bridge owing to a rise in sea level. The conditions in the two areas will be rather different and by the natural selection of the fittest individuals, each population would change to match up to its own particular environment. If they are isolated for any length of time the two groups will become so different that they will not be able to interbreed when they meet. They are then separate species.

At a cellular level, this development of new species is carried out by genes. Genes carry the instructions for the building of the body of the animal from one generation to the next and their various combinations (and sometimes changes or 'mutations') give to a population a 'gene pool' of potential characteristics, some of which may be masked, waiting for circumstances to bring them to prominence when conditions change.

The beautiful thing about this theory of evolution is that it is not at all like the brutal struggle that 'Darwinism' might suggest. For evolution also 'smoothes' a population – it irons out all the eccentrics that do not fit the workable pattern. By keeping the soup of the gene pool topped up, however, new forms may exist ready to come to dominance as soon as conditions change, as they constantly do.

More shore birds are to be seen on page 232, sea birds on page 238. Some of the waders nest on moorland in summer (pages 162, 165), others on such unimproved grassland as they can find alongside lowland rivers and pools (pages 149, 210).

Birds of the shore and saltings

From a birdlife point of view, Britain has a favoured coast. The variety and numbers of birds seen in estuaries as well as on the open shore along many parts of the coast are staggering. This is true particularly of waders. 'Wader' is not so very appropriate a name for these birds, nor is the alternative general name of 'shore bird'. They are birds of seashores and lakes, but they often nest on open ground far from water. In Britain many waders nest on moors and move back to estuaries and lowlands, or migrate to the Continent, when the moors become cold and inhospitable in autumn.

Physically, waders usually have a longish bill, which is used to probe for worms and other food in soft ground or mud. The different lengths of bill allow each species to exploit a different depth of mud on the shore, although all will also feed from the surface – it is, after all, less effort – if food is available. The young birds have (with the exception of the oystercatcher) to fend for themselves from hatching. Waders usually have a rapid flight with quick wingbeats.

Our shores and estuaries are the best places to look for waders in winter. Some estuary regions, particularly the Dee, Ribble and Morecambe Bay stretches in the north-west, the Wash in Norfolk and the Solway Firth in Scotland, attract large numbers – possibly over half the total number of waders in Europe.

In these places, the birds have to cope with conditions that are quite different from the moors and their other breeding places. Winter brings colder and shorter days, and the tide may be out only during darkness. Waders may often be seen feeding in the moonlight or on cold, dark, misty mornings following the ebb of the tide.

Oystercatchers, dunlins and knot (shown on the next page) select favourite feeding areas on the shore, but the bar-tailed godwit (also next page) has a more opportunist strategy: it follows the tide out, and is chased back when it turns. At the turn of the tide, the oystercatchers are the first to hurry up the beach: they occupy ground on the beach itself, well out of reach of the high tide – a prime spot – for a roost. Close by, knot may form their own group, while another part of the patchwork may be occupied by sanderling (next page) and dunlin sharing space. The bar-tailed godwits occupy any land that is left within the 'roost' and can sometimes be seen standing with water up to their chins.

These birds often have alternative night roosts away from the beach as it would not be a good strategy to fall heavily asleep with the sea restlessly washing a few feet away!

Shelduck are commonly seen on estuary flats. They are found all round our coast except where there are steep cliffs. They feed on hydrobia (a small snail) in muddy ooze, sifting the shells from the mud with a swinging action–a comb of projections along the edge of the bill filters them out. As well as nesting in sand dunes and old rabbit burrows, they may find crannies under buildings, or holes in trees. They tend to feed at ebb tide, following the water down.

They have traditional moulting areas off Germany and, for example, in Bridgwater Bay in Somerset. After moulting they return to their breeding grounds. They have a nasal *ak-ak-ak* call. 60 cm.

Dunlin are the most abundant and widespread of all our waders. In winter large numbers come here from Russia – you will see them as flocks wheeling over the water or probing the mud head-down, and with a round-shouldered look. Some stay on in summer to breed here on moors beside lakes and bogs, in the Pennines, and maybe Wales and Dartmoor. A hoarse nasal *dzee* call. This is often recommended as the 'basic' wader, on which to base comparisons with others. As with other waders, the nest is a shallow depression in the ground. 17–19 cm.

The estuaries of Britain are of international importance as feeding grounds for hundreds of thousands of wintering waders and waterfowl. This flock of bar-tailed godwits and knots has just joined a small group of oystercatchers at the water's edge on the Solway Firth, on the west coast of Scotland.

Shelduck
Tadorna tadorna

Little tern
Sterna albifrons

Curlew
Numenius arquata

Redshank
Tringa totanus

Snipe
Gallinago gallinago

Dunlin
Calidris alpina

Oystercatcher
Haematopus ostralegus

Greenshank
Tringa nebularia

Ringed plover
Charadrius hiaticula

Common sandpiper
Actitis hypoleucos

Golden plover
Pluvialis apricaria

Oystercatchers (and ringed plovers to some extent) usually rely on the tides to expose their food. Other waders can find alternative feeding grounds. They nest round the coast, but have recently spread to farmland (where they feed on earthworms). All birds gather at the coasts in winter and a southerly movement takes some British breeding birds to Spain; our resident birds are joined by others from Iceland and Scandinavia.

Each day oystercatchers take their own weight of mud worms and shellfish, especially mussels (oysters were probably also eaten in past centuries when they were more common). The birds either stab the mussels open or smash the shells; the youngsters learn their parents' method. Call a piping *kleep* and penetrating *pic-pic-pic*. The nest is a scrape on sand or shingle. Oystercatchers are unlike other waders in that they do provide their young with food, both parents tending them on the nest. 43 cm.

Some sandpipers winter here; most are seen on passage in spring and autumn, often in estuaries but in other places too. A few sandpipers breed in Britain, by boggy upland streams. They make a scrape nest on the ground, usually in streamside vegetation. These birds have an un-waderlike habit of bobbing their tail all the time. They are often seen perched on a rock, and can be mistaken for a dipper (see page 186). A shrill *twe-wee-wee* when disturbed, and an easily recognised *kittiweewitt* ('willy wicket') courtship call. 20 cm.

Ringed plovers search the bare sand, pecking at invertebrates. They have a *too-lee* call. (See also page 236.) 19 cm.

Curlews are resident and breed on moors, bogs and lowland heaths and occasionally on wet grassland where they may form large flocks. In winter they move to the coast, to shores and estuaries. Their long bill is often used for probe feeding, but they will take surface prey as well.

They have a distinctive *coor-lee* call (curlew) but other bubbly calls when breeding. The males circle the nest sites with a display flight which includes switchbacks. 55 cm.

The way in which bird flocks coordinate their movements is interesting. Nervous birds often fly up from a feeding flock and settle again nearby. The trigger that makes the entire flock take off may be when the number in the air at the same time exceeds a certain proportion. Thus cummulative individual reactions to a real or supposed threat aid the flock as a whole. On the other hand, a general response to *any* individual reaction among the birds of a flock wheeling in the air at top speed over the surface of the mud would lead to instant and total chaos!

The salt marshes

Many of these birds can also be seen on the salt marshes or on the grazings that have been created from them by dyking and draining. Saltings of any kind are a habitat with a simple structure, and few species of breeding birds can be expected. It is interesting to note that, back from the sea, skylarks, meadow pipits and other song birds are numerous. Oystercatcher and lapwing may breed on the saltings but the density of breeding birds is generally low. However, there may be quite a few redshanks breeding, and sometimes mallards and shelduck can be seen. Some saltings have colonies of black-headed gulls and common terns.

You see golden plovers in winter on salt grazing or on marshy wet grasslands in the lowlands, often with lapwings. They are joined in October by birds from Iceland and the Continent.

Most golden plovers now breed on flat moor tops, over 200 m. The display flight is interesting to watch: the males fly low and slowly over the ground with flicking wing beats and sometimes switchback high off the ground. A drifting *pee yor yor* whistle. 38 cm.

Compare this little tern with the common tern alongside. This bird is small with white forehead and yellow bill. Now quite rare, with only a few small colonies. A summer visitor. 24 cm.

A few greenshank breed in the Highlands, usually on moorland slopes, but they are often seen on passage, migrating in spring and autumn, though a few may stay to winter in Britain. Their call, a 3-note fluted *tue-tue-tue* is easy to recognise. 30 cm.

Skeins of flying geese are easy enough to see, but until radar we had little knowledge of the vast movements of birds of all kinds in the winter night sky – the occasional sighting of a flock across the face of the moon being the only clue. Canada goose: page 200.

Shore birds from far afield

The mud of estuaries is very rich, containing the nutrients drained from an entire river system. As a result, estuaries are amongst the most productive of all ecosystems. The giant flocks of birds seen feeding on the mudflats and salt marshes of some our estuaries are, in sheer numbers, the nearest thing we have to the profusion of grazing animals in the African game parks.

The geese and other birds shown here are winter visitors, migrants from breeding grounds elsewhere. Migration is now an accepted fact of bird life, but only recently has the complexity of these journeys been understood.

Bewick's swans (named after an eighteenth century wildlife engraver) are migrants from Arctic Russia. They are seen on inland lakes in the south of Britain and are smaller than mute swans, distinguished by a rather variable patch of yellow at the base of the bill – each individual swan has its own pattern. 120 cm.

Another somewhat similar swan, the **whooper** breeds in Iceland and the Arctic tundra; it is about the size of a mute swan and has a wedge-shaped yellow patch at the base of its bill. Its name comes from its loud, goose-like trumpeting call. This migrant is seen mainly in the north of Britain. 150 cm.

Whooper and Bewick's swans on the Ouse Washes at Welney in Norfolk. Both these swans nest in northern Europe and the Arctic tundra (although the whooper has bred in Scotland) and spend the winter in sheltered bays and lakes further south. If the winter is particularly harsh, numbers are further swelled by swans moving across from continental Europe.

Wild geese can be divided into 'black-necked' or 'grey' types. The brent and barnacle geese are 'black-necked'; the bean, white-fronted, pink-footed and greylag geese are 'grey'. All geese are gregarious and often form large flocks.

Brent geese can be of two different races. The dark-bellied brents breed in high Arctic tundra in Siberia and overwinter around the North Sea, including the coast of south-east England. The light-bellied brents breed in Greenland and Canada and overwinter in Ireland, north-east England and Denmark. Both races eat eel grass and enteromorpha weed, but will also devour grass and farmland crops, much to the farmers chagrin. They have a quiet *rroukk* call. 60 cm.

Barnacle geese are thick-set bulky birds easily recognised by their contrasting black, grey and white plumage. They are winter visitors to western Scotland and Ireland, travelling from Greenland where they breed. They may be found in large, noisy flocks, feeding on grass. They fly in long 'v' or diagonal lines. Call a dog-like *gruk*! To 65 cm.

White-fronted geese have a white patch on the front of their faces. They winter in western Scotland, south-west England and Wales, travelling from their breeding grounds in Greenland and Siberia. They are gregarious geese that traditionally grazed saltings but have now spread to farmland. Call, a high-pitched *kow-lyow*. To 75 cm.

Pink-footed geese are the smallest of the 'grey' geese. They form huge flocks in central Scotland and Lancashire where their entire population from

Greenland and Iceland overwinters. They will graze a range of grasses and cereal crops. They are very noisy and have a variety of *ung-unk* and far-carrying *wink wink* calls. To 75 cm.

Bean geese are very similar, but larger to 84 cm, and quieter. Often found feeding by lakes inland.

The greylag goose is the ancestor of our domesticated farm goose. Wild populations breed in the Scottish islands, but feral greylags are widespread, breeding in most parts of Britain. The numbers of wild birds is boosted in the autumn by migrants from Iceland that settle mainly in central and eastern Scotland. They feed on a range of waterweed, grass and farm crops. They have a call like the domestic goose, a clanging *unnk*. To 90 cm.

Only small numbers of wigeon breed in Britain, in the Scottish Highlands, but large flocks from Iceland and Europe congregate in estuaries in winter; nowadays they are also seen on inland lakes and flood meadows. They are grass-eaters, but take almost any plant food. A whistling *whee-oo* voice. 48 cm.

There are two species of godwits in Britain: bar-tailed and black-tailed. Bar-tailed godwits breed in Scandinavia and Siberia and pass through Britain in spring and summer; some may stay on for the winter, others fly on to Africa or southern Europe. They have no white wing-bars, in summer their bellies are chestnut-red and they have striped tails. Call is *kirruck-kirruc*. 36 cm.

Black-tailed godwits are winter visitors to the coast of southern Britain or may be simply

passage migrants. A handful breed in the Ouse Washes and elsewhere. They have a white tail with a broad black band. Their voice is a loud *wicka-wicka* call. 40 cm.

Sanderling are less common than the knot, with which they may be confused. They are found on sandy beaches where they dash up and down the beach following the waves and feeding on shellfish and worms with a frequent *wick wick* call. They overwinter in Britain or may pass on from their Arctic breeding grounds to Africa. 20 cm.

Knot are most numerous on the Lancashire and north Cheshire coast. Others may be seen on the Humber and Wash estuaries. They leave in mid-March to breed in Greenland and Siberia, returning in July. Usually silent, but have a *knut* call.

Knot remain in huge flocks, blanketing the flats, rising with a rush of wings if disturbed, twisting and turning over their feeding ground. They feed on crustaceans and worms in the estuary mud. 25 cm.

Grey plovers breed in the Arctic tundra, unlike their relatives the golden plovers, that breed in Britain. Usually seen singly or in small groups, separate from other birds, feeding well spaced out, on the mud usually on southern saltings. They have a diet of shellfish and crustaceans. Call is a *tee-oo-ee*. 28 cm.

Turnstones choose rocky and shingle shores – they flick through the rafts of seaweed with their short bill, or probe the mussel beds. A sharp call and twittering *wiik*. Usually in small groups but may roost in larger flocks. Winter visitors. 23 cm.

Bean goose
Anser fabalis

White-fronted goose
Anser albifrons

Pink-footed goose
Anser brachyrhynchus

Barnacle geese
Branta leucopsis

rent geese
anta bernicla

Wigeon
Anas penelope
female

male

Bewick's swan
Cygnus columbianus

Greylag goose
Anser anser

Black-tailed godwits
Limosa limosa

Bar-tailed godwits
Limosa lapponica

Sanderling
Calidris alba

summer
plumage

Grey plover
Pluvialis squatarola

Turnstone
Arenaria interpres

Knot
Calidris canutus

Bird migration

Through the ages, the sudden appearance and disappearance of birds in spring and autumn attracted great interest, resulting in some bizarre explanations. For centuries it was thought that swallows and martins hibernated at the bottom of muddy ponds and the ancient Greeks went so far as to believe that one species changed into another.

For most of us, bird migration is summed up not by the cuckoo, but by the picture of those intrepid travellers, the swallows, perched wing to wing along telephone wires, ready to leave when the chill autumn winds begin to blow. A great many other British birds migrate, although it may not at first be apparent since the total population of birds seems to remain largely the same. Within the birds' range there may be rather different local populations: some migrate long distances, others not so far, others do not migrate at all. The ones that stay put are usually located at parts of the bird's geographical range where winter conditions are not so extreme. The time of migration is also complex. There are of course the early spring arrivals, such as the chiffchaff, and last autumn leavers, such as the swallows and martins, but there are birds arriving and

departing almost throughout the year. While some British lapwings remain in this country, for example, many drift south at the end of their breeding season before many lapwings that breed in northern Europe have even built their nest.

There could be various reasons for these migrations, not least the reaction to climatic change. Some birds migrate to favourable breeding grounds and some, like the shelduck or Canada goose, migrate to areas where they moult.

How these birds navigate when they migrate is a fascinating puzzle that has

no simple answer. They certainly use the sun and stars and must have a very accurate internal clock to do this. More recently, experiments on pigeons and other birds have revealed an acute awareness of the earth's magnetic field, which would explain how they can navigate in cloudy skies. Since World War Two, radar has played a valuable part in unravelling the mystery of migration. We can now follow the flocks of birds as they migrate, cataloguing their movements and mapping their flight-paths.

A flock of brent geese.

A salt marsh is a developing habitat, and the plants zone themselves from dry land to open mud (bottom right). Though rooted in salty soil, they are all by origin land plants. Expect to see skylark, meadow pipit, maybe little owl – see page 144.

Salt marshes

Salt marshes form in sheltered estuaries and along shallow coasts where silt is deposited rather than being carried away. Out on the tide-swept mud grow seaweeds and also eel grass, one of the few flowering plants to grow actually in the sea. That mud is fertile and holds abundant hydrobia and other shell-fish: it is an important feeding ground for waders and other birds.

Where sediments are reasonably firm, glasswort and seablite can take root. Then follows a process of continuing colonisation: sea aster and purslane grow and the plants begin to form a closed community, hiding the mud. Where the marsh is banked so high that dousing by the tides occurs only a few times a month, a colourful carpet of flowers grows – with sea lavender, sea plantain and sea pink (thrift). This is the 'middle marsh'. Although they seem to have one foot in the sea, these salt-marsh plants are very definitely land plants: they cannot make use of soil water that is too salty. They need to retain fresh water and so some of them are fleshy succulent plants similar to many plants commonly found growing in deserts.

Creeks cut through the salt marsh, and the continual erosion caused by the scour of the tides along them means that a salt marsh rarely becomes permanent dry land unless helped by man. Sea banks to protect such areas have been built fitfully since Roman times and are still being constructed. The original aim was to secure good grazing for livestock – salt-marsh plants (succulents and others) and the grasses that grow with them are excellent fodder; in fact, the best natural grazing in Britain is on Romney Marsh in Kent, which even produced its own breed of sheep. In recent years many salt marshes have been 'reclaimed' for arable farming, housing and other uses, such as land for power stations, and the ancient grazing marshes that do remain have often been deep-drained and ploughed for arable crops or fodder grasses.

Rushes and reeds indicate the highest and least salty reaches of the salt marsh.

Thrift (sea pink) **can withstand grazing** and eventually forms a turf. A typical plant of the 'middle marsh', it can also be found growing on some mountains and sea cliffs. April–October; 5–30 cm.

Sea lavender (not related to garden lavender) with flat-topped heads of purple flowers is found in the middle marsh. July–September; 8–40 cm.

Sea aster, like a fleshy Michaelmas daisy, is also found in the middle marsh. Occasionally seen inland, alongside well-salted motorways in the north, its seeds are spread by the rushing traffic. It is a tall plant that towers over other marsh plants. July–October; 15–100 cm.

The fleshy leaves of sea milkwort crowd along its prostrate stems. Its small pink flowers do not have petals but a five-lobed calyx. It is a relative of the primrose. June–August; 10–30 cm.

Sea plantain is found not only on salt marshes but also on cliff tops exposed to salty wind and by mountain streams. June–August; 5–20 cm.

Sea purslane grows as a low shrub or sprawling plant which traps silt. It is found fringing muddy creeks where there is more air in the soil, but is often covered by the sea. It has minute green flowers. July–September; to 80 cm.

Common cord grass is a natural hybrid, first seen growing in Southampton Water last century. It is a cross between a native cord grass and one from North America. It was vigorous and became very widespread, growing further out on to the tidal mud than other grasses. It can smother the salt-marsh flowers and in some places has supplanted the eel grass on which some wild geese and other birds rely. Note its head of stiff upright spikes. July–September; 15–50 cm.

Glasswort and seablite are the first colonists of mud. They are annuals, that is not surprising for plants that live on such unstable 'soil'. Both these plants have succulent segmented stems and very small green flowers. Both July–October; to 30 cm.

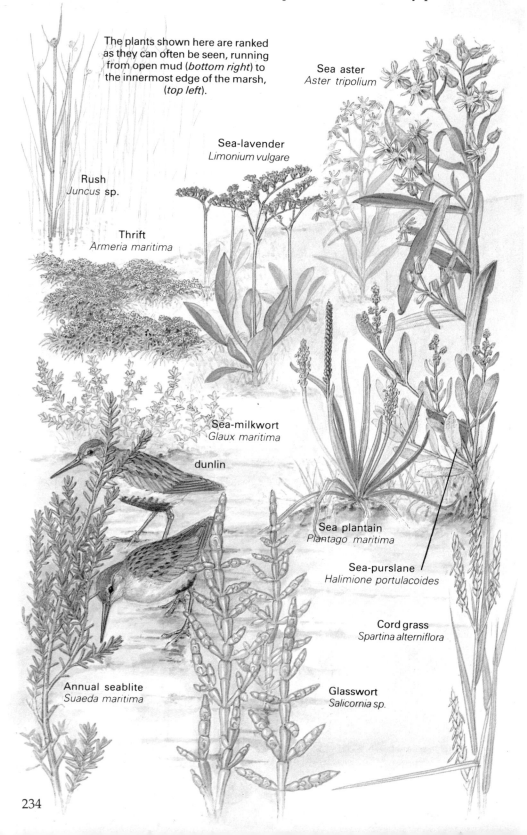

The plants shown here are ranked as they can often be seen, running from open mud (*bottom right*) to the innermost edge of the marsh, (*top left*).

Sea aster
Aster tripolium

Sea-lavender
Limonium vulgare

Rush
Juncus sp.

Thrift
Armeria maritima

Sea-milkwort
Glaux maritima

dunlin

Sea plantain
Plantago maritima

Sea-purslane
Halimione portulacoides

Cord grass
Spartina alterniflora

Annual seablite
Suaeda maritima

Glasswort
Salicornia sp.

Sand dunes

In Scotland, the mosaic of turf and sand that fringes many beaches is called a 'link', from which the term 'golf links' is derived. Links are stabilised sand dunes found all over Britain, built up by on-shore breezes carrying loose sand grains inland that pile up in the sheltered lee-side of any small obstacle. As time passes more sand accumulates, a ridge grows and marram grass, which has a dense mesh of underground stems (rhizomes), arrives to bind the sand together. Close on its heels, the dune, although still mobile and sandy coloured, will bloom

with other plants such as stork's bill and sea bindweed. When mosses and lichens appear on the ground, giving it a grey appearance, you know the dune has become stable.

The plant life of a 'grey' dune can be surprising. Where the sand is made up of particles of quartz and other rock, heather and other indicators of acid soils may be seen. If, however, the

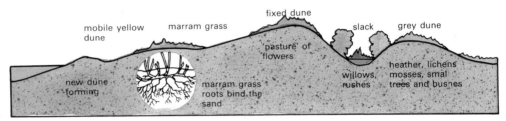

sand contains large amounts of broken limy sea shells, chalkland plants may be seen, often close-cropped by rabbits to form a turf. Look for 'slacks', damp hollows between the dune ridges; they often become colonised by willow scrub, surrounded by rushes. If walkers make a new path and break through the thin stabilising crust of the dune, the wind will swiftly punch through the breach and 'blow out' a large area. On the bared sand, the slow process of colonisation then has to begin again.

One of the first flowers to colonise is sea rocket. It grows in low mounds or clumps and helps the embryo dunes to form. An annual, with fleshy leaves, it flowers June-September; to 40 cm tall.

Sand couch-grass is often also seen on the embryo dunes. Its ability to grow up the soft dune is limited, so it gives way on older dunes to marram grass.

The leaves of marram grass are stiff, pointed, and rolled inwards to lessen water loss. Look at eroded areas in the dune to see its layers of underground stems (rhizomes) binding the sand.

Shelduck often nest in rabbit burrows in the dunes (see page 230).

Stork's bill is one of the wild geranium family. It takes its name from the seed-pod shape. The flowers may be purple to white, opening in early morning to be self-pollinated, the petals dropping by mid-day. June-September; 30 cm.

Sea bindweed has succulent kidney-shaped leaves. The stems creep over the sand and may become buried and help to bind the dune. The trumpet-shaped pink and white flowers are up to 3 cm across. June-September.

Biting stonecrop (wall-pepper) takes its name from the taste of its leaves. It is common not only creeping over sand dunes in mats, but also on walls. July-August; to 10 cm.

Marsh helleborine is one of the many orchids found in 'slacks'. It is also found in fens and marshes. July-August; to 50 cm.

Creeping willow has wiry stems that carry catkins at ground level. It is also found on heathland. Catkins appear in March. Stems to 2 metres.

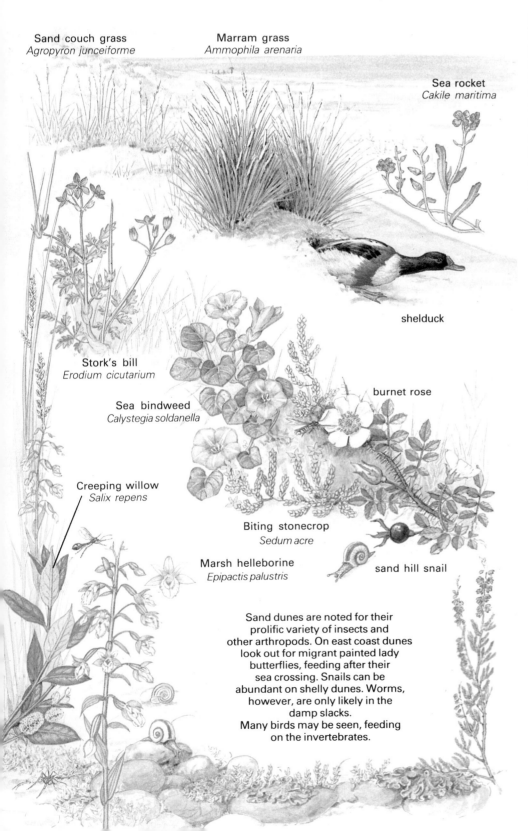

Sand couch grass
Agropyron junceiforme

Marram grass
Ammophila arenaria

Sea rocket
Cakile maritima

shelduck

Stork's bill
Erodium cicutarium

Sea bindweed
Calystegia soldanella

burnet rose

Creeping willow
Salix repens

Biting stonecrop
Sedum acre

Marsh helleborine
Epipactis palustris

sand hill snail

Sand dunes are noted for their prolific variety of insects and other arthropods. On east coast dunes look out for migrant painted lady butterflies, feeding after their sea crossing. Snails can be abundant on shelly dunes. Worms, however, are only likely in the damp slacks.
Many birds may be seen, feeding on the invertebrates.

235

Although shingle beaches are commonplace, permanent shingle features not much disturbed by the tides have a definite identity and age: the largest of all (at Dungeness in Kent) is 4,000 years old. They are irreplaceable features of the countryside.

Shingle beaches

The general impression of a shingle beach is of a long sterile expanse of smooth pebbles of an infinite variety of sizes thrown up at random by the sea. Look a little closer and you may notice that there is in fact some order to this chaos. The pebbles tend to be ranked in size, with the larger at the back of the beach where they have been flung by the powerful incoming storm waves, and then left, for the retreating backwash is too weak to move them far. Pebbles can be of flint, semi-precious agate, granite, sandstone and limestone. Many contain fossil fragments. Many pebbles are from

rock outcrops far away along the coast. Although some shingle is still being eroded from cliffs today, the bulk is a legacy of the scouring glaciers of the last Ice Age.

On undisturbed shingle beaches there are many plants that take advantage of this less salty coastal habitat. Any salt on the pebbles is washed away by rain which clings to their surface and provides a reasonable supply of fresh water for plants. The yellow horned-poppy with its enormous 30 cm-long seed pods is one of the first colonisers of shingle, with the prickly sea holly not

far behind. On the 'strand line' there may be sea-kale, and at the back of the beach in the sheltered lee-side of a shingle bank you may find shrubby seablite, a relative of the annual seablite, an early colonist of estuary mud.

Although almost a quarter of our coastline is fringed with shingle, much of it is under scrutiny by the building industry for extraction. If the pebbles are removed, not only do all the shingle plants disappear, but the pits left behind may alter the sensitive and vital freshwater levels of what is left and the whole area may dry out.

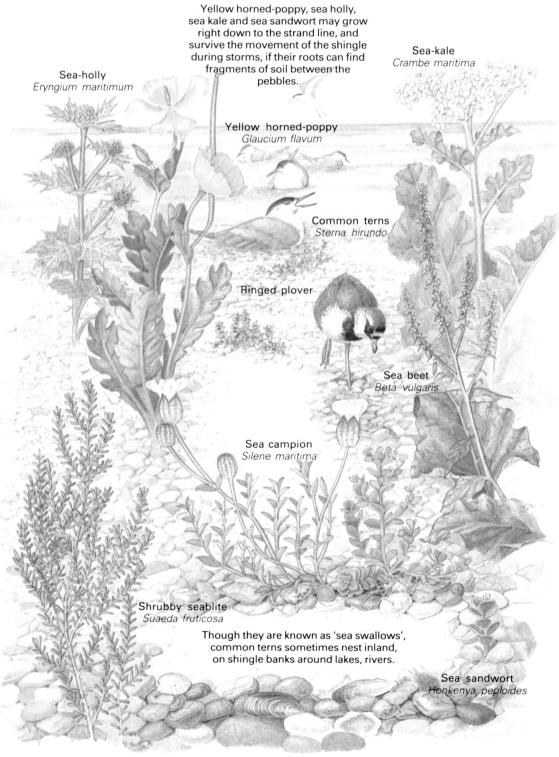

Yellow horned-poppy, sea holly, sea kale and sea sandwort may grow right down to the strand line, and survive the movement of the shingle during storms, if their roots can find fragments of soil between the pebbles.

Sea-holly
Eryngium maritimum

Sea-kale
Crambe maritima

Yellow horned-poppy
Glaucium flavum

Common terns
Sterna hirundo

Ringed plover

Sea beet
Beta vulgaris

Sea campion
Silene maritima

Shrubby seablite
Suaeda fruticosa

Though they are known as 'sea swallows', common terns sometimes nest inland, on shingle banks around lakes, rivers.

Sea sandwort
Honkenya peploides

Yellow horned-poppy has long scythe-shaped seed pods that develop from attractive yellow flowers. It overwinters as a dandelion-like rosette of leaves. June-September; to 80 cm.

Sea holly is now becoming rare due to its sensitivity to human disturbance. It has waxy leaves and a large system of fleshy roots to conserve water. July-August; to 50 cm.

Sea-kale has large roots and cabbage-like leaves. Often found on the strand line on the east end of the south coast, and elsewhere (but not in Scotland). May-August; to 50 cm.

Shrubby seablite is a perennial shrub found along the south and east coasts as far north as Lincolnshire. It occurs above the high tide mark where there is good drainage. July-October; to 1 metre.

Sea campion is a plant of fixed shingle where it forms cushions or mats. It is also occasionally found on mountains. May-July; to 25 cm.

Like many shingle plants, sea beet has a long tap-root to collect any fresh water from rain or dew. It is also common on salt marshes. Rare in Scotland. June-September; to 1 metre.

Common terns are one of few seabirds that nest on pebble beaches. They lay their eggs in small hollows. They fly low, and hover over the sea before plunging after shrimps and small fish. A common tern colony will often act as one: mobbing human intruders, sometimes flying unexpectedly and silently out to sea in what may be called a 'dread', from which they return in a short while. These terns have in recent years been dispossessed by gulls, which occupy the breeding sites before the terns arrive (they arrive from mid-April on and leave between July and October to winter on the coasts of west Africa). They have *kree-err* and *kikikikik* calls. 35 cm.

Ringed plovers (with a ring of black across their chest and eye) are active birds, running ceaselessly in their search for sand hoppers and shellfish. They call with a whistling *too-lee*. Usually they nest in scrapes in amongst pebbles but sometimes they nest inland, perhaps because of disturbance by holidaymakers on the coast. After breeding they join other resident birds in large coastal flocks on estuaries.

Like others of the plover family they are often seen 'pattering' – they stop running and 'tremble' the mud with their foot. It may be that this brings worms to the surface, perhaps because they think it is raining. But why should worms living in wet sand and mud worry about rain? The name 'plover' does, however, mean 'rain bird'! 19 cm.

Compare the sea ivory here with other lichens shown on pages 18 and 116. It is interesting that ancestors of many of today's vegetables are to be found amongst the specialised plants of cliffs and shingle. The bird life can be exceptional (overleaf).

Sea cliffs

Sea cliffs provide rather special habitats for plants and animals. The rock of the cliff face obviously plays a part in what you see, and while the white cliffs of Dover support one array of vegetation, another quite unlike it will be seen on the red cliffs of Devon. However, they all have to cope with exposure to winds and salt sprays. So it is not surprising to find that some of the plants of salt marshes such as thrift and sea plantain are also found growing on cliff ledges and crevices.

On an exposed hard-rock cliff, soil patches are likely to be shallow, and the chemical composition of the soil altered by the salt spray that reaches them. In some places, the soil may be enriched with the droppings of sea birds. The result is not a profusion of many and different interesting flowers, however, but often rank growths of weeds such as dock. If the pollution from the droppings is severe, no plants other than algae will grow.

Out of reach of the spray, you will find plants you might expect to see inland in open habitats, but there are some surprises. In the wetter west, bluebells are seen on some cliff ledges.

The woody shrubs of cliffs are likely to be severely wind-pruned. On the flat clifftops of the Lizard peninsula in Cornwall and some other places, rather unusual heaths can be found.

Lovage is a stout stemmed and celery-scented perennial, a Scottish culinary speciality not found south of Northumberland. It is one of the umbellifers. July; 20–90 cm.

Rock samphire is fleshy, quite tall and found round the coast clockwise from Suffolk to the Hebrides. An umbellifer. June-August; to 30 cm.

Wild cabbage is the ancestor of cultivated cabbage and kale. Like its garden relatives it has leaf scars at the bottom of its thick, rather woody stem. It has a preference for limy soils and is localised to southern England and south Wales. May-August.

The sea spleenwort is typically found on cliffs in the north and west. It is a fern.

The lichen sea ivory is found growing profusely on granite and other quartz-like rocks. It is one of the lichens that create the top 'grey' lichen zone.

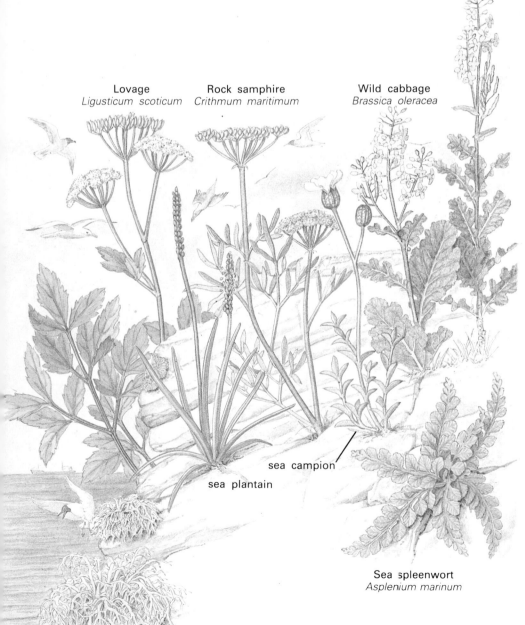

Lovage
Ligusticum scoticum

Rock samphire
Crithmum maritimum

Wild cabbage
Brassica oleracea

sea campion

sea plantain

Sea spleenwort
Asplenium marinum

Sea ivory lichen
Ramalina siliquosa

Lichen zones on the cliff

Lichens are abundant on rocky coasts where they arrange themselves in three colour bands, from the low tide mark to the splash zone and beyond. They are particularly noticeable if you look back at the shore from a boat.

The upper *grey* zone is only slightly influenced by the salt spray. Sea ivory is one of the lichens growing here.

The splash zone is dominated by three or four orange lichens. This *orange* zone gives way, at about high tide mark, to a *black* zone; black lichens colonise rocks down to low water mark, but are often overlooked. Many appear as just a black film on the rock, growing between the seaweeds.

Though seemingly very tough, the lichens are as sensitive as any other life to outside disturbance.

When the oil tanker *Torrey Canyon* broke up on the rocks of the Cornish coast in 1967, the lichen zones were destroyed by the oil pollution along 200 miles of coastline. They have now recovered, however, and the grey, orange and black zones can again be seen.

The gull family (which includes kittiwakes) are easily recognised birds; some are regularly seen inland – see page 144. Other clans are the auks (guillemots and puffins), shearwaters (fulmar). Gannets belong to the booby family! Cormorants form a separate clan.

Birds of the cliffs

Some cliffs around our coasts attract vast numbers of nesting seabirds occupying, it seems, every available ledge and cranny. A search with binoculars will reveal that the birds are sharing out the cliff. At the top, puffins excavate holes with their broad beaks or occupy deserted rabbit burrows. Gannets choose the high cliff, above the guillemots, razorbills and kittiwakes.

These cliff-nesting birds do not simply divide the cliff vertically between them, they also seek their own kind of place on it. Guillemots happily nest on tiny ledges where the rock is steepest, but razorbills feel more secure with a roof over their heads, and seek out rock crevices or crannies between small boulders. Neither of these builds a nest. They lay their eggs straight on to bare rock. The kittiwake does make a nest, however, plastering fronds of seaweed and grass on to seemingly smooth vertical rock faces.

At the nest sites, the pairs are fiercely territorial, defending their eggs and young against all intruders. In the open sea, where the majority of these birds feed, they appear to mingle happily. Squabbles are forgotten and they dive and fly together in search of food for their young. It is interesting to compare this version of territorial behaviour with that of the blackbird and other garden birds: see page 54.

Puffins are not only bizarre-looking birds; their life-style is also unusual. They winter at sea and in spring they land to dig out nest holes with their bills and form large colonies on clifftops.

They are sometimes seen with many fish held in their bills when they are taking food back to the nest. Strangely, these fish are often head to tail, like sardines in a tin. The bird probably zig zags through the water after its prey (they dive down from the surface), which would explain this unexpected sight. Call is a growl – *aargh*. 30 cm.

Ground-nesting birds are always at risk from rats, foxes, stoats and other predators. This is a hazard faced by many of the birds shown on this page. Such birds seem to have a very weak defence against aggressive predators, especially when on the nest. Predators may be one reason for the sometimes dramatic falls in seabird numbers. Other possible causes may be declines in fish stocks and wholesale deaths from oil pollution.

British puffins seem to have declined since the end of the last century, especially in the south west, on Lundy Island, Grassholm, in the Irish Sea area and in south west Scotland. Much of the decline has taken place since 1962; the causes remain obscure. Some think that the small organisms and fish that the birds feed on may be becoming poisoned with traces of long-life pesticides and other harmful chemicals washed down into the sea in rivers. Although some puffins become oiled and die, not as many do as, for instance, guillemots. Some colonies (on Lundy for example) have been eliminated by rats, but this does not apply to all areas. However, in the north of Britain, there now seems evidence that colonies are increasing.

The real or main reason for their decline may be changes in the ocean waters of the Atlantic, which may be affecting the food supply of the birds. The seas around southern Britain warmed up in the 1940s and 50s, but started to cool again in the 1960s. Perhaps conditions are improving again for the puffin.

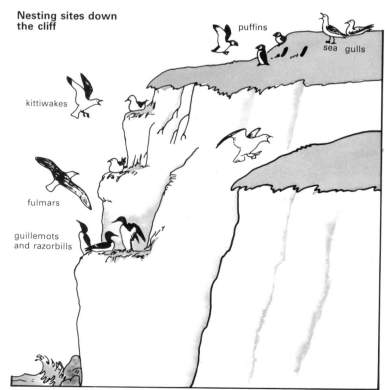

◀ A pair of gannets 'skypointing' whilst changing over at the nest. This display ensures that the change-over takes place only when one partner is clearly intending to leave and the other is there to take over, so that the egg or chick is not left unattended and put at risk from other birds, including marauding gulls.

Guillemots are our most numerous seabirds. They spend much time feeding from the surface of the sea and are therefore at risk from oil spills. Colonies are jammed on to cliff ledges. They face into the cliff, to protect themselves from the spray.

Some guillemots are bridled, with a white eye ring – a race common in the north, rare in the south. Flight is rapid, whirring, and close to the sea. They fish by plunge-diving from the surface, swimming with the wings underwater. Call is a growl-like noise. 42 cm.

Razorbills are rather similar to guillemots in build and flight, but can be identified by their deeper bills and darker plumage. They fish by plunge-diving from the surface. 42 cm.

Cormorants are relatively uncommon. They breed in colonies on western rocky shores but can be seen elsewhere, especially outside the breeding season and can even be found inland on lakes. They fish shallow, inshore waters, often catching flatfish. Silent, except when breeding when they are raucously noisy. 90 cm.

Shags are rather similar birds, but smaller with a greenish-tinge to their plumage.

Eider ducks are usually seen out to sea. One of the most numerous ducks in the world: we have 20,000 of them breeding around Scotland. They have colonial nesting sites on rocky shores, usually in exposed positions. The ducks (females) line their nests with a thick mass of down – feathers plucked from their breasts. When this eiderdown is collected, as it often still is in Iceland, the duck will pluck another lining for the nest. They are very handsome birds; noisy when courting. 60 cm.

Nesting sites down the cliff

puffins

sea gulls

kittiwakes

fulmars

guillemots and razorbills

There is considerable overlap between species, but each has a broad positional preference

In recent decades, fulmars have spread round the coast, and are now seen wherever there are cliffs. Until the 1870s they were seen breeding only on St Kilda and their spread may be linked with a change in their feeding habits. They now take squid, fish and offal from fishing boats, where previously they ate only fish. They are superb gliders, skimming the surface of the waves at speed. Their call is an *ug ug* plus gruntings. They may be confused with gulls but are members of the petrel family. You can see the difference in the way they hold their wings stiffly; gulls 'stroke' the air as they flap. They lay one egg on a cliff ledge. To 45 cm.

A century ago, only 50,000 pairs of gannets nested around Britain. Now we have a total of around 150,000 pairs at St Kilda and five other huge colonies. They are our largest breeding seabird, flying over the waves in 'shearwater' manner with wings held stiffly, frequently gliding. They plunge into the sea, often from 10 metres or more. These birds are strongly territorial; although nesting cheek-by-jowl, they 'own' the area they can reach with their tail while on the nest. This results in an even scatter of birds over the colony, which is noticeable from a distance. Harsh *urrah* call. 95 cm.

The kittiwake is Britain's most numerous gull but it is rarely seen inland. It has black legs and a lemon bill. Nests on small ledges on steep cliffs; or even on window sills of coastal warehouses. Call: *kitti-wa-aa*. 40 cm.

Great black-backed gulls are sometimes seen with flocks of other gulls. Their bill is yellow with a red dot and they have pink legs. Deeper voice than herring gull and goblin-like chuckle. They

Oil pollution and sea birds

The worst thing to do when you find an oiled seabird is to wrap it up warmly, scrub it with washing up liquid and feed it with sprats. This treatment could be as lethal as a shotgun. The internal chemistry of a bird like a guillemot is so delicate that even the short journey in a plastic bag to a 'bird hospital' can kill it. When a sea bird is contaminated by oil, it will suffer from many problems. It loses buoyancy and cannot float and may drown. Its oiled feathers are no longer a good insulation; it can lose heat and die of a chill. It can be poisoned by swallowing the black mess while trying to clean itself.

Seabirds and other waterfowl float with feathers waterproofed by oils from special glands. Buoyancy is obtained from the layers of minute air bubbles that are trapped by the waterproofed mesh of barbules on the feathers; they form a 'hull' as effective as the solid hull of a ship. Washing a bird can remove the oil, but without the feathers being preened to recreate this buoyant layer, the bird will drown.

The care of oiled birds is obviously a job for experts. A bird that does recover from the first shock will need careful feeding for a week or two at least, beginning with glucose and gradually small pieces of fish until it can resume its natural diet. It also needs a lot of time and commitment. The washing of an oiled bird takes two people: one to hold it and another to soap it. At least an hour is needed to wash out all the detergent.

have a rather large head and are predatory, preying even on other gulls. They are more open sea living than other gulls, but can also be seen around ports. Less tame than other gulls. 80 cm.

Herring gulls are large with pink legs and a red spot on their yellow bill. The young have brown plumage and do not usually look like the adults until the fourth year. They move, roost and feed in flocks, breeding in colonies on low ground more often than on cliffs; sometimes nowadays they may be seen on house roofs. Call is the familiar *kee-ow kee-ow kee-owk owk owk*. They feed on a range of food, from fishing offal to rubbish picked from tips. 60 cm.

Lesser black-backed gulls are closely related to, and are rather like, herring gulls and will nest with them. They are migratory, but a few remain in winter. They have yellow legs and bill with red dot. Call like herring gull's, with chuckle. Nest in colonies usually near the coast. 55 cm.

Common gulls are medium-sized, grey-backed and with yellow-green bill and legs. They breed in small colonies inland, sometimes by moorland lakes. Seen on farmland in winter with black-headed gulls. A *kak-kak-kak* and high *kee-ya* call. 40 cm.

Herring gull
Larus argentatus

Lesser black-backed gulls
Larus fuscus

Great black-backed gulls
Larus marinus

Kittiwakes
Rissa tridactyla

Guillemots
Uria aalge

Razorbills
Alca torda

Fulmars
Fulmarus glacialis

Gannets
Sula bassana

Cormorants
Phalacrocorax carbo

Gannets, above, can be recognised by the striking contrast between white body and black wing tips. By and large, we show here the summer plumage of the birds; they may appear somewhat different in winter.

Puffins
Fratercula arctica

Common gull
Larus canus

Eider duck
Somateria mollissima

Beachcombing

Holiday beaches with their ice-cream stalls, hot-dog stands, bustling promenades and acres of bronzing bodies seem to owe little of their atmosphere to nature. When holidaymakers leave, beaches are often littered with debris of all kinds from plastic bottles to aerosol cans, which no doubt grind down in time to some kind of rusty plastic mud. At the tide marks, scraps of seaweed rot with a fruity, salt smell and tar binds pieces of wood, shells, sand and pebbles into sticky lumps. Out of season, when holiday resorts are left to hibernate and bronzed bodies are replaced by an occasional muffled walker, little lives among man's squandered summer flotsam and jetsam. But in summer on a deserted beach, beachcombing can be one of the most delightful pastimes. That smell of salt, sand and seaweed, the unending variety of rubbish that accumulates and the way beachcombing seems naturally to turn into a happily solitary amusement, seem to satisfy some primeval instinct within most of us. Look out to sea as you browse and prod: you may catch a glimpse of dolphins and seals or even the fin of a basking shark. Above all, relax and enjoy the tranquillity, forget the ice-cream and hot-dogs – at least for a while.

Common porpoise
Phocoena phocoena

Grey seal
Halichoerus grypus

whelk eggs

Mermaid's purse

Wood gribble wo and shipworm ho

Treasure there may be, of a kind. Look for pebbles of semi-precious stones, onion-ringed agate, for example. However, they will probably be pitted and discoloured on the surface. A century ago, an average of six vessels a day came to grief around our coasts – storms often throw up interesting relics still. Dead oiled birds should be reported to the RSPCA (address in phone book). Keep an eye out for the marker ring on its leg and report the number. Watch out also for seal tags – one is shown on the rock *far right*.

Sand hoppers spend the day under cover of rotting weed on the strand line. They may share their seashore habitat with terrestrial animals such as woodlice and beetles. At night, sand hoppers scavenge, moving down with the tide. To 12 mm.

Eel grass is the one flowering plant that grows on inter-tidal mud, where it often forms underwater meadows. 25 cm.

Cuttlebones are the internal supports of soft-bodied cuttlefish, mollusc relatives of shellfish.

Look for blue-rayed limpets from deep water, washed ashore on the holdfasts of kelp. 2 cm.

Jellyfish, animals of the open sea, dry up and die if stranded. Some species have tentacles that can inflict a sting.

Some worms build their own characteristic patterns of tubes on rock, shells and even seaweeds.

Atlantic or grey seals are our most common British seal. They are found in large breeding colonies or 'rookeries' on rocky shores on the north and west coast. They can grow to over 2 metres long and to a weight of over 300 kg. Like all seals, they are clumsy on land and will come ashore only to breed or to bask in the sun.

The common seal is found on the less rocky east coast and is rather smaller than the Atlantic grey seal, about 1.5 metres long and 100 kg, and has a flatter nose than the grey. Common seals spend more time ashore and have special 'hauling out' places at low tide.

The two species produce their pups at different times of the year, September to December in the case of the Atlantic or grey seals and May to June for the common seals. They are suckled for three weeks, sometimes in the water as the pups can swim immediately, then they are left to fend for themselves. Both species dive for fish and shellfish and may stay submerged for up to half an hour.

Look for porpoises. Out to sea you may see schools of them arching in and out of the waves some hundreds of metres out. Basking sharks, which can reach ten metres long, sometimes wander into shallows. They are quite harmless and feed by straining plankton from the sea water.

The egg capsules of the whelk are pale yellow, sponge-like masses, several hundred in each lot. The dried, empty egg sponge is often seen on the high tide mark amongst other jetsam.

Tunnels bored in wood may be the work of ship worms (which are really shellfish) or of the gribble – a water-louse-like animal. Tunnels in stone are usually made by the piddock shellfish.

Mermaid's purses are the empty egg cases of skates, rays or dogfish, which are all coastal fish. All egg cases to 10 cm.

Tar spot lichen covers rocks down to low water mark with a thin film that looks rather like tar. Dried tar, however, will smear and stain when rubbed or when dabbed with detergent.

Common seal
Phoca vitulina

Basking shark
Cetorhinus maximus

Dead seabird covered in oil,
with identification ring

Tar spot lichen
Verrucaria maura

eel grass
washed up

seal tag

limey tubes of
serpulid worms

jelly fish

oyster shell

holes made by
Common piddock
Pholas dactylus

cuttle-fish bone

Sand hopper
Talitridae family

kelp

thread worm

Blue-rayed limpet
Patina pellucida

A common seal pup. A single pup is born in mid-summer, usually on a sandbank at low tide. The pup is able to swim from birth but will be closely attended by the mother, who will sometimes allow it to rest on her shoulders. The largest concentration of common seals in Britain is to be found in the Wash estuary.

Much of the animal life shown in this book may, at some time or other, be seen in a garden. We have an estimated 300,000 varied hectares of garden in Britain. Compare that total with the nature reserves, page 250. No comment is needed!

Gardens

Gardens are an artificially created environment for native and exotic plants, each varying with the tastes, aims and abilities of its owner. Some may veer towards the wild state, enjoying little in the way of cultivation and providing a haven for insects, birds and other small animals. Others are nurtured to a degree where even individual blades of grass seem to be regimented to a pattern of tidiness that owes little to nature and offers a somewhat inhospitable environment for wildlife. In between these two extremes, however, are the majority of gardens where trees are pruned back, bushes trimmed and a patchwork of grassland and bare soil created. A garden is a habitat 'held' back from further development, and the wildlife you see reflects not only the kinds of plants growing, but the degree of disturbance from pesticides and other sprays, from dead-heading of the flowers and other factors.

Red admirals, small tortoiseshells and peacock butterflies regularly visit

Ichneumon flies are parasites and can be very important regulators of insect populations in the wild. The ichneumon here is 12 mm, and is often seen at lighted windows. Its eggs are laid inside the bodies of moth caterpillars. The grubs eat their prey from inside and weave cocoons inside their host's body, which by this time is usually dead. The ichneumon, which often chooses the caterpillars of the large white butterfly as its prey, has grubs that weave small yellow cases and these can often be found with the tattered remains of the caterpillar skin.

Spotted flycatchers arrive from Africa in mid-May when insects are plentiful. It is a solitary bird that can be seen perched alertly, then twisting and fluttering after insects, to return usually to its perch, unlike its pied cousin, which usually flies to a different perch. It nests in a hole in a tree or under cover against a wall and has a high-pitched *zee* call and a two-part song, *zee-it zee-it* followed by a trill. To 14 cm.

The robin is essentially a bird of woodland edges and glades which has successfully exploited the 'habitat' created by our garden lawns and shrubs. It has even learnt to take advantage of feeding opportunities created when the garden is dug.

The familiar house sparrow (compare with tree sparrows on page 50) is related to the tropical weaver birds, which explains its rather untidy domed nest built under the eaves, in holes, in nest boxes, or any other suitable place where it may produce four broods a year. The house sparrow is found throughout the world. It is not our commonest bird but is widespread wherever there are human settlements of any size. It has *cheep* and *chirping* calls. 15 cm.

A garden environment suits the holly blue butterfly and you will see it hovering around holly in the spring. It has a hesitant flight and settles high up with its wings closed. The female is distinguished from the male by having a blacker front edge to the forewing. The eggs, which are laid on holly and possibly some other shrubs, hatch in June. Adults fly in autumn and again lay eggs, this time always on ivy. The over-wintering stage is the chrysalis and this is attached to the ivy leaves. 30 mm ws.

Because of today's pesticides, cabbage whites are not as common as they were. There are two kinds, both of which lay on plants of the cabbage and mustard family in gardens. The butterflies

gardens to feed at the flowers, but rarely breed in them. Whites do, however; and the holly blue, the only woodland butterfly to lay its eggs regularly in gardens.

Gardens do not often contain sufficient trees to attract true woodland birds, but an interesting bird of woodland glades which has colonised gardens is the spotted flycatcher. It does show a preference for gardens with some tall trees; an echo of its origins. The collared dove is another recent addition to the list of typically 'garden' birds.

have an uneven flapping flight and settle often. The large white female has two dots on the forewings, the male none. The caterpillar is yellow and black, and hairy. The small white female has two dots, the male only one or none at all and the caterpillar is smaller and velvety green. The large white overwinters as a chrysalis, the first generation flies and mates in May, the second is on the wing from August to October. In the case of the small white, the butterflies fly from May to July and the second brood may overlap with this, flying from August to September. Large whites 60 mm ws; small whites 40mm ws.

The spread of the collared dove across Europe is particularly well documented. At the turn of the century it was found in Asia and south-east Europe, but in the 1930s it began to spread its range north-west. Birds bred in Holland in 1947 and in Britain (in Norfolk) in 1955. They can now be found everywhere near man, where food is easy to come by: they take grain and seeds of all kinds. They have an astonishing breeding rate, raising five or even more broods a year. Note the collar. The song is an abruptly ending three-note *coo cooo cuk*. Nests of twigs in a tree, often an evergreen. 32 cm.

Spotted flycatcher
Muscicapa striata

Holly blue butterfly
Celastrina argiolus
female

Feral rock dove
Columba livia

Collared dove
Streptopelia decaocto

House sparrow
Passer domesticus

male

Yellow ichneumon
Netelia testacea

female

Small white butterfly
Pieris rapae
female

Small white caterpillar parisitised by ichneumon grubs

Large white butterfly
Pieris brassicae
female

Cabbage white ichneumon
Apanteles glomeratus

large white caterpillar

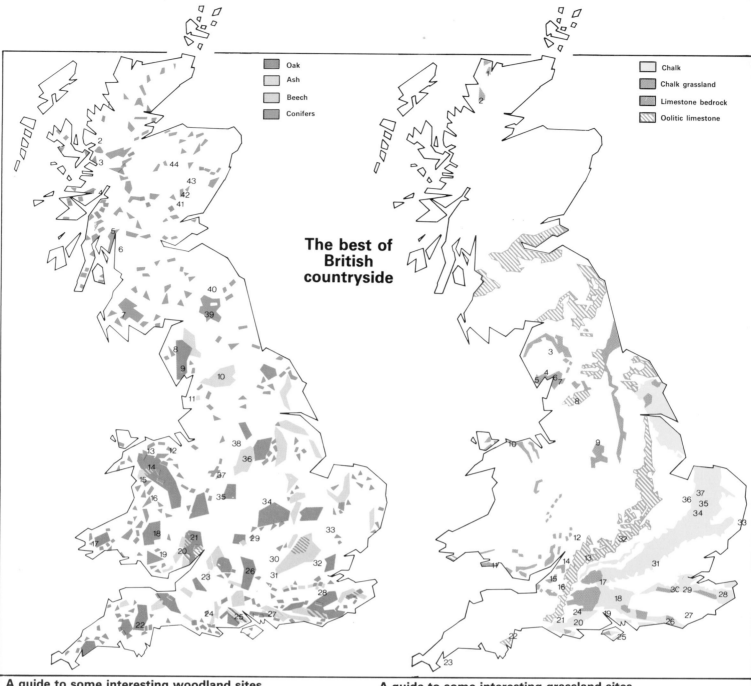

Oak
Ash
Beech
Conifers

Chalk
Chalk grassland
Limestone bedrock
Oolitic limestone

The best of British countryside

A guide to some interesting woodland sites

1 Inverpolly, Ross-shire. Birch and hazel wood with rowan and alder. NC 10 13

2 Beinn Eighe, Ross-shire. Pine woods with holly and rowan. NG 92 72

3 Rassal Ashwood, Wester Ross. Ashwood with birch, hazel and rowan. NG 84 43

4 Arriundle Wood, Argyll. Sessile oak wood with birch, holly and rowan. NM 84 64

5 Loch Lomond, Argyll Forest Park, Argyll. NS 20 06

6 Loch Lomond, Dunbartonshire. Sessile oak woods with Scots pine. NS 40 90

7 Glen Trool Forest Park, Kirkcudbrightshire. Conifer plantation. NX 40 79

8 Borrowdale Woods, Cumbria. Upland sessile oak woodland. NY 27 20

9 Grizedale Forest, Cumbria. Conifer plantations. NY 37 15

10 Malham Woods, Yorkshire. Deciduous woodlands. SD 98 67

11 Eaves Wood, Lancashire. Ash woodland. SD 46 76

12 Clwyd Forest, Clwyd. Conifer and mixed plantation. SJ 17 61

13 Snowdonia Forest Park, Betws-y-Coed, Gwynedd. Spruce plantation. SH 76 57

14 Coedydd Maentwrog, Gwynedd. Sessile oak wood. SH 67 42

15 Coed Ganllwyd, Gwynedd. Sessile oak woodland, some pedunculate oak, and ash. SH 72 24

16 Coed Rheidol, Dyfed. Sessile oak woodland. SN 74 78

17 Slebech Forest (Narberth), Dyfed. Conifer plantation. SN 05 14

18 Talybont Forest, Powys. Mixed plantation. SO 06 17

19 Cwm Clydach, Powys. Native beech woodland, sessile oak and wych elm/ash. SO 21 12

20 Craig y Viliau Woodlands, Powys. Small-leaved lime and whitebeams in upland limestone grassland. SN 19 15

21 Forest of Dean. Pedunculate oak with ash limestone woodland. SO 90 10

22 Wistman's Wood, Devon. Relict pedunculate oak wood. SX 61 77

23 Selwood Forest, Somerset/Wiltshire. Conifers with oak and ash woodland. ST 79 42

24 Cranborne Chase, Dorset/Wiltshire. Pedunculate oak/hazel coppice. ST 96 19

25 New Forest, Hampshire. Mixed oak and beech woodland and conifers.

26 Savernake Forest, Wiltshire. Replanted oak and larch. Ancient oaks and beech. SU 23 66

27 Kingley Vale, West Sussex. Yew woods the 'best in Europe'. SU 82 11

28 Scords, Wood, Kent. Oak, beech, ash woodland and alder carr. TQ 48 52

29 Chiltern Beechwoods (Aston Rowant), Oxfordshire. Plateau beechwoods. SU 75 98

30 Burnham Beeches, Buckinghamshire. Beech with pedunculate oak, birch and holly on gravels. SU 95 85

31 Windsor Forest, Berkshire. Mixed broad-leaved woodland; conifer plantations. SU 93 73

32 Epping Forest, Essex. Ancient woodland of pollarded beech. Also pedunculate oak with hornbeam coppice. TQ 42 98

33 Breckland Forest, Norfolk. New forest of pine but also some hardwoods. TL 85 90

34 Bedford Purlieus, Northamptonshire. Fragments of pedunculate oak woodland. TL 04 99

35 Wyre Forest, Worcestershire/Herefordshire. Sessile oak woodland. SO 75 76

36 Charnwood Forest, Leicestershire. Mixed oak woodland. SK 49 14

37 Cannock Chase, Staffordshire. Sessile oak, birch and alder woodland. SJ 98 18

38 Derbyshire Dales Woodland, Derbyshire/Staffordshire. Ash woodland. SK 14 53

39 Kielder Forest Park, Northumberland. Conifer plantation. NY 62 93

40 Holystone Woods, Northumberland. Sessile oak wood. NT 93 01

41 Tummel Forest, Perthshire. Extensive plantations and other woodland. NN 86 59

42 Caenlochan, Tayside. Common birch, and examples of montane willow scrub. NQ 70 20

43 Morrone Wood, Aberdeenshire. Sub-alpine wood with common birch and juniper. NO 13 90

44 Aviemore, Inverness-shire, Glen More Forest Park. Spruce plantation; remnants of Scots pine. NH 97 09

A guide to some interesting grassland sites

1 Durness, Sutherland. Coastal limestone outcrops. NC 35 70

2 Inchnadamph, Sutherland. Limestone outcrops. NC 27 29

3 Upper Teesdale. Hay meadows NY 87 28

4 Orton Meadows, Westmorland. Grazed grasslands on limestone soil and hay meadows. NY 62 09

5 Humphrey Head, Lancashire. A low limestone headland. SD 39 73

6 Gait Barrows, Lancashire. Limestone pavement with woodland and scrub with grasses and flowering plants in the grykes. SD 48 77

7 Hutton Roof, Westmorland. Limestone pavement including patch scrub and grassland species in the grykes. SD 55 78

8 Malham, Yorkshire. Habitats merge with upland conditions but include limestone grassland and limestone pavement. SD 89 66

9 Derbyshire Dales, (Lathkill Dale, Miller's Dale, Cressbrook Dale). Ash woodland on the slopes to open limestone grasslands. SK 14 52

10 Great Ormes Head, Caernarvonshire. Limestone grassland grazed by sheep, other habitats include scrub and rock outcrops. SH 75 82

11 Gower Peninsula, Glamorgan. Carboniferous limestone supports a variety of plants including rare species. SS 38 87

12 Rodborough Common, Gloucestershire. Cotswold grasslands managed by regular burning. SO 84 03

13 North Meadow, Wiltshire. Lammas land managed as a hay meadow. SU 09 94

14 Avon Gorge, Avon. Woodland, scrub and limestone flowers. ST 56 74

15 Brean Down, Somerset. The steep grassland slopes have rock outcrops rich in flowers. ST 28 58

16 Shapwick Heath, Somerset. Mown meadow grasslands and acidic bogs or mires. ST 43 43

17 Martin Down, Hampshire. Chalk heath and scrub. SU 04 19

18 Butser Hill, Hampshire. High chalk hill and very steep grazed chalk grassland slopes. SU 72 20

19 New Forest heathlands, Hampshire. Dry to wet heath and valley mire. SU 27 09

20 Morden Bog, Dorset. Dry heathland area with pines and scrub. SY 91 91

21 Hod & Hambledon Hill, Dorset. Chalk downland hill with rich chalk grassland flora, insects and butterflies. ST 85 10

22 Berry Head, Devon. Devonian limestone headland. SX 94 56

23 Lizard Downs, Cornwall. Variety of heathland and coastal habitats; rare and local plants. SW 71 20

24 Purbeck Heaths, Dorset (Studland Heath, Hartland Moor, Arne Heath). Lowland heathland rare plants, birds, reptiles and insects. SZ 00 83

25 Crompton Down, Isle of Wight. Chalk downland with maritime flora. SZ 36 85

26 Castle Hill, Sussex. Grazed chalk grassland on steep slopes. TQ 37 07

27 Ashdown Forest, Sussex. Wet heathland contains rare plant species. TQ 45 31

28 Wye & Crundale Downs, Kent. Chalk grassland on steep slopes. The Devil's Kneading Trough is a chalk combe feature. TR 07 45

29 Box Hill, Surrey. Chalk grassland and scrub. TQ 17 51

30 Chobham Common, Surrey. Dry heathland and damp valleys. SU 97 65

31 Aston Rowant, Oxfordshire. Grassland and scrub in the Chiltern Scarp. SU 72 97

32 Pixey & Yarnton Mead, Oxfordshire. Alluvial meadow grasslands managed as hay meadows. SP 48 10

33 Monewden Meadows, Suffolk. Old grassland meadows with fritillary field. TM 22 57

34 Devil's Dyke, Cambridgeshire. Chalk grassland. TL 60 63

35 Wicken Fen, Cambridgeshire. Fenland relict. TL 55 70

36 Barnack Hills & Holes, Cambridgeshire. Limestone grassland on spoil of ancient quarry. TF 97 04

37 Ouse washes, Cambridgeshire and Norfolk. Meadow grassland; area noted for wildfowl. TL 39 75

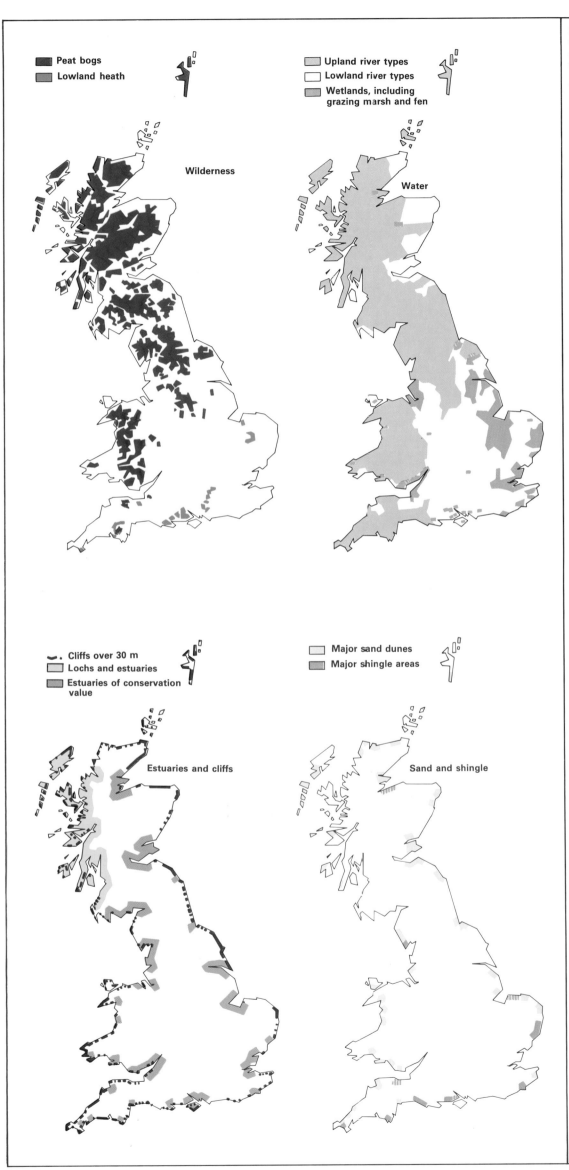

Peat bogs
Lowland heath

Wilderness

Upland river types
Lowland river types
Wetlands, including grazing marsh and fen

Water

⌒. **Cliffs over 30 m**
Lochs and estuaries
Estuaries of conservation value

Estuaries and cliffs

Major sand dunes
Major shingle areas

Sand and shingle

Most peat bogs are found on uplands where rainfall is high and drainage poor, and where the water flows over granite or sandstones which do little to neutralise the acid formed by decaying vegetable matter. Raised peat bogs built by layers of sphagnum moss occur for example, in Cors Tregaron nature reserve near Aberystwyth. Lowland heath is found where the soil is acidic and well drained. The main areas in Britain are in the Hampshire and London basins, parts of Dartmoor and Exmoor, the Lizard Peninsula in Cornwall and the Brecklands and east Suffolk Sandlings.

Britain's topography and geology broadly divide our river systems into upland and lowland types. Upland rivers tend to be faster flowing and subject to dramatic spates after heavy rain or sudden thaws of snow. They flow over predominantly acidic rocks and therefore contain few mineral nutrients. There are few plants growing in the rivers themselves other than mosses. Lowland rivers on the other hand meander across fertile soils and have rich assemblages of plants and animals. They are, however, subject to the various forms of enrichment and pollution near towns and cities. See pages 174–175.

Spectacular sheer cliffs are formed along our coasts when horizontally-bedded hard rocks such as limestones and shales are worn down by the erosive force of the waves. These cliffs are sometimes colonised by large numbers of breeding seabirds. Where a river flows into the sea, large estuaries may form with extensive areas of salt marshes and mudflats, providing important winter feeding grounds for wildfowl and waders. On the west coast of Scotland the estuaries have steep cliffs and deep inlets. They are drowned glacial valleys formed during the last Ice Age.

Britain's most extensive shingle deposits are found along the south and east coasts with well known examples of Chesil Beach in Dorset, Dungeness in Kent and Orfordness in Suffolk. Sandy beaches in contrast are scattered all around our coastline often backed by sand dunes. The longshore drift of sand and shingle is caused by the direction of the waves as they pound the shore, which in turn depends upon the coastal contours and winds. On the east coast the drift is from north to south. On the south coast the movement is from west to east.

245

Countryside and the law

Country footpaths and walkers' rights

The best way of seeing the countryside is, of course, on foot. But remember when walking along any part of the 120,000 miles of footpaths in England and Wales you have certain rights and obligations under the law. In Scotland the laws are different and if anything give the walker more rights.

In judicial jargon footpaths can be established in two ways. They can be either 'presumed' by being walked for a period of twenty years without interruption, or 'dedicated' by compulsory order or with the consent of the landowner.

The local Council supervises the footpaths in its area and is obliged to signpost them when they leave a road. Up to date maps with footpaths marked can be consulted at local Council offices and the Ordnance Survey large scale maps will also show most paths.

Footpaths are dedicated for people only (and dogs kept on the path); bridle paths are for use by people, horses, bikes and pets. You may *not* take motor vehicles onto footpaths unless by permission of the landowner. Remember that although there is no statutory footpath width an estimate of two people walking side-by-side is regarded as an acceptable guide. The owner of the land through which the footpath runs is responsible for the upkeep of gates and styles.

It is illegal to block a path with wire or other obstructions and 'Private' or 'Keep Out' notices have no legal sanction on the path itself. If the path is blocked then the walker has a right to bypass the obstruction but must not cause damage doing so. If a footpath is ploughed up then the farmer is obliged to return it to a usable condition as soon as is practicable, ideally within two weeks. If crops are sown over the path then the walker has the right to walk across the field along the line of the footpath. If you walk around the edge of field you will be trespassing. In practical terms the laws of trespass are relatively simple. Trespass is not in itself an offence. If you stray from a path, the landowner has the right to ask you to leave and can use 'the minimum possible force' to make you do so. If you cause any damage whilst trespassing the landowner is at liberty to sue you for damages.

For a more thorough treatment of this subject see *Rights of Way: A Guide to Law and Practice* by Paul Clayden and John Trevelyan, published by the Commons, Open Spaces and Footpaths Preservation Society and The Ramblers' Association.

Commons

The rights of access to common land are complex, almost every common having idiosyncratic local history to protect it. Generally, common land is open to local people (*not* the general public) who after registering with the local Council have rights to take certain things from the land, such as wood, fish and grazing. Country commons are registered by County Councils and maps of them can be viewed at their offices. Other commons may have special provisions for access. For instance those administered by District Councils; those within town and city boundaries; National Trust commons and certain large commons such as Epping Forest which were opened by special Acts of Parliament.

Where access is permitted, byelaws dictate obligations for the public, prohibiting, for example, motor vehicles, making camps or lighting fires.

Seaside

It may be surprising to learn that there is no general right of access to the land between low- and high-water marks. By-and-large, this area belongs to the Crown Estate Commissioners (with the exception of Cornwall) who allow public access to most areas excepting those used by the Ministry of Defence. The beach, above high water, may be privately owned and the public has no right of access to it, nor are there any general rights for the public to cross private land to get to the foreshore except via public rights of way.

Protected species

Various laws have made it an offence to interfere with certain of our endangered species, and also laid down rules for the treatment of wildlife as a whole. The following is a precis of these Acts.

Birds

All wild birds, their eggs and nests (while in use) are protected, except for 13 'pest' species:

Collared dove	House sparrow	Rook
Crow	Jackdaw	Starling
Feral pigeon	Jay	Woodpigeon
Great black-backed gull	Lesser black-backed gull	
Herring gull	Magpie	

Unless you have a licence, it is unlawful to:

- Kill, injure, take (and even to ring with a marker ring) any wild bird unless it is a pest species. You must, therefore, have a licence for a 'bird hospital' of any kind, although there will be no fuss if you take an injured bird into care and try to help it.
- Use certain cruel or indiscriminate methods of killing or capturing wild birds (*including* pest species).
- Take, damage, or destroy the nest of a wild bird unless it is a pest species or unless it is done with the permission of the landowner in the course of some accepted legal activity, e.g. farming or forestry practice.
- Sell or show any wild bird (some wild birds bred in captivity are exempt).
- Sell the body of a dead wild bird of *any* kind except for *some* sporting birds.
- Sell the eggs of any British species of wild bird.
- *Disturb* any *specially protected* wild bird while it is nesting, or disturb its young even if they are feeding for themselves: this applies to any disturbance caused by photography.

Some birds, because they are rare, have special protection. Offences against them carry heavier penalties (maximum fine £1,000 per offence or even per bird is possible). Wild birds which receive this special legal protection at all times are:

Avocet	Golden eagle	Red kite
Barn owl	Golden oriole	Red-necked phalarope
Bearded tit	Goshawk	Redwing
Bee-eater	Green sandpiper	Roseate tern
Bewick's swan	Greenshank	Ruff
Bittern	Gyr falcon	Savi's warbler
Black-necked grebe	Harriers (all species)	Scarlet rosefinch
Black redstart	Hobby	Scaup
Black-tailed godwit	Honey buzzard	Serin
Black tern	Hoopoe	Shorelark
Black-winged stilt	Kentish plover	Short-toed treecreeper
Bluethroat	Kingfisher	Slavonian grebe
Brambling	Lapland bunting	Snow bunting
Cetti's warbler	Leach's petrel	Snowy owl
Chough	Little bittern	Spoonbill
Cirl bunting	Little gull	Spotted crake
Common quail	Little ringed plover	Stone curlew
Common scoter	Little tern	Temminck's stint
Corncrake	Long-tailed duck	Velvet scoter
Crested tit	Marsh warbler	Whimbrel
Crossbills	Mediterranean gull	White-tailed eagle
Dartford warbler	Merlin	Whooper swan
Divers (all species)	Osprey	Woodlark
Dotterel	Peregrine	Wood sandpiper
Fieldfare	Purple heron	Wryneck
Firecrest	Purple sandpiper	
Garganey	Red-backed shrike	

Wild plants

Wild plants protected under the Acts are:

Alpine gentian	Ghost orchid	Snowdon lily
Alpine sow thistle	Killarney fern	Soldier orchid
Alpine woodsia	Lady's slipper	Spiked speedwell
Blue heath	Mezereon	Spring gentian
Cheddar pink	Monkey orchid	Teesdale sandwort
Diapensia	Oblong woodsia	Tufted saxifrage
Dropping saxifrage	Red helleborine	Wild gladiolus

Unless you have a licence, with the exception of damage caused by customary and lawful practice, eg in the practice of 'good' farming or forestry, it is not lawful to:

- Uproot *any* wild plant without the permission of the landowner, ie you can lawfully only dig up wild plants on your own land or with permission.
- Intentionally uproot or pick any flower on the list of protected species, or even collect their seeds. These plants are rare, and unlikely to be seen by accident. Some orchids, for example, are reduced to a handful of blooms on a scatter of sites in a county – and the location of these sites is a closely guarded secret. The monkey orchid is one such plant, and to try to safeguard its existence, day and night watches are kept on it when it is in flower, with the Nature Conservancy and various voluntary organisations organising this 'orchid watch'.

Mammals

Protected mammals are: all bats (15 species in all), common dolphin, bottle nosed dolphin, otter, common porpoise and red squirrel.
Unless you have a licence, it is unlawful to:

- Kill, injure, take, possess or sell a specially protected wild animal, though exceptions may be made, for example when property needs protection.
- Damage or destroy or obstruct access to the animal: in other words it is illegal by the letter of the law to block off the holes

to dens or burrows of protected animals. It is also unlawful to disturb the animal unless it is in a house, or the disturbance is by lawful activities such as good farming practice. However, bats are a special case and are protected at all times unless they happen to be living within the area of the house itself. Today many bats find refuge in the roofs of modern houses.

- Sell any protected animal.
- It is unlawful to deliberately kill or capture certain animals other than protected species without a licence. These include: badgers, pine martens, dormice, hedgehogs and shrews.
- It is also illegal to use certain cruel or indiscriminate methods to kill or capture *any* wild animal.

Other Animals

Some other animals receive the same special protection as the specially protected mammals. They are:

Reptiles	sand lizard		(though now
	smooth snake		extinct in
Amphibians	great crested		Britain)
	newt		swallowtail
	natterjack toad	**Moths**	Some moths are
Fish	burbot	**Snails, Crickets**	also protected,
Butterflies	chequered	**Spiders**	as are some
	skipper		very rare,
	heath fritillary		crickets, spiders
	large blue		and snails

Conservation and wildlife organisations

Amateur Entomologists Society (AES)
355 Hounslow Road, Hanworth, Feltham, Middx. TW13 5JH. 01 894 9007
Holds meetings, study groups and passes on information about entomology via a quarterly bulletin. It is particularly interested in the encouragement of young people and novices.

Association for the Protection of Rural Scotland
14a Napier Road, Edinburgh EH10 5AY.   031 229 1890
Concerned with the protection of Scottish rural scenery and amenities. Information service, meetings. An annual report is issued to all members.

Botanical Society of the British Isles
c/o Department of Botany, British Museum (Natural History), Cromwell Road, London SW7 5BD.   01 589 6223.
This Society promotes all aspects of plant conservation but is particularly interested in British flowering plants and ferns. Organises surveys of British plants and communicates information via its regular journal, Newsletter and other publications. Members can be amateur or professional botanists.

British Association of Nature Conservationists (BANC)
Dept. of Landscape Architecture, Sheffield University, Sheffield S10 2TH.
0742 78555.
Provides a forum for debate about all aspects of nature conservation. Through its quarterly journal 'ECOS' it reviews the conservation scene and disseminates information on a cross section of issues and views. It holds an annual conference and has regular meetings as well as commissioning special reports on important conservation issues.

British Bee-keepers' Association
National Agricultural Centre, Stoneleigh, Warwickshire CV8 2LZ
Through meetings, conferences and its monthly publication, 'Bee Craft', this association aims to 'further the craft of keeping bees'.

British Butterfly Conservation Society
Sternes, York Road, Beverley, East Yorkshire HU17 7AN
Encourages interest in butterflies through meetings and exhibitions, and via its members publication 'The News'. Its aims are to protect British butterflies both by field conservation and captive breeding and release.

British Deer Society
The Mill House, Bishopstrow, Warminster, Wiltshire BA12 9HJ
Its main objectives are to study deer in Britain and promote the spread of knowledge in all aspects of deer biology and management. It produces a magazine 'Deer' and organises conferences and meetings.

British Ecological Society
Burlington House, Piccadilly, London W1B 0LQ.   01-434 2641
Promotes all aspects of ecology. It publishes a quarterly Bulletin and separate journals of, 'Ecology', 'Animal Ecology' and 'Applied Ecology'.

British Entomological and Natural History Society
c/o The Alpine Club, 74 South Audley Street, London W1
Encourages the study of natural history with particular emphasis on entomology and insect conservation. Organises meetings, exhibitions and supplies information.

British Herpetological Society
c/o Zoological Society of London, Regent's Park, London NW1.
01 205 7635
Involved with the conservation and captive breeding and release of European reptiles and amphibians. Through its publication 'British Journal of Herpetology' members are kept informed of research, meetings and exhibitions.

British Lichen Society
Dept of Botany, British Museum (Natural History), Cromwell Road, London, SW7 5BD
Aims to encourage interest in the study of lichens. It produces a magazine 'Lichenologist' three times a year and a bulletin twice a year.

British Naturalists Association
c/o The Society for the Protection of Ancient Buildings, 55 Great Ormond Street, London WC1.
Concerned with preserving wildlife and the natural beauty of conservation areas and sanctuaries. It produces specialist publications and a magazine 'Country-Side' three times each year.

British Ornithologists Union
c/o Zoological Society of London, Regent's Park, London NW1.
01 586 4443
A rather learned body whose aim is to advance the science of ornithology. It produces a quarterly publication called 'Ibis'.

British Pteridological Society
42 Lewisham Road, Smethwick, Warley, West Midlands B66 2BS.
Is concerned with the study and conservation of ferns. It produces an annual magazine 'The Fern Gazette', and a Bulletin, as well as holding conferences and recording fern distribution.

British Trust for Conservation Volunteers (BCTV)
26 St Mary's Street, Wallingford, Oxon OX10 0EU.   0491 39766
Young people over 16, undertake practical conservation work on nature reserves and other wildlife sites. The Trust co-operates closely with the RSNC, local authorities and other wildlife organisations. It produces a quarterly magazine 'Conserver' and produces handbooks on conservation techniques.

British Trust for Ornithology (BTO)
Beech Grove, Station Road, Tring, Herts HP23 5NR.   044282 3461
Appealing especially to the serious ornithologist. Undertakes ambitious surveys and research programmes and is involved in the Bird Ringing Scheme with a team of professional biologists. The Trust produces a quarterly journal 'Bird Study' and a newsletter 'BTO News'.

Commons Open Spaces and Footpaths Preservation Society

25a Bell Street, Henley-on-Thames, Oxfordshire RG9 2BA.   0491 573535
Concerned with the preservation for public use of commons and village greens, bridleways and footpaths. It publishes a Journal three times a year and pamphlets on preservation issues.

Council for Environmental Conservation (CoEnCo)

c/o Zoological Society of London, Regent's Park, London NW1. 01722 7111
Concerned with nature conservation in its widest sense: pollution, waste disposal, recreation and preservation of listed buildings. It has an information service which deals with queries on environmental matters from government, public and the media. Produces a monthly newsletter 'Habitat'.

Council for the Protection of Rural England (CPRE)

4 Hobart Place, London SW7W 0HY.   01 235 9481
Promotes the improvement, protection and preservation of the English countryside. Publishes a magazine 'Countryside Campaign' three times each year. Very lively!

Council for the Protection of Rural Wales, (Cymdeithas Diogelu Harddwch Cymru) (CPRW)

31 High Street, Welshpool, Powys SY21 7JP.   0938 2525
Activities and aims similar to (CPRE). Produces a news letter three times each year.

Countryside Commission

Dower House, Crescent Place, Cheltenham, Glos., GL50 3RA.
0242 521381
(Welsh Office, 8 Broad Street, Newtown, Powys.)

Countryside Commission for Scotland

Batleby, Redgorton, Perth, PH1 3EW.   0738 2721
Designates National Parks, AONBs and proposes long distance footpaths and bridleways. Encourages setting up of country parks and picnic sites. They are the principal official bodies concerned with the countryside as an amenity.

Dry Stone Walling Association

The Old School, Pont-y-Glas, Oswestry, Shropshire.   0691 4019
Fosters the interest in dry stone walling and dyking. It produces a bulletin for members and operates a register of recommended craftsmen.

Farming and Wildlife Advisory Group (FWAG)

The Lodge, Sandy, Bedfordshire.   0767 80551
Aims to reconcile the interests of farming and conservation. There are 62 county groups which contain representatives of all the major conservation groups and National Union of Farmworkers. Produces a series of Information Leaflets on conservation and farming.

Fauna and Flora Preservation Society

c/o Zoological Society of London, Regent's Park, London NW1.
01 722 7111
Takes a major interest in the flora and fauna of the British Isles.

Field Studies Council

62 Wilson Street, Loncon EC2A 2BU.   01 247 4651
A charitable organisation which runs its own residential field centres in various parts of the country. Courses on aspects of wildlife and the countryside are run for all ages.

Forestry Commission

231 Corstorphine Road, Edinburgh EH12 7AT.   031 334 0303
Official government organisation concerned principally with producing timber commercially. From its establishment in 1919 up until quite recently, the Commission bought up and planted great tracts of land and planted them with hundreds of square miles of fast-growing exotic conifers. This regime almost totally destroys any indigenous wildlife and completely changes the landscape. Recent policy has been to encourage wildlife and to open its forests for recreation. In its consultative document 'Broadleaves in Britain', the Commission seems to have changed its outlook and is advocating wider planting and conservation of broadleaved trees. Some wildlife and conservation groups think the Forestry Commission could do more to protect semi-natural habitats.

Friends of the Earth (FOE)

877 City Road, London EC1V 1NA.   01 837 0731
Acts as a pressure group for rational use of natural resources and attacks environmental abuse by legal means. It is particularly active in fighting for habitat protection. A quarterly supporters bulletin is available.

Friends of the Lake District

Gowan Knott, Kendal Road, Staveley, Kendal, Cumbria LA8 9LP.
0539 821201
Campaigns to protect the landscape and beauty of the Lake District and Cumbria. Produces a quarterly bulletin and a monthly newsletter.

Greenpeace

6 Ensleigh Street, London WC1.   01 387 5370
Well known for its non-violent action in international wildlife issues such as whaling, sealing and dumping of radioactive waste.

The Institute of Terrestrial Ecology (ITE)

One of the several research units under the umbrella of the National Environment Research Council, on a par with such as the Medical Research Council. It undertakes fundamental research into aspects of the ecology of animals and plants at six research stations throughout Britain. It publishes summaries of research and other reports.

The Mammal Society

c/o Linnean Society, Burlington House, Piccadilly, London W1V OLQ.
0296 668659
Concerned with the collection of data and study of mammals, their movements and distribution.

Marine Biological Association of the United Kingdom

The Laboratory, Citadel Hall, Plymouth, Devon PL1 2PB.   0752 21761
Advances the marine zoological and botanical knowledge and researches the life, conditions and habits of ocean life. Provides information and issues a journal.

Men of the Trees

Crawley Down, Crawley, Sussex RH10 4HL.   0342 712536
Advocates the planting and protection of trees throughout the world. It produces a twice yearly magazine 'Trees'.

National Shire Horse Society

East of England Showground, Peterborough PE2 0XE.   0733 234451
Promotes the old English breeds of Shire horses. Every year it holds the National Heavy Horse Show.

National Trust

42 Queen Anne's Gate, London SW1H 9AS.   01 222 9251

National Trust for Scotland

5 Charlotte Square, Edinburgh, EH2 4OU.   031 226 5922

National Trust for Northern Ireland

Rowallane, St Field, Ballynahinch, Co Down BT24 7LH.   0238 510721
The oldest voluntary conservation body in Britain. It now owns about one per cent of our total land area and ten per cent of our coastline (400 miles). Apart from its historic buildings, monuments and so on, it safeguards considerable areas of our most beautiful countryside. The Trust is financed by voluntary contributions and the subscriptions of members. It also runs a National Trust Junior Division.

Nature Conservancy Council (NCC) (England)

Northminster House, Northminster, Peterborough PE1 1UA   0733 40345
NCC (Scotland), 12 Hope Terrace, Edinburgh EH9 2AS.   031 447 4784
NCC (Wales) Plas Penrhos, Penrhos Road, Bangor, Gwynedd LL57 2LQ.
0248 355141
The NCC was established by Act of Parliament in 1973 as the successor to the Nature Conservancy which was set up in 1949. It is a government funded organisation which is responsible for the National Nature Reserves and Sites of Special Scientific Interest (SSSIs). The NCC is governed by a Council whose members are appointed by the Secretary of State for the Environment.

The Otter Trust

Earsham, nr Bungay, Suffolk.   0986 3470
Actively promotes the reintroduction of otters into areas of Britain where pesticides and other problems have removed them. They own a 47 acre otter haven in Norfolk and a breeding facility at Earsham.

Ramblers' Association

1–5 Wandsworth Road, London SW8.   01 582 6826
Protects the public's rights of access to the 120,000 miles of public footpath through England and Wales. It also encourages the care and preservation of the countryside as a whole. It produces a members' magazine 'Rucksack' three times a year.

Royal Society for Nature Conservation (RSNC)

22, The Green, Nettleham, Lincoln LN2 2NR.   0522 752 326
This is the United Kingdom's largest voluntary organisation concerned with all aspects of wildlife conservation. It runs nature reserves (see Countryside Conservation and Protection Areas) and coordinates the activities of 46 local Nature Conservation Trusts (see below). It produces an illustrated quarterly magazine 'Natural World', free to members, which is a forum for all those interested or involved in the whole range of conservation work.
Watch: The Watch Trust for Environmental Education is sponsored by the RSNC and *The Sunday Times*. It is a national club for 8 to 18 year-olds, with more than 15,000 members and 250 area groups.

Nature Conservation Trusts in the UK associated with Royal Society for Nature Conservation

Avon Wildlife Trust, 209 Redland Road, Bristol B36 6YU   0272 603076

Beds & Hunts Naturalists' Trust, 38 Mill Street, Bedford, MK40 3HD. 0234 64213

Berks, Bucks and Oxon. Naturalists' Trust, 3 Church Cowley Road, Rose Hill, Oxford, OX4 3JR.   0865 775476

Urban Wildlife Group (Birmingham), 11 Albert Street, Birmingham B4 7UA. 021 236 3626

Brecknock Naturalists' Trust, Chapel House, Llechfaen, Brecon. 087 486 688

Cambs/Isle of Ely Naturalists' Trust, 1 Brookside, Cambridge, CB2 1JF. 0223 358144

Cheshire Conservation Trust, c/o Marbury Country Park, Northwich, Cheshire, CW9 6AT.   0606 781868

Cleveland Nature Conservation Trust, The Old Town Hall, Mandale Road, Thornaby, Stockton on Tees, Cleveland TS17 6A.   0642 608405

Cornwall Trust for Nature Conservation, Trendrine, Zennor, St Ives, Cornwall, TR26 3BW.   0736 796926

Cumbria Trust for Nature Conservation, Church Street, Ambleside, LA22 0BU. 0966 32476

Derbyshire Naturalists' Trust, Estate Office, Twyford, Barrow-on-Trent, Derby, DE7 1HJ.   0283 701743

Devon Trust for Nature Conservation, 35 New Bridge Street, Exeter, Devon, EX3 4AH.   0392 79244

Dorset Naturalists' Trust, 39 Christchurch Road, Bournemouth, Dorset BH1 3NS.   0202 24241

Durham County Conservation Trust, 52 Old Elvet, Durham, DN1 3HN. 0385 69797

Essex Naturalists' Trust, Fingringhoe Wick, Nature Reserve, Fingringhoe, Colchester, CO5 7DN.   020628 678

Glamorgan Trust for Nature Conservation, Glamorgan Nature Centre, Foundation Rd, Tondu, Bridgend, Mid Glamorgan CF32 0EH.   0656 724100

Gloucestershire Trust for Nature Conservation, Church House, Standish, Stonehouse, Glos. GL10 3EU.   045 382 2761

Gwent Trust for Nature Conservation, The Shire Hall, Monmouth, Gwent NP5 3DY.   0600 5501 (9–1 Mon–Fri)

Hants. & Isle of Wight Naturalists' Trust, 8 Market Place, Romsey, Hants S05 8NB.   0794 513786

Herefordshire & Radnorshire Nature Trust, Community House, 25 Castle Street, Hereford, HR1 2NW.   0432 56872 (9.30–12.30 only)

Herts & Middlesex Trust for Nature Conservation, Grebe House, St Michael's Street, St Albans, Herts. AL3 4SN.   (0727) 58901

Kent Trust for Nature Conservation, 125 High Street, Rainham, Kent, ME8 8AN.   0634 362561

Lancs. Trust for Nature Conservation, Dale House, Dale Head, Slaidburn, Lancs, BB7 4TS.   02006 294

Leics/Rutland Trust for Nature Conservation, 1 West Street, Leicester, LE1 6UU.   0533 553904

Lincs. & Sth Humberside Trust for Nature Conservation. The Manor House, Alford, Lincs LN13 9DL.   05212 3468

London Wildlife Trust, 1 Thorpe Close, London W10 5XL. 01 968 5368/9

Manx Nature Conservation Trust, Ballacross, Andreas, Isle of Man (Honorary Secretary)   062488 434

Montgomery Trust for Nature Conservation, 18 High Street, Newtown, Powys, SY16 2NP   0686 24751

Norfolk Naturalists' Trust, 72 Cathedral Close, Norwich, NR1 4DF 0603 25540

Northants Trust for Nature Conservation, Lings House, Billing Lings, Northampton NN3 4BE   0604 405285

Northumberland Wildlife Trust, Hancock Museum, Barras Bridge, Newcastle-upon-Tyne, NE2 4PT   0632 320038

North Wales Naturalists' Trust, 154 High Street, Bangow, Gwynedd, LL57 1NU   0248 351541

Notts. Trust for Nature Conservation, 33 Main Street, Osgathorpe, Loughborough, Leics LE12 9TA   0530 222633

Scottish Wildlife Trust, 25 Johnston Terrace, Edinburgh, EH1 2NH 031 226 4602 (see also separate entry)

Shropshire Trust for Nature Conservation, Agriculture House, Barker Street, Shrewsbury, SY1 1QP   0743 241691

Somerset Trust for Nature Conservation, Fyne Court, Broomfield, Bridgwater, Somerset, TA5 2EQ.   082345 587/8

Staffordshire Nature Conservation Trust, 3A Newport Road, Stafford, ST16 2HH.   0785 44372

Suffolk Trust for Nature Conservation, Park Cottage, Saxmundham, Suffolk.   0728 3765

Surrey Trust for Nature Conservation, 'Hatchlands', East Clandon, Guildford, Surrey GU4 7RT   0482 223526

Sussex Trust for Nature Conservation, Woods Mill, Shoreham Road, Henfield, West Sussex BN5 9SD   0273 492630

Ulster Trust for Nature Conservation, 11A Stranmillis Road, Belfast, BT9 5AF   0232 682552

Warwicks Conservation Trust, 1 Northgate Street, Warwick, CV34 4SP 0926 496848

West Wales Naturalists' Trust, 7 Market Street, Haverfordwest, Dyfed 0437 5462

Wilts Trust for Nature Conservation, 19 High Street, Devizes, Wiltshire. 0380 2463 or 5670

Worcs. Nature Conservation Trust, Hanbury Road, Droitwich, Worcestershire WR9 7DU   0905 773031

Yorkshire Wildlife Trust, 20 Castlegate, York YO1 1RP   0904 59570

Royal Society for the Protection of Birds (RSPB)
The Lodge, Sandy, Bedfordshire, SG19 2DL.   0767 80551
The largest organisation concerned with the conservation of birds and their habitats. It has over 360,000 members kept in touch through their magazine 'Birds'. It has been the major driving force in persuading Parliament to pass legislation to protect birds and is actively involved in enforcing these laws. The Society runs its own reserves (see Countryside Conservation and Protection Areas).

Royal Society for the Prevention of Cruelty to Animals (RSPCA)
Addresses and telephone numbers of local offices may be found in the telephone book.

Royal Entomological Society (RES)
41 Queens Gate, London SW7 5HU.   01 584 8361
Society for amateur and professional entomologists which encourages the study of insects. It holds meetings and symposia and publishes a number of journals and a series of identification guides.

Royal Forestry Society of England, Wales and Northern Ireland (RFS)
102 High Street, Tring, Herts HP23 4HH.   044 282 2028
Concerned with the furthering of knowledge and practice of forestry and arboriculture. Publishes books, pamphlets and a quarterly 'Journal of Forestry'.

Royal Scottish Forestry Society (RSFS)
18 Abercrombie Place, Edinburgh EH3 6LB.   031 557 1017
Similar aims as RFS. Publishes a quarterly magazine 'Scottish Forestry'.

Rural Preservation Association (RPA)
The Old Police Station, Lark Lane, Liverpool 17.   051 728 7011
Primarily concerned with the enrichment of the urban environment. It also advocates the preservation of the countryside as a whole. Produces a twice yearly magazine 'Natterjack'.

The Scottish Field Studies Association (SFSA)
Kindrogan Field Centre, Enochdhu, Blairgowrie, Perthshire PH10 7PG. 025081 286
Holds courses to study all aspects of natural sciences, natural history and conservation at its own residential field centre.

Scottish Ornithologists Club
Scottish Centre for Ornithology and Bird Protection, 21 Regent Terrace, Edinburgh EH7 5BT.   031 556 6042
Concerned with the study of Scottish ornithology and the protection of rare birds. It holds conferences and meetings and has an information service and library. It produces a quarterly journal 'Scottish Birds' and an annual 'Scottish Bird Report'.

Scottish Rights of Way Society Ltd
52 Plewlenes Gardens, Edinburgh EH10 5JR.   031 447 9242
Preserves and defends Scottish public rights of way. It also undertakes the setting up and maintenance of guideposts. Produces maps and a booklet.

Scottish Wildlife Trust
25 Johnston Terrace, Edinburgh EH1 2NH.   031 226 4602
The national organisation of Scotland concerned with all aspects of wildlife conservation. It liaises with the government and landowners on wildlife issues and arranges lectures for public information. It runs over 40 nature reserves and produces a journal 'Scottish Wildlife' three times a year.

Tree Council
Agricultural House, Knightsbridge, London SW1 7NJ.   235 8854
Promotes the planting and cultivation of trees in Britain.

Ulster Society for the Preservation of the Countryside (USPC)
West Winds, Carney Hill, Hollywood, Co. Down BT18 0JR.   02317 2300
Concerned with a wide range of activities to do with conservation and improvements of the Northern Irish countryside. It holds lectures in association with Queens University, Belfast and New University of Ulster, Coleraine. A journal 'Countryside News' is produced twice yearly.

Wildfowl Trust
Slimbridge, Gloucester GL2 7BT.   045 389 333
Sir Peter Scott set up the Trust in 1946 to study and conserve wildfowl. It now runs seven reserves throughout the country and has the most comprehensive collection of wildfowl to be found anywhere in the world.

The Woodland Trust
Westgate, Grantham, Lincs NG31 61L.   0476 74297
A registered charity which buys up areas of broadleaved woodland to protect them.

World Wildlife Fund (WWF – UK)
11–13 Ockford Road, Godalming, Surrey GU7 1QU.   04868 20551
Is an international charitable organisation which, in the United Kingdom, concerns itself with the relationship between agricultural policy and habitat loss, badgers and bovine tuberculosis, and the problems of grey seals and fisheries amongst many others. It also works on international issues such as trade in endangered species and the exploitation of resources in Antarctica.

Countryside conservation and protection areas

National Parks of England and Wales

The term National Park is something of a misnomer since they are neither national nor are they parks. They are areas within which special planning controls cover development of all kinds, and into which national grant money is channelled for various pruposes. They were first provided for in 1949 in the National Parks and Access to the Countryside Act which also announced the setting up of Areas of Outstanding Natural Beauty (AONBs).

The National Parks are administered by committees, or by boards of the local county councils advised by the Countryside Commission, and were all established between 1950 and 1957.

Brecon Beacons (Parc Cenedlaethol Bannau Brycheinog)

It is an upland area of flat-topped mountains, lush valleys and moorland covering 1344 square kilometres of South Wales. The majority of the upland is grazed by sheep and in some areas herds of wild ponies may be seen. Information centres include: Abergavenny, Brecon and Llandovery.

Dartmoor

This last great wilderness of Southern Britain covers 945 square kilometres of Devon. Within its boundaries lie three national nature reserves and two forest nature reserves. The best-known and most interesting forest reserve is Wistman's Wood. The park is very wild in places and has many quaking mires and tussock bogs. The northern part is a military training area. Information centres include: Exeter, Newton Abbot, Okehampton and Plymouth.

Exmoor

Exmoor is England's smallest National Park at 686 square kilometres comprising mostly high heather moorland cut by deep combes. Its northern boundary is the coastal cliffs which face the Bristol Channel. The moorland supports herds of red deer. Information centres include: Minehead, Lynmouth, Lynton and Combe Martin.

Lake District

The largest (2248 square kilometres) and most famous of our National Parks. Its habitats range from coastal sand dunes, and upland moor to England's highest mountains and largest natural lakes. On the fells are found red deer and rare mountain plants such as alpine lady's mantle and alpine saxifrage. The forest museum at Grizedale introduces the visitor to the area's woodland wildlife. Information centres include: Ambleside, Keswick and Broughton in Furness.

North York Moors

Encloses an area of 1432 square kilometres. At its heart is the largest area of heather moor in the country. Around this are rolling limestone dales noted for their rich flora and fauna. Along the North Sea coast runs the Cleveland Way which takes in the whole of the park's coastline. Information centres include: Middlesborough, Northallerton, Saltburn and Whitby.

Northumberland

The Northumberland National Park covers the bleak open country of the Cheviot Hills in the north, the heathland at the Simonside Hills and the valleys of Redesdale and North Tyne in the South. Its single nature reserve contains one of Britain's best examples of blanket bog. The whole area is being rapidly afforested with conifers. Information centres include: Newcastle-upon-Tyne, Otterburn, Rothbury and Hexham.

Peak District

Covers an area of 1400 square kilometres of pastured hills, broad valleys, moorland and wooded dales. The southern limestone region is known as the 'White Peak', the northern Gritstone region the 'Dark Peak'. It is the most visited of our National Parks and most densely populated. Information centres include: Bakewell, Buxton, Ashbourne, Manchester and Sheffield.

Pembrokeshire Coast (Parc Cenedlaethol Penfro)

The smallest of all our National Parks at 583 square kilometres. Its primary asset is the 272 km cliff line some of the finest in Europe. Here lies the nature reserve of Skomer Island supporting puffins, razorbills, and manx shearwaters. On Romsey Island is a breeding colony of grey seals, and Grassholm Island is a RSPB reserve. Information centres include: Pembroke, Fishguard, Tenby, St. David's and Milford Haven.

Snowdonia (Parc Cenedlaethol Eryri)

Encloses 2171 square kilometres of North Wales. Habitats range from sand dunes and marsh on the coast to moorland and mountains inland. In its several upland nature reserves arctic and alpine plants can be found including the early-flowering purple saxifrage. Fine examples of native ash and oak woods are found at Coed Camlyn and the Vale of Ffestiniog among others. Information centres include: Bangor, Machynlleth, Caernarvon and Conway.

A magnificent view over Derwentwater in the Lake District National Park.

Yorkshire Dales

Comprises 1761 square kilometres of high fells, moorland and lush green dales. The moorland varies from thin vegetation in the south to tussocky highland in the central and northern area of the park. There are two nature reserves at Ling Gill and Colt Park and the famous limestone pavement above Malham Cove. Information centres include: Harrogate, Ilkley, Skipton and Richmond.

National Park Direction Area Orders (Scotland)

Scotland has no National Parks but instead it has five National Park Direction Area Orders which together cover about six per cent of Scotland. These areas have stronger development controls, and any proposals for building must be submitted to the Countryside Commission for Scotland.

Loch Lomond and the Trossachs covers 829 square kilometres of Loch, hillside and moorland. There is a National Scenic Area around Loch Lomond.

Glen Affric, Glen Cannich and Strathfarrar takes in 673 square kilometres of wild highland northwest of the Caledonian canal.

Ben Nevis, Glen Coe and Black Mount covers 1580 square kilometres of the Western Highlands and moorland, through which runs the West Highland Way.

The Cairngorms covers 466 square kilometres of central Scotland, some of the highest most spectacular mountain scenery in Britain.

Loch Torridon, Loch Marle and Little Loch Broom covers 2072 square kilometres of northwestern coast and lochs.

Forest Parks

Set up in Scotland and governed by the Forestry Commission, who have, in these areas, tried to make commercial afforestation more compatible with recreation.

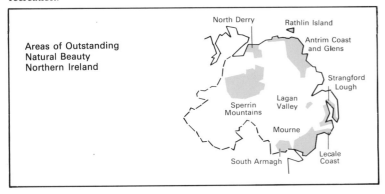

Areas of Outstanding Natural Beauty Northern Ireland

Areas of Outstanding Natural Beauty (AONBs) and National Scenic Areas (Scotland)

There are over 33 AONBs which cover some 14,300 square kilometres 9.6% of the total area of England, Wales and N. Ireland. They are considered as no more or less crucial than National Parks, but have local planning restrictions only and have no grants. They can be remote, little visited Scottish lochs, or busy commercial recreation grounds such as the Cotswolds or the South Downs. There are 15 National Scenic Areas in Scotland, which are broadly akin to AONBs.

Sites of Special Scientific Interest SSSIs

Set up by the Nature Conservancy Council, these are the cream of the British countryside – areas of land identified as being of outstanding interest for their plants, animals or geology. SSSIs are legally protected but the status of the site may be changed overnight by the action or sometimes inaction of the owner: over this there is little control.

The supervision of SSSIs is part of the role of the Nature Conservancy Council (NCC). Each owner or occupier of a prospective SSSI is notified of intention to register the site as a SSSI. This status does not give the NCC any power of decision over the use of the land, but it is hoped that it will ease the processes of consultation. SSSI status does not change the rights of access to the land, nor is SSSI status publicised, although local conservation and planning groups should be aware of it. The hope is that the assessment of the SSSI will encourage the landowner to respect the site.

The NCC provides guidelines for management and use which will protect the site in question.

Category	Number	Area in hectares
National Nature Reserve	195	150,003
RSPB Reserve	93	43,728
Nature Conservation Trust Reserve	c.1,400	44,090
Woodland Trust Reserve	102	1,214
Forest Nature Reserve	11	2,448
Local Nature Reserve	105	14,371
Wildfowl Refuges additional to those covered by other categories	44	11,180 266,034
Bird Sanctuaries	16	–
Biological SSSI	3,166	
Geological SSSI	984	
	4,150	1,470,900

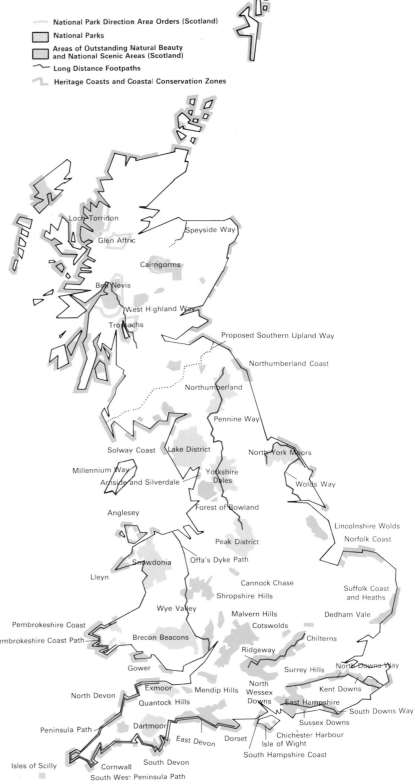

Heritage Coasts and Coastal Conservation Zones

As a result of studies by the Countryside Commission, it was decided that certain coastal stretches of outstanding beauty and interest should be designated. These areas are protected in a similar way to AONBs.

National Nature Reserves

Established under Act of Parliament which also established the Nature Conservatory Council (NCC) which runs them for the benefit of their plant, animal or geological interest. Some are completely open to the public others have limited access. Part of the spirit of the Act was that such places should also serve as research areas for the benefit of conservation as a whole.

RSNC (Royal Society for Nature Conservation) Reserves

The Society and local Trusts manage about 1500 nature reserves throughout the country totalling around 44,000 hectares. More than half are SSSIs. These reserves cover all habitats, and are occupied by a wide range of plants, animals and birds. The Trusts are now employing conservation officers and are becoming much more involved in local planning liaison and advising other local conservation groups.

RSPB (Royal Society for Protection of Birds) Reserves

There are over 95 RSPB reserves in England, Scotland and Wales, totalling over 47,000 hectares. Most of them are open to the public, although non members sometimes have to pay an admission charge. A full list of reserves can be obtained from the RSPB (see Conservation and Wildlife Organisations).

The declining countryside

The wildlife and wild plant interest of the countryside (which is a thing quite separate from its green appearance, and attractive view) lies in the habitats which have been established by, and matured over, centuries of traditional and for the most part slowly changing farming practices and policies.

Such places are at risk from modern land use, and a large proportion of them measured both by number and by area has been changed and their interest lost in recent years. The following information taken from the Nature Conservancy Report on Nature Conservation in Great Britain (1984) indicates the extent of this change.

The price of a cup of tea?
The Gross National Product, (GNP) the 'turnover' of a country, is an indication of its wealth. The GNP of the United Kingdom in 1981, was £210,788 million.

	£ million	%
Agriculture, forestry and fishing	4,867	2.3
Petroleum and natural gas	11,972	5.7
Other mining and quarrying	3,455	1.6
Manufacturing	49,916	23.7
Construction	13,545	6.4
Gas, electricity and water	6,670	3.2
Total output industries	90,425	42.9
Total service industries (including tourism)	118.525	63.8
	(6,925)	(3.3)
Adjustments	210,788	100.0

The amount spent 'officially' – direct by Government funding of the Nature Conservancy Council, for example or via the Local Authorities was of the order of 0.01% of the GNP. That is the cost of two cups of tea per person per year! To be generous and leave room for every possible error, let us say five cups of tea per year. Is this enough to safeguard our wildlife?

Loss of hedges
By using air photos taken over the last 25 years estimates can be made about hedge loss over this time. About 500,000 miles of hedge existed in England and Wales in 1946–7; by 1974 some 140,000 miles seemed to have disappeared. Of this, 120,000 is probably due to changes in farming methods following the amalgamation of fields. Some apparently 'lost' hedges have in fact been

Pattern of land use in England and Wales, and Scotland

	England (hectares)	Wales (hectares)	Scotland (hectares)
Arable land	5,278,186	263,397	1,125,868
All grass (5 years old and over)	3,170,596	845,031	562,647
Rough grazing	1,189,172	531,428	4,272,566
Woodland	175,945	31,654	65,711
All other agricultural land	136,352	13,022	35,517
Inland waters	72,779	12,950	160,321
Urban area (1971 est.)	——1,650,000——		225,000
Broadleaved woodlands (productive)	469,000	61,000	76,000
Coniferous high forest (productive)	395,000	172,000	831,000
Unproductive woodland (scrub and felled woodland)	91,000	10,000	71,000

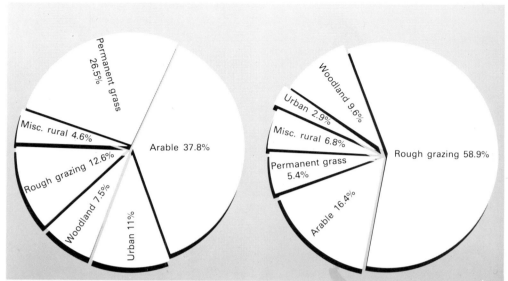

The pattern of land use in England and Wales, and Scotland shows not only the tragically small amount of traditional woodland, downland and other areas of countryside when compared to agricultural and urban land, but also contrasts the differences between the lowlands where land is richer and in almost every way more easily exploited, and the uplands of Scotland which are poorer and more inaccessible. A more comprehensive land use break down is shown below left.

coppiced and since 1974 have grown back again. Coppicing is a harsh system of hedge management and is not beneficial to wildlife or plants. With no protecting shrubs and trees, hedge plants wither in the full sun and the cut hedge offers no shelter to animals for years until the cut stumps grow.

Loss of hay meadows
95 per cent of ancient hay meadows now lack significant wildlife interest as a result of field drainage and the use of herbicides and fertilisers. In a survey in the old counties of Huntingdon and Peterborough in 1971, of

13,544 hectares of *permanent* grassland, only 4% were found to be still botanically rich.

Loss of limestone pavement
Limestone pavements in northern England: 45% damaged or destroyed, largely by removal of weathered surfaces for sale as rockery stone, and only 3% left undamaged.

Loss of upland open moorland
Upland grasslands, heaths and blanket bogs: 30% loss or significant damage through coniferous afforestation, hill land improvement and reclamation, burning and over-grazing.

The irregular dark lines show the pattern of hedges removed to make large fields which are more accessible to the modern machinery, the tracks of which can be seen in the adjacent cleared fields. This aerial photograph is of Wickham Skeith, Suffolk, and was taken in 1976.

The loss of some of our most precious habitats is an appalling catalogue of destruction. In 50 years 53% of our semi-natural woodland has gone; in 180 years 92% of our chalk grassland; and over the last 300 years we have destroyed 99.8% of the East Anglian fenland. The loss of lowland heath, county-by-county is shown below.

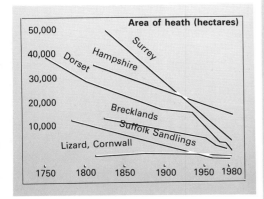

Area of heath (hectares)

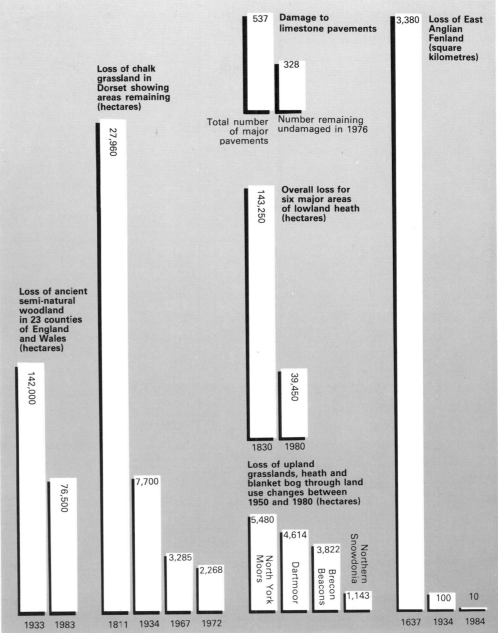

Loss of chalk grassland in Dorset showing areas remaining (hectares)

27,960

7,700

3,285

2,268

1811 1934 1967 1972

Loss of ancient semi-natural woodland in 23 counties of England and Wales (hectares)

142,000

76,500

1933 1983

Damage to limestone pavements

537

328

Total number of major pavements

Number remaining undamaged in 1976

Overall loss for six major areas of lowland heath (hectares)

143,250

39,450

1830 1980

Loss of upland grasslands, heath and blanket bog through land use changes between 1950 and 1980 (hectares)

5,480 North York Moors

4,614 Dartmoor

3,822 Brecon Beacons

1,143 Northern Snowdonia

Loss of East Anglian Fenland (square kilometres)

3,380

100

10

1637 1934 1984

Loss of old grassland

Since 1940, 80% of sheep grazing land on chalk and limestone has suffered changes due mainly to ploughing or 'improvement' which has led to the disappearance of wild flowers, butterflies and bird life. Some grazing has been lost through becoming 'scrubbed up' when sheep are removed. It is usually on slopes too steep to plough.

Loss of woodland

The bulk of the woodland converted to plantation has been planted with conifers, with consequent reduction of loss of wildlife interest. Woodland totally destroyed has mostly been grubbed out to create more farmland. Ancient woods are those on sites wooded since at least 1600 and often dating back to the original wildwood. In the table below semi-natural woods are those with tree and shrub layers of species native to the site.

County	Surviving area of ancient semi-natural woodland in 1983	Converted to plantation during last 50 years*	Totally destroyed during last 50 years	% converted to plantation or destroyed in the last 50 years
Avon	2810	1040	141	30
Bedfordshire	1648	943	178	40
Buckinghamshire	6809	2642	299	30
Cambridgeshire	2035	763	222	33
Cornwall	3246	2928	119	48
Essex	7252	1372	931	24
Hertfordshire	3431	2111	462	43
Humberside	767	308	110	35
Leicestershire	1614	1067	341	47
Lincolnshire	2868	3351	261	56
N. Cumbria	2524	1559	269	42
Norfolk	1410	1395	144	52
Northamptonshire	2634	3931	694	64
Northumberland	3588	3194	323	50
Oxfordshire	5656	2884	270	36
Shropshire	4133	6382	641	63
Somerset	5687	4489	426	46
Suffolk	3022	1347	483	38
Surrey	4712	2428	840	41
Clwyd	3032	2402	379	48
Gwent	3249	5568	925	67
Gwynedd	3415	3174	376	51
Pembrokeshire	1244	1286	44	52

All figures in hectares

*In a small number of instances the base maps for the earlier period were up to 80 years old.

A short list of declining bird species

Birds, general	Reason for decline
Grey partridge	reduction of habitat, changes in farming
Rook	ploughing of grasslands
Yellowhammer	reduction of habitat variety, modernisation of farming methods
Cuckoo	reduction of habitat variety, modernisation of farming methods
Yellow wagtail	draining of wet meadows (and their 'improvement')
Redshank	draining of wet meadows (and their 'improvement')
Lapwing	draining of wet meadows (and their 'improvement')
Barn owl	reduction of habitat variety, modernisation of farming methods
Long eared owl	unknown
Sparrowhawk	long life pesticides and reduction of habitat variety
Nightjar	destruction of heath plus other factors
Nightingale	loss of good coppice
Bittern	die back of reed beds as a result of water pollution and disturbance
Kingfisher	long life pesticides, hard winters, river engineering

Birds, upland	Reason for decline
Raven	plantations on uplands, disturbances with improved sheep grazing
Dunlin	plantations plus drainage of bogs
Grouse	changes in patterns of use of heather moor; loss of moor to conifers, etc

253

Index

Floret – small individual flower in a compound flower head, eg the 'petals' of dandelion are florets
Flote grass (sweet grass) – **176**
Flower – the reproductive part of flowering plants. Has rings of green sepals and coloured petals surrounding the female pistil (the carpels, = ovary + style) and male stamens (carrying pollen anthers).
Flower head – collection of flowers, often as distinctive as the individual flowers themselves. See, eg **92, 94, 120**
Flush – seepage of (rich) ground water
Fly – general word for winged insect, but **true flies** are Orders of insects with two wings: see hoverflies **48, 102, 110**; flesh flies etc **110**; robber flies **142**; dung flies 142.
Flycatcher – pied **61**, spotted **50, 242**
Fog – Yorkshire fog, a grass **120**
Food chain – ladder-like ranking of food and feeder, see 42, 98, 138.
Footprints – shown **56, 58**
Forest – area of (waste) land set aside for hunting, subject to Medieval Forest Law 12, 15; often with trees. In general speech, a large area of woodland. **High Forest** has a special meaning 12, 66
Forest bug – a green shieldbug **48**
Form – hare's resting place
Fossil – relic of (usually extinct) animals or plants in rock
Fox – **42, 56**, 138. See also 220
Foxglove – **36**; not found on limy soil
Foxtail – grass **120**
Freshwater – not salt, of rivers, lakes
Freshwater shrimp – **180●**
Fritillary, snakeshead – 149●
Fritillary butterfly – pearl-bordered, silver-washed 44.● They lay their eggs on violets
Frog – amphibian **198**. Marsh and edible frogs from Europe may be found in south-east England.
Frogbit – a free-floating plant **192**
Froghopper – a plant bug **110**
Fruit – ripe ovary containing seeds. Some are dry, others fleshy. A berry is strictly a fleshy many-seeded fruit, eg gooseberry, tomato. Sloes and blackberries are 'drupes' with the seeds enclosed singly in the stone or pip. Nuts are dry fruits with a woody wall
Fry – young of fish 186
Fulmar – gull-like seabird **238**
Fumitory – family of scrambling plants, see **96**
Fungus – plural fungi. Some have extraordinary links with green plants (mycorrhiza). See 18, 40, 42, 124. Fungi are mainly shown on **40**; honey fungus **18**, woodland fungi **62–64**; ear fungus **82**; mushrooms **122**; heathland fungus on **166**
Furze, gorse – **166**, 128; **needle furze** is another name for whin. Mostly ACID

Gad fly (warble fly) – **142**
Gall – swelling of plant tissues caused by insects, fungi **18, 64, 86**
Game – sporting animals. Game birds include: pheasant **16**; grouse, ptarmigan **162**. Game fish include trout **182**
Gannet – **238**
Gardens – as habitat 242.
Garlic (wild garlic, ramsons) – **34, garlic mustard**, jack by the hedge, also smells of garlic
Gastropod – snail mollusc
Gatekeeper (hedge brown butterfly) – 98, **100**
Gault – (chalky) clay
Gean (wild cherry) – **28**
Gene – base unit carrying the inherited characteristics within a cell 229
Gentle – anglers' name for fly larvae
Genus – group of similar species in classification of plants and animals 106
Geometer – group of moths with caterpillars which loop or 'measure' their way. See thorn, magpie moths **46**
Geranium – family of plants 92
Germination – of tree seeds 23, 26
Gill – spore bearing part of fungus; oxygen-obtaining organ of aquatic animals
Glasswort (samphire) – **234**
Globe flower – buttercup **150**
Glow-worm – a beetle, **106**
Gnat – two winged (true) fly. The larger types often suck blood and are called mosquitoes
Goat – feral goats can be seen **162**
Goat's beard (Jack-go-to-bed-at-noon) – dandelion-like flower **94**
Goatsucker (nightjar) – **bird 170**
Goby – seashore fish **226**
Godwit – straight-billed wader **232**
Goldcrest – our smallest bird **70**
Goldenrod – plant of dunes, woods, grassland, wastes **34, 61** ACID
Goldfinch – **144**
Goosander – sawbill duck **202**
Goose – see **232**; the Canada goose is shown on **200**
Goosefoot – family of plants including fat hen, glasswort, seablite
Goosegrass, see cleavers
Gorse – see **Furze**
Grass – petal-less flowering plants, monocotyledons, with narrow leaves. See page **120**; also wood melick **62**, common bent **64**; moorland grasses 158, **160**. In woods 15
Grasshoppers – insects, shown **142, 165**. See also **bush cricket**
Grassland – with the exception of some mountain slopes etc, this would revert to woodland if ungrazed. Some grassland is old 118, **148, 150**. Grassland plants can be seen **120, 122, 150** etc. Described as a habitat 138, 144, 148, 150, 210
Gravel pits – are often of interest 190 ff
Grayling – fish relative of trout; brown butterfly of arid places **168**
Grazing – effects of in woods, grassland, heath etc 15, 118, 126, 132, 134, 138, 158. Salt marshes also provide grazing 234
Grebe – little **200**; great crested **210**
Greenbottle – fly **110**
Green drake – angling fly 188
Green hairstreak – butterfly **140**
Greenfinch – **112**
Greenfly – see **Aphid 110**
Green oak moth/roller – 18, **48**
Green seaweeds – of upper shore **222**
Greenshank – a wader **230**
Greenweed – gorse-family plants, eg petty whin **166**
Greenwood – Romantic name for woodland
Gregarious – living, flocking together
Gribble – marine wood borer **240**
Ground layer – in a wood, below the field layer, with mosses, fungi etc. Animals of the ground/soil **104**
Ground beetles – carnivorous beetles **106**
Ground elder – umbellifer family plant **36**
Ground hoppers – grasshopper family, **142**
Ground ivy – plant of shady, damp places **88**
Groundsel – plant **96**
Grouse – game birds; the grouse family includes ptarmigan, capercaillie. **158, 162**
Grub – (soil dwelling) insect larva
Guelder rose – shrub of heavy soil **28**
Guillemot – seabird of auk family **238**
Gull large black/grey and white seabirds. See **238**; also black headed gull **144**

Habitat – the 'address' of an animal or plant, its living place – the complex of soil, climate and so on, to which it is adapted. See 42 etc
Haemoglobin – the red oxygen-carrying substance of blood
Hairstreak – small butterflies of grass (green **140**) woods (purple, black **44**)
Haltere – reduced hind-wing of true flies
Hanger – hillside wood, especially on chalk slopes in the south **62**
Hard water – freshwater containing much dissolved mineral salt, in chalk areas
Hardhead (knapweed) – plant **122**
Hardwood – broad-leaved tree and its timber
Hare – (mammal) brown **146**, blue **162**
Hare's tail (a cotton grass) – **160** ACID
Harebell (known as bluebell in Scotland) – bellflower of dry open places **166**, 148
Harrier – marsh harrier (bird of prey) **212**
Harvestman – spider-like arachnid **108**, with undivided body, not web-spinning
Harvest mouse – small mouse, 11 cm, with long tail; nest **114**; see also page 30.
Haw – fruit of hawthorn **82**
Hawfinch – woodland bird of finch family
Hawkers – large dragonflies **196●**
Hawkbits – dandelion-like plants **122**
Hawk's beard, Hawkweed – dandelion-like plants **94**
Hawthorn (may) – shrub or small tree of hedges, scrub, woods. Common (quickthorn) **28**, 60, 76, **82**; Midland● also 34, 128
Hay – 118, **149**
Hay fever – and grass pollen 120
Hazel – shrub, often coppiced 12, 14, **28**, 32, 60; 76. Cob nuts **114**, 56
Heath – a classic community on acid soil or peat, with heather: 71, 158, 168, 170 etc
Heather (ling) main member of family of plants described **160**; see **158** 71, ACID
Heath butterfly – a brown butterfly **140**
Heather(ing) – binding of hedge **78**
Hectare – 10000 square metres = 2½ acres
Hedge, hedgerow – 76 ff, **90, 132**. Life of hedges 98 ff.
Hedgehog – **146**, 247. See also 30
Hedge brown (gatekeeper) – butterfly **100**
Hedge sparrow (dunnock) – **112**
Helleborine – orchid **62, 124, 235●**
Hemiptera – scientific name for bugs 106
Hemlock – poisonous umbellifer **92**
Hemp-agrimony – of watersides **212**
Hemp-nettle – **136**
Herb – a green, non-woody plant that dies down to rootstock or low rosette or survives winter as seed.
Herb bennet – wood avens **32**
Herb layer – field layer of wood 12
Herb paris – **34**, indicates old woods 63 ● ALK.
Herbicide – manufactured 'weed' killer
Herbivore – an animal which eats plants or parts of them: herbivorous = sustaining itself on plant matter: 42, 98, 138 etc
Heron – family of birds, grey heron **200**
Hibernation – winter strategy of animals see, eg 114, 146, 198
High forest – close-growing timber wood, tall woodland 12, 66
Hip – fruit of wild rose **86**
Hive bee – semi-domesticated bee **102**
Hobby – short tailed small bird of prey
Hogweed (cow parsnip)– **92**
Holdfast – attachment of seaweeds **222**
Holly – evergreen shrub or small tree 15, **26**, 62, 76
Holly blue – butterfly **44, 242**
Holm oak – **20**
Holt – otter's riverside den 184
Honey bee (hive bee) – **102**
Honeydew – sweet exudation of aphids, caterpillars, consumed by ants, moths 110, 138. On lime, sycamore 26, 24
Honey fungus – **18**
Honeysuckle (woodbine) – **84**
Hop – native climber **84**
Hornbeam – native tree **26**, 128
Horned-poppy – **236**
Hornet – large brown-yellow wasp **102**
Horntail (wood wasp) – stingless insect **102**
Horse – grazing of 118
Horse chestnut – **80**
Horsefly – blood sucking fly **142**
Horse-radish – **94**
Horseshoe vetch – yellow flower of the pea family **148**, important to butterflies 140 ALK.●
Horsetails – primitive plants **192**
House – loosely used in some names, of species seen but not limited to houses, eg house spider, house fly
Hoverfly – family of interesting true (2 winged) flies **48, 102, 110, 142**
Humblebee – bumblebee
Hybrid – offspring from cross breeding of parents of different species, varieties or races. Rarely fertile 20, 34, 234
Hydrobia – small snail found in estuaries. Food for many wildfowl **229**
Hymenoptera – Order of insects including bees, wasps, ants, ichneumon flies
Hypha – plural hyphae. Fungal feeding thread
Ice Age – Britain icebound down to the Thames 9 ff, 12
Ichneumon flies– family of parasitic insects with long antennae 98, **242**
Improvement – drainage, fertilising etc of fields to increase yield, often does great damage to wildlife 118, 172
Indigenous – native to that area
Inflorescence – flowering head of plant
Ink cap (lawyer's wig) – fungus **40**
Insect – Class of arthropods. Adults have a body divided into head (carrying a *pair of antennae)* a thorax (carrying *three pairs of legs* and maybe *two pairs of wings)* and an abdomen. Insects have complex life-cycles, with the larva either undergoing a complete metamorphosis (change) to become adult as in beetles, butterflies, or an incomplete metamorphosis, already resembling the adult, as in grasshoppers, bugs etc 106, 180
Intertidal – zone of shore 218
Introduction – non-native species of plant or animal, released by man and now established in the wild (naturalised). If accidentally escaped and not yet naturalised, known as **casual.**
Invertebrate – general name for all animals without backbones. Numbers in woodland 49
Iris – wild, 65, **208**. See also **flag iris**
Irruption – movement of birds for food 70
Ivy – evergreen climber **18, 36; Ground ivy** is another plant **88**

Jack – a young pike 182
Jackdaw – bird of crow family **144**
Jack-go-to-bed-at-noon (goat's beard) – **94**
Japanese knotweed – **92 (Japweed** is a naturalised string-like seaweed)
Jay – shy bird of woods **50**
Jellyfish – found on shore **240**
Juniper – native conifer **30**, 64, 71

Kale – cabbage type crop 16
Keck, kek – cow parsley **36, 92**
Kelp – seaweeds found below low tide mark **222**
Kelt – salmon after spawning, very weak
Kestrel – a small falcon 90, **112**
Key – fruit of ash tree **23**
Kidney vetch – of grassland **122**, ALK.
Kingcup (marsh marigold) – **65, 154, 208**
Kingfisher – **184**
Kite – buzzard-like bird of prey; rare
Kittiwake – small gull **238**
Knapweed (hardhead) – of grassland **122**
Knot – small wader **232**
Knotgrass – of dock family **96**

Lacewing – **110**
Ladybirds – small beetles **110**
Lady's mantle – rose-family flowers producing 'magic dew': **150, 164**
Lady's smock (cuckoo flower) – **149, 209**
Lady's tresses – orchid **71** ACID.
Lambs' tails – hazel catkins **28**
Lammas leaves – oak buds may renew growth in summer
Landscape – origins see, eg 10–15; protection 250
Lapwing (peewit) – wader, **144, 210**
Larch – deciduous conifer 67, **68**, 128
Lark – small brown song birds – see **skylark** and **Woodlark**
Lateral line – of fish **182**
Latex – 'milk' of, eg sowthistle
Laurel – **30**; spurge laurel 62
Laver – seaweeds (red and green) **222**
Lawyer's wig (ink cap) – fungus **40**
Lay or layer – a hedge 78. A layer is also a level of vegetation in a habitat: in a wood there are canopy, underwood, field and ground layers 12–15, 20, 38, 63
Leaching – removal of nutrients and salts by rain soaking down through soil
Lead – poisoning of swans 184
Leaf miner – larvae of moths and flies which eat out tunnels within leaf **18, 86**
Leather jacket – larvae of crane fly
Leech – aquatic, blood sucking worm
Legume – seed pod of pea family plants, general name for peas, beans etc
Lepidoptera – butterflies and moths
Lestes a damselfly **196**
Lettuce – daisy family plants; sea lettuce is a green seaweed **222**
Leucobryum (pin cushion moss) – **38, 61**
Level – wet grassland in Somerset 204
Ley – grass sown as a crop, for grazing or silage.
Lichen – pronounced li-ken or litchen: primitive plants, with body of fungus and algal elements. Good indicators of air pollution, acid rain. **18●, 116**, 202
Lily – plant family, eg bluebell, asphodel
Lily-of-the-valley – 34, **63●**
Lime – native tree, the small-leaved lime found only in old woods 20, 22, **26, 60●**
Limestone – rock containing much calcium carbonate; chalk is a pure form. Such rock makes alkaline soil, and encourages varied plant growth. See **148, 150**
Limy – of soil rich in calcium
Limestone pavement – landscape feature **150**
Limpet – 224; blue-rayed **240**. River limpet **180**. Slipper limpet **228**
Ling – another name for **heather 160** ACID
Linnaeus, Carolus– originator of systematic method of notation of plant and animal names 106
Linnet – a small finch of scrub etc **112**
Litter – decaying twigs, leaves etc
Littoral – zone on the sea shore
Liverwort – primitive plants **38**
Lizard – reptiles: common lizard **168**
Loam – soil of good quality
Lobelia – water lobelia **202**
Lobster – crustacean, relative of crabs
Lodgepole pine – 67, **68**
Longhorn – family of wood-eating beetles **106**
Looper – caterpillar of geometer moths
Loosestrife – purple **208**
Lords and ladies – see arum
Louse – 1) Small parasitic insects. 2) **Plant louse** is another name for aphid. 3) often used in name, eg woodlouse
Lousewort – of moors, heaths **166** ACID.
Lousy watchman – dor beetle **142**
Lovage – umbellifer of cliffs **237**
Lugworm – **228**
Luminescence – light created by living things: glow-worm 106, honey fungus 18
Lungwort – leafy tree lichen
Lupin – (blue) pea-family flower, often seen as garden escape
Lyme grass – greyish grass of seashore 215

Machair – a natural grassland 215
Maggot – legless larva of, eg flies
Magpie – bird of crow family **112**
Maiden – standard timber tree
Mallard – a dabbling duck **200**
Mallow – roadside flower **94**
Mammal – vertebrates with hairy bodies. Young are born live and fed on milk
Management – use and care of a habitat or site for farming or other purposes. Of woods 12–15; hedges 78; fields 118, road verges 90; rivers 172 etc
Mandrake – white bryony **84**
Maple, field maple – **24**
Marble gall – **18**
Marbled white – a 'brown' butterfly **140**
Marestail – a flowering plant 154, **187**
Marigold – corn **136**; marsh marigold = kingcup **65, 154, 208**
Marram – dune grass **235**
Marsh – waterlogged mineral (not peaty) soil; cf **fen.** See page 204
Marten, pine – stoat-like mammal
Martin – birds: house, sand martins **188**
Mason wasp – related to potter wasp **170**
Mast – nut crop of, eg beech
Master tree – see purple emperor butterfly 44
Mat grass – of moors, heaths 158, **160**
Mating behaviour of beetles 110, butterflies 140, 142; dragonflies 196. spiders 108. See also birds
May – hawthorn, especially blossom **82**
Maybug (cockchafer) – **48**
Mayfly – order of insects with aquatic nymphs **180, 188●**
Mayweed – of daisy family **136**
Meadow – field of permanent grass kept for hay, often alongside a stream See 118, 122, 204, **149**
Meadow pipit – bird of rough-land habitats 66, 70, **144, 165**
Meadowsweet – waterside flower **208**
Medick – small yellow clover
Mercury – see dog's mercury●
Mere – shallow pool, often infilling
Merganser – sawbill duck, eg goosander **202**
Merlin – small falcon 70, **162**
Mermaid's purse – egg case of dogfish **240**
Metamorphosis – change from larva to adult: see **Insect**
Microspecies – differing from close relatives in small ways only
Midland hawthorn – see hawthorn●
Migration – regular movement usually between breeding and wintering grounds: moths 46, butterflies 100, birds 232. See also irruption 70
Mildew – mould-like fungus
Milfoil (yarrow) – **122**
Miller's thumb (bullhead) – fish **187**
Millipede – many-legged arthropod **104**
Mimicry – **102**
Mining bee – solitary bee **102**, 168
Miner – of leaves **18, 86**
Mink – naturalised mammal **184**
Minnow – freshwater fish **182**; a minnow reach is where they can be seen 172
Mint – water mint **208**
Mire – general name for marsh, or bog
Mistletoe – semi-parasite of trees **18, 60**
Mistle thrush – **54**
Mite – small arachnids **108, 194**
Mole – **146**
Mollusc – phylum of shelled animals, snails, slugs, octopus, squid
Monkshood (wolfbane) – **130**
Monocotyledon – one of the two divisions of the flowering plants with one seed leaf, leaves with parallel veins, flower parts in 3s or multiples, eg grasses, orchids, pondweeds
Moonwort – fern of grassland **150**
Moor – (usually high) open ground, with acid soil, kept open by grazing 158ff
Moor-grass – purple 158, **160** ACID
Moorhen – **200**
Mor – raw, acid humus of, eg heathland
Moschatel (town hall clock) – **60**
Mosquito – large blood sucking gnat **194**
Moss – a class of primative green plants, but with stem 'leaves', and spore cases **38, 61, 116**
Moths – close relatives of butterflies, but without club-ended antennae **46**; also see green oak roller etc **48**, chinese character, brimstone, ermine **82**, cinnabar, silver Y **130**; burnet **142**; antler **162**; emperor **165**; china mark moth **194**
Mountain – habitat **164**
Mountain ringlet – butterfly **165**
Mountain ash (rowan) – **26**, 26, 71 ACID
Mouse – small rodents: longtailed field or wood **114**; house **162**; harvest 30, **114**
Mouse-ear – grassland plant **122**
Mugwort – roadside plant **92**
Mull – decayed humus-soil
Mullein – great **94**
Muntjac – smallish deer **58**
Mushroom – field, horse **122**
Mussel – bivalve shellfish **224**; fresh-water mussel **194**
Mustard – cabbage-family plants, eg charlock **136**; hedge, treacle **94**
Mutation – gene change resulting in new character, eg in peppered moth **46**. See also evolution 229
Mute swan – the most common swan **184**
Mycelium – feeding threads of fungus
Mycorrhiza – association of fungus with plant roots 40, 124
Myrtle – bog myrtle **160** ACID
Myxomatosis – disease of rabbits 140

Narcissus – wild, see **Bluebell 32**
Narcissus fly – hoverfly **48**
National Parks Wildlife Trusts, etc – 247 to 251
Native – plant or animal whose natural range includes Britain
Natterjack – protected toad **198**, 247
Natural – not influenced by man: see, eg of woods, trees 12, 71
Naturalised – alien species holding its own in competition with native species wild in the countryside
Natural selection – 229
Nature reserves – area in which management protects habitat, species: 250
Neaps – smallest tides of month 218
Necklace shell – predatory seasnail **228**
Nestling – downy chick, young bird
Nettle – stinging **36, 88**. See also 100
Newts – tailed amphibians **198**; 247
Niche – role of species in an ecosystem; in part, an 'address' in the habitat, but also a part in the living scheme. A niche is occupied by a **species**: 42, 182
Nightingale – songbird, of the thrush family; **54**; found especially in coppice 14, (70)
Nightjar (goatsucker) – bird **170**
Nightshade – family of poisonous plants: woody (bittersweet) **84**; black **96**; deadly 62 ALK. (Enchanter's **32** not related)
Nipplewort – daisy family flower **94**
Nocturnal – active by night
Node – where leaves arise from stem
Norfolk broads – **212**
Nut – dry fruit with woody wall **28**, etc
Nuthatch – small song bird **52**, 70
Nutrient – plant 'food', obtained from soil: mineral and other substances 42. Effect of nutrient to water 174, 190, 202
Nymph – young insect resembling adult
Nymphalid – see **Butterfly**

Oak – we have two native species which play a major role in the story of the countryside: 12, 14, **20, 60, 61**. Oaks are host to many animals 18, 44. See also 128
Oak apple – a gall **18**
Oarweed – large brown seaweed **222**
Oat – wild grass **120** and crop **134**
Old man's beard (wild clematis) – **84**
Oil – effects of pollution by, 180, 220, 237, 238
Oligotrophic – nutrient-poor
Olive – plant family including ash tree; anglers' flies, certain mayflies
Open ground – see succession 128; 'weeds' on **94, 96**; grasslands 122, 148, 150 etc; grassland plants, origin of 170
Opium poppy – 136
Orache – goosefoot family weeds **96**
Orange tip – 'white' butterfly **101**
Orb web – spider **108**
Orchid – family of plants, main entry **124**; early purple **32●**; bird's nest, white helleborine **62**; lady's tresses **71**; marsh helleborine 235
Organic – of living organisms
Orpine – fleshy plant of dry places **130**
Osier (withy) – shrubby willow **24**
Osmia bees – as pollen collectors **116**
Otter – native mammal **184**, larger than European otter of zoos. Protected 247
Ouzel – ring ouzel, black migrant thrush
Owl – tawny **50**; long-eared **70**; barn **112**; little **144**
Ox-eye daisy – of neutral soil **122**
Oxlip – true **60**;● false also described
Oyster – marine bivalve
Oystercatcher – large wader **230**
Oxygen – prime requirement of all living things. See **Photosynthesis**. In water 176, 180; effect of pollution 174. In rock pool 226

Painted lady – migrant butterfly **100**
Palm – sprays of hazel, pussy willow, yew to decorate church at Easter
Pan – hard sub-soil layer 170
Panicle – (loosely) branching flowerhead of, eg many wild grasses
Pannage – commons right of pig grazing
Pansy – violet-like plants, field **136**
Pappus – tuft on, eg candelion seeds
Parasite – an animal or plant gaining nourishment from a living organism, and living on or in it. Many fungi are parasites: also, eg dodder **170**, ichneumon fly 98, **242**. Cuckoo is also regarded as a parasite.
Paris – herb paris **34●**
Park – originally enclosed for grazing deer; then other estates, especially with an open wood-pasture appearance 15, **10**
Parr – young salmon 186
Parrot toadstool – grassland fungi **122**
Parsley – name of many flowers of the **Umbellifer** family. See **Cow parsley 36, 92**
Parsnip – cow (= hogweed) **92**
Parthenogenesis – 'virgin' reproduction of, eg aphids 110; violets are self fertile 32
Partridge – grey, red legged **144**
Passage migrant – bird passing through, en route to elsewhere
Passerines song or perching birds: see **song bird**
Pasture – grazing for sheep and/or cattle. Pastures may be permanent grass, or ley 118, 134, 148. See also wood pasture 12–15; heaths and moors are also grazed 152 ff
Pea – plant family with characteristic flowers and pods. See, eg **gorse, restharrow, clover, medick, trefoil** in this Index. (Also peas – similar to garden peas – and **vetchlings**, which are akin to **vetches)**
Peacock – vanessid butterfly **100**, often seen in gardens
Peacock – seashore tubeworm **228**
Peat – 'soil' of semi-decayed plant matter. Bog peat is acid 156, **160**; fen peat may be somewhat alkaline if the water contains minerals to neutralise acid decomposition products 204, **208**
Pedunculate (common) **oak** – see **Oak**
Peewit (lapwing) – a wader **144, 210**
Pellet – undigested waste coughed up by predatory and insect eating birds **50**
Pellitory-of-the-wall – **116**
Peppered moth – **46**
Peppermint – 208
Pepper-saxifrage – grassland flower **149●**
Perch – gregarious freshwater fish **182**
Peregrine – large falcon
Perennial – plant which continues living from year to year
Perennial rye grass – **134**
Periwinkle – see winkle; also name of creeping plants with purple flowers
Persicaria – see Redleg **96**, a weed